Third World Politics

Third World Politics

A Comparative Introduction

Second Edition

Paul Cammack, David Pool, and William Tordoff

The Johns Hopkins University Press • Baltimore

Published by
The Johns Hopkins University Press
2715 North Charles Streeet
Baltimore, Maryland 21218–4319

Library of Congress Cataloging-in-Publication Data

Cammack, Paul A. (Paul Anthony)
     Third world politics : a comparative introduction / Paul Cammack,
David Pool, and William Tordoff. —2nd ed.
          p.   cm.
     Includes bibliographical references and index.
     ISBN 0–8018–4750–8 (alk. paper). —- ISBN 0–8018–4751–6 (pbk. :
alk. paper)
     1. Developing countries—Politics and government.   I. Title.
JF60.C36   1993
320.9172'4—dc20   93–13687
                                                        CIP

A catalog record for this book is available from the British Library.

To Anamaria and Daniela Cammack, Hannah, Thomas and Lydia Pool, and the memory of Dora Tordoff

Contents

List of Maps

Changes in Country Names

Throughout the text, the name by which the country was known at the date relevant to the discussion is used. Changes of name usually occurred at independence; post-independence changes are indicated in brackets.

Present	*Pre-independence*
Benin (1975)	Dahomey
Botswana	Bechuanaland
Burkina Faso (1984)	Upper Volta
Burundi	Ruanda-Urundi[1]
Cameroon	{ French Cameroons
	British Southern Cameroons[2]
Cape Verde	Cape Verde Islands
Central African Republic	Oubangui Chari
Congo	French Congo[3]
Côte D'Ivoire	Ivory Coast[4]
Djibouti	French Territory of the Afars and Issas[5]
Equatorial Guinea	Spanish Guinea
Ghana	Gold Coast and British Togoland
Guinea-Bissau	Portuguese Guinea
Lesotho	Basutoland
Malawi	Nyasaland
Malaysia (1963)[6]	Malaya
Mali[7]	French Soudan
Myanmar (1989)	Burma
Namibia	South West Africa
Rwanda	Ruanda-Urundi
Saharan Arab Democratic Republic[8]	Spanish Sahara\Western Sahara

Somalia\Somali Democratic Republic	{ British Somiland { Italian Somaliland
Tanzania (1965)[9]	{ Tanganyika { Zanzibar
Thailand (1939)	Siam
Togo	French Togoland
Zaire (1971)	Belgian Congo[10]
Zambia	Northern Rhodesia
Zimbabwe	Southern Rhodesia\Rhodesia

Notes:
1. Ruanda–Urundi was a Belgian-administered UN trust territory which became independent in 1960 as two separate states.
2. The Southern Cameroons, a British-administered UN trust territory, joined the Republic of Cameroon following a plebiscite in 1961; the people of the Northern Cameroons opted for integration with Nigeria.
3. Often referred to as Congo–Brazzaville.
4. In 1986 the Ivorian government instructed international organisations to use the French language designation in all official documents.
5. Often referred to as French Somaliland.
6. Malaysia was created in 1963, when Singapore and two British-controlled territories in Northern Borneo – Sabah and Sarawak – joined Malaya in a federation. Singapore subsequently withdrew (in 1965) to become an independent city-state.
7. The Mali federation was formed by Senegal and Soudan in 1959, but survived for less than three months after being granted political independence by France in June 1960. France then recognised the separate independence of Senegal and Soudan, and the Union Soudanaise changed the name of Soudan to the Republic of Mali.
8. Or the Sahrawi Arab Democratic Republic. Its international status is disputed by Morocco, which claims the territory.
9. The United Republic of Tanganyika and Zanzibar came into being on 26 April 1964, as a consequence of the union between Tanganyika and Zanzibar; the name 'United Republic of Tanzania' was officially adopted a year later.
10. Often referred to as Congo–Léopoldville and subsequently (from 1 July 1966) as Congo–Kinshasa.

Preface

This is a revised and extended second edition of the text first published in 1988. Firstly, sections on East and Southeast Asia have been added to those already covering Africa, Latin America and the Middle East. For the most part, these new sections centre on four selected case studies, chosen to limit the amount of background historical material required, and to maximise our ability to address important comparative themes: South Korea, Taiwan, Indonesia and the Philippines. Where particular themes justify our doing so, we have ventured outside this set of four cases. We include this new material, with apologies for our lack of regional expertise, in the conviction that the comparative scope of the text is thereby strengthened. Secondly, we have expanded the introductions and conclusions to each chapter, to allow a fuller discussion of the comparative themes advanced. Thirdly, we have converted all footnotes to Harvard references within the text, provided considerably extended suggestions for further reading for each chapter, and listed all the works to which we refer in a single bibliography. We feel that these changes have considerably enhanced the teaching value of the text as a self-sufficient introduction to Third World Politics. In conjunction with the sources discussed in the Further Reading sections, it provides a suitable basis for a semester-long or year-long introductory course. We hope that it will also prove valuable both for teachers of comparative politics who have previously concentrated primarily on the United States and Western Europe, and wish to add a broader comparative dimension, and for area specialists, familiar with some but not all of the regions we discuss, who may weight their teaching towards one or two particular areas, but welcome the potential for broader comparison.

As in the previous edition, Paul Cammack is responsible for the sections on Latin America, David Pool for those on the Middle East, and William Tordoff for those on Africa. For this second

edition, Paul Cammack was responsible for the final editing, and
wrote all the sections on East and Southeast Asia with the
exceptions of Chapters Four (William Tordoff) and Five (David
Pool).

We thank our publisher, Steven Kennedy, for his encouragement,
and Ray Bush, Diane Elson, Barry Munslow, Georgina Waylen,
Ralph Young and anonymous readers for their extremely helpful
comments and suggestions. The final responsibility, as always, is
ours.

Paul Cammack
David Pool
William Tordoff

Introduction

This text provides an introduction to politics in the Third World which is thematic and comparative, and places politics in its historical, social and international contexts. Our approach is based upon comparison within and across regions, rather than upon generalisation with relatively little concern for regional specificity and historical background. We believe, as regional specialists ourselves, that the history and politics of different regions are sufficiently distinctive to make such an approach essential. Although useful in other ways, the term 'Third World' is somewhat misleading if it suggests a shared and uniform history. The framework we adopt allows us to compare and contrast four major areas of the world outside the core capitalist economies and the former socialist bloc, and it is this exercise which is our primary concern.

However, if there is a danger in excessive generalisation and the imposition of a false uniformity across space and time, there is an equal and opposite danger in the insistence that everything is utterly unique. Regional specialists are particularly prone to feeling that the historical and cultural characteristics of the region they study are so distinctive that comparisons across regions are of far less value than prolonged and detailed study of a single one. Many are inclined to argue, too, that any national or regional analysis requires a thorough knowledge of relevant languages and cultures, and to insist that almost any attempt to generalise is either misleading or premature. We have some sympathy for this view, and readily recognise that the enterprise undertaken here would be entirely impossible if we could not draw upon the work of such specialists. But there is nothing more likely to deter potential students of Third World politics than the false claim that nothing can be achieved without an apprenticeship served in in-depth study of a single region. We feel that a comparative approach based upon a wide range of accessible sources is particularly appropriate at an

1

introductory level, and an extremely valuable basis for more advanced study.

While the claim that many of the constituent features of politics and the driving forces of change around the world are unique and specific to each region is not to be dismissed out of hand, it should still be tested against the available evidence. Comparison here plays a double role. Where similar features and processes appear to exist, we are impelled to look for common causes. On the other hand, where sharp contrasts appear, we may be able to locate all the more precisely specific local factors which account for the differences observed. In other words, comparison does not lead inevitably to generalisation. It should also promote a better understanding of the features of particular regions which are genuinely distinctive and of significant explanatory value. In pursuing a comparative analysis sensitive to regional difference, we hope to have avoided both the devil of too detailed regional specialisation, and the deep blue sea of excessive generalisation.

We wish to emphasise, at the same time, that this text is consciously *introductory* in character. While it is comprehensive and self-sufficient as an introduction to Third World politics, it offers only a first step towards the study of the regions and themes discussed. Ideally students will go on to more ambitious comparative analysis of particular themes, or to more detailed and intensive study of one or another particular region. We seek to equip and stimulate them to do so.

In urging the comparative study of Third World politics at a broad introductory level we are also influenced by practical considerations. As teachers of politics with backgrounds in regions outside Europe and the United States, we are constantly aware of the restricted curriculum, insularity and inappropriate level of generalisation of much teaching of politics. It is quite possible to graduate in political science and pursue studies at post-graduate level without acquiring the slightest knowledge of the politics of any region of the Third World. Programmes which offer even optional specialist coverage of more than one or two particular regions are in a minority, and the balance of regional options available varies greatly from country to country (with Africa favoured in Britain, for example, Latin America in the United States, and East and Southeast Asia in Australasia) and from institution to institution. In Britain the dearth of funding for post-graduate studies which require disciplinary training, language acquisition and prolonged field-work abroad has been such in recent years that the flow of such specialists, always rather sluggish, has slowed to a trickle.

Offsetting this somewhat bleak picture, however, is the fact that there is now available an immense amount of English-language material upon which students of comparative Third World politics can draw. This ranges from book-length regional or national histories and case studies to essays on specific topics and comparative themes in such professional journals as *Comparative Politics*, *Comparative Political Studies*, and the *Journal of Commonwealth and Comparative Politics*. In addition, such regional journals as the *Journal of Modern African Studies*, *Pacific Affairs*, the *Journal of Latin American Studies*, and the *Middle East Journal* offer valuable and easily accessible material for particular regions. For contemporary coverage, these can be complemented by such weeklies as *West Africa*, the *Far Eastern Economic Review*, *Latin America Weekly Report*, and *Middle East*. At one level, this text represents a modest attempt to open up this literature both to beginners in comparative politics and to single area specialists.

In addition to the problem of regional specialism versus cross-regional generalisation, students of comparative Third World politics face a problem of premature and excessive theorisation. Ever since the notion of 'political development' was conceived and built into a major sub-discipline of political science from the 1950s, studies of the various regions which collectively make up the Third World have been swept by successive waves of theory, each bidding to displace its predecessor. As a result, a vast amount of theoretical baggage has been accumulated, of varying quality and utility. The writers of such an introductory text as this must decide at the outset whether to address this material directly. We have elected not to do so, in part because it has been ably done elsewhere [Roxborough, 1979; Randall and Theobald, 1985], in part because it is our experience that an attempt to introduce such theories directly alongside introductory empirical material and comparative thematic analysis leads very quickly to overload. We make occasional references to this literature within the text, and readers familiar with it will recognise some affinities and influences. It will also be clear to such readers at some points that one or another of us finds some elements of such theorising less than convincing. However, we have not sought to draw particular attention to points of agreement or disagreement, on the grounds that such digressions are superfluous to our central purpose, and irritating and distracting to readers at present unfamiliar with the debates in question. On the basis of our own experience, we would rather have students go on to evaluate the merits of such approaches for themselves as they move beyond an introductory level of study.

Our material is drawn from Africa, East and Southeast Asia, Latin America and the Middle East, four important and historically contrasting regions. The authors are individually specialists in the politics of Africa, Latin America and the Middle East, and an earlier edition of the text covered these three regions only. We have now included East and Southeast Asian material in order to extend the comparative scope of the text. Each chapter follows the same basic structure. After a brief introduction which sets out the topic and raises a number of comparative issues, sections follow on Africa, East and Southeast Asia, Latin America and the Middle East in turn. Then a lengthier conclusion compares and contrasts the evidence from the different regions, and draws out the points that seem appropriate.

The first chapter explores the historical background of the four regions covered in the book, with a primary focus on the related but separate issues of colonial rule and incorporation into the global capitalist economy. A brief review of the kind we offer cannot do justice to the rich and varied histories of the regions considered, or of their relations with the rest of the world. It is not intended to do so. Rather, it aims to give a sense of the historical particularity of each region, and to draw attention to the scope for comparison, and its limits. It does make sense to talk, at a broad level of historical generalisation, of the emergence of a global capitalist economy. Indeed, it is impossible to make sense of the contemporary world, and the relationships between its various parts, without doing so. But there is no universal pattern of incorporation, to which the historical experience of every nation-state can be mechanically fitted. Equally, independent nation-states have emerged through distinctive cycles of colonisation, colonial rule and decolonisation in different parts of the world. Some sense needs to be given of the broad parallels and contrasts between the activities of the Spanish and Portuguese in Latin America, the British and French in Africa and the Middle East, the Dutch in Southeast Asia, and the Japanese in East Asia.

In the opening chapter, as elsewhere in the book, we do not seek to be comprehensive. We have struggled against the powerful temptation to include a sufficient mass of detail to make us impregnable against the remonstrations of other regional specialists, or to mention in parentheses every possible case which might qualify the arguments we make. No doubt our knowledge and judgement can be faulted, despite our best efforts. But we have set out deliberately to offer a selective account, aimed at identifying the features of each case which seem to us most significant, as a prelude to comparison and further independent reading. The final sections of each chapter are pitched at a level appropriate to the amount of detail that has gone before, and should be treated as a basis for discussion rather than a set of definitive conclusions. They provide a starting-point, not an end-point.

After the initial historical chapter, five chapters take up standard themes in comparative politics, looking in turn at state–society relations, party politics, the military, social revolutions, and women. The last plays a double role, looking back over the issues considered thus far from a gender perspective, and introducing the international and global issues with which the final two chapters are concerned. The latter deal in turn with international politics and the international political economy. We preface these substantive chapters here with a brief discussion of current issues in Third World politics.

Current issues in Third World politics

The first issue in Third World politics today must be the appropriateness or otherwise of the term 'Third World' itself. The term, first used in the early post-war period, quickly came to combine a number of related ideas. In the first place it assumed the existence of a bipolar global system, shaped by antagonism between the 'First World' of developed capitalist states, and the 'Second World' of developing socialist states led by the Soviet Union. In this context, the idea of a 'Third World' expressed the existence of a large group of states around the world, growing as decolonisation gathered pace, outside either of these two groupings, with a shared history of colonisation or informal imperial control, and characterised by varying degrees of poverty and underdevelopment. In addition, the term recognised, in the context of the promotion of the Cold War on a global scale, that these states were under pressure to declare themselves ideologically for one or the other of the leading power blocs, and accordingly adopt appropriate economic strategies and political forms. In this connection the idea of the 'Third World' contained within itself the parallel idea of a 'third way' which would avoid either an unconditional alliance with either bloc, or the adoption of borrowed models of economic and political development. This thinking was particularly strong in the 1950s, as reflected in the Bandung Conference (discussed below in Chapter Seven), and the non-aligned movement to which it gave rise. In ideological terms, its two leading components were nationalism and developmentalism.

For obvious reasons, the term 'Third World' now seems less appropriate than it might once have been. The collapse of the 'socialist states' set up in Eastern Europe on the periphery of the Soviet Union in the wake of the Second World War, and the subsequent collapse of the Communist regime in the Soviet Union and the break-up of the Union itself, have largely done away with the 'Second World' as a separate entity; and they have entirely removed the Cold War as a defining feature of global politics. As a result, it is harder to attach any precise meaning to the idea of a 'third' world, or the option of an independent 'third way' of development. Additionally, the varying trajectories of different countries and regions within the 'Third World' over the last fifty years, and notably the vast accumulation of wealth in a limited number of oil states and the achievement of rapid economic development in East and more recently Southeast Asia, have called into question the usefulness of the blanket term 'Third World' to cover developing nations, if they are assumed to be uniformly poor and underdeveloped.

These are substantial arguments. But it is vital to distinguish between the difficulties which were always present in the term, and those which have arisen as circumstances have changed. From the perspective of developing countries, the idea of a bipolar world was always a distortion. The influence of the Chinese revolution was always powerful, particularly in East and Southeast Asia, and although it has evolved and perhaps fundamentally mutated in character, Communist China has survived the Soviet and East European break-up. Additionally, the global influence of the Soviet

Union has often been grossly exaggerated. For the great majority of 'Third World' states, the issue has not been to find a 'third way', but to find a 'second way' which preserves some independence from the dominant capitalist economies of the developed world. As we shall see below, this is as crucial an issue today as it has ever been.

Where economic development is concerned, a number of states, mostly in East and Southeast Asia or Latin America, have found their way to a relatively autonomous form of **capitalist** development; in as many cases again, however (among them, Korea in the 1950s, Vietnam and Cuba in the 1960s, Angola, Chile and Mozambique in the 1970s and after, and Nicaragua in the 1980s), states have been denied by military and economic pressure the right to seek relatively autonomous paths of **socialist** development. In this sense imperialism has remained as powerful a force as it ever was, preceding, accompanying and out-living the brief period in which it seemed possible to hold out the hope of a 'Third World'.

At the same time, however, unity around the idea of a nationalist and developmentalist path out of underdevelopment and colonial rule was itself short-lived, and far from all-embracing. The moment of unity around such ideas – reflected by the emergence of such figures as Lumumba, Nasser, Nehru, Nkrumah, Perón and Sukarno on to the international stage – was brief, in part rhetorical, and marked by internal contradictions. And for each such figure there was a Somoza, a Syngman Rhee, a Tubman or a King Idris elsewhere, or a Mobutu or Suharto waiting in the wings. In the same way, the idea of a common condition of colonialism, poverty and underdevelopment was as misleading in some ways in the 1950s and 1960s as it is now. Variations between rates of growth and levels of urbanisation and industrial development in the wealthiest states of Latin America and the poorest in Africa were quite as striking then as other disparities are today.

To an extent, then, the Third World was always a mythical construct. As our adoption of a method of regional comparison in this text makes clear, we do not subscribe to the idea of an entirely homogeneous Third World uniformly marked by poverty and underdevelopment. On the other hand, our continued use of the term is justified by the fact that the period to which we devote most attention, from the post-Second World War years to 1992, is almost exactly that in which it was in current usage and broadly valid in terms of the location of issues of development within the bipolar structure defined by the Cold War. The regions we consider may now be moving out of that specific historical context. They certainly face, in the 1990s, a situation very different from that which attended the wave of decolonisation in the two decades after the Second World War. We may profitably conclude, therefore, by considering the extent to which the ideas of 'Third Worldism' have been displaced as a consequence of the changes which have taken place.

We can best do so by returning to the central ideas of nationalism and developmentalism. By the 1980s these had been displaced by quite different concepts, each external to the Third World in its origins and implications. While nationalism was undergoing an intensive revival particularly in the post-socialist states of Eastern Europe, it had been displaced in much of the Third World by a new commitment to liberal democracy, reflected in a wave of democratisation of virtually global proportions. At the same time the national sovereignty of Third World states and their ability to pursue interventionist national development strategies were being undermined by the promotion, by international agencies and leading Western governments, of strategies of structural adjustment centred on liberalisation and privatisation. This double shift, from nationalism to liberal democracy and from internally defined developmentalism to externally imposed structural adjustment, provides a measure of the extent to which the idea of indigenous strategies of economic and political development has gone into decline. Third World countries are increasingly conforming to ideals and standards defined externally. And where the processes of democratisation and structural adjustment coincide, the formal institutions of Western liberal democracy are often being adopted in the absence of the state capacity, social conditions and levels of economic development which have sustained them elsewhere. This raises questions as to the appropriateness and durability of the processes concerned.

Democratisation

The new states emerging to independence in the 1950s and 1960s did not always attach a high priority to the institutionalisation of liberal democracy. In many cases liberal democratic systems were adopted only very shortly before independence, and previous traditions of colonial rule had done very little to prepare the way for them. As a result new political élites lacked experience with democracy, and felt little commitment to it. In addition, they frequently attached greater importance to other goals, such as the consolidation of the authority of new national governments, or the use of state power to further personal and group interests. Also, many doubted that their developmental goals could be achieved within a framework of multi-party politics. Radicals felt that in conditions of limited social and economic development democratic electoral systems gave conservatives too much scope to mobilise support, in the countryside in particular, to block progressive initiatives. Conservatives, in contrast, feared that democracy would unleash uncontrollable demands from below for more radical change than they were willing to contemplate. Many of these considerations applied just as strongly in long-independent Third World regimes in Latin America and elsewhere, where the pressures of post-war social and economic change were putting the few established democracies under threat. Finally, although departing colonial powers sought, if sometimes half-heartedly, to establish democratically accountable regimes, the circumstances arising from the expansion of the Cold War into the Third World soon bred as keen a concern for order as for democratic accountability. With few forces strongly committed to it and many ranged against it, democracy proved fragile in the Third World. In a majority of cases, it gave way to military regimes, or systems in which elections continued to determine the choice of government, but the holders of state power made sure that there could be only one winner. In a number of the latter cases, mostly but not only in Africa, this situation was recognised through the creation of single-party regimes. In a small but significant minority of cases the overthrow of dictatorships or decadent colonial regimes led to the establishment not of liberal democracies, but of revolutionary socialist regimes. Chapters One to Five below consider in turn the historical legacies and patterns of state–society relations which hindered the widespread adoption of democracy, the resulting fragility of competitive party politics, and the record of military and revolutionary alternatives.

Since the 1960s, much has changed. In Africa, military and single-party regimes alike have proved unequal to the tasks they have assumed. In Latin America, the wave of authoritarian regimes that came to power in the 1960s and 1970s, with the intention of transforming the politics of the sub-continent for ever, has spent its force. In each case, the consequence has been a sharp upward re-evaluation of the merits of liberal democracy as a political system which at least holds out the promise of upholding the rule of law and making it possible to remove incapable governments from power, and attract foreign support and aid. For reasons which have much to do with the consequences of internal conflict and unremitting external pressure, many socialist regimes around the Third World, previously committed to single-party rule, have also recently adopted multi-party systems, though Cuba, for many the flagship of revolutionary commitment in the 1960s, has refused to go down that road. In East and Southeast Asia, where the democratic legacy is weaker, and authoritarian governments have enjoyed more considerable success in promoting long-term econom-ic development, liberalisation and democratisation are under way in a majority of cases, though opposition forces still face considerably greater obstacles than they do elsewhere. Even in the Middle East, where Western-style liberal democracy has never had more than a tenuous foothold, pressure for democratisation has been greater in recent years than ever before.

The issue of the relative weakness of liberal democracy in the Third World in the past and its prospects for the future runs through many of the chapters which follow. At the outset, two particular points should be borne in mind. Firstly, although the process of democratisation can be termed global in scale without undue exaggeration, it does not follow that it has the same character, depth, or intensity in each of the regions studied. As we shall see in more detail below, it often has quite different roots and significance from case to case: while it is appropriate to use the concept of Western-style liberal democracy in the case of Latin America, 'political liberalisation' may be a more apt term to use to describe the movement towards multi-party politics which is occurring in many of the former one-party authoritarian-ruled states of Africa, East and Southeast Asia, and the Middle East. In consequence, it may well be better to view the wave of democratisa-tion in the 1980s and 1990s as a temporary conjunction of somewhat different processes of change than as a single one with a single meaning. Secondly, although the move towards liberal democracy across the Third World is more substantial than it has been before, and much hope is invested in it, few of the problems which prevented its widespread acceptance and successful institutionalisation earlier have as yet been resolved. Rather, the alternatives to it have temporarily fallen by the wayside. Liberal democracy has as much to prove in the Third World as it ever had, and its future is very much in the balance. This is particularly so because of its relationship with economic development, to which we now turn.

Structural adjustment

If the political prospects of the Third World came in the early 1990s to be tied closely to the fortunes of democratisation, its economic prospects were even more closely linked to the fortunes of increasingly widespread programmes of structural adjustment. This marked a substantial change, and a backward step, from the aspirations of the 1950s and 1960s. Although there were often variations in the strategies employed, Third World states took it for granted in that period that it was appropriate to pursue rapid economic development in order to improve the quality of their citizen's lives, and to bridge the gap between the rich countries and the poor. It was accepted, too, that state intervention on a large scale in pursuit of these ends was appropriate and legitimate. Despite conflicts of interest between developing and developed countries, and shifts in patterns of trade and investment which brought more rapid growth to the richer countries and actually widened the gap which development sought to bridge, those were decades of substantial growth in the Third World as in the world economy as a whole.

However, in the wake of the global crisis which gathered in the inflationary 1970s and hit home in the 1980s, Third World developmentalism, with its goal of an independent national industrial economy superintended by an active state, was largely eclipsed. The industrialised countries were never excessively keen to promote balanced industrial development in the Third World. But while they were themselves largely committed to Keynesian-style interventionism as part of a larger process of post-war reconstruction and social pacification, they tolerated a degree of interventionism in Third World states seeking to hasten the process of economic development. In the 1970s the crisis of such interventionist policies in Britain and the United States gave rise eventually to policies under Thatcher and Reagan which cut back on state intervention and propounded the merits of the free market, while allowing the swelling US deficit to destabilise world trade and financial flows. Coming in the wake of the wave of enormous financial instability set in motion by the devaluation of the dollar and the boom in irresponsible lending in the 1970s, these policies brought to those Third World countries most closely tied in to the Atlantic economy the worst of all possible worlds. The upshot was that by the 1990s international institutions, such as the IMF and the World Bank, backed by the US government and its faithful junior partner in London, were urging more single-mindedly than ever before the adoption of policies which would 'adjust' the economies of the Third World to the existing distribution of wealth and power in the global economy, and the exigencies of unstable world markets. The alternative of 'adjusting' the practices of the minority of wealthy capitalist countries and the pattern of global investment, production and trade in order to make space for Third World development, as canvassed by proponents of a New International Economic Order, was pushed firmly off the agenda.

The thinking behind programmes of structural adjustment is that Third World economies will eventually prosper if they remove obstacles to the free play of market forces both in the domestic market and in international trade. They are intended, in other words, to draw Third World economies ever more fully into the global capitalist economy. As a consequence, they necessarily subject them to its disciplines and expose them to its periodic fluctuations. Taken together, therefore, they provide a test of the ability of capitalism on a global scale to meet the needs of the peoples of the world. In evaluating this issue, two points should be borne in mind. First, the version of global capitalism being tested is a particularly uncompromising kind, designed to maximise global competition and reduce to the minimum the scope for state intervention to mitigate its effects. In this sense, it is more reminiscent of efforts, in the wake of the First World War, to restore stability to the world economy by returning to the gold standard and free trade than it is of efforts at domestic intervention and international developmentalism (as practised in Europe and East Asia) after the Second World War. Second, the countries which have adopted programmes of structural adjustment are precisely those which have tied themselves most closely to the Atlantic economy in the past, and have suffered the most damage as a consequence of the extreme instability of that economy. The majority of the countries which have become testing grounds for World Bank-inspired programmes of structural adjustment are in Africa and Latin America. If the capacity of the state to lead the process of economic development in these countries is low, it is in part because of the previous effects of exposure to global capitalist forces. The implementation of policies of structural adjustment places as many demands upon the state as the previous policies of state intervention, and weak states, further weakened by the short-term effects of adjustment, may not be equal to the task. The Third World economies which have proved able to maintain their own course of development – those of East and Southeast Asia – have not been obliged to accede to similar demands for adjustment. By and large, they are more oriented to Japan than to Europe and the United States, and increasingly drawn into a distinctive Asian–Pacific regional economy. In addition, they have maintained a capacity for state intervention, and a willingness to impose limits on the workings of pure market forces both in the domestic economy and in international trade and financial flows. It may be that despite their stated commitment to longer-term goals, programmes of structural adjustment are functioning as mechanisms to impose the costs of previous global disorder upon Third World economies too weak to resist, while the foundations for future success continue to be laid elsewhere.

In line with our comparative regional and historical approach, we seek to draw attention to the very different ways in which our four regions have experienced the global economic crisis of recent decades. Alternative patterns and strategies of economic development are considered in Chapters One and Two, and recur as a minor theme in Chapters Three to Five. Gender-related aspects of those patterns and strategies are addressed at length in Chapter Six, while Chapter Seven covers such international issues as orientations to foreign investment, and attempts to create regional economic blocs. Finally, Chapter Eight addresses four specific issues which seek to highlight central aspects and consequences of the regional experience of economic change over the last two decades.

Further Reading

Approaches to the study of political change in the Third World are usefully reviewed in Roxborough [1979] and Randall and Theobald [1985]. Brett [1985] provides a valuable account of the international context since the Second World War. For Africa, Tordoff [1992] is comprehensive; in addition, Young [1982] and Chazan *et al.* [1992] give a good idea of established themes and the emergence of new approaches over the 1980s. Steinberg [1987] covers the history of Southeast Asia up to the 1980s, and has an extensive bibliography. Pye [1985] surveys East and Southeast Asia, with an emphasis on culture; Higgott and Robison [1985] combines evaluations of competing approaches with case studies of Southeast Asian political economy. Drakakis-Smith [1992] covers East and Southeast Asia in a useful brief introduction, with an emphasis on development. For Latin America Skidmore and Smith [1992] is a reliable comparative history; Wynia [1990] covers politics since the Second World War, and Abel and Lewis [1984] provide a stimulating collection of analytical essays. For the Middle East Mansfield [1991] is an accessible modern history, and Richards and Waterbury [1990] a very useful comparative introduction.

1

The Heritage of the Past

1. Introduction

As noted above, the term 'Third World' came into common use in the context of decolonisation and super-power rivalry in the two decades after the Second World War. But at the same time the Third World, as then defined, was the product of a much longer historical process – more than five hundred years of commerce, conquest, colonisation and economic penetration carried forward by competing European states, later joined by the United States and Japan. We cannot give a comprehensive account of that process here. Rather, we draw attention to its central features for the four regions – Africa, East and Southeast Asia, Latin America, and the Middle East – which provide our subject matter throughout the book. Additionally, we seek to draw out some implications for economic and political change in the period since the Second World War, with which we shall be concerned in later chapters.

In some ways the impact of commercial competition, colonial rule and capitalist expansion upon the four regions with which we are concerned was uniform; but in others it took different forms, with significant historical consequences. As far as colonisation was concerned, the similarities from region to region arose from two broadly common features of the enterprise of colonisation itself: the goals of colonising powers were economic and strategic, and each of these goals required a degree of direct control over the territories and populations claimed; and the resources deployed were generally scanty, considering the magnitude of the enterprise. This meant that successful colonisation would require the creation of local systems of rule, and the building of alliances with at least some groups from among the colonised peoples. Contrasts from region to region

15

resulted from such factors as differences in location and timing, the nature of the indigenous society, and the administrative practices favoured by the colonising power. The character of economic and strategic goals and the balance between them depended in part upon the geographic location and the timing of the launching of colonial enterprise, while the ability to implement economic goals in particular depended quite heavily on the nature of the society encountered. At the same time, the administrative arrangements adopted by different imperial powers had quite substantial consequences for post-independence politics in the territories concerned.

We shall return to these themes at the close of the chapter. Before embarking upon case studies of the four regions examined, however, we draw attention to the broad characteristics of each, and the contrasts between them. Colonial rule came late to Africa, mostly towards the end of the nineteenth century, enduring for six decades into the twentieth – and beyond in such cases as Zimbabwe, Namibia, and the Portuguese possessions. Rivalry between the great powers played an important part in explaining the timing of colonisation, and differences in the way in which those powers organised themselves administratively in Africa have had vital consequences for the nature of post-colonial society and politics. Our emphasis here, therefore, is squarely upon the character and legacy of colonial rule. In East and Southeast Asia the extent of prior cultural and institutional development and the greater array of competing influences demand a broader focus. Emphasis is placed upon the varying outcomes of accommodation between different local patterns of social organisation and the new pressures brought to bear by the European powers and their later rivals, with case studies of the Dutch in Indonesia, the Japanese in Korea and Taiwan, and successive Spanish and American rule in the Philippines. Latin America provides a sharp contrast. On mainland South America new élites won independence from Spain and Portugal early in the nineteenth century, bringing colonial rule to an end before 1830. In the wake of early independence came a particular role within the emerging world capitalist economy which was to differentiate the region sharply from the developing centres of industrial capitalism in Europe and North America, as it became (haltingly at first) a supplier of minerals, foodstuffs, and other raw materials to the hungry industrial centres of the advanced nations.

It was this, rather than the direct impact of recent colonial rule, which was to shape twentieth century politics in the region. For Latin America, therefore, we focus upon the experience of early independence and the development of the export economy. Finally, the history of the Middle East in the nineteenth and early twentieth centuries was dominated by the slow decline of the extensive Ottoman Empire, its collapse after the First World War, and the granting of mandate powers to Britain and France over its dependent territories. We concentrate on that sequence of events, with particular attention to the impact of mandate rule, and the resilience of Islam.

The twin historical processes of the emergence of a global capitalist economy and a system of independent states have been closely intertwined, but they have not run in parallel, and neither should be seen as a single process with a single universal logic. They have had markedly different characteristics from region to region. Within a general focus on commercial and capitalist expansion and colonisation, then, we seek to differentiate as appropriate between the regions studied. At the same time, we begin in this chapter our enquiry into topics that will concern us throughout the book: the record of economic and political change in the Third World over recent decades, and the implications for the future. How far can we detect, in the recent past experience and present character of the regions we study, specific legacies which derive from the more distant past? And how far have these affected the political and economic experience of these regions, after 1945 in the case of Latin America, and after independence elsewhere?

2. Africa: the colonial legacy

Many different forms of sociopolitical organisation existed in pre-colonial Africa, ranging from centralised kingdoms with quite strong bureaucracies to stateless societies. Though urban communities existed in parts of pre-European Africa, particularly in the western Sudan, most Africans lived in the rural areas, with their horizons limited by the family, kinship group and clan. They were engaged in a constant struggle with a harsh environment and migrated frequently from one area to another in the face of war, disease, drought and economic need [Iliffe, 1979: Ch. 2].

European contact with Africa long preceded the establishment of European rule – the Portuguese began to trade to the west coast in the fifteenth century. Together with rival European seafarers, they established a pattern of coastal trading (in gold and ivory, and – especially from the seventeenth century – in slaves) which had the effect of diverting African trade away from the trans-Saharan route linking West Africa with the Maghreb. In the nineteenth century this pattern began to change: the slave trade was supplanted by legitimate commerce, and the interior of the continent was gradually penetrated by explorers and missionaries, culminating in the period of European empire building, especially following the Berlin Conference of 1884–5 (see Map 1). The various European powers – Britain and France, Belgium and Portugal, Germany, Italy and Spain – established (or were confirmed in possession of) colonies and protectorates, mostly drawing the boundaries between them arbitrarily and with scant regard for traditional allegiances. The map of Africa came to resemble a patchwork quilt.

Though strategic considerations were sometimes important and 'civilising' and other altruistic – if arrogant – motives on the part of some colonisers cannot be entirely discounted, the prime motive for the establishment of colonies was economic. The European powers were anxious to secure easy access to the raw materials needed to fuel the manufacturing industries established in Europe following the industrial revolution and to obtain a protected market for their manufactured goods; moreover – as the British showed in 1900 in Ashanti and the Germans a few years later in Tanganyika – they were prepared if necessary to fight in order to gain these objectives. The colonies became dependent on foreign private capital, and foreign trading companies monopolised the import–export trade and the purchase of farmers' produce. A pattern of external economic dependence was thus established that was to persist after political independence was achieved [Rodney, 1972: 162].

Though colonial rule, until the Second World War and beyond, was everywhere authoritarian, bureaucratic and paternalist, and rested ultimately on superior force and technology, the colonial powers differed (often widely) in their specific policies and overall approach to colonial development. Common features included the small number of European administrators in relation to the size of the population being administered, the paucity of the resources made available to them by the colonial powers (especially before the

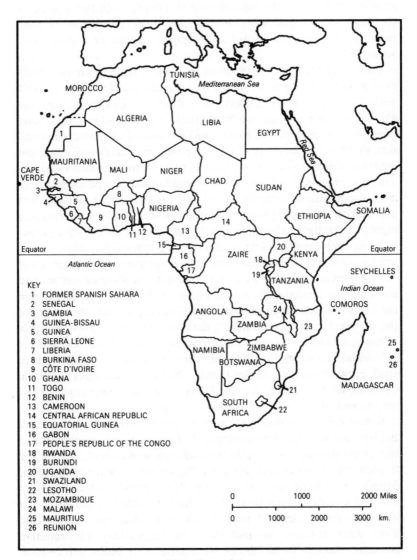

TUNISIA
Mediterranean Sea
MOROCCO
ALGERIA
LIBYA
EGYPT
1
Red Sea
MAURITANIA
MALI
NIGER
CHAD
SUDAN
CAPE VERDE
2
3
4
8
5
NIGERIA
ETHIOPIA
SOMALIA
6
7
9
10
14
11 12
13
Equator
15
16
ZAIRE
20
KENYA
Equator
Atlantic Ocean
18
SEYCHELLES
17
19
TANZANIA
Indian Ocean

KEY
1   FORMER SPANISH SAHARA
2   SENEGAL
3   GAMBIA
4   GUINEA-BISSAU
5   GUINEA
6   SIERRA LEONE
7   LIBERIA
8   BURKINA FASO
9   CÔTE D'IVOIRE
10 GHANA
11 TOGO
12 BENIN
13 CAMEROON
14 CENTRAL AFRICAN REPUBLIC
15 EQUATORIAL GUINEA
16 GABON
17 PEOPLE'S REPUBLIC OF THE CONGO
18 RWANDA
19 BURUNDI
20 UGANDA
21 SWAZILAND
22 LESOTHO
23 MOZAMBIQUE
24 MALAWI
25 MAURITIUS
26 REUNION

ANGOLA
24
ZAMBIA
23
COMOROS
NAMIBIA
ZIMBABWE
25
BOTSWANA
26
MADAGASCAR
21
SOUTH
AFRICA
22

0   1000   2000 Miles
0   1000   2000   3000 km.

Map 1 *Africa*

1940s), and the sense of European superiority which they were able to instil in the subject (especially rural) people, with the result that the hold of colonial rule came to be more psychological than military. The Second World War helped to shatter this myth of superiority.

Following the Berlin conference of 1884–5, the French eventually established eight colonies in *Afrique Occidentale Française* (AOF), with headquarters in Dakar, and four in *Afrique Equatoriale Française* (AEF), based on Brazzaville. Each colony had its own governor and budget and (from 1946) its own elected assembly, and was divided for administrative purposes into *cercles*; it acquired substantial territorial autonomy under the *loi cadre* reforms of 1956. The governors were subject to the overall direction and authority of a governor-general (one for AOF and one for AEF), who in turn was subject to the Minister for Colonies in Paris. The system was highly centralised, characterised by parallel administrative structures in each territory and staffed by a remarkably mobile public service. Other unique features of the system (following the Brazzaville conference of 1944) were first that African political parties and trade unions tended to be either linked with (or to function within the orbit of) metropolitan parties and unions; second, that some of the political parties – notably, the *Rassemblement Démocratique Africain* (RDA) – were interterritorial parties with sections in individual territories; and third, that Africans were allowed to send representatives to the French National Assembly and the Council of the Republic in Paris (a right long enjoyed by inhabitants of the '*quatre communes*' of Senegal).

British colonial policy was more pragmatic than the French, and British rule was also less centralised. There was no counterpart to the 'metropolitan axis' of French colonial policy and, within the framework of policy laid down by the Colonial Office in London, British colonial governors (in the pre-1939 period especially) were allowed greater discretion than their French counterparts in initiating policy deemed suitable for their individual territories. They were assisted, in each case, by legislative and executive councils, though these bodies were limited in both composition and competence until after the Second World War. Up to that time, the cornerstone of British policy was 'indirect rule', an approach which entailed the British administration (and the District Commissioner in particular) ruling through indigenous political institutions

– the chiefs and their councils. As a result, existing communal divisions were accentuated and the educated élite was largely excluded from power-sharing.

By contrast with British colonial rule, Belgian rule was extremely centralised, strongly paternalist and subject to close European supervision. In the Congo it sought to arrest social and political change through the creation of a materially prosperous and contented people, educated (mainly by missions, Protestant as well as Catholic) to the primary level. This attempt failed and civil war followed the precipitate grant of independence in 1960.

Portugal was the only other European power with an extensive African empire. Germany was stripped of its colonies after the First World War; Italy was ousted from Ethiopia during the Second World War after a brief occupation and was left with no colonies of its own, though it administered Libya and part of Somaliland on behalf of the United Nations until 1951 and 1960 respectively; Spain was under little pressure to grant independence to Spanish Guinea and Spanish Sahara, both of which were very thinly populated; and South Africa, which had been mandated to administer South West Africa/Namibia by the League of Nations after the First World War, continued in illegal occupation of the territory after the Second World War in defiance of the United Nations. For its part, Portugal claimed to be undertaking in Africa a non-racial, Christian civilising mission, but in fact it exploited its colonies economically and subjected them (in the educational sphere, for example) to long years of neglect; racial discrimination, forced labour and tight bureaucratic control were key features of Portugal's highly authoritarian rule. In the post-war period – and especially after the outbreak of the African colonial wars in 1961 – Portugal, still an underdeveloped country in European terms, looked to its colonies to supply it with cheap raw materials and to import more than a third of its cotton manufactures.

Nowhere in colonial Africa was there any sustained and meaningful preparation for independence. The Belgians resisted independence until a very late hour; the French fought a bloody colonial war in order to 'keep Algeria French' and, in the mid-1950s, accepted territorial autonomy as a means of preventing independence in AOF and AEF; in the 1950s also, Britain battled against a Kikuyu-based nationalist movement, known as 'Mau Mau', in Kenya; and Portugal fought a bitter and protracted war in a bid to retain its African colonies, as did South Africa in relation to Namibia. Britain did more to prepare its non-settler colonies for independence than any of the other European powers, but preparation began very late, and, as Bernard Schaffer pointed out, was 'all along rivalled and hindered by other values, which were predominantly bureaucratic' [Schaffer, 1965: 59].

After the Second World War, when jobs were scarce and inflation was rampant, anti-colonial nationalism spread quickly and was channelled into political parties and interest groups. These were led in most colonies by a thrusting petty-bourgeoisie of primary school teachers, clerks and small businessmen who often indulged in socialist rhetoric and were impatient to change places with the colonial élite. In some cases – in areas of substantial white settlement such as Algeria and Southern Rhodesia, and above all in Portuguese Africa and Namibia – African demands for significant constitutional change leading to the transfer of power went unheeded and violent conflict followed. In the majority of cases, however, even to talk of an independence 'struggle' is somewhat misleading. In both French- and English-speaking Africa, most nationalist movements were willing to enter into power-sharing arrangements with the regimes which they aimed to displace and brought their countries peacefully to independence under the tutelage of the colonial government itself.

Since Africa was subject to rule by several powers, the colonial legacy has varied from one part of the continent to another. Generalising, one can say in the first place that the economies and communication networks of the African colonies were largely developed in accordance with the needs of the colonial power. Primary products – whether cash crops such as cocoa and coffee or minerals such as copper and bauxite – were exported to European markets in their raw state at prices which fluctuated widely and sometimes (in the 1930s and 1940s) fell dramatically; in return, the colonies imported manufactured goods from abroad, mainly from the 'mother country', at prices subject to the inflationary pressures of the European domestic economies. Trade was monopolised by large European companies, while Asians in East Africa and Lebanese in West Africa tended to monopolise distribution; the result was that the great majority of indigenous (African) entrepreneurs had scope only at the lowest levels of business activity.

Secondly, the imposition of colonial rule integrated the African territories more fully into the global economy, but it did not necessarily alter fundamentally the domestic economic structure. In countries with predominantly agricultural economies (the vast majority), disruption was greatest where (as in Portuguese Africa and parts of French Africa) plantation agriculture was introduced, and least where (as in the Northern Territories of the Gold Coast and much of Upper Volta) peasant farmers grew yams, millet and other crops to meet the needs of their extended families and to market any surplus. The smallholder production of cash crops – undertaken, for example, by cocoa farmers in the Gold Coast and Nigeria, and coffee farmers in the Ivory Coast and Tanganyika – was potentially more disruptive of the domestic economic structure than predominantly subsistence agriculture. This was because, in certain contexts, it stimulated the emergence of the rural capitalist farmer who employed wage labour, invested his profits in urban property and even (as in the Akwapim district of the Gold Coast) bought land. A sizable manufacturing industry was developed in colonies (such as Southern Rhodesia) where there was extensive European settlement, and substantial mining was undertaken in a large number of countries – for example, copper in the Belgian Congo and Northern Rhodesia – though ownership, production and control were vested in European- or South African-based companies. The more radical pre-independence political parties were committed to ending foreign control over the economy, but on coming to power found themselves hampered by the lack of trained and experienced personnel.

Thirdly, colonialism – through its handmaiden, capitalism – had a differential impact on African countries, accentuating differences caused by geography and geological good fortune. It resulted in the juxtaposition within the modern state of advanced economic regions, characterised perhaps by the mining of bauxite, copper and diamonds, or the growing of cash crops such as cocoa, coffee and tea, and deprived areas where the people eked out a meagre living on marginal, badly irrigated land. In these latter areas educational and health provision was inadequate. There was also a sharp rural–urban divide, accentuated as more and more rural dwellers migrated to the towns in search of jobs.

Fourthly, traditional social values and institutions were undermined during colonialism; this was a universal phenomenon, though the erosion was uneven. It was more marked in Francophone than in Anglophone Africa and its impact was less in predominantly agricultural communities than in the urban areas.

One result in the post-independence period was that central and local politicians – for example, in Nigeria, Senegal and Zambia – were able to win popular support by appealing to those ethnic, regional–linguistic and other vertical divisions in society which linked the new states of Africa to their colonial past. Industrialisation – in the form of extractive and manufacturing industry – did shake up the traditional social and economic organisation, but it was the advent of a booming oil industry in a country like Nigeria (where production reached two million barrels a day by 1973) that was to prove especially disruptive.

A final colonial legacy that might be mentioned was constitutional and political. In the terminal phase of colonial rule, Britain and France introduced ministerial systems and other features of modern democratic government under constitutions modelled substantially on those of the metropolitan countries. The constitution of the Fifth French Republic, which was tailor-made for General de Gaulle, was fairly easily adapted to the needs of the new Francophone states. It facilitated an easier transition to an executive presidency, with the president supported by a dominant or single party and unencumbered by a strong legislature, than occurred in Anglophone Africa, where the Westminster-style constitution stressed the virtues of parliamentary government and the two-party system.

There was continuity as well as change in many of the other post-independence governmental arrangements in Black Africa: the old structures were certainly extended – notably, by the almost universal creation of a large number of parastatal bodies – but were rarely transformed. This was even true of ex-Portuguese Africa, despite governmental commitments to socioeconomic transformation on Marxist–Leninist lines. As far as most African leaders were concerned, their attitude was understandable: they had sought to take over rather than dismantle the inherited institutions of state, and they were content for the most part to operate within the framework of control which the colonial powers had established.

3. East and Southeast Asia: the meeting place of empires

East and Southeast Asia has seen competition over centuries between rival creeds, empires and powers. It has felt the influence

of Hinduism and Buddhism as they spread from the Indian sub-
continent, then the expansion of Islam from the Arabian peninsula,
and successive waves of Catholic and Protestant evangelism from
Europe. In terms of regional geopolitics, it has been drawn into the
fields of force exerted by China, India, Japan, and Russia. In global
economic and strategic terms, it has been the object of the
commercial and colonial ambitions and power politics of Portugal, Spain, the Netherlands, Great Britain, France, and the United
States. The resulting interplay of external and internal forces has
woven complex cultural and political patterns on a background of
settled agrarian kingdoms based upon the cultivation of rice on
irrigated land, coastal communities linked by trade, and upland- or
island-based peasant cultivators of various kinds, often in small
states or stateless societies.

In Korea and Vietnam prolonged Chinese influence left a legacy
of Buddhism and Confucianism, while in maritime South East Asia
Brahmanist and Buddhist influences were mostly overlaid or
displaced by Islam as it spread along trade routes and coastal
regions from the fifteenth century. Portugal broke into the spice
trade by seizing key trading points between 1509 and 1515; the
Spanish settled in the Philippines in 1565, linking China and
Spanish America through Manila; and the Dutch created the
Vereenigte Oost-Indische Compagnie (VOC) or East India Company in 1602, and set up its headquarters at Batavia (Jakarta) on
the island of Java in 1619. This gave them a major role in long-
distance trade in the Indian Ocean until they were displaced after
Singapore (founded as a free port by the English East India
Company in 1819) became the dominant trading centre.

For the most part, colonisation came much later, but in the half-
century after 1860 it spread across virtually the whole region. The
French established Cochinchina in southern Vietnam between 1862
and 1867, and made the north their protectorate in 1885; the British
seizure of southern Burma led to the annexation of the whole in
1886, while the passage of control over the Straits Settlements from
the English East India Company to the Colonial Office led to steady
expansion, and the consolidation of the Federation of Malaya in
1895. After the VOC was taken over by the state in 1799, the Dutch
extended their authority outwards from Java to create the Netherlands East Indies, which was eventually to become Indonesia. The
Philippines won freedom from a decadent Spain in 1898, but were

annexed forthwith by the United States, delaying independence for nearly fifty years.

The most significant development in the late nineteenth century was the emergence of Japan as a colonising power, at the expense of China. By 1910 Korea and the island of Taiwan were both under direct Japanese rule. Elsewhere the process of colonisation was nearing completion. By the same date Cambodia and Laos were French protectorates, Britain had extended its authority over the Malayan states outside the federation, and only Siam, under the modernising rule of King Chulalongkorn (1868-1910) survived as an independent entity.

The division of the region along these lines was followed by an intensification of export development, a process which took place later than in Latin America, but earlier and more intensively than in either Africa or the Middle East. Export production developed on the basis of peasant labour in Burma, Korea, Taiwan, Java and the Philippines, and through the exploitation of imported labour in Sumatra and Western Malaya. The policies of the colonial powers in this period broke old connections and fostered new ones. In some cases, as in French Indochina, the Dutch East Indies, and the Philippines after 1902, protective tariffs were introduced in order to orient trade towards the imperial power. In others tighter ties were created, as with annexation to India in the case of Burma, and to Japan in the cases of Korea and Taiwan. Education in the home country was offered to a tiny minority, and attempts were made to create a new sense of identity through increased use of a common language for the population at large. In the Philippines this was English, until – under the Commonwealth of 1935 – it was officially replaced by Tagalog; in the Dutch East Indies, it was 'Indonesian', developed by official fiat out of the lingua franca, Malay, and adopted in the 1920s. In Korea, however, an attempt to impose Japanese failed, despite the insistence that Koreans should adopt new Japanese names. In other ways colonial practice and experience varied widely. Decolonisation, mostly concentrated in the period following the Second World War, broadly confirmed the divisions arising from colonisation itself (see Map 2). A comparison of Korea, Taiwan, Indonesia and the Philippines will illustrate the range of experiences in the region, and some of the contrasts between East and Southeast Asia.

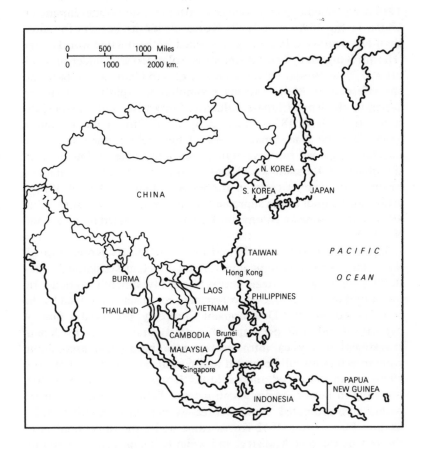

Map 2 *East and Southeast Asia*

Korea avoided conquest by China in the seventh century, but until 1895 remained in a tributary relationship strengthened by shared adherence to Confucian principles of rule. From 1392 to 1910 it was ruled by the Yi dynasty. After invasions from Japan and China in the 1590s and 1620s Korea closed its borders for more than two centuries, becoming renowned in the outside world as the 'Hermit Kingdom'. This self-imposed isolation came under pressure after 1850, as Western states gained access to China and Japan, and the subsequent Meiji reforms prompted a rapidly modernising Japan to challenge Chinese influence. Successive trade treaties, the first with Japan in 1876, forced an opening of the economy, and in 1895, after the Sino–Japanese War, China relinquished its claims, and Korea gained full sovereignty and independence. Immediately the object of Japanese and Russian rivalry, it became a Japanese protectorate when victory in the Russo–Japanese War of 1904–5 established Japan as the supreme regional power. It was annexed in 1910, and remained a colony until Japan was defeated in the Second World War.

Japanese rule between 1910 and 1945 transformed Korea through direct large-scale economic intervention aimed at satisfying Japan's developmental and strategic needs. Heavy investment in agriculture, much of it on land allocated to Japanese colonists or retained by the state-owned Oriental Development Company, produced a flow of exports of rice (50 per cent of output) and cereals to Japan. Investment in physical infrastructure was sharply increased, along with spending on public health and education, and from the early 1930s Japan developed and exploited Korea's industrial potential, investing in power, communications and light and heavy industry within a co-ordinated 'Japan–Korea–Manchuria Resources Mobilisation Plan'. From 1942 Korea came under the direct control of the Japanese Home Ministry, and while Koreans were drafted into the Japanese army, over 250 000 Japanese troops were stationed in Korea.

The Japanese surrender was followed by the declaration of the Korean People's Republic, based upon local committees and democratic provincial assemblies in which Korean Communists played a prominent part. However, while Soviet troops occupied the country north of the 38th parallel, US troops occupied the south, outlawed the People's Republic, recalled the long absent Syngman Rhee and other exiles, and armed and expanded the Japanese-trained police force as its main instrument of rule, suppressing a popular uprising in October 1946. After the Soviet Union rejected a US-inspired UN plan for nation-wide elections, voting confined to the south was followed by the creation of the Republic of Korea there in August 1948 under Syngman Rhee, and of the Democratic People's Republic of Korea in the north under Kim Il Sung a month later.

Taiwan was similarly transformed by Japanese rule. Known to passing Portuguese sailors as the 'beautiful island' (Ilha Formosa), it came under Manchu control in 1683 after brief occupations by the Dutch and by Ming forces fleeing from mainland China. After two centuries of largely nominal Chinese rule it became a province of China in 1886, only to be ceded to Japan after defeat in 1895. The Japanese swiftly imposed order on a society previously dominated by independent warlords, and pursued a policy of infrastructural investment and intensive agricultural development which generated a flow of food exports to Japan, dominated by rice and sugar. These efforts were accompanied, as in Korea, by investment in public health and education, and after the First World War by indus-trialisation, stepped up in the 1930s with the introduction of heavy industry. The incorporation of the island into Japan's war effort as a forward base for southward expansion, the defeat of Japan, and the reassertion of nationalist Chinese control after the Chinese revolution created a virtually new society between 1940 and 1949.

With the departure of the Japanese in October 1945 the nationalist leaders in China declined to restore Taiwan's status as a province, placed the island under military rule, sharply curtailed public investment and systematically plundered the economy, transferring assets of all kinds to mainland China. A local rebellion broke out in February 1947, followed by harsh military reprisals which brought the deaths of 10 000 Taiwanese, including the core of its political leadership. In the wake of these events the Governor-General was removed and provincial status was granted, but the triumph of Mao Ze-Dong's revolution on the Chinese mainland in 1949 brought Chiang Kai-shek and perhaps two million of his followers on to the island. The new nationalist government there-after maintained the fiction that Taiwan was the temporary seat of the nationalist government of the whole of China, pending the recovery of the mainland through the defeat of the victorious Communist forces. As a result the Chinese constitution of 1946 remained in force, along with the exceptional powers taken by Chiang Kai-shek thereafter, and the island was governed by the surviving members of the National Assembly elected on the mainland in 1947, a situation which was to endure into the 1990s.

In contrast to Korea and Taiwan, **Indonesia** (an archipelago of nearly 1000 inhabited islands, with nearly two thirds of the population of 180 million on Java, and half the remainder on Sumatra) owes its unity to the long commercial and colonial presence of the Dutch. After the assets of the VOC were taken over by the state, successive Dutch governors (and British administrators during a brief period of British control) subjected Java to formal colonial rule, and extended it to Sumatra and the surrounding islands. Thirty years of warfare from 1873 eventually defeated the sultanate of Aceh on northern Sumatra, after which the statelets and chieftaincies of the 'outer islands' were swiftly brought under Dutch administrative control.

In its slow evolution from trading organisation to quasi-government, the VOC sought where possible to assert authority and extract a tradeable surplus by varying arrangements with hereditary rulers, members of the existing ruling élite, and appointed Chinese tax-farmers and agents, all recipients of tribute in labour or goods from the peasantry. Coffee, which was first introduced in the Sundanese Priangan district of West Java, became the most successful export, while elsewhere sugar, rice and other crops were grown. After 1799 the Dutch sought to replace hereditary rulers with a system of European residents placed in authority over Javan regents and district heads, and to move from a system of tribute to taxation, but financial difficulties and widespread revolts in the 1820s forced them to step back from this attempted process of modernisation. A new Governor-General, Johannes van den Bosch, restored stability after 1830 with the 'Culture System', which created a modern sugar industry linked to Dutch-owned mills by returning to the old system of extraction of tribute by Javan intermediaries. He also introduced the production of coffee by forced labour on Sumatra. The rapid expansion of plantation agriculture on Java after 1870 eventually prompted modernising reforms in which regents lost their rights to peasant labour for personal services and fixed shares of peasant output. Dramatic increases in sugar production followed, taking output to 750 000 tons per year by 1900. On Sumatra, the large-scale introduction of tobacco after 1863 laid the basis for the East Coast Residency, a major source of varied agricultural exports thereafter.

Dutch rulers responded to quickening development with the 'ethical policy' of basic welfare provision and Dutch-language education for sections of the élite. Initial tolerance of moderate opposition turned to repression as the nationalist movement grew in strength and shifted towards a policy of non-co-operation with the authorities. In 1926 a Communist revolt was defeated, and Sukarno, the founder of the Indonesian National Party (PNI) in 1927, was exiled in 1933. Stability was maintained until Japanese occupation in 1942 allowed exiled leaders to return to create mass organisations and a military force with Indonesian officers. Sukarno claimed independence in August 1945, but social revolution, civil war, Dutch reoccupation, guerrilla resistance and UN intervention ensued before it was accepted by the Dutch on 27 December 1949.

Unlike Korea and Indonesia the **Philippines** felt little influence from China or India, despite connections through trade; the first significant external influence came in the fifteenth century as Islam penetrated the southern islands of Mindanao and Sulu. On the eve of Spanish colonisation the archipelago was inhabited by scattered communities almost entirely devoted to hunting, fishing and shifting cultivation, organised in kinship groups (*barangay*) under local chieftains (*datu*). The Spanish landed in 1521, settled in Cebu (1565) and Manila (1571), and found themselves facing Muslim rivals to the south, as they had in Spain until 1492.

Manila quickly became a vital entrepot linking Mexico and Macao, with the crown licensing two galleons each year to exchange American silver for silk and other goods from China, but insistence on monopoly and a single annual sailing limited the impact of the trade. Extensive evangelisation cemented Catholicism in the dominant position it has retained since, while the introduction of property rights over land, with the Church itself a major owner, created powerful landed élites drawn from immigrant Spanish and Chinese, and from village leaders recognised as local chiefs (*caciques*).

The declining economy weakened further after brief British occupation of Manila in 1762 was followed by local rebellions, and the licensed galleon trade ended when Mexico achieved independence in 1820. Thereafter, development proceeded almost in defiance of Spanish rule, as the Spanish provided the numerous clergy and a swollen bureaucracy, and hired mercenaries to subdue the Muslim south. A British adventurer introduced modern sugar production on the island of Negros in 1857, Philippine-born Chinese *mestizos* moved into planting sugar, indigo and rice, often on lands leased from the Church, and immigrant Chinese came to dominate internal trade. Filipino nationalism, fuelled by persistent discrimination against native-born clergy, grew rapidly after the execution of three nationalist priests in 1872. Then, in a dramatic sequence between 1896 and 1901, the colonial regime executed José Rizal, a moderate reformer, after a revolt in which he was not involved, and was overthrown by a broader élite-dominated movement in 1898. The newly independent state was annexed by the United States (then at war with Spain), and taken over after two years of bitter warfare in which nearly 200 000 Filipinos died. The US army soon completed the incorporation of the Muslim sultanates to the south, and its colonial administration put political power in élite Filipino hands, setting up an elected legislature in 1907 and extending its powers thereafter, before creating a Commonwealth in 1935, with a promise of full independence ten years later. Its policies tied the increasingly sugar-based Philippine economy to its own, and allowed the greatly strengthened landed oligarchy, to which it allied itself, to dominate the political process. Japanese occupation in 1942 produced a collaborationist independent republic in 1943 but also led to widespread popular resistance and peasant rebellion. Upon the defeat of the Japanese, the US government finally granted independence in 1946.

As these accounts suggest, the last phase of the age of empire in the region was dominated by Japanese expansion southwards, and decolonisation after the Second World War. The Japanese advance after their surprise attack in December 1941 on a series of targets from Pearl Harbour to the Philippines, Hong Kong, Singapore, Malaya and Thailand (as Siam was re-named in 1939) brought about an irreversible shift of power in the region [Anderson, 1966]. After 1945, of course, Japan could no longer sustain its attempt to construct an empire across Southeast Asia. But the Europeans had been evicted except in French Indochina (where the Vichy government chose to co-operate with the Japanese), the myth of European invincibility had been punctured, and a process of European eviction which began in a small way in the Philippines at the turn of the century rapidly accelerated. War also subjected millions to forced labour drafts, and unleashed local currents of nationalism and militarisation. Before the end of the 1940s, the independence of India, the Chinese revolution, and the emergence of the Soviet Union as a world power provided new models for anti-colonial struggle and post-colonial development, and transformed the pattern of power politics in the region.

The different patterns of colonial rule and exploitation would have distinct consequences for later political and economic development. Korea and Taiwan experienced late and intensive development under Japanese control, the defeat of the colonial power and of local attempts to assert independence, the installation of a new ruling power of external origin, and the imposition of land reform under external pressure. This course of events laid the basis for continued economic development, but blocked the emergence of any form of democratic politics. In Indonesia the changes brought about by the Dutch, though substantial, were less far-reaching, and their attempt to return after the departure of the Japanese altered the course of internal conflict without resolving it. Only after two decades would a new military-backed élite consolidate its authority and impose a model of authoritarian development. Again, however, this proved incompatible with any move towards democracy. In the Philippines, US colonial practice and subsequent influence substantially strengthened the traditional landed class and its clientelistic politics. Here the resulting social structure proved inimical to both economic development and democracy. In the region overall, therefore, prospects for economic development varied, while the political legacy of colonial rule was strongly authoritarian.

4. Latin America: early independence and the export economy

In Latin America, as elsewhere, levels of social and political organisation varied widely from area to area at the time of colonisation. In contrast to the experience of other regions, however, Latin America saw the early subjugation of the indigenous population in the most advanced and densely settled areas, and a long process of intermixing and assimilation which left the Catholic religion of the Spanish and Portuguese colonists dominant, and rendered ethnicity comparatively weak as a basis for collective identity and resistance to colonial rule. Liberal–Conservative conflicts, in which religion and the Church played a major part, were significant in the late nineteenth and early twentieth century in some areas, but religion and ethnicity have played a relatively minor role in social and political conflict in the area in the contemporary period. A further striking contrast is provided by the early independence achieved by those areas under Spanish and Portuguese rule. In the early decades of the nineteenth century – well before the systematic colonisation of Africa had even begun – independent states had emerged in all the territory in mainland Central and South America previously ruled by the Iberian powers, and the process of state formation was completed with the US-sponsored separation of Panama from Colombia in 1903 (see Map 3). Some major sources of political identity and political conflict elsewhere in the Third World – ethnicity, tribalism, religion, and opposition to colonial rule – have been weak in Latin America. Despite this, the region is recognisably a part of the Third World. In order to understand the strong parallels between Latin America and the other regions considered here, one needs to examine the way in which the economy of the region developed during and after the colonial period. Economic development took a distinctive form which shaped societies quite different from those of the developed world, and structurally similar to those whose experience of colonial rule generally stretched well into the present century.

Significant variations existed in population density and levels of social organisation throughout the region at the time of the first contacts with Spanish and Portuguese colonists (around the end of the fifteenth century). Two distinct and well-developed civilisations existed in what is today Mexico (the Aztecs in the central region, and the Maya in the Yucatan peninsula), while the Inca had built up an extensive empire in the Andean region. In contrast, the dense forests which covered much of tropical and central Brazil sheltered thousands of largely separate groups, living a far more rudimentary life. The remnants of these groups still inhabit the Amazon region, and fight a desperate battle against the encroachment of 'Western civilisation'. Further south, in Chile and Argentina, the indigenous inhabitants quickly adopted the implements of Spanish warfare, and kept the European colonists at bay until well into the nineteenth century. The result was that they were in the end largely

Map 3 *Latin America*

exterminated rather than assimilated, and Chile's small Mapuche community is the last remnant of these proud and powerful peoples.

In the areas of densest settlement and earliest contact, even where present-day societies reflect the survival of indigenous inhabitants, the demographic impact of colonisation was catastrophic. A population perhaps numbering 25 million in Mexico and Central America was reduced to 1 million within a century of contact, partly as a result of war, but primarily as a consequence of the fatal impact of Western diseases to which the indigenous peoples of the Americas lacked immunity.

The primary purpose of colonisation (in the sixteenth century as always) was economic gain. The fortunes of the colonists and the impact of colonisation varied in accordance with the availability of exploitable resources, both natural and human. If the finely worked gold seized from the Incas and Aztecs first aroused the avarice of the Spanish adventurers in the early sixteenth century, it was the fabulous silver mines of Mexico and of Potosí (in present-day Bolivia) which proved the greatest source of wealth in the colonial period. They were equally a source of misery, as the populations of the surrounding regions were forced to render onerous tribute in the form of labour in the mines. With the passage of time, complex economies arose – centred upon the mining areas, but also involving surrounding regions as suppliers of foodstuffs and other essential goods to the mines themselves and to the expanding urban centres where commercial and bureaucratic activities multiplied. In due course similar developments occurred in Brazil, with the creation of a prosperous sugar-exporting plantation economy in the north east of the country (around the settlements of Salvador and Recife), and in the eighteenth century with the shift of the centre of gravity of the economy to the state of Minas Gerais, where gold and diamonds were discovered at the end of the seventeenth century. However, initial economic exploitation on any appreciable scale was delayed by the attractiveness of Portugal's other interests in Africa and Asia, and the absence of lucrative opportunities for trade. Only in the later sixteenth century did a minor trade in 'brazil wood' (a source of natural dye-stuffs) give way to sugar production. A further contrast with Spanish America, which was to prove of major significance, was the early abandonment of attempts (led by settlers in the struggling southern colony of São Vicente, today São Paulo) to capture and enslave the indigenous inhabitants of the country, and the switch to negro slavery, made possible by Portugal's extensive African trade. The endurance of slavery to 1888 had a social and political impact which was matched only in Spanish Cuba, where it spread dramatically in the nineteenth century with the rapid extension of sugar production on the island.

Over three centuries of colonial rule the present-day nations of Latin America adopted the role of suppliers of primary commodities to an already industrialising Europe. Even so, Latin America owes its present character not primarily to its colonial experience but to developments which took place in the nineteenth century. The first of these was the coming of political independence. The second was the development of the 'export economy' on a much extended scale, as the industrial revolution in Europe gathered pace and transformed the international economy, of which Latin America was already an integral part.

With the minor exceptions of British Honduras (Belize) in Central America and three small British, French and Dutch colonies on the Caribbean coast of South America (today Guyana, French Guiana and Surinam), the whole of Central and South America fell under the rule of either Spain or Portugal. Among the most significant consequences were the early development of commercial exploitation, the adoption of Portuguese in Brazil and Spanish elsewhere as common languages, the ascendancy of the Catholic Church, and the reproduction throughout the region of élitist and absolutist conceptions of social organisation and rule. Overriding all these in importance, however, was the early departure of the Spanish and Portuguese. The early mercantile development of Spain and Portugal had given them an initial advantage over other European powers in the area of trade and colonisation, but by the end of the eighteenth century the combined effect of economic backwardness and military overextension, resulting from the dogged attempt to sustain the Hapsburg empire across Europe, had greatly weakened Spain, while the extent of Portugal's overseas empire masked a chronic weakness at home. In the later eighteenth century, both Spain and Portugal were seeking to reorganise the administration and exploitation of their colonial possessions, but in the period of the Napoleonic Wars both countries suffered occupation and invasion, the temporary triumph of the Liberals over the monarchy, and the loss of their American possessions. In the case of the Spanish possessions, the four separate vice-royalties of the late colonial period split further to produce fourteen independent states by the 1830s; in the case of Brazil the flight of the Portuguese royal family to Rio de Janeiro in 1807 and the subsequent declaration of Brazilian independence by the Portuguese prince Pedro I in 1822 were factors in the survival of the territory as a single independent state. The overall impact of early independence was the establishment, across the Atlantic from Europe, of a new group of distant, relatively impoverished and underpopulated states, just at the moment that the industrial revolution was gathering pace. For fifty years (during which momentous changes took place in Europe), the primary concern in the majority of these states was the restoration of order and authority in the wake of wars which began over the issue of independence, and continued as the succession to power was disputed. Across most of the continent the resulting destruction (along with the disruption of colonial patterns of production and trade) undid much of the relatively modest economic development achieved during the colonial period. Where a relatively rapid and peaceful transition to independence and stability was achieved, as in Chile and Brazil, the new élites (generally based upon the land) saw the rapid development of the export economy as the key to prosperity. Nowhere could a pattern of industrial revolution parallel to that under way in Europe be set in motion, and early experiments with protectionism were soon abandoned.

The unique combination of early and uninterrupted political independence and early and substantial incorporation into the international capitalist economy, through the production and export of primary commodities, gives Latin American political development its distinctive character within the Third World. The development of the region under independent political rule as a supplier of primary commodities was part of a single global process dominated successively by the rise of Great Britain to industrial pre-eminence, rivalry between the leading capitalist economies from the late nineteenth century on, two World Wars centred on Europe on either side of a prolonged depression, and the subsequent emergence of the United States in a position of unrivalled supremacy within the capitalist world. Naturally, no understanding of Latin America or the development of the Third World in general can be gained without reference to that global process. At the same time, the complementary development of each region has its own complex internal dynamic. In the case of Latin America, where some of the complicating factors present elsewhere – ethnicity, tribalism, religious conflict, Great Power rivalry and colonial rule in the modern period – were weak or absent, this internal dynamic arose primarily out of the secular struggle during the process of export-led development between the different class forces which it spawned.

In Western Europe the process of rapid industrialisation weakened the formerly dominant landed élites, generally absorbing them or subordinating them in one way or another to the rising industrial bourgeoisie. The complementary process of export-led development (experienced to one degree or another throughout the Third World, but most strongly in Latin America) gave new strength to revitalised landed classes. The first problem they faced was to restore order and reassert their authority in the wake of the gaining of independence. The second was to organise production for export. Even where order was rapidly restored, there were great discontinuities with the colonial period. The products which became the basis of expanded export economies in the nineteenth century were rarely the ones which had dominated colonial trade. Brazil's steadily declining mining economy was eclipsed by coffee and plantation labour; in Chile, a varied export structure of wheat, copper and silver was submerged after the War of the Pacific (1879–82) by the development of nitrate mining in the newly-acquired northern territories; Argentina, a poorly-developed source of hides, tallow and other products of a primitive free-ranging cattle economy at the end of the colonial period, eventually prospered as a result of the highly organised production of wheat and beef; Uruguay developed a modern and prosperous wool industry which displaced a poorly-organised cattle-ranching economy. In each of these cases the development of new products in new areas meant the rise of new élites, and necessitated the forging of alliances in which previous élite groups were either divided, incorporated, or deposed. As the types of production undertaken varied, so did the relations of production involved. For example, the development of coastal plantation agriculture in Ecuador (for cocoa) and Peru (for sugar and cotton) made coastal entrepreneurs dependent upon reserves of labour in the highlands, while the continued reliance in Brazil upon slavery made the powerful coffee élites of the centre-south dependent upon the support of the sugar barons of the north east, for without it the monarchy and the system of slave labour it upheld could not have been maintained. One consequence in Brazil (which persisted after the end of slavery in 1888 and the fall of the monarchy in 1889) was the sharing of national power between a number of regional élites, reflected in the adoption of a federal system in 1891. In contrast, the absence of major centres of regional power in Argentina after independence allowed an early process of centralisation, leading to the unchallenged supremacy of Buenos Aires and the cattle and wheat economy by the end of the nineteenth century.

Although the general picture across Latin America was the emergence of powerful groups associated with new or expanded export sectors, there were considerable regional differences. The greatest of them was between land-based export sectors on the one hand and mineral-based sectors on the other. Where the export products came from the land, élites combined economic and political power. Where export-led development was based primarily on minerals – as in Chile, in Mexico, and in Venezuela after the belated discovery of petroleum – élites tended to preserve power by acting as allies of foreign investors, rather than by taking direct control of the export sectors. A second consequence of this pattern of development in Chile and Venezuela, of considerable significance later, was the relative backwardness of agriculture, neglected in view of the flow of foreign exchange from the exploitation of minerals.

For a period, export-led development brought relative peace, stability and prosperity to Latin America. But it did so at the cost of introducing a pattern of development which had serious internal and external drawbacks. Internally, it condemned the majority of the population to a level of exploitation which threatened stability in the longer term. This was particularly so where the most dynamic expansion was taking place. The expansion of the export sector frequently meant the destruction of peasant communities as the land was taken over by large-scale commercial agriculture, or the imposition of harsh regimes in mining camps drawing their labour from displaced peasantries. Externally, it meant the entrenchment everywhere of a pattern of development complementary to (and dependent upon) the industrial development of Western Europe and the United States. The problems arising out of the internal tensions generated were seen most dramatically in the Mexican revolution in 1910, in which some two decades of intermittent warfare saw first the overthrow of the old élite based upon the Diaz dictatorship, and (at a cost of over a million lives) the victory of a newly consolidated northern bourgeoisie over the peasant armies of Emiliano Zapata and Francisco 'Pancho' Villa. Similar tensions (though on a less dramatic scale) were everywhere apparent after the First World War, which disrupted patterns of trade and growth, and provoked considerable unrest. Rising urban middle-class groups were assimilated in Argentina, and were challenging for power elsewhere, when the external dependence of the export economies was ruthlessly exposed in the wake of the 'crash' of 1929 and the ensuing depression. After 1930 the export-based economies and the ruling groups they had sustained could not be put back together again. The dividing line which came in Africa with decolonisation, in Asia with the ending of the Second World War and in the Middle East with the withdrawal of the European powers from direct control, came in Latin America with the collapse of the export economies in 1930.

The high hopes for steady economic growth and progress towards democracy which had been nurtured as export-led development proceeded were shown after 1930 to have been based upon an illusion. The depression not only revealed the shortcomings of the previous model of growth, it also left Latin American states ill-prepared to play a more active role in charting a new economic course. And by pulling down one set of political systems before export-led growth had matured sufficiently to provide the basis for another, it launched the region into half a century of political instability in which democracy would be precarious where it survived at all.

5. The Middle East: from empires to states

The contemporary Middle East emerged from the Ottoman Empire after the First World War when the mandatory system was established and the states of the area took their current form. The social and economic structures of the independent countries were formed through a lengthy process of change in the nineteenth century, as the Empire crumbled, and through the impact of the mandatory form of government, a disguised and short-lived colonialism. Of the Arab states, the Arabian peninsula and North Yemen remained free of imperial and colonial rule, the Gulf states had British advisers but not direct rule, and Iran (or Persia, as it was sometimes called) was an Empire in its own right. The Ottoman Empire extended across the Middle East to the Persian Empire in the east, to Ethiopia and Sudan in East Africa, into the Balkans and across North Africa. It was based on tributary relations rather than fixed territorial unity, with tribal leaders, provincial governors and military commanders paying regular tribute to Istanbul, the centre of the Empire and seat of the Ottoman sultans. Pre-colonial society had elements of both hierarchical and communal organisation. The heads of villages, pastoralist clans, and urban craft and merchant guilds were in principle responsible to the local representatives of the Ottoman state but frequently unresponsive to the demand for tax and dues.

In the nineteenth century, European expansion transformed the nature, territorial extent, political form and economic base of the tributary state (see Map 4). Balkan nationalism and constant military pressure from Russia, the recipient of new western technology, had cut off one of the main sources of Ottoman military strength – the levy of slaves from the Caucasus who were converted to Islam and trained to serve the Ottoman dynasty as soldiers, governors and bureaucrats. Originally they were insulated from society and owed allegiance to the state, and the demise of the institution had a weakening effect on the army in particular. The spread of Western trading companies and the establishment of European colonial rule in Africa eroded the grip of Middle Eastern merchants on long distance commerce across this trading cross-roads of the world. Furthermore, traditional craft and manufacture were hit by the influx of goods from the rapidly industrialising West. These developments seriously weakened the economic base of the state, and consequently its capacity to combat external military pressure and centrifugal forces organised around provincial military commanders, local governors with dynastic ambitions and well-armed tribal groupings. At the beginning of the nineteenth century Muhammad Ali asserted his autonomy in Egypt, and most of North Africa was effectively controlled by ruling families from the local Ottoman military and administrative establishment. These autonomies not only reduced the territorial extent of the Empire but also further eroded its financial base through the denial of tribute.

During the nineteenth century, the Ottoman Empire, and formally component parts like Egypt, attempted to restructure

43

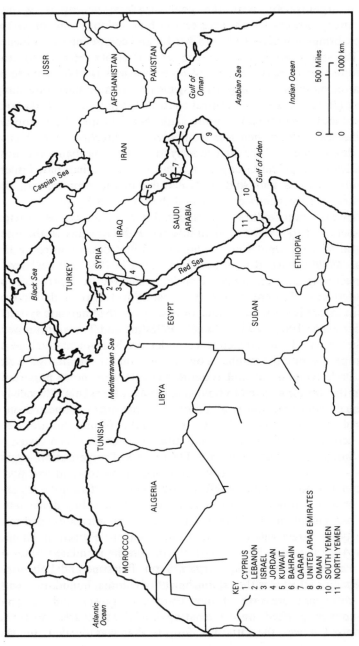

Map 4 *The Middle East*

KEY
1 CYPRUS
2 LEBANON
3 ISRAEL
4 JORDAN
5 KUWAIT
6 BAHRAIN
7 QARAR
8 UNITED ARAB EMIRATES
9 OMAN
10 SOUTH YEMEN
11 NORTH YEMEN

state organisation with the goal of strengthening it against predatory powers which were establishing colonies and protectorates, bringing settlers to North Africa, and competing for influence in Palestine and Lebanon. The reform effort began with the introduction of educational and legal measures for the purpose of creating modern armies, generating greater revenue and establishing more efficient systems of central control. Despite these efforts both Egypt and the Ottoman Empire sank into debt and the European embassies changed their role from advice to direction. In each case the development of private property in land was probably the most politically significant long-term change, with urban-based merchants, officials and soldiers benefiting in the Empire, and the members of the ruling dynasty and their allies in Egypt.

Egyptian indebtedness and nationalist rebellion against foreign advisers and the later Ottoman alliance with Germany in the First World War, brought France and Britain into direct control in the Arab Middle East. Britain occupied Egypt in 1882 and declared a Protectorate, and Britain and France divided the Arab provinces of the Ottoman Empire during the First World War, a division of spoils recognised by the League of Nations as the 'mandate system', under which Iraq, Syria, Lebanon, Palestine and Transjordan were to be prepared for independence under the benevolent tutelage of Europe. Despite the emphasis on preparation for eventual self-rule, the underlying social and economic effects were more important than the 'training' given to politicians and civil servants. The newly-created states (previously a collection of provinces connected only by rule from Istanbul and a dominant Arabo–Islamic culture) were the heirs to massive areas of land, title to which had been vested in the Sultan or the Ottoman state. The process of privatisation, begun in the mid-nineteenth century, continued in the colonial and post-colonial periods, to the benefit of tribal chiefs, urban notables and merchants, top bureaucrats and members of the ruling dynasties.

Colonial rule in the Middle East and North Africa divided into two types: direct rule by Italy in Libya and the French in Tunisia and Algeria, and indirect rule in Egypt and the mandated states of the Fertile Crescent (Iraq, Jordan, Syria, Palestine and Lebanon). One major effect was the establishment of colonial boundaries, with the attendant creation of new centres of power and national economies grafted on to existing social structures. For the colonised it was the Ottoman Empire that was divided; for the incipient Arab nationalist movement it was the Arab nation. Nationalities were left straddling boundaries: the Kurds were divided between Iraq, Iran and Turkey; in Lebanon, Arab Sunni Muslims were attached to Mount Lebanon's multiplicity of Christian and Muslim sects; and pastoral nomads accustomed to shifting across the deserts of the Middle East were entrapped within new state boundaries, and found traditional trading routes like those of Mosul–Aleppo and Damascus–Baghdad increasingly disrupted. Egypt (with its longer history as a political entity) was less affected in this respect by the coming of colonial rule.

More broadly, the colonial period hastened the integration of the states of the region into the international economy, subjugating them economically to the coloniser. Dependency was created not only by the export of a single product (cotton from Egypt, oil from Iraq, phosphates from Tunisia and Morocco, wine from Algeria) but also by the direct grip of Western trading companies on these key exports. Prices were determined by Western market forces, over which the local producer had no control. In a bid to break this economic stranglehold some of the largest landowners and nationalists in Egypt organised the independent Misr Bank and attempted to use it as a vehicle for indigenous industrialisation.

The colonial state established the social basis for the post-colonial regimes. The monarchies of Jordan and Iraq were created by the British, and urban notables, former Ottoman officers and the leading families of the tribes, already converted into large landowners, were recruited into the 'façade' of political institutions. One further effect of the colonial period was the strengthening of the state. Armies, ministries, police and local government were established, along with an educational system to supply the necessary personnel, although the poverty of these societies typically limited access to the educational system to areas surrounding the urban centres. The expansion of the state carried with it a political thrust to erode the autonomy of village heads and tribal leaders. Police posts, the standing army and the secular judiciary impinged on customary tribal authority and the authority and status of the Muslim religious men, while the village primary school teacher threatened the values, status and financial position of the traditional village teacher of the Koran. The salience of agriculture in the economy, limited industrialisation, and the lack of absorptive capacity in other spheres tied the graduates from educational institutions to a career within the state apparatus, either the army or the bureaucracy. At the same time the political power of the landed and mercantile sectors blocked the extraction of state revenue from agriculture: those who became salaried officials were better off than the peasantry and landless, but considerably worse off than the large landed and merchant families.

In certain cases, particular combinations of social forces enabled autonomy from the state to be perpetuated. In Iraq, alignment with central politicians and strong representation within parliament secured the local political power of tribal leaders and their interests in land: they had their own armed bodyguards and exercised judicial authority over their tribesmen through the Tribal Disputes Regulation. In Lebanon, the rural *zu'ama* (*s. za'im*: landowners and local leaders) combined with import–export merchants and Beirut financiers to establish a state which was powerless. Most Lebanese provided votes for the *zu'ama*, who gave services and protection in return. In Syria and Egypt, the landowners predominated. In Egypt, geography and history combined to diminish the power of provincial autonomies: the peasantry was highly concentrated along the Nile, organised for production for the market and ethnically homogeneous. In Syria, as in Lebanon and Iraq, however, minority sects and ethnic groups lived in mountainous zones and followed cultural imperatives (deriving from a history of persecution) to maintain solidarities against an expanding state.

One general pattern, then, was the dominance of landlords within a new context of parliaments and cabinets which helped to preserve and expand their power. The social base of the new regimes brought about major political conflicts in the post-colonial period. Landlords with massive concentrations of land determined policy, one consequence being very limited industrialisation. The establishment of the state apparatus, the expansion of schools, the creation of a small working class and the burgeoning numbers of landless in the rural areas provided counter-forces to the domination of the landed. Entrants to educational institutions found graduating difficult, and opportunities for employment limited, while the primitive conditions of the small working class enhanced the appeal of the Middle Eastern Communist parties. Landless labourers and poor peasants (many previously owners of land) migrated to the towns, where they eked out a living in the margins of urban life, selling chewing gum, biros or cigarettes. With students, they became the nucleus of the urban demonstrations mobilised by various socialist and nationalist parties and organisations. These general social and economic divisions were cut across by religious and ethnic politics, and complicated by colonial practice, as two examples will illustrate.

In the **Lebanon**, the initial alliances made by the French had enduring consequences. During the nineteenth century, the Maronites of Mount Lebanon were the beneficiaries of the development of Beirut as a port and the related expansion of mulberry bushes and silkworm-rearing. Although the largest factories were initially French-owned, by the 1860s silk was an important source of wealth for merchant families and peasant-workers. The factories employed women and it was apparently easier for Maronite than Muslim women to work in them. With mulberry growing in peasant hands, a relatively wealthy peasantry emerged, and overthrew the traditional feudal system in a communal uprising in 1859–60. A second set of developments concerned education. The Maronite church was linked to Rome, and Protestant evangelisation between 1810 and 1830 stimulated a response from French Roman Catholic missions. Consequently by the time of the French mandate the Christian communities (Greek Orthodox, Greek Catholic and Maronite) had far higher levels of education and modern skills than other communities. Colonial competition, trade and the disintegration of the Ottoman Empire through the nineteenth century furthered the differentiation of communities although certain leading families of the Druze and Sunni Muslim communities were also beneficiaries of mission education and economic development. The establishment of the French mandate further enhanced the general position of the French Catholic-educated Maronite community. Despite tensions between Maronite Lebanese nationalists and the French authorities, when the Maronite heartland of Mount Lebanon was united with the Sunni coastal towns and the Shi'a Beqa valley the political institutions of presidency and confessional parliamentarianism (fixed quotas of representation for each sub-sect of the community) ensured a dominant political role for Christians in general, and Maronites in particular.

In **Iraq**, members of the heterodox Shi'a community had not been appointed to positions in the Ottoman bureaucracy nor recruited to military schools because of the intolerance of the orthodox Sunni Empire. As a result, the level of secular education among the Shi'i was generally lower than in the Sunni community. When the British established the Iraqi mandate the Shi'i were rarely recruited into the new state institutions. Landlords in both communities were supported, but while Sunni Arab nationalists were branded as 'extremists' by the British authorities, Shi'a nationalists were even more prejudicially tagged as 'fanatics'.

However, the spread of colonialism was not complete. The multi-ethnic empire of **Iran** was never directly colonised, although it had a lengthy history of foreign interference and periods of military occupation. Until the middle of the nineteenth century its tribes, villages and towns were relatively isolated from each other and, because the Qajar dynasty failed to establish a centralised bureaucracy, they had a high degree of administrative autonomy. The Qajar shahs had no standing army, and depended for coercive power on tribal levies, who owed more allegiance to their tribal leaders than to the rulers. Royal power inhered in the ability of the shah to manipulate and mediate between the different segments of Iranian society. Military defeats and humiliating treaties forced the shahs to grant economic concessions to foreign commercial concerns (one, the grant of a 50-year monopoly to the British Major Talbot to distribute and export Iran's tobacco, in return for a personal gift of £25 000 for the Shah and a 25 per cent share of profits for the state, caused an uprising), and toward the end of the century the dynasty was increasingly squeezed between foreign powers and companies and the traditional commercial and trading classes. The new intelligentsia created through the impact of the West was animated by secular ideas but alienated from the Qajars because of the subservience of the latter to Western interests. These two forces – the merchants and the intelligentsia – played an important role in the 1905–9 Constitutional Revolution, during which Iran was effectively partitioned into two zones of influence by the Anglo–Russian Agreement of 1907, with the Shah left a swathe of territory in the centre; in 1911 Britain and Russia occupied the country. In 1926 the Iranian state asserted itself through the person of Reza Khan, a colonel in the Russian-officered Cossack brigade, who became Shah, founded the Pahlavi dynasty, and set about establishing a strong centralised state based on a standing army and a modern bureaucracy. He introduced secular reforms in law and education and launched a programme, funded by increased oil revenues, to modernise the economy.

Britain and Russia invaded again in 1941, removed Reza Shah because of his pro-German sympathies, and remained in occupation until after the war. Reza Shah was then replaced by his son, Mohammed Reza Pahlavi. If the legacy of Reza Shah was a stronger, centralised state, the legacy of foreign intervention was an anti-Western nationalism (at times dormant) which unified the broad range of Iranian classes.

The creation of a pro-Western regime in Iran was echoed in the general policy pursued where mandate powers were granted in the Middle East. Where they could, the mandate rulers granted independence to successor regimes based on conservative élites, generally highly restricted constitutional monarchies. Iraq under King Faisal (1932), Egypt under King Farouk (1937), and Libya under King Idris (1951) are examples of this practice. Subsequent revolutions, in 1952 in Egypt, in 1958 in Iraq, and in 1969 in Libya, overthrew the monarchies and brought regimes hostile to Western influence to power.

Finally, the relationship between Islam and nationalist responses to the spread of imperialism and foreign influence demands particular attention. The Turkish, Arab and Iranian nationalisms which developed during the late nineteenth and twentieth centuries never wholly obliterated the appeal of Islam. Indeed, as a more secular set of nationalisms developed, nationalists frequently drew on Islam as a source of cultural authenticity to oppose an encroaching West, which had inflicted military defeat, debt and, finally, the humiliation of direct political control. This was a massive reversal of history for peoples proud of their past and the achievements of successive Islamic empires. Of the wide range of remedies which were sought, the most popular were those which drew on solidarities of the past to confront this shift from victor to vanquished. Muslim fundamentalism and Islamic modernism, secular Arab and Iranian nationalism and a less coherent but nevertheless popular entwining of nationalisms and Islam can (and do) mobilise the populations of the Middle East. Such consciousness of the past, both national and religious (even when manipulated by political leaders), has been a significant factor in limiting the level of cultural penetration by the West. The contemporary power of these indigenous sources of political mobilisation was very evident in the combination of Islam and nationalism which overthrew the Shah of Iran in 1979.

6. Conclusion

As this review shows, the history of the emergence of the contemporary Third World is extremely varied and complex. While it makes sense in some ways to see it as a single global process, this should not obliterate the specificity of that process in each region and each country. Even when particular processes may be considered to be global in scale, they translate at local level into very different outcomes as a consequence of differences in intensity and timing, and interaction with different constellations of local factors. Given this inescapable complexity, the focus on four contrasting regions provides a useful starting point, making comparison possible without descending so far into minute local detail as to make it impossible to grasp the broader significance of events.

Our survey suggests that three issues have to be distinguished for analytical purposes, even though they are closely entwined in practice. These are the development of a global economy, inter-state rivalry, and the particular historical phenomenon of colonial rule. In each of the regions studied, the balance between these elements has been different; and variety in (and between) each region in matters such as natural resource endowment, climate, demography, and previous economic, social and political history also generates widely varying outcomes. In the end, there is no substitute for a detailed and intimate knowledge of such matters. What we attempt here is a preparatory survey, the first essential of which is to recognise that we are concerned with a single complex historical process. The shaping of the Third World is part of the same story as the shaping of the modern industrialised world. This does not mean that every development in the regions we study should be seen as being imposed from outside. However, due weight must be given to external military, technological, economic and political factors. The central process involved is the emergence of a vigorous and dynamic international capitalist economy and the spread of its effects outwards from a core in Western Europe (and later the United States and Japan). Although the pattern of conflict between states is partly an outcome of this process, it has had a dynamic of its own which cannot be discounted; and although direct colonial rule has in one sense only been a specific outcome in certain parts of the world of these other broader processes, its impact has been such that it merits separate treatment.

The relationships between direct colonial rule, incorporation into the global economy and involvement in conflicts between the great powers vary considerably from region to region, but are linked by a common logic. In the crucial formative period between 1860 and 1914 the republics of Latin America, freed from Spanish and Portuguese rule a generation earlier, yet lying outside the major theatres of great power presence and rivalry, turned to export-oriented development under new and generally land-based élites who were able to preserve their political independence, along with direct control of the state. In East and Southeast Asia, where the leading European powers had maintained a long competitive presence, rivalry after the Napoleonic Wars led to the expansion and modernisation of colonial rule, along with rapid development of new export sectors. Thus export-led development proceeded in Latin America in the absence of colonial rule, and in East and Southeast Asia through its intensification. In the 1880s Africa was subjected to a new wave of competitive colonisation, involving among others states, such as Germany, in the early stages of capitalist modernisation. Here, though, great power rivalry and the search for markets dominated, and the link with intensified production for export was not so immediate. By the turn of the century a challenge to European global domination appeared, from Japan in East Asia and the Pacific, and the United States in the Pacific and the Caribbean. And throughout the period, the slow sinking of Egypt and the Ottoman Empire into debt made space for the first European incursions in the Middle East, but kept thorough-going colonisation at bay. It also fostered the expansion of private property in land, paving the way for the emergence of great landed proprietors. Against this varied background, successive global events in the twentieth century produced waves of change. The First World War brought the end of the Ottoman Empire, and under mandate rule the strengthening of new landed élites throughout the region continued, to conclude with a general, though not universally successful, effort to establish 'traditional' (often newly-minted) monarchies to which power could be handed. The 1929 crash and ensuing reorganisation of the international economic system brought down the political regimes established in the era of export-led development in Latin America, bringing some of the first 'Third World nationalists' to power. The Second World War destabilised colonial rule everywhere, bringing about a decisive shift in Asia as a consequence of Japanese expansion and defeat, swiftly followed by Indian independence and the Chinese revolution. The Dutch accepted defeat in Indonesia in 1949. The French left Indochina in 1954, leaving behind a divided Vietnam. The British left Burma in 1948, and Malaya in 1957 (with an enlarged Malaysia created in 1963, including parts of Borneo, and Singapore, which left in 1965 to become an independent city state). The immediate effects of the war also extended to the Middle East, where Lebanon and Syria came under Free French control in 1941, and won independence in 1946. Third World nationalism spread on a number of fronts in the 1950s, with anti-colonial wars against France in Indochina and Algeria, a major First World–Third World confrontation over Suez in 1956, and the overthrow of pro-Western monarchical regimes in the Middle East. As the era of colonialism moved to its conclusion, a hasty transfer of power took place across Africa, largely to new élites which had emerged in the colonial period itself.

If one of the remarkable features of colonial rule has been the achievement of large effects from the deployment of small resources, this is partly because it has been just one local manifestation of the broader global processes of change discussed above. Colonial rulers have never lacked allies, from the first Spanish incursions into the Americas to the mandate period in the Middle East. In large part, these allies have been conservative, but perhaps the most striking testimony to the power of the forces driving the process forward is the imprint of the colonial legacy on its fiercest and most radical opponents. The opponents of colonial rule in Africa were for the most part the direct products of colonial penetration and rule in its political and economic manifestations, and they sought not to destroy but to take over the new regimes. In general, there has been no going back from colonial rule to an earlier age. The same is true for Latin America, where in many countries much of the population is European in origin. Latin American political traditions and aspirations are thoroughly Western; liberal democracy has not fared well, but it remains the central point of reference. In Africa, where competitive democratic regimes did not generally long survive independence, they had not long preceded it either, and the types of regime consolidated in the post-colonial period bear a close enough resemblance to colonial systems of rule to suggest a degree of continuity. Colonial rule was not liberal-democratic, and if liberal democracy has not flourished in Africa it is more, in most states, because it was not planted or tended than because it has been violently uprooted since independence. In East and Southeast Asia too, modern forms of government often bear a strong colonial imprint. In contemporary South Korea and Taiwan, for example, the influence of Japanese institutional practice is stronger than previous indigenous traditions, while in Southeast Asia the tendency has been for indigenous practices and institutions to survive far more strongly through to the present, but to reflect at the same time the influence of lengthy but less transformative colonial rule.

In a sense, too, the legacy of colonialism goes deeper still. In the cases of Siam and Iran, for example, imperialist intervention gave rise to a process of internal modernisation which created regimes strong enough to reach an accommodation which preserved national independence. It also led to a domestic process of militarisation and authoritarian rule. And, as Reza Khan discovered in 1941, it laid down a rule for survival which was to be confirmed repeatedly in the future: friendly authoritarian regimes will be backed, often unconditionally, whereas regimes hostile to the West, however anti-authoritarian, will be subjected to remorseless attack.

The 'colonial legacy' is strongest, then, where it has been carried forward or absorbed by its adherents and its opponents alike, taking on a momentum of its own beyond the immediate intentions and goals of the colonisers themselves. Much of the instability of the contemporary Third World can be traced back directly to periods and practices of colonial rule. Contemporary problems are often the unforeseen outcome in the longer term of short-term solutions to immediate challenges. The French authorities who introduced silk farming into the Maronite areas of Mount Lebanon did not intend to bring about the conflicts that have engulfed the area since the middle 1970s, any more than the British authorities who shipped hundreds of thousands of Tamil labourers to Malaya, Ceylon, and further afield, or devised indirect rule as a means of governing in Africa, intended to make the regions concerned ungovernable after independence. But the connections are there. It is a mistake to attribute too great a capacity to bring about particular ends to any actor in the Third World, but it remains the case that colonial rule and other aspects of Western intervention left a legacy which contributed to later instability. This arose in large part out of the contradictions between the conscious strategies of the European nations and their citizens, and the dynamic economic forces which they represented and carried with them. Marx drew attention well over a century ago to the 'progressive' side of capitalism and even of colonial rule, and there have been dynamic forces at work whose effects have ranged far beyond the intentions of their human agents. But at the same time the social and political strategies of colonial rulers and of entrepreneurs, merchants and traders abroad have been divisive and deeply conservative. While colonial rulers and the advanced guards of Western industrial society introduced progressive forces into the Third World, they also created divisions and conservative alliances which made the effects of those forces anything but progressive – the satisfaction of their own interests depended upon their doing so. In Latin America conservative landowning groups were strengthened in the course of the nineteenth century, often as a result of direct alliances with foreign interests; in Africa, some of the colonial authorities looked to amenable traditional rulers and, in settler communities, to minorities to shore up their control; in the Middle East selective support was given to chosen minorities, and a decaying landowning class was resuscitated as a suitable instrument for the purposes of the mandate powers; similarly conservative alliances were constructed in Southeast Asia. Only in East Asia did successive external interventions occur in such a way as to weaken the grip of traditional power-holders, again with significant consequences for the future. Turmoil in the Lebanon, instability in Nigeria, Malaysia and Sri Lanka, revolution in Algeria and Iran and even rapid economic development in Korea and Taiwan are not simply unpredictable long-term consequences of humdrum decisions made by harassed and pragmatic officials, merchants and adventurers abroad. A deeper logic underlies them, which can be traced ultimately to interactions between the global dynamism of expanding capitalism, the attempts of particular individuals, groups and nations to control, direct and benefit from it, and the conflicts which these processes generated.

Further Reading

Wolf [1982] is a superb introduction to the broad sweep of European expansion. For Africa, Oliver and Fage [1962] is a useful short history; Iliffe [1983] discusses the emergence of capitalism; Brett [1973] is a thought-provoking study of colonial rule in the inter-war period; Gifford and Louis [1982] and Hargreaves [1988] offer accounts of post-war colonial rule and decolonisation. Hodgkin [1956] is still valuable as an account of nationalism in the colonial period. Collier [1982] is a good comparative essay on post-independence political development. Hall [1981] is a standard history of Southeast Asia; Pluvier [1974] gives a general account of decolonisation. These sources should be supplemented with Henderson [1968] for Korea, and Sutter [1988] for Taiwan. For Latin America Lockhart and Schwartz [1983] surveys the colonial period, Lynch [1973] covers the independence period, and Albert [1983] discusses export-led development up to 1930. Collier and Collier [1991] attempts a theoretical and historical analysis of political development in twentieth century Latin America, and includes masses of detail in the process. For the Middle East Hudson [1978] is a good general account, and Owen [1981] covers economic developments up to the First World War. Ayubi [1991] offers a wide-ranging and informative discussion of the politics of Islam.

2
State and Society

1. Introduction

Whereas the Spanish and Portuguese colonies in Latin America had achieved political independence by 1830, the contemporary state system in Africa, East and Southeast Asia and the Middle East (with exceptions such as Ethiopia, Thailand and Egypt) is of relatively recent creation. In the post-Second World War period new state governments in these regions tackled the problem of welding together a variety of people who were at different stages of educational development, and divided along ethnic, regional and other cultural lines. In Latin America, relatively long-established states faced the challenge of responding to new demands arising out of the collapse of export-led development after 1930, and the political emergence of the middle and working classes. Spanish was the *lingua franca* of Latin America (outside Portuguese-speaking Brazil) and Roman Catholicism was the main religion. Most people in the Middle East were Arabic-speaking and predominantly Muslim. In East and Southeast Asia ethnically and linguistically homogenous societies such as Korea contrasted with plural societies such as Malaysia, Indonesia and the Philippines, which had been brought under a single state only as a consequence of colonial rule. Finally, Africans were divided by a myriad of vernacular languages and a colonial legacy of seven languages of European origin – Afrikaans, English, French, German, Italian, Portuguese and Spanish; the African people were Christians (Protestant and Catholic), Muslim and animist. Africa was also divided by artificial boundaries which resulted in the eventual creation of more than fifty states – more than twice the number in any other region; not surprisingly, some of the smallest of these

56

(such as the Gambia and Lesotho) were hardly viable. In addition to these regional variations, the social context within which the state operated changed as urbanisation, industrialisation, and the demand for educational and other services created new challenges and new social forces.

This chapter examines the relations between state and society in each of the four regions and explores the factors which make some states (such as Taiwan) strong and others (such as the Lebanon) weak. Among these factors are the length of time that the state has existed, its political heritage and institutions, its social complexity and economic base, the relationship between the state itself and leading social groups, and the nature of public recruitment and administration. The failure of programmes of national development involving substantial state intervention in large parts of the Third World has cast doubt in recent years upon the capacity of Third World states to do more than seek to ensure their own survival from day to day [Migdal, 1988]. Broadly speaking, a regional contrast can be drawn in this respect. African states have generally proved unable to secure either political stability or economic development; those of Latin America and the Middle East have enjoyed mixed fortunes; and those of Southeast and especially East Asia have proved most successful.

Political leaders in the Third World are subjected to powerful and often contradictory pressures. The machinery of state may be poorly developed, and only partially under their control. They may put the institutions and resources they do control to a variety of uses, ranging from the courting of powerful national and international allies or the fostering of a sense of national identity to the promotion of progressive social change or the strengthening of their own political bases and the advancement of their own interests by means of factional appeals. In some cases it may prove almost impossible for the state to establish any degree of authority at all; in others the potential for the accumulation of resources at the centre may lend itself either to the furthering by state action of the goals of identifiable social groups and coalitions, or to the pursuit of an agenda primarily of interest to the state and state officials themselves. Attention must be paid, therefore, not only to the degree to which the state has the capacity to achieve its goals (its strength or weakness, or the balance of power between the state and social groups), but also to the character of the techniques used to extend and consolidate state power, and the extent of overlap between the goals of the state and those of particular social groups. Consideration of these relationships raises a number of questions. Will the socially homogeneous state necessarily be stronger than the state which is socially pluralistic? Is there a direct correlation between social sophistication and state stability? How far do horizontal (class) and vertical (ethnic, communal, religious, linguistic, or regional) divisions in society explain political behaviour in each region? Why do politicians recruit support on a class basis in some states, but not in others? Where they do not, are they afraid that such an appeal will undermine their élite position, or are communalism, religious sectarianism and other vertical divisions in society simply more important than class? In Africa, the Middle East, and parts of Southeast Asia a significant role is played by communalism, and by competition between communal or sectional groups for a share of state resources. It is important to note, however, that though politicians may play upon the regional– linguistic, ethnic and religious identifications of their followers in order to gain support, their motivation may be self-interested, class- oriented and economic rather than primordial. In some cases, such as Iraq, one particular regional group has managed to seize and maintain control of the state by building upon such loyalties. Often, however, communal competition for scarce resources has escaped the control of political leaders, and produced a weak and over- extended state. In East Asia and in parts of Southeast Asia, in contrast, states pursuing capitalist development have been able to maintain a measure of ascendancy over foreign or domestic capitalist interests, enabling them to define national developmental goals and pursue them over long periods of time [Johnson, 1987: 156]. In Taiwan a strongly developmental state emerged on the basis of a new leadership transplanted from the mainland. In Indonesia and South Korea effective developmental states were eventually created after the failure of regimes, under Sukarno and Syngman Rhee respectively, which were quite different in their orientations to foreign and domestic élites, but equally unsuccessful in establishing their authority. These states have enjoyed a sufficient degree of autonomy to allow them to set goals and have them respected, while generally retaining the support of the business community. Else- where the separation between state and society has been so great that it has become a source of weakness and eventual collapse. In

Indochina in the 1960s, for example, reactions to a general tide of revolt against dominant classes and their foreign allies led to the emergence of states which were generally highly autonomous, but weak because they had no local social roots, and relied heavily on foreign support. Here, as in the Philippines under Marcos, autonomy did not bring the capacity to direct social change. On the contrary, leaders became so detached from existing social forces that they became isolated and eventually ineffective. In Latin America, where political conflict has revolved more around the need to create new coalitions to push forward development after the collapse of export-led development than around the need to consolidate newly independent states, such coalitions, developed around the state, have reflected class alliances rather than communal allegiances.

In each of our four regions we identify a 'patronage' kind of politics, whereby those in control of the state reward their supporters, and these supporters (the 'clients') themselves act as patrons to dependants at lower state levels. It has sometimes played an important part in the construction of dominant-class or cross-class alliances, but it can also be used as a weapon against the state, or as a means of building parasitic political machines which exploit state power to no social purpose. Although clientelism exists in all four regions, its social roots, institutional significance and political consequences differ. This raises two questions. Is patronage politics necessarily hostile to economic development, or to democracy? And how does it relate to the question of class? As we shall see, the role it plays varies, depending upon who controls it, and to what ends it is directed.

2. Africa: weak states under siege

The anti-colonial African nationalists achieved independence for their states within artificial, colonial-imposed boundaries. Some of these states (notably Sudan and Zaire) were immense in area, and Nigeria was huge in population, while others including the Gambia in West Africa, Rwanda and Burundi in East Africa, and Lesotho and Swaziland in southern Africa, were so small in both size and population as to be hardly viable as independent states. With the exception of Egypt (which for most purposes can be classified as part of the Middle East) and Ethiopia, the new states therefore lacked the deep historical roots of those in Latin America, and East and Southeast Asia. Several of them, however, including Dahomey (now Benin), Ghana and Nigeria in West Africa, contained within their borders what had once been powerful centralised kingdoms. The survival of a traditional unit such as Buganda within modern Uganda often fanned sub-national loyalties, while the absence of such loyalties facilitated (as in Tanganyika) the process of nation-building. However, sub-national loyalties might also flourish where, as among the Ibo in Eastern Nigeria and the Kikuyu in Kenya, there was no centralised traditional unit upon which they could build. In short, communalism in Africa took various forms and was widespread; it constituted a formidable challenge to the leaders of the newly independent states.

The new rulers – who had next to no experience of operating a governmental system on a national scale – adapted to their own purposes the structures of power established within the former colonial state. Their inheritance normally included the essential machinery of government (notably a legislature, executive and judiciary at the centre and – in Anglophone Africa above all – the rudiments of a representative local government system at the base). As noted in the previous chapter, adaptation generally proved easier in Francophone African states than in Anglophone states which initially adopted Westminster-type constitutions. However, within ten years at most of independence, the latter had been discarded in favour of executive presidential systems. Though Anglophone countries retained 'residual' legislatures and ministerial structures as a legacy of the colonial past, the one-party state became a well-nigh universal feature of the African scene. Nigeria was the most important exception to this pattern in the period before and after the first phase of military rule; it was also exceptional in its adoption of a federal constitution. Within this framework, the national president exercised extensive (and often dictatorial) powers.

Unfortunately, the new state rulers did not also inherit the state capacity needed to work either these institutions, or the new institutions (such as the large number of parastatal bodies) which they themselves created. Trained and experienced personnel were in short supply, and in some cases the shortage was critical. In Zambia (formerly Northern Rhodesia), at independence in 1964, few of the country's 109 African graduates possessed administrative experience at a senior level, and it was possible for a chief clerk to become a permanent secretary overnight. In Mozambique, the exodus of expatriate managers in 1974–5 and the dearth of Africans with management skills meant that the extensive measures of nationalisation undertaken by Samora Machel's government floundered, and flagging industrial output was not revived. This acute shortage was partly the result of the slowness with which African regimes had adopted Africanisation policies, and reflected above all the inadequacy (or sometimes the irrelevance) of colonial educational provision. In the Belgian Congo, for example, the primary educational net was spread very wide, but secondary and higher education was badly neglected – in 1960, when the Belgian Congo became the newly independent state of Congo–Leopoldville (now Zaire), there were only sixteen graduates in a population of over thirteen million. In Northern Rhodesia (which, like the Belgian Congo, had a large copper industry), next to no attention was given to technical education. In Portuguese Africa the record was abysmal: according to official government statistics, the illiteracy rate in 1959 (after some 500 years of Portuguese presence) was over 95 per cent in Mozambique, Angola and Guinea–Bissau, and nearly 80 per cent in Cape Verde.

Understandably, therefore, the governments of the independent African states gave education a high priority. In Zambia, educational expenditure rose from K13 million in 1963–4 to K85 million in 1973; primary education doubled during this period and secondary, technical and university education expanded even faster. In 1974 Tanzania, one of Africa's poorest countries, set the end of 1977 as the date for the achievement of universal primary education (UPE); though this target was not met, it was well within sight by the scheduled date. In Nigeria, educational objectives changed several times. At independence the emphasis was on secondary, tertiary and vocational rather than primary education. The number of universities increased from one (at Ibadan) before independence to thirteen by 1975 and twenty-one by 1985. During the 1970s the military (mainly for political reasons) shifted the emphasis to primary education; the enrolment of children was up from 3.5 million in 1970 to 13 million by 1980 [Stevens, 1984: 11]. While such educational measures (and corresponding initiatives in health and the other social services) were desirable in themselves, they were adopted at the expense of more directly productive, job-creating sectors. In view of the sharp downturn of their economies in recent years, most states have had to cut capital expenditure and have been unable to maintain high levels of recurrent expenditure on the social services generally.

This situation is serious because urban migration (already marked in the colonial period) proceeded apace after independence: in 1960 no tropical African city had a population of over one million; in 1985 there were 28 such cities. Today, the urban population of many states exceeds 40 per cent. The consequences of this urban drift are manifold. One is the reduction in the number of people to work the land, thus contributing to a fall in food production which, since 1975, has lagged behind population growth (about 3 per cent a year); moreover, it is a very young population – about half consists of children. Other consequences are urban problems of housing, sanitation and unemployment, and rising crime rates; and – through subsidies to keep the price of food and other produce artificially low – the distortion of government policy in favour of often politically volatile urban dwellers, at the expense of rural producers.

At independence most African states were still dependent for foreign exchange on agricultural or mineral exports. New state leaders, anxious to end their dependence on primary produce, sought to diversify their economies, with industrialisation as a favoured strategy. Unfortunately, the new manufacturing industries that were established in many states (mostly in the towns) tended to be capital-intensive and dependent on the importation of costly machinery from abroad; they therefore created only a limited number of jobs.

The severe developmental imbalances inherited by most states also persisted after independence: in Ghana, the Côte d'Ivoire, Nigeria and Uganda, for example, the contrast was sharp between the underdeveloped northern part of each country and the more prosperous south. In Namibia, socio-economic problems were compounded by the South African administration's policy of working through ten population groups in a bid to preserve white dominance, which had to a large extent served to direct inter-ethnic and intra-ethnic competition into racial channels. However, the diversion was never complete: the underlying conflict between the non-white groups remained, became evident in the 1989 campaign for elections to the Constituent Assembly, and was carried over into the post-independence period. Again, this conflict stemmed from a north–south divide – the imbalance between the populous, over-crowded and under-developed northern part of the country, inhabited by the Owambos (who had borne the brunt of the guerrilla war) and the more economically developed regions to the south. The Owambos continued to migrate southwards in large numbers, looking for work in the mining towns and Windhoek, the capital, where many of them eked out a precarious existence in insanitary compounds in Katutura township [Abdallah *et al.*, 1989: Chs. 2 & 3; Tordoff, 1992: 76–7].

In most African states, social conflict was expressed in terms (ethnic or regional–linguistic) which the people could understand and the political leaders could exploit; it was not only between one region and another, but was also evident within a particular region – in Zambia's Copperbelt Province, for example, the bustling Copperbelt towns were ringed by depressed rural areas. However, the real competition was over educational opportunity, jobs and government contracts, and the provision of roads, bridges and hospitals. Ethnic-linguistic or regional–linguistic competition also tended to obscure the growing importance of class inequalities in Africa. These had been slow to emerge: it was not until the first twenty to thirty years of this century that pioneer capitalism penetrated the rural areas of Africa on any scale [Molteno, 1974: Ch. 3; Iliffe, 1983]. Thereafter, it gained momentum: in the Gold Coast, for example, cocoa farmers purchased land in the Akwapim district, while further inland in Ashanti many of the early leading cocoa farmers were chiefs and rich merchants. Alongside such instances of rural capitalism, pre-capitalist relations often persisted, partly because land remained abundant and labour was still migratory over much of the continent (though not everywhere – Burundi, Ethiopia, Ghana, Kenya, Nigeria, Rwanda and Togo are countries with low per capita arable land and high population growth).

Despite isolated peasant protests (as in Buganda in the 1920s), there was little organised resistance to early African capitalism, one reason being the part played by religion (both indigenous and imported) in easing the transition. Cases in point were the Christian ministry which Albert Atcho, healer and entrepreneur, established in 1948 at Bregbo near Abidjan in the Côte d'Ivoire, and the work of the Mouride brotherhood of Senegal among their peanut-growing Wolof followers. In the subsequent period, thoroughgoing capitalism sometimes provoked a sharper response – as occurred in Kenya from 1952, Zanzibar in 1964, and Ethiopia in 1974, when southern tenants and labourers seized the land from their (predominantly) Amharic landlords. In Tanzania, government policies adopted in the wake of the Arusha Declaration of 1967 checked the spread of rural capitalism, but it made headway among (for example) big African cattle-owners in Botswana and large farmers in Zimbabwe.

From an early date, rural capitalists invested their profits in urban property. The post-1945 period, however, saw the burgeoning of African urban capitalism in its own right in a number of colonies. Following the achievement of political independence, the growth of manufacturing industry (mainly of an import substitution variety) was marked in most of the richer countries of tropical Africa, and was especially rapid in Nigeria during the oil-boom years of the 1970s. Most early manufacturing enterprises were started by foreign firms, which were already dominant in extractive industries. State participation became increasingly common from the mid-1960s as the new state governments sought to end or reduce foreign control of the economy. Prime examples were the Zambian government's assumption of majority ownership of Zambia's copper industry in 1969–70, and the Nigerian federal government's acquisition (on an incremental scale) of part ownership of the Nigerian operations of the foreign oil-producing companies in the 1970s. However, foreign control persisted: after as before 'nationalisation', foreign-based multi-national corporations (MNCs) were able to maintain their position by using a variety of devices, including transfer pricing, patents, and management and sale contracts. For some countries state participation was not a viable option: post-independence Namibia, for example, remained heavily dependent on three South African-dominated mining companies.

State participation in the economy was accompanied by the creation of a large number of semi-public ('parastatal') enterprises which were made responsible for running industrial ventures, either on their own account or jointly with foreign companies. The Nigerian National Oil Corporation (NNOC) was thus established in May 1971 to engage in all phases of the oil industry from exploration to marketing. Such parastatals mushroomed in all states, irrespective of their governments' ideological leanings, but had, for the most part, such a poor record of performance that many state governments adopted privatisation measures (with 'encouragement' from the IMF and World Bank). Virtually everywhere, the state has played a vital role in stimulating the growth of African capitalism, and the ruling élite has benefited enormously. This was revealed by experience in Zambia where the economic reforms of 1968–72 resulted in an enormous expansion of the parastatal sector (and therefore of the bureaucracy) and opened up massive new opportunities for citizen entrepreneurs. A substantial middle class emerged and the political members of it articulated class interests in their capacities as members of the bourgeoisie. However, they continued also to play upon regional–linguistic divisions (even in urban areas) in order to win popular support. Extrapolating from Zambian experience, we can say that in most of sub-Saharan Africa class consciousness is most highly developed among the emergent middle class and that the latter's advance has been fastest in urbanised and industrialised states which adopted a capitalist (or state capitalist) strategy of development. While class identifications have not yet emerged sufficiently to structure political conflict in most states, it is noteworthy that middle-class leaders have been in the forefront of recent moves to achieve political and economic democracy.

Africa's other identifiable classes are the peasantry and what may loosely be called the urban proletariat. Elements of the peasantry in individual states may well react to exploitation by urban élites by either ceasing to produce for the market or by smuggling their produce across the state borders (as Senegalese peanut-producing peasants did in 1969–70). However, they are too scattered and disunited a force to be able to organise and sustain concerted resistance; they tend to be divided by particularistic loyalties and do not yet see themselves as an obviously or directly exploited class. For their part, urban workers earn high wages by comparison with the great majority of the rural people, but often retain close social links with them. Despite a relatively high level of cohesion, organised labour has 'represented a reformist and economistic, rather than radical, voice' in most countries [Baylies and Szeftel, 1982: 212]. Among the reasons for this limited ability to show political solidarity as a class are the continuing practice of seasonal migration in many states and the prospect of upward mobility.

Moreover, the fact that factional politics have (as in Kenya) penetrated labour organisations and other modern interest groups also militates against the development of class consciousness. Predominantly in Africa, therefore, we are dealing with a kind of 'patronage politics', with economic resources used as political currency to enable the leadership to buy support for their policies. Patron–client linkages may reflect the intense communalism to which many states are subject; but they may also serve as a cement – the cement of material interest – holding a weak state together. They do not inhibit the process of class formation and, as far at least as the middle class is concerned, the process of class consolidation.

3. East and Southeast Asia: variations on state autonomy

The distinctive feature of state–society relations in East and Southeast Asia – a broad contrast with Africa which is as apparent in different ways in Indonesia and the Philippines as in Taiwan and the two Koreas – has been the ability of the state to raise itself as an independent force above social groups and classes. This capacity arises from a combination of historical circumstances: the dislocation which resulted from Japanese colonisation or occupation followed by expulsion; the subsequent pattern of competition between external powers; the extent of both revolutionary movements and authoritarian responses; and the weakness of landowners and capitalists, to say nothing of the working class, throughout most of the region. But relative state autonomy has not always meant state strength. In North Korea and Taiwan, in South Korea under Park, and in Indonesia's 'New Order', it produced states capable of directing economic development and controlling political activity over decades; in Indonesia under Sukarno, South Korea under Syngman Rhee, and the Philippines (as in Cambodia and South Vietnam under puppet presidents backed by the United States) it produced weak states unable to direct economic or political change.

State–society relations throughout the region reflect the outcome of attempted state-building emerging out of a context of class conflict, social revolution, and foreign intervention, explored here in studies of Taiwan, South Korea, Indonesia and the Philippines.

Successful revolution in China created as a by-product an author-itarian regime in Taiwan capable of very substantial reform and development; in Korea, intense social conflict and Western inter-vention created opposing revolutionary and counter-revolutionary states, the latter initially repressive, corrupt and incompetent. In Indonesia, an uprising against the reimposition of Dutch control produced in turn a weak parliamentary system, a radical nationalist regime under Sukarno, and a long-lasting authoritarian regime under Suharto, while in the Philippines the breakdown of the regime of conservative oligarchy was followed by the rise of the Marcos dictatorship. In each case external powers played significant roles, but the underlying dynamics came from indigenous sources.

The case of **Taiwan** represents an extreme example of the elevation of the state above society. As noted above, Chinese rule had been virtually nominal prior to Japanese control between 1895 and 1945. For all that the population was Chinese in origin (divided between the majority Fukien and minority Hakka, with only 1.5 per cent accounted for by the original Malay inhabitants), the restora-tion of Chinese rule in 1945 essentially imposed control by a foreign power. The initial placing of the island under military rule, the slaughter of most of the local political élite after the uprising of 1947, and the massive influx of mainlanders in 1949 (amounting to perhaps a quarter of the total population) created an entirely new state, and a largely new society. The state was literally imported from the mainland: soldiers, bureaucrats and politicians predomi-nated among the immigrants, and immediately took positions of authority.

A number of factors then reinforced the ascendancy of the state over society. The first was the security issue, arising out of the threat of invasion from the mainland, regional instability associated with the Korean and Vietnam Wars, and the insecurity generated by US rapprochement with China, leading to diplomatic recognition in 1979. This served to justify a large standing army and mass conscription, a continual state of martial law (temporary provi-sions introduced on the mainland before 1949 remained in force until replaced by a stringent National Security Law in 1987), and severe restrictions on labour organisation. Secondly, Chiang Kai-shek weakened local élites by adopting the comprehensive land reform he had never implemented on the mainland. Rent reduction, the sale of public lands, and the forced sale of private land to establish a maximum holding of just under three hectares of irrigated land made 60 per cent of rural residents owner-farmers by 1953, and provided the new regime with a base of support in the countryside.

Thirdly, the style and success of industrial development placed the state in a position of strong authority over local capital. The state-owned enterprises of the Japanese period initially remained in state hands (giving the government control over more than half of industry in the 1950s), and the initial policy of import-substituting industrialisation benefited those state industries and mainlander interests closely connected to the incoming regime. After 1959, when a shift to export promotion began and the economy was selectively opened to foreign capital, state intervention remained substantial, although now oriented to different ends. Of equal significance for relations between the state and domestic capital was the absence of large Taiwanese industrial concerns. In contrast to patterns of industrialisation in South Korea, the basic unit behind industrial growth in Taiwan was the small 'family' enterprise based upon the pooling of capital and direction of labour, the key feature of which is 'joint ownership of property by males in the group' [Sutter, 1988: 26–7]. Fourthly, the close relationship between the state and the ruling party, and the enduring control over the party and the political system by an ageing group of mainlanders (explored further in the following chapter), limited the scope for the political representation of indigenous interests. As a result, no local social class or political organisation could threaten the dominance of a remote and powerfully authoritarian state. The state and its allies from the mainland ruled over a numerous class of small and intensively competitive capitalists largely unrepresented in the political system, a working class subject to close supervision and denied the right to organise, and a peasantry practising increasingly intensive farming on small plots of land.

The case of the **Philippines** presents a striking contrast. The blend of formally democratic institutions under oligarchic control, and continued US authority after 1935 gave rise to an irresponsible political system dominated by factionalism and organised from top to bottom on the basis of patronage networks financed by sharing state funds among the political class. Japanese occupation sharpened divisions within the élite, while the popular war against it turned into a social movement against the landed oligarchy. The ability of the state to appeal to security issues after independence was limited by the lack of a credible external threat and by nationalist opposition to the subservience to US security interests represented by the Military Bases Agreement of 1947, which established the Clark and Subic Bay bases on Philippine territory. Despite land hunger, and peasant rebellion led by the Hukbalahap (originally the 'People's War Against Japan') in Central Luzon, the government turned its back on land reform, preserving the social ascendancy of landowners and further limiting its popular appeal. Free trade agreements with the United States and the placing of US and Filipino citizens on an equal legal footing limited the scope for state intervention to promote economic development, and the distribution of wealth and income remained grossly unequal.

By the time Ferdinand Marcos first won election in 1965, a weak state was confronting domestic élites themselves weakened by backward agriculture and industry. The patronage system was becoming a source of serious inter-élite conflict, while failing to stem rising rural and urban discontent. But after initial reformist rhetoric and selective reform, Marcos set out to extend the politics of patronage, bringing it under central control and making it the key feature of the regime, to the personal advantage of himself and his cronies. Whole sectors of the economy were handed over to key allies (sugar to Roberto Benedicto, the coconut industry to Eduardo Cojuangco and Juan Ponce Enrile), while government resources were diverted to fund vast patronage machines, notably the Ministry of Human Settlements run by Imelda Marcos from 1981. Backed consistently by the United States, Marcos bought himself re-election in 1969, established martial law in 1972 to avoid stepping down in 1973 as the constitution dictated, and maintained himself in power through a blend of corruption, manipulation, repression and murder until 1986. The regime was fabulously successful in amassing personal wealth for Marcos and his cronies, but incapable of achieving political legitimacy or economic development, because the national economy was undermined and devoured by the 'political economy of patrimonialism' [Wurfel, 1988: 258]. The Marcos regime became so detached from social forces and interests as to be a hyper-autonomous personal empire, as weak as the Taiwanese system was strong.

In North and **South Korea**, foreign intervention, social conflict and war stimulated the establishment of strongly authoritarian states. In each case, the effect of the Korean War (June 1950–July 1953) confirmed and strengthened the character of regimes which had already taken shape. In their occupation zone south of the 38th parallel, occupying US forces eventually repressed all popular movements pressing for reform, and built up Syngman Rhee and the anti-Communist right without regard for local preferences. At the same time they responded to reform north of the 38th parallel by cutting rents to a maximum one third of the crop, and selling formerly Japanese-owned land to tenants. Syngman Rhee, an exile in the United States since his release from prison in 1904, took power as President in 1948 as a virtual outsider, heavily dependent on the police force and the terrorist 'youth groups' created under US occupying forces; and his eventual (reluctant) decision to dispossess Korean landowners completed the ascendancy of the state over existing social classes. However, the highly centralised, repressive, corrupt and patronage-ridden regime he developed resembled that of the Philippines under Marcos more than that of Taiwan. The sweeping National Security Law of 1948 was used to purge the Assembly, the military, the press, and educational establishments, a process which intensified once war broke out between North and South. During and after the war suspected opponents of the regime were murdered wholesale, the assembly was cowed into ceding further powers to the virtually autocratic president, and the army was built up into a major power in the state. Even so, the regime remained prey to factionalism, and riddled with corruption. Vast amounts of US aid were used to favour its friends, while ministers (129 in thirteen years) were allowed to amass personal fortunes in their brief spells in office.

The collapse of Rhee's anachronistic regime in 1960, following massive student demonstrations in the wake of gross electoral fraud, was followed by a democratic interlude swiftly terminated by a military coup in May 1961. Its leader, General Park Chung Hee (1961–79), modernised and intensified the authoritarian character of the Syngman Rhee regime by disciplining new capitalist interests, and subjecting them to bureaucratic rather than personalistic control. Whereas Syngman Rhee had reverted to the politics of the Yi dynasty which exiled him, Park (a graduate of Japan's Manchurian War College in the early 1930s) practised the statism, developmentalism, anti-communism and contempt for civilian politicians learnt from Japan's imperial army. The state strongly supported capitalist development, but kept individual concerns at sufficient distance to allow it to direct and co-ordinate development, proving willing not only to repress emerging sources of opposition (initially largely confined to disenchanted students, with working class opposition late to develop), but also to impose its discipline on its own supporters. In sum, a weak autonomous state was replaced by a strong one.

A similar transition took place in **Indonesia**, against a background of far greater social and political heterogeneity. Java, Sumatra, and the remaining outer islands experienced divergent patterns of development and relations with the colonial state under Dutch rule, and moved further apart under Japanese occupation. The 1945 republic had little authority in Sumatra, and never controlled the outer islands, on which the Dutch set up the state of East Indonesia prior to attacking the republic in July 1947. Indigenous political forces were divided between Muslim associations, communists and nationalists, and along regional lines. They also split over collaboration, neutrality or opposition to Japanese rule, confrontation or negotiation with the Dutch, and differing responses to the social conflicts precipitated in the course of resistance to restored imperial control.

Building on the leadership role granted him under the Japanese, Sukarno sought to create a personalised and centralised authoritarian regime able to absorb all competing forces. Claiming to be 'a convinced Muslim, a convinced communist and a convinced nationalist', he promoted the doctrine of *Pancasila*, the 'five pillars' of Nationalism, Social Justice, Democracy, International Cooperation, and Belief in One God. He further supervised the writing in 1945 of a constitution establishing a unitary state headed by a president selected by an advisory council and empowered to veto the acts of the legislature. He then withstood the radical youth groups (*pemuda*) who led the insurrections against British and Dutch forces, a Communist-backed rebellion in Madiun (central Java), and capture by the Dutch, to keep the presidency after the negotiation of independence in 1949.

The outward appearance of strength was deceptive. The new state was bankrupt, and lacked an organised bureaucracy or military apparatus. While it faced few strong countervailing forces (landowners, weak under Dutch rule, were further weakened by peasant pressure between 1946 and 1948), it was competing with multiple unstable alternative centres of power. Sukarno was forced to accept a federal system (until 1950) and a parliamentary government under which the bureaucracy was colonised and expanded by competing parties, while local army commanders backed successive regional revolts. He responded by governing through an independent cabinet under a state of martial law from 1957, making an alliance with the army, restoring the 1945 constitution by decree in July 1959, and having himself made president for life under the system of 'Guided Democracy'.

This proved a half-way house to a stronger state of a quite different character. Based uneasily on the army, the Communist Party, and a hybrid parliament incorporating appointed 'functional groups', the regime became increasingly unstable. While the army monopolised key state resources and moved into more conservative national and international alliances, Sukarno sought to preserve his nationalist programme and personal ascendancy by extending his mass base. In the middle 1960s the regime collapsed under the weight of internal contradiction, economic crisis and radical mobilisation, to be replaced by a 'New Order' constructed by General Suharto, the head of the army's élite Strategic Reserve (*Kostrad*), who formally assumed the presidency in 1968 after two years of de facto authority.

The New Order 'is best understood as the resurrection of the state and its triumph *vis-à-vis* society and nation' [Anderson, 1983:487]. Suharto had made his whole career in the security apparatuses of the successive Dutch, Japanese and Indonesian states, and made the strengthening of the state his primary goal. The main obstacle to authoritarian state power – the Communist Party and associated urban and rural activism – was eliminated by a deliberate and sustained massacre between 1965 and 1966, and economic nationalism was abandoned in favour of close ties with the United States and foreign capital. Resulting flows of aid were used to cement the ascendancy of the state, and to create new economic conglomerates linking the politically weak Chinese community to regime insiders. Sukarno's 'functional groups' were expanded to give the regime a permanent appointed majority, and built into a tightly controlled state party, *Golkar*, dominated by members of the bureaucracy; opposition parties, amalgamated into two groupings and strictly controlled, were banned from organising in the countryside; and the army was allocated the dual function (*dwi fungsi*) of development and national security, yet kept at one remove from the centre of state power by the strong presidency and the special security apparatus surrounding it. In all of these cases, the state achieved considerably more autonomy than was common elsewhere in the Third World. But the consequences of such autonomy varied just as considerably, and somewhat different situations (examined further in the following chapter) existed in the early 1990s in each case. In Taiwan, the mainland majority built into the system at the outset disappeared in 1991, as the ageing of the generation of 1949 took its course, leaving the first Taiwanese-born president facing a Taiwanese-dominated legislature; constitutional reforms in the same year forced the resignation of all members of the National Assembly and Legislative Yuan who had been elected on the mainland, leading to the election of truly representative bodies in December 1991 and 1992 respectively. In South Korea, an independent party of business arose for the first time to challenge the state-centred factions hitherto dominant in politics, though it suffered considerable harassment from the state machine, and failed to prosper. In Indonesia, signs of friction emerged between Suharto and the financial conglomerates and the army as he manoeuvred for a sixth successive presidential term. Finally, in the Philippines, where President Aquino (from the old landed élite) passed power on to Fidel Ramos (Minister of Defence under both Marcos and Aquino herself) in 1992, the struggle to restore the authority and legitimacy of the ravaged state continued to be dogged by the legacy of irresponsible government dating back to colonial times.

4. Latin America: class, clientelism and the state

Three factors discussed in Chapter One in relation to Latin America – the early achievement of political independence, the development of export-oriented economies from the mid-nineteenth century, and the relative insignificance of potential complicating factors such as ethnicity, tribalism and religious conflict – combine to give a particular stamp to the theme of state and society in this region. The shaping impact of export-led development and its breakdown after 1930 has been considerable, and undiluted either by the impact of recent decolonisation or by conflicts provoked by ethnic or religious rivalries. In the circumstances the nature of the state in contemporary Latin America and the dynamics of change from country to country are best understood in the context of the changing relationship through the twentieth century between the countries of the region and the international economy, the development of internal social forces, and the resulting political conflicts.

This is best seen in terms of three different phases. The first, of export-dominated development, extends to 1930. The second, marked in most of South America by a turn to industrialisation, continues into the 1950s or beyond. The third phase, dominated by the 'internationalisation of capital', or the movement into the region of manufacturing multinational firms, and its impact upon the rest of the local economy, has endured into the 1990s, in the countries where it has been reached. It may be succeeded, in one or two of the most advanced countries of the region, by the emergence of relatively powerful economies with a capacity to compete inter-nationally across a diverse range of export goods. The long history of political independence in the region, the early incorporation of its economies into the international market, and the relatively advanced degree of development achieved, make this framework fruitful where Latin America is concerned. As noted in Chapter One, there were significant differences between the various Latin American states in the period of export-led growth. Beyond these differences, however, there were equally decisive similarities, which can be taken as defining the character of the state in an export-led economy.

First, these states generally ran an open *laissez-faire* economy, and embraced enthusiastically the roles of suppliers of raw materials and purchasers of manufactured goods. Secondly, they depended upon exports of primary commodities not only for economic growth, but also for the generation of revenues to finance the limited activities of the state itself. In the absence of well-established income or land taxes, the bulk of revenues were drawn either directly from exports, or from the imports which exports financed. Thirdly, the increasing complexity of economic administration and social change brought with it the rise of an urban professional class, often directly employed by the state or tied to the export sector, which became an important factor in national politics. Fourthly, the working class in town and countryside was excluded, repressed or ignored. States of this kind generally reached maturity around

1910, were shaken by severe economic fluctuations and increasing social and political unrest during and after the First World War, and prospered again during the middle 1920s, only to be toppled in the wake of the depression beginning in 1929.

The economic impact of the depression of the 1930s was severe in Latin America, reducing export revenues by 50–80 per cent across the region, and causing sharp falls in GNP. Its impact went far beyond this economic setback, however, for three reasons. First of all, it changed the nature of the international economy. The central capitalist countries reversed policies in the areas of investment, finance and trade, thus removing the conditions which had made export-oriented development possible. This meant that there could be no return to the previous pattern of growth. Secondly, the demise of purely export-led growth robbed the élites associated with it of their legitimacy, and their ability to rule by consent. They became the targets of broad oppositional movements which either led directly to their removal from power, or to the reconstitution of existing regimes on a narrower and more repressive basis. Thirdly, given the structure of the export-led state, the drop in foreign exchange revenues led directly to a fiscal crisis. This was particularly severe in its political implications where the regime had been broadened, as in Argentina, to give new middle-class élites a share in power through the medium of expanded public employment.

The depression gave rise to a period of instability in Latin America similar to that experienced after independence, leading eventually to the emergence of a new and more interventionist role for the state. Throughout the region, control of the state was disputed between badly weakened old élites and new forces aiming to steer economic development in new directions, or even to overthrow old regimes entirely. In some cases (notably in Central America but also in Peru and Argentina) the old élites were able to reassert control, generally on the basis of repression. Where radical reform was attempted – as in Chile's brief 'socialist republic' of 1932, Grau's revolutionary nationalist administration of 1933–4 in Cuba, or the three-year rule of *Acción Democrática* in Venezuela between 1945 and 1948 after the belated departure of the military successors of the dictator Gomez – it generally proved fragile. The classic case of unsustainable reform was El Salvador, where brief reform-oriented experiments in 1930, 1944, 1960–1 and 1979–80 were succeeded by the swift reimposition of authoritarian rule.

Reform was carried furthest in Guatemala for a decade after 1944 (to be cut off by US intervention) and Bolivia, where the old regime (restored in the 1940s after a period of hectic experiment) was toppled in 1952 by a revolution which in turn largely lost its initially considerable reforming content by 1956. Until the Cuban revolution in 1959 introduced a radical alternative, new and relatively stable state forms appeared only where counter-élites (clearly differentiated from the old exporting sectors, but committed to capitalist industrialisation rather than more radical reform) were able to rally an urban and largely working-class following but at the same time to control its mobilisation.

The styles of political mobilisation combined with state control adopted by these counter-élites gave rise to the term 'populist' to describe them. It has been so widely used that attempts to give it precise meaning have generally foundered, but for our comparative purpose here we can identify populism as a political response to the depression in Latin America. Its policies and politics make most sense if seen as a direct contrast to those of export-led development. Reliance on exports gave way to a process of 'import-substituting' industrialisation, based upon the local manufacture of the most easily produced of formerly imported goods – textiles, processed foods and beverages – and complementary state investment in infrastructural and heavy industrial projects. The greater involvement of the state in the promotion of industrialisation entailed the abandonment of *laissez-faire* principles. The promotion of industrial production and the simultaneous need to enlarge the internal market made for a temporary alliance between an industrial bourgeoisie dependent upon the state and a working class newly mobilised through the state itself. At the same time, the expanded role of the state allowed it to build a considerable base among the professional classes. To tie workers to the regime, they were organised in state-controlled unions (and to a lesser extent in pro-regime parties) while autonomous alternatives were crushed. Finally, the old élites were either excluded, or incorporated in minor and subordinate roles.

The 'classic' case of political mobilisation of the urban working class behind a project for import-substituting industrialisation came under Perón in Argentina. Perón cultivated a backing among workers while Secretary of Labour in the 1943–6 military government which ousted the old regime, and he used their support to win the presidency in 1946. He destroyed independent challenges to his leadership and set out deliberately to channel the loyalties of his followers towards himself and his wife Evita personally. Peronism may be taken as a reference point for other populist experiments. In Brazil under Vargas the landed élites were retained as an important (though subordinate) element in the populist alliance, and the workers never played so dominant a part. In Mexico, exceptionally, the previous defeat of the landed élites in the revolution (discussed in Chapter 5) meant that land reform and the incorporation of the peasantry could be a part of the 'populist' settlement of the 1930s, though Cardenas (1934–1940) was careful to keep peasants and workers separate, and equally tied to the state. In Peru rival civilian and military populists clashed around 1930, and the return of the old regime allowed the civilian populist party APRA (American Popular Revolutionary Alliance) to survive only as an opposition force. Lastly, in Ecuador the scope for a developmental urban coalition was too slight to allow the indefatigable Velasco Ibarra to do more than seize and lose power on five successive occasions. The appeal of populism can be gauged from the fact that it was essayed (generally with limited success) in other countries where unstable processes of reform and conservative reaction had developed: Ibañez in Chile, Rojas Pinilla in Colombia, Perez Jimenez in Venezuela and even Batista in Cuba provide examples of this tendency.

In the long run, states organised along these lines suffered a number of serious weaknesses. Their leaders were vulnerable to attack from direct representatives of capitalist interests wary of state intervention and working class mobilisation. In addition, it became increasingly difficult to combine policies of investment with improvements in the living standards of the urban population. Export sectors could be taxed heavily, but in the end declining production meant shortages of all-important foreign exchange. Equally, it proved difficult in the long run to contain the ambitions of the organised working class within the bounds laid down by populist regimes. There was a tendency therefore for populist regimes to find growth flagging, state investment subordinated to boosting consumption, capitalist allies subverting their programmes or withdrawing their support, and lower-class constituencies turning to more radical solutions. Only in Mexico was this outcome avoided, as a result of the greater autonomy of the state, its successful incorporation of the peasantry, and its more comprehensive co-optation of the working class.

In the larger Latin American states, populism was successful in creating a temporary stability and a reorientation of economic development. As the latter proceeded, however (and particularly as foreign multinationals began to invest on a large scale in these countries), it became a victim of its own success. Given the unequal distribution of income and the widespread poverty, such goods as cars and domestic appliances were available initially only to a relatively small proportion of the population; at the same time, the introduction of their manufacture required large capital investments, and drew domestic manufacturers into complementary sectors where start-up costs were also high. Opportunities for new investment in the production of widely consumed wage goods were reduced as 'import-substitution' in these areas became virtually complete. There was therefore a need to channel funds more towards investment than towards consumption, to increase the rate of accumulation both for private industry and within the productive state sector itself. This coincided with a political crisis provoked by the radicalisation of groups initially mobilised from above, the emergence of challenges from excluded groups, and the incapacity of élites outside the 'populist' alliance to generate an electorally viable alternative. It was this political crisis – reflected in the end in the inability of populist leaders to govern and the equal inability of their conservative civilian opponents to rally the popular support to take over from them – which brought the military to power for protracted periods in both Brazil and Argentina. The emergence of these military regimes can therefore be traced back to the political and economic crisis set in train by the depression.

Other Latin American states, also among the most highly developed of the region, reached the same situation – military rule for protracted periods – by a different route. In both Chile and Uruguay, pressure for reform eventually overwhelmed the forces of conservatism, but provoked a highly authoritarian response, bringing particularly repressive military regimes to power. Each country had reached a state of political crisis. In Uruguay, the traditional *Blanco* and *Colorado* parties had been unable to find an answer to economic stagnation and mounting social unrest, while the leftist *Frente Amplio* (Broad Front) gained adherents and the young turned increasingly toward the urban guerrilla movement of the

Tupamaros; in Chile, the apparent stability of civilian rule masked a cycle of exhaustion of successive political alternatives, as regime followed regime with none able to return from opposition to a second period in power. The process of polarisation along class lines went further here than elsewhere, and in 1973 Allende's civilian opponents themselves called upon the military to intervene.

These militarised 'bureaucratic authoritarian' regimes have been seen by one influential analyst, the Argentine social scientist Guillermo O'Donnell, as representing foreign capital in alliance with the largest national monopolies and oligopolies; ruling through technocracies, both military and economic, rather than through representative civilians; seeking to remove key policy issues from the 'political' arena and to demobilise the previously mobilised working classes; and excluding the latter both politically and economically from participation in the regime [O'Donnell, 1977]. This is a fair description, if one bears in mind that the origins and dynamics of these regimes differ, and that there have been major differences in economic policy. Whereas Brazil pursued industrial development along lines similar to those followed in Mexico, the deliberate stimulation of industry through widespread government intervention was reversed, with catastrophic consequences, in Chile, Uruguay and Argentina. Also, O'Donnell and others were initially inclined to overestimate the ability of such regimes to provide a basis for long-term rule.

If changes in the character of the state and state–society relations arising out of the proliferation of military rule in the most advanced states of the region were the most striking characteristic of the 1960s and the 1970s, their character from 1979–80 onwards was shaped by military withdrawal and a marked shift to economic liberalisation. This led to the restoration of civilian politics of a conservative or cautiously social democratic character, as in Argentina (1983), Brazil (1985), Uruguay (1985) and Chile (1990). This in turn brought the countries concerned into line with a trend first apparent in Colombia and Venezuela after 1958, and subsequently experienced in Ecuador, Bolivia, and Peru: the emergence (after a period of sometimes severe upheaval terminating in a period of protracted military rule) of a 'self-limiting' party political system dominated by parties committed to a moderate consensus and prepared to discipline their own forces in order to maintain it. This theme is explored further in the following chapter.

As we have seen, communalism, religious sectarianism and other forms of primordial attachment are relatively insignificant in Latin America. Even so, there are significant social bonds which cut across class differences, and they have played an important role in the politics of the region. Ties linking lower-class individuals as clients to higher-class individuals as patrons (typically involving peasants and landowners) can be seen as weakening (and even obliterating) any tendency for horizontal bonds of class loyalty or solidarity to develop. It is possible to trace the impact of clientelism in urban settings as well. Networks of contacts based upon common regional origins, kinship and the like play an important part in integrating migrants, for example, into city life and work. However, the most significant aspect of clientelism, with regard to relations between the state and society, is the part it plays in the organisation and the activities of the state itself. Patronage practised through the ability of the state to reward (in conjunction with its equal ability to punish) plays a vital part in Latin American state and party politics, and at times this is seen as weakening the significance of class as an organising and explanatory factor in politics in the area. This is a mistake. In Latin America, as elsewhere (in the Lebanon, for example), clientelism – viewed from a social rather than an individual perspective – is a means by which one class perpetuates its domination over another; at the level of the state, it is a means by which a political project favouring one set of class interests over another is defended or advanced. It owes its prevalence to the consequences of dependent development: the survival and strengthening of the landed classes; the existence of a numerous peasantry; the weakness of the urban bourgeoisie, its dependence upon the state and its need to create a political base through expansion of the bureaucracy; the weakness of urban workers; and finally the divisions within the dominant élites. The fact that political loyalties do not neatly echo horizontal class distinctions may weaken class as an indicator of political attachment, but it does not rule out an explanation rooted in class interests and practices.

5. The Middle East: communalism, class and state power

The Arab Middle East has a range of states which share a common historical heritage, with populations which are largely Muslim and

Arabic-speaking. The contemporary state system, however, is a relatively recent creation, dating from the division of the Ottoman Empire into French and British mandates. Egypt is an exception: it had established autonomy from the Empire by the beginning of the nineteenth century. It has functioned as an established political entity longer than Germany or Italy, with an historic seat of power in Cairo from where rulers have taxed and administered a stable population living in a limited area along the Nile delta and valley. Egypt is also relatively homogeneous with a small Christian minority. As a consequence, Egypt has been a relatively strong state: it has undergone three succession crises and dramatic shifts in policy without significant domestic political turmoil.

At the other end of the spectrum is Lebanon, a state which has been extremely weak and where power has inhered in society. The lack of either an integrative or coercive capacity brought more than fifteen years of civil strife, foreign invasions and interventions and created a stateless society. In between these two poles are Syria and Iraq, which are ethnically and religiously heterogeneous but where the power of the state has been asserted in a context of intense social and political conflict against ethnic and regional rebellions and uprisings. There are, then, factors other than social heterogeneity which contribute to state weakness. Of particular importance is the evolution of class forces and the way in which these have interacted with communalism, ethnicity and sectarianism.

The formation of a cohesive social order has been a major task for many Middle Eastern governments. Prior to the creation of the contemporary state system, religious communities had organised their own affairs: Jews, Muslims and Christians each had their own legal system and were communally responsible for the payment of special taxes to the Ottoman Sultan. The geographic isolation of some minorities (particularly the non-Sunni Muslim sects) compounded social autonomies. With some exceptions, ethnic groups and minority sects have inhabited particular regions: the Kurds in the mountainous north-east of Iraq; the Alawites in the mountains of north-west Syria; the Druze in the southern Syrian hills and the Lebanese Shuf district; and Shi'a Muslims in southern Iraq, south Lebanon and the Beqa valley. Because Sunni Islam was the orthodoxy of the Arab and Ottoman Empires, Sunni Muslims have tended to predominate in urban administrative centres. Even though rural migration has changed this pattern, newcomers to the towns have tended to settle together in urban quarters.

One further legacy of the past is that non-Sunni Muslim minorities, like the Alawites, Shi'a and the Druze, were generally excluded from the reformed late-Ottoman educational, administrative and military systems. As a result, members of the minorities were less educated, lacking in administrative experience, and hardly represented in the officer corps. This imbalance was perpetuated during the period of European control as the mandatory authorities recruited those with experience and education. Within this general pattern, it is necessary to point out two exceptions. Firstly, the French authorities in Syria recruited minorities into the Syrian army because urban Sunni Muslims were identified with nationalism. Secondly, Mount Lebanon had acquired a high degree of autonomy during the nineteenth century and both Maronite and Druze leaders, religious and civil, participated in the administration of their own regions. With these exceptions, at independence communities had become politically stratified: orthodox Sunni Muslims had greater representation in (and access to) administration, government and the army.

Because communal groups are located in different regions, economic development has also had an impact on the socio-economic differentiation of Middle Eastern communities. The more peripheral any community to the urban centres of trade and commerce, the less have traditional patterns of stratification changed. It is possible to identify two distinct and parallel processes of stratification: those within ethnic and sectarian groups and those between them. We have mentioned how the growth of Beirut as a port and the expansion of the Lebanese silk industry (sponsored by French entrepreneurs in Mount Lebanon) increased the economic opportunities of the Maronites in the Lebanese mountains and initiated internal social diversification. The position of the community as a whole was enhanced by Christian educational mission activity and favour shown to the Maronite Catholics during the French mandate. By the middle of the twentieth century the Maronites ranged from millionaire bankers and businessmen through an educated middle- and lower-middle class, to a relatively prosperous peasantry. In contrast, the peripheral Lebanese Shi'a community experienced less radical change and was divided between a handful of large landlords and a poor subsistence peasantry. The Alawites of Syria were largely middle and poor peasants and landless labourers working the land of absentee urban Christian and Sunni Muslim landowners. One writer has called the Alawites a 'class-sect' because their position in Syrian social structure has correlated with sect membership [Batatu, 1981]. A combination of various legacies of the past and the process of the uneven regional impact of economic development has informed communalism with both a social and political content. Any analysis of the impact of ethnicity and sectarianism on Middle Eastern politics based simply on communal identity or solidarity is misleading. Communal groups have been restructured internally, as have relations between them, and they have functioned within new national, social, economic and political systems. Social change and class formation, within and across communities, have dramatically altered the nineteenth-century pattern of communal separateness.

As far as class is concerned, discussion has to begin with the first class which had national power: the landowners. In Iraq, Syria, Egypt and (to an extent) Lebanon, this class was not only very wealthy but also controlled the political system. Landownership was highly concentrated. In Egypt, before the 1952 land reform, the top 1 per cent of landowners controlled 72 per cent of Egypt's cultivated area. The position was similar in Syria up to 1963 and Iraq up to 1958. The peasantry were generally owners of small plots or sharecroppers, and were in perpetual debt to their landlords whose domination of the post-independence parliaments enabled them to block any threat to their economic and political privileges.

Varying combinations of rural overpopulation and pressure on the land, rural poverty, the mechanisation of agriculture, landlord oppression and the possibility of slightly better employment prospects in the towns led to a large-scale migration from the countryside. The twelve major cities of Syria increased their population by 57 per cent between 1960 and 1970, and between 1927 and 1966 the population of Cairo increased threefold. In Lebanon, Beirut became encircled by what was called the 'belt of misery' as the rural poor joined the Palestinians in the shanty towns. Although Middle Eastern states became more urbanised the change involved the translation of rural deprivation into visible urban poverty. Most of the new migrants were underemployed or employed in casual or menial tasks. It has been estimated that in the early 1980s 48 per cent of Egypt's population was living in absolute poverty and 20 per cent of employed urban dwellers were servants [Waterbury, 1983: 211]. The position of rural migrants in Syria is somewhat less stark, and in Iraq it has been ameliorated by the flow of oil revenues. The migration of labour to the oil-producing states has not radically altered the position of the urban poor. Iran's oil revenues only increased the flow of migrants from the rural areas and although casual work in construction provided employment, the urban infrastructure was not sufficient to absorb the inflow: in 1977 45 per cent of urban families in Iran lived in one room and Teheran (a city of 4 million people) had no proper sewage system. Those living on the margins of urban life found little time for politics, but when they have, their participation has been violent. The burning of Cairo just before the 1952 revolution and the mass support for Ayatallah Khomeini in Iran came from this underclass.

Another marked change in Middle Eastern societies has come about through the expansion of education and state employment. The radical and reformist parties and groups (the main opposition to landlord power) sprang from this class and it was their military counterparts in Egypt, Syria and Iraq which ended landowners' rule. In Egypt, primary school enrolment increased from 1.5 to 4.2 million between 1952 and 1977, secondary from 182 000 to 796 000 and further education from 51 000 to 453 000 [Waterbury, 1983: 222]. In Iran, between 1963 and 1977 enrolment in primary schools increased from 1.6 to over 4 million, in secondary from 370 000 to 740 000 and in colleges (at home and abroad) from 42 000 to 230 000 [Abrahamian, 1982: 431]. Far greater expansion has taken place in the towns than in the countryside, and (except in Lebanon where private schools predominate) the state has been the engine behind these developments. Most of the secondary and further education graduates have been employed by the state, in part because of the absence of any other opportunities, and in part because of the governments' desire to placate this stratum which has produced opposition leaders and parties. Despite such co-optation, only the upper echelons of this stratum receive a salary commensurate with their education and employment expectations.

Although there has been a substantial shift in employment patterns, large numbers are still employed in agriculture. In 1978 the percentage share of the labour force in agriculture was as follows: Egypt 51, Iran 40, Iraq 42, Syria 49. In Lebanon the share was only 12 per cent [Weinbaum, 1982: 27]. Small peasants who are owners and tenants are the largest proportion, and about 80 per cent are subsistence or near-subsistence farmers. Despite the expansion of education, most are illiterate. The countryside, however, is highly diversified with significant differences of income. An International Labour Organisation (ILO) report on Egypt has pointed to the impossibility of delineating income groups in rural Egypt because of the diversity: landownership, agricultural and urban wage labour, crafts and services, government employment. Like the middle strata, then, the peasantry is not monolithic: there are prosperous peasant owners, subsidised by the state, selling their produce to the overpopulated towns; urban absentee, small, but highly capitalised farmers exporting produce to Europe; subsistence peasants scraping a living; peasants who have to work because their landholding is not sufficient; and landless labourers. In Egypt, despite extensive land reform, the ILO report asserted that the incidence of rural poverty was high, 'affecting 35 per cent of the households and 41 per cent of the population in 1977', and that poverty had not diminished over the previous 15 years [Hansen and Radwan, 1982: 99–111].

Despite this, there has been quite considerable social and political change in the Middle East since independence. In some states like Iraq and Syria, upper levels of the middle strata have seized power from the landowners, and have been able to assert the power of the state over entrenched autonomies of political leaders of communal groups. Where the dominant landowning group was multicommunal, this process has been somewhat easier. In Iraq, where the biggest landlords were Sunni and Shi'a, there have been less sectarian political repercussions, although Kurdish demands for autonomy and national rights have resulted in civil strife as the post-1958 regimes have attempted to establish a strong centralised state. The post-Gulf War uprisings in the Shi'a south and the Kurdish north in 1991, however, suggest that the authoritarian centralism established by the Ba'th was a fragile creation. In Syria, where the landlords were overwhelmingly Sunni Muslim and urban, the architects of the land reform (the Ba'th party and Ba'thist military officers) were preponderantly of the rural minorities, particularly Alawite. The result has been a series of urban uprisings spearheaded by the Muslim Brothers, an Islamist political movement drawing its support from Sunni Muslims. Because the urban landlords and merchants are generally Sunni Muslim, political conflict in Syria has been multi-faceted, involving communal, class and ideological struggles. Such violence has led the political leadership to recruit only those who can be trusted into strategic military, security and political positions, and these have often been friends and relatives who have generally been members of the same sect. Even though the policies of the post-1970 regime in Syria have not favoured the minorities in general or the Alawite community in particular (indeed, from the early 1970s the regime has sought to conciliate the urban merchants), the regime is perceived as narrowly sectarian.

It is in **Lebanon** that the most complex and destructive relationship between communalism and class has been reflected in politics. After independence, the political system was organised on a religious basis. Seats in parliament were allocated on a 6:5 ratio of Christian to Muslim, the president had to be a Christian and state employment was distributed proportionately between sects. It is, however, a distortion to view Lebanon as a wholly Christian-dominated state. For every six Christian deputies there were five Muslim, and although the president was a Christian and had extensive powers, the prime minister was a Muslim. Cross-sectarian alliances were built into the system: because the president was elected by the Assembly any presidential aspirant had to gain support from Muslim deputies, and mixed sect multi-member constituencies promoted electoral cooperation between candidates. Factional alliances between members of the political élite and the exchange of electoral votes for patronage were as significant as sectarianism. Control of patronage sustained the dominance of the political leaders, known in Lebanon as the *zu'ama*. Most of these had more in common with each other than they did with their co-religionists: they came from established families, were generally wealthy and attended the best schools and universities.

It was essentially a class alliance which underpinned the political structure. Businessmen, bankers and import–export merchants (with a vested interest in a *laissez-faire* economy) and traditional landlords (with a vested interest in maintaining control over the peasantry and curtailing the powers of the state) combined to establish a state which did not intervene in the economy, and provided minimal welfare and social security. Health care, social welfare, housing and employment existed almost wholly in the private domain. Deputies provided patronage in these areas in exchange for votes and political support. In doing so, they enabled a small ruling group to stay in power.

In Lebanon, the Christian communities were generally more prosperous, better educated and greater beneficiaries of the *laissez-faire* economy. The Muslim communities did less well. The Shi'a were generally rural, poor and under the dominion of large landowners, many of whom went into commercial mechanised farming during the 1960s and forced their peasants into seasonal labour. Lebanon, then, had a social system wherein Christians were better off than Muslims but at the apex of the system was a religiously mixed group of businessmen, merchants, bankers, land-owners and politicians.

Underlying the political crises which led to the 1975 civil war was the breakdown of the patronage system. Large numbers migrated to the urban areas as a result of the expansion of commercialised farming and Israeli air raids on southern Lebanon in reprisal for Palestinian attacks. With a quarter of a million Lebanese arriving in the coastal cities the individualistic patronage system ceased to cope with much broader social demands. Demands for welfare, housing, education and employment, as well as for an army which could defend the state, were converted by the Muslim leadership into a demand for a change in the confessional allocation of political and bureaucratic positions. Their solution was greater Muslim repre-sentation. What was at base a social crisis became a political crisis with a sectarian face. The more privileged Christian communities saw these demands as a threat to their advantaged position and to a system out of which they had done relatively well. The Phalange party (representing the less opulent Maronites and ideologically committed to a strong state and Christian hegemony) became the vehicle for the Maronite response to the crisis. The civil war, with all its barbarities and criminality, brought an overt sectarianism to a deep social crisis which a weak state could not manage. The state did not even have any coercive capacity: that inhered in localised sectarian and political militias and, at times, criminal gangs.

In conclusion, the Middle East exhibits a range of state–society relations. In certain cases the centre holds, as it has done in Egypt and Iran. In other states, like Syria and Iraq, although social change has informed internal conflicts with ethnic and sectarian dimensions, strata and sections of classes have emerged supportive of a central state against fissiparous tendencies. Even where external forces have protected minorities against state oppression, as happened in Iraqi Kurdistan after the Gulf War, care has been taken to ensure the survival of state boundaries. These post-independence developments have taken place within the context of large-scale social and political upheaval: the overthrow of landlords and monarchies, the beginnings of industrialisation, a rapidly expanding urban society, the decline of agricultural production and rapid population growth. Only Lebanon, based on the formal acceptance of religious division as an essential component of the political system, fell apart.

6. Conclusion

In Africa and the Middle East political leaders routinely invoke communal differences that are readily understandable to the rural majority in their competition for power and access to economic resources. However, they do so with varying goals and results. In Iraq and Syria, the fusion of nationalism, anti-landlordism and communalism has produced long-lived and authoritarian centra-lised regimes; in the Lebanon a political settlement apparently based on communal principles actually protected the interests of merchant and landed élites until accelerating social change destroyed the patronage system revolving around the *za'im*, and led to the virtual collapse of a state which had been kept weak as a matter of deliberate policy; in the vast, landlocked and mostly arid country of Chad in central Africa, the writ of the central government, defied by rival warring leaders, has never fully run. In East and Southeast Asia patronage politics have been kept much more under state control than in Africa in particular. In Taiwan, where the new state established in 1949 had no ties to local society, and in South Korea and Indonesia, where the military made a particular effort to extend the authority of the state after periods of acute instability, the politics of patronage was controlled, and harnessed to a particular model of economic development. In the Philippines, in contrast, it took on a destructive logic of its own which eventually brought down the Marcos regime. In Latin America, the scope for appeals to communal interests has rarely existed, but the discriminatory use of state resources has played an equally significant part in attempts to build support for governments through patronage politics. While Mexico has been very successful in harnessing patronage in order to consolidate central political power and reinforce the dominance of a particular class alliance, Brazil, Uruguay and Argentina have seen patronage politics decay, as it did in the Lebanon and the Philippines, into a major source of instability.

In part, the regional differences noted here can be explained by the relative levels of industrialisation from case to case. At the time of independence in Africa and the Middle East, neither region had much industry other than of an extractive kind, and the educated element had little prospect of employment outside agriculture, the state sector, and limited opportunities in law and medicine. Industrialisation was therefore taken forward by the state, in the absence of a well-defined national bourgeoisie. The result of this was that where new industrial classes arose, they did so as a result of favourable political ties with states which were sources of development funds and other privileges. Factors such as these have led Sklar to advance, in respect of Africa, the controversial proposition that 'class relations, at bottom, are determined by relations of power, not production' [Sklar, 1979: 537]. Similarly, control of oil revenues by the state in much of the Middle East has given the state a predominant role. In each case, ironically, this has been as much a source of weakness as of strength. Schatz has characterised the resulting parasitic attitude of entrepreneurs in Nigeria as 'pirate capitalism', while Anderson notes that the flow of revenues from oil in the Middle East has often precluded the development of efficient systems of taxation which would have allowed states to exert control over local classes, and promote more balanced economic development [Schatz, 1984; Anderson, 1987].

In the larger Latin American countries the level of economic development and of indigenous industrialisation was generally higher, and tended to gather pace after 1930. The state played an important part in promoting industrial development in the wake of the collapse of primary exports during the depression, often through innovative alliances which brought the working class into politics for the first time. At the same time exporters and new industrialists resisted state intervention and working class mobilisation when these began to threaten their interests. They succeeded in blunting the early reformism of the post-revolutionary state in

Mexico, and in securing military intervention against populist regimes in Argentina and Brazil. Although the extent of state capacity varied in the region, populist regimes generally proved too timid to challenge existing power relations (particularly in the countryside), relying on measures of redistribution rather than fundamental reform.

In East and Southeast Asia, in contrast, the state has generally proved far more able to direct the process of capitalist development. It has done so by the use of authoritarian methods which have not yet proved compatible with any measure of liberal democracy. But the significant point here, from a comparative perspective, is that patronage has been used to reinforce the authority of the state rather than being allowed to undermine it, and individual capitalists have been as subject to state direction as other citizens. As a consequence, personal enrichment through political ties has tended to lead, more often than elsewhere, to capitalist investment and accumulation. This has happened because government policies have been consistently oriented to long-term capitalist development. This suggests an important corollary to Sklar's argument: only if relations of power are attuned to the logic of capitalist production will they promote class formation and economic development.

On the surface, at least, class constitutes a more important basis for interest-group appeals and for political cleavage in the industrialised countries of Latin America than in the predominantly agricultural societies of Africa and the Middle East, or the state-dominated regimes of East and Southeast Asia. But in all cases clientelism is used to perpetuate the dominance of ruling élites over other classes in society. There is, in short, no incompatibility between class and a patronage system of politics. The prevalence of patronage politics hinders the emergence of independent political organisation among the peasantry and the urban working class, often reflecting the success of one form of class politics, rather than the absence of any class politics at all. Continued economic development, to the extent that it occurs, will not necessarily reduce the significance of communalism. As Melson and Wolpe conclude, an individual's 'acquisition of a new socio-economic identity need not mean the elimination of his prior communal point of reference' [Melson and Wolpe, 1971: 28]. As we have seen, such identities are as likely to be self-reinforcing as to be mutually incompatible.

At the same time, it is to be expected that where the state has taken a distinctive leading role in promoting economic development, success over the longer term will eventually lead to the emergence of demands from some sectors of business for an independent voice. This was beginning to happen in Nigeria and Zambia in the 1970s before economic crisis slowed the process. It was also true in Latin America in the later years of both populism and military rule, and was a major reason for the collapse of each. Similar developments have been taking place in East Asia since the late 1980s. In Taiwan, the autonomy of the ruling Kuomintang, weakened by the forced retirement of the mainland representatives, was further threatened by the rise of 'money politics' as, within the party, Taiwanese politicians looked for wealthy backers and responded to their political demands. Similarly, the emergence in the 1992 presidential elections in South Korea of an independent party of business led by the owner of the Hyundai group, and promoting his candidacy for the presidency, was an indicator of a growing separation between the state and the large conglomerates whose development it had fostered. At the same time, its relatively poor performance, in part a consequence of the ability of the government to place obstacles in its way, suggested that the supremacy of the state may not be immediately in peril.

We may return finally, then, to the question of the relationship between patronage politics, economic development, and democracy. From our review of comparative cases, it appears that the character of economic development in different Third World states depends on whether those states control or are controlled by the politics of patronage, and the use they make of it where it is under their control. A state firmly in control of the levers of patronage may use them to boost long-term economic development, as in the East Asian cases, and in Indonesia and Mexico for long periods of time, or it may use them increasingly for personal enrichment which adds little to the development effort. Where social groups connected to the state but not controlled by it are able to take charge of patronage resources, it is very unlikely that development will result, as other more direct routes to enrichment are too easily available. As far as the political process is concerned, the prevalence of patronage politics, whether orchestrated by private interests or by the state, generally has negative consequences for democracy. At best it may allow electoral systems to survive by giving a built-in advantage either to the government itself or to powerful and generally conservative social classes, thereby producing a degree of stability at the cost of the democratic content of the political system. At worst it will allow the government to assert itself so entirely that no discernible element of choice remains, or convert the political arena into a combat zone between antagonistic factions each bent on controlling the state as a source of direct enrichment. In the following chapter we shall examine the implications of these factors for the character of party politics in the regions studied.

Further Reading

Migdal [1988] offers a provocative introduction to the broad comparative issues raised here. For Africa, Rodney [1972] is an early and influential attempt to apply a dependency perspective. Allen and Williams [1988] offer a more recent collection with which it may be compared. Rothchild and Chazan [1988] and Sklar and Whitaker [1991] offer contemporary perspectives, and Herbst [1990] offers an excellent case study of Zimbabwe. For East and Southeast Asia the collections by Deyo [1987], Taylor and Turton [1988] and White [1988] are excellent points of departure. Golay [1969] is valuable for the post-war period in Southeast Asia. However, the themes discussed here are best approached through country case studies, among which Amsden [1989] on South Korea, Gold [1985] and Wade [1990] on Taiwan, Hawes [1987] and Doronila [1992] on the Philippines, and Robison [1986] on Indonesia are particularly useful. For Latin America Cardoso and Faletto [1979] is the best dependency account. Archetti [1984] offers a related set of readings. Malloy [1977] and Collier [1979] reflect the extensive debates of the 1970s; Cammack [1991a] offers a more recent perspective. For the Middle East Luciani [1990] provides an essential collection; Owen [1992] is an excellent comparative essay; Waterbury [1983] and Hinnebusch [1990] are good case studies of Egypt and Syria respectively. There is also a substantial journal literature, covering all the regions studied here, from which the following are recommended: Amsden [1979], Anderson [1983], Anderson [1987], Baylies and Szeftel [1982], Cotton [1992], Doner [1992], Frieden [1988], Robison [1988], and Schatz [1984]. On clientelism, Clapham

[1982] is a useful collection; further case studies for comparison are Doronila [1985] on the Philippines, Johnson [1986] on the Lebanon, Lawson [1989] on Syria, Purcell [1981] on Mexico, and O'Brien [1979] on Senegal.

3

Political Parties and Participation

1. Introduction

The extent to which newly independent Third World states have adopted the formal institutions of liberal democracy has varied from area to area. In terms of political traditions and practices, Latin America is perhaps the most thoroughly 'Westernised' of the areas we examine: practically every country in the region has experimented with liberal democracy, though few have sustained it for long. In Africa, where the period of political independence has been brief, colonial rulers generally attempted to establish institutions shaped in the image of those of the mother country before departing the scene, but these did not long outlive their departure; they soon gave way to a more authoritarian politics reminiscent of that practised under colonial rule, either through military intervention or through the establishment of single parties closely tied to the state. In East and Southeast Asia, where democratic experiments have been far less common, authoritarian parties equally closely linked to the state have been the norm. Even in periods of electoral continuity, severe restrictions have been imposed upon political competition, while state employees have often been enrolled in dominant parties, and state agencies have made systematic use of patronage in order to maintain pro-government majorities. Finally, the penetration of Western political institutions and practices has perhaps been least substantial in the Middle East; in the Gulf states autocratic rulers have made minimal concessions even to the formalities of democratic politics, while elsewhere parties have tended to be inseparable from broader movements tied closely either to particular communities, or, again, to elements within the state.

94

In every region, of course, there is more variety than this brief survey suggests. Nigeria, with its alternation between democratic politics and military rule, and the Philippines, with its blend of clientelism and repression, are in some ways closer to the Latin American pattern than to regional norms; parallels for Mexico's extraordinarily successful ruling party, in power continuously since 1929, can be found only in East and Southeast Asia; and the dynamics of Lebanese politics, to which the representation of sub-national collectivities is central, bear comparison to similarly multi-ethnic states such as Malaysia and the former Yugoslavia.

Overall, the most striking feature of party politics in the Third World is the prevalence of 'parties of the state', formed after power has been obtained by means other than electoral competition, or transformed into bureaucratic arms of government after power has been won in elections. Such parties have often seemed essential instruments for the pursuit of national integration and economic development in divided and underdeveloped societies. But when ruling parties depend heavily on state resources for their ascendancy the prospects for democracy are poor. A ruling party founded after power has been gained by means other than electoral victory lacks authority to set the political agenda, and the legitimacy to attract independent and principled support. As a result, it runs the danger of being dominated by the executive, and either being subordinated to purely formal status, or being used simply as an agency to regulate state employment – or worse, to mobilise support for the regime while lacking any input into the process of policy formation. In such circumstances the ruling party itself ceases to represent vital social interests, opposition becomes a hopeless cause, and the prospect of alternation in power and thus stable democracy in the longer term becomes remote. Meanwhile, parties outside government seeking to compete are liable to remain weak as a result of their lack of access to public resources. Feeling unable to compete on equal terms in the electoral arena, they may be tempted to seek routes to power other than through the ballot box.

However, despite the enormous advantages they enjoy, parties of the state are subject to decay over time, and vulnerable in the longer term to internal corruption, disintegration as a consequence of economic failure, or even displacement as a result of the emergence of new social forces and political movements during the process of development. Much depends, in this respect, upon whether they are dominated by a single individual or generation, and whether they have found mechanisms to renew leadership at the top and throughout the party over time. Secondly, when parties enjoy a monopoly of power, it is difficult to maintain internal discipline and at the same time ensure that the party and leadership are responsive to the needs and demands of ordinary citizens. In such circumstances, apparently secure majorities may often be the illusory product of blatant and subtle forms of control and manipulation, liable to be swiftly overturned by popular mobilisation once the balance of power tips away from the state machine. Such failures have often given rise in the past to military intervention and rule, which we discuss in the following chapter. Over recent years, however, they have tended to lead to attempts to establish democratic political systems, in a global trend which has transformed the character of party politics and of government in the Third World.

In Africa, a general crisis of the developmentalist states of the post-independence period has resulted in the collapse of Marxist and non-Marxist single-party regimes alike, and a return to multi-party politics; in Latin America, a transformation during the 1980s established a near-universal pattern of highly competitive but somewhat unstable democratic regimes. In East and Southeast Asia such changes are less advanced, but the fall of Marcos in the Philippines, the restoration of democracy in Thailand, the launching of limited processes of liberalisation in Taiwan and South Korea, and the strains associated with the prospect of the eventual departure of Suharto in Indonesia – all contribute to a marked change of tone in the region. To a limited extent, pressures for democratisation have also emerged in the Middle East and Arab North Africa. Here, though, they retain a distinctive character arising on the one hand from challenges to Gulf State autocracy, and on the other from a renewed politics of fundamentalist mobilisation, spreading from Iran to the Lebanon, and into Egypt and Algeria.

The record of party politics in the Third World is not impressive. Civilian rule has proved frail, and where civilians have exercised power it has been for the most part in the shadow of the military or through non-democratic agencies such as personalist movements or single parties closely tied to the state. However, as noted above, current trends suggest that competitive party politics may be more widespread in the future than it has been in the past. Our focus, therefore, is on the origins and nature of parties in our four regions, the implications of their close links (for the most part) with the state, the nature of the forces stimulating a move to more competitive politics, and the prospects for the future. We do not assume that Western-style democracy (an imprecise concept in any case, given the differing historical records and current variations between the United States, Great Britain and continental Europe) represents a norm to which Third World political systems must necessarily tend. Nor do we assume that democracy and economic development go together in the Third World. In the East Asian cases often held up as examples of successful economic development, authoritarian rule has been the norm, while elsewhere it is not yet clear that liberal democracy can be sustained if the programmes of economic liberalisation and structural adjustment that have proliferated around much of Africa and Latin America are continued. We approach the issues of political parties and participation, then, with the primary purpose of assessing, in the light of past practice, the current prospects for democratisation around the Third World. How substantial are the changes which are occurring from region to region? And what obstacles remain to the introduction or consolidation of genuinely competitive liberal democracy?

2. Africa

With the main exception of Liberia's True Whig Party (which was founded in 1860 as the Whig Party) modern political parties in Africa were essentially post-1945 creations. In nearly every case, their origin was extra-parliamentary, though in other respects they often differed sharply from each other– for example, in leadership, structure and the social basis of support. While some parties – like the Convention People's Party (CPP) in the Gold Coast and the Parti Démocratique de Guinée (PDG) – sought to appeal to the lower-middle strata of the population, others – such as the Northern People's Congress (NPC) in Nigeria and the Parti Progressiste Nigérien (PPN) in Niger – had a narrower appeal, the NPC being at the outset the mouthpiece of the native authorities. However, the early categorisation of parties into 'mass' and 'élite' was always inexact, and the divisions between the parties were never clearcut. It became even more meaningless in the post-independence period as power came to be concentrated in the hands of a single, ruling party and (very often) in the party leader who became state president. There were often sharp differences between one single party and another, depending (for example) on whether they rested on a *de facto* or a *de jure* basis, on the amount of intra-party competition which each allowed, and on the quality of their leadership. Until the 1970s, the great majority of African states were reformist rather than revolutionary and, under the broad umbrella of 'African socialism', were ideologically weak. A new pattern emerged in the 1970s when Marxist–Leninist regimes assumed power in the former Portuguese colonies of Angola, Guinea–Bissau and Mozambique; their commitment to a more scientific form of socialism than any that had previously existed was shared by a number of military regimes, notably those in Somalia and Ethiopia following coups in 1969 and 1974 respectively.

The political party, whatever its ideological basis and whether enjoying a monopoly of power or (as continuously in Botswana, the Gambia and Mauritius) competing for power with other parties, is a most resilient political structure. Thus in Uganda, after a military interregnum of nine years (1971–80), the two former leading parties – the Uganda People's Congress (UPC) and the Democratic Party (DP) – were revived. The UPC again formed the government, but was disbanded by the military following a second coup in July 1985. This was the normal fate of ruling parties when military regimes were established, though the latter might create political parties of their own in a bid to increase their legitimacy; they did so frequently in Francophone Africa.

Parties in Africa have been called upon to play a number of roles, mostly concerned with nation-building and policy-making. The first is the integrative function. In Nigeria the makers of the 1979 constitution looked to the registered political parties to inculcate national values in place of communal or parochial values, while in post-independence Mozambique the Frente de Libertação de Mozambique (FRELIMO) mounted an intensive political education campaign in areas which had been barely penetrated by guerrilla activity during the liberation struggle. In neither case was the attempt notably successful, thereby reflecting the difficulty which virtually all parties faced in the post-independence period in winning sustained support for issues and causes which lacked the obvious appeal of anticolonialism.

Secondly, as noted above, the party has a legitimising role. In a multi-party context, each party seeks to win maximum support at a general election. Provided that the election is free and fair and allows the country's adult citizens to play (however briefly) a full part in the political process, the winning party will confer legitimacy on the successor government. This condition was satisfied in successive elections in Botswana, the Gambia and Mauritius, in Ghana in 1969, Ghana again and Nigeria in 1979, Zimbabwe in 1980 and Namibia in 1989. However, it was not satisfied in Nigeria in 1983, when corruption was rampant, in Sierra Leone in 1973 and 1977, when the main opposition party was prevented from nominating candidates, and in Uganda in 1980, when the election was blatantly rigged in favour of the UPC.

In the one-party context, elections have been used by the ruling party to demonstrate that it has a mandate for its continuance in office, and for its policies. This tended to be easily achieved in most of Francophone Africa where a massive vote was recorded in favour of an approved list of party candidates. In English-speaking Africa the presidential election – in which electors voted 'Yes' or 'No' for a single candidate put forward by the party – was more meaningful in this respect than the parliamentary elections which revolved round local rather than national issues and in which voters were restricted to a choice between rival candidates of the single party. In Tanzania, however, in successive five-year elections from 1965 many sitting MPs – 33 out of 241 in 1990 – and a number of ministers were defeated; to an extent, the same happened in Kenya, Zambia and (in Francophone Africa) the Côte d'Ivoire.

A third potential role for the political party is the formulation and execution of policy, to examine which we take the case of Tanzania and (briefly) that of Zambia. From 1964 onwards President Nyerere of **Tanzania** was personally responsible for a number of important foreign and domestic policy initiatives, such as the Arusha Declaration of January 1967. As occurred also in Zambia, the president was careful to associate the ruling party with major policy pronouncements, thus ensuring at least formal party support. For some years after 1967, the president, party and cabinet worked out together the policy implications of the demo-cratic socialist path which Nyerere had mapped out in the Arusha

Declaration. Hartmann argues that from the mid-1970s the party and government showed a tendency to pursue policies independently of each other, with the president sometimes acting as initiator, sometimes as mediator, and sometimes in support of one side or the other [Hartmann, 1983]. This is possibly so, though the extent of the divergence of viewpoint between party and government can easily be exaggerated. What is certain is that the party – *Chama cha Mapinduzi* (CCM) following a merger between the Tanganyika African National Union (TANU) and the Afro-Shirazi Party (ASP) of Zanzibar in 1977 – was at its weakest when facing up to the harsh economic realities with which the cabinet had to grapple as economic conditions in Tanzania deteriorated.

One must not, however, dwell too much upon policy differences between government and party since there were overlapping links between them: cabinet ministers could, and did, serve on the party's national executive committee (NEC) – ten of them out of 29 in 1983, for example. Neither cabinet nor NEC were monolithic bodies and each contained a diversity of viewpoints [Liviga and van Donge, 1983]. Nyerere moved individuals freely from one sphere of activity to another in an attempt to make optimum use of scarce manpower and this had the effect of blurring the distinction at senior levels between politics, administration and even university. This mobility between jobs and the presence in the presidential entourage of men (and a few women) drawn from a wide variety of institutional backgrounds – the party, cabinet, administration, university, defence forces, trade union and co-operative movements, and the Bank of Tanzania, among others – makes it extremely difficult to say whose influence on policy-making was dominant at any one time. However, Nyerere was always 'his own man' and certainly in the period up to 1985, when he vacated the state presidency, the policy lead which he gave was always important; he reluctantly accepted the need to reach agreement with the IMF, and the outlines of Tanzania's agreement with that body were worked out before he left public office. It is also probably true to say that his retention of the chairmanship of CCM (until 1990) served as a brake on the pace at which the government (under Ali Hassan Mwinyi) could adopt economic liberalisation measures.

In **Zambia**, as in Tanzania, government was characterised by executive dominance. The effectiveness of the central committee of the ruling United National Independence Party (UNIP) was by no means commensurate with the increased formal power which was conferred on it by a constitutional amendment in 1975. Facilities existed for joint decision-making with the cabinet (said to occur over the setting of agricultural producer prices, for example), but in other respects its direct impact on policy (other than broadly on political issues) was limited. The main policy initiatives were taken by President Kaunda and his advisers in State House.

In Afro–Marxist states the extent to which vanguard-type parties exercised important policy-making functions is open to question, given the high concentration of power in the hands of the ruling élite; these parties, too, faced the challenge of burgeoning state bureaucracies. In these, and in African states generally, the initiative in the execution of policy passed increasingly to state officials. One reason for this loss of initiative was often the run-down of the local party organisation. This did not occur in Zimbabwe, though land seizure was the only area of government decision-making in which the Zimbabwe African National Union-Patriotic Front (ZANU-PF) became involved; this apart, the civil service was 'the key element in matters of most concern to people in the rural areas' [Herbst, 1990: 241].

A fourth party role is to mobilise the people for economic development through self-help; this was a task for which, in those states which became independent in (or about) 1960, the party was believed to be pre-eminently suited. In fact, it tended to be a weak mobilisation agent in these states and the initiative passed to the central government – for example, to civil service regional and district directors of development in rural Tanzania from 1972. Afro–Marxist states placed a high valuation on political participation and created new structures, such as the 'dynamising groups' in Mozambique, to encourage it. However, except in the short term these experiments were not successful.

All parties, whatever their origin and ideological orientation, can also be expected to play a reconciliation role by accommodating different interests and mediating conflict, as UNIP frequently did in Zambia. However, in this sphere too, the initiative in many states passed to the president and his personal representatives at regional and district levels.

In the fifth place, the patronage functions of political parties have remained important in nearly all states. In Zambia there is plenty of evidence to show that the slogan 'It pays to belong to UNIP', first used on the Copperbelt in 1965, was not an empty one. In respect of access to markets, the grant of trading licences, and the allocation of building plots, for example, UNIP members received preferential treatment, and members of the opposition African National Congress (ANC) were often discriminated against. Szeftel concludes that 'given the relative scarcity of state resources, the monopolisation of patronage for UNIP members constituted a major asset for the Party in building and maintaining support' [Szeftel, 1978: 278].

The final party role we identify is that of political communication, which is a corollary of political competition and remains, potentially, an important party function. However, the reluctance of local party leaders to communicate unpopular messages is probably one reason why many governments often prefer to use non-party channels of communication – the Tanzanian government, for example, has relied substantially on the bureaucracy, while the government of Senegal, both before and after independence, has used Muslim leaders to put over its rural administration policies. In Malawi, on the other hand, the president and government have made use of the extensive organisational network of the ruling Malawi Congress Party (MCP) to explain their development strategy to the rural people.

Judged by the functions which they perform, African political parties have been in decline since independence, being run down in most states in favour of the burgeoning state machine. However, the moves since the late 1980s to establish multi-party systems of government have resulted in a dramatic change in Africa's political climate, and promise to give political parties a new lease of life. They came about when urban residents under middle-class leaders reacted angrily against the repression, corruption and gross economic mismanagement of one-party rule. At the beginning of 1990 constitutional provision for a multi-party system of government only existed in four mainland sub-Saharan African countries – Botswana, the Gambia, Senegal and Zimbabwe – and the Indian Ocean island of Mauritius, a member-state of the Organisation of African Unity (OAU) with a population mix similar to that of many states in the Caribbean. To this number could be added Namibia, on its becoming independent in March 1990, and Algeria, Egypt, Morocco and Tunisia in North Africa. Nigeria and Uganda were committed to the restoration of democratic civilian government.

The pro-democracy movement took root in one-party states of varying ideological persuasion and led to the removal in February 1991 of Mathieu Kérékou's dictatorial military regime in Benin, thus opening the floodgates of political reform throughout Francophone Africa. The defeat of Kaunda and UNIP in Zambia later the same year speeded up the ongoing process of reform in Anglophone Africa. Even the socialist states in Lusophone Africa and the Horn were not exempt: they renounced their commitment to Marxism–Leninism and held, or pledged themselves to hold, multi-party elections; one such election in Cape Verde resulted in the defeat of President Aristides Pereira, one of Africa's most respected leaders, and the ruling party early in 1991. Only a few states (including Burundi, Djibouti, Equatorial Guinea, Malawi and the Seychelles) held out against the democratic tide, maintaining – as President Daniel arap Moi had done in Kenya – that multi-party politics would intensify ethnic rivalry and prove politically destabilising. The leaders of a number of other states, such as Gnassingbe Eyadema in Togo and Mobutu Sese Seko in Zaire, sought to limit the extent of political reform. In Nigeria, in some contrast to the general pattern, a process of change was taking place in the early 1990s in which an outgoing military regime, led by General Ibrahim Babangida, attempted to construct a workable two-party national political system before stepping down. Here the perceived problem was the persistent tendency to breakdown of an imperfect competitive system, most recently experienced under the civilian regime of President Shehu Shagari between 1979 and 1983. In an ambitious piece of political engineering, the Babangida government founded two parties, 'one a little to the left, the other a little to the right of centre', in the words of the President. They were provided in advance with matching party headquarters, and carefully drafted political manifestos. However, it proved virtually impossible to contain the expressed wishes of the Nigerian electorate within the guidelines laid down by the military, and by late 1992 the timetable for transition was running into difficulty.

Our concern here is with the impact of this reform movement on party roles. It is likely that the greatest effect will be on the electoral role of parties. Multi-party competition will take place in countries which have never previously experienced it or where it is but a distant memory, with varying outcomes. In a few instances, as in Benin and Zambia, the result will be the defeat of the incumbent authoritarian regimes and the enhancement of the legitimacy of the successor governments. Elsewhere, the impact will be more muted, suggesting that it would be rash to expect too much of inter-party elections. As the October 1990 elections in the Côte d'Ivoire showed, it is possible to 'manage' electoral competition in such a way as not seriously to threaten the ruling party's monopoly of power. Evidence from Senegal points in the same direction, even though a more meaningful democratic experiment has been conducted in that country as reflected in national elections in 1978, 1983 and 1988. Alongside the Parti Socialiste's superior organisation and the professionalism of its campaigns must be set electoral regulations which did not allow the opposition parties to form a coalition, and the fact that the ruling party had the whole weight of the government machine behind it [Coulon and O'Brien, 1989]. In Kenya, where presidential and parliamentary elections were held in December 1992, a split in the opposition and electoral malpractice assured President Moi and the Kenya African National Union (KANU) of another term in office. There may, in other words, be less to democratisation than meets the eye.

3. East and Southeast Asia

In East and Southeast Asia alike, the tendency for the state to dominate over social interests has been fully reflected in party politics. Parties have generally been virtually inseparable from the state, executives have enjoyed considerable ascendancy over legislatures, and levels of political competition have been low. For some commentators, this reflects specific regional cultural traditions and concepts of power, whether associated with the values of Confucianism in the cases of Taiwan and South Korea, or with Javanese traditions of leadership in the case of Indonesia [Pye, 1985]. However, too great a reliance should not be placed on cultural explanations for the weakness of democracy. The authoritarian politics practised in the region have always responded directly to the perceived interests of ruling groups; they have reflected the influence of regional models of successful development, notably that of Japan; and they have generally been responses to current issues of internal and external security rather than to ancient cultural values. Although they have been installed and maintained with high levels of repression, they have still faced quite considerable opposition, suggesting that there is no particular innate disposition to accept such forms of politics. Finally, the character and dynamics of state ascendancy in fact vary substantially from case to case, reflecting more a temporary combination of circumstances than a permanent trait of regional culture. In Taiwan, where the state has certainly dominated, its dominance arises from the external character of the ruling élite and its alliance-building strategy in Taiwan itself. In Indonesia, the authority of the Suharto regime rests in part upon the memory of previous instability, and the massacre of half a million political opponents in 1965, and in part upon the elaborate bureaucratic state party, *Golkar*, in which a large part of the population is enrolled. In South Korea, despite the authoritarian character of the state, levels of opposition have always been high, with the government party rarely assured of even a bare majority of the vote. The ideologies through which East and Southeast Asian states and ruling parties have sought to justify their rule are generally modern rather than traditional, whatever their more distant sources of inspiration, drawing on such ideas as developmentalism, self-reliance, and anti-communism. Where the focus has been on consensus, this has frequently entailed a refusal to associate the state too directly with any particular communal tradition, as in the Indonesian doctrine of *pancasila* devised by Sukarno, with its emphasis upon worship of one (unspecified) god. Ideologies of rule which have claimed links with traditional models have generally been cynical, fraudulent, and unsuccessful, most notoriously in the case of Marcos's attempt to impose a form of 'democracy' allegedly based on the pre-colonial pattern of *barangay* organisation. Elsewhere, excessive emphasis upon traditional cultural patterns misses the extent and significance of the successful modernisation of forms of state authority.

The character and strength of ruling parties across the region varies widely. In **Taiwan** the KMT (Kuomintang – National People's Party) plays a leading role within the state system. According to Sutter, the KMT and the state are often inseparable:

The party forms cell and branch organizations in all aspects and at all levels of the government administration, the judiciary, the armed forces and the legislatures. Through these branches and cells, the party enforces political loyalty. Practically all leaders in these state institutions are party members. Political careers of the party members show substantial crossover between party and state positions, and state funds have been channeled into the support of party-related activities. [Sutter, 1988: 56]

The combination of party ascendancy and strong central executive control depends upon the cell structure and internal discipline of the party, and has been facilitated by the special circumstances arising from the fact that the two leading representative bodies, the Legislative Yuan (Parliament), and the separate National Assembly charged with the election of president and vice-president, were dominated until recently by mainland majorities in place since 1949.

A somewhat different situation obtains in **Indonesia**. The ruling party, *Golkar* (*Golongan Karya*, or Functional Groups), as its name suggests, is in fact less a political party than a corporatist body organised by the state. As such, its particular character derives from its domination not by the representatives of private interests, but by the military and civilian bureaucracy. Dating in embryonic form back to Sukarno's period, it was expanded by Suharto in an effort to free the state from the pressure of private interests. Liddle describes it as 'an electoral vehicle given its present form in 1969 in order to deny a parliamentary majority to other parties,' whose seats 'are filled with men or women who have or have had bureaucratic careers or are in other ways connected to the bureaucracy' [Liddle, 1985: 72]. Here the party is a subordinate part of a larger system dominated by the president, the military, and the bureaucracy. State control is secured by a simple expedient: in a formally competitive political system given its shape by the forced fusion of opposition parties in 1971 into two entities, the PDI (*Partai Democrasi Indonesia* – Indonesian Democratic Party) and the Islamic PPP (*Partai Persatuan Pembangunan* – Development Unity Party), the supremacy of *Golkar* in Parliament is ensured not only by the immense advantage it derives from its favoured position as a party of the state, but also by the president's power to nominate one fifth of the members of parliament from among the military. In addition, the president and vice-president are elected every five years by a People's Consultative Assembly made by combining the members of Parliament with an equal number of delegates, giving the government an appointed 60 per cent majority even without the members elected by *Golkar*. In fact *Golkar* has proved a successful electoral machine, winning between 62 and 64 per cent of the vote in 1971, 1977 and 1982, 73 per cent in 1987 and 68 per cent in 1992, while the enlarged People's Consultative Assembly has easily elected and re-elected Suharto to successive presidential terms.

Despite its deserved reputation as a highly authoritarian political system, **South Korea** has not been characterised by such emphatic electoral domination by either official presidential candidates or ruling parties; the 'ruling party' has generally been weak and of peripheral significance. Parties were slow to form after the declaration of the Republic in the south. Syngman Rhee kept his distance from the Korean Democratic Party, founded in 1945 by conservative landowning élites from the south-west, and forced it into opposition. He relied upon the National Association for the Rapid Realisation of Korean Independence, NARRKI (founded in 1946, and renamed the National Society in 1948) as a political vehicle, along with the police and youth groups. In the 1948 and 1950 elections a majority of candidates ran as independents, and thereafter moved freely between parties described as 'fluid, rootless associations among opportunistic individuals' [Henderson, 1968: 274]. Rhee founded the Liberal Party in December 1951, *after* he had begun in earnest his campaign to destroy the power of the Assembly, and used it as a political arm of the executive within a broader strategy of intimidation intended to crush all political opposition. It was opposed from 1955 by a re-founded Democratic Party (linking conservative opposition in the north-east to that in the south-west) which elected 79 representatives in 1958, and was kept from power in 1960 only by the immense fraud which led to the fall of the Rhee regime. The Liberal Party split into two immediately after Rhee fell, opening the way for military intervention in 1961.

Under President Park the task of creating a new ruling party was handed over to the Korean Central Intelligence Agency, after an interim period in which thousands of politicians were banned, and a new 1962 constitution removed the right of the assembly to challenge decisions of the Supreme Council for National Reconstruction. Despite the enormous advantages it enjoyed, the resulting

Democratic Republican Party could deliver only 46.7 per cent of the vote for Park in presidential elections in November 1963, giving him a narrow victory over a divided opposition. Likewise, a highly distorted electoral system was required to give the party a majority in the new assembly, where a mere 32 per cent of the vote gave it 63 per cent of the seats [Henderson, 1968: 188]. After failing to build an effective party (opposition candidate Kim Dae Jung polled 46 per cent of the votes in the presidential election of 1971), Park moved in 1972 to introduce the even more restrictive Yushin constitution, which made the presidential election indirect and gave the president the right to appoint one third of the assembly. A regime that had begun in 1962 by banning coffee drinking on the grounds that it was politically dangerous ended by passing legislation in 1974 banning all public criticism of the ultra-authoritarian constitution. Clearly, the ascendancy of the regime owed far more to repression and manipulation than to the efforts of its ruling party. As Han comments, 'Park was personally suspicious of both the pro-government and opposition parties and considered them as a necessary evil at best and a threat at worst' [Han, 1989: 276]. The ruling party in South Korea has been far less substantial and far less successful than its counterparts in either Indonesia or Taiwan, a fact reflected in the more recent process of democratisation discussed below.

In the **Philippines**, parties have been weak in periods of democratic politics, and weaker still when used to mobilise support for authoritarian rule. Attempts to modernise the political system and create an effective ruling party responsive to executive control never overcame the legacy of irresponsible factionalism and landowner power bequeathed by US colonial rule. The oligarchy opted in the 1935 constitution for a strong executive and a weak legislature, and the first president after independence, Manuel Roxas, set the tone by engineering the expulsion of opposition deputies and senators in order to secure passage of the amendment demanded by the United States to give US citizens equal rights with Philippine nationals over the exploitation of national resources and public utilities [Doronila, 1992: 46]. Between 1946 and 1972 party politics were characterised by fraud, corruption, and fluidity of the kind experienced in South Korea under Syngman Rhee, as rival factions competed to control executive power. With governments unable to maintain support, and oppositions anxious to gain power at all costs, a peculiarly

Philippine pattern of alternation in power emerged in which ruling-party politicians ran as opposition candidates and won: Roxas left the Nacionalista Party (founded in 1907) to form the Liberal Party in 1946; Liberal Minister of Defence Magsaysay left the ruling Liberals for the Nacionalistas in 1953; and Liberal senator and party president Ferdinand Marcos switched to the Nacionalistas to run against Liberal President Macapagal in 1965. All three were elected. Throughout the period votes were openly bought and sold, and opposition representatives routinely switched to the winning party once elected, in order to secure a share of government patronage for their constituents [Wurfel, 1988: 94–8].

As fraud, violence, and the level of electoral corruption peaked with Marcos's second presidential victory in 1969, civic pressure mounted for a constitutional reform, a prospect welcomed by Marcos as he was ineligible for re-election to the presidency after his second term. A constitutional convention which first met in June 1971 had made only limited progress when Marcos intervened in September 1972 to declare martial law, and suspend the activities of Congress. In the resulting 'New Society' competitive party politics was replaced by a sham form of direct democracy based upon local assemblies of around 500 families (*barangays*) headed by appointed captains, which were called upon to endorse a hastily revised constitution in carefully supervised public votes. While individual opposition leaders remained prominent, the old patronage-based parties quickly fell apart, and Marcos made no immediate move to replace them. However, rather than reform and modernise the party system, Marcos moved instead, in conjunction with his wife Imelda, to strengthen official powers of patronage at every level. Successive referendums 'confirmed' the popularity of martial law, and in 1976 a Legislative Advisory Council was created, along with provisions for the election of an interim assembly, the *Batasang Pambansa*. For elections to this new body, eventually held in 1978, Marcos created a new government party, the KBL (*Kilusan Bagong Lipunan*, or New Society Movement), based upon the *barangay* youth movement and the patronage networks controlled by the Minister of Local Government (the party's secretary-general), and by Imelda Marcos as governor of Metropolitan Manila and Minister for Human Settlements. Massive fraud kept the leading opposition movement LABAN (*Lakas ng Bayan*, or People Power) from winning a single seat, but the KBL was too much of a personal vehicle for the Marcoses and their cronies to become a viable political party in its own right.

The unfolding of the process of democratisation in these four cases largely reflected the relative strengths and weaknesses of state parties in each case. At one extreme, in **Indonesia**, there was no evidence in the early 1990s that either *Golkar* or the system of bureaucratic domination upon which it rested were losing their grip, although it was likely that the presidential term to which Suharto was elected in March 1993 would be his last. In **Taiwan** the KMT remained in control, although the opposition had made considerable headway in recent years. Here the rise of opposition reflected in part a successful political reform which made the system representative for the first time. As noted in the previous chapter, the Taiwanese political system came to depend upon the results of national elections only in 1992, when the remaining mainland members of the Legislative Yuan seated after 1949 finally lost their seats: the KMT only then embarked upon the effort to maintain its position through elections. The ruling élite succeeded in the 1980s in carrying through two important changes in the character of its rule in preparation for this challenge, by emerging from domination by Chiang Kai-shek and his son to come under Taiwanese leadership, and by allowing the creation of a minority opposition party. The Democratic Progressive Party contested the 1986 elections and gained over 22 per cent of the vote. A series of reforms in the early 1990s then placed political relations on the island on a new basis, reforming national security legislation, ending the state of 'civil war' with China, and repealing the 'Temporary Provisions' of 1948 which kept the 'senior parliamentarians' from the mainland in their seats. In December 1991 the KMT took 71 per cent of the vote in elections to a newly reconstituted 325-member National Assembly (twenty of whom, representing the mainland, were appointed), to 24 per cent for the Democratic Progressive Party. In December 1992 elections for the reformed 161-member Legislative Yuan gave the KMT 53 per cent to 31 per cent for the leading opposition party. The drop in the KMT vote was significant, and in part reflected serious splits within the party itself. At the same time, it had successfully negotiated a transition to a fully electoral system after more than forty years of disguised dictatorship.

In **South Korea** the degree of control exercised under pressure for change was much less substantial. Even before the assassination of

President Park by a senior aide in 1979, South Korea's ruling Democratic Republic Party was winning less than a third of the votes in National Assembly elections, though still taking a majority of seats. Park's successor, former head of military security Chun Doo Hwan, founded his own Democratic Justice Party, and introduced a new constitution which continued to ensure him an artificial majority. In 1982 and 1985 the DJP won over half the National Assembly seats with a little over a third of the vote, but opposition within the Assembly and mobilisation among students, intellectuals, business and workers forced a constitutional reform which went beyond government plans for cosmetic change. In mid-1987 the official candidate for the presidency, Roh Tae Woo, accepted opposition demands for direct presidential elections, political amnesty, and associated reforms. With opposition forces divided between the 'two Kims', veteran political dissident Kim Dae Jung and the more moderate Kim Young Sam, Roh was able to win the presidency with under 36 per cent of the vote. However, the DJP secured only 125 of the 299 Assembly seats in 1988 (with 34 per cent of the vote). Loss of control was avoided only by a subsequent merger between the DJP and Kim Young Sam's Reunification Democratic Party. This in turn led to the selection of Kim as presidential candidate, and a split in the party. In the ensuing elections, held in December 1992, Kim Young Sam emerged victorious with just under 42 per cent of the vote, as a consequence of a split in the opposition vote between veteran oppositionist Kim Dae Jung (33.4 per cent) and Hyundai boss Ching Ju Yung, whose United People's Party came in third with a disappointing 16.1 per cent of the vote. It remained to be seen what the impact upon the governing party would be of adopting as its leader a moderate oppositionist, and electing the first civilian president for thirty years. At the same time, the defection of Kim Young Sam, the retirement of Kim Dae Jung from politics after his defeat, and the first emergence of a business party suggested that it would be as difficult for the opposition to reorganise itself as it would be for the government to maintain its hold on power.

The popular movement in the **Philippines** which ousted Marcos in 1986 was the direct result of outrage at electoral fraud, reflecting his continued failure to create a viable party of the regime. However, the departure of Marcos was not followed by a strengthening of party politics in the wake of democratisation. The organisations which contributed most to the downfall of Marcos were not parties but movements: the opposition alliance UNIDO, founded in 1980 by Salvador Laurel, the National Movement for Free Elections, NAMFREL, and CORD, the Coalition of Organisations for the Restoration of Democracy. In 1992 Corazon Aquino was succeeded as president by Fidel Ramos (Defence Minister in the Marcos and Aquino governments) at the head of a coalition which could win only 23.5 per cent of the vote, narrowly defeating an independent, Miriam Santiago, and a former stalwart of crony capitalism, Cojuangco, with Imelda Marcos in fifth place. Despite democratisation parties were as weak nearly half a century on from independence as they had been at the outset. In the region as a whole the path of opposition remained a hard one, despite the progress which had been made.

4. Latin America

Until 1930 Latin American political parties were fairly similar to their European counterparts. There was a strong commitment, often a century or so old, to the formalities of political practice in the Western world: in legislatures modelled on European lines grave gentlemen in frock coats confronted each other in elaborate parliamentary rituals, volumes of learned debates were printed, and party loyalties were intense and enduring. Parties were élitist and loosely organised; electorates were small; nowhere did women have the vote before 1932; civil liberties were periodically curtailed by the oppressive hand of government; rebellion and civil war sometimes interrupted the normal squabbles of party politics; and here and there lengthy dictatorships appeared, while party politics and functioning congresses were a mere façade. However, all of these elements could equally well be illustrated out of the experience of Western Europe. Latin America becomes distinctive in party political terms only in the modern period. Liberal democracy as practised in Western Europe and in North America remains the goal to which all participants in the political system claim to aspire, and in that sense Latin America falls more squarely into the Western political tradition than any other region of the Third World; but modern political parties have failed until very recently to develop along typical 'Western' lines, or to move to the centre of the stage as they have done in Western Europe since the Second World War. Here we discuss why this should be so.

Although party traditions and systems vary in the region, there are few cases of independent parties competing for and alternating in power. In Colombia, Nicaragua, Paraguay and Uruguay, liberal and conservative parties over a century old still survive. However, Colombia experienced civil war and military intervention after World War II, and its democracy since 1958 has been limited by artificial constraints on competition, very low rates of participation, and frequent resort to government under state of siege. In the other cases continuity is only apparent, as each country has known lengthy periods of dictatorship, and in Stroessner's Paraguay and the Somozas' Nicaragua the survival of old labels concealed a dominant single party in an authoritarian regime. In Cuba, Mexico, and Nicaragua, more fundamental breaks with the past have taken place, but the post-revolutionary regimes created new single or dominant parties. Mexico has been governed since 1929 by a dominant party, now called the PRI, and opposition parties have never been allowed more than a minor share of the vote; Cuba adopted a single-party state model along Soviet lines in the wake of the 1959 revolution, in combination with a continuing experiment in popular participation, and retained it after the demise of the Soviet Communist Party; and in Nicaragua the Sandinista party adopted a pluralist system, and made history by stepping down after losing elections to a loose opposition coalition in 1990, but retained a substantial foothold on areas of state power.

Elsewhere new parties which emerged after 1930 could not establish either free political competition with majority participation, or stable civilian rule. In Argentina, Bolivia, Brazil, Ecuador and El Salvador a single party or coalition has tended to dominate. In Chile until 1973, in Cuba until Batista's 1952 coup, and intermittently in Peru, party politics has been competitive without achieving full participation, stability or sustained alternation in power. Venezuela, as we shall see, scarcely experienced democracy before 1958. In summary, the record of democracy in Latin America in the modern period is poor. Apparent continuity frequently masks *de facto* single-party rule, and breakdown and military intervention have been frequent.

Two important developments have taken place since the early 1960s. The first was the seizure of power by the military for long periods of time, reflecting a deep crisis at the level of civilian politics, and bringing to an end even such enduring democracies as Chile and Uruguay. The second was the establishment, in the wake of military withdrawal between 1979 and 1990, of competitive systems across virtually the whole region. By 1990, with elected presidents in power across the region, Latin American politics appeared more comparable to contemporary North American and Western European politics than it had done for many years; it could no longer be argued that democracy was 'impossible' in the region. Three questions arise. Why has democracy been so fragile in the past? What was the character of the democracies established? And were the prospects for stability and continuity in party politics better than before?

Civilian rule in Latin America has often come to an end as a result of civil war, revolution, or military intervention. Such breakdowns have reflected not only major social tensions, but also internal weaknesses in the party systems themselves. In many cases these have been dominated by parties of the state, with similar consequences to those observed elsewhere in the Third World. Examples may be drawn from Argentina, Brazil and Mexico. In **Argentina**, the Peronist Justicialista Party, founded after Perón's election victory of 1946 and the crushing of the independent pro-Peronist *Partido Laborista*, never functioned as an effective party in Perón's lifetime. Endowed with an ambitious ideology advocating a 'third way' between capitalism and communism, it was hampered from the start by Perón's refusal to allow it any organisational or political autonomy. It remained a hollow shell activated at elections, and a vehicle for the distribution of state patronage dispensed by the Peróns. It showed signs only in the aftermath of Alfonsín's electoral victory for the Radicals in 1983 of transforming itself into a coherent, autonomous and democratic party, but the election of Carlos Meném to the presidency in 1989, its first genuine electoral success, paradoxically threatened to reverse this process by reasserting the practice of virtually independent leadership unconstrained by party control.

Similarly, the parties which dominated in **Brazil** between 1945 and 1964, the Social Democratic Party (PSD) and the Brazilian Labour Party (PTB), had their origins within the authoritarian state of the *Estado Novo* (1937–45). The PSD was literally the party of the dictatorship, created when Vargas summoned the state governors and local executives of the *Estado Novo* and formed them into the party in 1945. It began life as a party of official patronage, closely wedded to the state. The PTB, also formed in 1945 at Vargas's instigation, was based on the bureaucracy of the official trade union movement, and intended as an instrument of state control. The tension arising from the conservatism of the PSD and the growing radicalism of dissident currents within the PTB was a major factor in the crisis which eventuated in military intervention in 1964.

Only in **Mexico** has a 'party of the state' governed continuously for a long period commencing before the Second World War. The Institutional Revolutionary Party (PRI), founded in 1929, established itself primarily as a result of its monopoly on linkages between the powerful executive and the population at large, gathered into separate official workers', peasants' and public employees' unions. It derived its ability to survive from the broader social base of the post-revolutionary regime, and the mechanisms for institutional renewal established as a reaction to the long personal dictatorship of Porfirio Diaz. For over sixty years the party has functioned primarily as a channel for the distribution of public goods, with politicians at municipal, state and federal levels playing the role of intermediaries. Deputies may not seek re-election after a three-year term, and administrative and 'political' positions are closely intertwined. Individuals move back and forth over time between appointed and 'elective' positions (the latter virtually appointed until recently in view of the near certainty of election for official candidates). The combination of enforced mobility and dependence on the state for advancement makes party members servants of the state rather than independent representatives, and the legislature and the party play a relatively minor role in the political system. Within these limits the PRI has been a highly successful ruling party, though its grip weakened considerably through the 1980s as the new 'technocratic' élite drawn from the Finance Ministry, which came to dominate the presidency, broke with the old popular alliances around which the party was constructed, adopting liberal economic policies and transforming the relationship between the state and the social forces formerly organised through the party.

In all three country cases, the dominance of 'parties of government' had a substantial effect on the nature of opposition parties and their attitude towards electoral competition. The PAN in Mexico, the divided Radical and Intransigent Radical parties in Argentina, and the UDN in Brazil were all model liberal democratic parties in terms of the ideologies they endorsed. They all despaired, however, of gaining power through the ballot box, and attempted at some stage to ride to power on the backs of the military, whether through armed rebellion, backing for coups, or acquiescence in the proscription of their rivals for power.

Thus one major cause of instability has been the creation of 'parties of government' after the acquisition of power, and the tendency for such parties to sustain themselves as monopoly suppliers of state patronage and as intermediaries between the executive, the bureaucracy, and the people, thereby limiting the prospects of opposition parties. Where these parties have additionally been the first to mobilise new social groups they have so dominated the political arena that the chances for opposition have been bleak. Even so, 'populism' is not the prime cause of political instability in Latin America. As noted above, it was itself a response to a loss (on the part of preceding élites) of the ability to rule by consent. Indeed, where strong populist movements failed to materialise, regime followed regime in a destabilising cycle of experiment and failure: as successive attempts to recreate a viable political regime foundered, a downward spiral to dictatorship ensued.

The clearest example of this was in **Chile**, where between 1932 and 1970 no government succeeded in securing re-election after stepping down from power. In the 25 years before the coup which instituted the Pinochet dictatorship, Chile was governed successively by the Radicals, the populist Ibañez, the Conservatives under Alessandri, the Christian Democrats under Frei, and the Popular Unity coalition under Allende. Each of Allende's predecessors saw his political backing evaporate by the end of his term; the rise and decline of the Christian Democrats made party alignments on the centre and the right highly unstable, and the Alessandri–Frei–Allende sequence produced a steady shift to the left, finally precipitating the coup of 1973.

In **Colombia**, where the Liberal and Conservative parties continued to dominate after 1930, the political system also disintegrated under opposing pressures for reaction and reform. While increasingly radical currents emerged within the Liberal

Party with the rise to prominence of Gaitán (until his assassination in 1948), the Conservative party came under the control of the arch-conservative Laureano Gomez. Social forces polarised over struggles for and against reform, and the army intervened in 1953 in the context of open civil warfare. **Venezuela**, lacking the experience of Chile or Colombia with democratic politics, lived through a similar cycle of destabilisation between 1935 and 1958. After the death of the dictator Gomez a sequence of military-led regimes wavered between repression and cautious reform, until a reformist coup in 1945 brought the Democratic Action party to power. Its attempt to launch a radical programme of social change centred on land reform brought a conservative reaction, and a counter-coup in 1948 which led (after a period of military rule) to an attempt by Colonel Marcos Perez Jimenez to set up a popular–authoritarian regime. Similar sequences leading to breakdowns of democratic politics can be witnessed in Peru and Bolivia. This suggests that while populism (with its authoritarian practices and its closeness to the state) was a flawed solution to the political crisis experienced across Latin America after 1930, it was more effective than any other political strategy in providing stability and promoting economic development.

In one way or another then, virtually every political system in Latin America broke down in the period after the Second World War, leading to military intervention, often of a protracted nature. Paradoxically, the cycle of military interventions across the region was to make possible a reordering of civilian politics which restored the prospect – for the first time since the 1930s – of stability within a context of respect for the rule of law. As we shall see in the following chapter, hard lessons were learnt from military rule and the shambles which resulted. The consequence (practically everywhere) was a greater willingness on the part of civilian parties to tolerate each other and to seek compromise, and a determination to make democracy succeed. There was also a general move toward the centre on the part of parties to right and left, and a conscious policy of exclusion of radicals, limiting of political agendas, and strengthening of discipline and hierarchy within parties. In other words, self-censorship took over from outside intervention, en-abling democratic political systems to survive at the price of slowing reform, containing radicalism, and placing the highest priority on establishing and obeying new 'rules of the game'. This general reorientation, apparent first with the restoration of democracy in Venezuela and Colombia, was followed in Ecuador in 1979, in Peru in 1980, in Argentina in 1983, in Brazil and Uruguay in 1985, and in Chile in 1990. It produced a range of 'self-limiting democracies' which (if they were to survive) could transform the face of politics in Latin America.

This raises the broader question of the character of democracy in Latin America after the general withdrawal of the military from power. The surviving democracies in Colombia, Costa Rica and Venezuela have tended to be dismissed as highly restricted, conservative, and élitist. In purely descriptive terms, that picture is not altogether misleading. The competing parties have tended to become more similar (and more centrist) over time; they have benefited from explicit agreements to share power or to exclude more radical opponents, and although the very high levels of participation and intense party loyalties of Venezuela contrast sharply with the low levels of involvement registered in Colombia, the Venezuelan system favours groups with vast financial resources, and offers limited opportunity for independent participation. For a considerable period, however, the limited and cautious nature of these democracies gave them, at a price, a degree of durability that was lacking in the more open and polarised systems of, say, Chile and Brazil before military intervention.

Peeler suggests that the common feature which explains the survival of democracy in each case is 'the ability of rival élites explicitly to accommodate one another's interests' [Peeler, 1985: 93]. This is helpful as far as it goes, but it begs the question of why élites were willing (and able) to co-operate here, when unable (or unwilling) to do so in other cases. This question can be answered only by identifying the class nature of the élites involved (representatives of different bourgeois interests), establishing the nature of programmes on which they co-operate (excluding radical alternatives in their joint interests), and asking why it has been possible for such programmes to be successfully implemented. The experience of deep social crises in each case (civil war in Costa Rica and Colombia, military intervention in Colombia and Venezuela, and intense political polarisation in all three cases) had the double effect of uniting previously divided bourgeois groups on a pro- gramme aimed at common survival, and persuading a significant majority of the population at large to accept (and support) a cautious democracy promising little in the way of immediate social and economic advancement, but committed to stability and the restoration of a state of law. After the traumatic events of the 1970s and 1980s elsewhere in Central and South America, similar developments are possible. If so, the prospects for Latin American democracy are bright in one sense, but dim in another: élite co-operation may secure democracy on a more stable basis than in the past, but at the same time the new forms of democracy may be too cautious to tackle the enormous social problems which are the legacy of decades of dependent development and years of harsh military rule. As Peeler notes, the stability of democracy in his three cases 'depended on the willingness of the democratising reformers to accommodate élite interests by forgoing major structural changes in economy and society' [Ibid.: 40–1]. Favourable conditions for growth in the 1960s and 1970s made it possible to ignore pressures for such change, but they have recently reappeared in both Colombia and Venezuela. In the longer run they will have to be resolved, there and in the new democracies, if even the most restricted and elitist forms of democracy are to survive [Cammack, 1991; 1993].

Indeed, it appeared in the early 1990s that the failure to address the need for reform was producing instability and breakdown in the new democracies, and in such established regimes as Venezuela, where social turmoil, unrest among the military and attempted intervention threatened the regime of President Carlos Andres Perez. The ubiquity of democratic reform elsewhere intensified the pressure on the Mexican regime, which had been promoting a controlled policy of liberalisation since the early 1970s, but which remained unwilling to allow liberalisation to spill over into democratisation. By the late 1980s the ability of the PRI to command a clear majority was rapidly disappearing, and a split in the party prior to the 1988 elections (producing the breakaway PRD – Democratic Party of the Revolution – led by the son of President Lázaro Cardenas) was followed by the PRI's narrowest victory in its history, accompanied by vociferous allegations from the opposition that it had been secured by massive fraud. Under newly elected president Carlos Salinas the party intensified its systematic use of state patronage, pouring government resources into local and regional elections on an unprecedented scale, but at the same time carried out an electoral reform which guaranteed any party winning over 35 per cent of the votes a majority of assembly seats – a sure sign that it felt itself to be losing its ability to command a majority. This admission of defeat recalled similar subterfuge in Brazil and South Korea, and suggested that the days of the region's most successful ruling party might themselves be numbered. There were similar signs of instability among the new democracies themselves. In Peru, President Fujimori, elected without significant party support in 1990 in a contest with another independent candidate, the novelist Mario Vargas Llosa, broke with the constitutional regime in 1992 to take dictatorial powers, then engineered elections for a new constituent assembly in which his supporters secured a majority. In Brazil, President Collor, also elected as an independent with little party support, this time in a run-off against 'Lula' (Luis Inacio da Silva), the leader of the PT (Workers' Party), took power in 1990 with plans to reshape Brazil's political and economic systems, but resigned at the end of 1992 in an unsuccessful bid to evade trial for corruption and impeachment in the Brazilian Senate. Each case signalled the weakness of parties, and the avoidance of issues of social and economic reform.

5. The Middle East

Political parties in the Middle East have ranged from loosely organised cliques of notables, through trans-state Pan-Arab and Pan-Islamic to the classic clandestine cell-based Communist parties which have been small in membership but politically important. There seems to be no overall general pattern in the historical evolution of parties other than that in some states parties of notables have given place to radical nationalist parties (as in Iraq and Syria in the 1960s), or to state-sponsored bureaucratic parties (like the Arab Socialist Union in Egypt and the Sudan Socialist Union). In the Maghreb, the pattern was similar to post-colonial political developments in sub-Saharan Africa: anti-French nationalist parties like the Neo-Destour in Tunisia and the National Liberation Front (FLN) in Algeria became state parties immediately after independence. In Lebanon, alignments of notables continued to be significant until the mid-1970s. In the kingdoms of Jordan and Kuwait the ruling families at times have allowed parties or groupings to function but ensured a central role for independent pro-regime tribal representatives in the assemblies. In the Libya of Qaddafi parties are banned on the grounds that the people should represent themselves directly, and in Saudi Arabia on the grounds that the state implements Islamic law, the major requirement of an Islamic polity.

In general, parties with some sort of ideology, structure and membership independent of the state have not flourished. Where such parties have emerged they have required an alliance with the military in order to assume power or they have been suppressed. In Iraq (1963 and 1968) and Syria (1963 and 1966) different wings of the Ba'th (Renaissance) Party came to power after military coups and have had a difficult and complex relationship with the officer corps as a result. One major factor in the development of this party–army relationship was the inability of the parties to make any political headway in an electoral system where landlords and tribal leaders held sway over the peasantry. Similarly, officers have sought civilian support and have organised party-like organisations. In Egypt, the Free Officers who came to power in 1952 banned the old political parties and formed nationwide organisations to mobilise, legitimise and control the civilian population. In Lebanon, parties came into their own only after the 1975 civil war and even then were essentially militias.

The early history of political parties in the modern Middle East reflected the broader constellation of social and economic power. In Iraq, Syria and Lebanon parties were first established in the Mandate period. In Syria, a loose party coalition of notables spearheaded the opposition to the French, although they were in a minority to the independents. In Iraq and Lebanon, prominent individuals formed loose political groupings. In the 1930s, however, ideological, organised political parties began to form. Some, like the Lebanese Phalange, the *Najjadeh* (Scouts) and Syrian Social National Party, were modelled on European fascist forms of organisation, and others, like the Syrian National Action League (one of the roots of the Ba'th party) were political clubs. They were established to mobilise various forms of nationalist opinion, and appealed to a new generation of the young and educated which the older nationalist blocs of the 1920s had ceased to attract. None of these new political organisations was able to compete with the landowners and tribal chiefs, who were factionally divided but conscious of a shared benefit arising from their large landholdings. Indeed, in Iraq a short-lived Shaykhs' Rights party was established. On independence, this pattern did not change. The assemblies of Iraq, Syria and Lebanon were controlled by independents or loose coalitions representing regional or local interests. Parties of this period were short-lived electoral lists controlling the peasant and tribal vote, or parliamentary factions coalescing around a cabinet minister who controlled and dispensed patronage. Against this entrenched ruling group socialist, nationalist and communist parties were unable to achieve any electoral success. In both Iraq and Syria these parties sought influence and allies in the officer corps. The 1958 coup in Iraq which swept away the monarchy and landlords presented the Ba'th with no greater political opportunity since the army refused to cede power to the parties. As a result, the party sought to recruit and place supporters in the army rather than rely on sympathisers. A short period of Ba'thist rule in 1963 was followed by a further five-year period of military rule until 1968, when a fully fledged Ba'thist government was established, although again after another military coup. Though dependent on military goodwill the civilian party was able to establish a degree of civilian control over the military and Saddam Husayn, a civilian party leader, held the levers of power. In Syria, the Ba'th came to power in 1963 after a coup by a group of Ba'thist officers organised in the Military Committee, which was separate from the civilian party. As a result, party politics in Syria was essentially intertwined with the internal politics of the officer corps.

In Egypt before the 1952 coup, party politics were somewhat more developed than in the other states. The *Wafd* (delegation) was a popular nationalist party and dominated Egyptian politics from the 1920s through the 1940s and generally won majorities in parliament when the palace did not exercise control. Like other pre-1952 parties the *Wafd* was a party of the Egyptian middle and upper classes, but unlike the others was able to appear as the party of the nation fighting for complete independence from the British. The 1952 coup by the Free Officers brought the banning of the political parties, although it was the well-organised Society of Muslim Brothers which was more of a threat. Subsequently the regime established a series of single-party organisations, although in the 1970s (when Anwar Sadat liberalised the political system, albeit under guidelines favourable to the government party) the Muslim

Brothers and the *Wafd* resurfaced, indicative of the engrained sentiment for parties in Egypt.

One distinct type of Middle Eastern political party has been that organised across state boundaries. The Ba'th party and the Arab National Movement have been orientated toward Arab unity and have been pan-Arab in structure and ideology. The Muslim Brothers have branches in most Arab states and both Iraq and Lebanon have had movements supportive of the Islamic regime in Iran. With the persistence of state boundaries such parties have tended to become based in a single state, or (as in the case of the Ba'th in Iraq and Syria) divided into separate national parties.

Middle Eastern politics, then, have to some extent reflected social and political change. Coalitions of landlords, urban notables and tribal leaders have given way to parties or state organisations whose core has been the modern educated middle strata. The evolution of party in the contemporary Middle East is linked to the way in which the monarchs and landlords were overthrown and to party–army relations. The Ba'th in Iraq and Syria and the single-party organisations in Egypt illustrate this evolution.

In **Egypt**, the political parties were not directly involved in the overthrow of the monarchy, and as a result the Free Officers sought to establish a supportive constituency by using the state which they had seized for these ends. Between 1953 and 1956 British, French and Israeli attacks on Egypt facilitated the mobilisation of national support for the regime, although the instrument employed was rather crude. The Liberation Rally was a bureaucratic mechanism for organising demonstrations and rallies, even though it did draw on popular sentiment. In 1958 the National Union was formed. This was more than an organisation for channelling national support against the former colonial power and a range of internal enemies; it was a more sophisticated bureaucratic machine, with an ideological justification supportive of its anti-party position: parties divided the nation and undermined national mobilisation for economic and social development. Such a rationale was hardly credible when the National Union was organised along the administrative lines of the Ministry of the Interior. Though the National Union was centrally controlled, the government passed a circumscribed power to those local élites who had not been affected by the land reform: the established middle peasantry. Because the National Union was established by the regime and the ideology of the regime was inchoate, everybody and anybody was recruited into the membership. When Nasser dissolved it, this moribund organisation died without a whimper even though it had a membership of six million. This number was hardly surprising, since membership meant 'the redress of grievance, protection of existing rights, the retention of social prestige, and attainment of minimal qualifications for co-optation into higher political echelons' [Binder, 1978: 42].

A more serious and more overtly corporatist attempt at forming a political party occurred in 1961–2. The Arab Socialist Union (ASU) was to represent the 'national alliance of working forces'. In so doing, it fell between two stools. On the one hand it aimed at national recruitment for regime support, and on the other required the mobilisation of militants committed to a regime which had formulated something like an ideology and at least a clear programme: the socialist transformation of Egypt. As Waterbury has pointed out, the ASU was to do everything: 'pre-empt all other political forces, contain the citizenry, and through the vanguard, turn it into a mobilisational instrument with a cutting edge' [Waterbury, 1983: 322]. He neatly condenses the contradiction in these goals with his account of the trial of Ahmad Kamil, former officer, security official and ASU apparatchik: 'organising Socialist Youth [a part of the ASU] or tapping phones . . . were routine activities that in Kamil's laconic rendering apparently had no qualitative difference between them' [Ibid.: 355]. It is indicative of the caution of the regime in recruiting those who were ideologically committed to transforming Egypt, that the recruitment of those at the top of the ASU was based on loyalty to President Nasser. The 'vanguard' could not survive because it was organised by those who had no sense of what a vanguard meant. In Moore's pithy summary, 'hardly a vanguard for recruiting the top political leadership, the party was a rearguard for retiring it' [Moore, 1974: 197]. Of 131 ministers, only two held party position before becoming ministers, whereas 83 held party positions after it.

The greater penetration of Egyptian society by the ASU was facilitated by the expansion of the state's control of the economy during the early 1960s. By the mid-1960s, one-third of the Egyptian work force was employed by the state and in the villages the state controlled the all important Co-operative Boards. It was not only republics which developed such organisations. In Iran, the Shah established the Rastakhiz party and used the state's bureaucratic and economic power to drum people into it.

The development of the Ba'th party is rather different. It emerged as a party independent of the state and attracted the new generation of young educated nationalists. In **Syria**, the entrenched power of landlords and the consequent electoral failure of the Ba'th caused it to seek alliances with nationalist officers and send young adherents to the military academy. Ideological and factional conflict within the party subsequently led to civilian party leaders seeking military support and Ba'thist officers seeking alliances with civilian party leaders. This tendency increased after the 1963 coup, when a Military Committee, organised separately from the civilian party intervened to establish a Ba'thist government. As civil party leaders amalgamated with military Ba'thists an intense power struggle developed, and party structure and membership radically changed. The party had been based on a cell system with tiers of local, provincial and national congresses. Since the congresses did have a say in defining party principles and electing the leadership, and since representation at congress was based on the number of full members, top political leaders recruited relatives and friends, thereby evading the internal party regulations which laid down strict guidelines for party membership. Those who were committed to the party and party principles were swamped by the new members. Not only did the party come under the control of the military but it shifted away from its original structure of a cadre party based on democratic centralism. Ironically, non-ideological members were recruited to resolve ideological divisions within the party over the significance of class analysis, and the relative weight to be given to socialism and nationalism, and to Syrian and Arab nationalism.

One further result of internal party struggle was the advancement of the rural minorities (particularly the Alawites) within the party. Because of its secularism the party had appealed to the minorities rather than to the Sunni Muslim majority, as it had appealed to those of rural and provincial origin rather than big town origin, because of its emphasis on peasant rights and land reform. Reinforcing this process was the fact that key members of the Military Committee were Alawites. The party became increasingly identified with the provinces and the rural minorities, and as the party became more influenced by Marxism and secularism, Ba'thist rule generated large-scale opposition from the towns, the merchants and Sunni Muslim fundamentalism. Party and state became increasingly one after 1970, when Hafiz al-Asad in a coup removed radical elements and attempted to use the state to conciliate urban Sunni Muslim Syria and attract back urban capitalists who had fled to Lebanon. This more pragmatic and conciliatory policy to woo the opposition was undertaken at the cost of a party life independent of the state, the military and the internal security forces, and it failed. The change in party structure and the process of recruitment (and, above all, the military connection) subverted the independence of the party from the state. Having sought a clientele in the officer corps, the Ba'th in Syria became a relatively passive client of the military.

In **Iraq** a somewhat similar development of the Ba'th party took place although there was not such a clear subordination of party to army. As in Syria, it appealed to young, educated Pan-Arabists. The party was small and weak in 1958 when the military overthrew the monarchy, but it did come to power in 1963 for nine months after conspiring with a group of non-Ba'thist officers. One factor in the overthrow of this Ba'thist regime was its attempt to establish a National Guard as a counterweight to the army, which alienated the officer corps. The Ba'th again came to power in 1968 (again through a military coup) and although Ba'thist officers were involved, the civilian wing of the party had a far greater degree of control. The first President after the 1968 coup was a retired Ba'thist officer, Ahmad Hasan al-Bakr, but power lay with Saddam Husayn, a civilian and provisional regional secretary since 1963. Saddam Husayn controlled the army by organising the promotion of officers who were his relatives or from his home town of Tikrit, and by establishing party control over the army in which only the Ba'th party could organise. Although the party has only around 40 000 full-time members, and party and state structures remain separate except at the upper echelons, the Ba'th does place members in key positions and attempt to recruit sympathisers who are technically and administratively able. Party committees have a role in formulating policy and government implements it. The Ba'th in Iraq (even when in power) is clandestine and conspiratorial and its relatively privileged members act as the eyes and ears of the regime. The semi-independent role of the party has been increasingly eroded by the more personalistic leadership role of Saddam Husayn, leader of the party, commander-in-chief and head of state. One effect of the 1991 war was the further attenuation of the party and deepening reliance of the President on special army units.

While Iraq and Syria have seen the mutation of independent parties into state-based ones, in other parts of the Middle East there has been the beginnings of an opposite trend, with the introduction of a process of partial political liberalisation. In Egypt, Tunisia, Algeria and Jordan measures have been introduced to open the political system to political parties. In all of these states such changes were promulgated as a result of economic crises which discredited the statist management of the economy, and the political structures associated with it, and ushered in a period of economic liberalisation. Political power remains in the hands of those who control the state, however, and the process of political liberalisation remains cautious and controlled. In all four of these states Islamic political movements have emerged and have generally been considered the major obstacle to extending liberalisation into democratisation. In Algeria, where the process of liberalisation went the furthest and the Islamic Salvation Front seemed on the brink of an electoral victory after the first stage of a two-stage election in 1991, the military intervened. This marked the end of the process of devolving power from the state but provided no test of whether an Islamic political movement there would have been incompatible with the emergence of party politics. It did suggest that the prospects for the broadening of the process of democratisation across the Arab world were limited.

6. Conclusion

Political parties in the Third World tend to be weak because they lack autonomy, authority and prestige. Where independence has been recent and opportunities for political organisation prior to independence have been limited, it is clear why this should be so. Under colonial rule parties were usually either élitist groupings closely associated with the colonial regime, hence lacking a popular base, or opposition movements denied the political space to develop on a broad basis. In the former case, adaptation after independence was made difficult by the need to conduct a hasty mobilisation among hitherto-neglected groups. In the latter, independence often brought with it both popularity and power, but the party tended to be weakened (paradoxically in some ways) by its close and immediate association with government.

In the transition from opposition to power, the resources of the movement were frequently stretched to the limit; the leadership often became remote, while the party lacked the substantial core of middle-level activists and workers it needed to establish itself soundly among the mass of a population eager for results. Key party activists had to be moved into administrative and governmental positions, and the tasks of political mobilisation and organisation were carried out (if at all) by less experienced party officials or by newly-appointed state functionaries. Power corrupted. State resources were used politically to shore up the regime, and the party tended to become above all a channel for patronage and the purchase of political support. It is no accident that parties in the Third World now tend to be agencies of the state rather than vehicles for the autonomous political mobilisation of the citizenry behind clearly-defined political programmes with strong ideological underpinnings.

A further factor causes problems for political parties in newly independent states. In a context of recent independence, opposition may appear (and be depicted) as verging on treason. Ruling parties are likely to mobilise around the themes of nationalism, independence, dignity and sovereignty. Calls for unity – stressing the danger of fratricidal conflict – are likely to predominate. In such a context, the problems of opposition (already made difficult by the close links between the ruling party and the state) are exacerbated.

It is not surprising, in the light of these problems, that parties in Africa, East and Southeast Asia and the Middle East tended to be swept aside, or swallowed up in the machinery of state. The Ba'ath parties of Syria and Iraq survived by tying themselves to the state in the form of the military; those of an increasing number of African states (typified in different ways by Zambia, Tanzania and the Côte d'Ivoire) succeeded by becoming unequivocally parties of government, rather than contestants among others of equal status in a competitive system. In East and Southeast Asia, parties of the state have been the norm: the degree of personalism and the balance of power between the party and other organs of the state have varied, but few independent parties have prospered.

It is perhaps surprising, at first sight, that Latin American parties should appear so similar to those in the other areas examined, despite the absence of recent colonial rule, and of the ethnic, religious and linguistic divisions which have made political mobilisation problematic elsewhere. We argue, however, that in some ways the history of élite-controlled, export-led development (and its crisis after 1930) can be seen as a functional equivalent to colonial rule and its demise. The rapid development of mass-based parties in Latin America after 1930, the tendency for mobilisation to take place primarily from within the state rather than outside it, and the frequency with which movements based within the state were successful in mobilising such a proportion of the population that peaceful competition within the electoral system seemed fruitless – these are all factors which offer immediate parallels with the record elsewhere.

All four areas have in common, then, a close identification of successful parties with the state. Success in such conditions goes along with both a lack of autonomy, and a weakening of the prospects for open competition for power. It is therefore the closeness of party and state which accounts most satisfactorily for the failure of competitive liberal democracy to develop out of existing party systems in the Third World. It also accounts for the fact that change tends to come (if at all) in violent or at least unconstitutional ways.

However, our case studies suggest that the party itself rarely plays a decisive role in political systems apparently dominated by a 'party of the state'. Taiwan's Kuomintang may be exceptional, precisely because it was essentially an external force for so many years. In other cases parties which have enjoyed considerable success over long periods of time, such as Indonesia's *Golkar* and Mexico's PRI, or the once independent Ba'ath parties of Iraq and Syria, have been arms of an independent executive, unable to set the agenda themselves.

A second conclusion to be drawn from our case studies is that regimes which have tried to govern through state parties have enjoyed very mixed success. In practically all the African cases, such parties have exhausted their efficacy and legitimacy, and in the early 1990s were in the process of modifying or abandoning their role. However, the phenomenon is by no means unique to Africa. Authoritarian states all over the Third World have found it difficult to establish and maintain such parties. The attempts of Nasser in Egypt, Peron in Argentina and Marcos in the Philippines show the difficulties facing personal leaders who want a party behind them but will not allow it any autonomy; in Brazil and South Korea, too, regimes much vaunted for their record of economic development have proved entirely incapable of creating parties able to win a bare majority of the vote, and relied instead on constitutional chicanery and manipulation of the opposition to perpetuate their control of key institutions.

If single or dominant parties turn out upon close scrutiny to have serious weaknesses, the move towards liberalisation and democratisation in much of the Third World is more easily understood. Care should be taken here not to generalise too broadly. As the previous sections demonstrate, the pace of movement towards democratisation is by no means uniform either across regions or within them. The dynamics of the process are quite different in such cases as Brazil, Mexico, Nigeria, the Philippines, South Korea, Taiwan, and Zambia, for example. However, a number of general points can be made. Overall, the record we have examined provides little support for optimism as regards the prospects for the new democracies as they emerge. Firstly, although we have stressed the internal dynamics of change, much of the pressure for democratisation comes from outside, and the resistance of ruling élites to meaningful reform remains strong. Secondly, where state-controlled clientelism has played a significant role the decline of parties of the state leaves a corrosive legacy of susceptibility to the attractions of official patronage which may not be easily overcome. The short-term use of official patronage to stabilise fragile new democracies may easily develop into long-term abuse. Thirdly, where authority has centred on leaders rather than organised parties, personalism remains a temptation for new presidents, even where they are backed by independent parties. Fourthly, in Africa and Latin America democratisation has all too often been associated with economic liberalisation, as a consequence of a broader questioning of the political, economic and social role of the state. In such circumstances it has been associated with an absence of state action or intervention to promote social and economic reform. Given the depth of poverty and inequality in much of the Third World, democracy in the absence of such reform may well prove unstable. Paradoxically, only a strong state can implement the structural adjustment policies prescribed by the IMF and the World Bank.

These characteristics combine to create a situation in much of the Third World in which an apparently democratic electoral system is being introduced in the absence of basic rights of political citizenship. Even if liberal democracy is defined narrowly, to exclude social and economic rights, it cannot function effectively in the absence of the following: freedom of opinion, expression, speech, assembly, and association within the rule of law; the right to cast a free vote and stand for office; competitive, free and fair elections; and institutional arrangements which make government responsive to preferences expressed in those elections. So long as the pressure for democratisation comes from outside, and personalism and state and private clientelism remain strong, while powerful social groups are able to assert their interests through extra-constitutional means, and poverty forces large proportions of the population into dependent relationships which effectively eliminate their freedom of political choice, the conditions for the exercise of effective political citizenship will not exist. Without them, many new Third World democracies will be democratic in name only.

Further Reading

Randall [1988] usefully compares Third World political parties across regions. The volumes of country studies edited by Diamond, Linz and Lipset on Africa [1988], Asia [1989a] and Latin America [1989b] provide a comprehensive set of essays on the politics of individual countries, with a focus on democracy and democratisation. Huntington [1991], Bermeo [1992], and Diamond [1992] offer general discussions of related themes. A number of West African cases are examined in O'Brien *et al.* [1989]. The background to the Nigerian case is also described in Uwazurike [1990]. Cohen and Goulbourne [1991] examine the links between democracy and socialist reform. Two articles by Liddle [1985, 1992] discuss the dynamics of the Suharto regime in Indonesia and the prospects for change; for similar material on South Korea and Taiwan see Cotton [1989] and Cheng [1989] respectively. Bresnan [1986] and Wurfel [1988] provide accounts of Philippine politics up to the end of the Marcos period. The wave of reform in Latin America from 1980 onwards is reviewed in Karl [1990] and Cammack [1993]. Rock [1985], Flynn [1978] and Valenzuela [1978] provide detailed accounts of the earlier politics of Argentina, Brazil, and Chile respectively. The cases of Colombia, Costa Rica and Venezuela are examined in Peeler [1985]. Malloy and Seligson [1987] reviews a number of cases, while Hagopian [1990] and Mainwaring [1991, 1992-93] explore the Brazilian case in helpful comparative perspective. Cammack [1988] provides background information on Brazil's party system since 1945. Perez [1992] examines Nicaragua's Sandinistas after the election defeat of 1990. For the Middle East, Makram-Ebeid [1989], Esposito and Piscatori [1991], Hudson [1991], Springborg [1987], Waterbury [1991] and Middle East Research and Information Project [1992a] provide material for comparison. For all the cases of democratisation current in the early 1990s, the contemporary sources listed in our introduction above should be consulted for subsequent developments.

4

The Military

1. Introduction

The military has played a central role in Third World politics since independence. There have been many attempts to explain military intervention but (in the main) they have proved inadequate to account for the great range of interventions. Some writers, like S.E. Finer, have pointed to the socio-cultural environment as the key factor. Finer has argued that a low level of political culture is likely to result in military intervention [Finer, 1981]. He gives limited independent criteria of a 'low' political culture, and cause and consequence are quite similar: military intervention itself seems to indicate a low level of political culture. In any case, there is little reason to think that either Zambia or Colombia has a political culture distinct from its neighbours, and every reason to doubt that Lebanon has a higher political culture than Egypt, or Malaysia than the Philippines. Yet these are the implications of Finer's approach. In contrast to Finer's broad focus on political culture, Janowitz focuses wholly on the characteristics of the military: the superior quality of its organisation and the shared values of the officer corps [Janowitz, 1964]. Yet the military has frequently been fragmented and has produced a wide range of political ideologies: nationalist, populist, monetarist, socialist, conservative and radical. The frequency of purges also casts doubt on such unity of organisation or values. Luckham focuses on the interplay between social forces external to the military itself and military structures [Luckham, 1971]. Other explanations have stressed *inter alia* personal ambition, corporate motives, class interests, regional and ethnic considerations, and the military's perception of the national interest.

133

Yet none of these theories has satisfactorily explained why the military has intervened in some states, and not in others.

There is no question that many Third World states, with underdeveloped political institutions and low levels of literacy, are much weaker in terms of political culture than the industrialised states of the West; to this extent, they are more susceptible to military intervention. But to explain why military intervention occurs in a state with a level of political culture manifestly higher than that of a coup-free state in the same geographical region entails looking at country-specific features. For example, the circumstances in which a particular state became independent may be a relevant factor – whether smoothly and constitutionally as in Sri Lanka, or following a protracted liberation struggle as in Indonesia; so, too, may be the many reasons for the decline, often over a longish period, of a government's legitimacy. These reasons may include political and\or economic mismanagement, authoritarianism, repression and corruption. The picture may be complicated further because a different meaning may attach to the term 'legitimacy' between one region and another, while within a particular region military personnel may have lower social origins than the political and bureaucratic élite, causing the former to feel alienated and resentful.

Psychological reasons for intervention may also be important: military officers who have participated in government in the past may not readily subscribe to a doctrine of civilian supremacy and, where opportunity offers, may intervene again to exercise their perceived 'right' to rule. And a successful coup in one state may encourage the armed forces in a neighbouring state to intervene. All these considerations have led Luckham to conclude that 'the words "coup" or "military intervention" are impoverished characterisations of the totality of a complex train of historical events' [Luckham, 1991: 11].

In looking at military intervention we need to consider, as well as social origin, whether those who seized power were senior officers or whether junior officers and other ranks were involved and\or took the initiative themselves; and also whether it was an exclusively army exercise or included naval, air force and police personnel. Again, it needs to be asked whether the take-over was easy or whether there were serious technical barriers to be overcome. Finally, it will be important to determine the objectives of the coup-makers since these will help to determine the nature of the subsequent military (or military-dominated) regime; at the same time, they might give some indication of how long the incoming regime intends to stay in office. Thus, one would expect a radical or revolutionary regime with transcendent goals to remain in power long enough to bring about fundamental socio-economic changes – far longer than a regime which merely sought to correct certain profound deficiencies in the old civilian order. In fact, of course, withdrawal will also depend on forces outside the military itself. If policies fail, leading for example to economic bankruptcy, civil protest may become so intense that the military is forced to hand power over to a civilian government; the same may happen or be accelerated if urban-based middle-class pressure for political liberalisation, supported by external financial institutions and agencies and Western donor governments, becomes strong and irresistible.

2. Africa

Since independence in and around 1960, the military has supplanted civilian governments in nearly half of Africa's states, and in many of these states (especially in Anglophone Africa) one wing of the military has subsequently been displaced by another: in Nigeria in July 1966, 1975, and 1985, and Ghana in 1978 and 1979. Many other states, including Gambia in 1981 and Kenya in 1982, have experienced serious coup attempts. Few states have escaped entirely; Botswana, a prime example, is not however obviously stronger in terms of political culture than states where coups have occurred or been attempted. While there is little doubt that a state with a weak political culture is susceptible to military intervention, which regimes survive and which are toppled by coups appears in part to be a matter of chance.

However, the element of chance must not be exaggerated since it is possible to explain on rational grounds the survival of civilian regimes; two explanations stand out. The first is the external dimension, which is especially important for French-speaking states. All the latter maintain military technical assistance agreements with France and several of them (including the core states of Cameroon, Gabon, the Côte d'Ivoire and Senegal, which developed tight security arrangements of their own) entered into defence agreements also. Moreover, most of the Francophone states still obtain the bulk of their military equipment from France and look to France for training and other support. Another aspect of the external dimension is the use of African armies (as distinct from French or other European forces) as an instrument of foreign policy in relations between African states. Available evidence suggests that short-term bilateral interventions (such as the dispatch of Senegalese troops to the Gambia in 1981) have been very successful, and that civilian regimes (often radical and frequently poor – such as Tanzania) have been more likely than military regimes to use their national armies on external military missions.

A second explanation for the survival of civilian regimes is the political skill shown by leaders such as Léopold Senghor of Senegal, Félix Houphouet-Boigny of the Côte d'Ivoire, Julius Nyerere of Tanzania and Kenneth Kaunda of Zambia. The converse would also appear to be true: the lack of political skill may precipitate a coup or encourage a counter-coup. Thus, the 1967 military takeover in Sierra Leone represented a failure of leadership on the part of Sir Albert Margai, the prime minister, and his advisers.

Considerable significance attaches to the case of Nigeria, where the military (led by a predominantly Ibo group of majors and captains) intervened in January 1966, and where a counter-coup was staged six months later by mainly Northern junior army officers and 'other ranks' drawn from all parts of the north. This case is instructive for a number of reasons. It shows first that the interaction of political and organisational variables differed over time: an army which had been predominantly non-political before the coup of January 1966 became politicised after it, as army discipline broke down and civil–military boundaries fragmented. Secondly, the coup leaders in January 1966 (as distinct from the army officers as a whole) were radically inclined and had clear military objectives: they sought to sweep away the old, conservative political order which rested on Northern dominance. Thirdly, ethnicity and regionalism became more important as vehicles of political expression after the January coup than they had been before it, and the flashpoint occurred when these vertical cleavages in society became intertwined with organisational tensions within the army. Finally, personal motives (such as the fear that promotion would be blocked) might have influenced both the conspirators in

January 1966 and those who staged the counter-coup the following July [Luckham, 1971].

Further lessons can be learned from other states where coups occurred, including Ghana, Uganda and Dahomey (now Benin). In Ghana in 1966, the military explained that it had intervened to get rid of an autocratic and corrupt regime which had bankrupted the economy, forged links with the Eastern bloc despite its official policy of non-alignment, interfered with the army and police, and established a private army – the President's Own Guard Regiment (POGR) – 'as a counterpoise to the Ghana armed forces'. There is no doubt that the protection of the military's corporate interest was particularly important.

In Uganda, in 1971, Major-General Idi Amin was strongly motivated by personal fears and ambitions, though corporate reasons were present on this occasion too – the military resented the preferential treatment given to the Special Forces (an élite unit equivalent to Ghana's POGR) and to a rapidly growing paramilitary police organisation called the General Service Unit. It is also possible that President Milton Obote's stated intention of establishing a socialist state in Uganda led elements within the army to *believe* that this would really happen and that their own socio-economic interests would be thereby prejudiced. In Dahomey, which experienced six military coups and counter-coups in nine years (1963–72), the backdrop to intervention was deep regional and ethnic animosities, a three-cornered struggle for political supremacy, a weak economy, a high level of unemployment, trade union resistance to austerity cuts, and a politicised military hierarchy presiding over a cleavage-ridden army.

These and other cases suggest that the factors to be taken into account in explaining military intervention in Africa are frequently multiple and complex. The 'mix' between them will differ from one state to another: thus, the corporate interests of the army seemed to count for less in Nigeria in January 1966 than they did in Ghana the following month, while the political leanings of the Nigerian coup-makers evidently counted for more. While certain generalisations about military intervention in Africa can usefully be made, each case is ultimately *sui generis*, to be understood only by studying the military organisation of the state concerned and the political and socio-economic context in which that organisation operated.

Against this background, we turn to the character of military rule once power has been seized.

In Uganda in 1985, the military regime headed by Lieutenant-General Tito Okello appointed as ministers a number of former members of Obote's ousted administration; among them was Paulo Muwanga (the ex-vice president) who became prime minister for a short period. This action was entirely atypical. Normally, on assuming power the military suspends the constitution, dissolves the civilian government and parliament, disbands the existing political party (or parties), and detains political leaders of the former regime. The military also establishes a new structure of control, with ultimate authority vested in a military council, thus providing (at least initially) a form of collective leadership. This council – possibly representative of the country's main regional–linguistic groups – rules by decree, but tends still to rely heavily (especially in economic matters) on the former bureaucracy, whose middle-class attitudes and values its members are likely to share. Populist radical regimes such as those of Libya under Colonel Muamar al-Qaddafi, Ghana under Flight-Lieutenant Jerry Rawlings, and Burkina Faso under Captain Thomas Sankara varied this structure by introducing people's defence committees.

Certain observations (which command wide acceptance) can be made about all military regimes, whether classified as 'caretaker' and pledged to restore constitutional integrity; 'corrective', intent on removing profound deficiencies in the old civilian order; or 'revolutionary' and committed to transforming the state's socio-economic structure (the main focus of this chapter being on non-revolutionary regimes). First, the military's hierarchical command structure and the habits of discipline and obedience of its members have led some military governments to believe that merely to issue a command is to have it obeyed; in Nigeria Major-General Aguiyi Ironsi's unification decree, number 34 of early 1966, abolishing regional civil services was a fatal error that contributed substantially to a counter-coup, in which Ironsi himself was killed, the following July. Military rulers have often also failed to appreciate that sensitive issues – like those of the census and revenue allocation in Nigeria – cannot be depoliticised. Secondly, the military's lack of an organised popular base and easy means of communicating with the people has led a number of regimes to forge an alliance with the police. Such an alliance worked quite well in Ghana during the first period of military rule (1966–9), though not in Nigeria under Ironsi.

In the third place, military regimes have sought to compensate for their relative isolation and lack of experience in government by gaining the support of groups not too closely identified with the previous regime. This is what the National Liberation Council (NLC) did in Ghana between 1966 and 1969; however, Ghana's second military regime (1972–8) looked more for support to the ordinary people in a manner reminiscent of the CPP. A fourth observation is that many military regimes have acquired civilian trappings in order to increase their legitimacy and reduce the stigma of illegality attaching to their assumption of power by force. In Egypt, Mali, Somalia, Togo and Zaire, for example, the military held presidential elections and sought to build up a national party linked to and controlled by itself. Fifthly, however, in a few cases 'civilianisation' has merely served to increase the difficulty, which all military governments face, of maintaining organisational cohesion. The danger is that army officers involved in government will become divorced from the army command structure, giving rise to conflict over policies. This occurred in Nigeria in General Yakubu Gowon's later years in office, when the Supreme Military Council deferred the return to civilian rule beyond the scheduled date (1976), while the army command favoured early withdrawal.

In the sixth place the military, despite its image of moral integrity and puritanical spirit, has not provided cleaner and more honest government than its civilian predecessor. In Ghana, the later Acheampong years (1975–8) were marked by massive corruption, while in military-ruled Nigeria the name of state governor had, by 1975, become a byword for corruption. Again, the human rights record of most military regimes has been no better (or worse) than the civilian governments which they supplanted; true, the record in Amin's Uganda and Jean-Bedel Bokassa's Central African Republic was appalling, but so it was also in Equatorial Guinea under Macias Nguema, a civilian ruler, while conditions in Guinea under Sékou Touré (1958–84) were not much better. A seventh observation is that even a military regime which had no obvious motive for intervention has sometimes been sucked into politics as the boundaries between the military establishment and its socio-political environment have become blurred. In Nigeria, the majors who staged the 1966 coup had political motives, but the army as a whole was not politicised; however, politicisation increased following the coup and led to moves to regionalise the army, and eventually to Biafra's attempted secession.

Most observers of the African scene are now agreed that African military regimes are no better equipped than civilian governments to play a developmental role. Take Nigeria, for example. During the first period of military rule in Nigeria (1966–79), sectoral performance was impressive in the building, construction, manufacturing and oil sectors, while the country's infrastructure (including transport and energy) benefited from heavy investment. On the other hand, performance in the agricultural sector was poor and, as the oil boom ended in the late 1970s, the government had to resort to large-scale borrowing. There was evidence of substantial maladministration and (despite Murtala Mohammed's efforts to check it in 1975) of corruption. Overall, the military's record was disappointing and was certainly no better than might have been expected of a civilian government similarly blessed with an oil bonanza.

In 1983 the military intervened again and inaugurated a second period of military rule in Nigeria, first under Major-General Muhammadu Buhari (to 1985) and then under Major-General Ibrahim Babangida. Plans for a transition to civilian rule were announced in 1986, but were subject to considerable delay. In the 1992 parliamentary elections, Babangida restricted competition to two government-sponsored parties, but deferred the presidential elections (scheduled for December 1992) to June 1993. If a civilian government eventually took over (as it was due to do in August 1993) its inheritance would be even less enviable than in 1979 at the end of the first period of military rule. The economy remained in a depressed state and external indebtedness was high; the standard of living of most people had declined and there was a greater awareness of social inequality (existing class divisions within Nigerian society were accentuated by the Nigerian Enterprises Promotion Decrees of 1972 and 1977); unemployment was widespread and corruption rampant. The predictable result was an unstable political situation.

In Ghana, the first military regime (1966–9) had a better political and economic record than the second regime under General Acheampong (1972–8). In most respects the latter's performance was very disappointing, despite the marked expansion of rice and maize production in northern Ghana in the regime's early years.

From the end of 1981 Ghana was ruled by a military regime headed by Jerry Rawlings who resumed the power which he had vacated voluntarily two years earlier in favour of Hilla Limann's elected government. Behind a populist façade, he undertook (from 1983) a series of economic liberalisation measures with IMF and World Bank support. This entailed breaking with the heavily urban-based economic strategies pursued by most previous Ghanaian regimes. Steady rather than dramatic improvement in the country's economy resulted. In November 1992 Rawlings, who had resigned from the air force, won the presidential election in a contest which the Commonwealth Observer Group described as 'clean and fair', but which the opposition parties alleged was flawed through electoral malpractice and the use of an out-dated voters' register; they boycotted the parliamentary election in December 1992.

To the north of Ghana in the poor, arid state of Upper Volta\Burkina Faso, Captain Thomas Sankara established in 1983 a regime which bore some resemblance to that of Rawlings. However, he failed to temper his idealism with realism: his urge to reorganise everything alienated even the peasantry (his chosen allies) and was socially destabilising. Sankara was killed in a successful counter-coup led by Captain Blaise Compaore in October 1987.

The evidence reviewed here suggests that African military regimes display no greater capacity in promoting economic development than their civilian counterparts; like nearly all of them, they are faced with bare domestic cupboards and mounting external indebtedness, and turn for succour to the IMF and World Bank. As Decalo has written, whatever the type of military regime under consideration, 'examples of Ataturk-style socio-economic transformation of new nations are extremely rare' [Decalo, 1990: 25]. On the political front, the record of the military in promoting political development has been no better than that of the civilian regime. In the past, because of the restrictions which military rulers have imposed on political party activity and representative institutions at the national and local levels, it has mostly been worse. This will probably remain true in much of Francophone Africa despite Kérékou's removal from power in elections in Benin early in 1991 and subsequent, mostly reluctant or enforced, moves to initiate political reform in the Congo, Togo, Zaire and elsewhere. To judge from past experience and present intentions, political liberalisation (resulting in multi-party elections and military withdrawal) is likely to be most meaningful in Anglophone Africa.

Finally in the social sphere, too, there is little to choose between military and civilian regimes. Non-revolutionary military regimes, made up mostly of officers with predominantly middle-class values, tend to reflect the same middle-class bias as non-revolutionary civilian regimes. They therefore promote policies which, though often entailing the redistribution of political and economic power among élites, maintain the socio-economic status quo. Any departure from this pattern can be a risky business, as Sankara's experience in Burkina Faso showed.

3. East and Southeast Asia

In *not* staging military intervention or seeking to play a major role in government, the Malaysian armed forces are an exception to the general pattern in Southeast Asia of military involvement in politics. Elsewhere in the region, the military's participation in government has varied, but it has generally been extensive. With the exception of Myanmar, where Ne Win's experiment in state socialist autarky resulted in economic and social stagnation, and the Philippines under Ferdinand Marcos, a common phenomenon has been impressive rates of economic growth. These and other points will be examined and illustrated in a series of brief case studies, beginning with Indonesia.

In **Indonesia** President Sukarno's refusal to adjust his policies, which entailed risky foreign ventures with crippling effects on the economy, led to his removal in a popular uprising sparked off by a military rebellion in 1966. General Suharto became first acting and, from March 1968, substantive president, and was committed to *pancasila* democracy, which was rooted in the traditional Indonesian ideals of consultation and consensus. His rule, like that of his predecessor, was highly personalised and authoritarian. The military became the undisputed base of his power, with representation in the Cabinet (ministers with military backgrounds held around a third of cabinet posts in 1983 and 1988), the People's Representative Council (to which the president could appoint 100 members), the higher echelons of the civil service, and the state corporations. Generals headed all the key provinces; even the Chief

Justice of the Supreme Court was a general [Crouch, 1991a]. The individual interests of military officers were safeguarded by allowing them to engage in commercial activities. Suharto's regime was not exclusively military in character; it was supported by a government-sponsored 'party' known as *Golkar* (discussed in the previous chapter), and two main opposition parties were allowed to exist.

The president's harsh methods in maintaining the military's domination brought sharp criticism both at home and abroad. External critics focused especially on the massacre of hundreds of thousands of 'communist' opponents in the period of military takeover, the regime's brutal seizure of East Timor from the Portuguese in 1975 and the cruel treatment to which its people were subsequently subjected. On the positive side Suharto slashed government and defence spending and, even more remarkably, maintained (as did Myanmar) a relatively lower military burden than the civilian governments of Malaysia, Taiwan and Singapore. He also reduced the rate of inflation from 650 per cent to 12 per cent in two years. He opened up the economy to Western aid and investment, and created a stable political climate conducive to economic growth, relying on resident Chinese businessmen with international market connections rather than indigenous entrepreneurs. In the 1970s the government benefited enormously from the large rise in the price of oil, the country's main export commodity. However, when the oil price collapsed in the mid-1980s, the government, with the help of civilian technocrats, set about creating an efficient non-oil sector geared to export-oriented growth rather than (as in the 1970s) to import-substituting industrialisation. Self-sufficiency in food production was also achieved.

Thailand has experienced a series of military interventions over the last sixty years, in a unique pattern of intervention arising from the absence of colonial rule and the mass movements associated elsewhere with its demise, and the emergence after 1932 of a distinctive 'bureaucratic polity'. A military–civilian *coup d'état* in that year subjected the previously absolute monarchy to constitutional controls, but the move towards democracy was only partial: elections were initially indirect, and while some representatives were elected, others were appointed. In the absence of a large middle class, the system worked to the benefit of both military and civilian bureaucrats who since 'have been the prime movers in political institutional arrangements under different constitutions' [Samuda-vanija, 1989]. Among them the army tended to have the upper hand, as 'the best organised, most concentrated, and most powerful of the branches of the bureaucracy struggling for power' [Wilson, 1962: 277]. In the 52 years to 1984 Thailand had sixteen prime ministers, but just six of them, all army officers, accounted for 44 of those 52 years; of the others one was a retired naval officer and nine were civilians [Bungbongkarn, 1991]. At the same time, military and civilian élites were often closely fused, and military-led regimes were not solely military in composition, but contained both civilian and military personnel.

In more recent years pressure for greater democratisation has increased, particularly after the democratic movement of 1973 which forced the departure of Marshal Thanom, and the author-itarian reaction of 1976. The monarchy, in the person of King Bhumibol, has emerged as a key arbiter of conflicts between élite factions. Changes of government have often come about through military interventions, frequently followed by the drafting of new constitutions. Such was the pattern of events in 1991. Following a coup, the military quickly took steps to 'normalise' the situation by withdrawing from direct rule and introducing civilian elements into government. It appointed Anand Panyarachun, a former diplomat and businessman, as prime minister and accepted his appointment of a cabinet made up (except at the Ministries of Defence and the Interior) of businessmen and technocrats. It again introduced a new constitution, under which a general election to the National Legislative Assembly was held in March 1992.

Following the election General Suchinda, the army commander, was made prime minister, though he was not an elected MP. In May 1992 the army brutally crushed a pro-democracy demonstration in Bangkok, massacring large numbers of the demonstrators. Amidst protest on a hitherto unprecedented scale, and the direct interven-tion of King Bhumibol, Suchinda had to step down. Panyarachun then returned temporarily as prime minister, and formed a government consisting mainly of politically neutral technocrats. He also began to weaken the hold which senior military officers had on the membership of the boards of state enterprises, especially the national airline. Reasonably free elections held in September 1992 then brought Chuan Leekpai, the Democratic Party leader, to power, but gave him only a narrow majority over the older political parties which represented the military and civilian bureaucracy rather than independent social forces. The military still claimed much of the credit for Thailand's rapid economic growth, and its hold within the country's 'bureaucratic polity' was far from removed.

Economic development was disappointing in the **Philippines** under the largely civilian administration of Ferdinand Marcos (1965–86), a United States-style lawyer–politician. Marcos needed the armed forces, which were developed on a United States' professional model, to fight the communists and Muslim insurgents; the military's influence increased during the period of martial law from 1972 to 1981. The armed forces became, in effect, a junior partner in government and maintained the president in power; this dependence remained after martial law ended. As with *Golkar* in Indonesia, Marcos attempted to strengthen the ruling party's links with the military.

The assassination in August 1983 of Benigno Aquino, a former senator and popular opposition leader, discredited the armed forces who were thought to be implicated; it prompted the formation of the Reform the Armed Forces Movement (RAM). From 1985 the latter received the backing of the United States which (until late 1992) retained military bases in the Philippines and provided the Philippine armed forces with training and equipment. With the economy in crisis – Aquino's assassination had sapped the confidence of business and the middle class – the legitimacy of the Marcos regime declined sharply. Marcos was overthrown in February 1986 following a military rebellion which sparked off a popular uprising, and fled abroad.

He was succeeded by Mrs Corazon Aquino (Benigno's widow), who was able to obtain the voters' overwhelming approval of the 1987 constitution emphasizing the concept of civilian supremacy over the military. Denied the right to continue participating in government, elements in the military associated with RAM attempted coups on six occasions between July 1986 and December 1989, seeking to destabilise and/or overthrow the government. Mrs Aquino sought to strengthen her position by appointing several retired officers to her administration; pre-eminent among them was retired General Fidel Ramos, who went on to win the presidential election of June 1992 by a very narrow margin, as described in Chapter Three.

Ramos had held high office under Marcos, but had eventually turned against him. He had been instrumental in Marcos's removal and Mrs Aquino's installation as president, and had then served in her administration as chief of staff and then defence secretary; his attempt to restructure the armed forces had met with limited success. He was, as the *Guardian* noted, 'the first military officer and the first Protestant to become president of this overwhelmingly Catholic country' [*Guardian*, 23 June 1992]. It is an open question whether he will be able to resist officer corps pressure to be allowed to participate in government.

This question does not arise in the case of **Myanmar**, since this country has been firmly under military rule since 2 March 1962 when General Ne Win staged a *coup d'état* to overthrow the government of U Nu. The coup makers pointed to economic, religious and political crises to justify their intervention; they also played on the fear that U Nu would give way to the sectionalist pressures of the Karens and other ethnic minorities. Ne Win emphasized a 'Burmese road to socialism' and stated that the aim was to unite the people and raise their standard of living in a controlled revolution based on self-reliance and the use of domestic resources. Foreign companies were virtually excluded from participating in the economy. The result of this experiment in state socialist autarky proved economically disastrous.

In 1974 a new constitution mitigated the absolutism of military rule and ushered in a second phase – that of 'constitutional dictatorship'. The armed forces were to have a less direct role in politics and were to share power with civilians. But such democratic trappings were not very meaningful. A one-party socialist state now existed under the leadership of the Burma Socialist Programme Party (BSPP), but the latter was never a viable governing party in its own right – the military would not allow autonomous institutions to develop. There was next to no outlet for the expression of opposition opinion and the ethnic minorities were given no hope, then or later, of securing any autonomy. Maladministration, inefficient management and corruption, among both civilian and military officers, provoked worker riots and student demonstrations in 1974–5 and an attempted coup by younger army officers in 1976.

In the early 1980s the military regime, in a reversal of previous policy, placed greater reliance on market forces and foreign aid, thereby giving a much-needed boost to the ailing economy. However, this improvement was not sustained and the country's foreign debt and the debt-service ratio rose alarmingly. Early in 1988 the United Nations granted Myanmar 'least developed country' status so that the government could obtain more grant and soft loan aid. In that year Ne Win, who had vacated the state presidency in November 1981, resigned as leader of the BSPP; however, his influence remained dominant. Two new administrations followed in quick succession; the second, headed by Dr Maung, a civilian politician, was overthrown by the military on 18 September 1988 following urban demonstrations against sharply rising prices. The coup leader was General Saw Maung, the Defence Minister, who became both head of state and government. The new regime tackled the economic crisis with considerable determination and established trading and commercial links with the outside world. But it continued the armed struggle against the ethnic minorities and communist insurgents, and followed up early steps towards political liberalisation (including the registration of over 200 political parties) with measures so repressive that Western governments and the Japanese government threatened to cut off aid. The government relented and held multi-party elections in May 1990. These elections revealed a widespread desire for political change: they resulted in a resounding victory for the opposition National League for Democracy (NLD) at the expense of the government-controlled National Unity Party (NUP), the revamped version of the BSPP. However, the military was unwilling to relinquish power to an elected civilian government and several leaders of the NLD remained in prison or under house arrest. General Maung's government adopted harsh methods to enforce its policies which (like those in Thailand) benefited the Western-educated, urban-centred élite rather than the peasant majority.

The contrast between Myanmar and Malaysia is sharp. In **Malaysia** (as noted above) the armed forces have accepted, apparently willingly, the principle of civilian supremacy, limiting their own role to matters of defence and security. If one reason for the military's disinterest in taking power is the effectiveness of civilian rule in achieving economic and social development, another, and perhaps more important, reason is (in Crouch's words) 'the communal make-up of society which places the Malay-dominated military on the same side as the Malay-dominated government and bureaucracy' [Crouch, 1991b: 136].

Of the states reviewed above, Indonesia and Thailand achieved high rates of economic growth, mainly by adopting capitalist strategies of development and emphasizing export-oriented industrialisation. This economic success has probably reinforced the belief among elements of the armed forces that they have a *right* to rule. In Indonesia this belief led the armed forces to formulate an ideology – *dwi fungsi* (Dual Function) – which 'asserts that the military does not have an exclusively military function but has an additional mission as a socio-political force with a permanent right – even duty – to participate in the political affairs of the nation' [Crouch, 1991a: 52]. In Myanmar Ne Win shared this view, despite his government's poor economic record; like Suharto in Indonesia, he instituted a regime which included civilians but in which the military was indisputably the dominant force. In Thailand, on the other hand, the military has rarely sought to rule directly following a take-over; more obviously than in Indonesia, representative government is on the domestic agenda. The country is making steady, if slow, progress towards a more democratic and plural political system without, however, (as yet) undermining the structural bases of military power. In Thailand, therefore, there is a civilian–military partnership rather than military domination.

In the Philippines under Marcos, military personnel were junior partners in a predominantly civilian administration which had a poor development record. Mrs Aquino sought to exclude serving (as distinct from retired) military officers entirely from her administration, but in this, in the longer term, she was only partially successful. In staging six coup attempts in a little over three years the Philippine armed forces probably did not so much seek to depose Mrs Aquino as to claim a stake in her government; they felt that this was due to them both because of their part in securing her accession in 1986 and because they had become accustomed to participating in government in the past. However, any claim by the military to participate in government was unconvincing. Despite geographical fragmentation and the lack of a strong sense of nationhood, there was not the same acute perception as in Indonesia that the armed forces stood between law and order and national disintegration; moreover, United States' support for its ex-colony was very strong. Nor was there, as in Thailand, the same real threat of external aggression. Again, the middle class is larger in the Philippines than in either Thailand or Indonesia where a trading (as distinct from an 'intellectual') middle class has been slow to develop. Discontent among members of the middle class was a factor in the overthrow of the Marcos regime. By contrast, in Indonesia the middle class, many of whose members are government employees, 'still seems too small to provide an effective base for civilian political movements demanding greater civilian participation in government' [Crouch, 1991a: 62].

In Malaysia the political, bureaucratic and military leaders are predominantly Malay, with very similar social origins and, it would seem, a common interest in maintaining a Malay-dominated multi-communal civilian government. The latter is also better suited than a military government would be to the needs of the Chinese and Indian entrepreneurial bourgeoisie – the non-indigenous communities make up over 40 per cent of Malaysia's total population. Successive civilian governments have provided sound administration and achieved considerable social and economic development, despite the racial riots of 1969 and periodic racial tension. In neighbouring Singapore the legitimacy of the government is very high – a tribute to Lee Kuan Yew's effective, if rather authoritarian, style of government. The state, which is underpinned by a well-equipped military machine, has achieved a high rate of economic growth.

The capitalist restructuring undertaken in Singapore is comparable in scope to that of South Korea in East Asia. The latter, too, has achieved a high rate of economic growth, though in this case in the context not only of authoritarian government but also of often corrupt and quasi-military government. As noted in Chapter Two, the origins of the model of successful growth lie unambiguously in the authoritarian regime established by General Park in 1961. Thus, South Korean experience, like that of Taiwan, reinforces much of the evidence from Southeast Asia that economic and social development is not the exclusive preserve of Western-style democratic governments. At the same time, the lesson of Myanmar under Ne Win is that military rule may result in underdevelopment rather than development.

4. Latin America

Despite improving levels of economic and political development, and steadily increasing professionalisation of the armed forces, the tendency for the Latin American military to intervene has not declined steadily over time. On the contrary, military intervention and prolonged military rule have been marked features of politics, particularly in the most highly developed states of the region. However, after a wave of protracted interventions in the 1960s and 1970s a retreat took place in the 1980s, leading to the restoration of civilian rule throughout the region. This cycle of prolonged intervention and general withdrawal is the focus here.

Despite the widespread militarisation of politics in the nineteenth century it is misleading to trace the roots of contemporary intervention back to that period. Recourse to arms on the part of groups contending for power in the decades after independence was a virtually continent-wide phenomenon, and armies were raised and dispersed as the rhythm of conflict rose and fell. But the 'men on horseback' who dominated much of the early politics of states such as Venezuela, Colombia, Bolivia, Peru and Mexico (where fighting during and after independence was most persistent) were rarely leaders of a professional army clearly set apart from civil society. Rather they were the leaders of regional forces (often closely associated with one or another set of economic and social interests) who took up arms to challenge other contending groups for power. The distinction between military and civil callings was blurred. As Little puts it, 'civilians were as ready to use force as the military, and just as successful commanders turned to politics so did leading politicians take to the field of battle' [Little, 1986: 11].

As export economies became established new élites came to frown upon such military adventurism, and sought order and peaceful compromise rather than the exclusive acquisition of power by force. Between 1880 and 1930, when the export economy was in its heyday, civilian rather than military domination was the rule; the alternative to highly restricted oligarchic democracy was the late imposition of order by a personal dictator committed to export-led development, such as Porfirio Diaz in Mexico or Gomez in Venezuela, rather than frequent military intervention. The armed forces of the different states were largely domesticated in this period, and played the role of willing allies of 'modernising' élites, in Central America, for example, as shock troops to force the peasantry off the land as commercial agriculture advanced. Only the few soldiers who seized power on behalf of modernising interests (as in Uruguay under Latorre and in Brazil in 1889) foreshadowed the distinctive twentieth-century tradition of intervention where civilian élites were proving incapable of handling the structural changes dictated by the evolution of the international economy, and the place of Latin America within it.

The later development of this largely new role was made possible by the professionalisation of the armed forces in Latin America between 1900 and 1930. This was achieved by the hiring of military missions from such sources as Prussia, France, and Britain, and by sending officers abroad for training. New standards of professionalism and changed patterns of recruitment and promotion created officers with an identity self-consciously different from that of their civilian masters, and at times resentful of perceived amateurism and elitism. Early evidence of this new mentality was seen in Brazil, Chile and Ecuador in the 1920s, as officers mounted successive rebellions. The increased visibility of the armed forces also reflected a growing political crisis in the civilian regimes under which the export economy had flourished, a crisis made far more intense by the collapse of these economies after 1929. In country after country, the old élites lost control of the situation, invariably bringing the armed forces closer to power. Only in Mexico, where the social tensions created by the rapid development of an export-based economy led to revolution and civil war before the crash occurred, did the consolidation in power of a capable new bourgeoisie lead to the marginalisation of the armed forces, a situation that remained unchanged in succeeding decades. Elsewhere, a new tradition of military intervention was born.

The twentieth-century pattern of military intervention has its roots, then, in the weakness of ruling civilian élites, rather than in factors wholly internal to the military themselves, or in historical traditions. When civilian élites have lost the ability to rule by consent the military has intervened, sometimes simply to guarantee the continued hold of those élites on power, but as frequently to force radical changes in the content of policy and in the nature of political authority. Their radicalism has generally had a single end, and clear limits. It has sought to reorient national development in order to take account of changed circumstances in the international economy and in national and international politics, while promoting capitalist accumulation and curbing the independent power of the working classes. This has occasionally meant bitter conflict with existing élites, while the strategies adopted towards the urban and rural working classes, ranging from authoritarian incorporation to the most violent repression and exclusion, have varied in accordance with the economic programmes adopted.

The common though not universal pattern, either immediately in 1930 or after conservative reactions had run their course, was for factions strongly opposed to ruling élites to force their way to power. This was true of Sanchez Cerro in Peru in 1930, the younger officers who surrounded Vargas in Brazil, the Argentine officers who seized power in 1943 and made way for Perón in 1946, and the 'military socialists' who took over in Bolivia from a civilian élite discredited by a failing economy and the catastrophe of the failed 'Chaco War' (1932–5) against Paraguay – launched, Malvinas-style, to distract attention from problems at home. Such officers were hardly democrats. They drew their inspiration largely from European fascism, interpreted as anti-imperialist, authoritarian, nationalist and statist, and fundamentally opposed in temper to the liberal democracy they associated with élite rule and foreign influence. They saw in European corporatism a solution to the problem of supplanting failed élites without letting power fall into the hands of dangerous radicals. This was a period in which the Communist party was influential in Latin America, along with the rival doctrines of socialism and anarcho–syndicalism, and to many observers it seemed that the belligerent and alienated masses might seize power and launch a revolution. Military intervention, therefore, tended to be both *radical* and *counter-revolutionary*.

The authoritarian, nationalist–developmentalist interventions of the 1930s and 1940s generally sought to break with the *laissez-faire* patterns of economic growth experienced in the past and checked by the depression. In doing so they generally moved fairly rapidly away from institutional control of government by the military itself, either through the emergence of a single prominent individual building a personal political base (as with Perón in Argentina), or through the forging of links with reform-minded political parties (as with the military society RADEPA in Bolivia in 1943). Only where the existing regime was heavily authoritarian was the 'democratic' content of military intervention likely to be high, as in Venezuela in 1945, where young officers brought AD (*Acción Democrática*, Democratic Action) to power.

However, the military rarely operated as a united force; competition for power between the military and civilians went on alongside intense factionalism within the military itself. Perón's period as president of Argentina between 1946 and 1955 saw the armed forces emerge as a strong base of anti-Peronism, but divide into factions urging rival liberal and corporatist alternatives. Within the civilian–military conflict that has marked Argentina ever since there has been an active struggle for supremacy within the military itself. This has meant that successive military regimes have sponsored very different 'projects', most notoriously between 1966 and 1973, when the successive regimes of Onganía, Levingston and Lanusse turned to authoritarian reconstruction, populist mobilisation and finally the restoration of Perón. Elsewhere factions have not always been so finely balanced. In El Salvador, for example, where the grip of the armed forces on government was virtually continuous from the ousting of the dictator Hernandez Martinez in 1944 until the 1980s, reformist alternatives emerging at intervals of fifteen to twenty years never survived for more than a matter of months. Military factions pressing for moderate reform held power briefly in 1944, 1960–1, and 1979–80, only to be removed by reactionary counter-movements on each occasion.

While some general regional pattern can be discerned since 1960, the dynamics and form of military intervention have varied quite substantially. Episodes of military intervention should not be examined in isolation, but set in the context of sequences of change in national politics. This does not prevent generalisation, but it recommends caution, and due regard for the particular circumstances of individual cases.

Since 1960 Colombia and Venezuela have survived as civilian regimes, while Peru experienced a strongly reformist military regime between 1968 and 1975, and (after an internal coup) a more orthodox conservative administration which handed power back to civilians in 1980. Brazil, a fragile multi-party democracy between 1945 and 1964, experienced 21 years of military rule thereafter, in a hybrid regime under which Congress was kept open but stripped of its power, while elections (made indirect for the presidency) continued on schedule. In Argentina (1966–73, 1976–83), Chile (1973–90) and Uruguay (1973–85) congress and parties were closed, but the form of rule varied: a series of military presidents in Argentina, a personal dictator in Chile, and a form of collegiate rule in Uruguay.

A number of common characteristics distinguish recent military regimes from their predecessors, suggesting that they represent a new departure. First, it has generally been the armed forces as an institution (through its high command) that has seized control, rather than individual rebel or relatively junior officers. Second, they have generally done so not with a view to a speedy return to civilian rule, but with the intention of ruling for the foreseeable future. In Argentina, Peru, Brazil, and Chile, between 1930 and 1964, sixteen military interventions gave rise to periods of rule of just over eight months on average; five interventions since 1964 accumulated over sixty years of military rule, an average of twelve years for each period [Little, 1986: 20]. This is linked to a third characteristic, born out of the 'Cold War' and the spread of counter-insurgency doctrines through United States training programmes: a pervasive concern with national security rather than external defence as the primary focus of military activity, and a consequent propensity to claim a permanent role in domestic politics. These characteristics arise from a common syndrome: the establishment of military regimes in response to a process of social mobilisation and polarisation too acute to be resolved by élite co-operation and compromise, and threatening to spill over into radicalism or socialism.

On other dimensions the degree of innovation is as marked, but less uniform. As regards economic policy, for example, the regimes of Chile, Uruguay, and Argentina after 1976 embarked upon ultra-liberal 'monetarist' policies aimed at eliminating previous 'artificial' industrial development and restoring the authority of the market, while Brazil continued to promote a model of state-led industrialisation. As regards internal security, all four of these regimes, along with El Salvador and Guatemala in Central America, created a far more elaborate repressive apparatus than had commonly been organised in the past, seeking to eliminate physically any perceived threats to their continuation in power. The use of repression and torture is not new, but its highly institutionalised and public application is, as is the range of targets (workers, peasants, political activists, trade unionists, and the student sons and daughters of urban élites). In contrast, the Peruvian regime from 1968 to 1975, while authoritarian in nature, was fundamentally reformist rather than reactionary, and sought (though without conspicuous success) to develop a broad base of social support.

In general, recent long-term military regimes in South America have adopted economic programmes already formulated before they came to power, or produced programmes in retrospect to justify what they have done. Whether reformist (as in Peru) or reactionary (as in Chile), they have claimed the ability to push through programmes where civilians have lacked the authority or tenacity to do so. They have depicted themselves as unconstrained by partisan political loyalties, able to take a long-term view, and willing to provide the space for technocrats to apply the policies necessary to secure economic progress without bowing to undue political pressure. However, they have invariably found themselves as deeply embroiled in 'politics' as their civilian counterparts, but lacking in the political awareness and skills to manage the situation.

The experience of recently departed regimes in Argentina, Uruguay and Chile suggests that the appeal of 'monetarism' lies not so much in its economic logic as in the illusory dream of removing economic management from the political arena. For the military its appeal undoubtedly derived from the attractiveness of an explanation for economic decline and political crisis which blamed two of the traditional whipping boys of armies everywhere – civilian politicians and the working class. However, the military proved to have a tendency to interpret economic policy (and their role with regard to it) in military rather than in economic terms, being more swayed by notions of 'mission', 'discipline' and 'sacrifice' than by the logic of economic argument. They often saw their task as 'seeing through' a necessary but unpopular policy, and were reluctant to abandon it in the face of manifest failure. This characteristic combined with the curtailing of debate and democratic control to make changes of course difficult: with opposition defined as treason, and the honour of the armed services at stake, alternative policies could not be freely canvassed and developed. Loyalty and respect for hierarchy made it institutionally difficult to question prevailing orientations from within, while criticism and comment from outside was disregarded. Finally, the military exploited power for their own corporate advantage. Spending on defence, salaries, and the acquisition of fancy hardware worked against attempts to cut the budget deficit, and created a privileged group determined to cling to power. The combination of newly privileged groups reluctant to abandon the political arena and dogmatic commitment to economic policies produced unpredictable results when a consensus was finally reached that those policies had failed, ranging from aimless drifting at the mercy of events (in

Brazil), to reckless adventure (as in the Argentine invasion of the Falkland Islands). Military governments whose programmes end in disaster are likely to prove particularly ineffective, lacking in authority, and hard to shift.

As for politics, lengthy military intervention tends to freeze the political situation, rather than achieve a renewal of civilian leadership. In Peru in 1980 with the return of Belaunde (president in the 1960s), in Bolivia in 1982 with the return of Siles Zuazo (president in the 1950s) and in Brazil in 1985 with the election of Tancredo Neves (prime minister in the 1960s) the military were replaced by the very forces they had expelled from power. Intervention generally fails to 'renew' civilian politics, while it politicises the armed forces themselves, so that leading officers come to consider themselves natural contenders for power. It creates particular bodies (primarily the expanded intelligence services or political police) which work for (and prolong) military incumbency. Finally, the material benefits of power, and the fear of reprisals for crimes committed while in office, breed powerful practical reasons for hanging on. As a result, military handover to civilians after prolonged rule has generally been marked by a triple crisis: an economic crisis exacerbated by drift and the protracted process of withdrawal; a crisis of political succession brought about by the persecution of civilian politicians and the suppression of popular alternatives; and a crisis of civil–military relations, arising out of the attempt to limit continuing military influence, and the need to investigate crime and corruption within the military institution itself.

Recent long-term military rule in Latin America, temporarily at least eradicated by 1990, provided a test of the ability of the armed forces in this area. The lesson to be drawn is that the negative features of military rule are not avoidable extras, but intrinsic to the military institution. Unfortunately, there is no simple correlation between the level of socioeconomic development and propensity for military intervention, and no guarantee that waves of intervention will not recur in the future. Civilian governments in the region therefore need to carry out reforms to make such intervention less likely. Stepan has usefully drawn attention to the need for institutional reform to establish democratic control over the military and its intelligence systems, by reducing military prerogatives and placing civilians in control of defence-related ministries

[Stepan, 1988: Chs 7 & 8]. While such reforms are needed, future stability may depend more upon far-reaching social and economic reform to eliminate the tensions which have produced breakdown and the conditions for intervention than upon purely institutional change. Neither institutional nor social and economic reform was initially much in evidence. Rather, the trend was towards the creation of a permanent supervisory role for the military, in 'hybrid civilian-military regimes' of the type openly advocated by Malloy [Malloy, 1987]. President Fujimori's personal coup which suspended Peru's new democracy in April 1992, and led to elections in November 1992 that were boycotted by the major opposition parties, may have only postponed the necessary effort to find more appropriate solutions. It contrasted with the more positive attempt by Chile's civilian parties and Christian Democratic government to unpick the set of restrictive institutional reforms through which General Pinochet sought to perpetuate the hold of the military on power [Loveman, 1991]. It remained to be seen whether either strategy would lead in the long run to a reduction in the level of military involvement in government.

5. The Middle East

In the contemporary politics of the Middle East the military has played a decisive political role. It was officers who brought down the monarchies of Egypt (1952), Iraq (1958) and Libya (1969), and ushered in an era of radical republicanism in each case. In Syria, from independence onward, there have been successive coups, and the main arbiters of political change have been factions within the officer corps. Although there have been degrees of civilianisation in Iraq and Egypt, officers in these states have been incorporated into key state institutions. The strongest domestic challenge to the Jordanian and Moroccan monarchies has come from the military. Only Tunisia, Lebanon, Saudi Arabia and the small Gulf states have remained immune from direct military interventions. All of these states have either very weak military establishments (like Lebanon), or a pattern of recruitment favourable to the ruling families. In Saudi Arabia, the military establishment is an amalgam of tribal recruits from the interior, historically loyal to the ruling Saud family, and a regular army with a number of princes in command positions. In Jordan, recruitment has been from bedouin tribes traditionally loyal to the king.

The 1950s and 1960s were the decades of intervention. Although the military remained politically important in the 1970s and 1980s, the officer corps was relatively quiescent. Military involvement in the affairs of state has historical precedent. In the Arab and Ottoman Empires, imperial rulers and provincial governors frequently became the prisoners of the local garrisons. Mamluk slave armies controlled most of the Fertile Crescent between the thirteenth and fifteenth centuries. It was the decomposition of the Ottoman Janissaries and their resultant control over many regions of the Empire that heralded Ottoman decline. Both Mamluk and Janissaries were very different from the contemporary military: they were recruited from slave outsiders in order that they would remain aloof from the wider society and wholly loyal to the Sultan. Only in the late nineteenth century did a formally organised army, paid for out of state revenue, come into existence. The collapse of the Empire during the First World War brought with it the establishment of new armies in the successor states of Iraq, Syria, Lebanon and Jordan. These armies were part of a new state apparatus which had the task of forging order in regions which had become increasingly autonomous from central control during the preceding century.

Although there has been a history of military involvement in the Middle East, it was only after independence that professional armies independent of external control came into existence. Not long after, the Arab officers moved into the political arena. These early interventions were the result of civilian mismanagement of affairs which directly and indirectly affected the army. The Iraqi army staged a coup in 1936, four years after independence, and three years after Syria became independent in 1946 there were three coups within one year. One common feature of these first coups was that the officers (with some justice) viewed civilian rulers as corrupt and incapable of handling the affairs of state. The Bakr Sidqi coup of 1936 came after the Iraqi army had been called in to quell Kurdish and Assyrian rebellions in northern Iraq and a widespread tribal uprising in the Shi'a south, a consequence of the machinations of politicians in Baghdad. The first Syrian coup involved the personal ambitions of various officers, reflected divisions over a pro-Iraq or pro-Saudi foreign policy, and was encouraged by the

CIA. Of greater importance was the defeat of the Syrian army in the 1948 war with Israel and repugnance at the chicanery involved in the provision of supplies to the front line. The Free Officers who removed the Egyptian monarchy in 1952 were also influenced by the 1948 defeat and the exposure of similar governmental scandals. Only the Jordanian army acquitted itself well in 1948, and it remained aloof from politics.

A second type of intervention that has been common in the Middle East is the reformist coup organised by politicised junior officers. Rarely has the high command intervened. In Iraq and Syria, for example, officers have intervened as members (or supporters) of political parties and movements. Such a pattern was set early in Syria when Akram Hourani encouraged young political supporters to join the officer corps. When his Arab Socialist party united with the Ba'th party, even though the latter endorsed civilian government, the Ba'th found itself inextricably linked to a group of politically active officers. As the army became increasingly pivotal in Syrian politics during the 1960s change of government by coup became the regularised mechanism of succession as officers of differing political orientations led their tanks on the presidential palace. The only way in which civilians could wield influence was through allies in the officer corps, but rather than controlling their supporters and sympathisers in the army, the party politicians became their clients. A similar pattern of military involvement emerged in Iraq during the 1960s. The Libyan coup of 1969 was led by Muamar al-Qaddafi, who joined the army with the aim of organising a group of 'free officers' on the Egyptian model to overthrow the monarchy.

One result of the politicised military was the greater weight given to ideological issues. Even where the motivation for a coup was one of political ambition, officers felt it necessary to dress their intervention with a heavy programmatic element rather than the usual clichéd attack on corrupt and venal politicians. The reformist model was set by Egypt in 1952, although it was to take a decade for that regime to move from pragmatism to a clear ideological programme.

In Sudan in 1989 and Algeria in 1991, military interventions occurred which suggest the beginnings of a new pattern. They involved different military reactions to the expanding domestic appeal of Islamic movements; both occurred simultaneously with prolonged economic and political crises; and both can be linked to the broader process of economic and political liberalisation, albeit in different ways. In Sudan, General Omar Hassan al-Bashir aligned his regime with the National Islamic Front and introduced Islamic law. In Algeria, in contrast, the military intervened to forestall an electoral victory for the Islamic Salvation Front. The general appeal of Islamic movements in the Middle East is a constant. Their contemporary expansion, however, has more to do with the reflection of the social consequences of unresolved economic crises. In Sudan, the problem has been compounded by the conflict between the Muslim north and the non-Muslim south and, in Algeria, by conflicts between Islamicists and secularists, liberalisers and statists. These interventions illustrate the continuing centrality of the military and its will to intervene in crisis situations. The officer corps has responded differently to the rising Islamic tide in these two cases. Whatever alignment the military takes, the history of previous interventions teaches that military rule is unlikely to resolve the underlying social and economic problems or the political and ideological cleavages associated with them.

Governments established by military interventions cannot all be described as military regimes. In many cases, officers have co-opted civilians, the proportion of officers has been low, and civil institutions have been established. Coup leaders like Nasser and Qadaffi, on the other hand, created a high degree of personal power. Rarely has the high command ruled as a junta. In Iraq and Syria, where the army has been persistently interventionist, only under Syria's Shishakli (1949–54) and Iraq's Qasim (1958–63) has the military been the major instrument of rule. In Iraq and Syria regimes have (at different times) been led by military 'strong men'. In Syria, between 1963 and 1970, there was a symbiotic relationship between the Ba'th party and the army, as there was in Iraq after 1968. Even after 1970, when the civilian wing of the Syrian Ba'th was eclipsed, it was a faction within the military which came to power and their ties were based on common kinship and sectarian group membership as much as military position. It is more accurate to describe Syria as being ruled by the clan of the president through special military forces than as a military regime.

Egypt comes the closest to an archetypal military regime in the period between 1952 and 1970. The Free Officers established the new Egyptian Republic and, although the military component of government varied over time, a high proportion of top political positions in central and local government was held by officers and former officers. Between 1952 and 1969, 33 per cent of political leaders were officers. Members of the Revolutionary Command Council held the key ministries after 1953 and, in the 1960s, as vice-presidents or deputy prime ministers, supervised blocs of subordinate ministries. At the upper echelon of the Nasser regime, military representation reached 83 per cent in the Presidential Council (the main advisory body to Nasser). To overemphasise military representation, however, underplays the supremacy of Nasser, since officers who held these key positions did so at the president's behest. Since the 1969 coup in Libya the military has remained exceptionally privileged but power is concentrated in the person of the president who relies on revolutionary committees and the popular militia as a counterweight to the army.

Given the range of military and quasi-military regimes in the Middle East it is not easy to identify any particular pattern of military rule. There is some linkage, however, between the character of the coup organisers and certain of the policies pursued. Where the traditional regime of landlords increasingly came to rely on a strong army, and where junior and middle ranking officers came from different social strata or from communities distinct from the ruling group, military rule has been reformist. This was the case in Iraq (1958), Egypt (1952), Syria (1963) and Libya (1969). Where the military has intervened in the context of domestic disturbance, military government alone (or in conjunction with civilians) has strengthened the power of the state. This pattern occurred in Iraq (1936) and Syria (1949).

The case of Syria is instructive, since there have been military regimes of both patterns, and it is also illustrative of the way in which class and sectarianism have combined to shape military rule. During the mandate period, the French created distinct administrative districts based on Syria's geographically compact sects, thereby enhancing the power of local tribal and religious leaders. When Syria became independent in 1946, it was left to the army to quell a messianic uprising in the poor Alawite mountains and a Druze revolt led by the tribal leadership in the south. Although the reputation of the army as a national and nationalist institution was badly tarnished by its defeat in the 1948 war, the three coups of 1949 restored it to the centre of politics. These military-dominated governments had no distinctive economic policies, but they did expand the power of the state: sectarian representation was abolished, a new civil law code was introduced and the role of religious leaders reduced. Under Shishakli, powers vested in tribal and sectarian leaders were abolished and the basis of a new statewide education system was founded. As the central state was strengthened against these semi-autonomous peripheral forces, the power of landlords was enhanced and a nascent peasant movement was crushed.

A second type of military rule emerged in the 1960s. It was partly a consequence of a changing pattern of recruitment into the officer corps resulting in greater representation of individuals from a rural and small town background. A distinct social gap emerged between these officers and the grand landowning families controlling parliament and cabinet. By the early 1960s, there was also a disproportionate representation in the army of the provincial Druze, Alawite and Ismaili minority sects. For them, a military career provided a channel of social mobility. Between 1963 and 1970, officers, largely from these minorities, ruled in harness with various factions of the civilian Ba'th party and (under the slogans of popular democracy and scientific socialism) introduced measures which favoured the rural hinterland at the expense of urban merchants and absentee landlords. In the rural areas, land was distributed to the peasantry and some state farms were established. Foreign trade, banking and commerce, almost wholly located in the big towns, were nationalised. The proportion of Sunni Muslims (the overwhelming majority) represented in cabinets declined considerably in the 1960s. Of greater importance (certainly in the eyes of many Syrians) was the increasing number of Alawites in the officer corps, and particularly their tenure of key command positions. This trend continued through the 1970s and 1980s and, despite the conciliatory economic liberalism of Hafiz al-Asad's post-1970 policies, the urban commercial classes (consisting largely of Sunni Muslims) have opposed the regime as narrow, sectarian and clannish. Such sectarian complications have been less apparent in Iraq, Libya and Egypt, although the bulk of the officers who took power were socially distinct from the ruling families, landlords and tribal chieftains.

In Syria the reformist measures introduced a greater degree of equity into society. The general performance of the military in economic development, however, has not been markedly successful, save where booming oil revenues have allowed governments to make mistakes without any significant economic penalty – as has been the case in Libya and Iraq. Even where reformist officers introduced a more equal distribution of wealth, the main beneficiaries of the dispossession of landlords and merchants have been the more wealthy middle peasantry, the urban state-employed middle classes, and the upper levels of the skilled working class.

A common feature of reformist military regimes has been the growth of the state through nationalisation and bureaucratic employment. For the Egyptian Free Officers, it has been argued that such growth derived from a political imperative: the need to create a constituency for the illegitimate accession to state power of a small group of unknown officers. Whether such a conscious motivation lay behind the policies pursued is unproven. It is, however, a pattern common to Iraq after 1958 and Syria in the 1960s. Factors other than the political mobilisation of support were also at work. Even though there was no evident decrease in the military component of the Syrian regime after 1970, government has encouraged the private sector. While there was a significant decline in the military component of Egyptian government during the Sadat era, there was a similar move to encourage private business. Under military government or not, both Syria and Egypt moved in the same economic direction, and in so doing began restructuring the class bases which they had originally created.

Military withdrawal from politics is not so distinct a phenomenon in the Middle East as in Africa, and Latin America in particular, since military and quasi-military regimes have tended to be linked to political parties, or to have a more or less indirect connection to sectarian groups, as indicated for Syria. In Egypt, there has been a 'demilitarisation' of cabinets and the establishment of a controlled multiparty system, but it has been exceedingly gradual, extending over a twenty-year period. Nasser established a state–party system and Sadat extended it, albeit within strict limits. Yet Egyptian leaders since 1952 have been military men: Nasser organised the Free Officers, Sadat was a member, and Husni Mubarak, who succeeded the latter, was a former career air force officer. In Iraq and Syria, the military is central to politics, but cannot be said to rule directly. The relationship between party and army (and between particular clans in both army and regime) is more important than the officer corps *per se*. In the case of Syria, since 1970 the core military support for the regime has lain with specially-organised forces loyal to president Hafiz al-Asad and parallel to the regular army. Although the regular army might be said to have withdrawn from politics, the political leadership has created its own military arm to secure the regime. Iraq did not go to such extremes until the accession of Saddam Husayn as president. Since then, he has presented himself as hero, ideologue and saviour of the nation. As a result the Iraqi Ba'th party has atrophied. With the army involved in a full-scale war with Iran and the UN coalition consecutively, President Husayn concentrated power in his own hands and, as occurred in Syria, created a distinct military organisation in the Republican Guard, guarding not the republic but the president and his entourage. Both Presidents al-Asad and al-Husayn, despite some degree of domestic popularity, use an efficient and ruthless set of security networks within party, army and Interior Ministry based on a handful of relatives and individuals wholly dependent on them for their positions. Military appointments and positions are vetted and (as a result) top military commanders do not have an independent power base even in the army.

The only sense in which there has been a military withdrawal from politics in Iraq and Syria is that power has accrued to the presidents, who (through the control of appointments in army, party and government) have become more pivotal in policy formation than factions within the officer corps. Despite the great power of the Iraqi president, the party there does have more of a role than in Syria. Saddam Husayn (unlike Hafiz al-Asad) was a civilian and his path to power was through the party. Even though military commanders sit on party policy committees there is little reason to think that they have any more weight in policy formulation than top civilian party members. The extent of 'civilianisation' in post-coup politics in the Middle East, then, is a consequence of increased presidential autonomy from the officer corps, and the imperative to incorporate technocrats and create a social base of support. This kind of civilianisation has, however, not generally decreased the role of the security services, most of which tend to be run by former officers or presidential relatives.

6. Conclusion

In all four regions, the armed forces have intervened extensively in politics to overthrow civilian regimes, although there are many states which have remained free from military intervention. As noted in the introduction, intervention can only be understood when placed in a historical context. It is inadequate to rely on general explanations since it is clear from the specific cases presented above that both the causes of the overthrow of civilian regimes and the reason for their survival are multiple. Latin American experience suggests that there is no correlation between the level of socio-economic development and military intervention: the latter has been most pronounced in the most highly developed states of the region.

A common reason for intervention in the four regions has been the inability of civilian regimes to manage political, social and economic crises. The different political crises resulting from the collapse of the export economies in the 1930s brought the Latin American military to the centre of politics. Whereas economic mismanagement, resulting often in negative growth rates, is almost invariably a leading cause of military intervention in African states, political mismanagement is a much more important cause in Asia (though not authoritarianism, which has been a constant in civilian and military politics alike). The overthrow in 1966 of Sukarno's predominantly civilian regime in Indonesia was an exception to this pattern – the fact that he had bankrupted the economy by rash foreign ventures was an important reason for his removal. In the Middle East and a number of African states tribal, ethnic and sectarian conflict has influenced intervention and has had an impact on the nature of military rule.

In Africa, Asia and the Middle East most coups have been staged by soldiers; the navy and air force have rarely taken part and only occasionally have held office in the military regime subsequently established. From time to time – as in Ghana in 1966 and Thailand in 1991 – the police have been brought into government, perhaps because they possess better political antennae than the military. In Latin America, the lead in intervention has been taken by the army, but personnel from the other services have participated more frequently – as in Argentina, for example. In this region, as in East and Southeast Asia, the coup-makers have tended to be senior officers (acting institutionally through the high command in Latin America). In Africa and the Middle East, on the other hand, middle and junior ranking officers (often radically-minded) have taken the initiative, though they sometimes handed over power to more senior officers once the coup succeeded, as in Nigeria in January 1966. In small states, such as Sierra Leone and Togo, the technical barriers to intervention have been slight. In several states in Africa coups have been successfully undertaken by a small body of well-armed soldiers, sometimes by other ranks rather than commissioned officers (Master-Sergeant Samuel Doe's takeover of Liberia in 1980 affords one example). Drawing again on Latin American experience, it is clear that the professionalisation of the armed forces does not by itself lessen the incidence of coups and that the latter might be precipitated if military personnel feel themselves discriminated against by urban-based political and bureaucratic élites who are higher up the social scale than themselves.

The military regimes which have seized power and inherited a crisis situation do not necessarily follow any clear political programme. As might be expected, government by armed-service officers is usually conservative, and is frequently reactionary and repressive – such is the case in Suharto's Indonesia, for example. Yet many Middle Eastern governments, which have been formed by coup-makers or as the result of a coup, have been radical. In Egypt, Syria, Libya and Iraq the officers removed the kings and landlords, established republics, redistributed land and nationalised industry and commerce. Such coups established the officer corps as the pivot of politics, but did not in all cases fundamentally alter the structure of society. In Africa, the maintenance of a social *status quo* is much more a common pattern, despite the radicalism of certain regimes, such as those of Burkina Faso under Thomas Sankara and Ghana under Jerry Rawlings; it was Sankara's ultimately futile attempts to dismantle the old social order and to short-circuit existing clientelist networks that led to his removal. In Africa, Ethiopia produced a *soi-disant* communist regime, while in Latin America only Peru has recently spawned a reformist military. In East and Southeast Asia, with the partial exception of Myanmar, right-wing radicalism has been marked. South Korea from 1961 and Indonesia from 1966 provide examples of military takeovers which initiated basic structural transformations; these were undertaken by the state within the framework of a capitalist economy. Myanmar's radicalism under Ne Win was of a state socialist rather than conservative kind, yet in some respects the effects were anti-socialist: in a society where parochialism and tradition remain strong, the spread of communism was checked and the power of the military–bureaucratic ruling class was consolidated.

In Africa, Latin America and the Middle East, there is little evidence for the argument that the military provides the order to spur economic development. The extent to which the economy performs well would seem to be a function of non-military factors. In East and Southeast Asia, on the other hand, many states with governments either led by the military or with military participation have achieved outstanding economic success. In a country such as Indonesia under Suharto, the military has provided a framework of order and stability (albeit often using repressive measures) favourable to economic development and has drawn upon technical advice in its pursuit of pragmatic economic policies. At the least, it would therefore appear that military regimes in the region, with the exception of Myanmar, have not inhibited economic development. At the same time, the very good economic record of Singapore and the creditable economic performance of Malaysia (both civilian-ruled states) suggest that the military does not have a monopoly in this sphere.

Viewing the regions we study at the time of writing in early 1993, a somewhat encouraging picture emerges. Despite the extensive involvement of the military in politics, and their obvious ability to use force against opposition, in all four regions there have been increasing pressures to civilianise and liberalise government. In Latin America, the generals have been in retreat in states such as Argentina and Chile, where they were accused of political and economic mismanagement and human rights abuses and, in Argentina's case, blamed for the costly and unsuccessful attempt to capture the Malvinas. In East and Southeast Asia, political 'modernisation' is the product of social forces unleashed by economic progress. In Africa, the democratic wave sweeping across the continent from the late 1980s has been directed against dictatorial, ineffective and corrupt governments, civilian as well as military, and has been led by predominantly urban élites, resulting in the removal of some regimes and the reform of others. In the Middle East, civilianisation has been marked in Egypt and has been more in evidence than political liberalisation in most states.

However, military and quasi-military regimes have tended to be linked to political parties; their rulers have incorporated more technocrats into government and created or strengthened their social bases of support. In Iraq, Syria and Libya, the fact that their presidents have accumulated power has increased their independence from the officer corps.

Though the military cannot be said to rule directly in any of these three states, it remains central to politics and early withdrawal is not in prospect. In Egypt, President Husni Mubarak is a former military officer, as were his two predecessors, and is likely to use the armed forces as a counter to the growing threat to his government from Islamic fundamentalism (already a major problem in Algeria, where it has prompted intervention). In Southeast Asia, the Indonesian military feels that it has a right, even a duty, to participate in government, while in Myanmar and Thailand the structural base of military power remains intact. It was noticeable in Indonesia in 1992, however, that as the 1993 elections approached President Suharto began to distance himself from the military, allowing public criticism of its role in the massacre of anti-government demonstrators in East Timor, and resisting pressure over the selection of a vice-presidential candidate for 1993. In Africa, some military rulers – like Kérékou in Benin – have been forced to withdraw, while several others cling precariously to power. Following presidential elections in November 1992, Ghana is still led by its former ruler – the ex-air force officer Jerry Rawlings – while Nigeria is in the protracted process of restoring civilian rule. Whether restoration will be permanent remains to be seen – it did not prove so in Ghana in 1969 and 1979, nor in Nigeria in 1979. The move to democratic, civilian politics is most advanced in Latin America. However, given the many coups that have taken place in this region over the past 60 years, it cannot be confidently predicted that the armed forces have withdrawn permanently to their barracks. In one way or another, it can be expected that they will retain an important role in each of the four regions which we have studied.

Further Reading

Approaches to the understanding of the role of the military in politics may focus on social factors, factors internal to the military itself, or relations between the two. Finer [1981] illustrates the first approach, Janowitz [1964] the second, and Luckham [1971] the third. As noted above, however, debates conducted at a broad general level have proved rather inconclusive. Most of the literature has concentrated on specific issues of practical significance, or on regional or national case studies. Clapham and Philip [1985] represents an attempt, combined with a range of case studies, to identify the problems encountered by the military once in power. Stepan [1988], primarily concerned with Latin American cases, contains an excellent general discussion of the means by which civilian authority over a previously interventionist military institution might be achieved. In addition, a number of regional and country case studies are recommended. For Africa, Decalo [1990] covers a number of cases. Cox [1976] is an excellent study of Sierra Leone. For the important case of Nigeria Luckham [1967] is outstanding, and Panter-Brick [1978] and Oyediran [1979] are valuable for subsequent developments. For East and Southeast Asia, Heinz [1990] and Selochan [1991] are useful collections, and Sundhaussen [1991] gives a wide-ranging overview. For Indonesia, Said [1991] covers the important immediate post-war period, and Crouch [1978] and Sundhaussen [1982] cover the army's rise and consolidation in power. On Myanmar, see Silverstein [1977]; on Thailand, Elliott [1978]. Among the extensive literature on Latin America, Loveman and Davies [1978], Angell [1984], Philip [1985], Lowenthal and Fitch [1986] and Remmer [1989] provide valuable overviews, the latter combined with a detailed analysis of the Pinochet regime in Chile. For studies of the internal organisation of the Pinochet regime and the process of military withdrawal and subsequent civil-military relations see Arriagada [1988] and Loveman [1991]. On Brazil, see Stepan [1971] and Alves [1985]; on Peru, Stepan [1978]. For the distinctive pattern of military intervention in Syria, see Batatu [1981]; for Iraq see Khalil [1989].

5

Revolution

1. Introduction

Revolutions are momentous events, involving fundamental social, economic and political change. Because so much is at stake they are usually violent and bloody affairs, and as much blood is shed again in conflicts between the revolutionaries themselves. Indeed, some of the revolutions we consider here would not be considered revolutionary in their outcomes by many who participated on the revolutionary side. This is certainly the case for the Mexican, Ethiopian and Iranian revolutions, in which groups with very different visions of the future first fought side by side and later slaughtered each other. The analysis of revolution is as contentious as the practice of it. Because revolution is such a contestable concept, and because revolutions have a strong ideological component to them, we introduce our chapter on Third World revolution by raising broader considerations of the topic.

Much contemporary thinking about revolution is drawn from the historical experiences of the 'great' revolutions of France, Russia and China. Specific features of these revolutions are frequently incorporated into general conceptions of what constitutes a revolution and what differentiates revolutions from other kinds of change. Such historically based criteria can lead to a dogmatic exclusivism in analysing revolutionary experience. Many Third World societies have borne a certain resemblance to the social and economic context from which the 'great' revolutions sprang: emergent capitalism, limited industrialisation, a small proletariat, and a predominantly agricultural economy with large-scale inequalities.

Thinking about revolution has been influenced not only by past revolutions, but by revolutionary theorists and practitioners following in a continuing ideological tradition. The theory and practice of revolution is so closely entwined because theorists and practitioners have been one and the same. Marx, Lenin, Trotsky and Mao immediately spring to mind: not only did they write about revolution, they struggled to bring it about. Their intellectual and political roles, their involvement in and accounts of revolution created a chain linking Marx's class analysis of the nineteenth century to twentieth century liberation wars in places as far apart as Vietnam, Angola and Nicaragua. Indeed, Third World writers on revolution like Amilcar Cabral, Franz Fanon, Ernesto 'Che' Guevara and Regis Debray have also been involved in revolutions. None of the movements with which these writers have been associated, however, were based on Marx's revolutionary proletariat. They have all been linked with peasant guerrilla movements and a tradition of people's revolutionary war of the kind propounded by Mao Ze-Dong, although none could be considered a Maoist. Although the intellectual lineage linking Third World revolutionaries to Marx is not a direct one, because it did originate with him, the authenticity of a revolution has frequently been assessed by the extent to which class actions were involved in the revolutionary process and the extent to which a revolutionary regime implemented socialism.

More recent developments in Eastern Europe (the demise of the communist state through popular pressure and uprisings) suggest that the processes usually leading to regimes based on Marxist–Leninist principles might equally be associated with the reintroduction of capitalism and liberal democracy.

The nature of the link between the revolutionary process and the regime which emerges from it draws attention to the utility of the distinction between revolution from above and revolution from below. Skocpol conceives revolution from below as an inherent part of 'social revolution'; for her revolutions are 'rapid, basic transformations of a society's state and class structures; and they are accompanied and in part carried through by class-based revolts from below' [Skocpol, 1979: 4]. In our examination of the experience of revolution in the Third World we consider how particular paths to revolution influence the outcome.

We have also taken into account the significance of external factors. Third World revolutions have been accompanied by high levels of external intervention, both in support of and in opposition to revolutionary movements. Since the Second World War, the United States has, at various times, advocated reforms by Third World regimes to head off revolution, condoned savage repression and directly intervened in the domestic politics of states undergoing upheaval. The Soviet Union and China have offered assistance to movements and helped consolidate regimes which appeared to them as revolutionary. External interventions were part of the Cold War. The declining capacity of communist states to intervene in support of revolutions and the hegemony of western capitalism might presage the end of the revolutionary lineage. On the other hand, the course and fate of Third World revolution have been inextricably linked to nationalism and national issues. This historical tradition has been undermined by the failure of regimes in Eastern Europe, but some of its major principles, particularly those of equality and opposition to exploitation, have had an enormous impact on the politics of the Third World. Finally, the tradition is not yet dead. Despite a current trend toward economic liberalisation, outposts of communism remain intact in Southeast Asia and in Cuba.

2. Revolutionary regimes in Africa

Of the many possible candidates for the designation 'revolutionary regime', very few states qualify. With the partial exception of Sékou Touré's Guinea, none of what Rosberg and Callaghy [1979: 5] described as the 'first wave' of socialist states (those which became independent in or about 1960) was revolutionary in the sense in which we have defined revolution at the outset of this chapter (most, like Nyerere's Tanzania, were 'populist socialist'). We had to wait until the 1970s before regimes emerged in Africa which could with any confidence be described as revolutionary in intent. Of the 'second wave' of socialist states, some – notably the ex-Portuguese-ruled states of Angola, Mozambique and Guinea–Bissau – emerged *from below* following a protracted liberation struggle under a leadership guided by a Marxist–Leninist ideology, while in others – especially in Ethiopia and to an extent in Somalia – 'revolutions' were imposed *from above* by military regimes. It needs to be stressed that the successful waging of a liberation struggle did not in itself guarantee that the consequent regime would necessarily be revolutionary. The ideological commitment of the national leadership was important, though Amilcar Cabral of Cape Verde put ideology into perspective when he stated that 'National liberation, the struggle against colonialism, the construction of peace, progress and independence are hollow words devoid of any significance unless they can be translated into a real improvement of living conditions' [quoted in Chabal, 1983: 66].

The historical experience of the peasantry (and the nature of its links with the leadership) may count for more. The context in which power is transferred, and the determination of the leadership to take firm control of the state apparatus, may also be important in shaping the kind of policies which are subsequently pursued. Thus, in Zimbabwe the fact that independence was ultimately achieved (in 1980) as the result of a negotiated settlement may have served to reduce the revolutionary zeal of Robert Mugabe's government. In this section we concentrate on the experience of Mozambique, Angola and Ethiopia.

The constraints within which the government had to operate when **Mozambique** achieved independence on 25 June 1975 were formidable. The predominantly agricultural economy was in a parlous condition, having been crippled by the long years of war and hit by rising oil prices. Economically, the country remained intensely dependent on the regional sub-system centring on South Africa, which it supplied with electricity and labour. The administrative structure was weak and the exodus of white managers, technicians, shopkeepers and traders meant that trained personnel (which was desperately short at all levels) was not available to sustain the extensive measures of nationalisation that were undertaken, or to revive flagging industrial output, or to underpin bold experiments in the state farming sector. The transportation, marketing and distribution systems were in a state of collapse.

At its congress in 1977, FRELIMO (which was formally converted from a front into a vanguard party) decided that agriculture should become 'the base and industry the dynamising factor for development'. However, in practical terms little was achieved and three years later production in all sectors was still below pre-independence levels. There were food shortages and food rationing in the towns, speculation and black marketeering, rapidly rising unemployment, and a prolonged drought in parts of central Mozambique. Acts of sabotage perpetrated by opposition groups, notably the Mozambique National Resistance (MNR–RENAMO) which was strongly backed by South Africa, forced the government to spend more on defence and security than the country could afford. This fact, and substantial expenditure in the spheres of health and education (in which the record was impressive) meant that the level of state consumption was high.

The fourth FRELIMO Congress in April 1983 therefore shifted the emphasis away from the big state farms (which had a poor production record) and in favour of private peasant production – peasants, for example, were paid higher prices for their produce. To help overcome the distribution problems, private trading was still permitted, though made subject to more stringent controls; the inefficient people's shops were abolished and consumer co-operatives were encouraged to handle the sale of food in urban areas. The Congress also took steps to reorganise and revitalise FRELIMO. The central committee was more than doubled in size (from 54 to 128), with a majority of its members now workers and peasants not directly linked to the central state apparatus.

However, conditions in Mozambique continued to deteriorate. The economy was critically weak and many of the people were starving, while the task of asserting military control over the whole country was daunting. It was in these circumstances that in March 1984 Mozambique signed a non-aggression pact with South Africa – the Nkomati Accord – on terms dictated by the white-ruled Republic: the South African government undertook to withdraw its support from the MNR and the Mozambican government agreed to stop backing the African National Congress (ANC), the leading South African nationalist movement. The two governments also agreed to promote closer economic relations between their two countries. However, South Africa cynically flouted this agreement and continued to provide enormous quantities of arms for the MNR. The result was to create a critical military situation in Mozambique, to play havoc with the Mozambican economy and to cause massive social dislocation as peasants, caught up in the fighting, were forced to abandon their homes – an estimated one million people sought refuge in neighbouring Malawi.

Given this record of continuing hostility towards Mozambique, it was understandable that most Mozambicans were not convinced by South Africa's plea of innocence over the death (in October 1986) of President Samora Machel in a plane crash just inside the South African border. The new president, Joaquim Chissano, was committed to continuing his predecessor's policies. Close relations with Zimbabwe were retained and troops from Zimbabwe and (for a time) from Tanzania joined the struggle against RENAMO. The latter's cruel tactics, coupled in 1991–2 with the worst drought that southern Africa had experienced in over 50 years, caused immense suffering. Renewed negotiations in Rome in August 1992 between the government and RENAMO (attended by both Chissano and Afonso Dhlakama, the rebel leader) brought the prospect of peace to a war-torn, famine-stricken country. In a desperate bid to obtain external assistance, the FRELIMO government renounced its commitment to Marxism–Leninism, and promised to hold multi-party elections in September 1993. An uneasy peace prevailed, and in November 1992 Zimbabwe postponed the withdrawal of its remaining 5000 troops.

The case of **Angola** shows that there are differences between revolutionary regimes, even when they originate in the same way: Angola, like Mozambique, achieved independence from Portugal in the mid-1970s following a prolonged liberation struggle. We take the similarities first and then the differences, though neither is a discrete category.

Like Mozambique, Angola entered independence under a government committed to Marxist–Leninist principles; the ideology was, however, somewhat eclectic, and was interpreted pragmatically to fit the Angolan context. The ruling *Movimento Popular de Libertação de Angola* (MPLA) announced in December 1977 that the movement would be transformed into a party – a change already made by FRELIMO. Power was centralised in the hands of the president (José Eduardo dos Santos following Agostinho Neto's death in September 1979), though predominantly elected bodies dominated by workers and peasants were subsequently created at national and provincial levels. The Angolan regime, again like that of Mozambique, inherited a shattered economy and a poor communications network, and was desperately short of skilled personnel (the government launched an ambitious educational programme). Sweeping nationalisation measures were similarly introduced, bringing some 80 per cent of Angola's enterprises under the state, thereby reinforcing the need for foreign technical assistance and equipment to run them.

But there were differences from Mozambique also. One of these stemmed from the fact that three nationalist movements had fought

for independence. This basic 'communal tripolarity', as John
Marcum has called it [Marcum, 1969: 10], had persisted throughout the liberation struggle and had been reflected in the 1975
constitutional arrangements that paved the way to independence. A
government of national unity had been established, but quickly
collapsed. The power struggle had been internationalised, the
decisive factor proving to be the massive Soviet and Cuban
intervention on the side of the MPLA, which was strongly
entrenched in the major urban centres. However, the southern-
based *União Nacional para a Independência Total de Angola*
(UNITA), led by Dr Jonas Savimbi, never relented in its bitter
opposition to the ruling MPLA, and central and southern Angola
were plunged into civil war. UNITA was backed by South Africa,
whose troops made innumerable incursions across the Angolan
border allegedly in pursuit of guerrillas belonging to the South West
Africa People's Organisation (SWAPO), who were fighting for
Namibia's independence, and by the United States.

Heavy defence expenditure placed a massive burden on the
economy and, as in the many other African states where it
occurred, reinforced external dependency. The economy was in a
mess, with continuing difficulties in production, marketing and
distribution, despite the fact that Angola's revolutionary rulers
(unlike those of Mozambique) sat astride a potentially very rich
country, with vast mineral deposits and fertile land and a relatively
low population (under a tenth of that of Nigeria but inhabiting a
larger geographical area). This potential was far from being fully
realised. Agricultural output was low: cash-crop production did not
reach the levels achieved before independence, when Angola had a
thriving commercial agricultural sector and was the world's fourth
largest producer of coffee. UNITA guerrilla attacks in the Central
Highlands region – the country's maize-producing and cattle-
rearing area – partly explained why the government could not
achieve self-sufficiency in food production and had to import food
on a substantial scale; these attacks also seriously disrupted the
country's transport and distribution system. Poor distribution
resulted periodically in acute food shortages in Luanda, the
capital, and other urban centres. There was also widespread
absenteeism and low productivity in industry.

Angola's revolutionary regime inherited important extractive
industries and this, too, set it apart from poorly-endowed Mozam-

bique; in other respects, however, Angola (like Mozambique) had a weak industrial base. The regime's policy was to tolerate foreign-owned enterprises so long as Angolan interests were respected. In the vital mining sector, the government renegotiated contracts with America's Gulf Oil Corporation to work the extensive oilfields in the Cabinda enclave (oil provided over 60 per cent of Angola's foreign exchange) and with the Angolan Diamond Company (Diamang) to mine the country's diamonds. Though the state acquired majority shareholding in both these undertakings, effective control (including day-to-day operations) remained with the foreign companies. Despite the regime's Marxist–Leninist commitment, Angola's trade was still overwhelmingly with the West; its government exercised further autonomy by refusing to allow the Soviet Union to establish a military base on its soil. Pressure from South Africa, Angola's near neighbour, was harder to withstand and, under the Lusaka Agreement of February 1984, Angola had to undertake not to harbour SWAPO guerrillas in return for a pledge that South Africa would withdraw all its troops from Angolan territory. This agreement was flouted by South Africa.

Four years later a new diplomatic offensive by the United States' government resulted in another agreement. Under the South African–Cuban–Angolan agreement of December 1988 South Africa withdrew its troops from Angola and Cuba repatriated its 50 000-strong force in stages (the operation was completed in May 1991). A period of intermittent negotiations, punctuated by heavy fighting, followed, but eventually – on 15 May 1991 – a cease-fire took effect; on 31 May, dos Santos and Savimbi signed the Estoril Accord, bringing a formal end to the 16-year-long civil war. A multi-party general election was held in September 1992. Savimbi refused to accept the results, which gave the MPLA a clear victory, and armed conflict broke out between the two sides, causing immense suffering among the civilian population. Peace negotiations, however, continued.

In **Ethiopia** the military did not so much instigate the revolution as act against the background of student and trade union protests. Socialism offered a way of putting maximum distance between itself and the old discredited order. Following its direct assumption of power in September 1974, the military (ruling through a co-ordinating committee or 'Derg') imposed tight control – censorship was reintroduced, strikes were banned and trade union leaders arrested, the university was closed, and a literacy campaign (*zemacha*), designed also to mobilise peasant support for the revolution, was launched in the rural areas. In 1975 the Derg extended state control of the economy by nationalising the banks, and insurance, industrial and commercial companies. It also nationalised urban and agricultural land (a significant proportion of which had been granted by Emperor Haile Selassie to the nobility), and sought to assert rural control through peasant associations. Some 30 000 associations were eventually established and made responsible for implementing the rural land reforms, but most were ineffective: peasants generally were reluctant to supply the cities with food. All urban land and all rentable houses and flats were nationalised, and urban associations (*kebeles*) were set up to administer the properties and improve roads, schools and other amenities in their neighbourhoods. Urban workers gained less from the revolution than the peasants, and resented the loss of their right to take strike action; students and professional groups in the urban areas were also alienated. Many students especially belonged to the Ethiopian People's Revolutionary Party (EPRP), a radical Marxist group which adopted the tactics of urban guerrilla warfare and was brutally crushed by the military during the 'Red Terror' of 1977–8.

Rural disaffection was much harder to deal with. While the rural land reforms won grass-roots support for the regime in certain parts of the country, they were bitterly opposed by local and provincial leaders. Outside secessionist Eritrea, against which the Derg fatefully despatched troops in November 1974, the main centres of opposition to the government were in the northern provinces of Tigray, Begemder and Wollo, in the south among the Afar and Oromo groups, and among the ethnic Somalis. New movements seeking autonomy or even secession emerged, prominent among them being the Tigray People's Liberation Front (TPLF) and the Oromo Liberation Front (OLF). Not only did the land reforms remain unpopular in the northern provinces, but the government policy of forcing many Amharas and Tigreans to settle in the agriculturally vital southern provinces offended the Oromos, who constitute by far the largest linguistic–ethnic group in Ethiopia, and resulted in increased support for the OLF. The Derg, under its leader Lieutenant-Colonel Mengistu Haile-Mariam, survived precariously with the help of Soviet military advisers and Cuban troops. The cost in human suffering of the regime's survival was very high; in 1984–5 this suffering was enormously compounded by severe drought, which spread to areas in the south of the country not previously affected.

In September 1984 Mengistu launched a ten-year Development Plan under which priority was to go to agriculture, with the intention of achieving self-sufficiency in grain by the end of the Plan period. The area given over to state farms, despite their poor production record, was to be doubled and the number of peasant households organised into producer co-operatives was to be increased from under 2 per cent in 1984 to over 50 per cent by 1994. The effect of the Plan was to exacerbate an already grim agricultural situation and to demoralise further the peasant community – it took no account of the better production record of individual peasant farmers.

After a long delay caused by the military's fear of restricting its own freedom of action, a Workers' Party of Ethiopia (WPE) was established in September 1984; the inauguration of the People's Democratic Republic of Ethiopia followed in 1987, with Mengistu as president. The party organisation was based on Soviet and Eastern European models and was centralist rather than federalist in structure. The WPE was a vanguard party dedicated to the building of 'scientific socialism'. However, virtually the same military clique dominated the party's top organs, and peasants and workers were only thinly represented. In consequence, the party did not enable the military regime to generate political support for the measures which it took.

The problem of communalism remained extremely serious. Government policies tended to benefit the Amharas and were reminiscent of those pursued by Haile Selassie; so, too, was the regime's response to the challenges which faced it – forcible (indeed brutal) repression was preferred to negotiation and compromise. A quarter of the 1984–5 budget was allocated to defence, compared with 10 per cent for agriculture. Reforms in the agricultural sector to satisfy external donors (notably the World Bank and the European Community) included better producer prices for grain and coffee, the abandonment of collective farms and the ending of the villagisation campaign. They were undertaken between 1988 and 1990, but came too late to save the beleaguered military government.

The latter's downfall was presaged with the formation in 1989 of the Ethiopian People's Revolutionary Democratic Front (EPRDF), a coalition of Tigrayan, Amharic and Oromo liberation movements, at the heart of which was the TPLF. As the Front's forces advanced on Addis Ababa Mengistu resigned on 21 May 1991, fled his bankrupt, poverty-stricken country and sought political asylum in Zimbabwe. Eight days later the Eritrean People's Liberation Front (EPLF), which had long co-ordinated military strategy with the TPLF, formed a separate provisional government in Eritrea. It remained in office until a UN-supervised referendum on Eritrea's independence was held in April 1993. The majority for independence was overwhelming. This was accepted by Ethiopia's new rulers. Each leader – Meles Zenawi of EPRDF and Issayas Afferwerki of EPLF – claimed that his movement had abandoned doctrinaire Marxism–Leninism and was committed to democracy.

Whereas in Mozambique and Angola the former liberation movement had to be transformed into a political party, in Ethiopia a political party to underpin the regime had to be created *de novo*. Nevertheless, the distinction between revolutionary regimes which emerged from below and those which were imposed from above was more significant in respect of their origin than their subsequent working. The similarities between the two categories of regime were as striking as the differences. Each based its policies on considerations of *realpolitik* as much as on Marxist–Leninist ideology, and in no case did revolutionary principle reduce external dependence, though instances did occur where a regime asserted some autonomy. Despite a commitment to mass political participation (especially on the part of Angola and Mozambique) each state remained subject to centralised, bureaucratic and (above all in the case of Ethiopia) repressive control; this accounted, in part, for the challenge posed by powerful linguistic–ethnic minorities and other opposition groups. These revolutionary regimes operated within a hostile regional and international capitalist environment and had to contend with serious drought conditions. But their leaders must at least share responsibility for poor regime performance – they adopted over-ambitious policies which were divorced from the reality of life in predominantly rural societies. They also diverted such limited resources as were available away from economic production and towards state maintenance and consolidation.

3. East and Southeast Asia

In comparison with other Third World regions, Southeast Asia has been marked by powerful and successful communist movements pursuing strategies of revolutionary guerrilla warfare, in some cases paralleling the experience of China. The wars were protracted, and confronted a succession of colonial regimes and invaders; in the final stages they involved a direct confrontation with the US. The establishment of communism in Laos, Cambodia (Kampuchea), Vietnam and North Korea, however, contrasts with the failure of similar movements in Malaya (Malaysia) and Indonesia. The account here will examine the contrasting fates of revolution in Cambodia, Vietnam, Malaysia and Indonesia.

The course and development of successful revolutionary movements in Southeast Asia are comparable in several ways. They were based on a poor, densely-concentrated peasantry, marked inequalities in landownership, a commercial/plantation agriculture developed largely under the impact of European colonialism, and the growth of a middle class influenced by nationalism and by both European and Asian Marxist thought and practice. At the heart of peasant and nationalist movements were communists, whose successful seizure of power (in Cambodia and Vietnam) was based, firstly, on mobilising and organising the peasantry and, secondly, on establishing a position of leadership over nationalist movements by incorporating them into secondary positions within united fronts. Their task was made easier by militarised foreign opposition to national independence movements influenced by communist ideas. Where communist movements mobilised support but ultimately failed (Malaya and Indonesia), their weakness lay in their identification with minority ethnic or religious groups (the Chinese in Malaya and the non-Muslim community in Indonesia) and in their secondary role to nationalist governments and movements. The difference between success and failure was often a function of a revolutionary situation occurring when communist strength coincided with anti-communist weakness. The Vietminh established control of North Vietnam after the battle of Dienbienphu in 1954 (a consequence of decaying French colonialism), but it took another twenty-one years to liberate the south (a consequence of the US replacing the French). In Cambodia, a strong nationalist leadership and the identification of the communist movement with the Vietnamese delayed the growth and success of communist revolution.

Distinctive patterns of Third World revolutions were established by the Cambodian revolution (led by Pol Pot), and the revolution in North Vietnam (led by Ho Chi Minh), which extended across all of Vietnam after the last American helicopter flew out in 1975. Each involved peasant guerrilla armies establishing liberated zones, introducing land reforms and finally conquering the cities. Both produced disturbing images of the consequences of revolution: the 'boat people' of Vietnam and the 'class genocide' of Cambodia.

French colonialism created the field for peasant and communist action, linking together the immiseration of peasants and the politicisation of intellectuals. As early as 1861 a writer on the French expedition to Indochina observed, prophetically: 'It would be more exact to regard each peasant fastening a sheaf of rice as a centre of resistance' [White, 1974: 91]. By the mid-twentieth century peasant resistance had become organised and armed. In Vietnam, a crucial development was the creation of two different agrarian zones, a factor in the prolonged nature of the revolution. In the north, there was an indebted, subsistence and densely-concentrated peasantry, as well as prosperous landlords whose emergence can be traced to the marketisation of land. In the south, peasant rice production was geared to export, and French land policy created an urban landowning class with two-thirds of productive land leased to tenant farmers who formed half of the rural population [Tate, 1979: 347–8]. In addition to rural inequality and poverty, a heavy burden of colonial taxation provided the spark for transforming a tradition of short-lived peasant rebellion into sustained revolt. French rule also disrupted Vietnamese rural society by uprooting peasants for plantation employment and drafting tens of thousands of Vietnamese to France during the First World War. Colonial practices like these went some way to dissolving the dichotomy between peasant and worker, and rural and urban dweller. It was the north that initially provided the fertile ground for guerrilla war and Vietminh leadership of the anti-Japanese struggle that made it possible to take advantage of the opportunity.

The impact of colonialism on Cambodian society was more a ripple effect of French rule in Vietnam. Cambodian peasant society was largely untouched, other than by taxation, but French rule brought with it Chinese and Vietnamese merchants and traders, and

Vietnamese labourers to work the export-oriented rubber plantations. This satellite relationship with Vietnam undermined indigenous development and was to create a strong anti-Vietnamese current within Cambodian communism after the victory of the Khmer Rouge in 1975. The leading role of Vietnam and Vietnamese communists also had an impact on the early Indochinese communist movement. Most of the Cambodian representatives to the Indochinese Communist Party were either ethnic Vietnamese or Chinese.

The expansion of communism in both Cambodia and Vietnam can also be linked to French colonialism. Most of the leaders of the early Vietnamese movement were educated or, like Ho Chi Minh, worked in France. The leadership of the Kampuchean Communist Party (KCP) was also French-educated. There was, then, a mix of ideological influences, including European Marxism and communism in its different guises, Asian Marxism, particularly Maoism, and the practical experiences of peasant-based guerrilla warfare against European and Japanese occupation and American intervention. In the cases of Vietnam and Cambodia, the different mixes of ideology and the nature, timing and experience of external intervention were crucial in shaping the outcome of revolution. Until the 1960s, Cambodian communism had limited success with the peasantry, and even then it was under the impact of the spillover of the guerrilla war in South Vietnam, and American bombings in Cambodia and influence over the Cambodian Lon Nol government.

For the case of **Vietnam**, the lengthy struggle of Vietnamese communists is a suitable starting point. Ho Chi Minh, a founder of the French Communist Party, established the Indochinese Communist Party in 1929. If one takes the fall of Saigon in 1975 as the culmination of the struggle, the process of establishing the revolutionary regime was one of the most protracted of all. Along with its appeal to and organisation of the peasantry, it was aided by support from the Comintern and temporary support from China, and facilitated by the crumbling of Kuomintang power and decay of French imperialism. The political benefits arising from external circumstances were not accidental. They were the subject of serious study by the leadership. For example, Ho Chi Minh, communist, nationalist and pragmatist, always chose to negotiate with the power likely to rid Vietnam of the stronger and immediate threat.

The tactical sensitivity of the Vietnamese leadership to the international context of revolution was paralleled by its use of united front tactics. The liberation of the North after the fall of the French garrison at Dienbienphu gave the edge to the communists at the heart of the Vietminh, the broad front of Viet nationalism. The growth of the Vietcong (the southern National Liberation Front – NLF), followed the same pattern. The liberation and unification of Vietnam resulted from nationalist outrage against US puppet regimes, the organisational power of the communists within the united front and the support and increasing preponderance of North Vietnam and the North Vietnamese Liberation Army (NVA). The massive American bombing, the disruption of peasant life through the 'strategic hamlets' programme (the re-grouping of peasants from their ancestral villages to areas supposedly defensible against Vietcong penetration), and US support for regimes which were corrupt, decadent and nepotistic were all factors in incorporating non-communist nationalists. The contradictions of US policy were encapsulated in the infamous statement of a US officer describing the outcome of the battle for Ben Tre: 'we destroyed the town to save it'.

In **Cambodia**, the development of the Khmer revolution followed a different course. The communist movement there had limited success, in part because of its early connection to the regional Vietnamese-dominated communist movement. A combination of factors similar to those operating in Indonesia also worked against the Kampuchean Communist Party. In Cambodia, the political order rested on a combination of imperial tradition, Buddhism and nationalism. In the twentieth century, these values were symbolised in the political leadership of Prince Sihanouk. He was of royal lineage, a social conservative but a nationalist. Through the 1960s he organised a coalition through his Sangkum party, based on the urban rich, bureaucrats, and an acquiescent peasantry, and followed a foreign policy of non-alignment. The political hegemony established by Sihanouk was deceptive. From an earlier position of an equality of poverty, by 1962 31 per cent of the Cambodian (Khmer) population owned less than one hectare per family (less than subsistence needs) and this proportion farmed only 5 per cent (approximately) of the arable land. As a consequence, many peasants were forced into tenant and debt relationships with a Cambodian rich peasantry and Chinese and Vietnamese money-lenders, respectively [Etcheson, 1984: 14–15]. Food shortages, urban speculation and the printing of money led to financial crisis and peasant immiseration, and a sharpening gap between the rural and urban sectors. The war in Vietnam intruded into this domestic crisis. Sihanouk's neutralism and policy of regional balance led to a close relationship with North Vietnam, antagonised the USA and resulted in the latter's support for an anti-Sihanouk Khmer group in South Vietnam. Sihanouk broke relations with the USA in 1965, after airstrikes against Cambodian territory, and cut off the country's major source of aid. In pursuit of alternative revenue, the Cambodian government began a rigorous taxation of the peasantry. Peasant uprisings brought brutal repression and created the opportunity for the KCP (some fragmented factions of which were established in the rural areas) to build greater peasant support. Further US interventions followed: Sihanouk was removed by a right-wing military dictatorship and his successor, Lon Nol, re-aligned with the United States. Simultaneously, the NVA and the southern Vietcong retreated into Cambodia under pressure from US bombing. As they made their way into the Cambodian interior to create new base areas and protect supplies they overran Cambodian army positions into which the Khmer Rouge (the armed wing of the Cambodian Communist Party) inserted their guerrilla units. The blanket bombing of rural Cambodia and Sihanouk's call from exile for national resistance to the Lon Nol regime paved the way for the Khmer Rouge to lead nationalist resistance and further mobilise the Cambodian peasantry. Domestic pressure in the USA weakened US support, and in 1975 the Khmer Rouge entered Phnom Penh, the same year that Saigon fell to the NVA and the Vietcong. The revolutionary forces ushered in very different regimes.

In **Vietnam**, the victory edged aside southern non-communist nationalists. In *Journal of a Vietcong*, Truong Nhu Tang, an urban, upper-class, French-educated intellectual, recounts his long involvement in clandestine political organisations, his imprisonment and torture under the pro-American Diem regime and his membership of the Provisional Regional Government in the liberated areas [Tang, 1986]. His departure by boat, after liberation, symbolised the problems of unifying Vietnamese communism and anti-imperialist nationalism. These problems were magnified in the integration of

the two different economies. Unification extended northern collectivist practices to the south. They were unpopular with those
involved in capitalist activities, and the result was the flight of the
'boat people'. Many of these were of Chinese origin, and had
dominated rural commerce and resisted the implementation of
revolutionary measures. In areas long under NLF control the land
issue had already been resolved. In other areas, a more pragmatic
approach was followed, sometimes after the collapse of collectives.
In the Mekong delta, where landlordism had developed under
colonialism, a stratum of prosperous peasants had been encouraged
by US advisers through land distribution. Reacting to low state
prices for their produce, they concentrated on their private plots.
The new government allowed private initiative and introduced a
mix of public and collective ownership and small-scale private
capitalism. In the early 1990s, however, the political and economic
structure of Vietnam remained state-directed.

In **Cambodia**, when the Khmer Rouge guerrillas came to the
cities, they made urban citizens become peasants. In the first days,
the Khmer Rouge compelled the urban residents to leave the towns.
Why this rustication took place is a matter of controversy. Different
explanations have been put forward: to rid the peasantry of
parasitic cities; to prevent urban famine after US aid was cut; to
counter the threat of the bombing of Phnom Penh. Whatever the
tactical thinking of the leadership, ideology played an important
role in shaping the implementation of a measure which was brutal
in its consequences. It was complemented by the most radical and
egalitarian of policies: the abolition of money. For an unpaid
guerrilla army drawn from a subsistence peasantry, money had
ceased to have much meaning. For the urban population, however,
the imposed peasantisation was catastrophic and brought in its
wake mass starvation. The onslaught against the cities went along
with the killing of members of the government and administration
of the Lon Nol regime. Research based on interviews with
Cambodian refugees in Thailand indicates that the 'class genocide', murder of a class, was not the programme of the regime. The
many deaths (estimated at one million) were the results of
complicated and rapid growth of the Khmer Rouge, the fragmented control of its military command structure, internal purges
consequent on the consolidation of power by Pol Pot's faction
and a revenge taken by peasants on the city dwellers. Those who

proved amenable to political re-education and did not die of hunger survived. The regime did not. In 1979, the Vietnamese army invaded and the Khmer Rouge retreated to the jungle.

In Malaya and Indonesia, powerful communist movements developed but were unable to resist colonial armies or indigenous regimes. In **Indonesia**, the Dutch colonialists easily contained the early wave of communist activities in 1926–7, and during the Second World War the PKI (Communist Party of Indonesia) did little to disturb the Japanese occupying forces. In contrast to the post-war situation in Indochina, the Indonesian communist movement was relatively weak, and the retreating colonial power did not require US support. After the war, it was a nationalist movement, the PNI, which spearheaded the drive for independence from the Dutch. After independence, the PKI faced two major obstacles. The first derived from the nature of the Javanese peasantry. Although it was poor and densely concentrated there was no exploitative landlord class, and religious and cultural cleavages (between mixes of animism and Hindu–Buddhism on the one hand, and Muslims on the other) made peasant politicisation difficult. Furthermore, the traditional Indonesian village structure, lacking the communal solidarities found in Indochina, was easily penetrated by government administration, a process begun by Dutch colonialism. The second obstacle derived from the nature of power in post-independent Indonesia. The PKI, like other Asian communist movements, followed united front tactics. The radical nationalism and neutralism of President Sukarno, similar to Cambodia's Sihanouk, marginalised the PKI. Squeezed by anti-communist Muslim leaders, the PKI supported Sukarno's measures and government, and as a consequence played a secondary role. The military coup which pushed Sukarno aside in 1965 did not create space for the PKI, as the Lon Nol coup did in Cambodia. After a poorly planned communist uprising, the military and the local opponents of the communists and their allies turned upon them and massacred them.

The communist movement in **Malaya** suffered a similar fate, but at the hands of the British army. In contrast to the PKI, the MCP (Malayan Communist Party) led an armed struggle from the Malayan jungle against the Japanese occupation, but failed to capitalise on this leading role when it resumed united front tactics in the urban areas after the war. Harassed by the British authorities, the MCP returned to the jungle in 1948 and launched a guerrilla war. The party was never able to mobilise anything like the force levels of the Vietminh, the Vietcong or the Khmer Rouge because of obstacles similar to those facing the PKI.

Malaya was divided between Malays, Indians and Chinese. Beginning in the 1920s, communist ideas spread among the Chinese community, but because of communal exclusiveness they never spread to other ethnic groups. Furthermore, rising prosperity among sectors of the Chinese population brought a combination of resistance and neutralism from its ethnic core. These communal and class cleavages undermined the mobilisational capacity of Malayan communism and facilitated the British military containment and crushing of the insurgency.

In Southeast Asia, those communist movements which were able, politically and militarily, to dominate the nationalist movement agenda and were unhindered by ethnic or religious cleavage among the peasantry successfully established communist states. Although the Vietnamese army removed the Khmer Rouge in 1979, the latter remained a formidable force within Cambodia and a challenge to the pro-Vietnam regime. Despite external challenges, these movements put down deep organisational and ideological roots. Elsewhere however, where other groups took the lead in nationalist movements, and the communist movement found itself confined to a minority without strong links to the rest of the population, it was isolated and defeated.

4. Revolutionary regimes in Latin America

Despite its turbulent history, Latin America has produced few regimes which could be described as revolutionary. In Mexico (1910–17) and Bolivia (1952) old élites were overthrown by popular uprisings attended by considerable violence, but the supporters of social revolution were soon pushed aside. More recently both Cuba (1958–9) and Nicaragua (1979) have seen dictators overthrown by widely-backed popular uprisings, and both embarked on socialist paths – Cuba through adherence to an increasingly orthodox Marxist–Leninist model which continued in place in splendid isolation in 1993, Nicaragua in a context of pluralism until interrupted by an opposition election victory in 1990. The Nicaraguan revolution was part of a broader revolutionary current in the region, initially inspired by the Cuban revolution, which saw guerrilla movements challenge incumbent regimes with varying success from the early 1960s onwards. Finally, the Maoist revolutionary movement Sendero Luminoso enjoyed considerable support and regional power in Peru throughout the 1980s, though without coming close to overthrowing the government, but was weakened in 1992 as a result of the capture of its leader, Abimael Guzman.

In Mexico and in Bolivia, a popular uprising overthrew a narrowly-based old regime; in both, workers and peasants played significant roles in the period of revolutionary upheaval, and seemed to make early and very substantial gains. But in both cases they lost out before too long to a middle-class-dominated coalition which had succeeded in seizing hold of the state. A party broadly representing these bourgeois or middle-class sectors (the PRI in Mexico, the National Revolutionary Movement – MNR – in Bolivia) established its ascendancy over mobilised workers and peasants, largely by dividing them against themselves, and subordinated their demands to its own. In each case, the successful party developed an ideology that was both nationalistic and anti-imperialist, but which displayed little that was remotely socialist in character.

We turn first to the case of **Mexico**. The Mexican revolution was a long, complex, untidy and bloody phenomenon, stretching over more than two decades. It was fought by the social forces produced by rapid export-led development and incipient industrialisation under the dictatorship of Porfirio Diaz (1876-1911): entrepreneurs and urban professionals demanding genuine liberal democracy, and led by Francisco Madero; peasants pushed off communal land by the encroachment of commercial farming, the best known being those of Morelos led by Emiliano Zapata; and workers in Mexico City and other major centres throughout the country. The names of the losers – Madero, Zapata, Francisco 'Pancho' Villa – are far better known than those of the winners – Carranza (assassinated in 1919), Obregon (assassinated in 1928) and Calles. After the failure of Zapata and Villa in 1915 to cement an alliance that would enable them to govern the country, Carranza, Obregon and Calles gradually imposed the ascendancy of a modern and commercially oriented northern bourgeoisie, paving the way for the reforms made by Cardenas (1934–40) to incorporate workers and peasants, in a subordinate role, into the revolutionary settlement. This 'triumph of the bourgeoisie' in Mexico, which has given rise to a long-drawn-out process of capitalist development under the unbroken rule of the PRI, owed much to the rift between peasants and urban workers, the latter embracing liberalism rather than socialism, and suspicious of the Catholicism and backward-looking communalism of the former. Many urban workers fought alongside the bourgeoisie, most notably in the 'Red Brigades' raised by Obregon from among the organised workers of Mexico City to fight against the forces of Villa and Zapata.

A number of characteristics of the Mexican revolution find parallels in the case of **Bolivia**. The Bolivian revolution began with the dramatic overthrow of the old regime between 9 and 11 April 1952, largely as a result of the defeat of the army at the hands of a militia dominated by the rebellious tin miners. It brought to power the MNR, a movement-based nationalist party tainted in the 1940s with suspicions of fascist leanings. In the immediate aftermath of taking power it could not stem the demands of workers and newly mobilised peasants for far-reaching reforms. In the months following the uprising the peasants threw landowners off the land and took possession of it for themselves, a situation recognised in a substantial reform programme launched in 1953. Meanwhile the workers (led by the militant miners' union, the FSTMB) had gained a dominant position: in the mining industry itself they were able to win the nationalisation of (Bolivian-owned) tin mines, and the introduction of a limited form of workers' control. It seemed that workers and peasants were calling the tune. However, within four years Siles Zuazo (successor to the first president of the revolution, Victor Paz Estenssoro) had imposed an IMF-backed stabilisation programme, cut miners' wages, and broken a strike called in protest. In later years the army was rebuilt, the MNR moved further to the right, and the radical impulse was entirely exhausted in a cycle which ended with the authoritarian dictatorship of General Hugo Banzer (1971–8).

One reason for this was that the land reform programme of 1953 gave the land to the peasants in individual plots. This had the effect of creating an impregnable electoral majority in the countryside, loyal to successive presidents, and willing to back the government so long as their new title to the land was honoured. As in Mexico, workers and peasants were divided, though here it was the peasants who first sided with the government. A second reason for the failure of radicalism was that many miners under FSTMB leader Juan Lechín rejected the Trotskyist Workers' Revolutionary Party (POR) and joined the MNR with the intention of forcing it to the left. This 'entryist' tactic failed, largely because the methods used to impose MNR control alienated many miners, and forced Lechín to rely heavily on the coercive power of government. Siles Zuazo was later able to make use of rival groups, historically at odds with the Trotskyist POR, to divide the workers further. The upshot was that the petty bourgeois nationalism of the MNR proved triumphant, and the radical impetus of the immediate post-revolutionary period was lost.

By 1958 the Mexican revolution had long lost its radical impulse, and the Bolivian revolution had rapidly followed suit. Additionally, US intervention in Guatemala had cut short an incipient process of radicalisation there. In no Latin American state was there evidence of anything which could be described as socialist, let alone revolutionary. This makes all the more remarkable the establishment and consolidation of a socialist state closely tied to the Soviet bloc in the small island of **Cuba**, 90 miles from Miami. The success and future course of the revolution is all the more surprising in that Fidel Castro launched his bid to overthrow the dictator Fulgencio Batista as a radical democrat rather than a Marxist revolutionary, and that the organised working class of Cuba played a relatively small part in the revolution.

During the first six decades of the twentieth century Cuba was shaped by the development of sugar for export on a massive scale, and the close involvement of the United States in its economy and its politics. Rural workers in the sugar industry (employed seasonally and forced to scratch a living from their own inadequate plots of land for much of the year) formed the bulk of the guerrilla army which came together in the two years after Castro and the handful of his comrades who survived an ambushed landing by sea from Mexico in 1956 headed into the remote Sierra Maestre. The urban working class, either enrolled in the pro-Batista 'yellow' unions or loyal to the pro-Moscow Communist party (known as the Popular Socialist Party, PSP), rallied late to the revolutionary cause. The dictatorship collapsed relatively early, before the struggle to overthrow it had turned into a nationwide civil war, and, unusually, the revolution radicalised *after* the entry of the victorious guerrilla army into Havana on 1 January 1959. It moved rapidly towards an explicit commitment to socialism and a far-reaching programme of collectivist agrarian reform and nationalisation once its leaders realised that substantial social reform would prove impossible otherwise. The Cuban revolution lacked Marxist–Leninist orthodoxy, even after its declaration of adherence to Marxist–Leninist principles. This was reflected in an internationalism based not upon the organisation of vanguard parties aimed at winning the proletariats of other nations to the revolutionary cause, but upon what was christened the '*foco*' theory: the idea that a group of committed revolutionaries could launch a guerrilla war from an isolated and defensible area away from major cities, and create a revolutionary situation by their heroic example. On the whole, this strategy (by no means a full reflection of the Cuban experience itself) proved a failure, generating or inspiring failed guerrillas in Guatemala, Colombia, Venezuela, and (most notoriously) Bolivia, where Ernesto 'Che' Guevara lost his life in 1967. On the other hand, it played its part in rescuing the idea of armed struggle from years of Stalinist neglect, and matured into a more sophisticated appraisal of the need for more organic links with the masses; in a modified form its influence was seen in the Nicaraguan revolution, and in wars of national liberation elsewhere.

Before the revolution, United States investment in Cuba was higher than anywhere else in Latin America. It had been most significant in the sugar sector, but the process of diversification had brought United States domination in most modern industrial sectors of the economy too. This (along with the virtual stagnation of the Cuban economy since levels of sugar production and exports peaked in the 1920s) enabled Castro to give his campaign against Batista a nationalist and anti-imperialist character. In a different way, **Nicaragua** falls into the same category. United States economic interest in Nicaragua was low – lower in fact than anywhere else in Central America. This was, however, a consequence of the close political involvement of the United States, and the decision to control the country, from the 1930s, through the proxy of the Somoza family. Somoza senior made his career as commander of the National Guard, set up by the Americans in the late 1920s in preparation for the departure of the Marines, seizing the presidency for himself once his American sponsors had departed; by 1979 his son Anastasio (the second of his sons to inherit the presidency) was the head of a multimillion dollar business empire which accounted for more than half Nicaragua's total GDP.

At the heart of the Nicaraguan economy was the agricultural export sector, based initially on coffee and, after the Second World War, on cotton and cattle as well. The expansion of the latter two commodities pushed formerly self-sufficient peasants off the land into precarious seasonal employment, and created the radicalised semi-proletariat which formed the backbone of the liberation struggle. From inauspicious beginnings along *'foco'* lines in 1961 the FSLN (Sandinista National Liberation Front) – named after the nationalist hero of struggle against United States occupation between 1929 and 1933, Augusto Sandino – developed in the 1970s into a mass movement. Divided into three currents which proved complementary rather than conflicting – endorsing respectively strategies of insurrection, prolonged popular war in the countryside, and proletarian organisation and revolution – it eventually won a position of unchallenged supremacy in the struggle against the Somoza dictatorship. Determined to cling to power at all costs, Somoza pursued a policy of outright refusal to accept any compromise, marked by the assassination of Conservative opposition leader Pedro Chamorro in 1978. It was in part the perception by the leaders of the FSLN that Somoza would not accept any compromise, and their insistence on the need to take up an armed struggle against the dictatorship, which enabled them to take the lead in opposition to the regime. The second factor which won them widespread backing was the orientation of their programme toward the needs and aspirations of the majority of impoverished workers and peasants in the country, and their insistence on the need for radical reforms.

The Nicaraguan revolution differed in several respects from its Cuban predecessor. In some ways it was more radical: the Sandinistas were clearly committed to socialism before they took power, and won popular support on that basis. Also, the process of political mobilisation went far further before the Sandinistas came to power (as a result of the far greater impact of the civil war) than in Cuba. However, the Sandinistas drew inspiration from a variety of sources, of which their own reading of Marxist theory was only one. They were responsive to social movements and grassroots organisation, and particularly to radical Catholicism and liberation theology, as witnessed by the presence of priests in the Sandinista movement and in the government. Finally, the post-revolutionary policies applied by the Sandinistas differed substantially from those applied in Cuba. They resisted the temptation to turn their backs on Nicaragua's orientation towards agricultural exports, whereas the Cubans initially launched an all-out drive to diversify and industrialise, before settling back in the end to the realisation that sugar would remain the engine of growth in the economy, as it does today. The Sandinistas refrained from moving against commercial export farmers, setting up state monopolies to export their produce but offering remunerative prices and guaranteeing that productive land farmed efficiently would be left in the hands of its owners. This strategy was made possible by the massive authority of the Sandinistas (and the head start gained as a result of the forced takeover of the properties of the Somoza clan, and of unused or underutilised land). And they chose not to rule through a single revolutionary party, but to allow opposition parties to organise and participate in elections. The fruits of these policies were seen in 1984, when Daniel Ortega was elected to the presidency with some two-thirds of the total number of votes cast.

These policies were consistent with the past commitments of the Sandinistas, and reflected a desire (perhaps utopian) to institute in Nicaragua a democratic brand of socialism subordinated neither to the West nor to the Soviet bloc. It soon became clear, however, that for Nicaragua, as for Cuba, the most pressing reality was the hostile international environment in which the newly-established socialist regime found itself. Cuba had moved early into the Soviet bloc. The same option was not open to Nicaragua, which became the target of unremitting hostility from successive US governments because of its attempt to pursue an indigenous experiment in democratic socialism. This hostility, expressed in actions that were illegal in terms of both international and US law, imposed enormous costs in terms of human life, physical destruction, and economic distortions arising from the need to pour resources into defence. As a result, support for the Sandinistas and their programme slipped back, allowing a US-backed coalition, UNO, to win a majority in the elections of 1990. However, the Sandinistas had brought about significant social and institutional change in a decade of rule, and the victorious UNO coalition, led by Violeta Chamorro, was far from united. It proved impossible to roll back the changes implemented under

Sandinista rule, and by early 1993 the UNO coalition had broken up, and Chamorro was governing with Sandinista support. The hope remained, therefore, that Nicaragua's democratic revolution would be resumed at some point in the future.

The four revolutions considered here have in common the fact that their leaders were drawn overwhelmingly from the petty bourgeoisie or the bourgeoisie, and that the working class – and particularly the urban industrial working class – played minor roles in them. In itself this is no more than a reflection of the historically shaped social structure of Third World countries, in which export sectors take the place occupied by advanced industry in the developed world. The leading protagonists in these revolutions came from the most advanced sectors of the export economy, or were created by it: the displaced peasants of the state of Morelos, and the mixed working population of the north of Mexico, along with the new bourgeoisie spawned by development; the tin miners of Bolivia; and the rural semi-proletariat in Cuba and in Nicaragua.

The prominence of petty bourgeois leaders recalls Amilcar Cabral's dictum that this class will necessarily take the lead in colonial revolutions, and suggests that even these revolutions in the politically independent states of Latin America may be approached in these terms. The different outcomes in Mexico and Bolivia on the one hand, and Cuba and Nicaragua on the other, confirm the precision of Cabral's argument that only where such leaders explicitly adopt a socialist programme conceived in the interests of the worker and the peasant majority ('commit suicide as a class') will the movement they lead turn in a revolutionary direction. It is instructive that this pattern did develop in the two countries most directly affected, well into the twentieth century, by North American economic and political imperialism: Cuba and Nicaragua.

A final feature worth noting is that in the four cases of Third World revolution considered here, the *ancien régime* that fell was particularly weak, with a narrow social base and an isolated and corrupt leadership. With the exception of Bolivia, the form taken by this leadership was a personal dictatorship. The presence of corrupt and isolated personal dictatorships in Mexico, Cuba and Nicaragua (reminiscent of similar regimes in Ethiopia and in Iran) suggests that personal rule may be as likely as colonial rule to give way to social revolution. The collapse in the mid-1980s of the Duvalier and Marcos dictatorships, in Haiti and the Philippines respectively, confirms the fragility of personal rule of this kind, whether 'traditional' or 'modernising' in intent. It also suggests (as does Cabral) that socialism is by no means the automatic outcome.

5. Revolutionary regimes in the Middle East

There is a wide gap between most Western analyses of revolutionary change in the Middle East and those of indigenous writers and politicians. Much of the gap is due to differing conceptions of revolution. Firstly, despite violent upheavals since independence, political change has been caused as much by national issues as by social or economic ones. Secondly, the process of regime change in most of the Arab states has been initiated by conspiratorial officer groups and lacked popular participation. Thirdly, regime change has not been followed by systemic and fundamental change in social and economic structures, nor has there been significant ideological innovation. The overthrow of the Shah of Iran in 1979 was the result of long-term structural causes and the revolutionary process was violent and bloody and involved massive popular participation. Yet, for most Western writers, the events in Iran lacked one other ingredient commonly associated with the outcome of revolutions: some progressive content. The regime which emerged was dominated by religious leaders whose goal was to establish a state based on Islamic law and clerical rule.

One of the major problems of analysing revolution in the Middle East, then, is the absence of clear revolutionary achievements. However, although the changes which have taken place do not fit with any general conception of revolution, they form a political pattern. Many of the monarchies which were established during the nineteenth and twentieth centuries were replaced by republics. Large landlords were displaced and their landholdings redistributed. Key sectors of the economy were nationalised, although recently some privatisation measures have been introduced.

Developments during the late nineteenth and early twentieth century explain the strong nationalist component of radical change. Political institutions became increasingly controlled by landlords and economic policy generally favoured the landed interest; industry and industrialisation were given limited attention and trade was largely in the hands of foreign companies. Furthermore, after the Second World War, the British maintained a military presence in many states of the area and, during the 1950s, the United States began to replace the European states as the defender of the West and pivot of anti-Communism, policies which necessarily involved support for friendly regimes. Internal problems of social and economic reform became intertwined with varying degrees of foreign control. One additional factor affecting domestic politics in the Arab states was the discrediting of governments by their failure to prevent the establishment of Israel in 1948 and the defeat of the Arab armies. In the aftermath of defeat, scandals about front-line supplies linked the Egyptian monarchy and Syrian regime to corrupt contractors. The defeat highlighted the impotence, corruption and inefficiency of civilian government and heightened the reform movement among a younger generation of nationalists. Jamal Abd al-Nasser, the organiser of the 1952 coup in Egypt, expressed the voice of the new generation when he wrote: 'We were fighting in Palestine, but all our thoughts were concentrated on Egypt. Our bullets were directed at the enemy trenches, but our hearts were hovering over the distant motherland, left an easy prey for hungry wolves to ravage' [Nasser, 1972: 17]. The ideas and movements which sprang up in the 1940s and 1950s were nationalist and reformist. It was in the process of consolidating power that more radical ideas were introduced.

The first upheaval took place in **Egypt** in 1952. It was nationalist in orientation and aimed at creating 'a strong liberated Egypt'. In the process, powerful ruling groups were attacked: the big landowners, the old politicians and high bureaucrats. Nasser explained the attack on these groups by reference to corruption, maldistribution of land and overspending on salaries. They were not considered revolutionary measures but 'steps necessary to redress and efface the traces of wrongs done in the past' [Ibid.: 40]. As one authority on the Egyptian economy wrote, the land reform was

seen as a serious aspect of the more fundamental problem of growing poverty and . . . overpopulation in the countryside, and it was conceived as an element of a 'development' package including industrialisation and land reclamation . . . The broad purposes were clear – to provide a solution to Egypt's economic problems, aggravated by a population explosion in a restricted area. [Mabro, 1974: 56–7]

The redistribution of land, the establishment of co-operatives, and the provision of credit and services through government agencies were aimed at solving Egypt's imbalance between population, resources and domestic capital rather than establishing a revolution. Although a concern for social justice was embodied in the land reform, the large numbers of landless did not benefit from increasing government regulation of the rural economy.

Again, industrialisation was aimed at diversifying the national economy rather than at establishing socialism. It was not until ten years after the overthrow of the monarchy that more radical economic measures were implemented. The National Charter of 1962 promulgated the principles of the 1952 revolution in very different terms: 'the ending of feudalism', 'the ending of monopoly and the domination of capital over government, the elimination of imperialism and traitorous Egyptian collaborators' were three of the six principles. Despite the radical tone of these principles, national unity was emphasised, as against class struggle: 'The Egyptian people refused the dictatorship of any class and decided that the dissolution of differences among classes should be the means to real democracy for the entire working forces of the people' [Nasser, 1972: 66].

The issue of participation is discussed above in Chapter Three. It is relevant to note that the post-1952 regime was locked in a contradiction which made the development of a revolutionary cadre extremely difficult. Ideology developed on a pragmatic and *ad hoc* basis. Ideological changes were announced by Nasser after consultation with his closest advisers. In such circumstances, members of the state political organisations simply shifted with the prevailing political wind. Only in the mid-1960s was an institute established for cadres of the Arab Socialist Union (ASU), and although the graduates from there played a radical role within the Union they were not able to transform the ASU, but became ensnared in factional conflicts and identified as factional supporters of Ali Sabri, a leading political figure. Indeed, the attempt to build a committed ideological cadre foundered on the absence of participation in formulating that ideology, with the result that such organisations lacked any autonomy from the central and local government structures and were part of the bureaucratic machinery.

That the 1952 overthrow had failed to put down any deep roots became increasingly apparent on Nasser's death. The ideology which had cohered during the 1960s became generally known as 'Nasserism', a reflection of the personalistic coloration which the Egyptian system had taken. Sadat's accession brought the dismantling of a whole range of state controls, the return of foreign capital and the resurgence of a new wealthy class, a consequence of the return to a market economy. One result of these changes was the re-emergence of certain elements of the old landed class among the new wealthy after the *'infitah'* (Arabic for opening).

In summary, a new political system emerged after 1952. The monarchy and a small number of large landowners were removed. Army officers, relying on the support of the upper and middle peasantry, shaped a new authoritarian system which relied heavily on the military, the security forces and the bureaucracy. Nasser was the pivot of the system, shifting powerful former members of the Revolutionary Command Council between key institutions. There was limited ideological clarity, which made it difficult to establish a core of committed cadres who could deepen the socialist tendency within Egypt. There was a concern for social justice and egalitarianism, but it did not extend to the poorest in the rural areas, nor to the growing urban poor. These problems were to be tackled through industrialisation, engendered by the twin pillars of foreign capital and extracting surplus from the agricultural sector. The goals and methods were reformist and developmental rather than revolutionary. And although sections of the peasantry were beneficiaries, they were also rather passive accomplices in a development process which was centralised and bureaucratically controlled. Development from above followed a political revolution from above. It should also be mentioned that although the new rulers lacked both revolutionary credentials and ideology and were gradualist, external pressures were a constraining factor on the new Egyptian regime, as the 1956 Suez invasion was to indicate.

Much emphasis has so far been placed on Egypt and the consequences of 1952 because the other self-styled revolutions in the Arab states followed a similar pattern and were influenced by 'Nasserism'. In Iraq, the monarchy was overthrown in 1958 by a group of officers after a prolonged period of nationalist agitation. The landlords were dispossessed and land redistributed. Although the regime which emerged was beset by conflicts between communists, Ba'thists and nationalists, by factions within the officer corps and by the spasmodic outbreak of fighting by the Kurdish national movement, the Hashimite monarchy and the landlord–tribal, shaykh-dominated political system was destroyed. In Syria, a more protracted political struggle took place between 1958 and 1966, removing the big landowning families from their positions. All of these changes can be categorised as political revolutions which fundamentally changed the political system and established a much stronger role for the state over the economy. They reflected a shift in the social basis of power away from the large private property-owners to salaried state-employed nationalists with a modern rather than traditional education. The political revolutions which overthrew the old landed class did not lead to a permanently established state capitalism. In the 1970s Egypt and (to a lesser extent) Syria opened their economies to private foreign investment, reflecting the unresolved problem of whether industrialisation should take place under the aegis of the state or of private control.

Iran has followed a very different pattern from the political revolutions in the Arab states. There is a superficial similarity in that the regime changed from a monarchy to a republic. The overthrow of the Shah in 1979 was one of the most spectacular political upheavals in the Third World. The Shah's regime was not a shaky monarchy but a powerful, centralised, autocratic state. It was not a revolution from above but one which had massive popular participation. Yet the outcome, a clerical, authoritarian regime, illustrates the paradox of a revolution from below in which there was mass participation but which resulted in one narrow and traditional sector predominating. Iran provides the paradox of a revolution which was theocratic and reactionary, in the true sense of a return to the past. The forces which overthrew the Shah came from all urban social classes, the different nationalities and ideologically varying political parties and movements. Islam was a major mobiliser and the clergy established an Islamic constitution and dominated the post-revolutionary institutions.

The causes of the revolution were the socioeconomic changes which occurred during the 1960s and 1970s, the alienation and politicisation of the different strata because of the Shah's autocracy, and the recrudescence of an Iranian nationalism triggered by the Shah's close relationship to the United States. The development of a capitalist agriculture along with a weakly implemented land reform programme, industrialisation, and the expansion of education, employment and services in the urban centres led to large numbers of rural migrants who participated in urban demonstrations when an economic crisis struck in the late 1970s. The urban middle class and intelligentsia were affected by inflation, food shortages resultant from decreasing agricultural productivity, and the level of repression. There was also strict censorship and supervision of higher educational institutions. Students were a particular target of the state, and in the movement to depose the Shah they played an important role.

The demands of this middle sector were for liberalisation and a secular brand of nationalism. The recent migrants from the countryside demanded better social and economic conditions and along with the bazaar (a mixture of merchants and traditionally organised craftsmen) supported the fundamentalist clergy's call for an Islamic state. The merchants had also been affected by the increased power of the state. The growth of large industry controlled by the royal family and a handful of other families, and the attempt by the state to take control of bazaar organisations, alienated the conservative, religious merchant class in Iran. Their historic connection to the clergy presented a dual threat to the regime, since their financial support made possible the clergy's independence of state control, even under the centralising Shah.

The social and economic changes which took place under the Shah were fuelled by a large increase in oil revenues, much of which went into the pockets of a few aristocratic and upper-class families and high state officials. Large sums were also spent on industrialisation and infrastructural development. The construction industry boomed, as did the numbers in education and salaried occupations, and urban employment. Excluding the unskilled labourers who flooded into the towns, the total size of the working class in the mid-1970s has been put at about 1.25 million [Abrahamian, 1982: 435]. Another million or more formed an urban sub-proletariat. This new working class was controlled by state-organised trade unions.

For Iranian Islamic and secular nationalists, the Shah's economic and foreign policies were symbolic of Iran's subjugation to foreign powers. In the economic sphere, foreign interests predominated. By the mid-1960s not one Iranian held a key managerial post in the oil industry. Foreign investment played a large role in economic development from the middle of the 1960s. American companies were involved in joint ventures with state and private companies in petrochemicals, steel, rubber, pharmaceuticals, construction and agribusiness. Increasing oil revenues did not alter Iran's dependence on the United States for arms. By the 1970s, Iran had purchased large stocks of military hardware and become the major pillar of the Nixon doctrine whereby regional states undertook to guarantee Western security. Oil wealth and the strategic concerns of the United States led to massive expenditure. Between 1972 and 1976 Iran spent $10 billion on armaments. At the time of the Shah's overthrow there was a further $12 billion in the pipeline. Most were bought from the United States and, by 1976, there were about 20 000 American military advisers in Iran. Many Iranians believed that such dependence on the United States went against the Iranian national interest and that the military expenditure was a gross waste of national resources. Co-operation with Israel went against the grain of Islamic nationalism and the general Third World nationalism of many Iranians, particularly the young.

At the apex of this system was the Shah, Mohammad Reza Pahlavi. He formulated policy in all key areas. The enrichment of his relatives under his protection; the squandering of oil wealth; the vicious role of Savak (the security police); the privileged position of the armed forces; the corruption of officials; the alignment with the United States – responsibility for all these was placed at the door of the Imperial Palace. Symbolising the Shah–United States connection was the historic role played by the CIA, which returned the young Shah to power in 1953 after he had left the country following nationalist pressures.

There was, then, a combination of social classes adhering to varying ideologies, of which an intertwined Islam and Iranian nationalism proved the most effective mobiliser. The most-often shouted slogans in mass demonstrations were 'death to the Shah', 'hang the American puppet', 'independence, freedom and Islam', and 'God is great'. It was the urban unskilled migrants from the countryside and fundamentalist students who formed the backbone of support for Ayatollah Khomeini, a puritanical fundamentalist who had never compromised with the Shah's regime. It was his followers among the clergy who established hegemony after 1979, in part as a consequence of his mass following and in part because of their positions in a semi-organised network of religious teachers and students throughout the country. The decentralised *komitehs* (committees) in Teheran and the provinces were controlled by Khomeini's clerical followers who organised the urban poor into *pasdaran* (revolutionary guards). In the period between the departure of the Shah and the establishment of the Islamic republic, the *komitehs* took over the running of the towns. Since the security police and military services had been utterly discredited through their support for the regime, the *pasdaran* were the major force for order, and played a key role in removing any political challenge to the fundamentalist group. Khomeini had swept to power with broad support, but his followers were able either to neutralise or divide the political organisations and groupings of liberal constitutionalists among the clergy, the Marxist Fidayin, the radical Islamic Mujahidin, the liberal National Front and the communist Tudeh.

The revolution removed what had seemed one of the most impregnable Third World regimes backed by the power of the United States. The determination of Khomeini and the bravery of tens of thousands of individuals mobilised by the personality of Khomeini, Islam, nationalism, liberation and Marxism ultimately brought to power a brutal and fanatical section of the clergy. What happened was revolutionary, but paradoxically the outcome was reactionary. In this case, revolution from below did not produce a social revolution but a thorough Islamicisation of governmental, administrative, legal and social institutions.

6. Conclusion

Rebellions, uprisings and mass demonstrations have been frequent occurrences in the Third World. Rarely have they been converted into revolutions. In our examination of the four regions, some emphasis has been placed on why revolutions have failed or produced reformist regimes, and on the difficulties of revolutionary consolidation. The reason for such a focus is the limited number of full-blooded revolutions which have systemically transformed state, society and economy, and the profound obstacles, both internal and external, to implementing revolutionary programmes.

Nationalism has been a salient feature of Third World revolutions. Economic domination and political subjugation by a colonial or foreign power have been factors in the historical development of most Third World states, and central in all of the revolutions which we have examined. The relative strength of revolutionary cadres within the nationalist coalition is one determining factor in the conversion of nationalism into a revolutionary force. Equally important is whether the social base of the coalition provides the opportunity for the revolutionaries to transform a nationalist movement. Creating liberated zones through military action and implementing reforms within them have proved particularly successful methods.

Common to three of the four regions are revolutions 'from below' led by intellectuals influenced by Marxist–Leninist ideas, mobilising a population in or from the countryside for guerrilla warfare against foreign occupation or personal dictators backed by external forces. 'Revolution from below', however, tells us little about revolutionary regimes. Similarities in the revolutionary process produce very different outcomes. In our examples from Africa, Southeast Asia and Latin America contrasting regimes within these regions emerged out of similar processes. In the Middle East revolutionary peasant movements are absent, but comparisons can be made between military-dominated, political revolutions from above in Ethiopia and Egypt: the former resulted in the introduction of revolutionary agrarian change and the latter in reformist land redistribution. Neither was able to engage the active support of the peasants. In Egypt, they became passive recipients of agrarian reform. In Ethiopia, they were forced into state farms and conscripted into the army for the war in Eritrea from which many never returned. Iran, the only Middle Eastern revolution which can be characterised as 'revolution from below', had a particularly idiosyncratic outcome.

Peasant-based communist revolutions appear to put down deeper roots and retain their ideological moorings more tenaciously than do liberation fronts more loosely influenced by Marxist–Leninist ideas. Cuba, Vietnam and Cambodia (prior to the Vietnamese invasion) followed egalitarian socialist paths. They all had single party organisations linked to ideologies which made them impervious to external pressures to modify their economic and political systems. In Nicaragua, the Sandinistas adopted a multi-party system and lost; in Angola and Mozambique ruling parties drawn from the liberation fronts have followed a similar path and opened their economies to foreign investment and an increased role for private capital. The death throes of the Mengistu regime in Ethiopia went along with announcements of similar reforms which were later implemented by the guerrilla-based successor government.

Whether or not revolutionary movements can form and consolidate regimes which pursue policies consistent with their earlier revolutionary programmes is partly a result of how the collision with non-revolutionary forces is handled, be it between peasants and city-dwellers, Islamicists and secularists, or communists and nationalists.

Establishing a revolutionary order is also the result of how the rejection of, or accommodation to, international economic and political pressures is managed. In most cases, anti-revolutionary regional states have acted with the backing of international actors. In Angola and Mozambique, civil wars occurred with anti-government forces backed by South Africa. In Nicaragua, anti-Sandinistas, using the territory of El Salvador, launched attacks on the new government there. In all three cases, the USA played either a direct or indirect supportive role. In Southeast Asia, the Vietnamese government invaded Cambodia to remove the Khmer Rouge and establish not a counter-revolutionary government but one which was friendly to Vietnamese communism. In Ethiopia, a civil war was one of the main factors bringing the regime there to an end. In this latter case, however, the anti-Mengistu forces sought an end to dictatorship, greater regional and ethnic participation, and independence for Eritrea, and had little external backing.

Whatever the varying causes of civil wars and regional conflicts in the post-revolutionary period, they were a massive drain on resources and, in certain cases, contributed to famine and starvation. They were an important factor in either dislodging regimes or altering their revolutionary trajectories, and remind us of Cabral's maxim that revolutionary words are hollow unless they result in a real improvement in standards of living. External threats and challenges can also have a unifying effect. The consolidation of clerical power in the Iranian revolution, which initially brought Iran to the brink of civil war, was helped by the opposition of the USA and the Iraqi invasion.

The extent to which regimes fulfil the promise of revolution (even by the minimal criterion of feeding their people) is an important factor in regime legitimacy. Third World regimes are particularly vulnerable to external economic pressures and the political destabilisation that these can cause. Nationalist mobilisation can go some way to offset the worst effects, as can the establishment of an organised system of political control. In the case of Vietnam and, more briefly, Cambodia, political organisation through a Leninist party facilitated the grip of communism and, surprisingly, the organisational ability of the clergy in Iran achieved a similar feat there. Of some importance too is the redistributional capacity of authoritarian political organisation. Where civil war did not follow the successful revolution – in Cuba and Vietnam for example – revolutionary legitimacy has been based on the provision of equal access to welfare and food, even if the revolutionary cadres have been greater beneficiaries.

Despite the demise of communism in Eastern Europe, the age of Third World socialist revolutions is not yet over. Cuba still adheres to the classic pattern of a single party and a dominant leader, and declares its continuing commitment to its own version of Marxist-Leninism. In Peru Sendero Luminoso maintains its attempt to implant Maoism in the Andes, while the Communist Party of the Philippines, the leading force behind the New People's Army, has recently been described as 'the most sophisticated Marxist–Leninist organisation still waging a full-blown armed rebellion anywhere in the world' [*Far Eastern Economic Review*, 14 January 1993: 18]. However, in early 1993 Castro was within sight of forty years in power, and would soon have to address the issue of succession, while Abimael Guzman, the leader of Sendero Luminoso, was behind bars in Lima, and José Maria Sison, once undisputed leader of the Communist Party of the Philippines, was in exile in the Netherlands, and rejected by the majority of his former followers. In the decades ahead, the greatest challenge to revolutionary regimes that have survived, and might yet emerge, will be to balance egalitarianism with some form of democracy, and to provide economic growth that ensures revolution is not associated with permanent poverty for societies which are largely peasant and agricultural. With the demise of the Soviet Union, there can be nothing in the future like the scale of support given in the past to a regime like that of Ethiopia; equally, such a regime could not have lasted so long without such support.

In the regions we have examined, whatever the outcome of the revolutionary process, the mobilisation of popular expression against domestic and external exploitation and control has been crucial, and is likely to remain so. Revolutions raise key issues of politics, usually in a violent way. Democracy (whatever form it takes), self-determination (individual or communal), equality (social and economic) and external subversion are not new issues in revolution. They have all been part of the classical revolutions. Revolutions in the Third World have raised many of these issues anew, and although the ultimate fate of revolutions may be controllable, the importance of such issues ensures that their initiation will not be.

Further Reading

General issues relating to the character of Third World revolutions are usefully discussed in Wolf [1969], Chaliand [1977], Dix [1983, 1984] and Goodwin and Skocpol [1989]. The ideas of Amilcar Cabral, 'Che' Guevara, and Ho Chi Minh are presented in Chabal [1983], Loveman and Davies [1985], and Fall [1967] respectively. Loveman and Davies also covers developments into the 1980s in several Latin American cases, while African cases are reviewed in Rosberg and Callaghy [1979] and Markakis and Waller [1986]. Otherwise the issues are best explored through case studies. Hellman [1983] gives a brief account of the Mexican revolution and a good analysis of its consequences; Knight [1984] focusses in more detail on the participation of the working class. Dunkerley [1984] covers both the Bolivian revolution and Guevara's abortive attempt to overthrow the regime in the 1960s. Fagen [1969] and Karol [1970] cover the Cuban revolution and Castro's first decade in power; Azicri [1988] covers the more recent period; Perez [1988] sets the revolution in its historical context, and Zimbalist [1992] assesses the situation in the early 1990s. Black [1981] and Vilas [1986] offer accessible accounts of the Nicaraguan revolution. For Angola, see Marcum [1969, 1978]; for Mozambique, Munslow [1983] and Hanlon [1984]. For Ethiopia, Clapham [1988], Harbeson [1988] and Keller [1988] offer good overviews. For Iran, Abrahamian [1982], Bakhash [1985] and Arjomand [1988] provide detailed accounts, and Behrouz [1991] and Moaddel [1991] examine class and factional conflicts in the Khomeini regime. On the class alliance behind the Vietnamese revolution, see White [1974]; for a graphic account of events in one area of the Mekong Delta, see Race [1972]. For Cambodia, Etcheson [1984] recounts the rise and fall of the Pol Pot regime. Other texts allow comparisons with cases of Indonesia and the Philippines: Kahin [1952], Anderson [1972], and Reid [1974] give good accounts of revolutionary movements in Indonesia after the Second World War. Kerkvliet [1977] examines the Huk rebellion in the Philippines, the story of the New People's Army into the mid-1980s is told in Kessler [1989], and Hawes [1990] analyses peasant revolution from a Philippine perspective.

6

Women in Third World Politics

1. Introduction

In previous chapters, we have covered broad historical issues, or focused on topics drawn from the traditional repertoire of comparative politics. In this chapter we complement the account given so far by examining aspects of social, economic and political change in the Third World from the perspective of gender. Beyond their differences, political parties and military regimes in the Third World have one thing in common: they are predominantly or wholly male-dominated institutions. Third World revolutions, too, have only been partially successful in challenging this pattern of male domination. Too often accounts of social and economic change in the Third World have ignored the issue of gender. In particular, they have often overlooked the part played in it by the subordination of women to the authority and designs of men, and the varied individual and collective responses of women.

Our decision to concentrate this material in a single chapter rather than to disperse it through the book does not signify adherence to the idea that the topic lacks connections with the other themes pursued, or is to be treated as an optional extra. On the contrary, it reflects our belief that a perspective focused on gender illuminates and materially advances our understanding of all the issues considered so far, and that the coherence, the theoretical importance and the critical power of such a perspective is best appreciated through a unified and extended treatment of the kind we attempt here. A direct focus upon gender relations is indispensable for a full understanding of the mechanisms by which the political and economic penetration and reshaping of the Third World has been carried through. It is also central to the dynamics of contemporary economic development and social and political change. In East and Southeast Asia young women are overwhelmingly the majority of workers in the 'global factories' which account for the dynamic economic performance of recent years; in Latin America they have organised on a massive scale to oppose human rights abuses and military rule, and to meet family and community needs generated by deep recession and reductions in state welfare provision. In each case they are responding to demands placed upon them as a consequence of family pressure, patriarchal authority, or 'traditional' views of the woman's role in society. But they are doing so, increasingly, not simply as passive victims, but as independent social and political actors, often extending or subverting traditional roles in ways which transform their character and social significance. As we shall see, the evidence assembled here suggests sharp variations in the degree of women's autonomy and the extent of change from region to region. It is all the more important, therefore, to recognise the range of experiences across the Third World, and to seek to identify the specific dynamics of change from case to case.

A focus on gender is illuminating in five ways. The focus on gender relations is valuable in itself; secondly, because it is a perspective which focusses upon personal relations and the lives of the majority of the population, it approaches the issues we consider from the underside of the state- or government-centred, macro-political point of view adopted thus far; thirdly, it is a *critical* perspective, and as such subjects any approaches which leave its concerns out of account to a vital and fruitful scrutiny; fourthly, it generates a framework within which the political and economic issues we have thus far considered to some extent separately for reasons of analytical convenience are seen 'in action' together in specific historical circumstances; and fifthly, it is particularly central to an understanding of the contemporary international division of labour and the working of the global economy. The isolation of 'politics' as a separate aspect of social reality is at best a necessary evil, and we have been at pains throughout to stress the range of internal and external social, economic *and* political factors shaping the Third World. Equally, as this chapter and those which follow demonstrate, a focus on the internal politics of Third World countries gives only a partial picture. It needs to be complemented by situating internal characteristics and developments in a global context. There is no better way to begin this task than by examining the interaction between domestic and international politics, and gender. We are able to draw here on a valuable and rapidly-growing literature which has begun to remedy a missing dimension to our proper understanding of the dynamics of that process.

Given the considerable and expanding literature, and the wide range of issues involved, an attempt to address the topic of women in Third World politics in a single chapter must necessarily be selective. We have chosen to focus on illustrative issues within each of the four areas upon which we concentrate, rather than to cover a single set of topics in less detail for all four areas. In relation to Africa (where the impact of colonial rule has been greatest and most recent) we concentrate upon colonialism and modernisation; for East and Southeast Asia (where there are interesting variations in the strength of patriarchal authority, and where women have played a vital part in the labour force responsible for rapid export-oriented economic growth) we look at women, work and family relations; for Latin America (where a dramatic process of political change in the 1980s has resulted in the departure of a number of long-lived military regimes and the virtually universal establishment of elected civilian regimes) we look at women, work and political participation; and for the Middle East (where long-established cultural patterns remain influential) we look at the impact and continuing significance of Islam. This approach enables us to draw attention to the variety of situations that exist around the Third World as far as gender relations are concerned.

2. Africa: colonisation and modernisation

In pre-colonial African societies, great variations existed in the social and economic positions of women, and little generalisation is possible. The impact of colonialism, however, was broadly uniform. Such status and independence as women enjoyed were diminished, and such rights as they possessed were undermined. The colonial rulers who came out to Africa from Europe carried with them Western conceptions of gender relations and responsibilities, at a time when these allowed only the most restricted public roles to women. What is more, the governing classes in the colonies were exclusively male, and disposed to assume that men in the societies they governed exerted authority over women, or to grant it to them where they did not. The combination of the imposition of 'Western' conceptions of the proper role of women and the organisation of family life and the creation of colonial economies tied into the international capitalist economy substantially worsened the situation of women. So, too, did the practice – in Botswana, Mozambique and other countries in central and southern Africa – of large-scale male migration to work in the South African mines.

This is not to say that women were particularly favoured in pre-colonial Africa. The development of African societies – partly under external stimuli but largely as a result of internal dynamics over centuries – led to a process of stratification which tended to undermine their status well before the colonial period. Etienne and Leacock identify a development from egalitarian through 'ranking' or transitional, to hierarchical or stratified societies, largely as a result of the development of trade [Etienne and Leacock, 1980: 7]. A parallel analysis is provided by Sacks, who discusses the shift from communal, to kin corporate, and eventually to class society, and sees as central to it the decline in the status of women from 'sister' – 'one who is an owner, a decision maker among others . . ., a person who controls her own sexuality' – to 'wife' – 'a subordinate in much the way Engels asserted for the family based on private property' [Sacks, 1979: 110]. In some cases (as among the Baganda), the process of subordination and the destruction of horizontal solidary associations among women was virtually complete before the colonial period proper began.

Among the Ibo of southern Nigeria and elsewhere, the effect of colonial rule was to accelerate and deepen the subordination of women. Disregarding differing family structures and roles, colonial authorities recognised and strengthened men as heads of families; women who had access to land under customary law or usage found their role and their entitlement were not recognised by colonial authorities; as export crops were developed, land, credit and technology were given to men; where education was provided, boys were favoured over girls, and girls were often trained only in suitable 'domestic' skills; and where Africans began to win access to jobs in colonial bureaucracies, positions with status became an exclusively male preserve.

The development of capitalism in Africa deepened already existing gender divisions and women's subordination. By the modern period 'in many (if not most) societies in Africa, few women had either individual or collective rights in land to maintain except access conditional upon becoming and remaining wives' [Roberts, 1984: 176]. In these circumstances, entry as wage-earners into the labour market opened up for women an apparent path to 'freedom', giving them an opportunity to escape from pre-capitalist male control over their labour and, at the same time, de-emphasising their role as child-bearers. However, while proletarisation forced women to find jobs (or to support themselves through petty commodity production) there was often, as in Tanzania, a lack of job opportunities. Colonial policies (and, indeed, post-independence state policies) gave high priority to male wage employment over that of females. Moreover, working conditions were riddled with sexual discrimination and women almost always received lower wages than men. To secure their subsistence, some women were forced into prostitution, with the result that 'women overcoming a position of subordination to men within the family, became subordinate to men in the market' [Bryceson, 1980: 27].

Thus, the advent of colonial bureaucracies and the development of export-oriented colonial economies led to a marked deterioration in the role and status of women in African societies; and to the extent that the new leaders of Africa after independence inherited the bureaucratic and economic structures of the colonial period, the position of women continued to deteriorate. To illustrate this, we examine four areas where the position of women was once favourable, but has deteriorated in the colonial and independence periods.

First, women had often enjoyed considerable autonomy in terms of family organisation and residential arrangements. They frequently lived in all-female residential compounds, extended families, or (in polygamous societies) in relatively independent and virtually female-headed households. In all of these circumstances women were more likely to enjoy a degree of autonomy or derive support from other women in the residential group. For example, mutual solidarity facilitated co-operative trading and production ventures among Ga women traders of Accra in Ghana. However, the introduction of the nuclear family as a norm meant that the advantages for women which stemmed from such family and residential arrangements and kinship ties were easily lost.

Secondly, women in pre-colonial Africa often had effective control of economic resources, in money or land. The extent to which agriculture was a female preserve has been well documented by Boserup, who describes Africa as 'the region of female farming par excellence' [Boserup, 1970: 16]. In many rural societies where women cultivated the fields, they would dispose independently, and on their own account, of any surplus remaining once household subsistence needs had been met. Out of these activities substantial trading networks controlled by women emerged, as surplus grain would be traded for sheep, goats or cattle, or vice-versa. Similar trade networks extended to urban areas. Again, Ga women traders were not accountable to their husbands for their business transactions, and would even charge interest (at rates of up to 30 per cent per month) for lending money to them. The heavy involvement of women in cultivation and trade had its drawbacks. It meant that women generally were subjected to a 'double shift', as they were still responsible for domestic tasks. Among the Nandi of Kenya, for example, the working day of the average woman was four hours longer than that of the man, and male work (here as elsewhere revolving around cattle) was less physically demanding. But direct involvement in production and control over the product gave women a degree of autonomy which was of considerable consequence.

As incorporation into a cash economy proceeded, one of two things happened. Either women were excluded from areas of production in which they had previously been involved, and relegated to the 'domestic' sphere, or the productive activities in which they continued to engage were deformed and devalued in a new context. For example, among the Kaonde community of Mukunashi in north-western Zambia (an area scarcely penetrated by the cash economy until very recently), the productive role and relative autonomy of women, who had cultivated crops in fields prepared by their men-folk, was eroded as the government-created agricultural board introduced ploughs and hybrid seeds and promoted the cultivation of maize as a cash crop, by men, on cleared, ploughed and demarcated fields, with guaranteed purchase of the crop. All agricultural extension workers were men, and parallel government schemes taught domestic skills in local schools for girls. Women were left to farm irregular plots with hoes and local seed, and found themselves increasingly relegated to a purely 'domestic' role as their production was no longer vital to the survival and reproduction of the family group [Crehan, 1984].

Similarly, among the Baule of the Ivory Coast, Etienne found that in the pre-colonial economy men had controlled the distribution of yams, while women had controlled that of cloth, intercropping cotton in the yam fields, spinning and dyeing thread for the men to weave, and engaging in or directing long-range trade of the resulting product. In the colonial era, the importing (and subsequent manufacture) of thread relieved male weavers of their dependence upon female spinners, and eventually the introduction of cotton as a cash crop with new seed and technology controlled by men broke the interdependent relationship between women and men entirely. In the wake of these developments, women lost land rights and control over production, and became labourers on fields owned by individual men. These trends were reinforced by the growing availability of manufactured cloth, purchased with the proceeds from cash crops, such as cotton, cocoa and coffee, controlled by men [Etienne, 1980].

Thirdly, women might play a key role in certain traditional societies. Thus, among the Akan in central and southern Ghana the importance of 'queen mothers' derived from the system of matrilineal descent and the supposition that 'blood alone can be transmitted by and through a female' [Rattray, 1929: 88]. The queen mother was something of a 'king-maker' in that she put forward the name of her chosen candidate for chief to the Stool elders who made the election and, in exceptional circumstances, she might even act as a war leader (as in the 1900 'Yaa Asantewa' war in Ashanti). In certain traditional societies (as in that of the Mende in Sierra Leone), a woman might even become chief in her own right. The decline of chiefly power, which occurred under colonialism (above all in French Africa) and was accelerated after independence, thus undermined the position of those women who had occupied positions of authority in traditional society.

Fourthly, even where men were clearly dominant in most spheres of public life, it was common for associations of women to control areas of interest to them, and to provide alternative structures of power, representation, solidarity and control. Such institutions have been described in some detail for the Ibo of south eastern Nigeria, and are of particular interest because of the decentralised political system under which the Ibo lived, and their relevance to the 'women's war' of 1929. Ibo communities west of the Niger were governed by a male *obi* and a female *omu*. The latter had her own council of elders parallel to that of the *obi*, and oversaw affairs of particular interest to women. Significantly, these were not confined to the 'private sphere', but centred upon the management and running of local markets, and the resolution of other public issues in which women were involved. When in the 1920s the British colonial administration, in pursuit of the policy of indirect rule, introduced male-dominated authorities and adopted regulations and controls which prejudiced the economic interests of female producers of cash crops, resentment among the women mounted. This resentment was brought to a head in late 1929, when successive incidents in Owerri province persuaded them that taxation established for men in 1928 was to be extended to their activities. As a result, women's solidary organisations were activated in widespread protests, demanding among other things the appointment of women as district officers and warrant chiefs. In the ensuing uprising tens of thousands of women mobilised over an area of 6000 square miles of Calabar and Owerri provinces; native courts were attacked and warrant chiefs ridiculed, as women drew upon networks and ritual traditions that had maintained their status in pre-colonial society. The movement was put down by force of arms, leaving over fifty dead. Remembered in colonial records by the dismissive term of the 'Aba riots', it is recalled among the Ibo themselves as *ogu umunwanyi* – the women's war [Ifeka-Moller, 1977].

To say that the role and status of women deteriorated in the colonial period and continued to decline following the achievement of independence is undoubtedly valid as a general statement. However, not only was this decline more marked in some spheres of economic activity than in others, it was also not universal. As Hill's studies of rural capitalism in West Africa (based on research carried out mainly in the early 1960s) showed, women might still play a key role in certain industries and even possess considerable entrepreneurial skills. Thus, in addition to the 111 men who owned kraals within, or nearly within, the Ashaiman-Dodowa area of the Accra plains, there were five women kraal owners, responsible between them for 482 cattle. One of these women, writes Hill,

> had once been a cocoa carrier at Aburi. Later she was a pig trader
> and then a cattle trader with the assistance of a Fulani on whose

death she turned to cattle-rearing. There are 222 animals in her kraals, about 50 of which are owned by her daughter; if it is true, as she insisted, that only 6 relatives have 17 animals in her herds and that she has given up caring for animals for private owners, it may be that she herself owns over 100 cattle. [Hill, 1970: 62]

Another of Hill's case studies pointed to the important contribution made to the local fishing industry by the 'wives' of the Ewe seine fishermen in south eastern Ghana. They cooked and provided for the men, but also bought the catch on preferential terms from the net-owner's 'company', preserved the fish (usually by smoking) and resold it, retaining any profit. A few women themselves owned nets, which were large and costly, while others – more than the men cared to admit – financed the purchase of nets out of the large profits which, in a good season, they made out of reselling the fish [Ibid.: 35–40].

Further evidence of women's activity in non-settler West Africa is to be found in the works of Arhin and Garlick. In his study of West African traders in Ghana, Arhin points out that modern markets were mostly operated by women, both because the apparatus of the modern state had brought peace to the market place and also because modern markets were for sedentary rather than itinerant traders [Arhin, 1979: 127]. Garlick, who also concentrates on Ghana, found that while most market women in Accra made very little from their trading activities, some of those who dealt in imported textiles in the mid-1950s 'had incomes of several hundred pounds a year and some had incomes running into four figures' [Garlick, 1971: 49]. In Kumasi, too, several women trading in imported cloth prospered throughout the 1950s. However, adverse political conditions towards the end of the decade began to work against them, and in the 1960s the rising price of imported textiles and import restrictions made necessary by the shortage of foreign exchange, coupled with a decline in the cocoa trade, knocked the bottom out of a once-flourishing business. This affords an example of how women suffered from exposure to modernisation, understood as increased integration into the global economy.

In the colonial and post-independence periods, then, women retained a foothold in certain spheres of economic activity, including aspects of the cattle and fishing industries, while losing it in others. Their management of what were mostly small-scale enterprises might make a vital contribution to the survival of the household, and provide a basis for some degree of power and prestige. Nevertheless, their position tended to be undermined as new and better opportunities were made available to men, and the significance and the standing of their production declined. The superior access of men to education, capital, and the employment of wage labour provided them with new opportunities and devalued women's work [Dennis, 1984: 11]. A case in point is provided by the deterioration in the material circumstances and the standing of the Ga women traders of Accra, mentioned above, as they met competition from men with access to imported goods, capital and extended trading networks; the women were pushed into less profitable areas of trade.

Clearly, then, women can be either excluded from production or reduced to inferior status as the nature of the economy changes and men move into new areas of activity. It has been argued that it is a general feature of the development process that new technology and opportunities are channelled overwhelmingly towards men, thus increasing their productivity relative to women. In combination with an ideology which preaches that woman's place is in the home, this leads to a reduction of opportunities and a lowering of status for women [Chaney and Schmink, 1980]. This process is strongly reinforced (even in the absence of direct colonial involvement) by the attitudes and practices of development agencies in the Third World. Male planners and 'experts' tend to ignore (or devalue) the direct contribution made by women to production; resources are channelled towards men; and women are the targets of programmes on 'home economics' rather than agricultural production techniques. Overall, women are driven back into the domestic arena, and hence 'domesticated' [Rogers, 1980]. Evidence from independent Zimbabwe suggests that this pattern of development is strongly entrenched. Under the Land Resettlement Programme land was being made over to individual males, while programmes for women were developed not by the Ministry of Agriculture, but by the Ministry for Community Development and Women's Affairs, and concentrated on home economics and small-scale craft and related projects. They lacked rights both over land and over the means of production [Jacobs, 1984: 48].

This depressing picture of the continuing decline in the standing of African women will only be halted when more women come to occupy positions of authority in society, notably as ministers and MPs. However, advance in this sphere is slow, especially in Africa's military regimes. In the run-up to independence and beyond, most 'mass' political parties – alike in Ghana, Guinea and Mozambique – had separate women's wings, enabling some of their leaders to achieve political prominence; nevertheless, post-independence cabinets have continued to be male-dominated institutions, with only a sprinkling of women ministers. Again, in the former Marxist– Leninist states of Angola and Mozambique (whose constitution declared the emancipation of women to be 'one of the state's essential tasks') the political rewards to women have not been commensurate with the important contribution which they made to the liberation struggle. Rather more has been achieved in the professional (non-technological and non-scientific) field as an increasing (though still inadequate) number of girls have proceeded to higher education, and have subsequently become secondary school teachers, middle- and senior-level civil servants, lawyers and doctors, and business executives. However, the numbers involved are still small and in this sphere, too, there is therefore a long way to go before social conditions will enable African women to compete on equal terms with men in the modern sector.

3. East and Southeast Asia: women, work and family

In this section and the following one we examine two related aspects of the consequences for women of changing patterns of paid work in the global economy. Here we ask what impact the dramatic increases in the last thirty years in the availability of paid work for women outside the home in East and Southeast Asia has had upon family relationships, and in particular upon the power and autonomy of young women within the family. In the following section, we examine the links between changing patterns of work in Latin America, and increased oppositional political participation. The entry of women into paid labour, and particularly manufacturing, has been greater in East and Southeast Asia than in Latin America; yet women in Latin America have been more prominent in politics in recent years, playing a vital role in many countries in the movements which brought an end to dictatorship during the 1980s. It appears that enhanced opportunities for employment are not in themselves enough to induce changes in political participation. In order to understand the different outcomes in these cases, one must explore the connections between family structures, social systems, national economies, and national political systems. As we shall see, there are some striking contrasts between East and Southeast Asia as regards family structure, but only in Latin America have aspects of all these elements come together in such a way as to prompt major changes in political participation.

The participation of women in the paid workforce is high in East and Southeast Asia by any standards. Women were 40 per cent of the workforce in East Asia in 1990, and 35 per cent in Southeast Asia, as they had been for more than two decades; this compared with 39 per cent in the world's developed regions, and 29 per cent in Latin America (compared to 24 per cent twenty years earlier). With 59 per cent of women of fifteen and over classed as economically active, East Asia was surpassed only by the Soviet Union (60 per cent); Southeast Asia (48 per cent) was closely followed by Sub-Saharan Africa (47 per cent), with Latin America running well behind at 32 per cent. Finally, women make up a larger proportion of factory workers in East and Southeast Asia than elsewhere in the world, contributing over a quarter of the manufacturing workforce [United Nations, 1991: Ch. 6].

In East Asia in particular, young women have been entering factory work for more than a generation without dramatic changes taking place in the character and extent of their political activity. This is largely as a consequence of the interaction between family structure, family employment strategies, and women's entry to paid employment. This is well illustrated by the comparable cases of Hong Kong and Taiwan, each strongly influenced by patriarchal Chinese traditions of family organisation and control. Sons inherit, daughters do not; daughters are under the father's authority until marriage; marriages are arranged; upon marriage women move into the husband's home and family; and within both the family and the community, decision-making is heavily male-dominated. Both Hong Kong and Taiwan have a largely Chinese population, and each received a substantial influx of population from China after the revolution: in 1951 three-quarters of Hong Kong's population of 2 million was of recent mainland origin. Although Hong Kong in particular has relatively high levels of female-headed households (in part because of male emigration and the practice of taking a second wife), family employment strategies are geared towards favouring sons who will stay in the family and provide later for their parents in old age. As a consequence, daughters often leave school after completing the primary cycle; they are sent out to work early, often from age thirteen; 75 per cent or more of their earnings are handed over to the family, to meet household expenses and pay to keep sons in private secondary education; and they may complete ten or more years of factory or other work before marriage, as parents are reluctant to surrender their earning power too soon. Hong Kong's 'working daughters' are used as a short-term resource to accumulate income which is reinvested in their brothers, until they leave home upon marriage to the similarly favoured son of another family. In the 1970s girls from working-class backgrounds found themselves entering textile or garment factories, or engaging in activities ranging from assembling light-bulbs for 20 to 80 cents a day, and hot-pressing the seams on plastic bags at the rate of $1 per 1000, to working on the assembly line of the US-owned Fairchild Semiconductor plant, where a starting age of twelve was common [Salaff, 1981]. In Taiwan in 1986 women accounted for 45 per cent of the labour force; 48 per cent of those women economically active were between the ages of 15 and 29; 58 per cent were unmarried; and 65 per cent were employed in manufacturing. Pressure on these young women workers was particularly intense, as a consequence of extremely intensive rhythms of work, long hours, the absence of minimal provisions for safety at work, the dissemination of factories through the countryside, isolation of young workers away from home in vast dormitories, and pressure from parents to continue to earn to contribute to family budgets [Arrigo, 1980; Gallin, 1990].

Because young women are not autonomous agents within the labour market, then, but rather resources mobilised by the family for a lengthy period between relatively early childhood and relatively late marriage, their high level of labour force participation has not had an immediate and dramatic effect on family and gender relations. Purely arranged marriages have become relatively uncommon, but marriage remains a strategic move which unites families, and considerable pressure is exerted to ensure that a suitable choice is made.

In both Hong Kong and Taiwan the relationship between work experience and gender politics is influenced not only by patriarchal traditions, but also by the interaction of these traditions with national economic structure and social and political factors. In both economies, factories tend to be small, and in Taiwan in particular family firms heavily predominate. The virtual absence of systems of social security makes long-term family survival strategies essential, and interacts with the high importance of education as a route to secure and well-paid employment. This combination of social factors reinforces the pressure to mobilise young women to provide funds to invest in the education of their brothers. Governments and national and transnational employers oppose the organisation of workers in effective trade unions, as part of a general strategy of maintenance of a low wage economy, and general political and democratic rights are either weak or absent. Britain's 150-year tenure in Hong Kong was not long enough for the issue of democracy to be raised until the 1997 handover to China was imminent: Salaff notes that, not surprisingly, neither the factory and shop women she interviewed *nor any of their family members* had ever qualified to vote [Salaff, 1981: 18]. In Taiwan labour militancy is low because 'the articulation of government policies and managerial practices appears to combine with family processes to inhibit the formation of class consciousness among the women' [Gallin, 1990: 180]. It should not be assumed that there will be no longer-term consequences, at the level of family or broader social and political relationships, of the increased importance of young female workers in the economy. But in the short term it appears that the situation of young women may have worsened, at least relative to that of their brothers, as their parents respond to changed circumstances in the international economy by withdrawing them from school earlier than they would otherwise have done, and seeking to dictate their pattern of employment for longer [Niehoff, 1987].

In recent years the Southeast Asian states have begun to rival the East Asian 'tigers' as sources of cheap labour, and to emerge as a result as the next wave of newly industrialised countries in the region. But in one significant regard, the situation of women in Southeast Asia is quite different to that in Hong Kong and Taiwan, where their position arises from the patriarchal tradition of the Chinese family. There is a tradition throughout Southeast Asia of relatively high female autonomy and economic importance which may in the sixteenth and seventeenth centuries have represented 'one extreme of human experience on these issues' [Reid, 1988: 629]. While these traditions of relative autonomy have not survived unscathed into the late twentieth century, significant contrasts with the East Asian cases described still remain. For example, family relations in north and northeastern Thailand are both matrilocal and matrifocal. A man moves into the family of the woman he marries, and until the 1920s, daughters inherited family land in equal shares. Despite the weakening of female inheritance rights as a result of the subsequent adoption of a new civil code advocated by foreign advisors, brothers tend to sell their land to their sisters. Children must earn money from the age of ten or eleven, and they keep control of it, though they make gifts of varying amounts to their parents. The youngest daughter may give virtually the whole of her wage to her parents, but she also inherits the house along with the obligation to care for her parents in their old age. Men and women from this region often migrate to Bangkok for factory work, but the decision is generally their own, and parents are as likely to discourage as to encourage them. Both men and women send money home, but women are more likely to do so than men; most send between a quarter and a half of their wages [Porpora *et al.*, 1989].

A similar situation is found among young women workers in a rural district in Central Java, Indonesia. Since the early 1970s a dozen factories have been established, literally among the rice-fields, to take advantage of extremely cheap local labour. By the late 1980s twelve factories were employing around 6000 workers, three-quarters of them local women under twenty-five. The decision to work in the factories is usually theirs rather than their parents', and even parents strongly opposed to such a course of action (because of a pressing need for the girl's labour at home) find it difficult to retain them once they reach fifteen. These young women prefer factory work to work in the family rice-field, even though wages are low (often less than a dollar a day). Also, they tend to retain much or all of what they earn, with scented soap being a favourite purchase [Wolf, 1990].

A final case from Malaysia [Ong, 1987] shows similar character-istics, and also suggests that access to factory work is leading to the exercise of far greater autonomy in regard to marriage. A wave of investment has taken place since the launching of the New Economic Policy in 1971. Nine Free Trade Zones were set up during the 1970s, leading to the creation of 80 000 factory jobs for young women by 1980, mostly in textiles and electronics, with many factories set up in rural areas to take advantage of very cheap labour. In one of these, outside the township of Telok in Kuala Langat, three Japanese factories draw upon female school-leavers often encouraged by their families to leave in search of factory work. The factories have waiting-lists of applicants all the time, and turnover is high, especially in micro-electronics where the pace of work is hard and close inspection of components through microscopes leads to deteriorating eyesight after two or three years. The area is one in which immigration from Java has been high for a century or more; women inherit, though they receive only half the share their brothers get; married women retain their own earnings as private wealth (in part as insurance against divorce, which is common); but, as elsewhere, sons are kept at school while daughters leave earlier, to work in the home or enter the factories. Daughters are more likely to contribute to family budgets than sons, though some make little contribution, but – as family finances are handled by mothers – they escape the control of brothers and fathers, and gain power within the domestic unit. Young women workers enter sexual relationships before marriage despite the Islamic prohibition of 'illicit sexual intimacy'; one, in a strong position because of her earnings, has her lover stay overnight in the family home. They use tactics such as departure to the house of the man they wish to marry, or the threat of it, to counter parental opposition to their marriage, and increasingly choose their own husband regardless of family pressure.

At least as far as family structure is concerned, then, the picture across East and Southeast Asia is not uniform. Whereas families in Taiwan and Hong Kong routinely send their daughters out to work and appropriate the greater part of their wages in order to cover household expenses and the costs of their brothers' education, in Indonesia, Malaysia and Thailand young women themselves make the decision to seek factory work either locally or further afield, and retain a considerably greater proportion of the wage for themselves. There is, however, another significant difference between the two sub-regions which must be taken into account before conclusions are drawn. Multinationals, especially in low-skill, labour-intensive sectors such as textiles, have been shifting their attention from East to Southeast Asia precisely because labour is far cheaper in the

Southeast Asian states. While in one sense migration and factory work are 'chosen' by the young women discussed above, they are at the same time a response to desperate poverty and extremely poor prospects at home. The young Indonesian women who seek local factory work may retain virtually all their wage, but they do so in a context in which a day's work will not buy two bars of scented soap. These young women come predominantly from land-poor families which cannot meet their household needs from their land alone, and receive from the factories in which they work a wage which is insufficient to provide for their own subsistence. Factories located in rural areas are able to pay such low wages (around US$0.80 per day in the 1980s) precisely because their workers remain at home, and depend largely upon their parents. In the Malaysian case, too, the only local alternative to factory work, except for the minority of women with substantial family farms, is casual labour.

Finally, the Southeast Asian cases share with Hong Kong and Taiwan the absence or weakness of effective trade unions and democratic structures which might allow female and male workers alike to seek to advance their interests. Labour unrest is virtually unknown in the rural factories of Indonesia, while in the similar rural factories in Malaysia 'opposition' to the new rhythms of factory work takes the form not of strikes or new forms of radical consciousness, but of episodes of spirit possession or hysteria, countered by the ritual cleansing of factory premises by traditional healers [Ong, 1987: Ch. 9]. These reflect the raising of the issue of control of female sexuality as a consequence of the greater freedom of movement and choice arising out of access to factory work, increased pressure from males in the family, and the resurgence of Islamic youth movements demanding purity and chastity from young women. On the other hand, in the textile factories of Bangkok female workers have consistently proved more likely to join unions and to engage in militant action than male workers. There is little evidence to suggest that young female workers are naturally 'docile', and willing to accept harsh conditions of employment without resentment or complaint. Rather, both in the small, family-run enterprises of Hong Kong and Taiwan and in the rural factories of Malaysia and Indonesia, they are in situations at work, between work and home, and in the national political system which make resistance to the conditions of work imposed upon them extremely difficult. The lack of strong patriarchal control within the family structure in the Southeast Asian cases does not prevent extreme levels of exploitation by local and international capital.

4. Latin America: women, work and politics

The distinctive process of modernisation characteristic of Latin America, proceeding from export-led development to limited industrialisation, has had a marked effect on the status of women. At the same time, their political participation until recently broadly followed the virtually universal pattern, with subordination and relative exclusion reinforced by the interaction of traditional Catholic ideas of female subservience with the legacy of the social dominance and practices of land-holding élites. In more recent years, however, the combination of social responses to deep economic crisis, widespread challenge to dictatorial rule, and the dissemination of feminist ideas, which began to circulate in the 1970s, has produced a marked shift in the character and extent of women's political activity, which we examine here.

As elsewhere, export-led development often weakened the relative status of women, largely as a consequence of the marginalisation or elimination of women's independent productive activities, and their forced entry into the labour market on unfavourable terms. As elsewhere, too, the balance of costs and opportunities in relation to female access to wage labour in the countryside depended and continues to depend upon the intersection of class and gender. A minority of women on relatively prosperous family farms are able to lead lives of leisure or run shops or small businesses; on poorer farms which must mobilise all available labour to survive, they contribute increasing amounts of unpaid labour; and the wives of the poor (without sufficient land to secure their subsistence) are forced to seek work as agricultural labourers, where they can find it, or as domestic servants. For all but the wives of the wealthy, a clear deterioration in status and increase in the burden of work takes place. This declining status is associated with the emergence of cash-cropping on peasant land, and the proletarianisation of a substantial proportion of the population; among the poor, men and women share the burden of proletarian status; but women bear the greater burden. They are subjected (either seasonally or permanently) to a double shift of work, and excluded from the leisure activities and consumption habits enjoyed by men. Here women turn to wage labour only as the family becomes unable to secure its survival otherwise, generally as it approaches landlessness. The work available is generally low in status, in domestic service or in labouring tasks, poorly paid, and additional to the burden of work already borne. Wage-earning by women is an index of poverty and a desperate struggle to survive, rather than a widening of opportunity. As in East and Southeast Asia, it rarely leads in such circumstances to greater political consciousness and participation.

Increased entry of women into the labour market does not necessarily mean enhanced status, then, either in terms of work or in terms of standing within the family and the community. This is the more so because women's participation in productive labour – particularly in the countryside – has consistently been under-reported in census data. What appears to be entry to the labour market may in fact be a shift from productive labour on one's own land to poorly-paid work outside. As this might well reflect reduced independence and autonomy, the implications for political partici-pation are again unfavourable.

At first sight the situation in Latin American cities looks equally unpromising. Although some opportunities have recently opened up for women workers in high technology factory work, those born in or migrating to the cities since the Second World War have frequently moved into 'informal sector' work, which tends to be precarious, poorly-rewarded, low in status, and lacking legislative protection in terms of minimum wages, conditions of employment, or workers' rights. A majority of migrants have been women, and for the most part young single women, and a major source of employment for such women on arrival in the cities of Latin America has been domestic service. Peru provides a case in point. Of the adult women who migrated to Lima between 1956 and 1965, 30 per cent entered work as domestic servants. They accounted for over 62 per cent of those who entered the labour market, and by 1970 there may have been as many as 90 000 servant women in the city. The majority were single, aged between 15 and 24, lacking education beyond primary level, and without children. They were generally recent migrants from small towns or rural areas within relatively easy reach of Lima itself, and from lower-class families. For these women, domestic service provided a bridge between life in the provinces and life in the city; but for the great majority, their 'career' ended in their mid-20s as they married and became full-time housewives [Smith, 1973: 193, 205]. As entrants into domestic service are often recent migrants, it can provide a basis for getting to know the ways of the city, and in a minority of cases can be combined with education or other forms of self-improvement. But it is generally an interlude between childhood and marriage. This is confirmed by similar statistics from Brazil, Argentina and Chile: most domestic servants fail to proceed to better jobs in the formal sector. Their time in well-appointed middle-class homes gives them aspirations which cannot subsequently be satisfied, while their isolation from working-class networks of support prevents their establishing contacts which might open other avenues. Whether in relation to the labour market or to political advancement, domestic service is a bridge leading nowhere [Jelin, 1977].

Most Latin American women who have entered the workforce have done so from necessity rather than from choice; for the great majority (especially those married and with children) opportunities in the formal sector are scarce. Hence the significance of the 'informal sector'. In the struggle to survive women seek to turn to account their 'domestic' skills, often engaging in a wide range of time-consuming and poorly-rewarded activities, generally carried on along with child care, food preparation and other household responsibilities. An account of one couple resident in Ciudadela Chalaca, a shanty town in Callao (near Lima) gives a vivid picture of the extremes of self-exploitation involved. Julio works full-time in a belt factory, works as a tailor from home at evenings and weekends, and sells as scrap tin cans and other metal collected by the six children. Helsomina has variously raised small animals such as guinea pigs, sold vegetables in the market, rewound into balls for subsequent sale scraps of wool gathered by her cousin in the textile factory where she works, brewed chicha for sale, bought food and other supplies in bulk for resale, and rented out space in her newly-acquired refrigerator. Taken together, such activities add enough to the income of the family to pay for materials to construct a solid house, and to educate a daughter as a secretary and a son as an electrician [Lobo, 1982: 37]. In Nezahualcoyotl, a suburb of Mexico City, an estimated 3000 unregistered domestic seamstresses sew up garments on machines that they themselves rent or purchase, picking up the cut material from downtown Mexico City and returning the finished garments. Pay is low, the business is clandestine, workers are subject to the impositions of inspectors who have to be bribed into silence, and they are unprotected by legislation of any kind. It is difficult to see in work such as this any element of 'emancipation' for the women who do it. It is better seen as a subsidy to capital from a vulnerable and highly exploited segment of the labour force. For most women, entry into the informal sector is a matter of desperation rather than choice, particularly in the period of deep recession of the 1980s and early 1990s.

These factors are partially offset by the fact that job prospects for women expanded from the 1970s onwards as new employers turned to women in preference to men in the most industrialised economies in the region. In Brazil, for example, after falling steadily throughout the century, the rate of female participation in manufacturing industry rose sharply in the 1970s. By the end of the decade, nearly a third of factory workers in the leading industrial state of Sao Paulo were women; and in the free trade zone set up on the Mexico–United States border as many as 85 per cent of employees were women. In such industries as these, wages may be good by local standards, though many times below those which multinationals would pay in the developed world. Here, as in East and Southeast Asia, the women employed are largely confined to monotonous, repetitive and demanding assembly-line jobs classified as unskilled. The work regime is harsh, and production targets qualifying for bonus payments practically unattainable. It is unusual for anyone to endure more than a couple of years of such employment, and in any case company practice is frequently to offer only short-term contracts in order to avoid legal commitments to long-term employees, and to lessen the prospect of labour organisation. Job security is low, therefore, turnover high, and prospects for promotion minimal. The women employed in these factories are overwhelmingly young and single, generally between the age of 18 and 24, for the most part resident in the family home, and are likely to be making a substantial contribution to the income of the household; in a significant number of cases, they will be the major (or only) wage-earner. Particularly in the recession-hit 1980s, they were working from necessity rather than from choice, while the majority still held to the view that it was preferable for women not to work outside the home [Tiano, 1990]. Their situation in relation to the family seems closer to the East Asian than the Southeast Asian cases discussed above. They are subject while active in the labour market to patriarchal controls within the family; the decision to take paid work may not be theirs, and they often do not control the wages earned. Their spell of employment in the 'global factory' will not present them with a life alternative; they will generally leave the factory and marry in their early 20s, perhaps returning to less well paid work in the future. Such work is therefore perfectly compatible with the patriarchal family and with a primary role as wife and mother. Some evidence suggests, too, that the preference of employers for women over men is a temporary one. By the mid-1980s only 60 per cent of assembly-plant workers were women; women workers were proving increasingly militant; and in conditions of deep recession and structural change employers were turning to 'the new docile, undemanding, nimble-fingered, non-union, and unmilitant male worker' [Sklair, 1989: 175].

The recession of the 1980s hit women workers as badly as men, not only in export-processing areas but across Latin America as a whole. In the absence of better opportunities, women sought work as domestic servants or street sellers in order to cope with the effects of higher unemployment and greater insecurity in such established male labour markets as construction. Other reasons were abandonment by male partners, or the rising relative cost of foodstuffs and previously subsidised state services as a result of IMF-inspired programmes of 'structural adjustment'. For many Latin American women in the early 1990s, resort to paid work of any kind available was part of a desperate attempt to provide for basic family needs, and stave off increasing impoverishment and malnutrition.

Greater access to the labour market, then, does not automatically generate substantial changes in the status of women. Within a dependent capitalist society still dominated by patriarchal attitudes and values, it may fit in with those attitudes and values rather than challenge them. If so, the participation of women in conventional politics may confirm rather than challenge the *status quo*. Patriarchal values have traditionally been strong in Latin America, and conventional avenues of political participation strongly male-dominated. The traditional Catholic cult of '*marianismo*' – the celebration of feminine spiritual superiority and the domestic sphere – has been powerful, and studies of women prominent in politics up to the 1960s argue that as voters they were generally conservative, and as active politicians (very much in a minority) they were channelled into (and generally welcomed) public roles which reinforced their image as 'mothers': one study characterised female politicians in Chile and Peru in that period as 'supermothers', transferring their caring and nurturing qualities deliberately and effectively to the public stage [Chaney, 1979]. Faced with evidence such as this, Western feminists have sometimes endorsed (though not without misgivings) the insistence of prominent women activists in Latin America that the 'separate sphere' inhabited by women is to be built upon rather than abandoned.

However, a combination of circumstances from the late 1970s on has led to the emergence of new forms of political activity by women. These were at first relatively unconnected, but they converged over time, and by the 1990s were beginning to coalesce into a powerful mass movement of regional scale, based upon movements rooted in organised urban communities, and increasingly informed by feminist thinking. The first element in this new situation was opposition to military dictatorship over the issue of human rights. The dictatorships arose in part in response to the radicalisation of a generation of students and young professionals, as well as the mobilisation of the peasantry and the working class, and launched a quite unprecedented wave of repression against their opponents. Central to this repressive effort was the practice of abduction, torture and clandestine murder of individuals identified as opponents of the regime, giving rise to a new class of citizens – the 'disappeared' – thought to be dead, or held in torture centres or prison camps, but of whereabouts unknown. Women took the lead in public opposition to these barbarities, in campaigns and public demonstrations of the kind sustained over years from 1977 onwards by the 'Mothers of the Plaza de Mayo' in Argentina, who walked in silent vigil in white headscarves around a central square in weekly protests which were at first ignored but which grew into a symbol of resistance to the regime. The setting up of permanent organisations, such as Chile's Association of the Relatives of the Detained and Disappeared, provided many women with their first experience of autonomous political activity, and gave rise to broader groupings and opposition movements with a clearly feminist content such as MEMCH83 and *Mujeres por la Vida* (Women for Life) in the 1980s [Schirmer, 1989].

Women also gained new political and organisational experience as a result of the economic consequences of dictatorship, recession, and the dismantling of welfare provision as a consequence of the adoption of liberal economic programmes. This was first evident in Chile, where monetarist policies were applied from the mid-1970s onwards, but was a general regional phenomenon throughout the 1980s. Women led the effort to develop community-based survival strategies around craft activities, soup kitchens, and health groups, and found themselves drawn into political activity through the need to organise to provide vital services, and often to lobby for resources from local government, and grants and aid from international charitable organisations. These activities gave rise to distinctive women's movements in urban communities [Waylen, 1992b].

Neither human rights campaigning nor local activities around survival initially drew particularly upon feminist ideas. Rather, each extended into the public sphere traditional ideas of women as mothers and providers. They were innovatory in the sense that they developed those traditional roles into platforms for public political and organisational activity and leadership. However, they often co-existed uneasily with feminist currents of thought, to which many of the women involved declared themselves hostile. At the same time, however, feminist currents of thought were growing in influence, and specifically feminist movements appeared in virtually every country in the region. Their ideas initially met with indifference or resistance from some women activists as much as from men, because they were seen as imported from the United States, oblivious to issues of class exploitation, and of dubious relevance to the situations of Latin American women outside the professional middle classes. But during the 1980s Latin American feminists confronted and analysed the circumstances of political and economic repression which marked their own societies, while activists in the human rights movements and in community organisations began to recognise and explore gender-related issues in their own areas of concern. As a result, new and original currents of thought and action began to develop, linking activities which had sometimes been separate. One index of the development of Latin American feminist movements is the growing size of the five successive regional meetings (*encuentros*) of activists organised between 1981 and 1990. The first, held in Bogotá (Colombia) brought something over 200 women together; the fifth, held in San Bernardo (Argentina) attracted approaching 3000 participants

[Sternbach *et al.*, 1992]. Another index is the creation of autonomous spaces within the political system and within existing political parties, and the achievement of reforms of specific interest to women. In this context, established parties have been slower to respond to new initiatives than more recently founded movement-oriented political formations, in which women have been actively involved in developing their own agenda from the start. The social democratic Party of the Brazilian Democratic Movement and the leftist Workers' Party contrast favourably in this respect with, say, Chile's Communist and Socialist parties.

Women's movements and feminist movements have proliferated across Latin America in the 1980s. Some tensions remain between them, and between the movements themselves and other arenas of political activity. Also, the combination of circumstances from which they have emerged – gross violation of human rights, harsh economic policies, and deep recession – has been extremely destructive. Nevertheless, individual and collective responses to those circumstances, in terms of ideas, organisation and action, have been dynamic and creative, and in practically every area of response we have considered, women have made the running. The question that arises is whether the resumption of 'politics as usual' in the wake of the general return to democracy will threaten the organisational gains that women have made, and lead to a redefinition of the political agenda to exclude many of the concerns that have been raised. The widespread granting of amnesties to draw a line under the issue of abuses of human rights, against the strong opposition of women's movements, is perhaps a portent in this regard.

5. The Middle East: women and Islam

Women's positions and their roles in the Middle East are widely attributed to the influence of Islam. The link between the subordinate status of women and Islam is complex and varied – in part because factors like regime ideology, power relations within the family, low literacy rates and employment opportunities also play a determining role, but also because Islam varies, and the way it is interpreted by individuals and regimes also varies considerably. The resurgence of Islamic fundamentalism in the Middle East and the establishment of the Islamic Republic in Iran have demonstrated that development does not necessarily bring secularism in its wake. Islam varies in several respects. There are different sects like Shi'ism and Sunnism, and different schools of legal interpretation. The weight and form of Islamic values also varies within particular social contexts: the folk Islam of the countryside is one of tradition and custom, and that of the urban educated more formal and intellectual. At the heart of Islam is the belief that the Quran is the word of God, and that the Quran and the *hadith* (the sayings of the prophet) comprise the basis of *sharia* (Islamic law). No distinction is made between religion and state, and the duty of the good Muslim ruler and the function of the Islamic state is the implementation of *sharia*. Since there are specific injunctions in the Quran concerning marriage and divorce, inheritance, modesty of dress and obedience to men, Islamic law enshrines the 'inequalities' of property inheritance, of legal witness and of rights in marriage and divorce. If, then, the historic legal practice of Islam has created a framework of cultural prejudice against women, the varying ways in which regimes frame their policy toward them is one index of the flexibility which Muslims have to interpret Islam. But even where reforms in personal status laws have taken place, change has generally been justified by reference to Islam. Turkey has been unique in replacing Islamic personal status by a wholly secular civil code. The most radical change in the Arab world took place in Tunisia in 1956 (although justification for the new laws was couched within an Islamic tradition, albeit radically interpreted). The necessity to justify change by reference to a pure or true Islam does set rather strict limits on the debate about women's position and role. Islamic feminists argue that the way the Quran has been interpreted is a deviation, and even a notable radical feminist such as the Egyptian writer Nawal al-Saadawi links her critique of women's subordination to a more pristine Islam. She emphasizes the broad ethical thrust contained in the Quran rather than the detail of the law and argues that Islam cannot be understood properly if it is taken simply as a conglomeration of unrelated precepts and statements. She makes the point that stressing sayings like 'And we have made you to be of different levels', or 'One above the other', or 'Men are responsible for women' is to isolate them from their general context and thus from the essential principles of Islam to support backward interpretations [Saadawi, 1980: vi–vii].

Whether such an approach to changing the position of women will provide only a straitjacket of apologetics is a question for the future, but the increasing political significance of Islam and the popular mobilising potential of the various Islamicist movements necessarily shape the context in which demands for reform can be made. Changing women's position is not simply a question of modifying customary and traditional practices, but an assault on the heart of religion: the Quran as the message of God communicated through the prophet Mohammed. There are, however, areas of law (other than personal status) which have been dispensed with. Civil and commercial law codes based on Islam have been replaced by secular codes. However, where popular or legal values relating to women and associated with Islam are operating in societies where men are in the ascendancy, change is more difficult. This is especially so when details of the law assign women an inferior position. Examining the real world of women in contemporary Islamic societies, it is nevertheless clear that Islam is not immutable. It is also clear that there is no unilineal progress whereby economic development goes along with secularism to the benefit of women, or even that economic exigencies necessarily bring increased employment opportunities for women. The contrast between Iraqi and Saudi Arabian policies illustrates how regime ideology can act as a determining feature. Both states have labour-short economies. In Iraq, women are encouraged to seek employment at all levels. In Saudi Arabia, women's activities in all spheres (employment included) are heavily restricted, even though the Saudi Arabian government finds that importing foreign labour undermines conservative social values which many want to retain. The Ba'thist government in Iraq has been avowedly modernist. Although women have increasingly moved into the labour market they are still very much dependent upon the goodwill of fathers and male relatives, and (given the high concentration of women in agriculture) still the source of cheap labour and subsidies to men working in urban centres. Although the Ba'thists have not radically changed personal status law, the new code promulgated in 1979 emphasised criteria other than that of Islamic principle, for the new amendments were based 'on the principle of the Islamic *sharia*, but only those that are suited to the spirit of today, and on legal precedents set in Iraqi courts . . . and on the principles of justice' [Rassam, 1982: 94]. These amendments guaranteed some rights for women in divorce, inheritance and marital choice, even though the extent to which the state would be able to intervene on behalf of women in such a socially sensitive institution as the family is questionable. Nevertheless it is in marked contrast to Saudi Arabia, where women are forbidden to work, study in proximity to men or drive cars, and have only recently gained access to higher education.

The contrast between these two societies is only partly a function of regime ideology. Iraq has undergone a prolonged process of change from the time of the late nineteenth-century Ottoman reforms, through colonialism and independence. It also has a much lengthier history of urbanisation and modern education, whereas Saudi Arabia has undergone intensive change over a short period.

Perhaps the most dramatic impact of regime ideology on Middle Eastern women came with the establishment of the Islamic Republic in Iran and the consequent implementation of Islamic law and emphasis upon fundamental Islamic values. On the surface, it reversed what had seemed a gradual improvement in women's legal position over the previous fifty years of Pahlavi rule. Reza Shah opened education to women, forbade discrimination in public places and abolished the veil, to the consternation of many. Although men's greater rights in inheritance and divorce were preserved, they were somewhat modified during the reign of Reza Shah's son, Mohammed. In 1967, the latter introduced the Family Protection Law, which gave the secular courts areas of jurisdiction over polygamous marriages and divorce; further measures extending these provisions were introduced in 1975. The Shah also launched campaigns against the wearing of the *chador* (the blanket-like outer garment). These reforms went along with a whole set of other secular measures, such as the replacement of the Islamic calendar with an imperial one. The clerical opposition to these changes was denounced as 'medieval black reaction'. The attack on tradition went along with the Shah's modernisation programme of industrialisation and agricultural reform. These latter processes, however, generally worsened the position of the great bulk of rural women, who were relatively untouched by the legal reforms or increased access to education. As Iran's national economy became more closely tied into the world economy, and Iran's food imports soared, women contributed less and less to the family's food supply. For example, increased meat imports (along with erosion and overgrazing) brought a decline in herding, and with it the disappearance of women's traditional tasks such as milking, wool processing and rug weaving. Although there was an expansion in national education and employment, village girls and women rarely had access to schools and jobs. The Shah's modernisation programme shrank the world of village women, making them more dependent upon men. Furthermore, as men migrated to the towns women were forced to undertake rougher work like shovelling snow and squeezing rainwater out of the dirt roofs of houses. Even where women gain access to the sphere of production in the course of development, the effect (in the context of patriarchal control) may be to worsen rather than improve their situation. In the village of Asiaback, studied by Afshar, carpet weaving was introduced in 1967 and substantially increased women's cash income, but in circumstances which increased rather than lessened their subordination. The rise in the contribution of women to the family income has not resulted in any improvement in their position. Women receive no payment for either spinning or weaving. The carpets are sold by the men in the local market where they buy yarn and dyes. Women have no access to markets, as they used to do, and do not own their produce nor their means of production. Neither are they able to sell their labour. Their ability to weave carpets has enslaved them even further in an unpaid relation of production which is kept separate from the money economy of the men [Afshar, 1985a].

A further consequence of the introduction of carpet weaving was that fathers became reluctant to lose productive workers, and thus tended to marry off their daughters later, at 18 or 19 rather than at 14 or 15 as before. In this case, the movement towards later marriage brought rural practice into line with the provisions of the Family Protection Code, but the effect was coincidental.

In other areas, the effect of the Family Protection Code has been minimal. One reason for this was that its provisions were ignored (as were the provisions within Islamic law which give women some limited rights of inheritance and ownership). Another reason, however, is that such practices as polygamous marriage and divorce were already rare, particularly in rural areas. In general, the villages were seldom bastions of the ultra-conservative Islamic orthodoxy as once preached by the Ayatollah Khomeini. The influence of the mullahs was often remote, religious observance could be lax, and social practices differed markedly from those prescribed. Even after the overthrow of the Shah, neither segregation nor the wearing of the *chador* were practised in Asiaback, for example [Afshar, 1985a: 70]. There is, then, a marked contrast between the legal reforms introduced and the practical consequences of the Shah's modernisation programme. A limited number of middle-class women did gain some social and economic benefits, such as increased access to university education. But these women were alienated from the regime in the same way as their male counterparts by the chaos and inefficiency of the modernisation, the high level of repression and the excessive United States presence.

With the establishment of the Islamic Republic, in some ways the cities proved less hospitable for women than the villages. Hostility, aggression, and physical attacks from fundamentalist males were frequent, and entry into the labour market made unattractive by the social and psychological pressures to which women were subjected. When the Iranian revolution broke out, there were high levels of female participation. Women, it seems, supported all groups: the secular *Fedayin*, the Islamic modernist *Mujahedin*, and the clergy. Middle-class and working-class women and students all joined the demonstrations and protests, and were frequently in the vanguard. Even some traditional village women (legitimated by religiously sanctioned opposition to the Shah) joined in demonstrations in nearby towns. Donning the *chador* for demonstrations became symbolic of both secular nationalist and religious opposition. The seizure of power by the fundamentalist wing of the clergy brought with it the implementation of an interpretation of Islam based on assumptions of women's natural and biological inferiority. Because of family dependence upon women's wages, and because many of the working-class women who supported Ayatollah Khomeini worked, no formal ban on female employment was introduced. Despite Khomeini's opposition to the extension of suffrage to women, which took place in 1962, women were not disenfranchised. Instead there was a concerted propaganda drive directed against urban-educated women – that is, those from the strata most likely to oppose the regime. Khomeini described women office workers as 'painted dolls who displace and distract men and bring sedition and degradation to the workplace' [Afshar, 1985b: 269]. One further direct pressure driving women back to the home was the ban on nurseries at work places. These were considered 'dens of corruption'. Such propaganda has placed on men the onus of stopping the 'shame' of their wives and daughters working. Although many women resisted the pressure to veil, those who were not modest in their dress were harassed by the *hizballahis*, members of the party of God. The obsession with women's modesty and the stress on the necessity for domesticity and marriage brought one Iranian feminist to comment that unmarried women are 'equated with terrorists', and to conclude that 'the effect of Islamic legislation has been to make women legitimate sex objects, excluded from most paid employment and chained with ever-increasing social and ideological ties to the uncertainty of Islamic marriage' [Afshar, 1985b: 269, 277].

Whether this Islam of Iran is the 'true' Islam or not is open to debate, but the Iranian experience illustrated that the fundamentalist clergy place a very great emphasis on the most conservative interpretation of Islamic textual sources relating to the position of women. Ironically, it is not only urban middle-class women who have been affected, but the urban poor and less well-off, and it is from these that the core of support for the clergy has derived. The regime appears to have greater control in the urban centres and although there is greater autonomy in the countryside it is here where the grip of family and class has contained women within patriarchy. In Iran, then, change in urban society produced improved access to employment and education, but the cities are more subject to the imposition of Islamic law and fundamentalist mores. Under President Rafsanjani, Ayatallah Khomeini's successor, however, there has been some slight modification of regime attitudes towards women's dress and the mixing of the sexes. In the villages, the prevailing values have sustained women's subordination as their roles changed with the expansion of capitalism and as industrialisation and construction in the towns attracted village men.

If the Iranian case illustrates the way in which regime ideology cuts against an improved position for women, developments in Egypt are less clear. As in Iran, a small but increasing number of women have sought employment in middle-class occupations and also as workers in textile factories. Interest in Egypt, however, has focused on the effects which the massive migration of Egyptian males from the countryside have had on the roles of the women left behind, particularly on the extent to which the absence of men has increased peasant women's independence. Recent research reveals rather mixed results. In general, though, it seems that migration has brought only limited changes in women's roles and positions. In most cases (in the absence of the male head of the family) an increasing burden falls on women, and girls are more likely to be taken out of the educational system than boys. Furthermore, male relatives from the extended family tend to make decisions concerning the spending of migrant remittances, the management of the plot of land and children's education. Yet increased autonomy depends very much on the stage women have reached in the reproductive cycle. At one extreme, the young childless married woman would be almost wholly under the public authority of the men of the family and the domestic authority of the mother-in-law. At the other, a mature woman in an established independent family – that is, one with sons or a son past infancy – would assume responsibilities for overall land management. In this case, she might control income from the land and her husband's remittances. Even so, it seems that such increased control is temporary. On his return, the migrant male resumes his patriarchal role. Women's resistance may well be tempered by the fear that his savings might be used for a new wife. In fact, this rarely happens, but it is a commonly expressed fear [Taylor, 1984: 10]. The power to divorce in Islamic law is the prerogative of the male, and can clearly be used to ensure male ascendancy. Yet in a study of another Egyptian village, one Egyptian sociologist has suggested the potential for change, albeit within the context of woman's subordinate position within the extended family. The migration of young men has provided the finance for earlier marriage, and has thus increased the number of nuclear families at an earlier age. Within such families women have greater influence and participate more in family decisions [Khafagy, 1984].

In summary, we can say that change has taken place in Muslim Middle Eastern societies. Girls and women have greater access to education and employment, although the length and nature of both tend to be determined by class position. In the rural areas, women have lost some of the small areas of independence, although there are varying effects on peasant women as a result of migration, be it to the towns or to oil-rich states. Contending interpretations of Islam do have an effect, but the growth of Islamicist movements –

be it to produce an Islamic Republic or enhance the influence of their adherents – is unlikely to provide greater independence from men for women. Large-scale participation in the overthrow of the Shah was legitimated by the clergy. Yet even in Iran, the policies of the fundamentalist clergy have been tempered by political and social realities. Because social and political realities change, however, gains made by women have not been permanent ones. In many respects the public position of women has become akin to a political weathervane, blown hither and thither by rival political forces competing for power and influence. A good example of this process could be seen in Saudi Arabia during the Gulf War, when a group of middle-class, educated women challenged the prohibition against driving by motoring into the centre of Riyadh. To conciliate conservative religious elements antagonistic to the massive presence of the Western soldiers, severe treatment was meted out to them and their husbands. In this case, greater freedom for women became caught up in the domestic repercussions of a global crisis.

6. Conclusion

The situations of women around the Third World have always varied greatly, and have become more varied in some ways as a result of different patterns and rhythms of development. The principal conclusion to be drawn from the comparative material studied here is that much more is explained by the precise combination of circumstances in particular cases than by any supposed universal characteristics of women, or of 'Third World' women. There are some powerful global forces at work – colonisation in an earlier period, 'modernisation' and the spread of capitalism in recent years, economic pressure arising out of imposed structural adjustment and privatisation in the contemporary period – but even these have varied greatly in their impact from region to region in accordance with the logic of capitalist expansion, and its interaction with established local patterns of social and economic development.

Our review of four regions of the Third World does suggest that 'Westernisation' and 'modernisation' are as likely to worsen as to improve the situation of women. Women have generally suffered a comparative loss of status as a consequence of colonial rule and modernisation, partly because of the marginalisation or destruction of pre-capitalist activities which they may have controlled, partly because of the gender-blindness or discriminatory character of colonial policy. While capitalist development and the diffusion of 'Western' attitudes and practices regarding gender relations are not necessarily linked, they have historically gone hand in hand in the Third World. These processes often interact with powerful local patriarchal systems, particularly in the Middle East and East Asia, which may sometimes hinder and sometimes facilitate their penetration of local society.

Where women first enter the paid workforce, the decision to do so should not automatically be celebrated as a sign of emancipation. It is as likely to be a sign of distress – prompted by approaching landlessness in a peasant economy for example, or increasing impoverishment as a consequence of crisis in the urban economy – as an autonomous choice in response to new opportunity. In many cases, particularly where national and international firms have deliberately set out to recruit young women as workers, the labour of available daughters will be mobilised. In this case the decision to enter the workforce is as likely to be taken by the father or the family as by the woman herself, particularly where patriarchal authority is strong, and where entry into paid work occurs at a very early age. In these circumstances, entry to paid work may prolong rather than undermine the subordination of women, particularly if much of the wage earned goes to the family rather than the woman herself, and is diverted in order to provide for the education and hence enhanced social and economic status of young men in the family, while young working women await marriage to a partner they may not be free to choose.

However, as the contrasts between East and Southeast Asia show, much depends upon the existing family structure and patterns of inheritance, and upon the character of the national economy and political system. Only where all these factors are negative, as in the East Asian cases, is prolonged employment likely to have little effect on the position of women. In Southeast Asia the relative weakness of patriarchal authority means that the decision to enter the labour market is often taken by the woman herself. In these extremely low wage economies, however, factories have often been placed in rural areas where poverty and the lack of alternative sources of employment combine to subject young women to high levels of economic exploitation, with little prospect for direct resistance to new forms of control. In East and Southeast Asian factories alike every effort is made to create within the public space of the factory the same age- and gender-based patterns of authority which characterise the family. But economic rather than social compulsion seems dominant in the Southeast Asian cases, suggesting that the key to the dynamic of change there lies more within the realm of relations between capital and labour than in gender relations.

In general it appears that where new activities into which women move are undertaken within the context of established and mutually reinforcing relations of authority, and respect and confirm relations of power within the family and society, their emancipatory effect will be limited. Where mutually reinforcing relations of authority are not so strong, more space is created for a challenge to private and public relations of power, and more substantial change may result. In these circumstances, even apparently 'traditional' aspects of the woman's role may become the basis for activities which subvert established relations of power.

These considerations help to explain some of the contrasts between the East and Southeast Asian and Latin American cases examined above. In East and Southeast Asia alike, responsibility for the provision of welfare, and especially for care for the sick and the old, have largely remained within the family, whereas in Latin America welfare systems, however limited, have in the past been more developed. Economic recession and policy change have recently increased the welfare burden, most of which has fallen on women. In Latin America the response has often been to organise such provision at community level, rather than to internalise it wholly within the family. As a result, it has led to increased levels of political organisation, and challenged the demarcation of 'private' and 'public' spheres of responsibility.

A similar point applies to the 'politics of motherhood', as reflected in the mobilisation of women around human rights issues. As many Latin American feminists point out, the dynamic of change in this area originated in the manner in which military dictatorships praised the family and glorified the traditional role of the mother, while instituting social and economic policies which tore families apart. In response, women turned the traditional private role of the mother into a basis for public mobilisation which challenged the legitimacy and authority of the dictatorships themselves. The basis upon which mobilisation takes place may in one sense be 'traditional', but the significance of the political activity which results, and the consequential effects in terms of organisational experience and an enhanced sense of political efficacy, are not.

There is evidence here to suggest, then, that feminist thinking and activity have the capacity to transform political practice. We may conclude by assessing the extent to which this is so, turning first to the politics of socialist revolution which was the subject of the previous chapter, then to grass-roots activism in contemporary Latin America.

Socialist–feminists argue that while the establishment of socialism leads to substantial advances for women (in comparison with their situation in capitalist society), organisation and mobilisation behind a separate feminist agenda is essential if such gains are not to be relegated to secondary status, or sacrificed as other priorities come to the fore [Molyneux, 1985b]. While there is a principled commitment to women's liberation in classical Marxist thought, sexual equality is not a first priority; male and female roles are seen as complementary rather than hierarchically ordered; the primary goal is initially the destruction of the traditional social order, which entails substantial changes in the status of women; and the goal once the construction of a new stable order commences is socialist accumulation, which may at first prompt measures to open education and employment to women, but is likely to lead at a later stage to attempts to promote motherhood and the nuclear family, and to deny the need for a specific feminist agenda for reform. Without such a separate agenda (which has to be created and fought for), specifically feminist goals will be forgotten, or denied priority.

This analysis is borne out by the experience of socialist states in the Third World. In Cuba in the 1970s a number of policies of strategic importance to women were weakened or abandoned in the drive for socialist accumulation and the development of the country's productive forces [Nazzari, 1983]. In Mozambique, FRELIMO initially saw the oppression of women as arising from the traditional social order. It attacked such practices as child marriage, forced marriage, bride price and polygamy, but advanced monogamy and entry into the paid labour force as an alternative, thereby increasing the 'double burden' which women suffered. At the same time the state-sponsored Organisation of Mozambican Women (OMM) initially called on women to mobilise to contribute to the consolidation of the revolution, but offered no programme relating to the particular needs of women themselves [Urdang, 1984]. The critique of socialist ideas from a feminist perspective corrects the tendency, within a socialist perspective, to associate the subordination of women exclusively with the capitalist system, and to overlook the independent impact of the structure of gender relations.

Many community or grass-roots activists share a socialist–feminist perspective. However, the Latin American women's movements discussed above have not developed within socialist regimes, but in either dictatorships or emerging democratic regimes, and their most significant impact has been as a critique and development of conventional modes of participation in liberal democratic politics. Feminist thinking has made a significant contribution to the development of grass-roots political activity by identifying the authoritarianism inherent in traditional Latin American gender relations, and using this analysis to illuminate the authoritarian practices present not only in dictatorships, but also in traditional political institutions such as parties and trade unions. This has made it possible in turn to identify and build upon common egalitarian, empowering and participatory practices in apparently diverse movements concerned with human rights, community improvement, and economic survival. Moser has noted the 'triple roles' ascribed to women as a consequence of their responsibilities for production, reproduction, and community management [Moser, 1992: 89]. It may be that the critique of existing political practice in socialist states and liberal democracies discussed here could only have come from a feminist perspective, precisely because of the accumulation of modes of exploitation which the 'triple role' entails, and the gender difference which is at its core.

Further Reading

For an introduction to some of the earlier debates and case studies on women in the Third World, see Etienne and Leacock [1980] on colonisation; Rogers [1980] on 'domestication'; Boserup [1970], Buvinic [1976], Wellesley Editorial Committee [1977] and Beneria

[1981] on economic development; Hafkin and Bay [1976] on Africa; Beck and Keddie [1978] on the Middle East; Pescatello [1973], Chaney [1979] and Nash and Safa [1980] on Latin America; and Arrigo [1980] and Salaff [1981] on East Asia. For Southeast Asia, see Heyzer [1986]. For more recent developments in the global economy, see Nash and Fernandez-Kelly [1983] for a critical perspective, and Joekes [1987] for a liberal view. See also the very useful collections edited by Afshar [1985, 1987]. On the more recent development of global restructuring and structural adjustment, see Ward [1990], and Afshar and Dennis [1992]. On Africa, Sacks [1979] gives a rich account of pre-colonial transitions. The *Review of African Political Economy* [1984] is a special issue on women, concentrating on rural themes. There are a number of good studies on Nigeria: Allen [1976] and Ifeka-Moller [1977] discuss the 'women's war'; Pittin [1984] looks at gender relations among urban workers; and Callaway [1984] considers the possible benefits of seclusion for Hausa women in the Muslim north. Oboler [1975] is a fascinating case study of the Nandi in Kenya. Bryceson [1980] examines proletarianisation in Tanzania. On East and Southeast Asia Ong [1987] on Malaysia, Porpora *et al.* [1989] on Thailand, Wolf [1990a, 1990b] on Indonesia, and Gallin [1990] on Taiwan are recommended. On Latin America, Aviel [1981] describes past patterns of political participation, and Miller [1991] provides a very useful overview in which all significant contemporary themes are covered. Jaquette [1989] is an essential collection on women's movements across the region in the 1980s. Fernandez-Kelly [1983] on women workers on the Mexican frontier, and Alvarez [1990], on women and gender issues in Brazil in the period of democratisation, are the best full-length country case studies. Tiano [1990] examines further the case of workers in Mexico's *maquiladoras*. Waylen [1992a, 1992b] covers political and economic issues in Chile, and relates them to more general debates. Schirmer [1989] examines human rights movements, and Sternbach *et al.* [1992] traces the development of regional women's networks through the 1980s. Molyneux [1985a] introduces the distinction between practical and strategic gender interests, and applies it to the case of Nicaragua. Moser [1991] develops the idea of the triple role, and relates it to material on urban Ecuador. On the Middle East, see Doumato [1991] on Saudi Arabia, and Mervat [1992] on Egypt. On the issues discussed in the conclusion, Molyneux [1985b] is a comparative discussion of the 'woman question' in socialist states; Nazzari (1983) offers a case study of Cuba. Moser [1992] contains a valuable extension and comparative discussion of practical and strategic gender interests.

7
The International Context

1. Introduction

A state's international bargaining position depends on its strategic importance, the character of the regime in control of the state, the personality and international standing of the leader, its economic resources and the extent of external control over them, and the alliances which the state makes with its neighbours and within the intergovernmental organisations to which it belongs. Virtually all Third World regimes have close links with the industrialised West, conservative and traditional regimes by choice and revolutionary regimes (which might in the past have gravitated towards the Soviet Union) out of military and economic need. The pull of the West is understandable: Western states (the United States particularly, and Western-dominated institutions such as the World Bank and the International Monetary Fund (IMF)) have the resources to assist in a way that the Soviet Union, with its shortage of foreign exchange, was never able to match; this was important for rulers who wished to survive – the state is the source of their own power and must be maintained. It is all the more important when no alternative global source of support is to be found.

Even those rulers who ally with the West out of choice rather than necessity may retain strong nationalist sentiments, leading them to take, for example, action in favour of indigenous entrepreneurs at the expense of foreign capital. However rulers, whatever their ideological orientation, who indulge in too strident a nationalism face the danger of cutting themselves off from external support; their foreign policy will be designed to strengthen rather than erode their domestic power base. Ironically, the rulers of a poor state may be more secure than those who rule a wealthy state but squander its resources, or whose policies create grave social inequalities; such rulers may survive only if they are underpinned by an external power.

The extent to which the Great Powers interest themselves in the affairs of Third World states will depend on the geographical location and strategic importance of the latter, and on considerations such as the size of markets and investments. States in 'the backyard' of a Great Power, such as the Latin American states in relation to the United States, are particularly susceptible to external intervention when the Great Power concerned feels it can intervene without international challenge or undue military and political cost, as the US invasions of Grenada and Panama demonstrated. Where strategic interests are thought to be high, even costly, controversial and internationally damaging interventions will still be maintained. This was true of US intervention in Indochina up to its defeat in Vietnam in 1975, and again in the 1980s, when the US government defied international law to maintain a blockade of Nicaraguan ports, and defied US law and its own Congress to pursue an illicit programme of funding to the armed opponents of the Sandinista government.

Where there is one dominant power unchallenged by contenders, as in Latin America, the situation is very different from one in which a number of powers seek to exert an influence. The latter has been the case in Southeast Asia since the Second World War: China, the Soviet Union and the United States have all pursued perceived interests in the region, either intervening directly or seeking to win particular states as clients, ever since the Chinese Revolution and post-war revolutions and superpower confrontations left China, Indochina and Korea divided between Communist and pro-Western forces. One response, prompted by US military involvement in Indochina and intensified as a consequence of the Vietnamese invasion of Cambodia in 1979 to remove the Pol Pot regime, and the resulting tensions involving China and the Soviet Union, has been a strong regional movement in favour of neutrality, first exemplified in the call for a Zone of Peace, Freedom and Neutrality launched by the ASEAN powers in 1971. Countries which have a commodity for export (notably oil in the Middle East) which is vital to the industrial and military wellbeing of one or more of the Great Powers are also vulnerable to intervention. For these reasons, Latin America, East and Southeast

Asia, and the Middle East have been of much greater importance than Africa to the Great Powers and the industrialised countries of the West. However, after 1974 the Horn of Africa became the cockpit of Great Power rivalry. The West also remained determined to protect its investments in South Africa and in Namibia, with its rich deposits of uranium, despite mounting international criticism of South Africa's repressive apartheid policies.

As the foregoing discussion suggests, intervention in the Third World is as much economic as strategic in its motivation. With the closing of the 'Cold War' and the break-up of the Soviet Union, the tendency for economic issues to predominate in international affairs has been strengthened. For Third World states in general, large transnational corporations and international financial organisations loom as large as foreign governments in global politics. Third World states have generally found it difficult to advance their common goals *vis-à-vis* multinationals and international institutions, in part because of a lack of receptiveness on the part of the leading industrial states, which have primarily been concerned with protecting and advancing their own interests, and in part because Third World states are often competitors between themselves for foreign markets and inward investment. As a result there is always a degree of tension between attempted regional co-operation and individual strategies aimed at gaining regional advantage. Mexico's negotiation of entry into an enlarged North American Free Trade Area with the United States and Canada in 1992 provides a case in point, as do the differing strategies pursued by, say, Iraq and Saudi Arabia with regard to oil. At the same time, projects for regional co-operation prove difficult to establish, as in ASEAN's case, as a consequence of radically different economic structures and strategies in different member countries – such as free-trading Singapore and more protectionist Indonesia. We assess in this chapter the impact of these different considerations from region to region, and their strategic and economic consequences.

2. Africa: the search for a new beginning

Until 1974, when military coups occurred in both Portugal and Ethiopia, Africa south of the Sahara was not a theatre of paramount concern for the two superpowers. With an eye primarily to Western security interests, the United States intervened in Congo–Leopoldville in the early 1960s, gave military support to Portugal (a NATO ally) in its fight against liberation forces in its African colonies, extended support to South Africa, and gave low-level backing (for a time) to the Smith regime in Rhodesia. After the Cuba missile crisis of October 1962 the volume of United States aid to Africa (which was already small) decreased further. The Soviet Union, for its part, encouraged 'progressive' leaders such as Nkrumah of Ghana, Sékou Touré of Guinea and Modibo Keita of Mali, but gave minimal amounts of economic (as distinct from military) aid even to the radical states.

In the late 1960s both the superpowers supported the federal government in the Nigerian civil war. In the next decade (as the influence of middle-level powers increased and the voice of the People's Republic of China carried greater weight in world affairs) bipolarity gave way to multipolarity. Soviet foreign policy was greatly affected by the Sino–Soviet split, and the Soviet Union's policy towards Africa (like that of the United States) became more pragmatically based than formerly. Both sides now recognised the complexity of African politics. Moreover, in both Angola and Ethiopia after 1974 the two superpowers avoided direct confrontation and opted instead for proxy conflict – the Cubans (it would seem of their own volition) became the Soviet surrogates in both countries, while the United States backed the dissident forces championed by South Africa in Angola, and from 1977 befriended Somalia rather than Ethiopia (its former ally) in the Horn of Africa. The latter became the cockpit of Great Power rivalry: both the United States and the Soviet Union had a strong strategic interest in the Indian Ocean. The close alliance forged with the Soviet Union by the Marxist–Leninist regime in Ethiopia enabled Mengistu to obtain the rapid build-up of armaments which was essential to counter the threat from Somalia in 1977–8 and to survive for a further thirteen years the challenge from the forces of communalism which his centralising, pro-Amhara policies had unleashed.

In southern Africa, the policy of the United States government was dictated by the very high level of Western financial investment in the Republic of South Africa, by strategic and mineral resource considerations, and by a desire to halt the spread of communist influence in the southern African sub-region. While condemning the white minority government's apartheid policies and stressing the need to moderate them, the United States administration supported South Africa's destabilisation policy towards Angola, even to the extent of making a public announcement early in 1986 that it would give military aid to the UNITA rebels. Unrealistically, the Reagan administration linked the withdrawal of Cuban troops from Angola with the independence of Namibia and refused to recognise Angola's MPLA government. It also took the view that 'punitive sanctions would hurt South Africa's economy, which is central to the region's stability and a major force for change domestically' [The *Guardian*, 3 April 1986].

However, a majority of members of the United States Congress did not share this view. Following a period of prolonged violence in South Africa's black townships in 1984–6 Congress, against the opposition of leading members of the Administration, imposed a string of sanctions under the 1986 Comprehensive Anti-Apartheid Act, to add to the existing arms embargo; they included a ban on trade, investment and air links with South Africa. The European Community, after months of argument, and the Commonwealth also voted in favour of sanctions, the combined effect of which was to increase South Africa's international isolation. Though welcomed by the ANC, sanctions sapped business confidence within South Africa and aggravated an already acute unemployment situation.

Faced with urban unrest and mounting debt problems, President P.W. Botha was afraid of being outflanked on his right; he therefore failed to undertake liberal reforms at home which would have given him an alternative source of support – on his left. The continued detention of Nelson Mandela and other ANC leaders and the fact that the ANC remained a banned organisation ruled out a negotiated settlement. A rapidly expanding African population continued to be denied even the partial representation which had been granted to Coloureds and Asians under the 1984 tripartite constitution. This, and the tight control of a repressive and often brutal state apparatus, added up to an explosive situation.

However, events changed unexpectedly. The battle for Cuito Cuanavale in Angola suggested that the military balance was turning against South Africa and led to a change of attitude in Pretoria. This, coupled with Gorbachev's desire to be free of Third World entanglements in order to concentrate on reviving the Soviet domestic economy, encouraged the United States to launch a new diplomatic offensive. It succeeded in bringing to the negotiating table representatives of South Africa, Angola and Cuba to find solutions to the vexed problems of Namibian independence and the Cuban military presence in Angola. By the end of 1989 agreements had been formally signed which, despite a number of hiccoughs on the way, facilitated the achievement of independence by Namibia on 21 March 1990, and the phased withdrawal of Cuban troops from Angola. These agreements were effectively guaranteed by the superpowers and (with F.W. de Klerk installed as South Africa's President and Nelson Mandela released from detention) led eventually to a peace agreement on 31 May 1991 between the Angolan government and UNITA. When multi-party elections between September and November 1992 gave a decisive victory to the government in Angola, Savimbi rejected the results and returned to armed opposition. The UN was powerless to impose a settlement.

If we exclude certain areas of the continent – notably the Horn of Africa and much of southern Africa – the predominant influence of external powers in Africa is exerted by neither the United States nor the Soviet Union (nor China, for that matter), but by the former colonial powers, especially Britain and France. Following independence, the 'mother country' was normally the new state's principal trading partner. African leaders sought to diversify their countries' trading links, the principal beneficiary being the European Economic Community (EEC); the volume of trade which even Africa's socialist states conducted with the eastern bloc's Council for Mutual Economic Assistance (Comecon) was still very small. In February 1975 African, Caribbean and Pacific (ACP) states joined together in signing the Lomé convention with the EEC; this convention has been renegotiated by the ACP countries on three subsequent occasions.

The extent of the influence of African states is circumscribed by their continuing economic dependence. This dependence was very real at the time that political independence was formally achieved, especially for those countries (such as copper-rich Zambia and Zaire) whose economies were based overwhelmingly upon the raw materials produced for export by multinational mining companies. From about 1965 onwards, a strong sense of economic nationalism led several African governments to take total (or majority) ownership of these extractive industries; however, the lack of indigenous managerial and technological skills meant that effective control still lay with the foreign companies. Many of the latter upheld their interests by using transfer pricing and other devices which worked to the disadvantage of the host countries.

President Nkrumah of Ghana believed that a united Africa, subject to a single government, was the only effective way of ending external dependency; he was convinced that without unity neocolonialism and racist minority rule in Africa would continue. The Organisation of African Unity (OAU), established in 1963, owed much to Nkrumah's statesmanship, but fell well short of his vision [Amate, 1986].

Since its formation, the OAU has registered some modest successes: it has provided a meeting ground for African leaders and has acted as an umbrella for sub-regional organisations and UN agencies, such as the Economic Commission for Africa (ECA); it has tried to settle interstate disputes and its liberation committee has to an extent helped several countries to throw off the colonial yoke. But there have been significant failures and numerous problems, of which some are due to the Organisation's cumbersome structure (which works against swift decision-making), its insecure financial base and its lack of a groundswell of popular support. The OAU also suffers from an excess of politics, as was shown in the secretary-general elections at the summit conferences held in June 1983 and November 1984. The underlying principles of the Charter have themselves contributed to the Organisation's difficulties. The clause stating that each independent African state has the right to join the Organisation has proved problematic in recent years, and difficulties have also arisen over the principles of non-interference in the internal affairs of member states and non-alignment; none of these principles has been strictly applied.

In respect of the major areas of activity established by the Charter, the Organisation's record is mixed. In promoting the liberation of southern Africa – always its principal area of concern – the OAU has worked through the African Liberation Committee (ALC), though never exclusively. Its moral backing always counted for more than its financial support. In settling inter-African disputes, the mediatory efforts of the OAU have counted for much less than the mediation of individual African heads of state – the Organisation's projected Commission of Mediation, Conciliation and Arbitration was in fact never formed. Under cover of the principle of non-interference, the Organisation has also failed to condemn the glaring atrocities which have occurred in several Black African states, and has been slow to act over explosive issues such as the Western Sahara and Chad. This is mainly because it is difficult for the Organisation (given the often divergent interests of its members) to agree on a common policy – most unanimity was achieved over attitudes towards South Africa.

From the 1970s the OAU has shown an increasing concern with economic affairs. Economic resolutions were passed at several of the annual summit conferences, but the Organisation has lacked the financial and other resources to implement them. It has also often had to give prior attention to urgent and frequently divisive political issues. None the less, the importance of economic co-operation is widely recognised and a large number of sub-regional groups exist in various parts of the continent for this purpose. The two major existing associations are the Economic Community of West African States (ECOWAS) and the Southern African Development Co-ordination Conference (SADCC).

ECOWAS was established by the Treaty of Lagos, which was signed in May 1975, as a 15- (subsequently 16-) nation economic community of predominantly English- and French-speaking West African states [Asante, 1985]. The Community began functioning in 1978 with its headquarters in Lagos, the Nigerian capital, and its members pledged themselves to work towards the free movement of goods and people throughout the community area. Co-operation has been hampered by a variety of factors, including the proliferation of currencies and of foreign exchange restrictions and controls in the West African region, the non-payment of subscriptions and the strong sense of economic nationalism on the part of several states, and over-dependence on Nigeria which is itself facing financial problems originating in the sharp fall in the price of oil in the early 1980s. Political events, too, have disrupted co-operation, a notable example being the civil war which erupted in Liberia in 1990 and led ECOWAS to take the costly step of dispatching a peace-keeping force – the ECOWAS Monitoring Group (ECOMOG) – to Liberia. As a result of these various impediments, only halting progress has been made in achieving ECOWAS's primary goals.

SADCC came into being in 1979, but was not formally established until April of the next year [Abegunrin, 1985; Anglin, 1985]. It has ten member states – Angola, Botswana, Lesotho,

Malawi, Mozambique, Namibia, Swaziland, Tanzania, Zambia, and Zimbabwe – which between them have a population of about 80 million. With substantial energy resources, rich mineral deposits and abundant agricultural land, the sub-region has great economic potential, but needs external finance, technology and manpower to supplement inadequate local resources in these fields. The stated aims of SADCC are to co-operate in designated areas in order to secure the equitable development of the sub-region as a whole and reduce the economic dependence of member states, especially on the Republic of South Africa. With the exception of Angola and Tanzania this dependence is extreme, especially in the fields of employment, trade and transport (six of the ten SADCC states are landlocked). The areas of co-operation are: transport and communications, agriculture, industry and trade, energy, manpower development, mining, tourism, and finance. Individual member states are to co-ordinate functional activities within a specific area: thus, Angola is responsible for co-ordinating energy and conservation, and Mozambique for co-ordinating transport and communications. The emphasis at present is on non-industrial areas of co-operation. A development fund has been set up, with finance supplied mainly by Organisation for Economic Co-operation and Development (OECD) governments (especially governments in the Scandinavian and Benelux countries); most of the technology comes from the same sources. SADCC relies heavily on external aid, even for co-operative projects, and this carries the danger that outside interests will influence (and may determine) project choice and long-term strategy.

SADCC's structure is still sufficiently flexible to allow a member-state to pursue policies which it conceives to be in its own national interest. Thus economic nationalism has led some states to retain (or develop) trade links with South Africa, thereby impeding the realisation of SADCC's aims, and has caused Zimbabwe to prefer the domestic production of coal-powered electricity to pursuing a policy of sub-regional energy integration; its attitude underlined the difficulty which SADCC will face in achieving the equitable distribution of benefits. The latter has already become an issue in relation to the planned production of steel by four SADCC states and, because of Zimbabwe's industrial dominance, may become a real problem when SADCC gives priority to industrial development. However, what happens in this and other spheres may be superseded by events in South Africa. If a democratically elected government is formed in the Republic, the situation in southern Africa would be dramatically changed and, in consequence, the whole character of SADCC would probably be transformed. For the time being, the touchstone of what can be achieved through groupings such as ECOWAS and SADCC will be the political leaders' perception of what is in their own and the national interest. Take, for example, the attitude of Félix Houphouet-Boigny, the veteran President of the Côte d'Ivoire. A lukewarm supporter of the OAU (whose meetings he never attends), he participates actively in ECOWAS, serving as an elder statesman of the group and playing a key role in removing misunderstandings between member-states. He is also a firm supporter of the annual Franco–African conferences, which deal with issues such as collective security and economic co-operation.

For all their shortcomings, sub-regional functional groupings have a better record than sub-regional political unions. Of the many attempts which have been made (both before and after the establishment of the OAU in 1963) to form political unions, only a small number have been successful: the union of Ghana and British Togoland in 1957, Italian and British Somaliland in 1960 (though the survival of this union became precarious in the early 1990s), Southern Cameroons and the Republic of Cameroon in 1961, and Tanganyika and Zanzibar in 1964. The parties concerned freely entered into these unions; however, except in the case of Tanganyika and Zanzibar, each union was achieved before the independence of one or both parties. In the exceptional case, Chinese and East German influence in Zanzibar was a factor taken into account by President Nyerere's government. Against these successes must be set a number of failures, important reasons in each case being institutional incompatibility and the perception of incumbent leaders that their political power base was being (or would be) eroded. These were the main causes of the early collapse of the Mali Federation formed in 1959 between Senegal and the French Soudan (later Mali), while they proved a major stumbling bloc to the formation of an East African federation in 1963 [Foltz, 1965; Hazlewood, 1979]. No comparable attempts at achieving small-scale political union have been made in the subsequent period and, with the main exception of Somalia, African states now accept the interstate boundaries established at independence.

3. East and Southeast Asia: emerging from the shadow of the Cold War

The impact of colonisation by diverse powers reinforced divisions in East and Southeast Asia naturally arising from the geographic dispersion of the region. In the early years after the Second World War these divisions were intensified, and new ones created, and regional identity and institutions were slow to emerge. The key features of the international context were the early grant of independence in South Asia, the successful Communist revolution in China, and the direct impact of the Cold War in Korea and French Indochina. The settling of the Chinese nationalist forces on Taiwan and the division of Vietnam and Korea on Cold War lines meant that in these areas international politics reflected global confrontation dominated by US–Soviet rivalry, hindering the emergence of a distinctively regional voice. The first sign that such a voice might emerge came with the Asian Relations Conference called by the Indian Council of World Affairs at Nehru's suggestion in 1947. Both here and at the later Bandung Conference the emphasis was developmentalist rather than regionalist. The 'Asian' label included the independent states of the Middle East, and an effort was made to bring Asian and African representatives together, rather than to create a purely Asian regional body [Stargardt, 1989: 565]. As Great Power diplomacy in the region overshadowed regional initiatives, and the most internationally prominent new states in the region continued to focus upon anti-colonialism (with an eye on Africa) and developmentalism, no regional association was firmly established until ASEAN was founded in 1967.

The different agendas of the great powers and the new states emerged clearly at the Geneva and Bandung Conferences in 1954 and 1955. At Geneva in 1954, where the United States, the Soviet Union, Britain, France, and China sought to resolve the status of Korea and French Indochina, issues of national independence were addressed in terms derived from confrontation between communist and anti-communist superpowers. The subsequent creation of SEATO (South East Asia Treaty Organisation), following the defeat of the French, tied the Philippines and Thailand into an anti-Chinese defence alliance dominated by the United States, and further extended the logic of Cold War politics into the region. In contrast the Bandung Conference, proposed by Indonesian premier Ali Sastroamidjojo and quickly endorsed by India and China, was explicitly pan-Afro–Asian in conception, and gathered together twenty-nine states of varying political, regional, and ideological character. For Nehru, its explicit purpose was to prevent the isolation of the People's Republic of China, and to preserve the option of non-alignment in the midst of tensions arising from the Cold War. India's alliance with China was soon to falter, but even so the Bandung Conference gave rise to the Non-Aligned Movement, and brought Nasser, Nehru, Nkrumah and Sukarno on to the international stage as leading defenders of a 'Third World' anti-colonial and developmentalist position with quite different priorities to those pursued by the Great Powers.

By 1967 the situation had changed. India's role in the international anti-colonial movement had weakened after the death of Nehru in 1964; the failure of Nasser's plans for pan-Arab union along with difficulties at home had tempered his international ambitions; Nkrumah was in exile after his ousting from power in 1966; and Sukarno had been edged aside by General Suharto. Hopes for pan-Afro–Asian internationalism had faded. Meanwhile sources of tension which had hindered the emergence of regional groupings in the early 1960s – the dispute between Malaya and the Philippines over Sabah in 1962 (which lingered on until the Philippines dropped its claim in 1992), the aggressive policy of confrontation (*confrontasi*) pursued by Indonesia against Malaysia from 1963 to 1965, and Singapore's withdrawal from the Malaysian federation in 1965 – had either faded or been resolved. On 8 August 1967 the Bangkok declaration created ASEAN, the Association of Southeast Asian Nations, with Indonesia, Malaysia, the Philippines, Singapore and Thailand as founding members. The five original members were joined by the oil-rich enclave of Brunei in 1984. At the outset security concerns were uppermost, as war raged in Indochina and indigenous communist movements threatened in Malaysia, the Philippines and Thailand. More recently the Association has been concerned with attempts to foster regional economic integration and development, albeit with limited success.

Along with a common commitment to anti-communism and a broad sympathy towards the United States, the countries of the ASEAN group were concerned to prevent the spread of war from Indochina into their own territories. They developed a somewhat awkward posture within which the presence of US bases (particularly important in the Philippines and Thailand) was declared temporary, and a general aspiration towards neutrality was announced. As a result of a Malaysian initiative, the ASEAN foreign ministers met in Kuala Lumpur in November 1971 to call for joint action to make the region a Zone of Peace, Freedom and Neutrality (ZOPFAN), but the US bases remained, and the Malaysian preference for formal guarantees from the US, the Soviet Union and China was resisted by Indonesia. Subsequent developments were largely dominated by events in Indochina. The communist victories in Laos, Cambodia and Vietnam in 1975 prompted a February 1976 Summit in Bali which produced the Declaration of ASEAN Concord and the Treaty of Amity and Co-operation in Southeast Asia. With military co-operation limited to a few bilateral initiatives, these documents endorsed the eventual goal of a Zone of Peace, Freedom and Neutrality but otherwise concentrated on measures of economic co-operation and integration in the areas of food and energy, large-scale industrial projects, intra-regional trade liberalisation, and joint initiatives on international commodity problems [Frost, 1990]. In both security and economic co-operation, subsequent progress has been slow.

The aftershocks of the Vietnam War have been a major source of security problems throughout Southeast Asia since 1976, primarily as a consequence of the flow of boat refugees from Vietnam since 1978, the Vietnamese invasion of Cambodia in the same year, China's invasion of Vietnam in 1979, and the continuing instability of Cambodia. In the late 1970s and the late 1980s in particular, heavy flows of refugees, primarily to Thailand, Malaysia and Indonesia prompted efforts to involve the major regional powers and the United Nations in co-operative solutions. While the refugee problem has been a persistent source of instability, the role of the ASEAN countries in negotiating an end to the Vietnamese occupation of Cambodia has given the association international prominence, and a degree of prestige. Despite a general antipathy towards the Pol Pot regime ASEAN opposed the 1979 invasion, and refused to recognise the Vietnamese-backed regime. Over more than a decade, the ASEAN states won recognition for this position in the United Nations and elsewhere, and played a leading part in negotiations to secure Vietnamese withdrawal and the return of the ASEAN-sponsored Coalition Government of Democratic

Kampuchea from exile. The signing of the Cambodian Peace Agreement in October 1991 represented a considerable success for the ASEAN countries, not least because they had proved able to act in unison throughout the period of negotiations despite the different perspectives on regional security among member states. At the same time, Indonesia did not drop its opposition to alignment with any of the major powers. It sought to keep links open to Vietnam throughout the period, and maintained its opposition to the presence of foreign bases in the region. As a result, there has been no move either towards joint ASEAN military co-operation, or to realisation of the Zone of Peace, Freedom and Neutrality. Instead, the Manila Summit of December 1987 called again for the 'early realisation' of ZOPFAN, and added a call for a Southeast Asian Nuclear Weapon Free Zone (SEANWFZ).

Progress in economic co-operation has been held back by differing levels of development and trade orientations between the ASEAN members (ranging from rich, liberal Brunei and Singapore and middling Malaysia to poor and protectionist Indonesia), competition rather than co-operation over primary exports, industrialisation, and the attraction of foreign capital, and the failure to liberalise trade in primary products through the GATT. By the late 1980s per capita income levels in Indonesia and the Philippines were comparable, but this reflected growth and structural transformation in Indonesia over twenty-five years, as against stagnation in the Philippine case. Malaysia was pulling away as an emerging NIC (newly industrialised country) in the wake of Singapore, with Thailand following closely behind. In all cases, growth in the 1980s was considerably below levels achieved in previous decades, and attempts to co-operate looked like being overshadowed by pressures to compete. The attempt to create an expanded and harmonised regional market illustrates some of the problems which have arisen. By 1987 industrial joint ventures had barely taken off, competition for foreign investment was causing ASEAN states to outbid each other, substantial non-tariff barriers to intra-ASEAN trade remained, and little progress had been made on preferential tariff arrangements between the partners. The Manila Summit agreed to act on all these fronts, most significantly by committing members to bring 50 per cent of intra-ASEAN trade under preferential tariff arrangements by 1992. In international negotiations, the four agro-exporters in ASEAN, Indonesia, Malaysia, the

Philippines and Thailand, had taken a direct interest in the Uruguay round of GATT negotiations, joining the Australia-led Cairns Group in 1986 in pursuit of free trade in agricultural and tropical products. Lack of progress on these talks, along with signs of a move towards protectionism in international trade, reinforced the concern of the ASEAN states over the emergence of competing trading blocs and the growing regional dominance of Japan, and made regional co-operation both more necessary, and harder to achieve. In response to these various pressures, the ASEAN states agreed in October 1992 to speed up progress towards the creation of an ASEAN Free Trade Area (AFTA), setting targets for a common effective preferential tariff of no more than 20 per cent by the end of the century, and of zero to 5 per cent by 2008, with accelerated cuts to 5 per cent or below by 2000 for cement, pharmaceuticals, fertilizer, plastics, chemicals and other goods accounting in all for a third of intra-ASEAN trade. However, the continuing problems of underlying structural incompatibility, reflected in provisions for exceptions in areas of particular national interest, were likely to make progress uneven.

By the time ASEAN celebrated its silver jubilee with the First ASEAN Congress in October 1992 a shift had taken place away from the conditions under which it had been founded. Cold War tensions had receded, while regional economic and security issues had gained greater weight.

Evidence of the weakening of the lines of force created by the Cold War came with the closures in 1991 and 1992 of US military bases at Clark Field Air Base and Subic Bay in the Philippines. These closures came as a result of nationalist opposition in the Philippines, changed security needs on the part of the United States, and the forced evacuation of Clark Field in June 1991, while talks on future leases were in progress, as a result of the eruption of Mount Pinatubo. With leases due to expire in September 1991, protracted negotiations were eventually concluded in July of the same year. Under this agreement Clark Field was to be returned to the Philippines by September 1992 (transfer of the ash-covered, evacuated and virtually unusable facility actually took place in November 1991). Subic Bay was to be leased for a further ten years, in return for a lump-sum payment and an annual commitment to US$ 203 million per year in aid. However, approval by a two-thirds majority of the Philippine Senate was required before these provisions could be ratified, and a contest of wills between President Aquino and the Senate ensued. A combination of nationalism, opposition to Aquino, and concerns at the continuing US refusal to confirm or deny the presence of nuclear weapons at the base provoked the 23-member Senate to reject the proposed Treaty of Friendship, Co-operation and Security by 12 votes to 11 on 16 September 1991. Aquino responded at first by threatening a national referendum on the issue, but backed off as the political risks and dubious legality of the initiative became clear. For its part the United States government asked first for four years to complete a phased withdrawal, then agreed in October 1991 to withdraw over three years. As controversy over the issue continued, and fears arose that a delay until after the 1992 elections would allow a new deal with a new government, President Aquino finally served a notice to withdraw within a year at the end of 1991, and despite the election of Fidel Ramos to the presidency the United States forces abandoned Subic Bay in September 1992. Their departure, along with the upsurge of nationalist feeling with which discussion of the issue was attended, signalled a significant shift in great power presence and influence in Southeast Asia. Although the major implications may appear to have been strategic, the combined economic implications of the devastation and dislocation brought about by the eruption of Mount Pinatubo and the departure of the large US population of the bases were substantial.

At the same time there were signs of movement towards the resolution of the anomalous situation of Taiwan, still seen by both China and Taiwan itself as a province of China. While China remained opposed to the independence of Taiwan, a position it shared with the conservative wing of Taiwan's ruling KMT, liberal Taiwanese-born members of the KMT advocated a 'two China' policy closer to the pro-independence line announced in 1991 by the opposition Democratic Progressive Party. The issue gained particular significance in 1992, as constitutional reform had eliminated the last members of the Legislative Yuan elected on the mainland in 1947. As a result, the December 1992 elections produced for the first time an assembly entirely chosen by the Taiwanese electorate. Pro-independence government and opposition forces turned out to be in the majority as a result of these elections, and it was likely that the issue of independence would gain in prominence, despite continuing Chinese opposition and its open threats of armed intervention.

As elsewhere in the Third World, however, the fading of Cold War tensions did not bring an end to instability and conflict in Cambodia. If the country was no longer a site of global confrontation, it still remained the most urgent regional issue, as an interim United Nations Transitional Authority (UNTAC) strove to oversee the withdrawal of foreign troops, the demobilisation of standing armies, and the repatriation of refugees, and to prepare for the democratic elections it was due to supervise in April 1993. Its relations with the Supreme National Council (representing the Hun Sen regime and the three opposition forces, the Sihanoukists, the Khmer Rouge, and the Khmer People's National Liberation Front) were made difficult by the scale of the problems faced, limited funds, and the refusal of the Khmer Rouge to lay down their arms until all Vietnamese troops had withdrawn. At the same time a renewed source of regional confrontation had arisen in the Spratly and Paracel Islands in the South China Sea. Competition in the area between China, Malaysia, the Philippines, Taiwan, and Vietnam, reflected in a race to claim and occupy different islands and reefs, was intense as a result of Chinese southward expansion and exploitation of presumed rich mineral resources, competition for access to those resources, and ASEAN concerns at the economic and security implications. Oil exploration from 1973 and Chinese expulsion of a South Vietnamese garrison from the Paracel Islands in 1974 were followed by Vietnamese reoccupation after the Communist victory in 1975, and competing claims from the Philippines and Taiwan. A new phase of conflict opened in 1988 when China occupied six islands in the Spratly group, and engaged the Vietnamese in naval conflict, leaving three ships sunk and 72 dead. In 1992 China claimed the islands in the area, and signed a contract with the Crestone Energy Corporation to explore for oil in a concession immediately to the east of an offshore Vietnamese block. Its rapid build-up of air and naval capacity prompted Philippine and Malaysian acquisitions of similar capacity, although on a much smaller scale.

Finally, there were signs of movement towards the eventual reunification of North and South Korea and the evolution of Vietnam from a hard-line communist state to a competitor for inward investment and entry to the ranks of the newly industrialised countries, along with the expansion of export-oriented industrial zones on mainland China. While it would still take some time for the aftershocks of the Cold War to subside, it was clear in the early 1990s that for the foreseeable future the most significant international issues in East and Southeast Asia would arise from regional economic rivalry, rather than from global military and ideological confrontation.

4. Latin America: in the shadow of the United States

For Latin America, the overwhelming presence of the United States to the north has been the most significant feature of the international context in the twentieth century. We first consider the role it has played, then turn our attention to the role of international organisations and multinational corporations in the region. Finally, we ask whether a collective Latin American voice independent of the United States is emerging in the region.

Since 1823, when President James Monroe warned the European powers to keep out of the Americas, the United States has claimed the right to exert exclusive authority in its own 'back yard'. Although its economic and military power was initially unequal to the task, a series of interventions around the turn of the century in Cuba, Puerto Rico and Colombia (in the latter case to sponsor the breakaway republic of Panama) signalled a willingness to intervene; in 1904 President Theodore Roosevelt announced that his country would exercise 'international police power' in cases of 'chronic wrongdoing or an impotence which results in a general loosening of the ties of civilised society' [Pearce, 1981: 11]. Over the following three decades Central America and the Caribbean became a familiar stamping ground for US troops, deployed at various times in Mexico, Cuba, Panama, Haiti, the Dominican Republic and Nicaragua, while the US government made and unmade governments throughout the area. In addition, Mexico (which had lost considerable territory to the United States in the nineteenth century) suffered intervention during the revolutionary period. At first such interventions were justified (as by President Taft in 1912) on moral and even racial grounds; inevitably, however, the strategic and economic self-interest which had been present from the start came to the fore as United States business interests followed the flag: looking back on his military career in 1935, General Smedley Butler described himself as 'a high class muscle man for Big Business, Wall Street, and for the bankers' [Ibid.: 20]. In the 1930s, when the 'Good Neighbour' policy announced by President Franklin Roosevelt in 1933 began to operate, emphasis was switched away from armed intervention to the promotion and support of local dictators, throughout Central America and the Caribbean, such as Trujillo in the Dominican Republic, Somoza in Nicaragua, Batista in Cuba and Hernandez Martinez in El Salvador.

During the Second World War and its immediate aftermath, a number of important developments occurred. The United States emerged as a world power, and began to define its interests (in global terms) in opposition to those of the Soviet Union as it perceived them, and to assess conflicts within the Americas in the context of the Cold War. Within Latin America it sought to extend its diplomatic and economic power further across mainland South America. It began to find ties with dictatorships south of its borders increasingly counter-productive, given the need to defend the values of democracy against the challenge of the Soviet Union, and to respond to pressure throughout the Third World for social reform and political freedom. However, it also found that its strategic and economic interests were frequently tied to anti-democratic forces, and in this context a number of serious dilemmas arose.

Nationalist governments which put United States economic interests at risk in their pursuit of social justice were denounced as communistic and Soviet-controlled – as with the government of Jácobo Arbenz in Guatemala, overthrown in a coup organised and funded by the CIA. But in the same period the United States threw its support behind democratisation in Brazil in 1945, and in Bolivia after the revolution in 1952. A consistent pattern seemed to be emerging when Colombia and Venezuela were prompted toward democracy under moderate leadership in 1958, but the situation in the region changed dramatically at the end of that year, when Fidel Castro swept to power in Cuba as Batista's dictatorship crumbled while the United States dithered in the wings. The consolidation of the Cuban Revolution and the country's rapid shift into the Soviet orbit were to be the major factors behind United States intervention in the region thereafter. For three decades the United States was the prisoner of its own perception that a confrontation between the superpowers was playing itself out in Latin America, and its policy was pulled in two opposing directions. On the one side was the intermittent awareness that social reform and democratisation were needed in the long run if the underlying conditions of poverty and repression which make revolution attractive were to be removed. On the other was the perceived need to support conservative allies and build up friendly armies in order to protect United States interests in the short term, and prevent radical opponents from gaining ground. This was a 'two-track' policy, in which one track persistently ran foul of the other.

One victim of this syndrome was the Alliance for Progress, launched by President Kennedy as a direct response to the Cuban Revolution. Its reformist impulse was rapidly lost as the armies built up across Central and South America and trained in the task of counter-insurgency tired of the moderate politicians sponsored by their paymasters, and took power for themselves, urging the need to adopt drastic methods to root out the guerilla movements which sprang up across the continent in the wake of Castro's success in Cuba. The threat these movements posed was rarely substantial, but the United States abandoned its commitment to reform, as the strategic perspective which had initially inspired it underwent a reorientation. In the wake of the botched attempt to defeat the Cuban Revolution at the Bay of Pigs, President Kennedy sponsored the overthrow of the democratically-elected President Bosch of the Dominican Republic, while his successor (President Johnson) supported and swiftly welcomed the coup which overthrew President Goulart of Brazil in 1964, and sent 20 000 troops to the Dominican Republic in 1965 to prevent Bosch from returning to power.

In Chile the Kennedy administration backed the Christian Democratic leader Eduardo Frei, in the hope that he would provide an attractive reformist alternative to socialism. To this end, millions of dollars were poured into the country to back Frei's presidential campaign in 1964, and in the wake of his victory he was encouraged to pursue land reform and other progressive measures. But his 'Revolution in Liberty' weakened under pressure from the right in the country and from conservative elements in his own party, the most committed reformers moved to the left as they saw their hopes frustrated, and in 1970 the Chileans elected Allende (by the narrowest of margins) as their president. The Allende government had been democratically elected, and was committed to a reform programme broadly similar to that adopted by Frei with

United States blessing in 1964, but still faced unremitting hostility from the United States. US agencies promoted economic destabilisation and funded civil disorder, while stepping up aid to the armed forces, and were rewarded in September 1973, when General Augusto Pinochet seized power at the head of a military junta. The bloodshed which accompanied and followed the coup, the curtailing of civil liberties and the widespread use of repression and torture, confirmed that (despite lip service paid to democratic reform) the United States would tolerate any regime, however harsh, which presented itself as fundamentally opposed to communism.

Developments such as these, in response to the Cuban revolution, set the scene for US relations with Central and South America in the 1970s and 1980s. Despite the rhetorical emphasis placed from the mid-1980s on support for democracy, the overriding goal was to prevent at all costs the appearance of another Cuba in the Americas. Sporadic attempts to promote or support reform broke down as old allies reacted with hostility, or new forces threatened too radical a departure from the status quo; in view of its record, it was difficult in any case for the United States to pose in the region as the agent of democracy and progress. In El Salvador and Guatemala, Presidents Reagan and Bush oversaw the brief installation of Christian Democratic regimes without control over unreconstructed military establishments, as part of an ideological campaign against Nicaragua, then acquiesced in the late 1980s in the return to power of the right amidst widespread violations of civil rights, large-scale cancellations of electoral registrations, and direct fraud. As for Nicaragua, the victory of the Sandinistas in 1984 in elections elsewhere regarded as free and fair was dismissed as fraudulent by President Reagan, and a policy of economic sabotage and military pressure was applied, with the intention of forcing the Nicaraguan people to choose between leaders favoured by the US government, or continued suffering imposed by a far more powerful adversary from outside. The defeat of the Sandinistas in the elections of 1990 was in large part a direct result of this pressure.

The United States is indisputably the major external governmental actor in Latin America, but by no means the only major international force. In the international economic orientation of the region, as important a role has been played by transnational corporations. Until the 1950s the major foreign corporations engaged in the region were concerned above all with the exploitation of natural resources, and primarily with minerals. The activities of primary commodity-producing transnationals (generally but not universally of US origin) produced a nationalistic reaction of particular intensity from the 1960s onwards, but at the same time the very governments which were reacting with hostility to those corporations concerned primarily with the extraction of raw materials were actively promoting the entry into their economies of a new wave of transnationals engaged in manufacturing. The result was a weakening of the hold of foreign corporations in the raw materials field, and their replacement with state monopolies or joint ventures of various kinds, and a shift of transnational activity into manufacturing – commonly on the basis of joint ventures either with the state itself or with private companies of indigenous origin. As a result, the issues involved in multinational investment have changed. Concern over the national control of sources and production of raw materials has tended to give way to an increasingly sophisticated process of bargaining with mining and manufacturing transnationals over such issues as investment programmes, rates of profit, levels of taxation, transfer of technology, and access to overseas markets. Access to technology, markets and foreign finance has enabled mining transnationals to accept nationalisation, often in return for generous compensation, but to continue to reap handsome profits from service contracts and other continuing links with their former properties. In recent years the high costs and technological demands of exploitation of new deposits have spawned a new wave of modern foreign-owned corporations in such mining economies as Chile and Peru.

The arrival of the major manufacturing multinationals in the region began in earnest after the Second World War with the arrival of European car manufacturers in Brazil, keen to break the American grip on assembly operations and on imports. Volkswagen was swiftly followed by Ford and General Motors, and over the ensuing three decades manufacturers moved into a number of countries in the region. The major economies of the region were able to play one company and one country off against another, sometimes acquiring commitments to long-term investment and to greater transfer of technology after short periods of in-country production. One consequence was the divergence of the interests of different countries on such issues. In Central America, individual corporations involved in the production of raw materials or agricultural commodities (such as bananas) may still present a substantial obstacle to national sovereignty; in the middle-ranking countries of the region, beset by deep economic crisis, the struggle to attract manufacturing investment may prove an unequal one; for the major emerging industrial powers of the region (Brazil and Mexico) access to foreign technology and investment is a key component in their development strategy. Advanced manufacturing industry in Mexico is still dominated by United States capital, whereas Brazil has attracted investment in fairly comparable proportions from the United States, Europe, and Japan; both Mexico and Brazil have found the goal of national independence an elusive one, as links with multinationals prove a necessary avenue to modern technology and international finance. At the same time, the high levels of capital investment (and foreign exchange spending) required to set up sophisticated modern industries commit them to develop these new industries as exporters and foreign exchange earners, and expose them to the competition of similar producers elsewhere (and the footloose global sourcing policies of the modern multinationals). Dependency, reduced in one area, is created in another. The debt crisis, discussed in the following chapter, was a specific consequence of the pressures generated in the course of the pursuit of development.

In the 1980s all the Latin American countries, their resistance weakened by recession, the outflow of resources following the debt crisis, the resulting crisis of state finances, and the need to boost exports at all costs, came under pressure to liberalise their economies and move public industries into the private sector. Here as elsewhere, though, the prospects for united co-ordinated action were limited by rivalries between competing economies, and divergent attitudes towards the reversal of state-led patterns of development. While Chile and Mexico changed course early and with enthusiasm as a result of changes in the internal balance of forces, change elsewhere was much more hesitant, and largely a consequence of external pressure or deep internal crisis. The cases of Argentina, Brazil, and Mexico are contrasted in the following chapter.

The difficulties caused for economic co-operation at the regional level by uneven industrialisation and divergent economic strategies are apparent in the role of regional and international organisations in the area. On economic issues, the most significant venture has been the creation of the Andean Common Market (or Andean Pact), set up under the Cartagena agreement of 1969. However, anticipated economic integration failed to materialise, as each of the participating countries entered long lists of exceptions and protected lines of production, greatly weakening the impact of general plans for reduced tariff barriers. Secondly, the apparent virtual unanimity of the early 1970s over the issue of strict national control over foreign investment disappeared, leaving the organisation in ruins. A decision was taken in 1971 that all member countries would adhere to a set of common practices – the most important of which related to maximum rates of profit repatriation, and protection of particular areas of production for national or joint ventures, or mandatory movement towards joint venture status – but as economic circumstances and governments changed, regional solidarity on the issue dissolved. Chile and Colombia broke with the organisation over Decision 24 (the foreign investment code of practice). Interstate rivalry, divergent economic policies, and anxiety to offer attractive terms to foreign investment precluded any consistent concerted action to establish better bargaining positions in relation to inward investment. The distinction between national and foreign capital is not so significant to policy-makers in these capitalist-oriented economies as the imperatives of global capitalist competition. National capital increasingly adopts the character of foreign capital and seeks links with it, with the result that transnationals embed themselves deeply into the national economy, reshaping it in their own image. As a result, the whole economy – rather than simply that part of it directly controlled by foreign capital – becomes internationalised. In the 1990s, the response to this situation was to seek once more to create larger economic groupings. However, it appeared that these would be competitive within the region rather than co-operative: the creation of Mercosur in 1991, bringing Argentina, Brazil, Paraguay and Uruguay together in a bid to create a common market by 1995 was followed in 1992 by Mexico's negotiation of entry into NAFTA, the North American Free Trade Area, along with Canada and the United States.

On broader international diplomatic issues, however, greater unity and a degree of separation from US interests has been achieved. One forum in which this has been clear has been the Organisation of American States (OAS), founded in 1948 and soon

enlisted by the United States into its global Cold War effort. For the
first two decades of its existence it proved to be highly subservient
to the United States, expelling Cuba after the revolution, for
example, and endorsing the invasion of Guatemala in 1954 and
that of the Dominican Republic in 1965. But in the 1970s Mexico's
long-standing independent foreign policy began to gather support
in the region, particularly as Brazil (committed to an independent
foreign policy from 1960) began to develop its links with Black
Africa. The first sign that a major shift had occurred came in 1979,
when the United States was unable to win support at the OAS for a
regional policy of hostility to the Sandinista regime in Nicaragua;
the subsequent emergence of the Contadora Group of Latin
American countries (led by Mexico and Venezuela and committed
to finding a peaceful solution to the Central American situation)
confirmed the United States' weakened diplomatic power. A second
came in the following decade, with the formation of an intra-
regional political grouping from which the United States was
excluded: in December 1986, Argentina, Brazil, Colombia, Mexico, Panama, Peru, Uruguay and Venezuela came together to form
the 'Group of Eight', re-named the 'Rio Group' after Chile,
Ecuador, Bolivia and Paraguay joined in October 1990 [Hurrell,
1992].

Over the 1970s and 1980s, then, economic interests diverged
sufficiently to make united action difficult, while the growing power
of states in the region reduced the historic predominance of the
United States. The evidence of the reorientation of the OAS, the
activity of the Contadora Group, and the emergence of the Rio
Group suggests that Latin America is beginning to find a voice of
its own; but the United States remains the major obstacle to the
establishment of an authoritative and independent regional perspective.

5. The Middle East: From the Cold War to the Kuwait Crisis

Analysing the international context of Middle Eastern politics
requires attention to three interrelated levels: the dynamics of
domestic politics and foreign policy; interstate politics; and the
struggle for global hegemony. The pivotal position of the Middle
East in oil production, the extent of reserves, the proximity of the

area to the Soviet Union and the volatility of interstate relations consequent on the disintegration of empires have produced a combustible combination of geological, geographic and historical features. In the twentieth century, these have been transmuted into material and perceived strategic interests in the pursuit of which powers external to the region have intervened extensively and as a result of which countless Middle Easterners have been killed.

In the past, the Western powers have sent crusaders and colonial armies. In more recent times, to ensure access to oil supplies the United States established a Rapid Deployment Force, renamed US Central Command in 1983, which became the core of the United Nations coalition force which drove Iraq from Kuwait in 1991. Imperial Russia and the Soviet successor state also sought to exert influence in a region on which it abuts. In turn, the West has been keen to contain Russia's influence in the area: in the nineteenth century by supporting the Ottoman Empire and, in the twentieth, by building regional alliance systems and backing regional allies.

In the contemporary period, tension and conflict between states in the region have facilitated the search by external powers for influence and allies, and marginalised the co-operative and mediatory potential of regional institutions like the Arab League and the Islamic Organisation Conference. The Arab–Israeli conflict and the Palestinian problem, and the tension between conservative monarchical and radical republican regimes in the 1950s and 1960s and between radical Islamic and conservative and secular ones in the 1980s, have resulted in Middle Eastern states relying on Eastern and Western Europe for arms and security. The alignment of states with different superpowers has been a further source of interstate tensions. Despite such external dependence, the area has been marked by fluidity in foreign alignments and some dramatic realignments.

After the Second World War France and Britain sought to defend their remaining economic and military interests against the rising nationalist tide. European reaction to nationalist regimes, symbolised in the British, French and Israeli invasion at Suez in 1956, undermined the Western policy of containing the Soviet Union. This was to be achieved through US-sponsored military pacts with the Northern Tier (Turkey, Pakistan and Iran), underlaid by the British-sponsored Baghdad pact with the Arab states, targeted at the Soviet Union's 'soft under-belly', but hostility between the

European powers and Arab nationalists opened the door to Soviet influence. In the jargon of the time, the Soviet Union had 'leapfrogged' the encirclement, but at the request of the states of the area. In the process, the Soviet Union became identified as a supporter of republican Arab nationalism, and of the Arab side in the Arab–Israeli conflict. The increased links between the Soviet Union and radical nationalism encouraged the more conservative Arab monarchies and Iran to seek stronger ties with the West, as it encouraged the United States to bolster Israel with economic and military aid.

Although the United States was able to support Israel (on the basis of a shared opposition to radical Arab nationalism) and the conservative Arab oil-producing states (on the basis of anti-communism), there were tensions with the latter because of US support for Israel. The global strategy of opposing communism and the Soviet Union confronted particular problems in the Arab Middle East: Arab states co-operating with the US were indirectly linked to Israel. Given that access to and security of oil was a central tenet of US foreign policy, balancing links to oil-producers with support for Israel proved problematic. The USSR had problems with the Arab nationalist states: it had recognised Israel's right to exist in 1948 and never withdrew recognition within the 1948 boundaries. A further constraining factor on deepening Soviet influence was the popular identification of the USSR as atheistic and anti-Islamic.

Despite such tensions, the superpowers supported their regional allies in the 1967 and 1973 wars, both of which threatened to embroil them directly in the conflict and transform a Middle East conflict into a global one. Ironically, the only way the superpowers could maintain a position to compete with each other was through the provision of military aid which, in turn, enhanced the ability of the states to act independently of them.

The 1967 war had two contradictory consequences. The fear of global confrontation led to a form of detente between the United States and the USSR and a freezing of the post-war status quo. Israel's victory, however, resulted in the occupation of Arab territory and created a group of states, aligned with the USSR, which opposed the post-1967 status quo. Egypt and Syria launched the 1973 war to draw the superpowers into the Arab–Israeli conflict, giving them no choice but to support their regional allies.

Developments during and after the 1973 war demonstrate two points made earlier. Firstly, the alignment of states in the region with any particular superpower was not fixed. Desperate to recover territory, Egypt turned to the US to secure Israel's withdrawal from its occupied territory. The United States government took the opportunity to take Egypt out of the Soviet orbit and ultimately out of the conflict with Israel. The Camp David Accords of 1978 and the Egypt–Israel Treaty of 1979, mediated by the USA, brought together the two strongest protagonists in the Arab–Israeli conflict. Indicative of the importance of the region, by the mid-1980s Israel and Egypt were the two biggest recipients of US military and economic aid.

Secondly, the relationship between the conservative oil-producing states and the US had become replete with tensions. Despite the fact that oil came largely from the Arab states, it was not until 1973 that US support for Israel affected US access to oil: an oil embargo was linked to Israeli withdrawal. The main producers of the 1950s and 1960s were non-Arab Iran, states under British protection like Kuwait and Bahrein, or states like Saudi Arabia whose major foreign policy goal was to prevent the radical republicanism of Nasser spreading to the Arabian Peninsula. The only real divergence of interests between the Arab oil-producing states and the United States concerned the role of the US in the Arab–Israeli conflict. Otherwise, they were agreed on combating communism, the influence of the Soviet Union and nationalist states aligned with the Soviet Union. The succession of President Sadat in 1970, his shift toward the West and his expulsion of Soviet advisers brought the 1973 oil embargo as a *quid pro quo* from the conservative oil-producing states, at a time when the changing relationship between demand and supply facilitated the politicisation of oil. The United States dependence on oil imports after 1970 heightened the sense of crisis and contradiction. The United States and Saudi Arabia had a vested interest in ending the major issue between them: the lack of a solution to the Arab–Israeli conflict and the Palestinian problem.

Events in and around the region, however, played into the hands of the United States toward the end of the decade, as the issue of Gulf security replaced the Arab–Israeli–Palestinian conflict as a key security concern. In 1979, the Soviet Union invaded Afghanistan at the request of a government which had come to power through a coup; in 1979, the Shah of Iran was replaced by an Islamic government, and in 1980 Iran and Iraq went to war. Fearful of a threat from an Islamic regime which was 'anti-imperialist', anti-monarchist and favoured the 'oppressed and the downtrodden', the Saudi government turned to the United States for the weaponry and support systems to withstand the Iranian challenge and the possible spill-over of the Iraq–Iran war. A regional conflict again provided the US with the opportunity to reconsolidate an influence over Saudi Arabia and marginalise the issue of US support for Israel. Although the fall of the Shah removed the local guardian of Western interests in the Gulf, the threat from the new regime in Iran allowed for a greater direct US role, albeit covert in nature. Advanced Warning Aircraft (AWACs) were supplied to Saudi Arabia under contract terms which made them wholly dependent on US personnel for their operation and maintenance.

While the Gulf states rejected American military bases and emphasised that the Palestinian problem and the Israeli enemy were major concerns, the United States government pressed a policy of 'strategic consensus': the USSR was the major threat to regional stability and the supply of oil. With the exception of Oman, the states of the area did not accept this image of an aggressive, expansionist Soviet state threatening the 'free movement of Middle Eastern oil', as expounded in the Carter Doctrine of 1980. Yet the very weakness of the sparsely populated and politically under-developed states of the Gulf precluded a capacity for self-defence against larger regional states, be it Israel, Iran or Iraq. This regional imbalance facilitated the growth of US power, the Israeli connection notwithstanding, but it required developing a capacity to project large-scale forces into the Gulf. Because of continuing resistance to US bases, the US established an 'over the horizon presence', building up Diego Garcia in the Indian ocean as a staging post, establishing pre-positioned supplies in Oman and undertaking joint military exercises with the Egyptian army. The provision of arms and aircraft to Saudi Arabia, and US involvement in developing the command and control infrastructure, gave the US what might be called 'quasi-bases' for the future. These develop-ments produced a partial solution to the US dilemma after the fall of the Shah: how to protect an overwhelming interest in the supply of oil from an area six thousand miles from its eastern seaboard in the face of a reluctance of key states in that area to provide bases because of domestic political repercussions. The 'over the horizon' presence and the development of the Rapid Deployment Force, later the Central Command under General Schwarzkopf, prepared the ground for the largest military intervention the Middle East has seen, and the largest troop movements outside of a world war. Again, a regional conflict produced the spark, underpinned by the complex interrelationship between regime, region and international factors.

The Kuwait crisis of 1990–1 had multiple roots: the Iraq–Iran war, the inability of the Gulf states to protect themselves against the stronger states at the head of the Gulf, tensions between oil-producing states over the supply and pricing of oil, and the provision of arms to one of the stronger Gulf states as a foreign policy instrument because of the political problems of direct intervention by the Western powers. Although issues of principle were at stake (a strong state occupying a weak state), the scale of the intervention can only be linked to the oil of the Gulf, the threat to Saudi Arabia, pivotal oil-producer, and the need to guarantee the rule of the House of Saud, whose oil-production policies had so favoured the Western economies during the 1980s.

As Iran had played a surrogate role for the West in containing radical Arab nationalism, during the Iraq–Iran war Iraq became a surrogate for regional and international powers opposed to the Islamic republic. Saudi Arabia and Kuwait were the principal financiers of Iraq and the bulk of the technology and arms in the later phases of the war came from the West. When the war ended the Iraqi government was in debt, had a great deal of reconstruction work to undertake, and had given priority to a military industrialisation and nuclear programme. The funding for these projects was based on income from oil, the allocation of which had been an important factor in legitimating its strict authoritarianism, and external credits, most of which came from states which eventually fought against Iraq. In the period preceding the Iraqi invasion Kuwait refused to forgive the Iraqi loans and cede control of two islands at the head of the Gulf (strategically placed to develop a capacity for exporting oil more distant from its border with Iran). Kuwait also rejected Iraq's claim to the Rumeila oil field and exceeded its production quota, thereby reducing the world price of oil and reducing Iraqi revenues. In response, Iraq threatened invasion, and then invaded. The invasion of Kuwait signified the occupation of a pro-western oil state by a regional state that was not amenable to control, and the removal of a buffer between that state and Saudi Arabia, the latter having the most accessible oil reserves in the world. As the Iranian revolution had provided an opportunity for the US, so the Iraqi invasion in 1990 delivered to the US what it had long desired: a request by Gulf states for a direct US presence. The participation of Egyptian and Syrian forces, particularly the latter, went some way to legitimating the attack on Iraq as more than a western intervention to protect oil interests. At the same time, the imperative of maintaining the US-led coalition's unity was an important factor in not delaying the decision to go to war against Iraq. The most important international development facilitating the political and military response to the Iraqi invasion was the decline of the Soviet Union as a world power. This was also to prove an important factor in shaping post-war developments. The lack of alternative superpower support for Iraq and the unexpected participation of Syria, previously dependent on Soviet diplomatic, military and economic aid, were direct results of Soviet decline.

The expulsion of Iraqi forces and the restoration of Kuwait, however, raised further problems. In the first place, the weakening of the Baghdad regime brought about uprisings in southern and northern Iraq and a further western intervention in the north to protect the Kurdish population in 'safe havens'. Such restrictions on the power of Iraqi central government brought to the fore general international concern over setting a precedent for limiting the sovereignty of Third World states and particular concern over the potential effects on the Kurdish population of Turkey, a NATO member and important participant in both the imposition of sanctions against, and the air attack on, Iraq. The uprisings in Iraq trapped the leaders of the coalition in a dilemma: a desire to remove the Iraqi leader without threatening the territorial integrity of Iraq and opening the door to a spill-over of Kurdish nationalism and an expansion of Iranian influence or control in southern Iraq. While the former had repercussions for Turkey, the latter was considered likely to threaten the Gulf states and Saudi Arabia. Although the intervention against Iraq eventually restored Kuwait as an independent state, it did nothing to establish a stable order in this important oil-producing region.

In the aftermath of the war, President Bush sought to deal with two other issues contributory to the political volatility of the Middle

East: the level of arms flowing into the region and the Palestine problem. In spite of speeches about the necessity to reduce and control arms supplies to the Gulf, it was not long before arms started pouring into the area again, fuelled by the US budget deficit and Saudi Arabian money. The US could not prevent arms flows from Russia and China, and in 1991 it supplied US$16 billion in arms to Saudi Arabia. Egypt and Israel received respectively arms worth US$ 3 billion and US$2.5 billion, also supplied by the United States.

As to the question of occupied Palestine, the linkage made by Saddam Husayn between Gulf security and the Palestine question by his missile attacks on Israel resulted in a renewed initiative by the United States to deal with the problem. Although the United States brought Palestinian and Israeli negotiators together in a series of meetings beginning at Madrid in 1991, it followed principles outlined at the Camp David meeting and confirmed in the Reagan plan, and similar to those of the Israeli government: no Palestinian state and no PLO representation. If such a framework were retained it was likely that the Palestine question would remain a source of instability.

The decline and break-up of the Soviet Union also had an impact on the broader Arab–Israeli conflict. We have mentioned the participation of Syrian forces in the Kuwait crisis. One consequence of this was Syria's attendance at the Madrid conference, where, for the first time, Syrians and Israelis negotiated together. The demise of the Soviet Union also had an impact on US–Israeli relations. Israel was unlikely to be the strategic ally of United States in the post-Cold War period. In the absence of a perceived communist threat, access to oil, and a diplomatic and military strategy to ensure that, would remain pivotal. The utility of Israel in the Gulf, foreshadowed in western pressure on Israel not to respond to Iraqi missile attacks, was likely to be marginal.

Predicting the future of the Middle East is a risky business. The past interventions and alignments of the superpowers have rarely secured their interests in the long term. Neither superpower has been able effectively to control its allies in the area and external alignment has been an important ingredient, along with continuing authoritarian rule, in mobilising opposition. Supplying arms secures influence for superpowers, but within circumscribed limits. It has rarely secured control over their use, and in times of war the superpowers have always resupplied their allies.

One result of the strategic and economic importance of the Middle East, allied with its oil-based purchasing power, has been the very large-scale military expenditure by the governments of the region. In terms of world military spending per capita, six of the top seven states are in the Middle East. Between 1962 and 1980 spending increased from $4.7 billion to $46.7 billion [Stork and Paul, 1983]. Fuelled by the Arab–Israeli conflict and the Shah of Iran's megalomania, and funded by the superpowers and oil wealth, the Middle East became one of the most heavily armed areas of the world. In Latin America, military expenditure is 6.9% of central government expenditure; in the Middle East it is 30.1%. Oil wealth not only buys arms, it buys armies. The costs of removing Iraq from the Saudi border and Kuwait were paid by the Gulf states. These levels of expenditure are a drain on resources. The result is highly dangerous in an area where volatile interstate relations are linked to interests identified by the external powers as vital. The Iraqi invasion of Kuwait and the response of the West underlined the continuing development of the Middle East, and the Gulf area in particular, as a politico–military powderkeg. First Iran then Iraq have been built up as the regional power, then smashed as they have run out of control. The US pursuit of a balance of power in the region has induced imbalances of power regionally in pursuit of short-term advantage, at the price of longer-term instability. In the wake of the Gulf War its hopes rested on Saudi Arabia, but the latter's political stability and pro-Western stance could not be guaranteed for ever.

6. Conclusion

Latin America has been subject to more external intervention than Africa, but because it has had the dubious privilege of being the preserve of a single power, the United States, this has not given rise to the large-scale confrontations, arms races and wars that have characterised East and Southeast Asia, the Middle East, and parts of Africa. The Middle East – because of its oil, strategic importance and religion – has become the cockpit of international competition, while divisions in East Asia along Cold War lines, and the merging of colonial wars of liberation, US imperialism and superpower confrontation in Southeast Asia, have made that region the site of persistent conflict since the Second World War.

Despite these differences in character and degree of external intervention, all four regions examined here have been deeply affected by the global confrontation between superpowers (importantly, including China). Even so, outside the special cases of Taiwan and the two Koreas, neither regions nor individual countries have been unchanging in their allegiances. African states differed widely in their external alignments and, except towards South Africa, did not share a common foreign policy. Their governments wished to assert their independence from outside control. Marxist-led Angola allowed an American multinational company to extract its oil and neither Angola nor Ethiopia (also under Marxist rule) would allow the Soviet Union to establish a military base on its soil, though the French were given this right by several African Francophone countries. In Southeast Asia, Indonesia has combined a pro-Western stance under Suharto with a refusal to tolerate bases on its own soil, and a reluctance to see superpower involvement in the region, while in the Philippines nationalist opposition, combined with changed US priorities, has seen the closure of US bases. In the Middle East, Saudi Arabia and the Gulf states turned to the United States to withstand the radical challenge from Iran, but refused to accept American military bases in their territories. Again, the Soviet Union was unable to prevent Egypt and Syria from going to war against Israel in 1967 and 1973. In Latin America, Cuba and Nicaragua have been the most prominent examples of states seeking a path of development in defiance of US preferences, and there has been a distinct shift towards regional independence, reflected in the refusal of the OAS to support the US position on Nicaragua, and the formation of the Rio Group as an independent grouping of Latin American states.

On economic issues, the picture is just as varied, and differences within and between regions have made co-operation difficult. There is a world of difference between the rich oil-states of the Middle East and the impoverished famine-stricken countries in the Horn of Africa, and between each of these groups of countries and the newly industrialising states of East Asia and Latin America. In Africa, the fact that a small number of states have oil and others have not has increased the differences in their levels of development. Uneven development – caused in Latin America by the extent of industrialisation which the various states have achieved – impedes effective political and economic co-operation at regional level. In Southeast Asia, competition between states for inward investment and differing orientations towards macro-economic policy have severely limited the prospects for economic co-operation within ASEAN. For similar reasons, the oil producers of the Middle East have not been able to sustain a common front on pricing and production policy. In West and southern Africa, too, economic nationalism has impeded sub-regional co-operation. In none of the four regions has the regionwide organisation – the OAU in Africa, ASEAN in Southeast Asia, the OAS in Latin America, and the Arab League in the Middle East – been a particularly effective body. Nonetheless, there have been some advances. In the Middle East the main expansion of Arab League activities has been in specialised functional areas like law, health, education and culture; in Africa, the OAU has served as a forum for the exchange of views between African leaders, and has shown most unanimity in its attitude towards South Africa; in Southeast Asia ASEAN has survived after a very tentative start, and has been most constructive and effective in international diplomacy related to the Cambodian situation; and in Latin America, the OAS was used by the United States as an instrument to further its own foreign policy until (in recent years) Brazil and Mexico emerged as industrial powers capable of challenging US dominance, and a general reaction took place against US dictation over Central America.

In the sphere of political unification, the results have been rather disappointing. The union between Egypt and Syria (leading to the formation of the UAR) foundered, as did the union in West Africa between Senegal and the (French) Soudan to form the Mali Federation. However, United Arab Emirates survives as a successful confederation of tribal societies in the lower Gulf, based on oil wealth. In Africa, the 1964 union between Tanganyika and the tiny state of Zanzibar has survived as the United Republic of Tanzania, if sometimes precariously; a number of other unions – such as that between Southern (British) Cameroons and the Republic of Cameroon in 1961 – have also survived, though the 1960 union between British and Italian Somaliland to form the Republic of Somalia has collapsed. In East Asia, the consequence of internal revolutions and Cold War politics has been the division of existing states, rather than the unification of separate entities, while in Southeast Asia the creation of larger unions, as in the Malaysian case or with Indonesian expansionism in the period of *confrontasi*, have led to tensions within the region. Particular attempts at aggrandisement have led either to partial failure, as with the departure of Singapore from the Malaysian Federation, or to the imposition of a brutal and genocidal regime of armed occupation and permanent repression, as with the Indonesian invasion of East Timor in 1975.

As to sub-regional functional associations, probably the best results have again been achieved in Africa: EACSO and its successor the East African Community (EAC) provided for many years (until the EAC finally collapsed in 1977) a wide range of common services between Kenya, Tanzania and Uganda, the member states. ECOWAS in West Africa and SADCC in southern Africa are more recent functional associations of considerable potential influence; a number of smaller groupings, such as the six-state Francophone CEAO, have already proved their worth. In Latin America, uneven industrialisation has worked against sub-regional economic co-operation, as the history of the Andean Group shows: it proved impossible to agree on reduced tariff barriers or the extent of national control over foreign investment. The recent linking of Argentina, Brazil, Paraguay and Uruguay in Mercosur suggests that economic co-operation may be possible at a sub-regional level. In the Middle East, the Gulf Co-operation Council emphasises economic co-operation between its (Gulf) member states, but is more political than economic. Functional co-operation elsewhere has been hampered by differences in foreign alignment and regime ideology. In addition, the temptation for individual countries to break ranks and tie themselves to developed country blocs, most recently exemplified in Mexico's negotiation of entry into NAFTA, tends to weaken regional co-operation among developing countries themselves.

As the period of Cold War confrontation draws to a close in the early 1990s, the issue of intervention is taking on a new face: the threat to the political and economic sovereignty of Third World states arising from the impact of global recession and an emerging pattern of supra-national intervention motivated by security, economic, and even humanitarian concerns. In the Gulf War, as in Panama on a much smaller scale, the United States intervened to chastise a regime it had previously encouraged and materially supported. But if Panama was an 'old-style' intervention, the Gulf coalition was new in the sense that it was formally constructed under the auspices of the United Nations. Successive interventions in the former Yugoslavia and in Somalia, along with the UN effort to oversee a peaceful settlement in Cambodia, suggest that international organisations may come to play a larger part in international disputes than they have in the past. As yet, such efforts have largely provided diplomatic cover for joint action by the advanced Western states, led by the United States. But the growing unrest in the Islamic world in 1992 over the scant protection given to the Muslim population of Serbia, in contrast to the massive effort mounted in defence of oil-rich Kuwait, pointed to tensions within the emerging 'New World Order'. In the following chapter we examine four aspects of international political economy which highlight issues of state capacity and national sovereignty.

Further Reading

For Africa, Harbeson and Rothchild [1991] provides a contemporary overview, and Mayall [1992] offers a concise survey of the period since independence. Amate [1986] explores the workings of the OAU, and Onwuka and Sesay [1985] offers a good collection on regional issues. Hazlewood [1979] explores the earlier failure of the East African Community. Anglin [1985] is a case study of SADCC, and Chan [1990] examines the impact of South African diplomacy in the region in the 1980s. For East and Southeast Asia Broinowski [1990] examines the workings of ASEAN in relation to a wide range of issues; its role in regional security is also examined in Simon [1987] and Liefer [1988]. Stargardt [1989] is an illuminating account of the development of a regional system in the immediate post-war period. For Latin America, Pearce [1981] is an accessible brief overview of the US role in the region. Two monographs by Schoultz [1981, 1987] explore US policy in relation to human rights and national security respectively. Atkins [1989] gives more detail on the role of the region in the international system. Hurrell [1992] examines the prospects for regional solidarity in the early 1990s; the prospects for economic integration may be further explored in Gitli and Ryd [1992]. Rabe [1990) examines the immediate post-war period in the context of Cold War anticommunism in the region.

For the Middle East, Kerr [1971] surveys the impact of the Cold War, and Tillman [1982] examines the role of the United States. The militarisation of the region is examined in Stork and Paul [1983], and Middle East Research and Information Project [1992b].

8

The Third World in the Global Economy

1. Introduction

The history of the Third World is to a large extent the history of its incorporation into a global economy dominated by Western Europe, the United States, and Japan. In their colonies, the imperial powers imposed taxes, deprived indigenous farmers of land, and sought to stimulate new 'needs' by introducing consumer goods, all in an effort to raise revenues and force local populations into providing labour for commercial farming and export-oriented production. In time the process of incorporation became largely self-propelled as new local élites sought to extend and deepen the process of development, and opportunities for survival entirely outside the market economy were eroded. In the twentieth century, mineral or agricultural export-based orientation began to give way to industrialisation, first in Latin America, then in East and Southeast Asia in particular. In the 1970s and 1980s dramatic global trends combined with particular regional situations to produce quite varied outcomes in the areas of the Third World we consider.

Since the United States, still the largest economy in the world, slipped from trade surplus to deficit in the later 1960s, the global capitalist economy has been increasingly unstable. The economies of East and Southeast Asia, tied more closely to the far more dynamic Japanese economy and less open to penetration from

Europe and the United States, responded to the declining competitiveness of these latter markets by embarking on a highly successful policy of export-led industrialisation. The larger oil producers, mostly in the Middle East, adopted a different strategy, which reinforced their dependence on primary commodity exports. In response to global inflation sparked off by the devaluation of the US dollar against gold, they forced the price of oil up by agreement among themselves. This strategy gave a massive twist to the destabilising forces already at work, unleashing the cycle of debt-based boom and bust in Latin America, dragging Europe and the United States into recession, and delivering a fatal blow to the relatively fragile economies of Africa. In the ensuing maelstrom the gains made by many of the most industrialised oil producers themselves were swept away, Africa's per capita income fell by as much as a quarter, and Latin America's hitherto modestly successful post-war growth came to a crashing halt. In the meantime, the economies of East and Southeast Asia continued to grow, reflecting the shift of economic power that was taking place from the Atlantic to the Pacific, and the advantage they derived from their relative insulation from the storms that were lashing the 'Western' capitalist world. Each region, therefore, had a different story to tell. We make no attempt to give a full account here. Rather, we focus on specific issues which illuminate some of the internal dynamics of each regional experience, and draw out their political implications.

For Africa, we focus on the recurrent famines of the last two decades. Throughout much of the Third World malnutrition and starvation affect substantial groups of the population. In part this results from population growth and pressure on resources and the environment over time, leading to situations in which natural disasters such as drought or flood can bring tragic consequences where the margin of survival is precarious. It also results from the impact upon domestic food production and consumption of the shift of resources into export crops and industry, and from international and national income distribution patterns which deny to hundreds of millions of people the ability to command an adequate diet. A further significant cause is the disruption to patterns of settlement, production and trade arising from war, and particularly from protracted civil wars which cause widespread displacement of peoples and disruption to existing patterns of exchange. In other words, the occurrence of famine is as much a consequence of local and global social conflict and political economy as it is of 'natural' disasters.

For the Middle East, we focus on the oil price-rises of the 1970s, and their effects for the oil producers themselves. Oil is the natural resource which fuels the global economy of energy-intensive consumption. After decades in which Western companies extracted it from production sites around the world with minimal benefit for the states and populations on whose territory significant deposits were found, a process of nationalist reaction led to the founding in 1960 of OPEC (Organisation of Petroleum Exporting Countries), increased local capture of revenues and control, and successive sharp price rises for crude oil in 1973 and 1979, intended to force a permanent shift in the terms of trade between oil producers and their customers. At first sight the oil price-rises of the 1970s seemed to represent a victory for primary commodity producers over their historically more powerful industrial customers. They seemed to overturn a pattern within which exporters of primary commodities were the victims of foreign control of production or marketing, and low returns to their national economies. But the temporary (albeit spectacular) gains of the oil states reinforced their nature as mono-dependent primary exporters, while the impact of the price rises on the international economy into which the producers were locked eventually had various negative consequences for the oil producers themselves. In addition, of course, many other Third World countries dependent on oil imports found themselves badly hurt by the rapidly rising price of oil, and the cycle of inflation and global recession to which it gave rise.

For Latin America, we examine the 'debt crisis', tracing its origins to the effects of the rises in oil prices on financial markets and on world trade. The debt crisis was largely though not exclusively a Latin American phenomenon, with Argentina, Brazil and Mexico, the three largest Latin American economies, accounting between them for the bulk of the commercial lending which spiralled from 1973 onwards as the huge reserves accruing to non-industrial Middle Eastern oil producers were placed on deposit in Europe and the United States. In the decade after the Mexican default of 1982 which brought the gathering debt problem to the centre of the international stage, these three leading debtors have moved, from a situation of deep economic crisis, to liberalise their economies and privatise large parts of previously state-owned industry. We examine the cases of Brazil and Mexico, the two largest debtors.

Finally, for East and Southeast Asia, where substantial economic growth has continued throughout this troubled period, we examine the destructive impact of this economic growth upon the local environment, an aspect of the process which tells us a great deal about the character and dynamics of the model of export-led industrialisation. The trail of destruction we document runs across the spectrum from the exploitation of primeval forest to modern heavy industry and nuclear power. At one extreme the vast forests of Kalimantan (Borneo) in Indonesia are disappearing as a result of internal migration, the large-scale industrial exploitation of forest products, and the resulting pressures upon shifting cultivators previously able to survive in the forest on a sustainable basis; at the other the river systems and urban environments of Taiwan and South Korea are being poisoned as a consequence of sustained rapid industrialisation without adequate environmental controls. The process of environmental destruction is not unique to East and Southeast Asia. However, it can be argued that it is an intrinsic feature of the dominant pattern of development in the region. The priority given to rapid growth has bred a relative lack of concern for environmental consequences; the emphasis upon export earnings has prompted the wholesale despoliation of existing natural resources; the willingness to acquire industrial capacity from all available sources has led to a willingness to import 'dirty' production processes excluded as a result of environmental pressures elsewhere; and, ironically, the sustained success in achieving continued growth has meant that the process of destruction has continued relentlessly, on a number of fronts, over a considerable period of time. Elements of the same syndrome can easily be identified elsewhere: the reckless destruction of the Brazilian Amazon; the high levels of pollution in the major industrial cities of both Brazil and Mexico; and the deliberate exporting south over the border into Mexico of environmentally harmful industries no longer welcome in pollution-ridden California. However, they come together in East and Southeast Asia in a particularly comprehensive way, and with an intensive rhythm which shows no sign of abating. Furthermore, they come as a consequence of developmental policies which are clearly imposed from within, rather than in response to external pressures.

2. Famine in Africa

There is no general shortage of food in the world. Nor is there an overall shortage in many Third World countries which experience chronic problems of malnutrition on a massive scale. Brazil, for example, is a major food exporter, yet between 25 and 30 per cent of its population suffers from malnutrition; this was also true of Zimbabwe prior to the severe drought afflicting southern Africa in 1991–2. Nor is it the shift from subsistence production to commercial agriculture and exports alone which leads to malnutrition – and, in severe cases, to famine – in the Third World. In the short term, it is the combination of this shift with highly unequal distribution of income which leads to hunger on a massive scale. Cuba, for instance, is heavily dependent upon imported food, but its distributional policies have eliminated hunger and malnutrition [Benjamin and Collins, 1985]. Dependence upon imported food, in combination with an inability to buy it on the part of substantial proportions of the population, creates a 'silent famine' of persistent malnutrition throughout large parts of the Third World. And where access to food is precarious, 'natural disasters' such as drought or flood or a plague of locusts, exacerbated by 'man-made disasters' such as civil war, can rapidly lead to crisis as small farmers without reserves lose their crops and animals, or labourers fail to find work and are therefore unable to afford food.

Crises of this kind have ravaged Africa since the late 1960s. In 1968–73 drought severely affected countries in the Sahel, the area stretching from Senegal in the west along the southern edge of the Saharan desert to Ethiopia and Sudan in the east. In 1983–5 drought was again widespread: it was centred in Sudan and Ethiopia, but extended also to Somalia, Mozambique and Botswana. In 1991–2 severe drought struck strife-torn Somalia and the whole of southern Africa. Drought is a historical phenomenon in Africa and most affected countries have learned to cope with one or two seasons of drought – as Botswana, for example, has done repeatedly and successfully [Holm and Morgan, 1985]. It is persistent drought, coupled with several other factors, which accounts for widespread famine – famine which resulted in the death of an estimated half-a-million people in 1983–5 and which put at serious risk some 18 million of the 130 million people affected in 1992.

Given the fact, noted above, that there is sufficient global food production to feed the world's population, the problem of hunger is as much one of distribution as of agricultural production. Nevertheless, production is important, particularly in view of the fact that from the 1970s the African population increased at a faster rate than food was produced. Drought conditions in many parts of Africa in the 1980s and early 1990s made it impossible to reverse this trend.

A historical perspective is essential. One of the constant features of colonial policy in Africa (as elsewhere) was to undermine the self-sufficiency of the indigenous population. Revenues had to be raised so that the administration of the colony should not be a drain on the resources of the metropolis. And beyond that, labour had to be forced or tempted into the mines or on to the farms of settlers, or into types of indigenous production that could be traded for profit. In short, the incorporation of African economies into national and international markets eroded self-sufficient peasant production. Take the case of Southern Rhodesia (now Zimbabwe). In the early years of the twentieth century, over 90 per cent of marketed food came from independent Shona producers. They were subject to increasingly onerous taxes but preferred farming on their own account to migrant labour. After 1908, however, a series of measures was taken to weaken African farming and to provide opportunities for white settlers. African farmers were forced off good land and denied access to remunerative markets; they eked out a precarious existence on overcrowded reserves. Many served as labourers on white settler farms, while others migrated to South Africa to work in the mines. By the end of the 1930s 'the agricultural economy of the Shona and the Ndebele, like that of the Kikuyu and most southern African peoples, had been destroyed' [Palmer, 1977: 243].

Even where the need to favour settler agriculture or mining operations did not lead to policies aimed at undermining African agriculture, the imposition of taxes and the extension of cash-crop farming could weaken the ability of the peasantry to survive. In Nigeria, for example, where white settler agriculture was never allowed to develop, the spread of cash-cropping in northern Hausaland (partly in response to the need to make tax payments), along with the weakening of the bonds of social responsibility between local rulers and their peoples, led to the undermining of 'precautionary mechanisms' such as the keeping of common foodstocks. As land was taken out of diversified food production and put under groundnuts and cotton, dependence on the market increased, leading to the 'atrophy of the defences of the poor' [Apeldoorn, 1981: Chs 8–11]. What happened in Nigeria was replicated throughout the African continent.

Policies which weakened the ability of populations to respond to crises of drought or famine were often pursued after colonial rule had given way to independence. Food production declined, while cash-crop farming was stepped up – it was undertaken by peasant farmers producing (for example) cocoa in Ghana, cloves in Zanzibar and coffee in the Côte d'Ivoire or by estate managers growing coffee in Angola and tea and tobacco in Malawi. After independence in 1964, President Banda's government adopted certain colonial-type measures which aimed to develop the estate sector of the economy [Vail, 1983]. Unfortunately, while cash-crop and plantation agriculture contributed to economic growth, they often did not benefit the poorer members of the farming community who had nothing to offer except their labour.

In the post-independence period, agricultural output in Africa has declined. A World Bank study published in 1981 attributed it to five complementary trends: a declining growth rate of agricultural production overall, bringing it below the rate of population growth in the 1970s; stagnant agricultural exports and a decline in the African share of world trade for many commodities; stagnant per capita food production in the 1960s, falling in the 1970s; commercial imports of grains rising at more than three times the rate of population increase; and, as a consequence of all these developments and a change in consumption habits, an increase in the overall level of food dependency [World Bank, 1981: 45]. These trends have been accelerated in the subsequent period: in mid-1992 the FAO estimated that some 10 million tonnes of food would have to be imported to meet Africa's needs, thus imposing a heavy burden on the foreign exchange reserves of fragile state economies. Many reasons have been given to account for the poor performance of African agriculture. They include: the preference of certain governments – for example, those of Mozambique, Nigeria and Zambia at various times – for huge, highly capitalised schemes which ultimately proved unsuccessful; the persistence on ideological grounds with rural experiments, such as *ujamaa vijijini* in Tanzania, long after they had failed economically; the bias against agriculture in government policy, and the diversion of scarce resources away from agriculture into massive defence expenditure, wasteful import substitution industrialisation and inefficient para-statal organisations. Bad farming practices have also been adopted over an extended period. In particular, there is a link between the spread of commercial farming and the preference for settled agriculture over nomadic pastoralism on the one hand, and the incidence of bad farming and grazing practices, sometimes resulting in 'desertification', on the other. These practices may be forced responses to circumstances which make survival impossible otherwise, as pastoralists and subsistence-oriented farmers are pushed on to marginal land. For example, the group hardest hit in the Ethiopian famine of 1972-4 – the Afar pastoralists – had been excluded from good riverside land in the Awash valley by the spread of commercial cotton and sugar cultivation, and obliged to shift their herds on to land which could not support them. This greatly reduced their ability to withstand the drought when it came [Sen, 1981: 104-5]. Again in northern Kenya, as a result of government attempts to increase food production by means of agricultural settlement, the Turkana and Boran pastoralists were made more, not less, vulnerable to drought [Hogg, 1987: 56-7].

Another important reason for poor agricultural performance is the failure of African governments to provide peasant farmers with market incentives, especially good prices for their produce. This may be because members of the ruling bourgeoisie 'divert surpluses from the peasantry to their own pockets, often with the aid of the state', thus giving a class dimension to famine [Lawrence *et al.*, 1985: 4-5]. If market incentives are absent, and if there is not also an adequate supply in the local shops of goods for the small farmers to buy, the latter may produce only enough to meet their immediate family needs. Another consequence will be a drift to the towns, thereby reducing the ratio of food producers to consumers. A policy of incentives to peasant producers alone, however, is insufficient. Even in areas of the Third World where a large majority of the population is rural, large numbers commonly depend (in part at least) upon earning a wage to survive. Loss of earning capacity can lead to starvation in the midst of plenty. As the proportion of rural dwellers depending on money income for survival rises, the problem becomes as much one of guaranteeing minimum year-round incomes as of providing incentives for peasant producers.

There is a further point of considerable importance: increased agricultural output cannot by itself combat famine. As Amartya Sen pointed out in his illuminating study, *Poverty and Famines*, effective distribution is also essential, since the availability of food within a particular country or region does not mean that all persons can gain access to it. Thus, the famine in Ethiopia between 1972 and 1974 was not accompanied by any significant reduction in food output and food prices rose little; even at its height in 1973 there was no abnormal drop in the consumption of food per head. It hit the north east (especially Wollo) in 1972-3 and provinces further south (particularly Hararghe) in 1973-4. The relative incidence of starvation was probably greatest among the pastoral people, who had lost some of their traditional dry-weather grazing land to commercial agriculture, as we saw above; many of their animals perished in the drought and the terms of trade of animals for grain turned against them. However, a majority of the famine victims in absolute numbers came from the agricultural community in the north-east [Sen, 1981: 111-2].

The situation in the Sahelian countries of Mauritania, Senegal, Mali, Upper Volta (now Burkina Faso), Niger and Chad was comparable in many ways to that in Ethiopia: both pastoralists who went south in search of fodder for their animals and paid employment for themselves, and agriculturists suffered severely from the drought, especially in 1973, the worst year. The number of those who died in 1973 alone was estimated at 100 000. Again, the critical factor was not so much the shortage of food – food supplies were adequate in nearly all the Sahelian countries to prevent starvation – but the inequality of distribution and the inability of many people to establish entitlement to it.

Additional lessons, some reinforcing those learned from the experience of 1973, emerged from the famines in Ethiopia, Somalia, Sudan, Mozambique and other parts of Africa in 1984–5, and the famines throughout southern Africa and in a number of states to the north, especially the Republic of Somalia, in 1991-2. In the earlier period (1984-5), all the signs of impending famine were evident in Ethiopia months (even years) before the main crisis occurred, but Western governments ignored the early warnings of the aid agencies. In the Sudan, the problem was accentuated both because the government's reluctance to admit that a problem existed (as in Ethiopia in 1973) caused food to be hoarded and its price to rise sharply, and because the continuing mass influx of refugees from Eritrea and Tigray into eastern Sudan coincided in 1984 with a severe drought which ruined more than 80 per cent of the harvest [Wallace, 1985: 64–5]. In both the Sudan and Ethiopia, food was available in the country, but the starving had no money with which to purchase it. And in both cases the problem was one of distribution across difficult and sometimes war-torn terrain with inadequate transport.

In the famine of 1991–2, a grim situation – above all in Somalia – was made worse by the slowness of most western governments, preoccupied with the Yugoslav crisis, in responding to the pleas for help of the aid agencies. The whole of southern Africa was suffering from severe drought. Even Zimbabwe and South Africa, which normally have surplus grain for export, became net importers. In 1992 Zimbabwe expected only 10 per cent of the normal yield of maize, a staple food. Zambia experienced one of the worst droughts of the century, but had no grain reserves and therefore needed to import almost a million tonnes of cereal. Botswana, with its long experience of drought conditions, again coped remarkably well, but had to increase the level of its cereal imports. In Malawi, whose central province and especially its densely populated southern province were badly hit by drought, the problem was compounded by the presence of a million refugees from Mozambique, by the need of this landlocked country to import and export its goods through the Tete corridor of Mozambique, thus risking attack by RENAMO rebels, and indirectly by the suspension of all non-humanitarian aid to Malawi by external donors in May 1992. In neighbouring Mozambique the long years of war had crippled the economy – this had also occurred in more richly-endowed Angola, where, however, the impact of drought had been less severe over most of the country – and rebel activities, as well as damaged roads and bridges, made immensely difficult the movement of relief aid to drought-stricken parts of the country. All regions of Namibia were affected by drought, but distribution was eased by an efficient road and rail network covering much of the country. The south of the island of Madagascar was severely affected by drought and locusts; some 80 000 people in the central and northern areas of Tanzania needed help; in Swaziland the dry weather from December 1991 onwards ruined crops in all parts of the country, while in Lesotho the cereal crop yield was 40 per cent of normal and impoverished pasture land led to the sale and slaughter of livestock. However, the country hardest hit (and the one which received most media coverage) was Somalia, located in the Horn rather than in Southern Africa. Here, famine resulted from a combination of severe drought and internal warfare: the downfall of the dictatorial regime of Siyad Barre in January 1991 unleashed vicious clan warfare, with faction fighters seizing relief supplies and hampering their distribution. This sad situation was slowly being eased by the presence of a United Nations' peace-keeping force.

Famine, then, is a multi-dimensional problem, which has created crisis conditions in Africa on three separate occasions since the 1960s. It is caused by a combination of natural disaster, social, economic and ecological conditions, and human intervention and failure. Among the latter can be listed the international capitalist exploitation of heavily-indebted Third World countries and the domestic exploitation of poor peasants by predominantly urban-based élites, the decline of domestic agricultural production and the inability of the economy to bring in emergency food surpluses through the normal channels of international trade. One can also point to poor or at best inadequate distribution systems, both within countries and between neighbouring states, and the lack of employment opportunities for rapidly expanding and increasingly urban populations. Finally, massive military expenditure and internal warfare (accentuated by external assistance for rebel movements, such as that given by South Africa to RENAMO) have lessened the capacity of African governments to prevent a severe drought from becoming a devastating famine.

When famine strikes, those who are most at risk are households with few cattle, and poor farmers forced by cash-cropping off good land on to tired and marginal land; and within these groups, women are more vulnerable than men. Without access to money earnings to enable them to enter the market to buy food in sufficient quantity to survive, the poor are obliged to adopt practices which worsen their situation: they slaughter or sell animals which could have provided future food or income, and consume portions of seed which should be retained for future planting. The greatest irony of the famine situation is that it is the producers of food themselves who lack access to food rather than wealthy members of the community and town-dwellers. In desperation, many of them leave their villages and trek long distances with their children to distant feeding centres; sadly the men and women, but the children especially, often arrive too weak to benefit from the food now available to them.

3. Petrodollars in the Middle East

Between November 1973 and April 1974, world oil prices rose fourfold. In 1979 a second sharp rise took place. The world is still living out the consequences. The initial success of OPEC was made possible by the dependence of the advanced Western economies as a whole upon imported oil, and the central role of oil as a source of energy in modern industrial society. It seemed to strike a blow for primary exporters against their generally more powerful international trading partners, and promised to bring about a permanent shift in power relations in the international market. To a certain extent, it did so. But, nearly two decades on, it is hard to say where the advantage now lies. In many ways the results have been negative for the oil producers themselves, while the worst hit have not been the advanced nations, but non-oil-producing Third World states. This is not to say that the oil producers were foolish to seek a better return for their oil. It suggests that the forcing up of prices in the short term was not in itself sufficient to overcome the liability of dependence on a single primary commodity, or to alter their subordinate position in the international economy. Indeed, their actions reinforced their status as primary producers, and increased their dependence on flows of goods and services from the advanced economies. It produced, therefore, in an exaggerated form, a set of circumstances which have bedevilled all primary-commodity-dependent countries in recent decades: rapid development requires foreign exchange for necessary imports of equipment and technology; efforts to boost export returns to provide the foreign exchange lead to a bias against domestic agriculture as land and investment is switched to exportable crops; foreign borrowing creates a need for further expansion of exports to meet repayment schedules; and the dependence eliminated at one level is continually recreated at another. This is a consequence of increasing integration into a capitalist-dominated international economy. But it is one in which Third World leaders and policy-makers, even in states

of a declared socialist orientation, have enthusiastically participated.

The change in the relationship between the oil-producing states,
the oil companies and the consumer nations since the early 1970s
produced one of the most dramatic reversals in contemporary
international economic relations. It brought to the centre of
international politics and finance a group of kingdoms which have
small populations, extremely limited agricultural potential, and in
the main scanty technically skilled personnel. Indicative of the
growth of these states was Saudi Arabia's increase in oil revenue
from $0.6 billion in 1965 to about $70 billion in 1979. The years
1973 and 1974 were the crisis years for the Western economies and
the Third World. There were gunfights in American petrol queues
and strict rationing of kerosene in impoverished states like Sudan.
The fall of the Shah and the Iranian revolution of 1978–9 brought
another jump in the price of oil. There were other factors at work
which caused the world recession: the collapse of currency agreements, uneven balance of payments spread among OECD countries
and growing protectionism. Even so, the higher price of oil was a
very important feature of the world slump of the 1970s and 1980s,
and it is ironic that the benefits for this new set of Third World
states had such negative effects on non oil-producing states in the
Third World. Although some of the latter, like Pakistan and
Bangladesh, were able to recoup some of the greatly increased
outflow of foreign exchange by exporting labour to the oil-rich
states, and a few others, like South Korea and Brazil, developed
their trade with OPEC countries, the broad effects were negative.

It was, however, a considerable achievement for OPEC to have
secured control over the pricing and supply of their natural
resources from some of the largest and richest multinational
corporations. Clearly, oil is a commodity unlike those possessed
by other Third World states. Initially, it was the domination by the
oil multinationals which made oil so cheap and caused the
industrialised states to be dependent on it as a source of energy.
By the 1970s OPEC had become the 'swing' producer, able to affect
the international price by its own production decisions, and was
able to increase prices. Within OPEC it was a handful of Arab states
in the Gulf, led by Saudi Arabia, which were the swing producers,
largely because they were 'low absorbers', that is, unable to spend
the vast revenues on their own development for reasons of

demography and geography. An oil-producing state like Nigeria with its 100 million population had no difficulty spending on development. On the other hand, states like Saudi Arabia, Kuwait and the United Arab Emirates, without agricultural potential, had small populations and large surpluses held in Western economies. In 1982 these were estimated at between $200 billion and $400 billion in the United States alone [Sowayegh, 1984: 177]. Furthermore these states had to import labour for development projects to such an extent that the United Arab Emirates and Qatar relied on non-nationals for over 80 per cent of their labour force [Smallwood and Sinclair, 1981: 151]. They also relied on imported consumer goods, manufactures, and civil and military technology. Between 1974 and 1980 imports from OECD countries increased by between 300 per cent and 400 per cent [Sowayegh, 1984: 177]. Even oil-producing states with a significant agricultural sector, like Iraq and Iran, had to import basic foodstuffs. Although OPEC members have gained control over their major export, there has not been any qualitative increase in their independence. The freezing of Iranian assets in American banks outside the United States during the embassy hostage crisis was a clear indication of the leverage held by recipients of oil investments. It is also important to point out that the price of oil is a function of demand. Depressed demand in the 1980s brought down the price of oil, just as increased demand in the early 1970s was an important factor in its increase. Since the oil-producing states depended on imports from the industrialised West, they were made to pay a high price for these as the OECD states recycled the oil surpluses through trade.

If some OECD states did not perform so badly after the oil price increases, much of the Third World, particularly the least developed states, was seriously affected. One of the main consequences of the two oil price increases and the subsequent world recession was to worsen sharply the import capacity of non-oil Third World states. In his address to the nation of 9 December 1981, President Julius Nyerere of Tanzania pointed out that 'for the amount of money with which we used to buy thirteen barrels of oil, we now only get one', and that his country had 'to give about four times as much cotton to buy a 7–ton lorry as we had to give in 1972, or ten times as much tobacco or three times as much cashew'. Thus, the poorer Third World countries were led into debt in the wake of the oil crisis, or sank further into poverty if they were unable to attract funds. They tended not to benefit from the surplus capital available, and to suffer further as the developed countries themselves changed the patterns of their imports to respond to the crisis.

The countries of the industrialised West attracted the OPEC surpluses, cut raw material imports, and concentrated on improving their trading positions with the OPEC states. Non-oil-exporting Third World states were excluded from this recycling process. Most of the surpluses were placed with Western financial institutions, in part a function of the large-scale expansion of Western banks, which were making most of their profits by the mid-1970s from overseas earnings. Ironically, the oil-producing states did rather poorly out of the process: one economist estimated that the rate of return on their investments between 1972 and 1979 was between zero and −3.4 per cent. For the Third World the result has been increased indebtedness with its attendant problems of high interest rates and debt servicing.

Many economists have recommended direct investment by oil states in other Third World countries as a means of enhancing economic growth, of reducing the necessity to borrow on the international capital market and of achieving a higher rate of profit for the oil states' investment. Recycling to the Third World has taken place through trade and migrant labour. OPEC's imports increased from $20 billion in 1973 to $226 billion in 1981, and with the erosion of OPEC's surpluses by the mid-1980s, trade had become even more central. The patterns of the 1970s did not favour the developing countries. In 1973 advanced industrial countries accounted for 77 per cent of OPEC's imports and non-oil developing countries for 16 per cent. By 1979 their respective shares were 75.5 per cent and 14.2 per cent [Sobhan, 1982: 719]. The fact that manufacturing is concentrated in a handful of Third World states limited the number of beneficiaries, even though it has been demonstrated that the expansion of OPEC imports from the advanced industrial states was a costly process, with OPEC 'importing inflation rather than real goods and services' [ibid: 735]. The weak trading relationship with the non-Muslim Third World has not been accorded much sympathy from Arab circles. Abd-al Aziz Sowayegh wrote of oil-importing Third World states that 'their development plans will . . . depend to a large extent on their ability to adjust to and comply with the new reality of limited, costly energy supplies' [Sowayegh, 1984: 23].

The oil-surplus states did give aid, some most generously. While United States aid was 0.27 per cent of GNP in 1985, in the mid-1970s Qatar gave 15 per cent, the UAE 11 per cent and Kuwait 8 per cent. Despite this high proportion of aid, derived from a depletable resource, the pattern of donations has benefited the poorer Arab states, other states with sizable Arab or Muslim populations, or states being weaned away from links with the Soviet Union. For example, between 1973 and 1977 Egypt, Syria and Jordan received 51.8 per cent of OPEC aid [Smallwood and Sinclair, 1981: 101]. The next largest recipient was Pakistan, with 9.5 per cent. Rather than giving for projects, the largest proportion during this period went for balance of payments' support. Because only a few of the OPEC states have surpluses, the pattern of OPEC giving has reflected the foreign policy goals of conservative states like Saudi Arabia, Kuwait, and the United Arab Emirates. The provision of Saudi aid to Sudan, Somalia and Egypt was based on their break with the USSR. In the case of Egypt, the later withdrawal of aid was a result of the peace treaty with Israel.

A further means of recycling was through remittances transferred by migrant workers. Given the small populations, the lack of skills and the magnitude of expenditure by the oil states, there was massive labour migration. The chief labour importers were Bahrein, Kuwait, Libya, Qatar, Saudi Arabia and the United Arab Emirates. In 1975 Saudi Arabia had 773 400 migrant workers, of whom 90 per cent were Arab, and the United Arab Emirates had 251 500, of whom 26 per cent were Asian. For the poorer states these remittances were an important source of foreign currency. By 1980 Egyptians were sending back $2.69 billion, Pakistanis $2.03 billion, Indians $3 billion, and Filipinos $376 million [Halliday, 1984: 9]. Annual remittances to Pakistan were equivalent to all its exports of raw cotton and cotton textiles, or one-third the value of all exports. Remittances were Egypt's largest foreign currency earner. Remittances help the balance of payments, but have a negative side. It is well documented that Pakistan and Egypt have lost highly educated technical, managerial and medical personnel, as well as skilled workers. Furthermore, remittances are frequently spent on consumer goods which are a further drain on foreign exchange. Remittances are also vulnerable to changing labour demands and economic down-turns in the oil-producing states, as well as to political crises. The demand for unskilled labour in the

Gulf declined as the construction boom came to an end, and declining oil revenues through the 1980s reinforced this trend. The Iraqi invasion of Kuwait and the massive flight of the immigrant workforce provided a poignant symbol of migrant worker vulnerability, as they huddled in temporary camps on the Iraq–Jordan border.

The consequences of the oil price increases were somewhat mixed, particularly when taken with the reactions of governments, banks and exporters in OECD countries. There has been increasing debt and decreasing raw material exports. Although the OPEC states have benefited and some quadrupled per capita income and spending on welfare, they did not benefit as much as they might have done. Reliance on imports for consumer goods and development projects has increasingly eroded capital surpluses. Surpluses of the 'low absorbers' have frequently gained a negative return and because they are so dependent on imports from, and investments in, Western capitalist systems, they have produced more oil than they require to stabilise Western economies. But the recession in the West and the over-production of oil in the mid-1980s led to a fall in the price of oil and cuts in production. Saudi Arabia, a state which can draw on foreign assets, was producing around 9 million barrels per day between 1979 and 1981, but by the summer of 1985 was producing only 2 million barrels. Between 1981 and 1985 its revenues fell from $108 billion to $47 billion per annum. The dual process of a falling price and production cuts also had its effect on OPEC solidarity. Member states have increasingly disagreed on pricing policy and production levels. While Saudi Arabia has been able to manage, budgets were cut from $84 billion in 1981–2 to $60.4 billion in 1984–5. Saudi Arabia had a per capita income 55 times that of Nigeria which, with its large population and their expectations based on the boom of the 1970s, found the drop in income a very bitter pill to swallow. The result was very sharp divisions at the regular OPEC meetings. In the 1970s the OPEC states became the 'haves' of the Third World, but by the 1980s OPEC itself had become divided between the 'haves' and the 'have-nots', with countries like Nigeria and Indonesia becoming indebted to maintain development programmes.

Finally, it should be noted that in none of the oil-rich states which benefited from the enormous flow of resources generated by the successive price rises of the 1970s was their allocation subject to the democratic accountability of ruling élites to the majority of the populations under their control. One of the consequences of the process of nationalisation of assets which preceded or accompanied the oil bonanza was that increased revenues flowed directly to the state. And in every case state power was in the hands of autocrats whose ability to ignore popular sentiment was enhanced by that flow of revenues. In the fabulously wealthy sheikdoms of the Gulf, autocracy translated into luxurious lifestyles for the minority who were citizens, and the means to procure an endless supply of cheap immigrant workers, imported for their labour but denied any of the rights of citizenship, from elsewhere in the region. In the larger economies of the region, resources were poured into often-inappropriate modernisation and capital-intensive industrialisation. And in both cases endless sums flowed into luxury projects to flatter the vanity of leaders, or into arms races which turned the region into a paradise for the international traders in weapons of war, and a graveyard for the hundreds of thousands of victims of successive armed confrontations funded and prolonged, if not directly caused, by interests associated with oil. Vast revenues from oil liberated leaders to pursue their own strategies of aggrandizement, but brought little if anything to the great majority of inhabitants of the region.

It seems likely that the Gulf oil-producing states will remain at the centre of the economics and politics of petrol through the 1990s. Oil exports from the ex-Soviet states halved between 1985 and 1991, and US production is in decline. The consequences of political crises and unstable inter-state relationships (some of which are partly a product of conflicts about production and pricing levels) in the Gulf area, however, suggest a considerable degree of unpredictability.

4. Debt and structural adjustment in Latin America

The 'debt crisis' of the 1980s was a consequence of the oil price rises of the 1970s and their repercussions first in international financial markets and later in the area of international trade. In the first stage, after 1973, the foreign currency earnings of the major oil states found their way into the United States and European money markets, and were channelled from there, in large part, to sovereign Third World states in large syndicated loans. US banks in particular competed aggressively for business in this area, convinced that sovereign borrowers were safe customers. There were six important characteristics to the lending which took place. First, it multiplied the amount of debt in the hands of Third World states. Second, the rate of borrowing far outran the rate at which foreign-exchange earning capacity could be developed; the debt would therefore need to be 'rolled over' (refinanced by new lending as it became due), in part, at least for the foreseeable future. Third, it went above all to the largest and most developed Third World states, with Brazil, Mexico and Argentina the leading recipients. Fourth, it came primarily from commercial sources rather than from the government and official lending agencies, which had been the major lenders before. Fifth, it was made at floating rather than fixed rates of interest, at times when inflation was rendering rates of interest low or even negative in real terms. And sixth, large numbers of banks were involved as a consequence of the raising of loans through syndicates; among them, the biggest lenders by far were the nine major US banks and two British banks (Lloyds and Midland). All of these banks accumulated obligations well in excess of their total capital reserves.

This was primarily, then, a business which involved the big banks on the one hand, and the big import-dependent developing countries on the other. In the mid-1980s the debts of Mexico and Brazil respectively were well over twice those of South Korea, the next largest borrower, virtually three times those of Argentina and Venezuela, and five times those of Indonesia and the Philippines. In addition, the Latin American debtors had proportionately greater exposure to commercial bank debt, and were therefore paying high rates of interest – 10.8 per cent in 1983, for instance – whereas low-income countries owing primarily to official lenders were paying 3.7 per cent [Dornbusch, 1985].

If interest rates had remained stable while the major borrowers had been able to expand their exports and foreign exchange earnings enough to meet the bulk of their repayment liabilities, and if banks had been willing to provide fresh money to cover remaining needs, a crisis could have been avoided. But such an outcome became impossible in the wake of the second phase of the oil crisis. After the second wave of price increases in 1979 real interest rates climbed until they reached record levels as the United States tried to finance its deficit without relaxing its tight monetary policy. Similarly tight monetary policies in the advanced countries around the world led to recession, falling demand for the exports of Third World countries, and sharply declining terms of trade for their products. The result was a fierce 'scissors effect' as interest rates floated up, raising the payments due on Third World debt, while export revenues dropped, reducing ability to pay. If new loans could not be secured, the major debtors were bound to fail to meet their obligations as interest and amortisation payments fell due. It was at this point that the significance of the shift towards commercial lending revealed itself. Just when new money was needed to sustain the stability of international financial markets, and when sovereign or official lenders would have been able to take a longer-term view and grant more credit, the commercial banks, concerned for the security of the massive loans they had made in the past, began to draw back. By the early 1980s oil prices were falling back, OPEC surpluses were beginning to dry up, and a shift was taking place to shorter-term loans. Before long, debtors found themselves borrowing to meet repayment demands, rather than to finance new investment.

The debt crisis proper broke on Friday, 13 August 1982, when the Mexican Finance Minister informed creditors that Mexico was unable to meet due payments on its debt. In the wake of this announcement, a number of fundamental and virtually unprecedented changes occurred in international financial markets. In a panic reaction, the banks cut off further lending to Latin America as a whole. Thereafter, for the best part of a decade, commercial lending was to be 'involuntary', prised out of banks involved in previous loans in order to enable debtors to meet payments as they fell due, and avoid the need to declare the loans bad and provoke a further collapse. It had hitherto been taken for granted by all parties that flows of money to developing countries would always be positive, with new lending outweighing the return flow of interest and principal due. But now, year after year, the flow was negative. The Latin American debtors had to pay out more than they were receiving, while levels of trade and export prices remained depressed. Had they been unable to repay, or chosen not to do so, the international financial system would have collapsed. As it was, Brazil and Mexico cut imports and living standards sharply, and diverted production to exports, achieving surpluses of US$13bn each in 1984. This meant austerity policies which brought recession in the domestic economy and severe cuts in the standard of living of populations already suffering hardship. The debtor populations, and particularly their poorer citizens who had gained least and had least say in the decision to borrow, were to pay the price of collective recklessness for which foreign banks and irresponsible leaders were jointly to blame. For the rest of the decade money continued to flow out, and even after a series of write-offs Brazil and Mexico still each owed around US100bn to the banks at the end of the 1980s.

Even so, despite widespread opposition to continued payment, calls from Fidel Castro for a general repudiation of all debts, and short-lived defiance from some of the minor but worst-affected debtors such as Peru, the Latin American debtors sought to pay up as best they could, and have continued to do so. Even in Argentina and Brazil, where civilian regimes have come to power which have no responsibility whatsoever for the reckless borrowing and unwise spending of their military predecessors, no attempt has been made to repudiate the debts. This is not in fact so surprising. The decision-makers involved, in Mexico as much as in Brazil or Argentina, were the beneficiaries and the representatives of a pattern of growth which was both highly dependent upon access to international markets, and highly unequal over time in its impact upon their populations. Even after the ending of military rule in Brazil and Argentina, none of the leaders of the major debtors, De La Madrid and Salinas in Mexico, Alfonsin and Menem in Argentina, or Sarney and Collor in Brazil, showed the slightest desire to break with the banks. Nor did they mount a noisy international campaign against the banks themselves; they were hardly in a position to have the issue of equity raised in connection with their own domestic policies. It is wrong to imagine that since the debt crisis broke they have been forced into adopting policies which they were reluctant to pursue. Rather, governments pursuing capitalist development and facing sometimes significant opposition from the left as they did so (from the Workers' Party in Brazil in particular, but also from the opposition coalition which was at least defrauded of its true vote in Mexico in the 1988 elections, and perhaps denied a victory by fraud) used the excuse of external pressure to justify the imposition of policies they were in any case set upon pursuing. The conservative regimes which have come to power throughout the region in the wake of the retreat of the generals, and their liberally oriented counterparts in Mexico, are unlikely candidates for a crusade against the fundamental character of the international order upon which they depend.

However, the debtor countries have not responded tamely to every demand from the banks and international organisations such as the IMF. Rather, they have sought to defend their own interests, and to reorient their economies in order to resume growth. As a brief consideration of the cases of Brazil and Mexico will show, they have done so with varying degrees of success. While successive military and civilian governments lost their way in Brazil in the 1980s and early 1990s, Mexico's successive leaders engineered a deliberate transformation in the Mexican economy and its international orientation over the same period. In each case, the result was the adoption in the 1990s of a liberal economic orientation which represented a sharp departure from the practice of the half-century since 1930. However, whereas Mexico adopted liberal policies as part of a planned programme of reform after 1982, Brazil adopted them hurriedly after the failure of successive economic reform programmes pursued from the mid-1980s onwards, only to step back from them again early in 1993.

Under De La Madrid (1982–8) and Salinas (1988–94), Mexico has carried out a radical internal reform and an equally radical reorientation of its relationship to the international economy. This has centred upon a clean break with the pattern of state-led capitalist development which was the legacy of the revolution, in favour of a whole-hearted embrace of the logic of the current international capitalist economy, reflected above all in entry to GATT in 1986, and negotiation for entry with the United States and Canada into a North American Free Trade Area (NAFTA) in the early 1990s. It had earlier decided against GATT entry in 1980, at the height of confidence in the guarantee of resources from the oil boom and against the background of a growth rate of 7.5 per cent per annum between 1977 and 1979. However, in the wake of the debt crisis and the concomitant collapse of the option of rapid state-led development fuelled by oil and foreign borrowing, the supporters of liberalisation and closer links to the US economy gained an opportunity to seize the initiative. Policies of wage cuts were combined with steady depreciation of the peso against the dollar, preserving and extending the international competitiveness of Mexican wage levels, and a number of major changes were made to Mexico's broader political economy. A programme of liberal-isation of imports was introduced in 1988, reversing the trade surplus but paving the way for a new wave of capital goods investment. In 1989 new rules were issued regulating the investment law of 1973, releasing ventures in all but a few strategic sectors of the economy (notably mining and auto parts) from the maximum limit of 49 per cent foreign ownership. Automobiles, capital goods, textiles, and processed agricultural goods were all opened up to foreign firms, provided that they drew on external sources of finance, and established production facilities outside the major industrial areas of the country. In 1990 the government reversed the 1982 bank nationalisation, launched an extensive programme of privatisation, and announced its intention (previously ruled out) of seeking a North American Free Trade Agreement with the United States and Canada. By the end of 1991 the bulk of the privatisation programme had been completed. The major item, Telemex, was in private hands, along with over one hundred of the major companies designated for disposal, as the Mexican state worked towards its target of an 86 per cent reduction in the extent of state ownership in comparison to the base year of 1982. Finally, the Chamber of Deputies approved in December 1991 a bill dismantling the state-owned *ejidos* and effectively privatising land-holding in the country. The government followed this move in February 1992 by allowing foreign share-holding (though not outright ownership) in large farms.

Under the Salinas government from 1988 onwards in particular, then, Mexico advanced deliberately towards a general economic liberalisation across a range of related policy areas. The new orientation of policy responded to the interests of a narrow domestic and international coalition, held together by a restruc-tured Mexican state. It rested upon the halving of real wages over a decade, which enabled Mexico to undercut Hong Kong, Taiwan and Singapore, and upon the gamble that the shifts in income and in institutional power this reflected could be maintained, while Mexico could continue to attract direct investment in manufactur-ing and cover its balance of payments deficit in the future. For good or ill, the character of Mexico's internal political economy and its relationship to the global economy had been transformed by purposive state action.

Brazil, like Mexico, persisted with a highly interventionist policy in the wake of the oil crisis, seeking to maintain the role of the state as a counter-cyclical source of capital investment. This policy became unsustainable in the late 1970s and early 1980s, as the evolution of the debt crisis brought to an end the ability of the state to perform this role. Brazil responded as Mexico did in the short term to the loss of access to foreign loans after 1982, cutting imports sharply and providing subsidies and fiscal incentives for exporters in order to force a balance of payments surplus to meet debt repayments. However, as the previous model faltered no clear alternative developed. Under Figueiredo (1979–85) and his civilian successor Sarney (1985–90) economic policy-making was marked by a loss of direction, rather than by the purposive adoption of a new course. Successive stabilisation efforts failed, while economic management lost any coherence it had previously possessed. President Fernando Collor, who took office in 1990, eventually opted for a liberal path after another failed attempt to bring about stabilisation, after his political support had dwindled almost to nothing, and after dropping his entire financial team. Whereas Mexico had advanced to a new liberal model, Brazil retreated toward it in disarray.

Under Sarney and Collor growth stagnated, with a sharp recession in 1990 wiping out previous gains. In the period from 1988 to 1991 Brazil's economy experienced no growth, and no recovery appeared to be in sight. At the same time, political problems were rapidly accumulating for Collor, who was eventually removed from office by a vote in the Chamber of Deputies in 1992, and sent for trial by Senate on charges of gross corruption over influence-peddling. He resigned his office in December 1992, on the eve of the Senate trial, to be replaced by Vice-President Itamar Franco, hitherto an opponent of liberalisation and privatisation.

As a consequence of this record, Brazil lost to Mexico its place as a favoured recipient of direct foreign investment. Of US$13.3bn directly invested in the top five Latin American economies in 1990, Mexico attracted 62.4 per cent, in comparison with the 3 per cent directed to Brazil [*Latin American Regional Report (Brazil)*, RB–91–02, 14 Feb. 1991: 4]. In these unfavourable circumstances a process of liberalisation began in 1990, in the absence of preparation over the previous decade. A programme of import liberalisation was adopted, to eliminate cumbersome bureaucratic procedures and intermediaries by the end of 1992, and reduce tariffs from an average of 32 per cent to under 15 per cent by mid-1993, and a long-promised privatisation programme was belatedly set in motion in 1991 after delays arising from legal challenges and popular opposition, with a large mining concern, USIMINAS, sold to primarily national interests in October of that year. Subsequent sales raised US$1.7bn in 1991, compared to the US$9.4bn raised by Mexico.

By the early 1990s, then, Brazil was finally moving in the direction of the liberalisation of its economy, under pressure from external actors, and in political and economic circumstances which still closely resembled those of the early 1980s. It continued to generate a large trade surplus, but had failed to take advantage of it to carry out institutional reforms which would have enhanced the prospects for successful liberalisation. As a consequence it undertook its turn to liberalisation in the worst possible circumstances: led by a deeply unpopular government lacking organised Congressional support, in the depths of a national and international recession, against the background of continuing monetary instability, and in the absence of interest from foreign investors. The country had fallen into liberalisation by default, as a last resort response after a decade of false starts and incoherent policy-making. Finally, as a consequence of the forced departure of President Collor, the twists and turns of policy-making did not end there. One of President Franco's first steps was to announce a three-month moratorium on the privatisation programme, and forbid the future involvement of the state pension funds which, in the absence of foreign interest, had been the keenest bidders in the past. If Brazil were to continue to move in the direction of liberalisation, it would be under the compulsion of external pressure, rather than as a consequence of a positive internal commitment to the process.

5. Environmental politics in East and Southeast Asia

Recent concern over the emission of 'green-house' gases, global warming, and the destruction of the ozone layer highlights the global implications of energy-intensive development policies pursued most destructively by the developed countries themselves, but also adopted with enthusiasm throughout the Third World. The issue is a sensitive one, on the one hand because the Third World contains virtually all of what is left of primeval rainforest (principally in Africa, Latin America and Southeast Asia), but on the other because the developed countries themselves have pursued development over centuries with little regard for the environment, and persist in practices which contribute far more to the degradation of the global environment than does deforestation. Secondly, international organisations and representatives from the leading industrial countries deplore environmentally harmful policies in the Third World while simultaneously urging upon them the opening of their economies to foreign investment and the development of their export capacity, both avenues which may lead to the exacerbation of environmental destruction. In the case of East and Southeast Asia, however, it cannot be said that environmentally destructive policies have been imposed from outside, or adopted in desperate circumstances in which they amounted to a forced choice. In fact the states of East and Southeast Asia examined here do not display the types of vulnerability we have discussed above in Africa, the Middle East, and Latin America: in some contrast to these cases, their economic destinies have been very much in their own hands. The region has been largely free from the famines which have ravaged Africa, despite dreadful exceptions such as the case of Cambodia, where the forced relocation of the urban population, combined with internal conflict in the Pol Pot period, caused starvation on a massive scale. In East Asia, successful agriculture combined with relatively good income distribution has kept food supplies and levels of nutritional intake across the population as a whole high. In Indonesia, too, large-scale investment in rice production converted the one-time largest importer of rice in the world to a surplus producer by the mid-1980s [Fox, 1991: 63]. At the same time, the East and Southeast Asian states, with the conspicuous exception of the Philippines, have avoided both the dependence upon primary exports which rendered the oil-producers of the Middle East vulnerable despite their temporary success in boosting prices, and the crisis of commercial debt-dependent development which has forced the major Latin American economies into liberalisation and structural adjustment.

The contrasts which these comparisons suggest are genuine. The patterns of economic development in East and Southeast Asia have been more successful than those observed in the other regions discussed here. However, the environmental record suggests that the developing states of East and Southeast Asia have paid their own internal cost for rapid economic development. Indeed, they have internalised these costs by voluntarily imposing them upon their own societies. They have pursued growth with scant regard for the environmental impact, and as a result the region provides examples of some of the most environmentally damaging development policies to be found anywhere in the world. These include the destruction of primeval rain-forest on a large scale, the recklessly intensive use of fertilizers and pesticides in agriculture, the large-scale dumping of untreated human sewage and industrial waste into rivers and coastal waters, the pollution of the air through uncontrolled industrial emissions and the high density of city traffic, and reliance upon nuclear power without proper regard for safe running of plants and disposal of contaminated materials. Here we examine these issues and the logic that connects them.

Deforestation has negative consequences of local, regional and global significance. It threatens or destroys the lifestyles of forest-dwelling peoples; provokes the leaching and erosion of soils, flash-flooding and desertification; reduces biomass stocks and species diversity; and leads to changing patterns of rainfall, and long-term climate change. It is a problem throughout the Third World, with Brazil, Indonesia and Zaire the sites of major forest loss in the 1980s. Although overall Amazonia remains the largest single mass of tropical forest, Southeast Asia has the greatest range of standing forests under threat. The Philippines is almost stripped of forest; Myanmar, Indonesia, Malaysia and Thailand figure among the ten countries where deforestation is taking place on the largest scale; Vietnam is still suffering the destruction caused by massive and indiscriminate use of napalm and chemical defoliants by the United States during the Vietnam War, and Cambodia is subject to uncontrolled and rapidly escalating logging.

World-wide, the major direct cause of deforestation is shifting cultivation (slash-and-burn agriculture). However, shifting cultivation is not in itself destructive of forest cover; it has historically proved to be compatible with sustainable exploitation and natural regeneration, if land is left fallow to recover after temporary use. It is therefore to other direct causes of deforestation and indirect causes of the intensification of unsustainable shifting cultivation that we must look in order to explain the greatly increased pace of loss of tropical rainforest. Among these are logging, often itself the source of widespread destruction for relatively low levels of extraction of valuable woods, and a means of opening up tracts of forest to further waves of entrants; large-scale clearing for mining, ranching and plantation agriculture; the widespread use of wood or charcoal as fuel, particularly in both rural and urban Africa, but also in industrial iron smelting in Brazilian Amazonia; and new settlement prompted by poverty, pressure on the land, agricultural modernisation and high population levels elsewhere (in Brazil and Indonesia in particular), involving individuals who lack the local knowledge and commitment to practice sustainable agriculture [Thomas, 1992: Ch. 7; Hecht and Cockburn, 1990].

It has been calculated that at least 1.2 million hectares of forest are lost each year in the Southeast Asian states of Thailand, Indonesia, the Philippines and Malaysia, with virtually half this loss occurring in Indonesia alone. The rainforests of the Philippines may not outlast the present century; the proportion of land under forest has fallen in the last thirty years from over three-quarters to under a half in Malaysia, and from over half to around a quarter in Thailand; and Indonesia's vast reserves, concentrated in the outer islands, are being cut at an accelerated pace to supply an intensive logging and processing industry which has recently been the recipient of enormous investment [McDowell, 1989: 310–11]. In addition, the Thai government and logging companies (many owned by the military) are rapidly expanding operations in Myanmar, and in areas of Cambodia held by the Khmer Rouge. Forest cover in Cambodia may have fallen from 73 per cent to less than 40 per cent since 1969, and the pace of cutting has increased enormously since 1990, perhaps to 1.2 million cubic metres of logs per year, at first as a result of competition for resources between the four factions engaged in fighting until the 1991 Peace Agreement was signed, and thereafter because of the factions competing for political support as the scheduled 1993 elections approached [*Far Eastern Economic Review*, 4 June 1992: 60–5]. The belated banning of the export of raw logs led to a surge of cutting at the end of 1992, and gave rise immediately to the proliferation of saw-mills, as processed logs were not affected. It thereby contributed to an intensification of the rate of destruction.

The case of the Indonesian plywood industry provides a dramatic example of the industrial development of logging, and its international ramifications [Potter, 1991]. The exploitation of timber in Indonesia has undergone two distinct phases under the New Order government since 1967. In the first, which lasted until 1979, twenty-year logging concessions of up to 600 000 hectares, largely in the outer islands of Kalimantan (Borneo), Sumatra and Irian Jaya, were granted to foreign or joint-venture companies (mostly Japanese, Korean or American, many in partnership with members of the Indonesian military or allies of the regime). By 1989, a total of 544 concessions covered 29 per cent of Indonesia's total land area. Traditional hand methods of extraction gave way to mechanised cutting under pressure from Japanese buyers, and the First Development Plan (*Repelita I*) gave priority to the export of logs to earn foreign exchange; by 1979 Indonesia had over 40 per cent of the world market for tropical logs. From 1977 government policy was oriented to the establishment of local processing, leading to a second phase (1980–9) in which the export of logs was eliminated, and Indonesia became the world's major plywood exporter. Over the decade 112 plywood factories were established, 65 of them in Kalimantan alone. Despite a drought and fire which destroyed over 3 million hectares of forest in East Kalimantan in 1982–3, production expanded rapidly. By 1988 capacity for plywood production was close to 10 million cubic metres per year, and forestry products (mostly plywood and sawn timber) accounted for 15 per cent of Indonesian exports. Exports of plywood approached seven million cubic metres, with Japan, China and Hong Kong, the United States, the European Community and the Middle East among major markets. Throughout the period, indigenous forest-dwellers have been 'relocated' elsewhere, while 1 750 000 migrants from Java have been brought in to settle on the outer islands under an extensive programme of transmigration. Migrants were often placed on poor land further damaged by mechanised clearing (resulting in loss of thin topsoils), and made matters worse by their own short-sighted and inappropriate methods of farming.

Logging to remove selected timber is, however, only one of a range of activities which threatens the forest, in which standing trees form only one part of a complex and interdependent ecosystem. The forest's vulnerability to varied economic exploitation is illustrated by the case of Malaysia, where all the major activities upon which economic development is based have destructive consequences. First, logging has virtually destroyed the timber stands of peninsular Malaysia, and is causing intense conflict in Sabah and Sarawak; second, rubber processing creates an acidic effluent which is largely dumped direct into the water supply; third, palm oil processing produces far more polluted waste, dumped in the same way; fourth, the dumping of worked tin and copper ores into rivers causes turbidity, rapid siltation, and toxicity, with devastating effects on fish stocks; and fifth, the high use of fertilizers and pesticides in agro-industry adds further to water pollution [McDowell, 1989: 317–18].

Serious problems arise when such various factors are combined in a single area. In the case of Indonesia's Jakarta Bay, pollution arising from the dumping of untreated sewage and industrial waste literally feeds directly into fish and shellfish harvested for human consumption. Bacteria from human excrement have been found at twenty-five times World Health Organisation recommended levels, along with especially high lead and cadmium pollution, and further contamination from copper, mercury and zinc. Further problems for coastal fishing arise when silt containing residues of fertilizers and pesticides is carried downstream [Rice, 1991: 171–5].

It is in South Korea and Taiwan, however, where first intensive agriculture then sustained industrial growth have had the most dramatic environmental consequences. In both countries, the process of deforestation is extremely advanced, and has given rise to problems with soil erosion, siltation and erratic river flow. In agriculture, the extremely heavy use of fertilizers and pesticides over decades has led to high levels of contamination of soils and water with heavy metals. Cadmium levels over fifteen times the legal upper limit of parts per million in the United States have been recorded in South Korea, while it has been estimated that 30 per cent of Taiwan's rice crop is contaminated with mercury, cadmium or arsenic [Bello and Rosenfeld, 1990: 97–8, 201].

The worst problems have arisen, however, as a result of urbanisation and industrialisation. Here, as in other areas, they arise directly out of the state's determination to avoid dependence on external interests. South Korea has responded to the threat to its growing energy needs – arising from the instability of global oil markets and the recurrent threat of higher prices – by basing the bulk of its electricity generation upon nuclear power. The construction of these plants offers a classic instance of the 'triple alliance' of foreign (mostly US) capital, the South Korean state, and the big domestic conglomerates, led by Hyundai. It has given rise to a small but determined environmental movement concerned at the failure to meet international safety standards, the record of nearly 200 accidents since 1978, the growing incidence of unsafe disposal of low-level waste, and the proliferation of leukemia and other radiation-related conditions in the vicinity of nuclear plants [ibid.: 104–11].

In Taiwan, the problem of industrial pollution has been as marked in rural as in urban areas, as a consequence of the deliberate dispersal of factories throughout the countryside. Taiwan's small enterprises have generally disregarded existing controls, as a consequence of which the lower reaches of Taiwan's rivers down the whole of the western coastline are heavily polluted. The dumping of untreated sewage into the river system compounds the dangers arising from industrial pollution, while the poor quality of air in Taipei presents a further hazard to health. Finally, Taiwan's nuclear programme is every bit as ambitious as that of South Korea, and every bit as dangerous: for example, radioactive metals sold as scrap have found their way into new buildings, where they continue to pose a hidden health hazard. It is scarcely surprising that cancer causes twice as many deaths as it did thirty years ago, while Taiwan boasts the world's highest rate of hepatitis infection, and asthma cases among children increased four-fold in the 1980s [ibid.: 195–214].

The environmental problems reviewed here have attracted international attention and condemnation. As Asia's largest producers and exporters of logs, lumber and plywood, both Malaysia and Indonesia have been widely criticised for their forestry policies, and have responded aggressively in their own defence. At the 'Earth Summit' (United Nations Conference on Environment and Development) held in Rio de Janeiro, Brazil, in June 1992, they led the call for the removal of obstacles to Third World development arising from protectionism and related practices, in order to make it possible for Third World producers to adopt environmentally sensitive patterns of production. Developing countries generally have consistently pointed to the hypocrisy – on the part of the advanced industrial countries responsible for by far the largest share of global environmental damage and unsustainable energy use – of pressing for the international regulation of forest conservation and use while continuing to be major users of Third

World exports implicated in deforestation, and refusing to bind themselves to similar action on energy use and greenhouse gas emissions. There is an equal measure of hypocrisy involved, too, in objections from the developed capitalist economies to environmentally damaging industrial processes adopted in the Third World, when as often as not these are acquired from or directly introduced by corporations based in Europe, Japan or the United States.

However, it remains the case that the governments of East and Southeast Asia have shown considerable capacity to impose their will in relation to other social and economic issues. Also, they have the means at their disposal to act against pollution and environmental destruction. Malaysia has had an Environmental Quality Act in place since 1974, but state governments decline to enforce federal statutes; South Korea has had environmental impact assessment legislation in place since 1982, but uses it merely to cosmetic effect. Shin Chang Hyun, the director of Seoul's independent Environment Policy Research Institute, comments that 'Laws and regulations are all there, but the government will to enforce them is simply missing' [*Far Eastern Economic Review*, 29 October 1992: 34].

One must conclude, in these circumstances, that the record revealed here is one further illustration of a particular 'strength' of the states concerned: the ability of their authoritarian regimes to impose their goals upon their citizens. Recent evidence from Taiwan suggests, however, that there are limits to this capacity on the part of the state, particularly as the grip of authoritarian control begins to weaken. An environmental movement has grown up on the island since the mid-1980s, and flourished as a slow move has taken place away from martial law in the context of the incipient process of democratisation. The movement rapidly developed a mass base, took on a stance of virtually permanent mobilisation, and succeeded in winning the suspension of plans for a fourth nuclear power plant and the closing of an ICI petrochemical plant whose discharged waste was claimed to be killing fish stocks. It also succeeded in blocking the construction of a massive titanium dioxide plant planned by US chemicals giant DuPont [Bello and Rosenfeld, 1990: 211]. Unfortunately, however, the consequence of the increasing success of the environmental movement has simply been a move to relocate variously in China, the Philippines, and South Korea.

There is some justice in the claim that criticism from the developed countries of environmentally damaging policies pursued elsewhere smacks of hypocrisy and double standards. However, the first victims of such policies are the citizens of states which deny their people the democratic channels through which they might seek less destructive alternatives. In other words, the situations we have examined reflect not only the relative success these states have achieved in insulating themselves from external pressures and recording high rates of growth, but also their success in insulating themselves from accountability to their own citizens in doing so.

6. Conclusion

Our examination of the issues of famine, oil, debt, and environmental politics confirms the need for a global perspective in the analysis of Third World politics. It also reveals the complex interlinking of issues, and the enduring pressures and disadvantages which Third World states suffer *vis-à-vis* the developed world. An historical perspective and a focus upon the manner in which Third World states are integrated into the global economy make indispensable contributions to our understanding of Third World politics today. At the same time, distinctions need to be made between the day-to-day decisions which individuals make in their own interests, the varying abilities of particular groups and countries to pursue and protect their interests in the world economy over the longer term, the broader consequences of outcomes which they cannot predict, and the enduring features of national and international political economy revealed by these outcomes. It is a mistake to believe that the development of the world economy is directed or in any sense controlled by *any* group of individuals or countries. Practically all the developments reviewed in this chapter were unintended and unforeseen by the major protagonists, whether they were bankers, oil shaykhs, or development planners in Africa or East and Southeast Asia. Frequently, as with famine or global recession, everyone loses.

The actions of Third World governments cannot all be explained by pressure from outside. A focus upon the nature and historical development of the global capitalist economy – as distinct from the current ability of particular states to exert influence over others (which is of course considerable) – shows that the process of incorporation into the global economy has created within most Third World states élites highly supportive of industrialisation and integration, and anxious to deepen it rather than see it reduced. They act under structural constraints, but in their own interests. Even in the most vulnerable of states, Third World leaders have not simply been the victims of either international market forces or the impositions of more powerful states. Events have taken the course they have (very often) because of a commitment on the part of Third World leaders to patterns of development which have tightened their links with the international market, with little regard to issues of social justice or sustainability. If in one sense these case studies illuminate different aspects and stages of the process of incorporation into the world economy, in another they show that perhaps the most lasting legacy of the 'West' in the Third World has been the creation of economies and élites oriented towards capitalist development, at once dependent upon and allied to the developed countries themselves.

In such circumstances, the major losers have always been those least able to take action to protect their own interests – the vulnerable sectors of the population either excluded from or victimised by the development policies pursued by ruling élites. In this respect it is of central importance that in every one of these four cases, élites have acted with relative impunity in pursuit of their own interests, while the majority of the population have lacked, or found themselves remorselessly stripped of, the means to resist. In other words, these four case studies point not only to some of the enduring structural features of the global economy, but also to the structural inequalities of power and access to resources in each of the regions studied. We will briefly explore these features of each in turn.

Famine has not been a single, sudden, devastating event, but a recurrent process in contemporary Africa. The signs of its approach have been in evidence well before it has struck, and the groups at risk have made successive efforts to avoid it, using the resources at their disposal until none remain. If they have been unable to avoid it, and if famines have been repeated, it is because they lack not only the entitlement to food, but also the democratic rights which would enable them to establish it. In this sense, as Watts concludes, 'in the long term, famine prevention in Africa will be rooted in the doubtless long and contradictory struggle for democracy' [Watts, 1991: 25]. In a similar manner, the accumulation of **petrodollars** in the Middle East and its consequences reflect not only the structure of international markets for primary commodities, but in some ways more strikingly the structure of state–society relations in the Middle East itself. The great majority of the population in the region had no say whatsoever in the concerted action which led to successive price rises, and little share in the benefits which derived from them. The accumulation of oil wealth had the effect of strengthening existing leaders and making them less accountable to their people. The same lesson can be drawn from the history of the **debt crisis** in Latin America. The heaviest borrowers were the military regimes of Argentina and Brazil, and Mexico, firmly in the grip of the dominant PRI. As in the case of the oil producers of the Middle East, the funds flowed in directly to the state and its dependent agencies, reinforcing the autonomy of already unaccountable élites. Finally, the various development policies which have led to widespread **environmental destruction** in East and Southeast Asia have been imposed by authoritarian governments upon communities which have often been well aware of the dangers to themselves and their environment, but have lacked democratic channels through which to resist these policies and pursue more appropriate alternatives. It appears, therefore, that the lesson drawn by Watts from the recurrence of famine, that 'the right not to be hungry and the emergence and consolidation of civil society in Africa are inextricably linked' [ibid.: 25], can be applied more generally to all our four cases.

If this is so, there are grounds for optimism in some parts of the Third World. Throughout the 1980s Latin American electorates in the new and old democracies alike grew increasingly hostile to successive governments which sought to impose the logic of structural adjustment. Opponents of such programmes came close to taking power in Brazil and Mexico, while throughout the region angry citizens expressed their discontent in social movements and spontaneous riots. In Africa, a comparable process of change was under way. In East and Southeast Asia, the overthrow of Marcos in the Philippines, the emergence of a powerful citizens' movement against environmental destruction in Taiwan, and the forcing of a transition to civilian rule in South Korea suggested significant moves towards greater accountability. Only in the Middle East, as the aftershocks of the Iran–Iraq War and the Gulf War continued to register their effects, did it appear that the regimes of the region were all firmly entrenched.

The situation overall brings us back to the question, posed in the introduction, of whether a genuine process of democratisation in the Third World could be compatible with economic policies of the kind implied by the current global balance of economic power, and pursued through Western-backed policies of structural adjustment. In the light of the case studies examined here, it is clear that the question can be replaced by two broader ones: are any of the broad patterns of development that have characterised the four regions of the Third World studied here likely to survive in any recognisable form if such a process of democratisation takes place? And does the dominance that the developed countries have enjoyed, and their ability to secure such benefits as they have secured from their relations with the Third World, therefore depend upon no such process taking place?

It should be clear, in the light of this discussion, that our depiction of the negative consequences of the promotion of export capacity under colonial and independent governments alike, and of preferences for high-technology, capital-intensive farming methods and industrial development, should not be read as a plea for a return to subsistence agriculture, low-technology industry and local trade. It is not the availability of technology itself that is to blame, but the distribution of wealth and power, the way in which resources are allocated, and the extent and character of national and international regulation of economic activity. Hunger has been with us throughout world history, but it is only in the present century that the resources to banish it have been available. At the same time, the same technological and productive advances that have the potential for the elimination of hunger and the satisfaction of other basic human needs have been a major cause of mass starvation in recent years, and are responsible at present for a potentially catastrophic process of global environmental destruction. Change will come, if at all, not from turning our backs on the advantages which technological change can bring, but by bringing the social, political and economic processes through which they can be realised, in the First World and the Third, fully under democratic control.

Further Reading

On famine, see Sen [1981], Dreze and Sen [1990], and, for a good discussion which links it to broader issues, Watts [1991]. On famine and war, *Review of African Political Economy* [1985] is an excellent collection. There are several valuable historical studies in Palmer and Parsons [1977] and Rotberg [1983]. Apeldoorn [1981] and Watts [1983] focus on the case of Nigeria. For further case studies, see Holm and Morgan [1985] on Botswana, Wallace [1985] on Sudan, Hogg [1987] on Kenya, and Jansson et al. [1987] on Ethiopia. On petrodollars in the Middle East, see Smallwood and Sinclair [1981] and Sowayegh [1984]; on the attempt to develop trade between the OPEC countries and their Asian neighbours, see Sobham [1982]. On the Latin American debt crisis, see Lever and Huhne [1985], Kaufman [1988], and Frieden [1991]. For Mexico, Sklair [1989] outlines the development of *maquiladoras* on the northern frontier, and Shaiken [1990] details the generalisation of new techniques of production throughout the region. For the failure of economic policy in Brazil in the same period, see Fishlow [1989]. For some interesting comparisons with African cases, see Sandbrook [1985]. On environmental issues generally, see Thomas [1992]; on the Third World, see Gupta [1988]. For a careful assessment of the prospects for sustainable development, of relevance to the issues of famine and environmental politics alike, see Redclift [1987]. For East Asia, Bello and Rosenfeld [1990] provide a graphic account; for Southeast Asia, McDowell [1989] discusses the policies of the various ASEAN countries, and Hardjono [1991] provides a good set of case studies for the central case of Indonesia. Brazilian policy towards Amazonia provides good material for comparison. Hall [1987] concentrates on the development of large-scale mining in the Carajás region, while Hecht and Cockburn [1990] discuss deforestation more generally, with specific attention to the social consequences.

Bibliography

Abdallah, A., Tordoff, W., Gordon, R. and Nyang, S. 1989. *Report on the Second and Third Tier Authorities*. Windhoek, Namibia: UNDP.

Abegunrin, L. 1985. 'The Southern African Development Coordination Conference: Politics of Dependence', in Onwuka and Sesay (eds), below.

Abel, C. and Lewis, C., eds. 1984. *Latin America, Economic Imperialism and the State*. London: Athlone Press.

Abrahamian, E. 1982. *Iran Between Two Revolutions*. Princeton: Princeton University Press.

Afshar, H., ed. 1985. *Women, Work, and Ideology in the Third World*. London: Tavistock.

Afshar, H. 1985a. 'The Position of Women in an Iranian Village', in Afshar (ed.), above.

Afshar, H. 1985b. 'Women, State and Ideology in Iran', *Third World Quarterly*, 7, 2.

Afshar, H., ed. 1987. *Women, State and Ideology: Studies from Africa and Asia*. London: Macmillan.

Afshar, H. and Dennis, C., eds. 1992. *Women and Adjustment Policies in the Third World*. London: Macmillan.

Ahmed, L. 1982. 'Western Ethnocentrism and Perceptions of the Harem', *Feminist Studies*, 8.

Albert, B. 1983. *South America and the World Economy from Independence to 1930*. London: Macmillan.

Allen, C. and Williams, G., eds. 1982. *Sociology of 'Developing Societies': Sub-Saharan Africa*. London: Macmillan.

Allen, J. van. 1976. ' "Aba Riots" or Igbo Women's War? Ideology, Stratification, and the Invisibility of Women', in Hafkin and Bay (eds), below.

Alvarez, S. 1990. *Engendering Democracy in Brazil: Women's Movements in Transition Politics*. Princeton: Princeton University Press.

Alves, M.H. 1985. *State and Opposition in Military Brazil*. Austin: University of Texas Press.

Amate, C. 1986. *Inside the OAU: Pan-Africanism in Practice*. London: Macmillan.

Amsden, A. 1979. 'Taiwan's Economic History: A Case of Etatisme and a Challenge to Dependency Theory', *Modern China*, 5, 3.

Amsden, A. 1989. *Asia's Next Giant: South Korea and Late Industrialization*. New York: Oxford University Press.

323

Anderson, B. 1966. 'Japan - the Light of Asia', in J. Silverstein (ed.), *Southeast Asia in World War Two: Four Essays*. New Haven: Yale University Southeast Asian Studies.

Anderson, B. 1972. *Java in a Time of Revolution: Occupation and Resistance, 1944–1946*. Ithaca: Cornell University Press.

Anderson, B. 1983. 'Old State, New Society: Indonesia's New Order in Comparative Historical Perspective', *Journal of Asian Studies*, 42, 3.

Anderson, L. 1987. 'The State in the Middle East and North Africa', *Comparative Politics*, 20, 1.

Angell, A. 1984. 'The Soldier as Politician', in D. Kavanagh and G. Peele (eds), *Comparative Government and Politics*. London: Heinemann.

Anglin, D. 1985. 'SADCC after Nkomati', *African Affairs*, No. 335, Vol. 84.

Apeldoorn, G. Jan Van. 1981. *Perspectives on Drought and Famine in Nigeria*. London: Allen & Unwin.

Archetti, E. *et al.*, eds. 1987. *Sociology of 'Developing Societies': Latin America*. London: Macmillan.

Arhin, K. 1979. *West African Traders in Ghana in the Nineteenth and Twentieth Centuries*. London: Longman.

Arjomand, S. 1988. *The Turban for the Crown: the Islamic Revolution in Iran*. New York: Oxford University Press.

Arriagada, G. 1988. *Pinochet: The Politics of Power*. Boston: Unwin Hyman.

Arrigo, L. 1980. 'The Industrial Work Force of Young Women in Taiwan', *Bulletin of Concerned Asian Scholars*, 12, 2.

Asante, S. 1985. 'ECOWAS/CEAO: Conflict and Cooperation in West Africa', in Onwuka and Sesay (eds), below.

Atkins, G.P. 1989. *Latin America in the International Political System*. 2nd edition. Boulder: Westview Press.

Aviel, J. 1981.'Political Participation of Women in Latin America', *Western Political Quarterly*, 34, 1.

Ayubi, N. 1991. *Political Islam: Religion and Politics in the Arab World*. London: Routledge.

Azicri, M. 1988. *Cuba: Politics, Economics and Society*. London: Frances Pinter.

Bakhash, S. 1985. *The Reign of the Ayatollahs: Iran and the Islamic Revolution*. London: Tauris.

Batatu, H. 1981. 'Some Observations on the Social Origins of Syria's Ruling Military Group and the Causes of its Dominance', *Middle East Journal*, 35, 3.

Baylies, C. and Szeftel, M. 1982. 'The Rise of a Zambian Capitalist Class in the 1970s', *Journal of Southern African Studies*, 8, 2.

Beck, L. and Keddie, N. 1978. *Women in the Muslim World*. Cambridge, Mass.: Harvard University Press.

Behrouz, M. 1991. 'Factionalism in Iran under Khomeini', *Middle East Studies*, 27, 4.

Bello, W. and Rosenfeld, S. 1990. *Dragons in Distress: Asia's Miracle Economies in Crisis*. San Francisco: Institute for Food and Development Policy.

Beneria, L. 1981. *Women and Development*. New York: Praeger.
Benjamin M. and Collins, J. 1985. 'Is Rationing Socialist? Cuba's Food Distribution System', *Food Policy*, 10, 4.
Bermeo, N. 1992. 'Democracy and the Lessons of Dictatorship', *Comparative Politics*, 24, 3.
Binder, L. 1978. *In A Moment of Enthusiasm: Political Power and the Second Stratum in Egypt*. Chicago: Chicago University Press.
Black, G. 1981. *Triumph of the People: The Sandinista Revolution in Nicaragua*. London: Zed Press.
Boserup, E. 1970. *Women's Role in Economic Development*. New York: St. Martin's Press.
Brett, E.A. 1973. *Colonialism and Underdevelopment in East Africa: The Politics of Economic Change, 1919–1939*. London: Heinemann.
Brett, E.A. 1985. *The Politics of Uneven Development*. London: Macmillan.
Bresnan, J., ed. 1986. *Crisis in the Philippines: The Marcos Era and Beyond*. Princeton: Princeton University Press.
Broinowski, A., ed. 1990. *ASEAN into the 1990s*. London: Macmillan.
Bryceson, D. 1980. 'The Proletarianization of Women in Tanzania', *Review of African Political Economy*, 17, January-April.
Bungbongkarn, S. 1991. 'The Thai Military and its Role in Society in the 1990s', in Selochan (ed), below.
Buvinic, M. *et al.*, eds. 1983. *Women and Poverty in the Third World*. London: Johns Hopkins University Press.
Callaway, B. 1984. 'Ambiguous Consequences of the Socialisation and Seclusion of Hausa Women', *Journal of Modern African Studies*, 22, 3.
Cammack, P. 1988. 'Brazilian Party Politics, 1945–1987: Continuities and Discontinuities', in Randall (ed.), below.
Cammack, P. 1991a. 'Democracy and Development in Latin America', *Journal of International Development*, 3, 5.
Cammack, P. 1991b. 'States and Markets in Latin America', in M. Moran and M. Wright (eds), *The Market and the State: Studies in Interdependence*. London: Macmillan.
Cammack, P. 1993. 'Democratisation and Citizenship in Latin America', in M. Moran and G. Parry (eds), *Democracy and Democratisation*. London: Routledge.
Cardoso, F.H. and Faletto, E. 1979. *Dependency and Development in Latin America*. Berkeley: University of California Press.
Chabal, P. 1983. *Amilcar Cabral: Revolutionary Leadership and People's War*. Cambridge: Cambridge University Press.
Chaliand, G. 1977. *Revolution in the Third World: Myths and Prospects*. Hassocks: Harvester.
Chan, S. *et al.*, eds. 1990. *Exporting Apartheid: Foreign Policies in Southern Africa, 1978–1988*. London: Macmillan.
Chaney, E. 1979. *Supermadre: Women in Politics in Latin America*. Austin: University of Texas Press.
Chaney, E. and Schmink, M. 1980. 'Women and Modernization: Access to Tools', in Nash and Safa (eds), below.

Chazan, N., Mortimer, R., Ravenhill, J. and Rothchild, D. 1992. *Politics and Society in Contemporary Africa.* 2nd ed. London: Macmillan.

Cheng, T. 1989. 'Democratizing the Quasi-Leninist Regime in Taiwan', *World Politics*, 41, 4.

Clapham, C., ed. 1982. *Private Patronage and Public Power: Political Clientelism and the Modern State.* London: Frances Pinter.

Clapham, C. 1988. *Transformation and Continuity in Revolutionary Ethiopia.* Cambridge: Cambridge University Press.

Clapham, C. and Philip, G. eds. 1985. *The Political Dilemmas of Military Regimes.* London: Croom Helm.

Cohen, R. and Goulbourne, H., eds. 1991. *Democracy and Socialism in Africa.* Boulder: Westview Press.

Collier, D., ed. 1979. *The New Authoritarianism in Latin America.* Princeton: Princeton University Press.

Collier, R.B. 1982. *Regimes in Tropical Africa: Changing Forms of Supremacy, 1945–75.* Berkeley: University of California Press.

Collier, R.B. and Collier, D. 1991. *Shaping the Political Arena: Critical Junctures, the Labor Movement, and Regime Dynamics in Latin America.* Princeton: Princeton University Press.

Cotton, J. 1989. 'From Authoritarianism to Democracy in South Korea', *Political Studies*, 37, 2.

Cotton, J. 1992. 'Understanding the State in South Korea: Bureaucratic-Authoritarian or State Autonomy Theory?, *Comparative Political Studies*, 24, 4.

Coulon, C. and O'Brien, D.B.C. 1989. 'Senegal', in O'Brien *et al.* (eds), below.

Cox, T.S. 1976. *Civil-Military Relations in Sierra Leone: A Case Study of African Soldiers in Politics.* Cambridge, Mass.: Harvard University Press.

Crehan, K. 1984. 'Women and Development in North Western Zambia: from Producer to Housewife', *Review of African Political Economy*, 27/28, February.

Crouch, H. 1978. *The Army and Politics in Indonesia.* Ithaca: Cornell University Press.

Crouch, H. 1991a. 'Military-Civilian Relations in Indonesia in the Late Soeharto Era', in Selochan (ed.), below.

Crouch, H. 1991b. 'The Military in Malaysia', in Selochan (ed.), below.

Decalo, S. 1990. *Coups and Army Rule in Africa: Studies in Military Style.* Second edition. New Haven: Yale University Press.

Dennis, C. 1984. 'Capitalist Development and Women's Work: A Nigerian Case Study', *Review of African Political Economy*, 27/28, February.

Dent, M.J. 1978. 'Corrective Government: Military Rule in Perspective', in Panter-Brick (ed.), below.

Deyo, F., ed. 1987. *The Political Economy of New Asian Industrialism.* Ithaca: Cornell University Press.

Diamond, L. 1992. 'Promoting Democracy', *Foreign Policy*, 87, 1.

Diamond, L. *et al.*, eds. 1988. *Democracy in Developing Countries: Africa.* Boulder: Lynne Rienner.

Diamond, L. *et al.*, eds. 1989a. *Democracy in Developing Countries: Asia.* Boulder: Lynne Rienner.

Diamond, L. *et al.*, eds. 1989b. *Democracy in Developing Countries: Latin America.* Boulder: Lynne Rienner.

Dix, R. 1983. 'The Varieties of Revolution', *Comparative Politics*, 15, 3.

Dix, R. 1984. 'Why Revolutions Succeed and Fail', *Polity*, 16, 3.

Dix, R. 1992. 'Democratization and the Institutionalization of Latin American Political Parties', *Comparative Political Studies*, 24, 4.

Doner, R. 1992. 'Limits of State Strength: Toward an Institutionalist View of Economic Development', *World Politics*, 44, 3.

Dornbusch, R. 1985. 'Dealing with Debt in the 1980s', *Third World Quarterly*, 7, 3.

Doronila, A. 1985. 'The Transformation of Patron-Client Relations and its Political Consequences in Postwar Philippines', *Journal of Southeast Asian Studies*, 16, 1.

Doronila, A. 1992. *The State, Economic Transformation and Political Change in the Philippines, 1946–1972.* Singapore: Oxford University Press.

Doumato, E.A. 1991. 'Women and the Stability of Saudi Arabia', *MERIP*, No. 171.

Drakakis-Smith, D. 1992. *Pacific Asia.* London: Routledge.

Dreze, J. and Sen. A. 1990. *Hunger and Public Action.* Oxford: Clarendon Press.

Dunkerley, J. 1984. *Rebellion in the Veins: Political Struggle in Bolivia, 1952–1982.* London: Verso.

Elliott, D. 1978. *Thailand: The Origins of Military Rule.* London: Zed.

Esposito, J. and Piscatori, J. 1991. 'Democratization and Islam', *Middle East Journal*, 45, 3.

Etcheson, C.E. 1984. *The Rise and Demise of Democratic Kampuchea.* Boulder: Westview Press.

Etienne, M. 1980. 'Women and Men, Cloth and Colonization: The Transformation of Production-Distribution Relations among the Baule (Ivory Coast)', in Etienne and Leacock (eds), below.

Etienne, M. and Leacock, E., eds. 1980. *Women and Colonization: Anthropological Perspectives.* New York: Praeger.

Fagen, R. 1969. *The Transformation of Political Culture in Cuba.* Stanford: Stanford University Press.

Fall, B. 1967. *Ho Chi Minh on Revolution: Selected Writings 1920–1966.* New York: Praeger.

Fernandez-Kelly, M.P. 1983. *For We Are Sold, I and My People: Women Industrial Workers on the Mexican Frontier.* Albany: State University of New York Press.

Finer, S.E. 1981. *The Man on Horseback: The Role of the Military in Politics.* 2nd edition, revised. London: Pall Mall Press.

Fishlow, A. 1989. 'A Tale of Two Presidents: The Political Economy of Crisis Management', in A. Stepan (ed.) *Democratizing Brazil: Problems of Transition and Consolidation.* New York: Oxford University Press.

Flynn, P. 1978. *Brazil: A Political Analysis*. London: Ernest Benn.

Foltz, W. 1965. *From French West Africa to the Mali Federation*. New Haven: Yale University Press.

Fox, J. 1991. 'Managing the Ecology of Rice Production in Indonesia', in Hardjono (ed.), below.

Frieden, J. 1988. 'Classes, Sectors, and Foreign Debt in Latin America', *Comparative Politics*, 21, 3.

Frieden, J. 1991. *Debt, Development and Democracy: Modern Political Economy and Latin America, 1965–1985*. Princeton: Princeton University Press.

Frost, F. 1990. 'Introduction: ASEAN since 1967 - Origins, Evolution and Recent Developments', in Broinowski (ed.), above.

Gallin, R. 1990. 'Women and Export Industry in Taiwan: The Muting of Class Consciousness', in Ward (ed.), below.

Garlick, P.C. 1971. *African Traders and Economic Development in Ghana*. Oxford: Clarendon Press.

Gifford, P. and Louis, W.R., eds. 1982. *The Transfer of Power in Africa: Decolonisation, 1940–1960*. New Haven: Yale University Press.

Gitli, E. and Ryd, G. 1992. 'Latin American Integration and the Enterprise for the Americas Initiative', *Journal of World Trade*, 26, 4.

Golay, F. *et al.*, eds. 1969. *Underdevelopment and Economic Nationalism in Southeast Asia*. Ithaca: Cornell University Press.

Gold, T. 1986. *State and Society in the Taiwan Miracle*. Armonk, N.Y.: M.E. Sharpe.

Goodwin, J. and Skocpol, T. 1989. 'Explaining Revolutions in the Third World', *Politics and Society*, 17, 4.

Gupta, A. 1988. *Ecology and Development in the Third World*. London: Routledge.

Hafkin N. and Bay, E. eds. 1976. *Women in Africa: Studies in Social and Economic Change*. Stanford: Stanford University Press.

Hagopian, F. 1990. 'Democracy By Undemocratic Means? Elites, Political Pacts and Regime Transition in Brazil', *Comparative Political Studies*, 23, 2.

Hall, A. 1987. 'Agrarian Crisis in Brazilian Amazonia: the Grande Carajas Programme', *Journal of Development Studies*, 23, 4.

Hall, D.G.E. 1981. *A History of South East Asia*. 4th edition. London: Macmillan.

Halliday, F. 1984. 'Labour Migration in the Arab World', *MERIP*, 123, May.

Han, S. 1989. 'South Korea: Politics in Transition', in Diamond *et al.* (eds), 1989a, above.

Hanlon, J. 1984. *Mozambique: The Revolution under Fire*. London: Zed Books.

Hansen B. and Radwan, S. 1982. *Employment Opportunities and Equity in a Changing Economy: Egypt in the 1980s*. Geneva: International Labour Organisation.

Harbeson, J. 1988. *The Ethiopian Transformation: The Quest for the Post-Imperial State*. Boulder: Westview Press.

Harbeson, J. and Rothchild, D. 1991. *Africa in World Politics*. Boulder: Westview Press.

Hardjono, J., ed. 1991. *Indonesia: Resources, Ecology, and Environment*. Singapore: Oxford University Press.

Hargreaves, J.D. 1988. *Decolonization in Africa*. London: Longman.

Hartmann, J. 1983. 'Development Policy-Making in Tanzania, 1962–1982: A Critique of Sociological Interpretations'. Ph.D. Dissertation, University of Hull, U.K.

Hawes, G. 1987. *The Philippine State and the Marcos Regime: The Politics of Export*. Ithaca: Cornell University Press.

Hawes, G. 1990. 'Theories of Peasant Revolution: A Critique and Contribution from the Philippines', *World Politics*, 52, 2.

Hazlewood, A. 1979. 'The End of the East African Community: What Are the Lessons for Regional Integration Schemes?', *Journal of Common Market Studies*, 18, 1.

Hecht, S. and Cockburn, A. 1990. *The Fate of the Forest: Developers, Destroyers and Defenders of the Amazon*. London: Penguin.

Heinz, W.S. *et al.*, eds. 1990. *The Military in Politics: Southeast Asian Experiences*. Hull: Centre for South-East Asian Studies, University of Hull.

Hellman, J. 1983. *Mexico in Crisis*. 2nd edition. New York: Holmes and Meier.

Henderson, G. 1968. *Korea: The Politics of the Vortex*. Cambridge, Mass.: Harvard University Press.

Herbst, J. 1990. *State Politics in Zimbabwe*. Berkeley: University of California Press.

Heyzer, N. 1986. *Working Women in Southeast Asia: Development, Subordination and Emancipation*. Milton Keynes: Open University Press.

Higgins, P. 1985. 'Women in the Islamic Republic of Iran: Legal, Social and Ideological Change', *Signs*, 10, 3.

Higgott, R. and Robison, R., eds. 1985. *Southeast Asia: Essays in the Political Economy of Structural Change*. London: Routledge and Kegan Paul.

Hill, P. 1970. *Studies in Rural Capitalism in West Africa*. Cambridge: Cambridge University Press.

Hinnebusch, R. 1990. *Authoritarian Power and State Transformation in Ba'athist Syria: Army, Party and Peasant*. Boulder: Westview Press.

Hodgkin, T. 1956. *Nationalism in Colonial Africa*. London: Frederick Muller.

Hogg, R. 1987. 'Development in Kenya: Drought, Desertification and Food Scarcity', *African Affairs*, No. 342, Vol. 86.

Holm, J. and Morgan, R. 1985. 'Coping with Drought in Botswana: An African Success', *Journal of Modern African Studies*, 23, 3.

Hudson, M. 1978. *Arab Politics: The Search for Legitimacy*. New Haven: Yale University Press.

Hudson, M. 1991. 'After the Gulf War: Prospects for Democratization in the Arab World', *Middle East Journal*, 45, 3.

Huntington, S. 1991. 'Democracy's Third Wave', *Journal of Democracy*, 2, 1.

Hurrell, A. 1992. 'Latin America in the New World Order: A Regional Bloc of the Americas?', *International Affairs*, 68, 1.

Ifeka-Moller, C. 1977. 'Female Militancy and Colonial Revolt: The Women's War of 1929, Eastern Nigeria', in S.Ardener (ed.), *Perceiving Women*. London: Dent.

Iliffe, J. 1979. *A Modern History of Tanganyika*. Cambridge: Cambridge University Press.

Iliffe, J. 1983. *The Emergence of African Capitalism*. London: Macmillan.

Jacobs, S. 1984. 'Women and Land Resettlement in Zimbabwe', *Review of African Political Economy*, 27/28, February.

Janowitz, M. 1964. *The Military in the Political Development of New Nations: An Essay in Comparative Analysis*. Chicago: University of Chicago Press.

Jansson, K., Harris, M. and Penrose, A. 1987. *The Ethiopian Famine*. London: Zed Books.

Jaquette, J., ed. 1989. *The Women's Movement in Latin America*. Boston: Unwin Hyman.

Jelin, E. 1977. 'Migration and Labor Force Participation of Latin American Women: The Domestic Servants in the Cities', in Wellesley Education Committee (ed.), below. Also published as *Signs*, 3, 1 (1977).

Joekes, S. 1987. *Women in the World Economy*. New York: Oxford University Press.

Johnson, C. 1987. 'Political Institutions and Economic Performance: The Government-Business Relationship in Japan, South Korea, and Taiwan', in Deyo (ed.), above.

Johnson, M. 1986. *Class and Clientelism in Beirut*. London: Ithaca Press.

Kahin, G. 1952. *Nationalism and Revolution in Indonesia*. Ithaca: Cornell University Press.

Karl, T. 1990. 'Dilemmas of Democratization in Latin America', *Comparative Politics*, 23, 1.

Karol, K. 1970. *Guerrillas in Power: The Course of the Cuban Revolution*. New York: Hill and Wang.

Kaufman, R. 1988. *The Politics of Debt in Argentina, Brazil, and Mexico*. Berkeley: Institute of International Studies.

Keller, E. 1988. *Revolutionary Ethiopia: From Empire to People's Republic*. Bloomington: Indiana University Press.

Kerkvliet, B. 1977. *The Huk Rebellion: A Study of Peasant Revolt in the Philippines*. Berkeley: University of California Press.

Kerr, M. 1971. *The Arab Cold War*. 3rd edition. New York: Oxford University Press.

Kessler, R. 1989. *Rebellion and Repression in the Philippines*. New Haven: Yale University Press.

Khafagy, F. 1984. 'Women and Labour Migration: One Village in Egypt', *MERIP*, 124, June.

Khahil, S. 1989. *The Republic of Fear: The Politics of Modern Iraq*. London: Radius.

Knight, A. 1984. 'The Working Class and the Mexican Revolution, c. 1900–1928', *Journal of Latin American Studies*, 16, 1.

Lawrence, R., Snyder, F. and Szeftel, M. 1985. 'Editorial: War and Famine in Africa', *Review of African Political Economy*, 33.

Lawson, F.H. 1989. 'Class Politics and State Power in Ba'ath Syria', in B. Berberoglu (ed.), *Power and Stability in the Middle East*. London: Zed Press.

Lever, H. and Huhne, C. 1985. *Debt and Danger: The World Financial Crisis*. Harmondsworth: Penguin.

Liddle, R.W. 1985. 'Soeharto's Indonesia: Personal Rule and Political Institutions', *Pacific Affairs*, 58, 1.

Liddle, R.W. 1992. 'Indonesia's Democratic Past and Future', *Comparative Politics*, 24, 4.

Liefer, M. 1988. *ASEAN and the Security of South-East Asia*. London: Routledge.

Little, W. 1986. 'Military Power in Latin America: An Overview', *Working Paper 4*, Institute of Latin American Studies, University of Liverpool.

Liviga, A.J. and van Donge, J.K. 1983. 'Tanzanian Political Culture and the Cabinet'. Mimeo.

Lobo, S. 1982. *A House of My Own*. Tucson: University of Arizona Press.

Lockhart, J. and Schwartz, S. 1983. *Early Latin America*. Cambridge: Cambridge University Press.

Loveman, B. 1991. 'Misión Cumplida? Civil-Military Relations and the Chilean Political Transition', *Journal of Interamerican Studies and World Affairs*, 33, 3.

Loveman, B. and Davies, T., eds. 1978. *The Politics of Anti-politics: The Military in Latin America*. Lincoln: University of Nebraska Press.

Loveman, B. and Davies, T., eds. 1985. *Che Guevara: Guerrilla Warfare*. Lincoln: University of Nebraska Press.

Lowenthal, A. and Fitch, S. eds. 1986. *Armies and Politics in Latin America*. 2nd edition. New York: Holmes and Meier.

Luciani, G., ed. 1990. *The Arab State*. Routledge: London.

Luckham, R. 1967. *The Nigerian Military: A Sociological Analysis of Authority and Revolt, 1960–67*. Cambridge: Cambridge University Press.

Luckham, R. 1971. 'A Comparative Typology of Civil-Military Relations', *Government and Opposition*, 6, 1.

Luckham, R. 1991. 'Introduction: The Military, the Developmental State and Social Forces in Asia and the Pacific: Issues for Comparative Analysis', in Selochan (ed.), below.

Lynch, J. 1973. *The Spanish American Revolutions: 1803–1826*. London: Weidenfeld and Nicholson.

Mabro, R. 1974. *The Egyptian Economy, 1952–1972*. Oxford: Oxford University Press.

McDowell, M. 1989. 'Development and the Environment in ASEAN', *Pacific Affairs*, 62, 3.

Mainwaring, S. 1991. 'Politicians, Parties, and Electoral Systems: Brazil in Comparative Perspective', *Comparative Politics*, 24, 1.

Mainwaring, S. 1992–93. 'Brazilian Party Underdevelopment in Comparative Perspective', *Political Science Quarterly*, 107, 4.

Makram-Ebeid, M. 1989. 'Political Opposition in Egypt: Democratic Myth or Reality?', *Middle East Journal*, 43, 3.

Malloy, J., ed. 1977. *Authoritarianism and Corporatism in Latin America*. Pittsburgh: Pittsburgh University Press.

Malloy, J. 1987. 'The Politics of Transition in Latin America', in Malloy and Seligson (eds), below.

Malloy, J. and Seligson, M., eds. 1987. *Authoritarians and Democrats: Regime Transition in Latin America*. Pittsburgh: Pittsburgh University Press.

Mansfield, P. 1991. *A History of the Middle East*. London: Viking.

Marcum, J. 1969. *The Angolan Revolution*, Vol I. Cambridge, Mass.: MIT Press.

Marcum, J. 1978. *The Angolan Revolution*, Vol II. Cambridge, Mass.: MIT Press.

Markakis, J. and Waller, M., eds. 1986. *Military Marxist Regimes in Africa*. London: Frank Cass.

Mayall, J. 1992. 'The Hopes and Fears of Independence: Africa and the World, 1960–1990', in D. Rimmer (ed.), *Africa Thirty Years On*. London: James Currie.

Melson R. and Wolpe, H., eds. 1971. *Nigeria: Modernization and the Politics of Communalism*. East Lansing: Michigan State University Press.

Mervat, H. 1992. 'Economic and Political Liberation in Egypt: The Demise of State Feminism', *International Journal of Middle East Studies*, 24, 2.

Middle East Research and Information Project (MERIP). 1992a. *Democracy in the Arab World*. Issue No. 174.

Middle East Research and Information Project (MERIP). 1992b. *Arms Race or Arms Control in the Middle East?* Issue No. 177.

Migdal, J. 1988. *Strong Societies and Weak States: State-Society Relations and State Capabilities in the Third World*. Princeton: Princeton University Press.

Miller, F. 1991. *Latin American Women and the Search for Social Justice*. Hanover: University Press of New England.

Moaddel, M. 1991. 'Class Struggle in Post-Revolutionary Iran', *International Journal of Middle East Studies*, 23, 3.

Molteno, R. 1974. 'Cleavage and Conflict in Zambian Politics: A Study in Sectionalism', in W. Tordoff (ed), *Politics in Zambia*. Manchester: Manchester University Press.

Molyneux, M. 1985a. 'Mobilization without Emancipation? Women's Interests, State and Revolution in Nicaragua', *Feminist Studies*, 11, 2.

Molyneux, M. 1985b. 'Family Reform in Socialist States: The Hidden Agenda', *Feminist Review*, 21.

Moore, C.H. 1974. 'Authoritarian Politics in an Unincorporated Society: The Case of Nasser's Egypt', *Comparative Politics*, 6, 2.

Moser, C. 1991. 'Gender Planning in the Third World: Meeting Practical and Strategic Needs', in R. Grant and K. Newland (eds), *Gender and International Relations*. Milton Keynes: Open University Press.

Moser, C. 1992. 'Adjustment from below: Low-Income Women, Time and the Triple Role in Guayaquil, Ecuador', in Afshar and Dennis (eds), above.

Munslow, B. 1983. *Mozambique: The Revolution and its Origins.* London: Longman.

Nash, J. and Fernandez-Kelly, M.P., eds. 1983. *Women, Men and the International Division of Labor.* Albany: State University of New York Press.

Nash, J. and Safa, H. eds. 1980. *Sex and Class in Latin America.* South Hadley: Bergin.

Nasser, J. 1972. *Nasser Speaks, Basic Documents.* London: Morsett Press.

Nazzari, M. 1983. 'The "Woman Question" in Cuba: An Analysis of Material Constraints on its Solution', *Signs*, 9, 2.

Niehoff, J. 1987. 'The Villager as Industrialist: Ideologies of Household Factories in Rural Taiwan', *Modern China*, 13, 3.

Oboler, R.S. 1975. *Women, Power and Economic Change: The Nandi of Kenya.* Stanford: Stanford University Press.

O'Brien, D.B.C. 1979. 'Ruling Class and Peasantry in Senegal: 1960–1976', in R.C. O'Brien (ed.), *The Political Economy of Underdevelopment: Dependence in Senegal.* London: Sage.

O'Brien, D.B.C., Dunn, J. and Rathbone, J., eds. 1989. *Contemporary West African States.* Cambridge: Cambridge University Press.

O'Donnell, G. 1977. 'Corporatism and the Question of the State', in Malloy (ed.), above.

Oliver, R. and Fage, J.D. 1962. *A Short History of Africa.* Harmondsworth: Penguin.

Ong, A. 1987. *Spirits of Resistance and Capitalist Discipline: Factory Women in Malaysia.* Albany: State University of New York Press.

Onwuka, R.I. and Sesay, A., eds. 1985. *The Future of Regionalism in Africa.* London: Macmillan.

Owen, R. 1981. *The Middle East in the World Economy.* London: Methuen.

Owen, R. 1992. *State, Power and Politics in the Making of the Modern Middle East.* London: Routledge.

Oyediran, O., ed. 1979. *Nigerian Government and Politics under Military Rule, 1966–79.* London: Macmillan.

Palmer, R. 1977. 'The Agricultural History of Rhodesia', in Palmer and Parsons (eds), below.

Palmer, R. and Parsons, N., eds. 1977. *The Roots of Rural Poverty in Central and Southern Africa.* London: Heinemann.

Panter-Brick, S.K., ed. 1978. *Soldiers and Oil: The Political Transformation of Nigeria.* London: Frank Cass.

Pearce, J. 1981. *Under the Eagle: US Intervention in Central America and the Caribbean.* London: Latin America Bureau.

Peeler, J. 1985. *Latin American Democracies: Colombia, Costa Rica, Venezuela.* Chapel Hill: University of North Carolina Press.

Pescatello, A., ed. 1973. *Female and Male in Latin America.* Pittsburgh: University of Pittsburgh Press.

Perez, A. 1992. 'The FSLN after the Debacle: The Struggle for the Definition of Sandinismo', *Journal of Interamerican Studies and World Affairs*, 34, 1.

Perez, L. 1988. *Cuba: Between Reform and Revolution*. New York: Oxford University Press.

Philip, G. 1985. *The Military in South American Politics*. London: Croom Helm.

Pittin, R. 1984. 'Gender and Class in a Nigerian Industrial Setting', *Review of African Political Economy*, 31, December.

Pluvier, J. 1974. *South-East Asia from Colonialism to Independence*. Kuala Lumpur: Oxford University Press.

Porpora, D., Lim, M. and Prommas, U. 1989. 'The Role of Women in the International Division of Labour: The Case of Thailand', *Development and Change*, 20, 2.

Potter, L. 1991. 'Environmental and Social Aspects of Timber Exploitation in Kalimantan, 1967–1989', in Hardjono (ed.), above.

Purcell, S. 1981. 'Mexico: Clientelism, Corporatism and Political Stability', in S.N. Eisenstadt and R. Lemarchand (eds), *Political Clientelism, Patronage and Development*. Beverley Hills: Sage.

Pye, L. 1985. *Asian Power and Politics: The Cultural Dimensions of Authority*. Cambridge, Mass.: Belknap Press.

Rabe, S. 1990. 'Dulles, Latin America, and Cold War Anticommunism', in R. Immerman, ed, *John Foster Dulles and the Diplomacy of the Cold War*. Princeton: Princeton University Press.

Race, J. 1972. *War Comes to Long An: Revolutionary Conflict in a Vietnamese Province*. Berkeley: University of California Press.

Randall, V., ed. 1988. *Political Parties in the Third World*. London: Sage.

Randall, V. and Theobald, R. 1985. *Political Change and Underdevelopment: A Critical Introduction to Third World Politics*. London: Macmillan.

Rassam, A. 1982. 'Revolution within the Revolution? Women and the State in Iraq', in T. Niblock (ed.), *Iraq: The Contemporary State*. London: Croom Helm.

Rattray, R.S. 1929. *Ashanti Law and Constitution*. London: Oxford University Press.

Redclift, M. 1987. *Sustainable Development: Exploring the Contradictions*. London: Methuen.

Reid, A. 1974. *The Indonesian National Revolution, 1945–1950*. Hawthorn, Victoria: Longman.

Reid, A. 1988. 'Female Roles in Pre-colonial Southeast Asia', *Modern Asian Studies*, 22, 3.

Remmer, K. 1989. *Military Rule in Latin America*. Boston: Unwin Hyman.

Review of African Political Economy. 1984. Special Issue on Women in Africa, Nos. 27–28, February.

Review of African Political Economy. 1985. Special Issue on War and Famine, No. 33.

Rice, R. 1991. 'Environmental Degradation, Pollution, and the Exploitation of Indonesia's Fishery Resources', in Hardjono (ed.), above.

Richards, A. and Waterbury, J. 1990. *A Political Economy of the Middle East: State, Class and Economic Development*. Boulder: Westview Press.

Roberts, P. 1984. 'Feminism in Africa; Feminism and Africa', *Review of African Political Economy*, 27/28, February.

Robertson, C. 1976. 'Ga Women and Socioeconomic Change in Accra, Ghana,' in Hafkin and Bay (eds), above.

Robison, R. 1986. *Indonesia: The Rise of Capital*. North Sydney: Allen and Unwin.

Robison, R. 1988. 'Authoritarian States, Capital-Owning Classes, and the Politics of Newly Industrializing Countries: the Case of Indonesia', *World Politics*, 41, 1.

Rock, D. 1985. *Argentina 1516–1982*. Berkeley: University of California Press.

Rodney, W. 1972. *How Europe Underdeveloped Africa*. Dar es Salaam: Tanzania Publishing House; and London: Bogle L'Ouverture.

Rogers, B. 1980. *The Domestication of Women: Discrimination in Developing Societies*. London: Tavistock.

Rosberg, C. and Callaghy, T., eds. 1979. *Socialism in Sub-Saharan Africa: A New Assessment*. Berkeley: Institute of International Studies, University of California.

Rotberg, R., ed. 1983. *Imperialism, Colonialism and Hunger: East and Central Africa*. Lexington, Mass.: Heath.

Rothchild, D. and Chazan, N., eds. 1988. *The Precarious Balance: State and Society in Africa*. Boulder: Westview Press.

Roxborough, I. 1979. *Theories of Underdevelopment*. London: Macmillan.

Saadawi, N. 1980. *The Hidden Face of Eve: Women in the Arab World*. London: Zed Press.

Sacks, K. 1979. *Sisters and Wives: The Past and Future of Sexual Equality*. Westport: Greenwood Press.

Said, S. 1991. *Genesis of Power: General Sudirman and the Indonesian Military in Politics, 1945–49*. North Sydney: Allen and Unwin.

Salaff, J. 1981. *Working Daughters of Hong Kong*. Cambridge: Cambridge University Press.

Samudavanija, C. 1989. 'Thailand: A Stable Semi-democracy', in Diamond *et al.* (eds), 1989a, above.

Sandbrook, R. 1985. *The Politics of Africa's Economic Stagnation*. Cambridge: Cambridge University Press.

Schaffer, B.B. 1965. 'The Concept of Preparation: Some Questions about the Transfer of Systems of Government', *World Politics*, 18, 1.

Schatz, S. 1984. 'Pirate Capitalism and the Inert Economy of Nigeria', *Journal of Modern African Studies*, 22, 1.

Schirmer, J. 1989. ' "Those who die for life cannot be called dead": Women and Human Rights Protest in Latin America', *Feminist Review*, 32.

Schoultz, L. 1981. *Human Rights and United States Policy Toward Latin America*. Princeton: Princeton University Press.

Schoultz, L. 1987. *National Security and United States Policy Toward Latin America*. Princeton: Princeton University Press.

Selochan, V., ed. 1991. *The Military, the State, and Development in Asia and the Pacific.* Boulder: Westview Press.

Sen, A. 1981. *Poverty and Famines: An Essay on Entitlement and Deprivation.* Oxford: Clarendon Press.

Shaiken, H. 1990. *Mexico in the Global Economy: High Technology and Work Organization in Export Industries.* San Diego: Centre for US-Mexican Studies, University of California, Monograph Series, 33.

Silverstein, J. 1977. *Burma: Military Rule and the Politics of Stagnation.* Ithaca: Cornell University Press.

Simon, S. 1987. 'ASEAN's Strategic Situation in the 1980s', *Pacific Affairs,* 60, 1.

Skidmore, T. and Smith, P. 1992. *Modern Latin America.* 3rd edition. New York: Oxford University Press.

Sklair, L. 1989. *Assembling for Development: The Maquila Industry in Mexico and the United States.* Unwin Hyman: Boston.

Sklar, R. 1979. 'The Nature of Class Domination in Africa', *Journal of Modern African Studies,* 17, 4.

Sklar, R. and Whitaker, C. 1991. *African Politics and Problems in Development.* Boulder: Lynne Rienner.

Skocpol, T. 1979. *States and Social Revolutions.* Cambridge: Cambridge University Press.

Smallwood, P. and Sinclair, S. 1981. *Oil, Debt and Development: OPEC in the Third World.* London: Allen & Unwin.

Smith, M. 1973. 'Domestic Service as a Channel of Upward Mobility for the Lower-Class Woman: The Lima Case', in Pescatello (ed.) above.

Sobham, R. 1982. 'Enhancing Trade Between OPEC and the Developing Countries of Asia', *Third World Quarterly,* 4, 4.

Sowayegh, A. 1984. *Arab Petropolitics.* London: Croom Helm.

Springborg, R. 1987. *Mubarak's Egypt: Fragmentation of the Political Order.* London: Kegan Paul International.

Stargardt, A.W. 1989. 'The Emergence of the Asian System of Powers', *Modern Asian Studies,* 23, 3.

Steinberg, D., ed. 1987. *In Search of Southeast Asia: A Modern History.* 2nd edition. Sydney: Allen and Unwin.

Stepan, A. 1971. *The Military in Politics: Changing Patterns in Brazil.* Princeton: Princeton University Press.

Stepan, A. 1978. *The State and Society: Peru in Comparative Perspective.* Princeton: Princeton University Press.

Stepan, A. 1988. *Rethinking Military Politics: Brazil and the Southern Cone.* Princeton: Princeton University Press.

Sternbach, N. *et al.* 1992. 'Feminisms in Latin America: From Bogotá to San Bernardo', *Signs,* 17, 2.

Stevens, C. 1984. *The Political Economy of Nigeria.* London: Economist Newspaper Ltd.

Stork, J. and Paul, J. 1983. 'Arms Sales and the Militarization of the Middle East', *MERIP,* 112, February.

Sundhaussen, U. 1982. *The Road to Power: Indonesian Military Politics, 1945–1966.* Kuala Lumpur: Oxford University Press.

Sundhaussen, U. 1991. 'The Military in Politics', in R.H.Taylor (ed.), *Handbooks to the Modern World: Asia and the Pacific*, vol. II. New York: Facts on File Publications.

Sutter, R. 1988. *Taiwan: Entering the 21st Century*. Lanham: University Press of America.

Szeftel, M. 1978. 'Conflicts, Spoils and Class Formation in Zambia'. Ph.D. Dissertation, University of Manchester, U.K.

Tang, T. N. 1986. *Journal of a Vietcong*. London: Jonathan Cape.

Tate, D. 1979. *The Making of Modern South-East Asia, Vol. II: The Western Impact*. Oxford: Oxford University Press.

Taylor, E. 1984. 'Egyptian Migration and Peasant Wives', *MERIP*, 124, June.

Taylor, J. and Turton, A. 1988. *Sociology of 'Developing Societies': Southeast Asia*. London: Macmillan.

Thomas, C. 1992. *The Environment in International Relations*. London: Royal Institute for International Affairs.

Tiano, S. 1990. 'Maquiladora Women: A New Category of Workers?', in Ward (ed.), below.

Tillman, S.P. 1982. *The United States in the Middle East*. Bloomington: Indiana University Press.

Tordoff, W. 1992. *Government and Politics in Africa*. 2nd ed. London: Macmillan.

United Nations. 1991. *Women in the World, 1970–1990*. New York: United Nations.

Urdang, S. 1984. 'The Last Transition? Women and Development in Mozambique', *Review of African Political Economy*, 27/28, February.

Uwazurike, P.C. 1990. 'Confronting Potential Breakdown: the Nigerian Redemocratisation Process in Critical Perspective', *Journal of Modern African Studies*, 28, 1.

Vail, L. 1983. 'The State and the Creation of Colonial Malawi's Agricultural Economy', in R. Rotberg (ed.), above.

Valenzuela, A. 1978. *The Breakdown of Democratic Regimes: Chile*. Baltimore: Johns Hopkins University Press.

Vilas, C. 1986. *The Sandinista Revolution*. New York: Monthly Review Press.

Wade, R. 1990. *Governing the Market: Economic Theory and the Role of Government in East Asian Industrialization*. Princeton: Princeton University Press.

Wallace, T. 1985. 'Refugees and Hunger in Eastern Sudan', *Review of African Political Economy*, 33.

Ward, K., ed. 1990. *Women Workers and Global Restructuring*. Ithaca: ILR Press.

Waterbury, J. 1983. *The Egypt of Nasser and Sadat*. Princeton: Princeton University Press.

Waterbury, J. 1991. 'Twilight of the State Bourgeoisie?', *International Journal of Middle East Studies*, 23, 1.

Watts, M. 1983. *Silent Violence: Food, Famine and Peasantry in Northern Nigeria*. Berkeley: University of California Press.

Watts, M. 1991. 'Entitlements or Empowerment? Famine and Starvation in Africa', *Review of African Political Economy*, 51, July.

Waylen, G. 1992a. 'Rethinking Women's Political Participation and Protest: Chile 1970–1990', *Political Studies*, 60, 2.

Waylen, G. 1992b. 'Women, Authoritarianism and Market Liberalisation in Chile, 1973–1989', in Afshar and Dennis (eds), above.

Weinbaum, M.G. 1982. *Food, Development and Politics*. Boulder: Westview Press.

Wellesley Education Committee, ed. 1977. *Women and National Development: The Complexities of Change*. Chicago: University of Chicago Press.

White, C.P. 1974. 'The Vietnamese Revolutionary Alliance: Intellectuals, Workers and Peasants', in J.W. Lewis (ed.), *Peasant Rebellion and Communist Revolution in Asia*. Stanford: Stanford University Press.

White, G., ed. 1988. *Developmental States in East Asia*. London: Macmillan.

Wilson, D. 1959. 'Thailand', in G.M. Kahin (ed.), *Government and Politics of Southeast Asia*. Ithaca: Cornell University Press.

Wilson, D. 1962. *Politics in Thailand*. Ithaca: Cornell University Press.

Wolf, D. 1990a. 'Daughters, Decisions and Domination: An Empirical and Conceptual Critique of Household Strategies', *Development and Change*, 21, 1.

Wolf, D. 1990b. 'Linking Women's Labor with the Global Economy: Factory Workers and their Families in Rural Java', in Ward (ed.), above.

Wolf, E. 1969. *Peasant Wars of the Twentieth Century*. New York: Harper and Row.

Wolf, E. 1982. *Europe and the People Without History*. Berkeley: University of California Press.

World Bank. 1981. *Accelerated Development in Sub-Saharan Africa: An Agenda for Action*. Washington, D.C.: The World Bank.

World Bank. 1989. *Sub-Saharan Africa: From Crisis to Sustainable Growth*. Washington, D.C.: The World Bank.

Wurfel, D. 1988. *Filipino Politics: Development and Decay*. Ithaca: Cornell University Press.

Wynia, G. 1990. *The Politics of Latin American Development*. 3rd edition. Cambridge: Cambridge University Press.

Young, C. 1982. *Ideology and Development in Africa*. New Haven: Yale University Press.

Zimbalist, A. 1992. 'Teetering on the Brink: Cuba's Current Economic and Political Crisis', *Journal of Latin American Studies*, 24, 2.

Index

CAMBRIDGE UNIVERSITY PRESS
Cambridge, New York, Melbourne, Madrid, Cape Town, Singapore,
São Paulo, Delhi

Cambridge University Press
The Edinburgh Building, Cambridge CB2 8RU, UK

Published in the United States of America by
Cambridge University Press, New York

www.cambridge.org
Information on this title: www.cambridge.org/9780521618670

First published 2009

Printed in the United Kingdom at the University Press, Cambridge

A catalogue record for this publication is available from the British Library

Library of Congress Cataloguing in Publication data
Nash, Kate, 1958–
    The cultural politics of human rights : comparing the US and UK / Kate Nash.
        p.   cm.
    Includes bibliographical references and index.
    ISBN 978-0-521-85352-1 (hardback) – ISBN 978-0-521-61867-0 (pbk.)
    1. Human rights–United States.   2. Politics and culture–United States.
    3. Human rights–Great Britain.   4. Politics and culture–Great Britain.
    I. Title.
    JC599.U5.N277 2009
    323.0941–dc22
    2008055954

ISBN 978-0-521-85352-1 hardback
ISBN 978-0-521-61867-0 paperback

The Cultural Politics of Human Rights

Comparing the US and UK

KATE NASH

CAMBRIDGE UNIVERSITY PRESS

The Cultural Politics of Human Rights

How does culture make a difference to the realisation of human rights in Western states? It is only through cultural politics that human rights may become more than abstract moral ideals, protecting human beings from state violence and advancing protection from starvation and the social destruction of poverty. Using an innovative methodology, this book maps the emergent 'intermestic' human rights field within the US and UK in order to investigate detailed case studies of the cultural politics of human rights. Kate Nash researches how the authority to define human rights is being created within states as a result of international human rights commitments. Through comparative case studies, she explores how cultural politics is affecting state transformation today.

KATE NASH is Reader in Sociology at Goldsmiths College, University of London and Faculty Fellow of the Center for Cultural Sociology at Yale Unversity.

UK laws

ATCSA   Anti-Terrorism, Crime and Security Act 2001
HRA   UK Human Rights Act 1998
PTA   Prevention of Terrorism Act 2005

Table of cases

LEGAL REFERENCES: US

Boumediene et al. *v.* Bush et al.; al Odah et al. *v.* United States et al. – F.3d (D.C. Cir. 2007).

Boumediene et al. *v.* Bush et al.; al Odah et al. *v.* United States et al. (549 S.Ct._ 2007).

Doe *v.* Unocal, 963 F. Supp. 880 (C. D. Cal. 1987); summary judgement granted, Doe *v.* Unocal, 110 F. Supp 2d 1294 (C. D. Cal. 2000); rev'd in part, remanded, Doe *v.* Unocal, 2002 US App LEXIS 19263 (9th Cir. 2002); vacated, reh'g granted en banc, Doe *v.* Unocal, 2003 US App LEXIS 2716 (9th Cir. 2003).

Filartiga *v.* Pena-Irala, 630 F.2d 876 (2nd Cir. 1980).

Hamdan *v.* Rumsfeld (126 S.Ct. 2749 2006).

In re Guantanamo Detainee Cases, 355 F. Supp. 2d 443 (D.D.C. 2005).

Rasul et al. *v.* Bush et al; al Odah et al. *v.* United States et al. (542 S.Ct 466 2004).

Sosa *v.* Alvarez-Machain (124 S.Ct. 2739 2004).

United States *v.* Alvarez-Machain, 504 U.S. 655, 657 (1992).

'FRIEND OF THE COURT' BRIEFS

Brief for the United States of America as Amicus Curiae in Doe *v.* Unocal, 2003 US App LEXIS 2716 (9th Cir. 2003).

Plaintiffs-Appellants Supplemental Brief in Opposition to Amicus Curiae Brief Filed by the United States in Doe *v.* Unocal, 2003 US App LEXIS 2716 (9th Cir. 2003).

Brief for the United States as Respondent Supporting Petitioner in Sosa *v.* Alvarez-Machain (124 S.Ct. 2739 2004).

Brief of Amici Curiae International Human Rights Organizations and Religious Organizations in Support of Respondent in Sosa *v.* Alvarez-Machain (124 S.Ct. 2739 2004).

Brief of Amici Curiae Lawyers Committee for Human Rights and the Rutherford Institute in Support of the Respondent in Sosa *v.* Alvarez-Machain (124 S.Ct. 2739 2004).

Brief of 175 Members of both Houses of the Parliament of the United Kingdom of Great Britain and N. Ireland as Amici Curaie in Support of Petitioners in Rasul *v.* Bush (542 S.Ct 466 2004).

LEGAL REFERENCES: UK

A and others *v.* Home Secretary (UKHL 56 2004).

A and others *v.* Home Secretary (UKHL 71 2005).

DD and Home Secretary; AS and Home Secretary (SC/42 and 50/2005).

Home Secretary *v.* E and another (UKHL 47 2007).

JJ and others *v.* Home Secretary (UKHL 45 2007).

LEGAL REFERENCES: EUROPEAN COURT OF HUMAN RIGHTS

Chahal *v.* United Kingdom (Application 22414/93) ECHR 54 (1996).

1   What does it matter what human rights mean?

The cultural politics of human rights disrupts taken-for-granted norms of national political life. Human rights activists imagine practical deconstruction of the distinction between citizens and non-citizens through which national states have been constituted. They envisage a world order of cosmopolitan states in which the rights of all would be fully respected. How likely is it that such a form of society might be realised through their activities? Is collective responsibility for human rights currently being shaped in cultural politics? If so, how, and with what consequences? If not, how is it that the vision of human rights activists is failing to take effect given the explosion of discourse on human rights in recent years?

A focus on what human rights mean to social and political actors, and on how these meanings impact on their institutionalisation, has been missing from the study of human rights.[1] And yet it is only through cultural politics that the ideals of universal human rights may be realised in practice. What I mean by 'cultural politics' is more or less organised struggles over symbols that frame what issues, events or processes mean to social actors who are emotionally and intellectually invested in shared understandings of the world. But cultural politics is not only the contestation of symbols. Cultural politics concerns public contests over how society is imagined; how social relations are, could and should be organised. It is only through

---

[1] Fuyuki Kurasawa's study of what he calls the 'ethico-political labour' of human rights is an impressive theoretical advance in terms of establishing the importance of struggles over meaning to the practices of human rights (Kurasawa 2007). Ultimately, however, it is disappointing that Kurasawa does not link this labour to changes in institutions of governance and states, but confines his analysis to movements in civil society.

practices that are meaningful to people that social life is possible at all: the social institutions that constrain our lives are nothing but routinised shared understandings of what is real and what is worthwhile. Although social actors rarely, if ever, imagine a fully formulated blueprint of a new society, even during revolutionary periods, in using or contesting symbols that are meaningful to them they are nevertheless engaged, more or less consciously, either in trying to bring one about, or, just as likely, in defending what already exists.

Human rights are the object of cultural politics concerning global justice. Globalisation raises difficult questions concerning how justice must now be rethought beyond the national frame which successfully routinised shared understandings of justice as relevant only to fellow citizens. Human rights are themselves globalising as they are deployed in strategies to end human rights violations or to condemn states which resist international pressure to comply with human rights norms. In images of suffering in the global media which are framed as issues of human rights, and in responses to violations which seek to extend capacities for global governance, human rights are themselves an aspect of globalisation. However, at the same time, human rights also seem to stand above globalisation, to represent a framework through which globalisation itself might be regulated and global governance organised. The comprehensive schedule of human rights developed by the UN and in regional systems of human rights seem to offer a framework for justice beyond states, a global constitution to guide the political development of the planet. This book is concerned with whether and how globalising human rights may become established as norms of global justice through cultural politics.

Although it is now common to think of human rights as essential to just global governance, it is important to note that it is only through states that human rights can be realised. States do not just represent dangers and obstacles to the realisation of human rights, as sometimes appears to be the case in the literature on human rights violations; they are absolutely necessary for the realisation of human rights in practice. In this respect, it is particularly important to consider how human rights are contested and defined *within* states. It is only with the collusion of state agents that human rights are violated, and only states can secure and enforce human rights within their own territories.[2] Even at the international level, human rights systems exist only by state agreement; it is states that act together in international organisations to create conditions for the realisation of human rights. States raise taxes to pay for international organisations, authorise personnel to act in them on their behalf, and maintain the military and police force that can, in principle at least, be used to enforce human rights.

States, like all other social institutions, are constituted as routinised social practices which establish that members of society 'know how to go on' in any particular situation. Language, symbolic communication organised into settled patterns of shared understandings as discourse, is the most important structuring dimension of institutions. This is equally the case in formal, bureaucratic organisations, such as those of the law and government, where face-to-face interactions are generally regulated by the tasks at hand, and by written materials that guide what is to be done, as it is in more loosely networked and informal spaces, such as those of social movements. At certain times conflicts arise about 'how to go on' in social institutions, over whether settled interpretations are fair, or accurate, or valuable. These conflicts often begin as a result of the activities of social movements, which challenge taken-for-granted understandings of routinised social life and militate for change in policy and legal documents which share in and reinforce those understandings. During periods of cultural political activity, common

---

[2] Although, in recent times powerful states have used a rhetoric of human rights to justify military intervention into other states, the legality of such measures is highly contentious, military intervention is never undertaken solely to secure human rights, but always primarily for reasons of security or economic advantage, and – as we have seen in Iraq and Afghanistan – it is also, unsurprisingly, ineffective (Chandler 2006; see also Cushman 2005).

interpretations are disrupted and become open to re-interpretation. Such conflicts may, where authoritative decision-makers allow it, or where they find themselves obliged to respond to contentious re-interpretations, result directly in changes in the law, or in government policy.[3]

'How to go on' in the face of contention over what are clearly stated in international law as universal human rights but which are in practice selectively applied and enforced within national states is currently highly contested. In this book I analyse precisely how cultural politics are constructing human rights in particular forms. I do so through a series of in-depth case studies comparing the US and UK. Both states have been and are currently prominent in extending human rights internationally; in both, within the national arena, the cultural politics of human rights practices is complex and hard-fought. Officials in these liberal-democratic states of long-standing clearly find it difficult, imprudent or unnecessary to adopt universal norms of human rights in practice, despite the fact that leaders of these states have been responsible for developing and promoting them in the international arena. In-depth study of the role of cultural politics is crucial to understanding their reluctance to realise human rights in practice and what it means for their future possibilities.

HUMAN RIGHTS CULTURE AND CULTURAL POLITICS

With the exception of anthropological studies, which are now moving beyond the debate over universalism and relativism in interesting

---

[3] I developed this understanding of cultural politics in *Contemporary Political Sociology*, where I drew on the work of post-structuralists, especially Laclau and Mouffe, and of sociologists, especially the work of Giddens on structuration theory (Nash 2000). This approach also has a good deal in common with that of American cultural sociologists, though I remain of the view that specifically in order to study social institutions we must understand culture as constitutive (rather than causal): whilst the cultural and the social may be separated analytically, symbolic meaning and social institutions are, in reality, so interrelated as to be indistinguishable. If culture is *constitutive*, it is not possible to identify an independent causal direction to its *influence* (see Alexander and Smith 2003).

ways, the importance of culture to the study of human rights has not been so much neglected as it has been routinely referred to as essential in literature on policy and politics without, however, being given rigorous attention in its own right.[4] It is above all in references to 'human rights culture' that the importance of linking inter-subjective and institutional dimensions of human rights is noted. 'Human rights culture' marks out a fairly well-established under-standing that culture is crucial to fostering the realisation of human rights in practice. However, it is invariably used to provide the *answer* to the problem of how human rights might be realised. In this study, in contrast, the concept of 'human rights culture' is the occa-sion for *questions* concerning the kind of research that is necessary to establish how the cultural politics of human rights is actually engaged. Rather than accepting that human rights culture is the ethical answer to the question 'how can human rights ideals be realised in practice?', it is important to think about how we might study the cultural politics of human rights and their effects on social institutions.

There has been no systematic study of human rights culture. However, the term has been widely used in a diverse set of inter-ventions in policy debates at the international and national level (Lasso 1997; UN 2004; see also www.breakthrough.tv). It has also been discussed by theorists of human rights from different disciplinary backgrounds (Rorty 1993; Klug 2000; Parekh 2000; Mertus 2004, 2005). 'Human rights culture' finds political and theoretical support because it marks the importance of inter-subjective understandings of human rights to their realisation, which are otherwise overlooked in policy debates and in academic studies of human rights. The common theme of the diverse uses of 'human rights culture' is that in order to be successful human rights must win hearts and minds. Mertus puts it well (drawing on the anthropologist Renato Rosaldo's

---

[4] Anthropological work on the meanings of human rights has been an inspiration for this project, especially for the way in which anthropologists treat human rights *as* culture (Wilson 1999; Cowan *et al.* 2001; Merry 2006).

definition of culture): human rights will only be established once human rights are one of the 'forms through which people live their lives' (2005: 212). Helena Kennedy, in the foreword to Klug's *Values for a Godless Age*, describes human rights culture as involving, 'not just aspirational principles, but a practical code for existence' which should not be left to lawyers, 'a new erudite priesthood, taking the life out of the debates' (Kennedy 2000: xiii).

Though 'human rights culture' is used in many different ways, across all its uses there is a kernel of agreement. What is needed to establish human rights is a shift in public sentiments: every single person must simply be respected and treated as an individual human being with entitlements, regardless of their gender, racial, ethnic or religious background. It should become unthinkable and intolerable that anyone should ever act against human rights, whether at home or abroad. Ignoring human rights must become ethically and emotionally repellent if human rights ideals are to become reality. Only then is there any real possibility of establishing and maintaining institutions that uphold human rights norms.

The concept of 'human rights culture' raises two main problems for investigation in this study. Firstly, supplying an *answer* to the problem of how human rights are to be realised, it tends to suggest an essentialist understanding of culture as a 'way of life' (even where there is the explicit attempt to break with this conception of culture (see Mertus 2004: 212)). Advocates of human rights culture must emphasise the stability and coherence of shared values, understanding and emotional commitments to human rights – even if this is more a future aspiration than a present reality. It is the stability and coherence implied by 'culture' that is precisely the value of human rights culture when it provides an answer to the question, 'can human rights be realised?'. However, there is general agreement amongst cultural theorists that culture is not stable, coherent or enduring in the way that advocates of human rights culture must assume (Cowan *et al.* 2001; Ortener 2006).

Secondly, the concept of 'human rights culture' does not enable the investigation of precisely *how* culture effects change. In particular, it has not been developed to engage with the question of precisely how it is that state officials, who are ultimately responsible for institutionalising and enforcing human rights, might be motivated to put human rights into practice. The answer that 'human rights culture' provides to the question of how human rights are realised seems to assume either that judges and politicians who make effective decisions concerning the realisation of human rights act as a result of cultural norms that are shared by the whole society; or that they act because of public pressure, itself shaped by shared cultural norms that are developed in civil society, the realm of sentiment and ethical values, which may then influence cold-hearted or anxiety-driven judgements of state officials.

In order to investigate the importance of culture to realising human rights ideals, I propose to replace the idea of 'human rights culture' with that of the 'cultural politics of human rights'. It is vital to preserve the insight of advocates of human rights culture that culture *does* make a difference to human rights. My approach is intended to expand and extend that understanding whilst avoiding reliance on a discredited essentialist definition of culture. 'Politics' could be used to sum up the principal theoretical difference between essentialist understandings of culture as a settled way of life and contemporary understandings of culture as inherently ambiguous, contested and structured by power. Cultural theorists have shown how power, and therefore politics, is inherent in all practices of symbolisation through which meaning is communicated. Culture structures institutional positions of authority which validate particular perspectives, creating hierarchies of subordination and obscuring or excluding recognition of differences and inequalities. It is not that there is no consensual stability to culture. To a large extent culture involves the reproduction of traditions, habits, perceptions and understandings. But culture is also inherently fluid and dynamic, a continually moving and 'changing same' (Gilroy 1993: 101). Constructed in relations of power, culture is always open to political challenge and contestation, whilst at the same time, caught in the inertia of repetition, it is resistant to intentional invention.

From the perspective of contemporary cultural theory, human rights are not just *supported* by culture: human rights *are* cultural. There is nothing meaningful in social life that is outside culture: human rights are cultural insofar as they are meaningful. Furthermore, there is also, then, no absolute distinction between practices of state and civil society: culture is not a distinct arena of society; it does not just involve the media, for example, or education, or religion. Culture, as Jeffrey Alexander puts it, 'is not a thing but a dimension, not an object to be studied as a dependent variable but a thread that runs through, one that can be teased out of, every conceivable social form' (Alexander 2003: 7). In so far as representations of human rights formed in civil society are influential on state practices, this is possible because human rights are meaningful on both sides of the analytic and socially sustained distinction between civil society and the state. What links officially sanctioned state practices and public pressure from civil society is cultural politics.

It is, of course, important to maintain an understanding of the specificity of different institutional practices, including those that are legal or governmental: different spheres of social life are created and sustained by different reflexive practices, including ceremonial rituals, formal and informal codes maintaining the distinctiveness of institutional settings, bodies of regulation that are specific to particular activities and so on. I develop the theoretical importance of these distinctions for the study of human rights in Chapter 2. Moreover, it is not that there is no value in distinguishing between state and civil society. Indeed, I will make use of just such a distinction in this book. But it is important to understand that human rights are not simply adminstered through state procedures, as if they always already existed as clear and distinct aims. As they are enumerated in international human rights agreements, the Universal

Declaration of Human Rights (UDHR), the International Convention on Civil and Political Rights (ICCPR) and the International Convention on Economic, Social and Cultural Rights (ICESCR), and so on, the meanings of human rights are relatively clear, even if their abstract formulations in these agreements allows a good deal of latitude for interpretation. These meanings are not, however, fixed; human rights are defined and redefined as policies are created and administered, legal claims dealt with and so on – both inside and outside state procedures.

FROM THE NATIONAL TO THE COSMOPOLITAN STATE?

Human rights can only be enforced by states. The case studies in this book focus on cultural politics of human rights *within* states as the most important spur to the formal realisation of human rights, at least in the advanced capitalist liberal-democracies with which I am concerned. But human rights are not, of course, solely, or even mainly the business of national states; in fact, it has been much more common to think of human rights as international. Human rights were initially developed in the international arena through diplomatic negotiations which led to the signing of treaties and conventions between states – most notably the UDHR and subsequent conventions derived from it (which we will explore more fully in the following chapter). In recent times, moreover, the networks of intergovernmental and non-governmental actors engaged in trying to bring about human rights in practice has become so significant within and across states that it has become common to refer to human rights as globalising (Brysk 2002; Coicaud *et al.* 2003; Mahoney 2007).

What does it mean to think of human rights as globalising? In one sense, of course, human rights are necessarily global insofar as, universal in form, they involve principles of justice for all human beings. It is with respect to their potential for institutional effectiveness, however, that human rights are increasingly considered to be globalising: the vast majority of states have committed themselves to precise and detailed international human rights agreements; and, as a result of human rights activism, interpretations of international law may deepen that commitment and at the same time extend it to include even those states that have not formally bound themselves to such agreements. In this respect, we might say that, because human rights are becoming increasingly institutionalised across the world, they now have the potential, historically unprecedented, to become effectively (as opposed to, or as well as, formally) global. For the first time in history human rights may become genuinely effective norms of global justice.

The potential of human rights to become effective norms of global justice can only be realised through state transformation. Although human rights are globalising, the national context is especially significant to the realisation of human rights. In fact it could be that it is *because* human rights are increasingly global that they have become so much more significant within states historically constituted as national. Compared to the international arena, predominantly a sphere of activity for elites, the national arena is much more populist: issues are addressed to 'the people' as democratically entitled citizens as well as to elites. What is important in the cultural politics of human rights – as we shall see very clearly in the chapters of analysis in this book – is how the global and national are entangled in human rights practices. There is (almost) a global human rights regime and state elites are under pressure from above and below to bring policies and practices into conformity with the principles of that regime. What human rights actually mean in practice, however, depends to a large extent on the cultural politics of human rights in the national context.

In order to clarify how the cultural politics of human rights may be contributing to the realisation of global human rights through state transformation, it is useful to make a working distinction between ideal-types of 'national' and 'cosmopolitan' states. Theorists of state transformation now generally take the view that states are not dissolving and nor are they becoming irrelevant in the face of processes of globalisation. States are rather adapting in order to manage flows of ideas, goods, services and people across their borders, becoming increasingly integrated into international networks that link them together in dense assemblages of shared norms and procedures connecting processes, insititutions and actors. Saskia Sassen analyses such processes of state transformation as 'denationalization'. For example, in specific cases, she says, the work of 'national legislatures and judiciaries' is now caught up in processes of globalisation which 're-orient particular components of institutions and specific practices . . . towards global logics and away from historically shaped national logics' (Sassen 2006: 2). Similarly, Anne-Marie Slaughter argues that states are now disaggregating across borders, as government regulators, judges and legislators network with their counterparts from other states and from supranational institutions like the EU, in order to share information, harmonise regulation and develop ways of enforcing international law (Slaughter 2004; see also Held 1995).

Where, like Sassen, theorists focus on political economy, they are generally critical of state transformation as it is currently being shaped by the de-regulation and re-regulation of national economies that leave workers unable to exercise much, if any, control over multinational corporations and flows of capital (see also Tonkiss 2007: Chapter 3). A focus on human rights, however, gives rather a different emphasis to the study of contemporary state transformation. The cosmopolitan state is a necessary condition of the full realisation of human rights as they are enumerated in international human rights agreements. This is *not* because human rights are inherently neo-liberal. On the contrary, as we shall see in Chapter 5, international human rights agreements actually encode a political order that much more closely resembles global social democracy than neo-liberalism. Moreover, how human rights are realised in practice, the kinds of social forms that are actually enabled by the cultural politics of human rights, is precisely the focus of this study.

The ideal of the national state as the basis of the global order is conventionally dated to the Treaty of Westphalia of 1648, but this is controversial.[5] As Craig Calhoun, for example, argues, nation-states hardly existed at this time, even in Europe; and certainly empires thrived for 300 years after the Treaty (Krasner 1999: 20; Calhoun 2007: 14; Lawson 2008). What we can say with a reasonable degree of historical accuracy is that the national state was hegemonic from the end of the Second World War, which saw the dismantling of formal European empires, until the end of the Cold War. As a political ideal, the national state was immensely significant during this time for anti-imperialist nationalist movements and minority nations who sought liberation from the majorities with whom they shared a state. In the case of established national states in North America and Western Europe, the ideal of the national state functioned more typically as a frame within which political activities were carried out and claims for justice were made. The national state also functioned in academic research, and to some extent also politically, as an ideal-type, a heuristic device against which to assess actually existing states. The ideal-type of the national state involves three main features:

1. Sovereignty – a state is to be free from interference by other states in its policy-making and law enforcement to enable justice as self-determination of the people;
2. For self-determination to be effective, states must have sole jurisdiction over what takes place within their own national territory, where jurisdiction concerns the 'power of the state to affect people, property and circumstances' (Shaw 2003: 574);

---

[5] Charles Tilly has suggested distinguishing 'nation-states', 'whose people share a strong linguistic or symbolic identity' from 'national states', which attempt to integrate large populations and territories, who do not necessarily share common cultural norms in the same way (quoted in Calhoun 2007: 56–7). Although 'nation-state' is the more common term, as states have generally *made* nations out of a diversity of groups sharing different languages and customs rather than being *found* by pre-existing nations I prefer 'national state'.

3. The political community is the people who make up the nation and, ultimately, they must consent to public policy made in their name – if not through elections, then by not rising up against the government or the state.

In the second half of the twentieth century, the national state was clearly staked out as a political ideal for persecuted and disenfranchised nations, as the taken-for-granted frame of political activities, and as the norm to which actually existing states everywhere should conform or against which their approximations might be assessed and criticised.

In comparison, since the end of the Cold War changes in state structures are evident along all three dimensions of this ideal-type as states become embedded in extended networks of global governance. The possibility that human rights may become effective norms of global justice depends on the direction and extent of these changes. Can the cosmopolitan state now displace the national state to become the ideal, the frame and the norm for political life in the twenty-first century? Drawing on research on changes that are judged to be currently taking place in state formation, and also on the work of political theorists on the progressive potential of those changes, the ideal-type of the cosmopolitan state may be characterised by the following features:

1. State sovereignty is transformed in international institutions of co-operative global governance and this is necessary to meet the policy problems increasingly thrown up by globalisation (Held 1995; Slaughter 2004; Beck 2006; Sassen 2006).
2. The legitimacy of policy actors depends upon the extent to which they conform to norms of international human rights and humanitarian law developed through international state co-operation (Soysal 1994; Jacobson 1996; Crawford and Marks 1998; Beetham 2000; Held 2002).
3. The legitimacy of public policy depends on the appropriateness of the scale at which it is made – from global to local – which in turn depends on the scale of the relevant policy problem and accountability to different political communities according to an 'all affected' rule (Held 1995; Gould 2004; Fraser 2005).

If globalising human rights are to realise their potential to become effective norms of global justice, the cosmopolitan state that puts international human rights agreements into practice must become, like national state before it, the ideal of the persecuted, the taken-for-granted frame of 'normal' political life, and the benchmark against which actually existing states are assessed. At the same time, however, the creation of human rights obligations in law and policy is absolutely necessary to the transformation of national into cosmopolitan states. The realisation of human rights and the formation of cosmopolitan states are mutually dependent, two sides of the same fundamental changes that are necessary to achieve a framework for global justice through human rights.

As we shall see in the following chapters, the cosmopolitan state is an ideal for human rights activists, even if they do not explicitly articulate it as a political goal in the way that nationalist movements invariably aimed (and in some cases still aim) to secure a national state. What part does this ideal play in the cultural political of human rights? Is a clash of ideals perhaps avoided as the cosmopolitan state is built incrementally and relatively unnoticed as an effect of particular legal judgements and government policies within the national state? Or is it rather that the national state remains dominant as the taken-for-granted frame within which 'normal' political life takes place, relatively unaffected by norms of human rights to which no more than diplomatic lip service is paid in international arenas? If so, what effect does this dominance of the national state have on human rights in practice?

The very real possibility that human rights may now play a role in state transformation arises because of their hybrid status as *intermestic*; they are both international and domestic at the same time (see Steinhardt 1999; Rosenau 2003). In conventional legal scholarship, human rights are conceived of as a matter for *either* international *or* national law. However, the reality of human rights practices is now much more complex. The intermestic status of human rights is nowhere more in evidence than the way in which international law, especially customary international law, is used in *national* courts – as we shall see in Chapter 3. In national courts, decisions that draw on customary international law confirm and extend its status *as* law whilst binding the national state to its observance in the particular case in question. Human rights are not just international: they are not solely the concern of international governmental organisations like the UN or the Council of Europe; nor are they only of value in international courts, like the European Court of Human Rights. Human rights are not transnational either; they are not simply ideas that *cross* national borders. Human rights are intermestic: legal claims to human rights which draw on international law in national courts disrupt and sometimes re-configure jurisdictional borders between the international and the domestic *from within states*.

What is at stake in the cultural politics of intermestic human rights is how conflicts over justice might be re-framed in cosmopolitan rather than national terms. In 'Reframing Justice' Nancy Fraser has analysed how arguments about justice, which until recently concerned only relations among fellow citizens within national states around the established topics of political representation, distribution and, more recently, recognition, are now exploding into debates over the very framework within which justice as such must be considered (Fraser 2005; see also Fraser 2007, 2008).[6] Conflicts over justice, Fraser suggests, always involve first-order questions about the substance of inequalities: representation, redistribution or recognition. But they also now involve second-order, meta-level conflicts over the frames of justice:

---

[6] Fraser's use of 'frames' involves two dimensions. Firstly, frames are schemas of interpretation that appear obvious, but which allow social actors to attribute relevance to events and persons in ways that are appropriate to their situations. A frame allows people to 'locate, perceive, identify, and label a seemingly infinite number of concrete occurences defined in its terms' (Goffman 1986: 21). Secondly, frames literally exclude some events, persons and processes, whilst including others as significant (see also Snow *et al.* 1986; Snow and Benford 1988).

1. 'What' is at stake in conflicts over justice – distribution of resources, recognition of cultural differences or political representation?
2. 'Who' counts as a subject of justice – now that it is no longer obvious that it is only citizens who count, whose interests and needs deserve consideration?
3. 'How' should conflicts over justice be decided – by what procedures, using which criteria, at what sites and by whom?

Struggles over definitions of intermestic human rights are amongst conflicts over justice that explode the previously taken-for-granted frame of justice as concerning citizens within the national state. In doing so, they potentially open up meta-questions along all three dimensions that Fraser has identified as relevant to issues of global justice. Are we living in a period in which definitions of human rights are being progressively expanded? If not, how is it that human rights, which appear to derive their legitimacy from international consensus on their content and form, are altered, and narrowed, as they become matters of concrete conflict within particular states?

What are human rights?

In conflicts over intermestic human rights the very content of claims for global justice is at stake. International human rights agreements are comprehensive, taking in all the concerns Fraser identifies as crucial to conflicts over justice: they potentially establish a framework for the re-distribution of global wealth; for the recognition of cultural difference within and across states; and for the securing of political rights to democratic participation. In this study we will particularly focus on conflicts over human rights concerning fundamental civil rights to individual freedom. These are very well-established as core human rights in international agreements to which European and North America states subscribe, which leaders of the US and UK were involved in creating, and which they continue to advocate. If *these* human rights are not validated and secured as a result of the cultural politics of intermestic human rights, it is extremely unlikely that any more extensive definitions of human rights will be possible in the US and UK. Nevertheless, in order to explore a range of questions concerning the 'what' of human rights in the intermestic human rights field in these states, in Chapter 5 we will also look at concrete possibilities of defining global justice in terms of social and economic rights. Social and economic rights are also quite well established in international human rights law though they are more disputed than civil and political rights at the international level.

Who is the subject of human rights?

International human rights agreements are very clear, as we shall see: the subject of human rights agreements is any individual human being in the world; distinctions between citizens and non-citizens with respect to fundamental human rights are not permitted in international law. However, in states historically founded on the distinction between citizens and non-citizens, interpretations of human rights commitments which apparently abolish that distinction in particular cases are highly contested. Again, how are international norms altered in intermestic cultural politics, by whom, and with what authority?

How are conflicts over human rights to be decided?

Conflicts over 'how' definitions of what human rights are to be decided are also highly contested in the cultural politics of human rights. In Chapter 2 we will consider how these conflicts are structured in the intermestic human rights field. They invariably result as challenges to activists' claims that human rights are already clearly established as law in international agreements.

It is through the cultural politics of intermestic human rights that the tensions inherent in the transformation from national to cosmopolitan state may – in principle – be worked out. The ideals of the national and cosmopolitan state are not necessarily contradictory.

Indeed, over 200 years ago, at the beginning of modern state formation in Europe, Immanuel Kant suggested that national states could be transformed into cosmopolitan states, of a kind. Kant proposed that, as a result of the exercise of public reason, states should bind themselves to peaceful co-operation with other states through international law, and cultivate the exercise of hospitality towards individual strangers (Kant 1991). Kant's model of the relations between republics with a 'cosmopolitan intent' is of discrete, sovereign states. Aside from this difference, however, his formulation is not so far from the optimistic solution for ameliorating the tension between the national and the cosmopolitan state that has been proposed much more recently by David Held: 'The principles of individual democratic states and societies could come to coincide with those of cosmopolitan democratic law . . . and democratic citizenship could take on, in principle, a truly universal status' (Held 1995: 232–3).

In her comparative work on post-national citizenship in Europe, Yasemin Soysal has effectively argued that long-term residents of European states who are not citizens and who have won social entitlements by appealing to international human rights agreements have altered national states in a cosmopolitan direction (Soysal 1994; see also Benhabib 2004; Sassen 2006). David Jacobson has made a similar analysis of post-national citizenship in the US in relation to illegal immigrants (Jacobson 1996). Soysal and Jacobson argue that long-term residents in Europe and the US who are not citizens have achieved post-national citizenship status for themselves and their families, thus blurring the sharp legal distinction between citizens and non-citizens within states along some dimensions – notably access to education, healthcare and employment. The status of refugees and asylum-seekers who have rights in the societies in which they are resident *only* as a result of the international human rights agreements is another example of a shift towards post-national citizenship, though they generally have access to minimal entitlements (the right to remain incarcerated, for example, rather than being deported, in the case of many asylum-seekers) compared to those of long-term 'denizens'. In some respects, then, it is clear that the absolute distinction between citizens and non-citizens is being called into question in practice as a result of uses of human rights within states. However, as Soysal herself argues, as it is states historically constituted on an absolute distinction between national citizens and non-citizens which administer international human rights agreements, progress towards a more flexible citizenship is complex and highly uncertain (Soysal 1994: 156–62; Soysal 2001). There have been changes in the practices of human rights since Hannah Arendt famously argued that human rights are actually enjoyed only by citizens of the most prosperous states, and that, as the end of the First World War indicated, the world finds 'nothing sacred in the abstract nakedness of being human' (Arendt 1968: 299). However, these changes are partial, paradoxical and in principle, and sometimes in practice, reversible (Castles and Davidson 2001). Progress in human rights can not be assumed – *especially* given the fact that the cosmopolitan project, including that of the realisation of human rights, has for so long been associated with the progress of history itself in Western thought.

What human rights actually *mean* in practice matters because it can not be *assumed* that increased activity around human rights, including their expansion in international law, necessarily results in a progressive movement from national to cosmopolitan states. In this study I focus on case studies in which, unlike those studied by Soysal and Jacobson, the distinction between citizens and non-citizens is in sharp relief in the cultural politics of intermestic human rights. These cases are not matters of routine administration concerning long-term residents within states. They are rather high-profile legal and/or media cases concerning a range of different 'non-citizens'. Such cases, I suggest, enable us to study precisely how the realisation of human rights, which would undoubtedly result in transformation from a national to a cosmpolitan state if it were a simple matter of 'applying' international law, are being contested in ways which make that outcome rather less than certain in reality.

COMPARING THE US AND UK

Because this book makes detailed, in-depth analysis of the cultural politics of intermestic human rights in the national context it is only possible to focus on a limited range of case studies. Nevertheless, appropriate comparison across at least two national contexts is necessary if it is to be possible to generalise the findings in any significant way. The US and UK make for a good comparison of the cultural politics of intermestic human rights because they share a number of similarities in terms of intermestic human rights cases. Cross-national comparison is facilitated by the fact that the US and UK are relatively similar along a number of dimensions that are important to human rights. Because of these similarities, the differences between two states are all the more striking.

Domestically, the US and UK have quite similar legal and political systems; they developed historically from the same roots and have continued to influence each other. They share, for example, a legal system based on common law – in contrast to continental Europe, even if the UK has, famously, no written constitution. Internationally, both the US and UK have been global leaders in human rights, and their politicians continue to present themselves as such. The US and UK took the lead in setting up the UN human rights system after the Second World War, and the US remains by far the largest contributor to the UN, even if it sometimes takes this role reluctantly. More recently – and notoriously – the leaders of both countries, key actors in the UN Security Council and allies in NATO, have used the vocabulary of human rights to justify military intervention, claiming to be acting in the name of the rule of law and of democracy in Afghanistan and Iraq. There has also been, and there continues to be, a good deal of exchange between the two countries, both in terms of the diplomatic and military 'special relationship' that is fostered by state elites, and also in terms of popular culture.

In terms of existing conditions for the cultural politics of human rights, however, the US and UK are rather different. In the first place, the US is the sole remaining global superpower (for the time being). It is embedded in global governance in that it is involved in all the most powerful international networks, but it is far richer and stronger in military and economic terms than any other state with which it shares these networks. This gives it a very particular role. In contrast, the UK, whilst similarly embedded in networks of global governance, is obviously far smaller and less powerful than the US as a state. Moreover, there is another very significant difference of scale between the US and UK with respect to human rights: the UK is networked into the only really effective international human rights system in the world, that of the Council of Europe and the European Union. The regional US equivalent, the Inter-American system of human rights, is practically without influence in US affairs (Moravcsik 1994: 54–5).

The US has long been a world leader in human rights.[7] At the same time, however, the US has also gained the reputation of being an 'outlier' in human rights. This reputation has undoubtedly been exacerbated by the 'global war on terror', but it has a much longer history. The US is an outlier in human rights because of the way in which US state officials resist binding domestic and foreign policy through international human rights agreements, which it nevertheless promotes for others, rather than because it is among the world's worst violators of human rights.[8] As contributors to Michael

---

[7] In fact, world leadership in terms of human rights dates back to the American Declaration of Independence, which framed the American state as a 'carrier' of liberal democratic norms for humanity before the French Revolution and the Declaration of the Rights of Man to which the origin of human rights is more usually traced (Calhoun 2007: 131; see Woodiwiss 2005 for an alternative account).

[8] This is not to say, of course, that the US has not been involved in human rights violations: as W. E. B du Bois argued in 1947, racial discrimination in the US may very well be understood as involving violations of human rights (Mazower 2004: 395); it is well-known that the US has been indirectly implicated in human rights violations, by supporting regimes that US elites know to be involved in torture and genocide (such as Pinochet in Chile in 1970s and Suharto in Indonesia in the 1980s); and there is also evidence to suggest that the US has been directly involved in such activities, especially through the CIA in Latin America (Chomsky et al. 1999). Nevertheless, the US is still by no means the world's worst state for human rights violations.

Ignatieff's collection *American Exceptionalism and Human Rights* show, there is a deep-rooted suspicion of international conventions of human rights in US political culture, accompanied by the belief that the US has a special destiny with respect to the discovery and legitimacy of fundamental rights elaborated by its own courts and institutions (Ignatieff 2005; Kahn 2005; Steiker 2005). US exceptionalism with regard to human rights is more than simply a matter of unilateralism, however, because the US is both a leader *and* an outlier in human rights. The International Convention on Civil and Political Rights (ICCPR) is perhaps the most famous example of US resistance to the human rights standards it recommends for others. The US was closely implicated in drawing up the ICCPR, which largely reflects an American understanding of civil and political rights. However, when the US finally ratified the ICCPR in 1992, almost twenty years after it came into force, it did so only with a reservation that allowed capital punishment, even for juveniles, though 'right to life' is the key provision of the Convention, and Article 6 (5) prohibits the imposition of the death penalty 'for crimes committed by persons below eighteen years of age' (Roth 2000).

The UK also has a mixed reputation in relation to international human rights, which has not been improved by the 'global war on terror' in which it has played the part of the US's closest ally. Nevertheless, as a member of the Council of Europe, the UK is unambiguously situated within the European system of human rights. This system – set up by the Council of Europe after the Second World War – was part of the revolutionary changes in the legal relationship between states and individuals of that period, allowing petitions by individuals against states, as well as by states against other states (Dembour 2006). It enjoys a high level of prestige and its rulings receive a good deal of publicity within member states. In 1998, the European Convention on Human Rights was finally incorporated into UK national law as the Human Rights Act (HRA). The cultural politics of human rights have been especially lively leading up to and since the HRA in the UK, with wide-ranging debate amongst lawyers, politicians and journalists over how human rights should be understood and enacted legally, morally and politically. It need only be noted here that the same government that has cultivated the 'special relationship' between the UK and the US in the global war on terror was also the government that passed the Human Rights Act.

US exceptionalism with regard to human rights is well-established. This exceptionalism is, however, strongly contested in the cultural politics of intermestic human rights 'from below', within the US. Indeed, I take it that because of its status and power in the international arena it is *only* 'from below' that resistance to human rights on the part of US elites could possibly be shifted at all. In the UK, the liveliness of the cultural politics of human rights in the last few years could result in fundamental state transformation. The UK could become more 'European', tending towards realising and extending global human rights norms in practice. It could, on the other hand, become more 'American', tending towards extending global human rights norms only as long as they have no real effect on domestic or foreign policy. As the following chapters indicate, the fact of being in Europe may not be enough to ensure that it is the 'European' path that is taken.

OUTLINE OF THE BOOK

In Chapter 2, I develop a methodology for the study of cultural politics of intermestic human rights using the concept of 'human rights field'. Cultural politics does not concern free-floating symbolic representations: it takes place in, is affected by and in turn affects the institutions that are constraining of social life. Social institutions are invariably hierarchical, but cultural politics does not necessarily only concern the furtherance of personal power and self-interest. Justifications in the professional settings with which we are concerned here also concern ideals which can, on occasion, be effective because they are persuasive to others within those settings, because they are made by actors with the authority to make effective decisions, or because they are accepted by others who are similarly oriented towards those ideals. The concept of 'field' enables the study of the cultural politics of intermestic human rights in a variety of settings that are crucial to defining and institutionalising human rights.

In the following chapter, then, I map out in some detail the four domains of the human rights field: juridical, governmental, activist and the mediated public. Law is especially important to human rights. In fact, the study of law and legalisation remains dominant in research on human rights, which is still largely undertaken by legal scholars. In the legal approach, human rights are seen as synonymous with human rights law. Such an understanding is obviously to be avoided, and finding out precisely how human rights are constructed as meaningful across different interrelated institutional settings is precisely the aim of this study. Nevertheless, it is important to note that the most vigorous cultural politics of human rights are very often centred on courts. This is reflected in the case studies chosen for this book, which take seriously legal claims to human rights and the counter-claims of governmental officials and their lawyers, which are also, though not exclusively, couched in legal terms, as a principal means through which human rights are being contested. It is because, as a matter of empirical fact, courts are one of the principal sites through which human rights are being extended that we must study how human rights are contested in law. The other principal site for the contestation of human rights is the media, though this, in contrast, is rarely studied by those researching human rights. In the media, meanings of human rights are often contested in terms other than those of human rights law or official governmental rhetoric. Translated from their legal meanings into popular political ideals, in the mediated public understandings of human rights are far more likely to privilege citizenship than they are to deconstruct it, and this has important implications for the success of human rights claims-making elsewhere.

This map of the human rights field enables exploration of how sites of contestation, which have previously been coded as national, may be transformed by human rights. How human rights are contested in courts and the media at any particular moment is influenced by professional justifications formed in relation to those settings. Where officials in the judiciary and government exercise state authority, these justifications put limits on what human rights effectively mean in practice, what they can and can not do. Studying cultural political engagements in the intermestic human rights field enables an understanding of how international human rights norms are brought into the national context, what is at stake for different actors in the field, and how human rights become meaningful in very particular ways, which are often rather different from those for which they were developed in institutions of global governance.

Chapters 3, 4 and 5 each take parallel case studies in order to compare the cultural politics of intermestic human rights in the US and UK. These case studies of intermestic human rights in the national setting involve the interpenetration of national and international along *at least one* of the following dimensions: human rights claims are made on behalf of non-citizens who may or may not be resident in the state in which they are made; they are made by organisations supported by transnational advocacy networks; they are addressed to national state elites (in courts or in the government), but they draw on international (as well as domestic) law. Each of the case studies in these chapters concerns the cultural politics of intermestic human rights in relation to state transformation in order to assess the real likelihood of a shift from national to cosmopolitan.

Chapter 3 is an analysis of how state sovereignty is affected by the cultural politics of intermestic human rights. Is state sovereignty being transformed in human rights practices? If so, how? In particular, the chapter examines sovereign decisions to suspend normal law in the name of national security. Both the US and UK have adopted security measures in the 'war against terror' that violate human rights by arbitrarily detaining terrorist suspects who are non-citizens. International human rights law requires that the distinction between citizens and non-citizens should be abolished with respect to fundamental human rights. National states, on the other hand, are supposed to exist for their citizens, not for humanity. Whilst national states exist to protect citizens' rights, cosmopolitan states are supposed also to provide equal protection for the rights of every individual human being.

Analysing the cultural politics of intermestic human rights in the US and UK around these sovereign decisions, what is most interesting is that in both states challenges to the violations of universal human rights resulting from 'exceptional' security measures were made predominantly in terms of national pride. In the US it might be supposed that this was because there is very little scope for legal challenges to human rights violations in international law within the US state, and to some extent this is the case. However, in the UK, both in courts and in the mediated public, technical *legal* understandings of European human rights law became entangled with sentiments of national pride, expressed by supporters of universal human rights as well as their opponents. Unexpectedly, in these cases universal human rights were defined by their defenders as linked to a properly functioning *national* state, not in terms of cosmopolitan ideals.

In Chapter 4, having identified the importance of national pride to the contestation of human rights in Chapter 3, we continue to explore the complex entanglements of cosmopolitan ideals, nationalism and human rights. Here, in contrast to the cases studied in the previous chapter, we examine the cultural politics of cases that are celebrated by the human rights movement as advancing the realisation of human rights as effective norms of global justice. The analysis particularly concerns how human rights activists and innovators in the judiciary try to effectively imagine a political community beyond the nation in order to realise human rights in practice. In doing so they are attempting to create a cosmopolitan state even if they do not explicitly name it as an ideal, focussing rather on the practical cases in question. In the US activists use the Alien Tort Claims Act (ATCA), which enables cases to be brought against foreign agents for human rights violations committed against non-American citizens in the national courts. These cases are immensely significant in the US context; drawing on customary international law in national courts, they are effectively the only way to introduce intermestic human rights into US political life. In comparison I investigate the cultural politics of the Pinochet case in the UK, in which lawyers similarly drew on customary international law in national courts, and which has been seen by many as a turning point in the progress of cosmopolitan law.

Around ATCA and Pinochet activists and human rights supporters were engaged in imagining a community beyond the nation, trying to mobilise sympathy in the US and UK for the civil rights of human beings in countries far away, and to gain support for action to realise human rights in practice. Using ground-breaking legal cases they attempted to create excitement and sympathy for human rights, to foster a global political community from within the state which would recognise obligations to realise international human rights encoded in international human rights law. We investigate the terms of this imagined global community, how and where it was justified, and how it was in competition with the visions of more conservative, or simply more cautious, actors in the human rights field. These actors responded in two main ways to the challenge: they either defended the national community along conventional lines, albeit with an emphasis on its place in the international community of states; or they re-imagined the national community in a new, and potentially rather dangerous form, that of cosmopolitan nationalism. What appears to be developing around the contestation of globalising human rights, then, in response to the model of global citizenship proposed by human rights activists and supporters, are varieties of nationalism which are either against or, at the very least, indifferent to the deconstruction of the distinction between citizens and non-citizens in practice, or which are for its deconstruction but in a politically strategic way that is at odds with the spirit of the universalism of human rights as such. The very definition of international law itself, how it is to be interpreted and practised in the national context, and therefore the possibility of state transformation from national to cosmopolitan, depends on how conflicts between these visions of political community are resolved.

Finally, in Chapter 5, we consider an attempt to construct solidarity through cultural politics. If it is difficult to imagine a community of global citizens, how much more difficult is it to imagine global citizens experiencing solidarity? Solidarity is a vital aspect of national citizenship: national states have enjoyed unrivalled success in organising solidarity as an expectation that material risks and resources should be shared amongst citizens. It is also a vital aspect of any possibility of global citizenship to be realised through cosmopolitan states. As an absolute minimum, global citizenship requires a restructuring of Northern states to allow fairer policies of trade and the re-distribution of wealth between North and South. In this chapter we will explore the prospects of constructing cosmo-politan solidarity beyond the nation in popular campaigns against global poverty: Make Poverty History in the UK and ONE in the US. These campaigns involved activists in powerful states using the media to put pressure on state officials to change international pol-icies that create poverty in other states. However, although there is detailed international human rights law covering the global distri-bution of economic resources, one of the notable features of these human rights cases, as opposed to those that took place in courts, is that they failed to get recognition as concerning human rights at all within the national settings of the US and UK. While the ultimate failure of these campaigns in terms of ending or even ameliorating global poverty is not attributable to the fact that they were not couched in terms of universal human rights, it is notable that they both failed to engage the structures of global governance in terms of human rights, and they also failed to transform those structures in a way that would alter the conditions of wealth distribution between North and South. Although very successful in mobilising popular support, these campaigns against global poverty have had no effect at all on state transformation.

Processes of globalisation call into question the frame of national justice that has linked states and national political communities. This is problematic when it leads to decreasing popular control over the state procedures through which justice is defined and put into practice. If calling the frame of national justice into question is to be productive rather than simply destructive of democratic gains over the long history of struggles for justice in the name of the nation, questions concerning what justice involves and how it is to be achieved must be extended to include the interests and values of human beings who are not fellow citizens, and who may not even be resident within the same state. There is no doubt that this is a very tall order. Human rights activists are trying to bring it about by piecemeal reform of the state through creative uses of human rights in different campaigns, and especially by bringing test cases in national courts. The success of this project depends on the reform of existing structures of states that have been formed as national, and on the authoritative decision-making of officials empowered to make definitions of human rights that have practical force. It depends on cultural politics.

2   Analysing the intermestic human rights field

Considering human rights in terms of a 'field' enables analysis of precisely how intermestic human rights are contested and defined and with what effects for global justice in practice. It enables the exploration of conflicts over what human rights are and should be, who has which entitlements, and how these conflicts are to be settled within and across relevant institutional settings. Legitimate conflicts in the human rights field are ended temporarily, if not finally resolved, through authoritative definitions that decide the limits and scope of how they are to be administered. As the result of these contestations is often regulation, policy or law, this understanding of the 'human rights field' links micro-social interactions to macro-institutional structures, conflicts over particular human rights cases to fundamental changes in state formation.

AUTHORITY AS POWER: THE INTERMESTIC HUMAN RIGHTS FIELD

Following Bourdieu, a field is a set of regularised social interactions in which the *value* of what is at stake is shared, and there is competition to gain status, power or material gain between actors properly designated as participants in relation to each other. These actors occupy objective positions in structures of power, with varying amounts of capital (economic, cultural, social) whose possession enables access to the specific profits that are at stake (Bourdieu 1977, 1991, 1992). What we are concerned with in this study, however, unlike Bourdieu, is not the outcome of conflict for the stratification of professionals involved in these conflicts, but the construction of *authority*, the ability to speak effectively, to define human rights in ways that impact on state formation. Effective speech is performative: it involves a particular kind of utterance in which words are also *acts* that alter reality to fit the declaration. The classic example, from the work of John Austin, is the promise; using the words 'I promise' sincerely is at the same time a statement and also the action of making a promise (Bourdieu 1991: 73–4). Effective speech takes different forms in different institutional settings. We will explore this point further in the section that follows on justifications. What is important here is that it is authority, the ability to make effective speech, which is the shared value, the stake of conflicts in the human rights field. It is not that actors in the human rights field share a belief in the value of human rights, or agree on what human rights mean, how they are defined legally, morally or politically. On the contrary, what participants agree on is that being able to decide *what it is that human rights mean* in practice is valuable for all of those involved. Of course, this authority is not definitive; in the human rights field, an authoritative definition of human rights rarely ends conflicts altogether. But the institutionalisation of an authoritative definition, whether in law, policy or in the mediated public, alters the terrain on which those conflicts take place, making it easier or more difficult to assert authority in other ways in the future.[1]

---

[1] An alternative body of social theory on which I might have drawn for this study is Foucault's work on authority (see Nash 2000: 19–30). I see Bourdieu's concept of 'field' as more useful here mainly because Foucault's critical analysis of power and domination is strongly oriented against any settled form of institutionalised regulation. Anarchism is the only ethical form of politics from a Foucauldian perspective. Foucault's own pronouncements on human rights confirm rather than qualify this conclusion (see Foucault 2000; and Chouliaraki 2006 for an alternative interpretation). In contrast, although I agree with Alexander (1995) that Bourdieu's social theory is similarly deficient in failing to distinguish democratic from authoritarian forms of states, I think the concept of 'field', supplemented with other methdological tools (see pp. 58–70), does allow for an analysis of how symbolic politics constructs authority which is agnostic about the legitimacy of that authority. Obviously, unless we rule out from the very beginning the possibility that realising human rights through state regulation may be desirable, such agnosticism is methodologically necessary.

The intermestic human rights field is made up of four domains: the sub-fields of the juridical, the governmental, the activist and the mediated public. Competition is engaged in distinctive ways within each domain for the authority to decide what human rights mean in practice. Competition is also engaged – often at the same time and in the same strategies – *across* different domains of the field. The most prominent sites for this competition are the media and courts. It is not that these are neutral arenas in which competition is staged. As I will discuss below, journalists and editors have their own stake in competitions over the authority to define human rights that take place in the mediated public, whilst in courts it is clearly the language of the legal profession that is dominant. Nevertheless, other actors in the human rights field have to engage in cultural politics in the media and in courts if they are to win authority over definitions of human rights. In this sense, the juridical, governmental and activist sub-fields converge in courts and in the mediated public.

The juridical sub-field

The juridical sub-field is the site of competition for monopoly over the power to determine law. According to Bourdieu the most important positions in the juridical field are theoreticians of doctrine on the one hand and practitioners on the other (Bourdieu 1987; see also Madsen and Dezalay 2002 for a more complex Bourdieuian analysis of law). In the intermestic human rights field, at least in the Anglo-American context with which we are concerned in this study, competition in the juridical sub-field is, however, most likely to be engaged between judges with different dispositions towards interpreting the law, and between lawyers representing human rights organisations on the one hand, and lawyers representing government on the other.

Law, like any other cultural practice, requires the interpretation of meanings. Like other cultural practices, it is primarily symbolic. The law requires interpretation and decision; it is not simply a body of texts that transparently leads practioners to a single rational outcome. To a greater or lesser extent in different cases, judges' decisions are underdetermined by legal doctrine (Fish 1994). Judges can legitimately disagree with each other's interpretations of the law even when, sitting together in the same courts or as cases proceed through the judicial system to higher courts, they hear exactly the same case. In this respect the law is different from other cultural practices which involve the re-iteration of meanings *only* insofar as the decisions that judges make are ultimately backed up by the force of the state.

For the sake of simplicity, we can speak of 'legal' and 'extra-legal' cultural politics in the juridical sub-field. Legal cultural politics here concern interpretations of legal doctrine. In the common law system the symbolic codes that are contested are the written texts of legal statute, and the precedents established by previous judgements that have decided what those statutes meant in a particular case. In any legal system, judges in the highest courts of appeal are appointed to have the final authority to determine what the law demands by virtue of their office. It is only when the law changes, or where there are fundamental disagreements about what the law means at the highest levels of the legal system, that those decisions may be revisited.

Extra-legal cultural politics in the juridical sub-field concern the way in which judges and lawyers seek to educate, influence and even to lead the public concerning what human rights mean and should mean *aside* from making legal judgements. For example, judges often accompany their legal summing up of cases with pronouncements on the general principles underlying their decisions, which concern how social life should be organised. Or they may use colourful metaphors or turns of phrase to make a point more vividly than legal language allows. Such declarations and pithy summing up of principles are much more likely to be widely quoted and commented upon in the mediated public than are the legal technicalities of the case. In human rights cases they invariably concern fundamental issues of definition concerning what, for whom and how human rights are, and should be, relevant, extrapolating from the particularities of the case in question.

Making human rights law

Human rights law is expanding. As it expands, new elements are introduced into the juridical sub-field, creating even greater indeterminacy in legal decision-making: scope for very different opinions concerning how human rights should be interpreted, which body of law is most appropriate to decide human rights cases, and even, on occasion, whether a particular case involves law at all. Because human rights are in the process of *becoming law* in court judgements as well as through legislation at both international and national levels, the stakes of these conflicts are particularly high: a judicial decision which denies that human rights apply, or which recognises only a very narrow definition of human rights, is a serious setback to the project of establishing human rights law, and therefore to the possibilities of realising human rights in practice.

The study of human rights has generally operated with a strict division between international and domestic law. However, intermestic human rights complicate the strategies and decisions of lawyers and judges around this division. Firstly, because human rights are increasingly legalised in ways which make the doctrinal international/domestic distinction upon which lawyers and judges have traditionally relied more complex. It is not that bodies of law have become doctrinally less distinct or discrete. It is rather that in intermestic human rights cases there is a proliferation of possibilities concerning which kinds of law could be applied in practice. State borders no longer mark an opposition between national and international law. Secondly, legal strategies and distinctions become more complex because the status of the human rights law *as law* is sometimes ambiguous or even in dispute for legal experts themselves.

Human rights law is made in three main ways. The first and least controversial is by multilateral conventions which are signed and then ratified by participating states. The most important international human rights conventions are the ICCPR and the ICESCR, both of which are derived from the UDHR, but there is in addition now a host of conventions which specify more limited aims: the Convention on the Elimination of All Forms of Discrimination Against Women, the Convention Against Torture and so on. In addition to the UN system of human rights which has been set up by these agreements, there are also regional systems, by far the most effective of which is the European. Member states of the Council of Europe have agreed to abide by the ECHR, and to make their national legislation conform to the decisions of the European Court of Human Rights in cases of dispute. Conventions are the least controversial way to make international human rights law, though the extent to which they are then binding on states is not always obvious. For some states, signing a convention involves 'automatic incorporation' into national law; international human rights agreements then become national law for those states and can be heard in national courts. For others, however, the convention must be enacted through the usual legislative methods separately from the signing of the treaty, and states do not always do this. In these cases, it applies to the state in question only as insofar as state officials adopt the application of international law within their states; it does not apply as domestic law (see Steiner and Alston 2000: 1000; Cassese 2001: Chapter 8). However, mechanisms for the enforcement of international law in the UN system are practically non-existent, consisting largely of 'naming and shaming' countries who are not making clearly documented efforts to comply with conventions in reports from UN officials and committees. (International Tribunals and the International Criminal Court do not hear human rights cases; they are set up to hear prosecutions of war crimes, which are related, but not the same.) Even the European Court of Human Rights can not force states to comply with its rulings.

The second main way in which human rights law is made is as customary international law. Customary international law is defined as established state practice, which states understand to be followed 'from a sense of legal obligation' (Steiner and Alston 2000: 70). The sources used to evidence customary international law include such a diverse array as 'newspaper reports of actions taken by states, and from statements made by government spokesmen [sic] to Parliament, to the press, at international conferences . . . from a state's laws and judicial decisions' and from multilateral treaties (Steiner and Alston 2000: 73). They also include judicial decisions and the teachings of highly qualified legal experts, and the resolutions and declarations of international governmental organisations like the General Assembly of the UN (Charlesworth and Chinkin 2000). It is not easy to establish the precise rules of customary international law, and lawyers must draw on these sources in order to do so. It is therefore unsurprising that court cases using customary international law generate acute conflicts in the human rights field about what such law might include or not include, and indeed, over whether it should be considered law at all (see, for example, pp. 121–2).

Clearly, then, international law is different from national law. Law is by definition predictable, equally applicable to all within its jurisdiction and, above all, backed by sanctions. While national law may not always exhibit these qualities fully (transgressors are not always punished, for example), international law is so far from realising them that it is often referred to as a mixture of 'soft' and 'hard' law. We can think of 'hard' and 'soft' law on a continuum, where the hardest law details very precisely what rules apply, specifying very clearly their content and also the degree to which they are obligatory; the hardest law also delegates interpretation and implementation of those rules to a court (Abbott and Snidal 2001). The continuum of international law *may* be shifting from soft towards hard legalisation. Claims for human rights which use customary international law, for example, and which are accepted by judges as involving sound legal reasoning, legitimate, clarify and extend its value *as law* through rigorous legal procedures. International human rights law may be considered as a kind of global constitution of human rights, to be applied across the world. It is, however, a constitution that is currently in formation, which is highly contested, and which may never function effectively as such.

Finally, human rights become law when they are adopted by states as a national constitution (or, as in the case of the UK Human Rights Act, a kind of quasi-constitution). The adoption of a constitution based on human rights is not always directly connected to signing or ratifying international conventions. In many cases it has been a response to changing political conditions, to national liberation from colonialism or the end of the Cold War, for example. Since the UDHR, however, the form of constitutions that have been adopted have been very much influenced by international human rights agreements (Boli 1987). By the same token, international human rights conventions have themselves been modelled on national constitutions. The form of the ICCPR, for example, resembles that of the US – though it also codifies important differences, as we shall see. Human rights agreements which are adopted as constitutional law are the most secure in legal terms, as 'hard' as national law itself; though they are, of course, still very much open to different interpretations.

We see, then, from this very brief sketch, how human rights law involves the interpenetration of international and national bodies of law in practice, even if they continue to be treated as doctrinally discrete. Lawyers and judges in national courts, with which we are concerned in this study, may refer to the intentions of international actors, to legal doctrine and precedent concerning human rights that has been decided in international courts, or even in other nations. We will be exploring the effects of interpenetration of international and national law in practice, and the conflicts it produces, more fully in the chapters of analysis that follow. Perhaps the sharpest conflicts arise where lawyers draw on customary international law, the most controversial type of international law, in national courts. We consider examples of such conflicts in detail in Chapter 4, in cases brought using customary international law in the US under the Alien Tort Claims Act, and in the Pinochet case in the UK. Conflicts over intermestic rights also arise, however, in human rights cases in national courts of the member states of the Council of Europe, where judges in courts of appeal must try to avoid decisions that conflict with the ECHR and with the case law of the European Court of Human Rights. In order to do so they make their arguments drawing on European human rights law as well as on domestic legal precedent. The case of the Belmarsh detainees, which we will consider in Chapter 3, involves just such interpenetration of national and international law.

From international to cosmopolitan law

Legal conflicts in the intermestic human rights field are engaged between traditionalists and innovators when innovators bring intermestic human rights cases into national courts. The conflicts are played out in the juridical sub-field, but they engage with wider conflicts over the authority to define human rights between government, human rights organisations and the media. Indeed, lawyers in these cases are generally employed by human rights organisations or by governments to take up their perspective in these legal conflicts. Such conflicts concern the very form that intermestic human rights should take, and sometimes even whether they are appropriately codified in law at all.

Traditionally international law concerned only international relations between states. It has not been concerned with jurisdiction over states' domestic treatment of individuals. In principle this paradigm was complicated after the Second World War, as liberal internationalism challenged the conception of justice on which classic state sovereignty was based. These changes to international law are sometimes known as the 'Nuremberg principles' because they were initially developed in the Nuremberg trials that followed the Second World War. Two major changes in international law came together in the legal aftermath of this war. Firstly, individuals became criminally accountable for violations of the laws of war ('just obeying orders' was no longer a legitimate defence for anyone, however lowly their position in the military or state hierarchy). Secondly, principles of human rights began to be developed, which prescribed limits to a government's conduct towards its own citizens, to apply in times of peace and war (Ratner and Abrams 2001: 4; see also Held 1995: 101–2).

This second principle was carried forward and extended with the UDHR, beginning international human rights law in the UN human rights system. According to the logic of the UDHR and subsequent international human rights law based on it, though this logic is only now being worked out in practice, individuals have human rights, and also the responsibility to uphold human rights, *regardless of citizenship status or residency*. As Article 2 of the UDHR has it:

> Everyone is entitled to all the rights and freedoms set forth in this Declaration, without distinction of any kind, such as race, colour, sex, language, religion, political or other opinion, national or social origin, property, birth or other status. Furthermore, no distinction shall be made on the basis of the political, jurisdictional or international status of the country or territory to which a person belongs, whether it be independent, trust, non-self-governing or under any other limitation of sovereignty.

However, with the partial exception of the European system of human rights, the balance of powers until the end of the Cold War meant that international law effectively maintained classic state sovereignty, being overwhelmingly concerned with keeping the peace between states (Held 2002).

Since the end of the Cold War, however, there have been the beginnings of what is sometimes called cosmopolitan law. In contrast to international law, and in conformity with the 'Nuremberg principles', cosmopolitan law reaches inside states, piercing nominal state sovereignty and enforcing claims against human rights violators (see Held 2002; Hirsh 2003). Cosmopolitan law requires states to pursue and prosecute those accused of acting in ways that violate human rights, not only regardless of the national citizenship of the victim or of his/her place of residence, but even regardless of where the violations took place. The practice of cosmopolitan law is most evident in international tribunals. In national courts too, however, with which we are concerned in this study, human rights lawyers are also working to create interpretations of existing law in order to further cosmopolitan law. According to Article 8 of the UDHR: 'Everyone has the right to an effective remedy by the competent national tribunals for acts violating . . . fundamental rights.' Although initially, when the Universal Declaration was made, states tended to interpret human rights obligations as applying only to individuals subject to their own jurisdiction, increasingly, where effective remedies are not possible in the domestic courts in which the plaintiffs are citizens, other states are finding themselves obliged in principle to make legal remedies for human rights violations possible. Juridical innovators in the human rights field try to realise the human right to legal redress on the principle of securing universal norms where fundamental human rights have been violated. They bring intermestic human rights cases in order to create the opportunity for cultural politics, both internally and externally to the legal system, in order to extend cosmopolitan law.

The governmental sub-field

The governmental sub-field involves competition between state officials for power to access and deploy the state's monopoly over legitimate violence: the crude physical forces of the police and the military, and the more indirect forces of economic power, achieved through taxation and regulation. It is difficult to be clear about the precise parameters of the governmental sub-field, as, unlike the juridical sub-field which is focussed on courts as the places where, ultimately, the law is decided, conflicts in the governmental sub-field are not focussed on outcomes in a particular institutional setting. Indeed, it is notable that, although actors in the governmental sub-field of democratic states are ostensibly there to represent 'the people', and this is the general principle that legitimates their authority in a democratic state, conflicts over human rights rarely reach the Legislature. The governmental sub-field is engaged wherever there are struggles involving government officials, whose objective positions give them the possibility of making effective decisions, whether in their own states or in international governmental organisations. Officials in the governmental sub-field engage in the cultural politics of human rights as the President or the Prime Minister, the Secretary for Defence, the Foreign Secretary and so on, or as political and legal advisors to those who occupy these official roles.

It may seem odd to talk about 'cultural politics' when we are considering the governmental sub-field, since its business is apparently nothing but politics. Competition in this field involves explicit, and unashamed, struggles over power, even if the actors involved invariably clothe those struggles in ideals. However, cultural politics is just as important in the governmental sub-field as it is elsewhere. The word 'politics' has many different meanings. In liberal-democracies it is most commonly associated with the party politics that takes place in formal democratic institutions. 'Cultural politics', on the other hand, concerning more or less organised struggles over what issues, events or processes mean to interested parties, and what these meanings make possible or impossible, is fundamental to all forms of social organisation, including the organisation and conduct of party politics. It is this more fundamental understanding of politics, as the struggle over what human rights mean, with which we are concerned here.

Cultural politics in the governmental sub-field concerns power over two main dimensions of governmental action concerning definitions of human rights. Firstly it involves the power to settle disputes over what form conventions of human rights are to take in discussions in international governmental organisations, and how and when they might be signed or ratified. Even states which have historically taken the lead in human rights, and which generally have the greatest influence over their form in the UN system, have not signed all the most important conventions. And when they do so, it is often on condition that they have been able to make reservations against certain Articles which effectively alter the form or the scope of the convention. For example, as noted in Chapter 1, the US signed and ratified the ICCPR with a reservation against Article 6(5), which prohibited the imposition of the death penalty for crimes committed by persons below eighteen years of age in order to be able to continue to execute juvenile offenders (see p. 22). A notorious example of a reservation the UK made against a human rights convention, which similarly negated a main purpose of that convention, was to the UN Convention on the Rights of the Child (CRC): it stated that in matters of immigration control, the UK would not be bound by the convention and would, in effect, accept no responsibility for upholding childrens' human rights.

Secondly, disputes in the governmental sub-field involve the authority to decide how far government policy should conform to or ignore human rights law. Of course, we know that many actions taken by government officials which deviate from human rights law do not result in overt or systematic conflict. Actors in the governmental sub-field often gain possibilities for action by *avoiding* conflict over human rights, by simply evading or obscuring their human rights responsibilities. Numerous examples have been discovered, principally by activists and journalists, of discussions 'behind closed doors' amongst government officials and their trusted supporters, which have led directly to human rights violations. Such secrecy is generally defended as necessary by the Executive where national security or foreign policy issues are concerned. The most notorious example in recent years was the discovery of 'the torture memos', initially uncovered by journalists and eventually obtained in their entirety through the actions of the American Civil Liberties Union. They are a series of memos, solicited by President Bush from government lawyers, giving him advice on what American interrogators may do to prisoners in the 'war on terror' without breaching the Convention Against Torture to which the US is a signatory, and on whether the prisoners in Guantanamo Bay are covered by the Geneva Conventions. According to the vast majority of human rights lawyers, the advice the President was given was wilfully inaccurate, and could only have been given because it was what the officials involved wanted to hear. As long as discussions were under the Executive's control, any, relatively minor, disputes which took place over these memos took place in secrecy, amongst officials of the Bush Administration, without the opportunity for other actors in the human rights field to participate (see Greenberg and Dratel 2005; Campbell 2007). They did not, however, remain secret for long.

In complete contrast, disputes between government officials or with others in the human rights field are sharpest if cultural political struggle comes into the courts. In such cases, government officials are often engaged directly in legal disputes, participating in their official capacities as respondents in cases brought by those with human rights claims against them. We will look at such a case in detail in Chapter 3, which concerns disputes between officials of the Bush Administration and the advocacy groups that took them to court over the arbitrary detention of detainees in Guantanamo Bay, and at the arguments of advocacy groups and the UK government in court concerning the Belmarsh detainees.

In addition, government officials may intervene in court cases in which they are not directly involved as litigants to try to influence decisions as 'friends of the court'. In important cases in appellate courts, 'friends of the court', or 'amici curiae', who are not parties to the case, are generally permitted to submit information to try to influence the court to take into account broader outcomes of the decision. Whilst 'friends of the court' often submit arguments based on legal texts and reasoning they fear may be overlooked by the court, they may also submit any information they feel is relevant. In the case studies researched here, for example, a friend of the court brief was submitted to a US Court of Appeal on behalf of the Bush Administration in *Doe* v. *Unocal*, the ATCA case we will be investigating in Chapter 4 (Brief for the United States of America as Amicus Curiae in *Doe* v. *Unocal*). There, in addition to presenting legal arguments, the Administration also put forward political reasons why the Executive should be free to pursue foreign policy and to ensure the security of the American people, arguing that it was being compromised by the arguments of human rights advocacy groups. Another example is that of the friend of the court brief submitted by UK parliamentarians in *Rasul* v. *Bush*, a case brought on behalf of Guantanamo detainees of British nationality but which presented arguments in general terms for fundamental human rights not to be imprisoned without a fair trial (Brief of 175 Members of both Houses of the Parliament of the United Kingdom of Great Britain and N. Ireland as Amici Curaie in Support of Petitioners in *Rasul* v. *Bush*).

There are also struggles over human rights law which do not involve the courts, do not take place in secrecy, and which take place entirely within the governmental sub-field. This happens where human rights law is taken seriously as guiding domestic public policy, and human rights are discussed and voted on in the Legislature. The instruments of international human rights law take the form of universal, abstract principles; very few Articles in international human rights agreements are absolutely prescriptive. Richard Bellamy notes that those that are listed in the ECHR and other human rights treaties in the form 'no one shall be' are absolute and unconditional. Many, however, are listed as 'everyone (or everyone in a certain category) shall be entitled to . . .', and these are subject to such limitations and conditions 'as are prescribed by law and are necessary, in a democratic society, in the interests of public safety, the protection of public order, health or morals, or for the protection of the rights and freedoms of others'. In some cases, conditions also include the protection of national security, the economic well-being of the country, and the prevention of crime and disorder (Bellamy 1999: 171). How domestic public policy is to be made in conformity with international human rights law therefore leaves a good deal of latitude for political disagreements and compromises concerning those interpretations.

Cultural politics in the governmental sub-field may be structured by the ritualised, and often ideologically inflected, antagonism of mainstream institutionalised political parties – the Democratic and Republican parties in the US, the Labour, Conservative and Liberal Democrat parties in the UK. However, there is often cross-party consensus on the fundamental issues that are raised by human rights. As we shall see, in debates over security and human rights, for example, or over state sovereignty, politicians generally judge the political stakes to be too high to allow for party politics.

In all cases, whether or not the usual mechanisms for party politics are available or not, whether struggles over human rights take place in the Legislature, in courts, or behind closed doors, actors in the governmental sub-field invariably *also* engage in struggles *outside* these settings, with each other and with others in the human rights field, in order to gain the authority to act. They make political speeches, lobby colleagues, attempt to influence the gatekeepers of the media, and through them the wider public, so that their interpretation of human rights will prevail. In these ways they engage in struggle to be able to use the authority of the official positions they occupy to confirm their preferred definitions of human rights. In this respect, whilst the possibility of achieving effective power in the governmental sub-field depends to a large extent on the objective positions that officials occupy there, it also depends on cultural politics that take place in the wider human rights field as well.

The activist sub-field

The sub-field of human rights activism differs from the juridical and governmental sub-fields in that it is located outside state structures. Authority in the sub-field of human rights activism is not exercised from official positions, as in the juridical or the governmental sub-field. Human rights organisations rather aim to achieve *indirect authority* when, by their extensive and up-to-date knowledge of human rights law, or their accumulated experience with international governmental organisations and with state actors at the international and domestic level, they are able to convince actors who do occupy positions of authority to speak effectively *following activist interpretations of human rights.* Human rights organisations exercise authority indirectly when they have been able to convince judges and politicians to resolve conflicts by adopting their understanding of how human rights should be put into practice.

Human rights organisations are seen as the main actors propelling the progressive realisation of human rights in the research on how human rights norms are expanding. According to the findings of those who work in this area, they achieve their aims by establishing transnational advocacy networks which influence the ideas, emotions, and therefore, eventually, the identities and practices, of state elites (Keck and Sikkink 1998; Risse *et al.* 1999). The constructivist premises of transnational network analysis are consistent with those of this study: human rights organisations contribute to the realisation of human rights by successfully contesting what human rights mean in a given situation, thereby achieving influence over the particular definitions of human rights that are put into practice. Moreover, theorists of transnational advocacy networks have accumulated some evidence for what they call the 'spiral model', which outlines a series of stages through which human rights organisations influence states to implement international human rights norms (Risse *et al.* 1999). However, as the name of the model itself suggests, this analysis tends towards rather a mechanistic view of change. According to the 'spiral model', recalcitrant members of state elites are 'socialised' into accepting international human rights norms by international society. The most common way the spiral begins is when domestic human rights organisations bypass their own repressive states and search out international allies – INGOs, international governmental organisations, and/ or 'great powers' – by means of which pressure can be brought to bear on state elites from above and below. According to the 'spiral model', progress is made through a series of stages, and may fail at any point: states elites move from repression of dissent, through denial of human rights absuses, to tactical concessions and acceptance of the validity of international norms, until, eventually, their behaviour is altered to comply with international human rights norms.

The theoretical model of the human rights field is preferable to that of the rather mechanistic 'spiral model' because the latter downplays how competition over the authority to determine human rights is *intrinsic* to human rights practices. Firstly, the theory of human rights field, unlike the 'spiral model' is open-ended, and does not specify a single, progressive, direction of change. Although theorists of transnational advocacy networks provide empirical evidence to support the 'spiral model' in the cases studied, it is far from clear that states which reach its highest stage will *always* act in accordance with international human rights norms. As we have noted, practices of human rights are *necessarily* subject to interpretation. It is true that there are gross violations which clearly transgress *any* interpretation of human rights norms, and it is with ending such violations by repressive states that theorists of transnational advocacy networks have been concerned. However, as we shall see in detail in Chapter 3, for example, Western states – which the model supposes are the leaders of international society in terms of expanding global human rights – do not have an 'all or nothing' approach to the adoption of international human rights norms. The arbitrary detentions in Guantanamo Bay, now in their seventh year, are challenged by human rights organisations as gross violations of human rights on the part of a state which prides itself on its exemplary status for the world as a human rights leader. Similarly, fundamental human rights have been violated in the UK in policies adopted in the name of national security. In focussing exclusively on how what they call 'repressive states' are transformed, theorists of transnational advocacy networks have not considered what happens in states that largely respect human rights when elites are tempted by what they perceive as new threats to their security. Then the contestation of what human rights might mean, which is intrinsic to human rights practices, and competition for the authority to determine what they *do* mean, becomes absolutely crucial.

Secondly, use of the theory of the human rights field enables the study of competition *between* state officials in the different sub-fields of the government and judiciary. Empirical analyses using the 'spiral model' consider the crucial roles that individuals in state elites often play in the successful institutionalisation of human rights: considering the evidence for such influences on their behaviour as fear for their reputation, moral conscience and so on. In this respect, these empirical analyses using the 'spiral model' do not treat the state as a black box. However, theoretically, the 'spiral model' itself does not direct attention towards the systematic and endemic conflicts between governmental and juridical officials over human rights, which are formative of the human rights field as such, and of definitions of human rights in practice.

My interest in this study is in how human rights organisations intervene in competitions over authority in the other sub-fields of the human rights field. I am, therefore, concerned with a more limited set of activities than those analysed by theorists of trans-national activist networks, with struggles that take place in the human rights field *within states*. The narrower focus enables a detailed analysis of the cultural politics of these struggles in the particular case studies chosen; and also of what is at stake for human rights and for state transformations in terms of pressure from below. I take it, however, that the methodology could be extended to study the international human rights field.

Human rights organisations are especially active in the juridical sub-field. There are both human rights organisations which specialise in the domestic arena (Liberty, for example, in the UK, and Human Rights First in the US), and those that are international (of which Amnesty International and Human Rights Watch are the best known). In the juridical sub-field they are able to claim indirect authority over human rights because of their their national or international prestige and the thorough knowledge and experience of human rights law they bring to bear. As well as actively bringing human rights cases, the advice of human rights organisations is sometimes also directly solicited by lawyers representing victims of human rights cases. In addition, they also invariably submit 'friend of the court' briefs in important cases in which they do not appear as litigants. Taking a wider perspective and with more expertise and experience than many of those involved in these cases puts them in a good position to exercise indirect authority relative to other actors in the human rights field once human rights cases come to court.

In the governmental sub-field, human rights organisations try to exercise indirect authority through government officals. They do so using a variety of means: through consultation documents that are requested by the government, for example; by producing independent reports on government policy to create conflicts between actors in the governmental sub-field that will open up debate and might enable them to influence its outcome; or by directly contesting existing policy in particular cases. In addition, international human rights organisations may also contribute to the monitoring procedures of international governmental organisations, in order to bring pressure to bear on governmental officials who are embedded in the extended networks of global governance.

Finally, human rights activists also try to exercise indirect authority in the intermestic human rights field through the media. In the first place they do so in order to make issues visible; to demonstrate that human rights violations are taking place that are of public concern. Then, using moral, as well as legal and political arguments, human rights organisations try to influence public opinion and to bring pressure to bear on juridical and governmental officials not to ignore or to continue to perpetuate those violations. In other words, human rights organisations use the media to create overt conflict in governmental and juridical spheres, or to intervene in conflicts that are already public in order to try to influence their outcome.

The mediated public

It is unusual to consider the media in relation to human rights (see Apodaca 2007). In some respects this is surprising: the media is obviously very important as a symbolic space for the struggle over human rights. This is immediately evident if we consider how actors in the human rights field strategise in relation to the media. Human rights organisations and political parties do so openly, employing professional press officers to enable them to create stories, present contributions to debates and 'spin' issues. All actors in the human rights field are, however, to some extent oriented towards the media. Even judges can not help but be aware of the impression they are making in the media. In the Pinochet case, for example – admittedly extreme in terms of the media attention it received – the Law Lords' decision was broadcast live on television for the first time, the judges' photographs and short biographies were published in newspapers, and there was intensive and extensive speculation in the papers and on television and radio, especially throughout the first year Pinochet was imprisoned in Britain, about whether they would send him to Spain for trial, or back to Chile to be freed.

In another respect, however, it is unsurprising that the importance of the media is under-theorised with respect to human rights: the media is now so hugely complex and pervasive, and its effects are so far-reaching, that it has become virtually indistinguishable from the social as such. Indeed, as Nick Couldry has shown, the media itself promotes its own centrality, paradoxically disappearing from the scenes it represents as if to reveal them as unmediated (Couldry 2000, 2003a). In addition, although it appears to be obvious that the media *does* have important social and political effects, precisely what they are has proved extremely difficult to pin down.

In this study I conceive of the media as an important space of symbolic struggle within the intermestic human rights field in which what is at stake is *influence* over other sub-fields, especially those of the state. News media – television, radio, newspapers, and increasingly the Internet – bring human rights issues into what John Thompson calls 'mediated publicness', the only kind of public life and public debate possible in complex societies (Thompson 1995). In the mediated public, human rights are contested and definitions of what human rights are or should be are introduced and consolidated, or emerge and then disappear, or are quite simply rendered invisible and therefore irrelevant. Although it would seem to be more consistent with the theoretical framework proposed so far to consider the media as a sub-field of journalistic practices, such an understanding is too narrow for my purposes here (Couldry 2003b; Benson and Neveu 2005). It is more useful to think of the media as forming a 'mediated public' because, as a space for the cultural politics of human rights, it provides a kind of 'meta-field' in which struggles for human rights are played out and in which all the actors in the human rights field are engaged. It is, however, much less than a 'meta-field' in that the actors who compete there understand that media practitioners themselves are involved in the struggle over the authority to effectively define human rights in practice. The mediated public is not democratic: conversations take place in the media amongst those whose voices are represented there, and they are represented in very particular ways. The concept of the 'mediated public' captures both dimensions well – the commonality of the symbolic space provided by the media, as well as the way in which journalistic practices structure media debates and frames issues and events within it. In addition, because of its link to Habermas's historically informed, but ultimately idealist, theory of the public sphere, the concept of the mediated public also directs us to pay attention to the influence of struggles in the media over authoritative definitions of human rights by state officials.

The mediated public is not the only symbolic space in which the cultural politics of human rights takes place between all the key actors involved in the human rights field. Courts have a similar, if more rigidly structured, function. The mediated public is, however, absolutely crucial in complex, large-scale modern societies. Most people do not themselves encounter or make claims for human rights, and no one has direct access to all the institutional places where human rights are discussed or decided face-to-face. The media is therefore an important source of information and understandings about human rights for everyone. It is obviously the most important source for those who are not professionally or personally engaged in the human rights field, the 'general public'. But it is also an important source of knowledge about how others understand human rights for those professionals involved in competitions for authority in the human rights field whose expertise and up-to-date knowledge is limited to one of its sub-fields.

The most obvious way in which media make issues of human rights public is literally by making them visible. The mediated publicness of different perspectives and of the actors who are engaged in promoting them is unequally distributed and of different value to different groups. In the case of human rights (as for other topics in which the state is implicated), the media routinely turn to actors in the governmental and juridical field in order to report on issues, frequently quoting them directly and offering analyses which treat them as authoritative in this area. In this way, by translating professional usages of the vocabulary of human rights into terms that are more easily and willingly grasped by readers and viewers, they reinforce the status quo. On the other hand, where issues have been raised by advocacy groups, or where their specialist knowledge and experience makes them especially valuable to journalists, human rights activists gain the opportunity to appear in public debate, and potentially to influence it, that is disproportionate to the power and influence otherwise wielded by 'ordinary people' in civil society, even when they have organised to bring about change (Thompson 1995: 247–9). By determining which perspectives on human rights are made visible, which 'voices' are heard, and which are given credibility, journalists and editors set agendas and frame human rights issues in ways that may influence the outcome of struggles over human rights.

The symbolic space the media provide for cultural politics of human rights is not, of course, simply there, blank and neutral, ready to be filled with the intentions of media practioners concerning human rights. Nor does the media simply relay messages to an already constituted public, existing in reality somewhere waiting for communication. The space of the media is itself structured. News media bring publics into existence by the way in which they frame news: 'we' find ourselves addressed by the way themes and topics are offered for our understanding and emotional response. In order to do so the media rely on general conventions of newsworthiness: which people and events are most interesting to their readers, listeners and viewers. In general terms – though the details may shift historically according to journalists' judgements – newsworthy events are those, for example, which concern powerful nations, and political elites or celebrities, which are anticipated and desired, and which promise disaster (Negrine 1989). To get our attention (and increase sales of media products or advertising), journalists and editors working in news media select and interpret from the uses of human rights elsewhere, and organise them into stories and staged rhetorical battles which they expect, on the basis of their expertise and experience in using those conventions, to inform, entertain, or merely distract us for a moment (Silverstone 1999). In this way, popular news media may create drama, emotion and interest out of (otherwise dry, abstract and boring) human rights issues, potentially constituting a public that might find human rights relevant, possibly even important.

However, a public is not simply the same as an audience. Following Daniel Dayan's definition, a public involves relative sociability and stability over time, commitment to internal debate, self-presentation in relation to other publics, a shared worldview, the possibility of translating desires and tastes into demands, and a reflexive awareness of the criteria establishing who belongs (Dayan 2001; see also Livingstone 2005). A public may overlap with an audience for a particular media output, or it may be formed across different audiences who nevertheless understand themselves to be sharing in debates which are addressed to elites who have effective authority and who are to be held accountable for their decisions by that public. News media constitute such a public where there is a consistency within the range of stories that are reported, within what is considered news, and also within the range of how they are reported across the media; and where there is the attempt to represent the interests and views, however imperfectly, of the public to elites.

The possibility that journalists may make human rights important in the mediated public gives those who create the news media a stake in competitions for authority in the human rights field. Like the other non-state actors with which we are concerned in this study, human rights activists, editors and journalists engage in cultural political struggles that *may* influence effective interpretations of human rights on the part of government officials and judges, so realising those interpretations in practice. Unlike human rights activists, influencing the state is only a secondary aim of media practitioners: the first aim is undoubtedly to create audiences. Nevertheless, traditionally in liberal-democracies the media has formed itself as 'the Fourth Estate': the watchdog for the people over state activities, and the forum within which public criticisms of the state are rehearsed. Thus, the media protects, represents and advocates the people's interests in relation to the state (see Keane 1991). Regardless of the individual intentions of a particular journalist or editor – and there are many who believe in it still (see Kovach and Rosentiel 2001) – this representation of the media as 'the Fourth Estate' gives a particular inflection to journalists' factual reporting as well as to journalists' arguments (in newspaper editorials, for example) which overtly argue in favour of or against government policies. On the one hand the media is there to educate and inform the public and to provide a platform for public debate. On the other hand, media practioners are bound, by the very form of news media itself, historically constructed as 'the voice of the people', to represent their unbiassed factual reporting as well as their arguments *as if* they were the peoples' protectors and advocates.

Conceptually the influence of the media is different in its effects from the authority of state officials, and also from the indirect authority of human rights activists, which depends on expertise and experience in the human rights field. It is influence which is indeed difficult to discern. It is not that social theorists should, or indeed do, naively take media producers at their word, and surmise that the media does, or has done in the past and could therefore in the future, represent 'the people' to the state. Let us take the example of the most influential theorist of the media in this respect, Habermas, who is often criticised for his idealist view of the public sphere. In fact, Habermas has shifted his view of the media from the critical comparison he made with the eighteenth century ideal of the public sphere in *The Structural Transformation of the Public Sphere* to a hugely complex account of the media and public in *Between Facts and Norms* (Habermas 1989, 1996). In his recent work Habermas sees the contemporary public sphere as *potentially* democratic and ethical: it is possible that mediated debate could – and it ought to – test the generalisability of solutions to conflicts in the court of public opinion; and these solutions could then – and they ought to – be filtered through the procedures of parliament and courts. For his theory of democracy to be anything more than a normative ideal, Habermas has a great deal theoretically invested in the claim that the media *could* enable the public to influence governmental policy, administration and legal judgement. Nevertheless, he is forced to conclude that precisely how and under what conditions the public using the media as a vehicle *is* actually able to influence state actors not only has not been established, but it is virtually impossible to establish using the current theoretical tools and methodologies available for the study of political communication.

What is clear is that, if we are not to think of people as the 'cultural dopes' of the media, we should not think of media influence as *causal*, but rather in terms of the 'reflexivity' of actors who interpret media representations and act according to their own understandings and judgements. Rather than thinking in terms of the causal influence of the media on the state, it is more useful to think in terms of how state actors reflect on what they think and do in the light of their own judgements concerning media practioners' – equally reflexive – self-representations as 'the people's advocate'. As media practioners try to influence the authoritative definitions of state officials, so too do other actors in the human rights field try to influence how the media represents their office, organisations or 'personality' and their perspectives on human rights. To investigate how actors in the juridical, governmental and activist sub-fields of human rights reflexively act upon media framing of issues, events, actors and processes concerning human rights – in their own sub-fields, in conflict with other actors across sub-fields, and by intervening in the mediated public – would, however, involve a research project which goes far beyond that in which I am engaged here.

For this study I have focussed on two much more modest tasks. In the first place, given that the media is the source of most people's information on how human rights are defined, I am interested simply in mapping how struggles over human rights which take place in and between the juridical, governmental and activist sub-fields are represented in the mediated public in ways which *create* meanings of human rights. The media arranges dominant and challenging perspectives on human rights – those of the traditionalists and the innovators engaged in the juridical sub-field, for example. In its factual reporting, the media *translates* definitions of human rights from the more or less technical ways in which they are used in other sub-fields into language which their readers, viewers and listeners will find interesting. In addition – in editorials and opinion pieces in newspapers, for example, or through TV documentaries or challenging interviews – media practioners also *evaluate* their own translations. They thereby potentially create a situation in which actors in the human rights field may have to respond to media representations of human rights, as well as to the technical definitions of other sub-fields.

Secondly, I am interested in mapping how closely dominant representations of human rights in the media *correspond* with authoritative definitions of human rights. The extent to which they correspond indicates a degree of influence, but it is not always clear in which direction, nor how that influence has been exercised. The clearest example of this – and it is one which exercises many theorists of the relation between media and politics (see, for example, Street 2001) – is where the strategies of populist politicians coincide with a media framing of events or persons. This is especially the case where it is a matter of new or unexpected stories, such that we would expect more conflict over how issues should be framed and discussed. An excellent example is analysed in Chapter 3. It concerns the way in which Prime Minister Blair – who led the government in passing the Human Rights Act – captured and led the conservative media agenda on human rights, whilst conceding practically all that was demanded by its campaign against human rights; and the way in which this was subsequently taken up by the new Conservative leader of the opposition who has gone still further in declaring himself in favour of restricting human rights. Was the Prime Minister influenced by the media to deny the validity of universal human rights in conditions of heightened security? Or were the media and leading politicians in both parties simply in agreement about their relative value in such conditions?

Alongside the courts, then, the media is absolutely crucial to how the meanings of human rights are contested, settled and insitutionalised. Using the idea of 'field' opens up the study of the cultural politics of intermestic human rights to encompass the cultural politics of human rights in the media, not simply in terms of cultural representations which affect those who directly view or listen to them but in relation to different institutional settings where what human rights mean, what they can do, is decided. The cultural politics of human rights does not take place in a homogenous and uniform space. It takes place rather across a range of heterogeneous and instititutional settings which are nevertheless interrelated through their focus on the same object, the authoritative definition of human rights. Actors pursue possibilities of institutionalising human rights, or resist their institutionalisation with means that they are partially formed by the contexts in which they act, and which differ across the human rights field. Most importantly, the human rights field works across the divide between state and civil society, with important practical consequences in terms of the possibilities of authoritative speech that differ from setting to setting. The outcome is not rational consensus but authoritative settlement that is more or less acceptable to those involved in the conflicts.

CULTURAL POLITICAL STRATEGIES: JUSTIFICATIONS OF HUMAN RIGHTS

Mapping the parameters of the intermestic human rights field enables analysis of the relevant actors engaged in the cultural politics of intermestic human rights and identification of the settings at which cultural politics is engaged. Use of Bourdieu's concept of 'field' does not, however, help us to analyse the *content* of the strategies that are used by interested parties engaged in the cultural politics of human rights.[2] Moreover, my use of the concept of 'field' for the study of globalising human rights makes for rather a different perspective on the social world than that for which Bourdieu intended it. Whilst Bourdieu is concerned with social stratification above all, with how social actors compete with each other to accumulate economic, social and symbolic capital, I am interested in the cultural politics of the authoritative decisions that are the *object* of competition in the human rights field; with the meanings of human rights that are produced in the competitive processes that take place there, and with their effects on the formation of social structures. According to my understanding, cultural politics allows for reciprocal persuasion, the construction of shared ideals and the imagining of a common political community, even across professional differences, possibilities for which Bourdieu's understanding of power, capital and class struggle arguably does not allow (Alexander 1995).

---

[2] Although good for 'thinking with' Bourdieu's cultural practice theory lacks methodological tools for analysing how the cultural politics of a field actually work in practice (Ortener 2006; Sewell 1992).

In order to pursue my analysis of the cultural politics in the human rights field, I therefore supplement Bourdieu's cultural practice with the idea of 'justification', drawing on the work of Boltanski and Thevenot. Boltanski and Thevenot developed the concept of 'justification' in order to analyse the rationales that actors use to end conflict, reach agreement and realise their aims in conditions of uncertainty. Justifications create symbolic equivalences between classifications of people and things and relate them to something general, 'common to all the objects brought together' (Boltanksi and Thevenot 2006: 32). They involve appeal to already existing mutual understandings of how things and people should be arranged, in order to extend that understanding to new situations. In this respect justifications are like frames: they simplify the world by encoding and patterning events, experiences and objects in particular ways. Justifications are necessary to co-ordinate collective behaviour once disagreements arise, but they are also necessary because such disagreements are an inherent possibility in ongoing social life.

Justifications are always strategic in that they are used as instruments to achieve agreement. This does not necessarily mean, however, that justifications are used strategically to achieve ends that are set in advance of the conflict in which they are engaged. Justifications *may* be manipulated in this way to defend and advance interests that are established and maintained prior to particular conflicts over the meaning of human rights. However, in appealing always to existing understandings, justifications often also involve the contention of fundamental values and interests.

Boltanski's and Thevenot's concept of 'justification' is compatible with Bourdieu's understanding of field in that justifications are used by actors to compete for authority in social settings. However, Boltanski and Thevenot break with Bourdieu in that they understand justifications to be free from particular institutional settings. In contrast, I follow Bourdieu in emphasising the importance of institutional settings. Whereas Boltanski and Thevenot are interested in constructing a complete typology of justifications across the social field, my aim is not to detail the entirety of justifications that are possible for human rights but rather to analyse the justifications that were *regularly* used in struggles for authority between significant groups of actors in the intermestic human rights field. It is Boltanksi's and Thevenot's methodology, rather than the conclusions of their investigations, that is useful to this study.

I found it useful to analyse justifications along two main dimensions (which may be more or less explicit in any particular case) (see Favell 2001). Firstly, the *value* of human rights must be justified: an answer must be given to the (implicit or explicit) question, why are human rights so signficant that they must override all other values in this particular case? Secondly, the use of human rights must be *explained*: claims about the 'facts of the matter' relevant to human rights have to be made, and some background must be supposed or elaborated about how those facts have come into existence and who is responsible for human rights violations. In addition, explanation is required to show how the normative value that is given to human rights might realistically be achieved; who is responsible for ensuring that human rights are respected in the future, and that justice is done for past wrongs.

Boltanski and Thevenot are certainly right that justifications as such do not rely on institutional settings. A good example of this in the cultural politics of intermestic human rights is the way judges make extra-legal justifications for their decisions in terms of general principles, as well as justifying those decisions in terms of legal reasoning. However, *successful* justifications in institutional settings are partially formed by the requirements of such settings, which prescribe appropriate 'tests of worth' for facts and values. Justifications gain authority by conforming to those requirements, and at the same time they reproduce the logics of the institutional settings within which they are made. Although judges may make extra-legal justifications for their decisions, it is on conventional legal reasoning as well as on their occupation of legitimate office that they rely for the authority of those judgements.

As we have seen, the intermestic human rights field encompasses a number of institutional settings in which the cultural politics of human rights are engaged. The way in which actors frame human rights as meaningful for their interlocuters tends to vary according to the institutional context in which they are situated, and the resources they have at their disposal because of that situation. Justifications are not entirely determined by institutional setting; the uncertainty inherent in any meaningful practice means there is always some ambiguity and play of interpretive possibilities. This is true even where it is a question of legal judgement: as we have already noted, the law is always open to more than one interpretation. Moreover, some institutions are more open to a plurality of types of justification than others: the legal setting appears to constrain the range of possible justifications more narrowly than does the media, for example.

Finally, it is also important to note that, although the concept of 'justification' may sound rationalist, justifications do not only work through their appeal to reason, but also through appeal to, evocation of, and indeed, creation of, emotion. Reason and emotion are not opposites. Reason as such requires certain emotions: calm, for example, and confidence in one's abilities to think something through. Practical reasoning requires other emotions as well; for example, trust in the actions of enabling others, and the ability to motivate co-operation (Barbalet 2002; Young 1996). Indeed, theorists of emotion have also shown how judgements of value are always suffused with emotion: what is considered an appropriate response to a particular situation or event is situated within ethical discourses that structure not only how we should *think* about that situation or event, but also how we should, and generally do, *feel* about it (Harre 1986; Nussbaum 2003). As well as depending on emotions to persuade, then, justifications which situate human rights, showing their relevance and value in a particular case, at the same time evoke emotions that are conventionally oriented towards the judgements they state or imply. As we shall see in the chapters of analysis that follow, national pride and shame are especially potent emotions in the cultural politics of human rights.

To summarise, then, competition within and between different arenas of the field of human rights is joined in justifications which explain and attribute value to human rights in different ways according to different institutional settings. In order to do so, they also draw on ethical 'emotional vocabularies'. In the following sub-sections I will briefly describe typical justifications in the field of intermestic human rights, and outline how I accessed them in the case studies that were analysed for this research. Although I have outlined what was distinctive about the justifications in each case, it should be borne in mind that, as the analysis detailed in the following chapters will show, they are not discrete areas: competition is engaged between, as well as within, these different domains of the human rights field. Justifications in one domain of the human rights field engage justifications in another, especially in courts and in the mediated public, which are the privileged sites of the human rights field.

Juridical justifications

As we have noted, the cultural politics of the juridical sub-field involves interpretation of the law and also extra-legal commentaries on those interpretations. In legal interpretations, the reality of human rights is explained and the ideals of human rights are defended or revised in terms of legal orthodoxy. Justifications for human rights must conform to conventional standards of legal reasoning in order to be authoritative. The 'tests of worth' demanded of authoritative actors are those of principle and precedent as set out in the texts that make up the law. Despite all the differing interpretations of these texts, the authoritative decision of judges as to what the law says is final. As Bourdieu points out, in no other setting is authoritative speech quite so effective. In making their decisions judges literally make the world according to their classifications (Bourdieu 1987: 838). The law allows for different interpretations, but once a judgement has been made in court, unless that decision is overturned by a higher court, it is the law.

In their extra-legal commentaries in juridical settings, judges use rhetoric that is not so closely tied to legal reasoning. Accompanying an authoritative statement of what the law requires, judges quite often also justify their decisions in terms of the general principles underlying that decision. Where intermestic human rights are concerned, such justifications are often strategic interventions for or against their globalisation through the procedures of national states. There is an excellent example of this kind of rhetoric, which was widely taken up in the media, in Chapter 3. In a case which challenged the arbitrary detention of terrorist suspects, Lord Hoffman resoundingly described the European Convention on Human Rights as simply reflecting 'quintessentially' British values of liberty. This was clearly an attempt to make human rights more appealing in a case in which national security was being opposed to international law in a national court (see pp. 97–8). In another example, analysed in Chapter 4, that is much more low-key and subtle, Justice Souter's opinion in *Sosa* v. *Alvarez*, described 'the door' as 'still ajar subject to vigilant doorkeeping', with reference to the possibility of using customary international law in ATCA cases in US courts in the future. In this case, the legal judgement *for* the obligation on US courts to enforce international human rights norms was accompanied by a metaphor that suggests that such human rights should nevertheless be viewed with suspicion by judges in national courts (see p. 116).

Analysis of justifications in the juridical sub-field was carried out on legal materials from the highest appellate courts involved in each case study, generally the Supreme Court in the US and the Law Lords in the UK. In *Doe* v. *Unocal*, which did not reach the Supreme Court, I analysed materials from the Court of Appeals for the Ninth Circuit and the Californian Supreme Court. I analysed the judges' decisions, legal arguments for the prosecution and defence, and 'friend of the court' briefs. I also analysed speeches made by judges outside the court where they were widely reported in the media and used by human rights activists (for example, the speech by Lord Steyn in which he described Guantanamo as a 'legal black hole' (Steyn 2003)). I was especially interested in the struggles between traditionalists and innovators in international law, and these sources proved rich sources for charting them in the juridical sub-field.

Governmental justifications

Government officials are, in principle, answerable to the electorate. As Bourdieu argues, political rhetoric therefore aims to gain the consent of the people to whom politicians are responsible as their elected representatives. In order to achieve their aims, however, politicians commonly present policies as if they *already* have that agreement or, even better, as if they were directly expressing the will of the people. Again authoritative political rhetoric is *performative*, bringing about the representation of the people it presupposes (Bourdieu 1991: 190–1).

As representatives of the people, governmental officials justify their actions 'in the name of the people'. The test of worth of such justifications may be evidence of popular support for their arguments (from opinion polls, for example). On occasion, however, the fact of having been elected is used as evidence that government officials represent the people; for example, against the claims of activists, lawyers and judges. However, the justifications of politicians for their actions may also have their worth tested in reference to international human rights norms to which the state has committed itself and to which government officials are supposed to be legally bound. In such cases justifications that they are 'acting in the name of the people' must take into account, and work between, national and international institutions. Elected politicians are first and foremost answerable to national voters; adherence to international norms is secondary. It is therefore relatively easy ordinarily for government officials to justify actions in the name of the (national) people which are at odds with the international norms of human rights. However,

if challenged in intermestic human rights cases, governmental officials may also have to show why state commitments to human
rights, which have also been made by elected politicians who act 'in
the name of the people', must now be ignored or overruled.

In order to create an archive for analysis of justifications in the
human rights field generally, I first created a timeline for each case
study. In each case this included the most important dates of legal
cases: the dates on which they were first brought, and of key judgements as the cases made their way through the courts of appeal.
It also included, in each case, key dates for other elements of the
human rights field. In the case of the governmental sub-field these
were: dates of important political speeches that were widely reported
in the media; of Executive orders and official announcements; dates
between which legislation was debated and at which it was enacted;
dates of relevant meetings of international governmental organisations in which officials participated; and of government reports
concerning human rights in the particular case at issue. I then conducted a search around each signficant date in the relevant documents for the governmental sub-field, in the week on each side of the
key date. These materials included: legal representation and friends
of the court briefs submitted in court cases; speeches by government
officials; government reports and consultation documents; press
releases and articles written for newspapers by government officials.

Activist justifications

Human rights organisations generally do not seek to monopolise a
specialist technical language, like law, nor to occupy existing official
positions, like political parties (though individuals involved with
organisations may build careers that lead them to official positions).
They do, however, compete very energetically with other actors in
the human rights field to achieve the authority to define human
rights. Indeed, this is their primary reason for existing. In order to do
so, human rights organisations use legal, political and also moral
justifications to explain the reality of human rights and to promote

and defend their value. Human rights activists in international organisations *invariably* justify human rights as *global* against the justifications of other actors in the human rights field for whom the national scale is almost always the most relevant to test their worth. As we shall see, this is not necessarily the case for those activists who work in national rights organisations even where human rights law is available to them.

Internationally, Amnesty International and Human Rights Watch are by far the largest human rights organisations, with the greatest credibility across the world. In the US, the Center for Constitutional Rights and Human Rights First (formerly known as Lawyers for Human Rights) have been crucial to legal strategies of the human rights movement. In addition, other national organisations are now beginning to use international human rights norms to put pressure on the US government, most notably the American Civil Liberties Union. In the UK, national organisations for civil liberties use European and domestic human rights law. Liberty (formerly the National Council for Civil Liberties), which is linked to the ACLU, has been very influential in this respect. In addition, for this research it was also important to study justifications produced by other, smaller organisations for specific case studies. For Chapter 3, I studied materials produced by the Council of American-Islamic Relations and the Muslim Public Affairs Committee, to find out if organisations set up to represent Muslims and to pursue Muslim civil liberties used human rights to contest the arbitrary detentions in Guantanamo Bay and Belmarsh. Earthrights Interrnational was key to the *Doe* v. *Unocal* case analysed in Chapter 4. The coalition campaigns against global poverty, Make Poverty History and ONE were compared with each other and with Jubilee 2000 UK and Jubilee 2000 USA in Chapter 5.

In order to create an archive for analysis of justifications produced by human rights activists I collected all the reports produced by each organisation relevant to the case studies selected for this research. I also analysed the legal materials they produced in each case. Finally, I collected and analysed press releases produced by human rights organisations in relation to the key dates of legal cases and of the governmental sub-field in the timeline created for each case study, as well as newspaper articles written by members of these organisations in their official capacities.

Mediated justifications

Journalists and editors have their own justifications for how they select and frame news stories about human rights, which have been formed, and are authoritative, within their professional field. As we have noted in Chapter 1, because the media has been historically constructed as the Fourth Estate in liberal-democracies, journalists are professionally positioned as the watchdogs and advocates of 'the people'. As well as providing entertainment, then, they also see themselves as informing both the public and government of the facts, and the values, at stake in cultural–political conflicts.

However, informing the public and government in the news media largely involves *reacting* to news that is made elsewhere. In factual reporting, as Herbert Gans put it, news stories tend to 'follow power' in that the most newsworthy sources, and generally the easiest for journalists to access, are those that make quotes available from government elites (Gans 2003). In 'informing' the public about human rights, the media tends to quote justifications of human rights made by a few government officials, who are widely known as 'household names'. In the case studies of intermestic human rights with which we are concerned here, journalists did, however, also draw on the expertise of human rights activists, who made themselves equally readily available for comment and analysis. Both in accessing 'official' and 'alternative' views, news articles tended to be constructed around quotes from individuals, with minimal analysis of institutional processes and wider political agendas. In this way, news items were invariably presented in realist terms, as a 'window' on what happened, whilst the criteria by which quotes and evidence were selected were obscured.

By comparison, in actively *creating* public opinion and influencing government elites, journalists often do offer their own explicit justifications for selecting evidence and subjecting statements concerning human rights to 'tests of worth' in terms of facts and values. There are two main ways in which journalists create news. The first, by investigative journalism, is quite rare. Investigative journalism uncovers and demonstrates elite hypocrisy, deceit and even criminality, and therefore contributes to demands that state officials should be genuinely accountable to citizens or to the law. Secondly, and much more commonly, news media try to influence both the public and elites through opinion columns and editorials. In both cases – unsurprisingly, given the time constraints under which news media operate, the lack of technical expertise of most columnists, and the number of different topics they must cover on a regular basis – these justifications are generally selected from those that have already been made by other actors in the human rights field, and reworked in more accessible and 'interesting' ways for the mediated public.

Both in producing information and influence, then, news media tend not to originate justifications for human rights but rather to *translate* the justifications of other actors into media products, representing them in the mediated public as 'neutral' information or in strongly worded and emotive arguments explicitly intended to influence the public and government officials. In this way, the news media do not simply stage the cultural politics of human rights, they also contribute to those cultural politics. They give greater weight to the perspectives of some actors over others in ongoing conflicts of cultural politics; and they alter justifications in 'translation' – simply by putting them into a new context, or by literally altering some of the terms and arguments of the debates.

The focus of this analysis is on newspapers as representative of the cultural politics of human rights in the mediated public. Newspapers had a number of advantages for this analysis: they share a similar agenda to national news broadcasting but their coverage of news tends to be more in-depth; they aim at niche markets so allowing analysis of a diversity of political perspectives on human rights; and they have the great advantage of being relatively easy to collect and to analyse.

However, comparing US and UK newspapers did present some difficulties. Journalists in the US tend to see themselves as bound by their professional code to avoid bias and to strive for an ideal of objectivity. Although, of course, journalists can not really be 'objective' – they can not provide a 'mirror' representation of the world – overt evaluation of events and figures in US newspapers is much more strictly confined to the opinion pages and to anonymous editorials than in the UK. In comparison with the UK press, US reporting balances perspectives to a far greater extent, avoids the use of sensationalist headlines and uses far fewer adjectives. Predictably perhaps, debate over the supposed neutrality of the press is also highly politicised in the US, with Republicans accusing the media of liberal bias, while commentators on the Left find the media guilty of conservatism. As a result, journalists and editors in the US are proud to be seen as taking a centrist line, even if this actually privileges the status quo (McChesney 2004). In contrast, the UK is notorious across the world for its sensationalist tabloids: populist mass circulation papers which barely gesture towards objectivity in news reporting, treating it largely as entertainment. Even journalists and editors on the quality newspapers in the UK, however, are not ashamed to be seen as politically partisan. Though the quality press in the UK also clearly works with some ideal of 'objectivity' in news reporting, even in the elite newspapers evaluative language is quite common in news stories, and headlines tend towards the sensational.[3]

---

[3] My aim in sampling media representations was to capture the *range* and regularity of justifications available in the mainstream of each respective mediated public. It was not to assess their quantity or dispersion, or their reception. I began the research looking also at Left-wing magazines in the US (*Mother Jones, Dissent* and *The Nation*) as the best way to access left, as opposed to liberal, contributions to the US debate, which were more likely to be included in the UK selection by virtue of differences between mainstream US and UK newspapers. In fact, however, I found: a) that these journals generally replicated the arguments of human rights advocates; b) as there was no direct comparison in the UK, it was difficult to situate them in the research as a whole. However, I may, as a result, have skewed my analysis, giving the impression that there are fewer occasions on which

In order to compare US and UK papers I made a selection from across the range of what was available in the mainstream, trying to balance like with like as much as possible, even where there were no direct equivalents. I analysed the news stories, editorials and commentaries around the key dates of the timeline created for the juridical, governmental and activist sub-fields. In addition, I also included dates at which news was created: when the detainees returning from Guantanamo to the UK were interviewed by journalists in March 2004 for example; and when the *New York Times* confirmed that detainees were being tortured there by interviewing officials at the prison in October 2004.

In the US newspapers, I analysed materials a week either side of each date in the timeline in the nationally distributed, agenda-setting the *New York Times* (the most liberal in the US by reputation), the *Washington Post* and the *Los Angeles Times* (liberal-centre), the *Wall St Journal* (conservative and finance-oriented), and the more popular (liberal-centre) national daily *USA Today*. In addition, as there are no national tabloids to compare with those of the UK, I also studied the mass circulation local papers the *New York Post* (conservative) and *New York Daily News* (liberal-centre). In the UK, I carried out the same analysis on national papers: the quality broadsheets the *Guardian* and the *Observer* (liberal), the *Daily Telegraph* and the *Sunday Telegraph* (conservative) and the *Financial Times* (similar to the *Wall St Journal*); and the tabloids the *Daily Mail* and the *Mail on Sunday* (conservative) the *Mirror* (centre-left) and the *Sun* (Murdoch-owned like the *New York Post*, and similarly sensationalist).

left-wing justifications of human rights are made in the US media, as they largely appear in these journals rather than in the mainstream (my thanks to David Hansen-Miller for this point). Another way to build on the research in this study would be to add broadcasting media to the sample of media analysed. In the UK news broadcasting standards tend to be set by the BBC, and therefore other TV and radio stations tend towards replicating its model of impartiality. In the US, on the other hand, Fox TV news has taken a considerable share of the market, as have right-wing 'shock jocks' on the radio.

3   Sovereignty, pride and political life

Sovereignty is central to national state formation, and to the possibility of its transformation; it is, therefore, crucial to the realisation of human rights. As we noted in Chapter 1, the understanding of sovereignty as the freedom of a state from interference by other states is a significant dimension of the ideal of the self-determining national state. By the same token, the transformation of state sovereignty in international institutions of co-operative global governance is seen as necessary to address policy problems that increasingly arise in globalisation.

There is a popular view, shared by theorists of human rights and others, that human rights are, as a matter of fact, *eroding* state sovereignty. For example, David Forsythe has said that human rights law is 'revolutionary because it contradicts the notion of national sovereignty – that is, that a state can do as it pleases in its own jurisdiction' (quoted in Krasner 1999: 105). Similarly, David Hirsh says that 'human rights are instruments that seek to limit the scope of state sovereignty' (quoted in Sznaider and Levy 2006: 659). Alternatively, it is argued that because sovereignty is not 'indivisible, illimitable, exclusive and perpetual' (Held, quoted in Bickerton *et al.* 2007: 5), but rather socially constructed, historically specific and mutable (see Biersteker and Weber 1996), it is better understood as transformed by human rights. Whereas sovereignty was once justified as the ultimate guarantee of state security, it is now justified only insofar as it provides the potential to protect human rights (see Montgomery 2002: 3; Sznaider and Levy 2006; Bickerton *et al.* 2007).

In the ideal-type of the national state, sovereignty is what authorises the state to have the 'last word' (Montgomery 2002: 5). Sovereignty is the ultimate authority: there is no authority over the sovereign which it must obey. On the contrary, sovereignty is obeyed *because* it is sovereign. Sovereignty is nowhere more in evidence, then, than in the state prerogative to suspend law in order to take action that would not ordinarily be legally permitted. Immediately following the events of 9/11, both the US and UK declared a state of public emergency.[1] A declaration of public emergency suspends the normal juridical order for a state to adopt exceptional measures. After declaring a state of emergency, US and UK authorities detained terrorist suspects who were not citizens without charge for an indefinite period – overriding fundamental rights to individual liberty that are foundational to the rule of law, and to global human rights.

Carl Schmitt is the theorist par excellence of sovereignty as the 'last word'. According to Schmitt's famous formulation, sovereignty is *created* by the decision that there is a state of exception: 'Sovereign is he who decides on the exception' (2005: 5). Following Schmitt's understanding, sovereignty is what states *do*; it is not something states *have*. Sovereignty cannot, therefore be eroded. The conditions under which sovereignty is exercised, and the way in which it is practised, can, however, be transformed. In the human rights field, the effective authority to have the 'last word' is precisely what is in question, disputed between the juridical, governmental and activist sub-fields and rehearsed 'on behalf of the people' in the mediated public. In the ideal of the national state, a distinction is made between internal sovereignty – the organisation of public authority in a state – and external sovereignty – the organisation of the inter-national system to prevent unwelcome interference in states' affairs. As we have seen, a clear distinction between the external and internal affairs of states becomes very difficult to maintain where it is a matter of intermestic human rights. Contestation in the human rights field is at its most acute when state prerogative is used to

---

[1] The President declared a public emergency on 14 September 2001 (Proclamation 7463). In the UK, the government declared a public emergency in order to derogate from the ECHR on 11 November 2001.

declare a state of emergency that overrides fundamental human rights which are now, on the face of it, a matter of global concern.

The sovereign decision is taken from within the juridical order: the law specifies – more or less clearly in the case of different states – legitimate procedures that must be followed in order to declare a state of emergency. In the US, Article 1 of the Constitution permits the President to suspend *habeus corpus* – the fundamental individual right not to be detained without trial – 'when in Cases of Rebellion or Invasion the public Safety may require it' (see Ackerman 2004: 1041). The US Supreme Court may then choose (it does not have to) to hear cases which subject the sovereign decision of the President concerning fundamental individual rights to judicial review, to determine its legality. There is debate over precisely what the Executive powers are according to the US Constitution. One interpretation of the Constitution is that the Legislature should be involved in deciding when the President is entitled to declare a state of emergency. It has not always been involved in the past, however, and it was not involved in President Bush's decision to declare a state of emergency following 9/11 (Ackerman 2004: 1053). In the UK the Executive must formally derogate from (opt out of) those Articles of the ECHR which specify the individual rights it wishes to override. It must inform the Secretary General of the Council of Europe, giving reasons for its decision, and there are a number of Articles from which it is not possible to derogate. In the European system of human rights, the sovereign decision may then be subject to judicial review by domestic courts (if a successful appeal is launched), and eventually, if no satisfactory conclusion is reached, the European Court of Human Rights may decide to hear a case in order to determine the legality of the sovereign decision.

However, as it creates measures which suspend 'normal' law, the sovereign decision is not *determined* by law or legal procedures. It is, as Schmitt says, at the limit of law and politics. It is extremely rare that there is a *total* suspension of the juridical order. Schmitt calls this 'an extreme exception' (Schmitt 2005: 7). Even in much less extreme situations, however, it is clear that sovereign prerogative of a state ultimately involves a particular person or group of people exercising the power to decide: (a) that a state of emergency is warranted; (b) what form suspension of the law will take. Where this sovereign power is located may be in question in principle, but insofar as, in the cases we are dealing with here for example, the Executive takes the prerogative, which is certainly legally and politically possible, it effectively acts as sovereign. Where the Executive exercises state prerogative in practice, it is only *after* the sovereign decision is made that the other branches of the state may question whether or not it is within the limits allowed by the law, and try to alter it procedurally.

Cultural politics is inherent to any sovereign decision. The fact that a sovereign decision ultimately depends on the will of the sovereign – in that it is not determined by bureaucratic procedures or legal reasoning – does not mean that it is not determined at all. *Before* the decision is taken to suspend certain features of the law, the sovereign Executive must evaluate the objective conditions that make exceptional measures desirable, if not necessary. In part this evaluation depends on how cultural politics have already structured those conditions: which actors and perspectives are most prominent; and how, therefore, the sovereign decision is likely to be received. In the cases we are dealing with here, for example, the Executive's evaluation of the objective conditions that made a sovereign decision desirable would undoubtedly have concerned not only the risks of *not* adopting exceptional measures (appearing weak in the face of security threats), but also the potential political *costs* of adopting those measures (how might doing so help political adversaries?), and also the political advantages of doing so (how might doing so strengthen the government's position in relation to its political enemies?). In addition, once the decision is taken, it must be publicly *justified*. The sovereign may decide when, where and how this justification will be made, but in liberal-democracies justification of the sovereign decision is impossible to dispense with altogether.

Evaluation before a sovereign decision must, therefore, also involve assessment of the relative difficulties of sustaining a policy which overrides fundamental human rights if there is sustained challenge to that policy. Since the very purpose of a sovereign decision is to override individual rights, it is only in the most repressive states that such challenges can be expected not to follow.

What form do the cultural politics of human rights take in cases in which sovereign decisions have been taken that violate fundamental human rights? How do human rights affect the conditions in which sovereign decisions are made and defended? In this chapter I explore the cultural politics of human rights around the sovereign decisions to suspend the fundamental rights of non-citizens suspected of terrorist activities in the US and UK. I focus on sovereign decisions which affect the rights of non-citizens in order to study the question 'who is the subject of human rights?' in concrete case studies of the cultural politics of intermestic human rights which problematise the distinction between citizens and non-citizens.

International human rights law requires that the distinction between citizens and non-citizens be abolished where fundamental human rights are concerned. In contrast, national states, ideally, have existed to serve citizens. What is most striking about challenges to the sovereign decision to suspend fundamental rights in the US and UK, however, is that they tended to be made using the rhetoric of nationalist pride rather than in universalist terms. Even supporters of human rights rarely offered a forceful cosmopolitan defence of international human rights. They tended not to justify human rights using arguments concerning humanity and the value of each and every human being, nor the fact and legitimacy of international human rights agreements. In both the US and UK – though in different ways – the value of human rights as a framework of universal principles regulating political life was secondary to the value of national pride in contestations of the sovereign decision to suspend fundamental rights for both defenders and opponents of human rights.

Nationalism is usually seen as intractably opposed to, and problematic for, cosmopolitan norms of human rights, to the point where nationalism and human rights are virtually never discussed together. The importance of nationalism is occasionally mentioned by theorists of transnational advocacy networks (Keck and Sikkink 1998: 202; see Jetschke 1999 for the most considered study of nationalism in relation to human rights I have come across), but its importance is rather implied than discussed in this literature. In this respect it is shame, the reverse of pride, which is the emotion that has been most frequently commented upon. It is assumed that shame accompanies the institutionalisation of human rights ideals by state elites where this is undertaken for principled rather than instrumental reasons (Keck and Sikkink 1998: 23; Risse and Ropp 1999: 245). The argument is as follows: if it can be shown that state elites accept that human rights norms are the right way to behave, rather just the most prudent, it must be because they have experienced the shame of being the leader of a 'pariah' state. In this understanding, shame operates at the international level: it is in what Keck and Sikkink call 'the world political system' that shame – implicitly national shame – is felt on the part of the leaders of states who then act according to norms of international rights rather than calculating the advantage they may gain by ignoring those norms.

Surely, however, it is unsurprising, given the historic identification of states and nations, that nationalist feelings are important in persuasive strategies to end human rights violations from within states? I found that national pride, far more than shame, played a crucial but very complex role in the cultural politics of human rights in relation to sovereign decisions to suspend the rights of non-citizens suspected of terrorism from within the US and UK. Both in justifications of the sovereign decision and in challenges to it, emotions of pride in the ideal nation, which is founded on the rule of law and which therefore respects and upholds fundamental individual rights, were entangled with fear for the bodies of the people of the real nation.

Georgio Agamben's famous distinction between *zoe*, or 'bare life' and *bios*, 'political life' is useful here to explore the cultural politics of national pride and fear that was evident in the case studies researched for this chapter. Inspired by Hannah Arendt's work on human rights, Agamben analyses how bare life and political life are collapsed in human rights, where the mere fact of having been born, as a human animal that is exposed to death, is supposed to be enough to give one entitlements in the political community of humanity (Arendt 1968; Agamben 1998). Both Agamben and Arendt are sceptical of this possibility, seeing no prospect of a political community of humanity. On the contrary, they argue that human rights are dangerously deceptive for just this reason, exposing those without state to persecution and destruction. What is useful here, however, is Agamben's distinction between bare and political life. What we see in justifications of the sovereign decision that opposes security and rights is the *separation* of bare and political life *both inside and outside the state*. Outside the state, those who are accused of threatening it may be reduced to nothing more than bare life, which, according to Agamben, can be killed without sacrifice (Agamben 2005: 4). What has been less remarked upon, however, is that *inside* the state, the sovereign decision to suspend fundamental rights creates a temporary separation of bare and political life in order to *protect* bare life: the cultivated ideals of political life are to be set aside to protect the vulnerable flesh and blood of the nation with which it is ordinarily entwined.[2] Through this separation, the sovereign decision promises to preserve both bare life and, ultimately, political life too. Following this logic, suspending fundamental individual rights is, ultimately, the only way to protect the very possibility of exercising rights at all. Externalising the bare life of non-citizens, and protecting

---

[2] Of course, deployment of the distinction between bare and political life, and, on occasion, its collapse and conflation, is strategic. The less than urgent response to the devastation of Hurricane Katrina is a good example of the separation of bare and political life *within* citizens. Thank you to Anna Marie Smith for prompting me to clarify this point.

the bare life of citizens, is ultimately the only way to secure the political life of the national community.

The following analysis charts the way in which sovereign justifications which separate and conflate the bare life and the political life of the nation were deployed and challenged in the cultural politics of human rights. In the US activists have found it virtually impossible to bring any significant pressure using human rights law to bear on the Executive. It is only by finding obscure national law concerning *habeus corpus* that activists have been able to challenge the sovereign decision legally. In the mediated public, supporters of human rights have tried to mobilise national pride and shame concerning international human rights. The national pride that has made a difference, however, is pride in the core values of America and the American constitution. It is not shame for the way in which the US fails to uphold international human rights norms but pride in the US as a political community founded on the rule of law, itself dependent on the lives of the American people, which has been effectively mobilised to challenge human rights violations.

In the UK, by comparison, because of the way the state is embedded in the European system, human rights have been relatively more effective legally in challenging sovereign justifications for arbitrary detention. However, although human rights are thoroughly institutionalised in the UK, the mobilisation of national pride has also played an important, though ambiguous, role in challenging the sovereign decision. Supporters of human rights have tried to mobilise national pride, to show how central human rights are to the political life of the nation. But this strategy, paradoxically, has had potentially dangerous effects for human rights as deconstructing the distinction between citizens and non-citizens in practice in the context of fears for national security.

AMERICAN EXCEPTIONALISM

Guantanamo Bay was *designed* to fall outside both international and national law, although this is not to say that it falls outside law altogether.[3] It is rather that in anticipation of legal and other challenges, the Executive decision to create a camp for arbitrary detention in Guantanamo deliberately carved out a space which law can not easily regulate precisely because it is exists in the interstices of international and national rules. Guantanamo Bay has been described by one senior judge as a 'legal black hole' (Steyn 2003). It is a black hole that exercises a gravitational pull on law, tying lawyers up in legal pedantry as they try to capture the sovereign decision to suspend the normal rule of law.

Guantanamo Bay was created outside international law. The White House announced shortly after the first wave of prisoners were taken there that they were not to be treated as prisoners of war under the Geneva Conventions since they were not conventional soldiers of a national state, but as 'unlawful' or 'enemy combatants' captured on the battlefield in Afghanistan. The policy had apparently been agreed as a result of secret memos, signed by the President in February 2002, that the Geneva Conventions would not apply in the war in Afghanistan, or in the global war on terror generally (Hersh 2005: 5). (It subsequently emerged that many had not reached Guantanamo from Afghanistan, but had been 'captured' elsewhere in the field of the 'war against terrorism'.) The Geneva Convention entitles individuals captured in war to give only their name, rank and serial number. Guantanamo Bay was designed as an interrogation camp. It was also created outside national law. There is provision in the Geneva Conventions for the treatment of 'illegal combatants', civilians who engage in armed conflict: they should be tried for crimes under domestic law, as common criminals, or for international war crimes (see HRF 2000: 9). However, as the camp was set up on territory that legally belongs to Cuba, from which it is leased by the US, the Bush Administration claimed that it was

---

[3] Guantanamo Bay was also a site of struggle over law. In this sense Guantanamo was both inside and outside law (Johns 2005; see also Comaroff 2007).

outside US jurisdiction. The prisoners were not, therefore, to have access to the US courts.[4]

Approximately 750 men and boys have been held in Guantanamo Bay since January 2001 (some 200 of whom have disappeared), without charge, without knowing the evidence against them, and without access to anyone outside the institution, including civilian lawyers, until 2004. At the time of writing, it is estimated that about 350 men remain. From the accounts of some of those released we know that many, if not all, have been tortured (see CCR 2004; HRW 2004a; Begg 2006).

Security vs. rights in the global war on terror

The US Executive constructed the sovereign decision that created Guantanamo Bay, in terms of a *choice* between national security, the prevention of further attacks, and the rights of terrorists guilty of the attacks. In the Military Order of November 2001 the President declared his intentions to identify, pursue and detain any non-citizen involved with Al-Qaeda who had been involved in terrorist activity against the United States. The Order stated that, given the 'extra-ordinary emergency', 'the principles of law and the rules of evidence generally recognised in the trial of criminal cases in the United States' should not apply to such individuals (Presidential Military Order 2001). Instead captured terrorists were to be tried in secret by military tribunals with greatly reduced standards of due process (including reliance on evidence that might have been gathered by torture, and which the defendant would have no right to see). A

---

[4] In the US there were two cases of 'accidental' citizens who have also been detained without charge and without trial: Yasser Esam Hamdi and Jose Padilla. The expression 'accidental' was used of Hamdi to justify treating him with less than full citizenship rights, even though he was formally a US citizen (see Nyer 2006). Both Hamdi and Padillo were accused of terrorist activities and imprisoned without charge as 'enemy combatants', but not in Guantanamo Bay. Hamdi eventually agreed to give up his US citizenship in return for deportation to Saudi Arabia in 2004. Padilla was found guilty of terrorist activities in a federal court in 2007. Their stories are outside the scope of this study, which focuses on the detentions of non-citizens in Guantanamo Bay.

guilty verdict could mean execution. The secrecy of the tribunals was justified in terms of security. It would be too dangerous to deal with such individuals in open court: intelligence sources would be compromised and judges who delivered 'guilty' verdicts would live in fear for their lives (see, for example, 'Bush Signs Executive Order Establishing Military Tribunals to Try Terror Suspects', *Wall Street Journal*, 14 November 2001). The necessity for summary justice at Guantanamo was justified, then, in terms of a choice between (our) security and (their) rights.

In his 'Address to a Joint Session of Congress and the American People' on 20 September 2001, the President announced a global war on terrorism. This war concerned both the real and the ideal nation. The sovereign decision to suspend law in the case of terrorists was justified on the basis that the ideals of the political life of the nation, America, lives only secondarily, as it were, through the bare life, the flesh and blood of vulnerable, frightened Americans. The test of worth of this justification appears self-evident after 9/11: terrorists have succeeded in their ongoing attempts to kill large numbers of Americans, striking with such force and cunning that much worse to come must be anticipated.[5] The Executive justified the global war on terrorism as necessary, not just for national security, but in order to safeguard civilisation itself. In the Address, the President said: 'Americans are asking, why do they hate us. They hate what we see right here ... a democratically elected government ... They hate our freedoms – our freedom of religion, our freedom of speech, our freedom to vote and assemble and disagree with each other' ('Address to a Joint Session of Congress and the American People', www.whitehouse.gov/news/releases/2001/09/20010920–8.html, last accessed 29 December 2007). The global war on terror, which precedes and exceeds any actual military conflict, is a war against those who hate America for exactly the same reasons that Americans are

---

[5] The possibility of future nuclear, chemical or biological weapons attacks was widely feared immediately following 9/11.

proud of and value 'our state': it is the very embodiment of civilised political life.[6]

Patriotism was also very much to the fore in the arguments, widely rehearsed in the mediated public, for the Military Order. Emphasis on protecting the 'flesh and blood' nation *avoided* rather than confronted the clash between the reality of arbitrary detention in Guantanamo and the ideal America, though it seems that it did not always do so with good conscience. This quote, for example, from Deputy White House Counsel Timothy Flanigan, reported in the *Wall Street Journal*, is more than a little defensive: 'The order's signed and nobody's ashamed of it' ('Bush Signs Executive Order Establishing Military Tribunals to Try Terror Suspects', *Wall Street Journal*, 14 November 2001). Discussion of the clash between the reality of Guantanamo and the ideal America as 'a nation of laws' was avoided by detailing the practical reasons why it was impossible to try terrorists in normal courts – the need for secrecy, and also the large numbers of prisoners who would need to be tried – but also by the judgement that, as those who would attack and destroy America, they are undeserving of the protection of its laws. As Vice President Cheney put it, 'They don't deserve the same guarantees and safeguards that would be used for an American citizen going through the normal judicial process' ('Bush Plans for Terrorism Trials Defended', *Washington Post*, 15 November 2001). This perspective is summed up in the words of the widely circulated phrase of venerable and uncertain origin, 'the Constitution is not a suicide pact' (see Barbara Ehrenreich's 'Our George and Theirs', *New York Times*, 20 December 2004).

America: 'a nation of laws'
Nevertheless, from the very beginning of the declaration of an emergency that suspended due process rights for suspected terrorists,

---

[6] It is because the global war on terror is so open-ended, without a clear enemy or goal, that critics fear that it – and therefore also the state of exception – is potentially unending, in time and space (Butler 2004; Agamben 2005).

the ideal of America as governed by the rule of law was the basis of challenges from across the political spectrum to the sovereign decision to suspend law. The defence of political ideals through the protection of bare life outlined in the Executive justification of the sovereign decision did not mean that political life of the nation simply vanished into bare life. Criticisms of the Military Order from legal experts and members of Congress were widely cited in the mediated public – although reporting was invariably balanced by arguments that such measures were required by the emergency situation. Interestingly, most of these challenges were not made on a strictly legal basis; the Military Order had clear precedents in US law, most recently dating from the Second World War, and it was widely argued in the mediated public that it was almost certainly technically lawful.[7] The objections to the Order were rather *moral*; finding their basis in intuitions of natural justice that imprisonment and execution without trial *must be* unconstitutional. They were also *political*, arguing that in making the Order the Executive was disregarding the separation of powers that is fundamental to American democracy, thereby acting unconstitutionally. Finally, they were geo-political; arguments concerned the security of American solidiers abroad if the Geneva Conventions were ignored.

It was the persistence of the activist organisation the Center for Constitutional Rights (CCR) that eventually led to a legal challenge to arbitrary detention at Guantanamo. In February 2002, CCR filed petitions for *habeus corpus* in *Rasul* v. *Bush* (Ratner and Ray 2004). After being defeated in the lower courts, *Rasul* v. *Bush* eventually reached the Supreme Court in 2004. The common law of *habeus corpus* (literally 'You have the body') is ancient, somewhat obscure, but absolutely fundamental; it stipulates that a prisoner must be

---

[7] Most prominently, in 1942 the Supreme Court affirmed the death sentences of six German saboteurs designated 'unlawful combatants' and captured on US soil during the Second World War which had been imposed by a secret military tribunal (Ex parte Quirin, *317 U.S. 1 (1942)*). This was widely reported in newspaper coverage of the Military Order.

brought to the court when ordered, and their detention must be legally justified, or they must be released. The Supreme Court decided against the Bush Administration that Guantanamo Bay was effectively under the jurisdiction of the US and that the prisoners did have *habeus corpus* rights in US courts. This decision was initially celebrated by lawyers as confirming that the US Constitution protects the fundamental rights of non-citizens, as well as of citizens (CCR, 'Supreme Court Rules Detention of Guantanamo Detainees can be Reviewed', 28 June 2004, http://ccr-ny.org; press release, last accessed 29 December 2007).

The Administration, however, was able to interpret the Supreme Court ruling as granting the prisoners *formal* but not *substantive* rights to bring *habeus corpus* petitions to US courts (Amnesty International 2005a: 45). As the Supreme Court had offered no advice to lower courts on how to treat those petitions, federal judges could simply throw them out. In fact, in January 2005, two judges in the same federal court passed completely contradictory judgements concerning *habeus corpus* petitions from Guantanamo prisoners. The Bush Administration appealed for a final decision to have the contradiction settled in its favour, and the Court of Appeals for the District of Columbia obliged in 2007 (following the Military Commissions Act), ruling that the detainees had no rights to *habeus corpus* relief in federal courts (*Boumediene* et al. v. *Bush* 2007).

In the other important Guantanamo case to reach the Supreme Court, *Hamdan* v. *Rumsfeld* in 2006, the Court found that, contrary to the arguments of the Bush Administration, it did have jurisdiction over military tribunals. It did so despite the wording of the very particular Graham-Levin amendment to the Detainee Treatment Act 2005, which had been passed in response to the judgement in *Rasul* v. *Bush*, to the effect that '[N]o court, justice, or judge shall have jurisdiction to hear or consider an application for a writ of *habeas corpus* filed by or on behalf of an alien detained by the Department of Defense at Guantanamo Bay, Cuba' (Section 1005, Detainee Act 2005). The Geneva Conventions did play a part in this decision: the

Court found that the military tribunals satisfied neither US nor international military standards of due process.

However, the decision in *Hamdan* v. *Rumsfeld* was also weak and ambiguous insofar as the Supreme Court did not rule that the detainees must be granted prisoner of war status, or that they should be brought within the US legal system. It required only that Congress should determine the form the trials for enemy combatants should take. Congress passed the Military Commissions Act in 2006 which explicitly stated that detainees deemed to be 'unlawful enemy combatants' should *not* be permitted to challenge their detention in US courts. In April 2007 the Supreme Court put off considering an appeal against the decision in *Boumediene* et al. v. *Bush* that the Military Commissions Act is unconstitutional, but it reversed itself and in June 2007 it announced that it would hear the appeal in the 2007–2008 Term. At the time of writing it has not been heard.

Guantanamo detainees now appear to have two routes to judicial review of their detention. The majority of the detainees must appeal to a military-only Combatant Status Review Tribunal. Set up following *Rasul* v. *Bush*, these tribunals have been widely criticised as governed by unacceptable standards of due process and as heavily biased towards determining that a suspect is an 'unlawful combatant' (Amnesty International 2005a: 47–51). If detainees do not appeal, or are unable to appeal, their cases will be heard by an Administrative Review Board each year to determine whether they should be released, transferred to the custody of another country, or continue to be detained (pp. 64–6). The minority of Guantanamo detainees, those who have been or will be charged with war crimes under the Military Commissions Act, must go through Military Commission Trials. These have been highly criticised on the basis that they allow evidence (including evidence gained by torture), procedures and broad and vague definitions that would not be permitted in any normal court of law, military or civilian (Amnesty International 2006a; Human Rights First 2007).

International human rights norms in America

What difference would international human rights have made to the prisoners in Guantanamo had they been applied? Prohibitions against arbitrary detention are fundamental to international human rights law. The President's declaration of a 'global war against terrorism' which justified the sovereign suspension of fundamental rights has created a context in which the laws of war have appeared more appropriate than international human rights law.[8] As we have seen, the disputed status of the prisoners under the Geneva Conventions has provided some basis for challenging arbitrary detentions in the US. However, it is hard to believe that court rulings in these cases would not have been much more straightforward and conclusive had they been judging the lawfulness of Executive measures according to the International Convention on Civil and Political Rights. Article 2 of the ICCPR states: 'Each State Party to the present Covenant undertakes to respect and to ensure to all individuals within its territory and subject to its jurisdiction the rights recognized in the present Covenant, without distinction of any kind'. Article 9 states: 'Anyone who is deprived of his liberty by arrest or detention shall be entitled to take proceedings before a court, in order that that court may decide without delay on the lawfulness of his detention and order his release if the detention is not lawful.' Moreover, the Human Rights Committee has stated that rights to minimal due process rights, such as *habeus corpus* and presumption of innocence, can *never* lawfully be suspended, even in states of emergency (Amnesty International 2002a; Human Rights Watch 2006; UN Human Rights Commission Report, 15 February 2006). As human rights pertain to

---

[8] This is despite the fact that terrorism is not a violation of military law or the laws of war (Ratner and Ray 2004: 71), and the armed conflict in Afghanistan ended with the establishing of a Transitional Authority in 2002 (Amnesty International 2005a). Moreover, according to Bruce Ackerman, the 'war on terrorism' is of doubtful legal meaning (Ackerman 2004: 1032–4). It does, however, have a cultural political meaning. The 'war paradigm' and the powers granted to the President following 9/11, when the country did appear to be literally preparing for war though war was never officially declared, have become very well entrenched in US political life.

human persons, in principle there is no detention anywhere, for anyone, to which international human rights do not apply (see Butler 2004: 98–9).

However, international human rights law was of no practical use to lawyers for the prisoners in Guantanamo Bay. The US ratifies human rights treaties, including the ICCPR, with the proviso that they are not *self-executing*; that is to say, they do not create rights directly enforceable in US courts (Buergenthal *et al.* 2002: 371). Officials justify this with the somewhat contradictory arguments that it would be undemocratic simply to import international law directly into US law, and, at the same time, that is unnecessary as US law already includes all the rights it covers except those against which there are reservations. As a result, it was deemed unnecessary for the ICCPR to be endorsed by the Legislature and there are no mechanisms for its enforcement in the domestic legal system of the US (Roth 2000). The ICCPR is of no use in providing *legal* checks on sovereign power in the United States; it can only be used to put *political* pressure on the Executive and Legislature to adjust policies to conform to international human rights. On the occasions when the Administration has felt it necessary to address its obligations under international human rights law, it has argued that they are irrelevant to Guantanamo because it concerns wartime detentions (Amnesty International 2005a: 32 and 37–8). However, not only is the legality of the 'war on terror' dubious in the extreme, but the ICCPR does not cease in times of war; it runs alongside international humanitarian law (p. 43).

Of course, human rights organisations, especially Amnesty International and Human Rights Watch did try to bring pressure to bear on the US government using arguments in international human rights law against arbitrary detentions and torture in Guantanamo Bay. They presented these arguments in 'friend of the court' briefs to the Supreme Court, in letters and memoranda to the US Executive and Legislature, directly to the public in press releases and reports, and in reports to international organisations, including the

Inter-American Commission for Human Rights, the EU and the UN Committee for Human Rights. National advocacy organisations also used arguments from international human rights law. In fact, the ACLU actually *increased* the resources it dedicates to international human rights during this time, employing more staff to work on human rights and preparing a shadow document for the UN Human Rights Committee on US violations of the ICCPR (ACLU 2004; ACLU 2006a). All the NGOs involved appealed to America's role as a *leader* of international human rights, as an example that other, presumably less principled regimes, would be tempted to, and actually had followed 'under cover' of the 'war on terrorism'; and to prudential arguments concerning the risks American soldiers would be likely to face if the US persisted with its policies at Guantanamo.

However, with the exception of Amnesty International and also, though to a lesser degree, Human Rights Watch, organisations campaigning for the civil rights of the prisoners in Guantanamo Bay, including the Center for Constitutional Rights, Human Rights First and the American Civil Liberties Union, relied much more on arguing from the 'core values' of American democracy and law, on the separation of powers and on fundamental rights to due process. For the most part arguments from international human rights and humanitarian law were secondary (see for example, CCR 2002; Human Rights First 2002, 2003a, 2003b; ACLU 2002, 2004, 2006b). On the rare occasions on which they engaged debate on Guantanamo, this is also true of Muslim Associations CAIR and MPAC which invariably represented their members and supporters, understandably, as good and loyal Americans. Amnesty International positioned itself much more as an outsider, as an international witness and advocate for the prisoners. Following a press conference accompanying the launch of its annual report in 2005 at which Irene Khan, Amnesty's General Secretary compared Guantanamo to the Soviet gulags as global symbols of human rights abuses, Amnesty was criticised by

President Bush and others as anti-American, and became an object of hate for the Right (see, for example, 'Amnesty's Amnesia', *Washington Post*, 9 June 2005). Even Amnesty did, however, on occasion appeal to national pride. Khan, for example, declared in response to the outcry over her comments that the US should: 'Reassert the basic principles of justice, truth and freedom in which Americans take so much pride. Make the USA a true force for good in a divided, dangerous world' (Irene Khan, 'Close Guantanamo and Disclose the Rest', 22 June 2005, press release, http://web.amnesty.org/library/ Index/ENGAMR511012005?open&of=ENG-USA, last accessed 29 December 2007; see also Amnesty International 2005a, 2005b, 2005c, 2005d, 2006a; and Human Rights Watch 2004b, 2004c).

What is it to be American?

There is no doubt that the cultural politics of the mediated public in the Guantanamo case turned far more on national identity, on 'what it is to be American' than on human rights. In populist and Right-of-centre arenas of the mediated public, the choice presented by the sovereign decision between 'our' security and 'their' (lack of) rights continued to be justified (see, for example, 'Terror and the Court', *Wall Street Journal*, 29 June 2004; 'Supreme Foolishness', *New York Post*, 29 June 2004; 'Supreme Court goes Overboard', *New York Daily News*, 30 June 2006). It was justified with reference to the ever-present danger faced by Americans, despite the lack of further attacks on US soil. In a speech on passing the Military Commissions Act, President Bush declared that 'It's important for Americans and others across the world to understand the kind of people held at Guantanamo . . . we have in place a rigorous process to ensure those held at Guantanamo Bay belong at Guantanamo . . . They are held in our custody so they cannot murder our people' (White House press release, 'President Discusses Creation of Military Commissions to Try Suspected Terrorists', 6 September 2006, www.whitehouse.gov/ news/releases/2006/09/20060906-3.html, last accessed 29 December

2007). We can call this the 'pride in our strength' position: America is great because it protects American lives and therefore, secondarily, American political life which depends upon it.

At the other end of the political spectrum, the liberal 'pride in our values' position is justified by the direct aim of preserving American political life. Increasingly, especially following the Military Commissions Act, criticising Guantanamo as unconstitutional led to accusations that the President was anti-American. The Center for Constitutional Rights, for example, was involved in a serious campaign to impeach President Bush, arguing that there are no other legal avenues to pursue against an Executive that will not accept the proper checks and balances of the democratic American system. The President is dismantling the American Constitution and must be stopped (CCR 2006a). Clearly, the strategy here is to encourage US elites to uphold values and principles of American political life by publicly disassociating themselves from the 'few bad apples': President Bush and his closest advisors.

Somewhere in between these two political positions is a straightforward belief and pride in America, virtually no matter what the government does. It is well summed up in the view of a columnist for the *New York Daily News*, who situated himself 'squarely in the middle' between conservatives and liberals following the *Rasul* v. *Bush* decision in the Supreme Court: 'We're Americans and we believe in laws, even for mad-dog killers' ('Top Court Right to Make US Play by its Own Rules', *New York Daily News*, 30 June 2006). This position – let's call it 'pride in our country because we are right' – is, of course, very far from guaranteeing that the highest principles of judicial procedure will be safeguarded. On the contrary, it may rather foster the complacency that assumes that 'we' don't violate human rights. However, in a relatively open and pluralist public this position does enable contestation of what *is* right, what 'America' means in terms of the core values of political life. 'Pride in our country because it is right' was, for example, explicit in the comments of Republican Senator for Arizona John McCain in relation to his Amendment to the Detainee Act which defined and listed permitted interrogation techniques, to give US troops clear guidelines and to show the world that the US does not practise torture. McCain justified his intervention in terms of national pride, arguing that 'it's not about who they are, it's about who we are' and 'we are better and different from our enemies' (quoted in 'Looking at Abu Ghraib's "Painful" Question', *New York Daily News*, 18 October 2005; and in 'Senate Supports Interrogation Limits', *Washington Post*, 6 October 2005).

Even when it has worked to challenge the cruelties and injustices of arbitrary detention and torture, however, there is generally a very clear limit to invocations of national pride as a way of securing rights for non-citizens. National pride, as we might expect, tended to reproduce a strong sense of the division between 'we Americans' and 'the rest of the world' in the mediated public. Challenges to the sovereign as a result of national pride did not lead to any sustained discussion of the logic of human rights: that there should be an end to discrimination between citizens and non-citizens in respect of fundamental rights; that all human beings should be treated equally before the law. A striking example of the limits of nationalism as a means of mobilising support for the rights of non-citizens comes from an editorial in the *New York Times* putting the case against the Bush Administration's position on Guantanamo as legally and morally wrong in the run up to the Supreme Court hearing *Rasul* v. *Bush* ('The Court and Guantanamo', *New York Times*, 19 April 2004). The *New York Times* is seen as ultra-liberal, even anti-American on the Right, and this article is one of the very rare occasions on which the ICCPR was cited in the mediated public as relevant to Guantanamo Bay. What is striking, however, is how the *New York Times* nevertheless strongly separates what is due to Americans and what is due to non-citizens, arguing that the prisoners are not claiming rights to have American courts review their cases but are, rather, 'seeking only the most basic elements of due process' and would be satisfied with a military tribunal. Not only is this inaccurate, given the form of military tribunals set up to try prisoners in Guantanamo, it is also surprising: why should it be necessary to insist that the rights of Americans and non-Americans are *not* identical, given that the whole purpose of the ICCPR is to insist that all individuals, regardless of nationality, are entitled to the same respect for fundamental freedoms?[9]

As we have seen, the legal judgements of the Supreme Court have made very little substantive difference to the detainees in terms of gaining them rights to a fair trial, and nor has political opposition to arbitrary detention in Guantanamo Bay had any real effect so far. On the contrary, at the time of writing those detainees who have not been released without charge or disappeared remain mired in legal pedantry as the Executive treats Supreme Court rulings as no more than tactical uses of the law which they must evade or combat. Many of the prisoners have taken their fate into their own hands, taking part in hunger strikes and riots and refusing to engage at all with the processes that have been put in place to judge them. There have been numerous suicide attempts; three of them successful so far. Where US law has made so little difference to the practical situation of the prisoners, it is perhaps unsurprising that international human rights have made even less difference. International human rights have virtually no legal purchase in the US courts, and nor have they proved effective in rousing public outrage or creating the political will to put pressure on the Bush Administration to act within international norms in granting prisoners a fair trial. Even where human rights *are* invoked in the mediated public sphere in the US they tend to be understood as 'special rights' for non-citizens, a set of second-class rights of last resort rather than the framework of universal principles of global justice within which the business of state should

---

[9] In fact, as Howard Friel and Richard Falk clearly demonstrate in their study of how the paper has reported issues of international law in relation to wars in which the US has been engaged – from Vietnam to Iraq – misunderstanding international law is the rule rather than the exception in the pages of the *New York Times* (Friel and Falk 2004).

be conducted. Guantanamo Bay is undoubtedly an international human rights scandal, and, for sections of the mediated public, an embarrassment and a blow to American national pride. It has not, however, led to serious, sustained discussion in the mediated public of what human rights mean, or to an understanding of the United States of America as bound by global standards of human rights.

HUMAN RIGHTS AT HOME IN THE UK[10]

In the UK, arbitrary detentions of suspected terrorists at Belmarsh and Woodhill prisons were comparable to those in Guantanamo in that the sovereign decision to suspend fundamental rights similarly created a space that was designed to fall outside national and international law. This was absolutely explicit in the UK Executive's declaration of 'a public emergency facing the nation' in November 2001 in order to be able to derogate from Article 5 of the European Convention on Human Rights. Article 5 forbids arbitrary detention, requiring that proper procedures of law should be followed if a person is detained, including telling them the reasons for their detention, charging them and bringing them 'speedily' before a judge. The declaration of a public emergency accompanied the 2001 Anti-Terrorism, Crime and Security Act (ATCSA) in order to detain around twelve men suspected of terrorism. Several more were subsequently added to the list, bringing the total to seventeen.

International human rights in the UK

As we noted in Chapter 2, in Europe human rights are far more thoroughly institutionalised than in any other system, including the UN: many of the member states of the Council of Europe have incorporated the ECHR into domestic law, and the European Court of Human Rights is effectively 'the constitutional court for civil and

---

[10] The phrase is that of the UK government, introducing the Human Rights Act 1998 (United Kingdom Government, 1997, *Rights Brought Home: the Human Rights Bill*, Cm 3782, London: TSO).

political rights' in Europe, hearing complaints from individuals as well as from member states (Buergenthal *et al.* 2002: 172).

This institutionalisation of global human rights certainly made one very clear difference between the conditions, and therefore the consequences, of the sovereign decision to declare a state of emergency in the US and the UK: the UK Executive was bound by an international human rights convention, the ECHR, even as it opted out of certain key Articles of the Convention. Firstly, when the UK incorporated the ECHR into domestic law as the Human Rights Act, the Law Lords (the UK Supreme Court) became legally bound to judge whether the Executive decision to declare a state of exception was justified. Secondly, derogation from the ECHR must be lawful according to the ECHR itself: the measures that are put in place to deal with the dangers presented must be *proportionate* to the situation; and they must be *compatible* with other human rights obligations under international law (Article 15, ECHR). The Law Lords were also, therefore, legally bound to judge whether the exceptional measures the UK government put in place were proportionate and consistent with the UK's other human rights obligations.

In December 2004 the Law Lords heard the 'Belmarsh detainees' case' on appeal against the decision of a lower court that their detention was lawful, despite the fact that none had been charged or had any prospect of being tried (*A and others* v. *Home Secretary* 2004). The Lords addressed whether the declaration of a state of emergency was justified, as they were legally bound to do. However, although all but one of the panel of judges were sceptical that there was a public emergency threatening the nation that would make such exceptional measures as arbitrary detention necessary, ultimately they declined to rule on the Executive's decision. Their principle justification for this reluctance was the 'traditional deference' of the courts to an Executive decision to declare a public emergency, given that such a decision is 'a pre-eminently political judgement' (Lord Bingham in *A and others* v. *Home Secretary* 2004, p. 17). For the most part the Lords in this case agreed that, as the

European Court has in the past accorded a large margin of appreciation to member states of the Council of Europe in their assessment of whether they face a public emergency, it was incumbent upon the UK court to respect the proper political functions of the Executive in making such a decision.

Although they refused to judge the declaration of public emergency as such in *A and others* v. *Home Secretary*, the Lords nevertheless ruled that the detentions were unlawful. In other words, they refused to rule on the state of emergency, but they did rule on the state of exception. They found that ATCSA was disproportionate – arbitrary detention was a poor solution to the threat posed by the suspected terrorists; and discriminatory because it targeted only non-citizens. In this sense, the logic of human rights was effective: all the judges agreed that it was not legal for the Executive to treat non-citizens differently from citizens, even when 'normal' law was suspended. In order to arrive at their decision, the judges referred to the case law of the European Court of Human Rights and to other international human rights law. They saw an important part of their task in reviewing a sovereign decision made by the UK Executive as anticipating what the European Court would have decided had it heard the case.

Sovereignty is not directly at stake in the Law Lords' ruling on whether the arbitrary detention of suspected terrorists in the UK is lawful. Unlike other Supreme Courts, the Law Lords have no authority to strike down law made by parliament. Nor, like other Supreme Courts, can they interfere directly with the prerogative powers of the Executive. Sovereignty is indirectly at stake, however, insofar as the UK Executive is required as a result of this ruling to review measures taken as a result of suspending the rule of law. Although the Law Lords can not strike down law that has been passed by the UK parliament, it is generally agreed that no Executive or Legislature would happily ignore a judgement from the highest national court that it was making law that is unlawful. Indeed, on introducing legislation to parliament, ministers are bound to declare that, in their opinion, it conforms to the ECHR.

In response to the Law Lords' ruling, the UK government did pass new legislation. The Prevention of Terrorism Act (PTA) 2005 granted the Executive the power to keep suspected terrorists under 'control orders' based on 'reasonable suspicion' founded on secret evidence. (At the time, the UK did not rule out the use of evidence extracted by torture, though it has now been officially banned following a ruling from the Law Lords (*A and others* v. *Home Secretary* 2005).) Whilst some of the control orders – amounting to house arrest – require derogation from the ECHR, so far the government has relied on those which appear not to require derogation, including curfews, electronic tagging, restrictions on communication and so on. The government declared its belief that the PTA is within the letter of the ECHR. However, far from the sovereignty of the Executive being checked, the opportunity presented by the new legislation has been taken to encroach still further on individual rights in the name of security. The PTA *extends* the powers of the Executive, whilst observing the letter of human rights law that there should be no discrimination between citizens and non-citizens: the control orders it has designed may equally be imposed on *citizens* as well as on non-citizens.[11]

The UK Executive has shown itself as determined as the US Executive in maintaining a policy of arbitrary detention that suspends key dimensions of the normal juridical order. Nevertheless, in so far as the Lords' decision did alter the terms of the sovereign suspension of normal law in the UK, it was as a result of international human rights norms. Technical, legal uses of human rights are cosmopolitan in so far as they abolish the distinction between

---

[11] The government has appealed various High Court rulings that control orders are not compatible with human rights, depriving individuals of liberty and of rights to due process that require derogation from the ECHR (Joint Committee on Human Rights Eighth Report 2007). On 31 October 2007, the Law Lords basically endorsed the control order regime, though they set limits to the curfews that could be imposed and ruled that suspects should have access to 'key evidence' against them (*JJ* v. *Home Secretary* and *Home Secretary* v. *E and others*). There will undoubtedly be further legal challenges to those rulings.

citizens and non-citizens in respect of fundamental rights. It is notable that, in contrast to the US, human rights norms were publicly justified by governmental officials as well as by human rights organisations and lawyers. At the same time, however, both in the US and UK, opponents and supporters of human rights share a similar orientation towards political life as based in the nation. In the UK, in court and in the mediated public, technical uses of human rights became entangled with, and eventually compromised by, sentiments of national pride.

European human rights and British liberties

The most striking instance of the entanglement of sentiments of national pride and of the vocabulary of human rights was the changing relationship between uses of the terms 'human rights' and 'civil liberties'. 'Human rights' made sense of the law in technical terms, and it was used in the mediated public to explain legal obligations and constraints which the UK Executive should respect, but from the very beginning of the case, when the Executive decided to derogate from the ECHR and ATCSA was passed in parliament, it was not the term 'human rights' but rather 'civil liberties', sometimes qualified as 'British civil liberties' or 'centuries-old liberties', that mobilised passionate defence. Opposition to the Executive decision to suspend rights was very frequently made, across the political spectrum, in terms of the glorious history of British freedoms. Such sentiments were resoundingly invoked in arguments by political opposition to Executive measures by both parties, by the leader of Liberty (e.g. Chakrabarti 2003) and most notably, and at some length, by Lord Hoffman in the 'Belmarsh Detainees' Case'. In what one commentator (Poole 2005) has described as 'tabloid history', Lord Hoffman constructed the European Convention as a modern-day protection of ancient British liberties, arguing that:

> Freedom from arbitrary arrest is a quintessentially British liberty, enjoyed by the inhabitants of this country when most of the

population of Europe could be thrown into prison at the whim of their rulers. It was incorporated into the European Convention in order to entrench the same liberty in countries which had recently been under Nazi occupation. The United Kingdom subscribed to the Convention because it set out the rights which British subjects enjoyed under the common law.

(A and others v. Home Secretary 2004: 50)

We see here a strategy on the part of human rights supporters to join human rights and British traditions together in an appeal to national pride. This strategy can be understood as an attempt to translate human rights into the vernacular of British political life. Sally Engle Merry has shown how cultural politics are necessary to bring human rights from the transnational sphere of global elites into local, everyday life. Merry describes processes by which 'human rights' can become political and legal tools in societies in which they have previously had no resonance. In order for human rights to make sense to ordinary people in a society, they must be translated into terms that make sense to them, that enable them to judge their situation in human rights terms, to see it as unjust and to take action against that injustice. Merry calls this process of translation and framing, 'making human rights vernacular'. One of the main roles of human rights activists is to mediate between legal understanding of human rights encoded in conventions, treaties and declarations and the language ordinary people use to understanding their own situation (Merry 2006).

In this case, the cultural political strategy to make human rights vernacular through an appeal to national pride was not successful. By the time of the Law Lords' judgement on ATCSA and debates over the PTA, rather than meaning the same thing, 'human rights' and 'civil liberties' had been quite clearly separated and opposed in many sections of the mediated public. Outside liberal and legal circles, in fact, European human rights were increasingly understood as *threatening* the ancient civil liberties of British citizens. They were understood to threaten both the bare life of British people and British political life by refusing to allow discrimination between terrorist suspects and British citizens. On the one hand human rights were seen as responsible for letting terrorist suspects loose in the country because the government was not allowed to deport them; on the other, human rights were seen as responsible for overturning centuries of entrenched liberties for British citizens.

Predictably opposition to human rights came from conservative sectors of the mediated public. However, it also came from the Prime Minister. In a speech following the terrorist attacks of 7/7 in which Tony Blair told the country that 'the rules of the game have changed', he also declared that human rights were creating obstacles to safeguarding national security and that it might be necessary to amend the Human Rights Act (Prime Minister's press conference, 5 August 2005, www.number10.gov.uk/output/Page8041.asp, last accessed 12 June 2007). In particular he proposed that foreigners suspected of terrorism should simply be deported. It is in contravention of European human rights law to send a person to a state where they are at risk of torture (*Chahal* v. *UK* 1996). Blair's suggestion that human rights law must be altered so that Executive measures to deal with terrorist threats will not be judged to be in violation of human rights has been widely taken up. Reforming or 'scrapping' the Human Rights Act, which incorporates the ECHR into British law and which was passed by the Labour government in 1998, became part of the Conservative Party's election manifesto in 2005. The *Sun*, the newspaper with the widest circulation of any paper in the UK, went so far as to run a campaign soliciting readers' votes to demand that the HRA should be repealed ('Time to Stop the Madness', *Sun*, 12 May 2006).

Although parliament can, in principle, repeal or alter the HRA, the UK must still comply with the ECHR, from which the HRA is derived. It would therefore be extraordinarily difficult even to alter the HRA, precisely because of the way the UK state is networked into the accountability structures of Europe. To avoid European censure for not complying with the ECHR, the UK would have to leave the forty-seven states of the Council of Europe and also the European Union (because signing the ECHR is a condition of joining). The UK would effectively become a pariah state in Europe (Bognador 2006). This seems a very unlikely course of action for any government. What the newly revived, and oft-repeated, opposition between 'our' security and 'their' rights does mean, however, is that although intermestic human rights are embedded in law in the UK, they are far from becoming part of the vernacular of political life. Human rights are themselves now in need of defence, as well as those unpopular non-citizens accused of terrorist activities whom human rights are supposed to protect.

Human rights have become highly politicised in the UK as a result of the Executive decision to suspend fundamental rights to liberty in the name of national security, and this makes their use as legal, technical instruments increasingly contentious. The government's problematisation of human rights, strongly supported in the mediated public by significant sections of the press, works to reinforce the sovereign decision of the Executive by devaluing the authority of the courts that judge intermestic human rights cases. It is a strategy of cultural politics which has been more successful than that of human rights supporters to link traditional civil liberties with human rights through national pride. By devaluing the authority of legal justifications that challenge the sovereign decision to suspend normal law, the Executive gains political support for policies which undermine human rights, and at the same time wins political popularity.

LEARNING FROM GUANTANAMO AND BELMARSH

Sovereignty is socially constructed: it is historically specific and justified differently according to the challenges which make political elites decide that exercising sovereignty is both desirable and possible. Sovereignty is always, however, by definition, effective: it is the authority to have the 'last word' where there is no higher authority. Threats to national security which justify sovereign decisions are surely the most difficult test of universal human rights applied to non-citizens: it is when 'we' feel threatened that 'their' fundamental rights are most likely to be violated. In the case of the sovereign decision to suspend fundamental rights in the US and UK because of the threat to national security of the 'war on terror', the viability of human rights to challenge that decision has been tested to the limit. In the cases we have examined in this chapter, far from state sovereignty being eroded or transformed so that it is only legitimate where it is couched in terms of the protection of fundamental human rights for all individuals equally, sovereignty is being exercised in ways that conform very closely to the ideal of the national state, discriminating between citizens and non-citizens in the name of the security of the nation.

In relation to the cultural politics of the human rights field, the research carried out for this chapter confirms that legal differences between the US and UK do make a difference. In both the US and UK there has been an Executive determined to use powers created by the declaration of a public emergency and willing to ignore the spirit of judicial rulings in order to do so. Moreover, in both cases the highest national courts have deferred to the Executive. Ackerman sees this as the historical norm when a public emergency has been declared (Ackerman 2004). However, American exceptionalism with respect to the significance of international human rights norms has been confirmed. Although advocacy organisations like the ACLU are now more than ever equipped to address domestic issues in terms of international human rights law (see also Mertus 2005: 328–9), human rights have only a very weak standing in US domestic courts. The only exception to this rule is cases brought under ATCA, which we will look at in the next chapter.

In contrast, in the UK, although the Law Lords were deferential to the Executive, and the Executive resisted the spirit of the juridical rulings, the deference was not so marked, and neither was the defiance. Whilst the terrorist suspects now under control orders in the UK have not been charged or tried – and this is certainly a violation of fundamental human rights – they are nevertheless living under a far less restrictive regime than that of imprisonment (which has, in Guantanamo Bay, been accompanied by torture, as arbitrary detention and secret trials very often are). The UK Executive was arguably more responsive to the rulings of the Law Lords, which was certainly bolder than the Supreme Court in its judgement that the sovereign's suspension of fundamental rights was unwarranted, because its authority is in part derived from the way it represents the European Court of Human Rights in the national context. In the UK the European Court of Human Rights functions as a constitutional court beyond the national. It is very unlikely, in a situation in which no other European state derogated from the ECHR because of threats from Al-Qaeda, that the European Court of Human Rights would support the UK Executive's decision to suspend fundamental human rights over the decision of the UK's highest court that such measures were warranted. Although this does not mean that the UK Executive has *less* sovereignty – the authority to have the 'last word' is not divisible in this way and, as we have already noted, neither the Law Lords nor the European Court of Human Rights have the power to strike down legislation made by the UK government – it does transform the conditions in which sovereignty is exercised. Authority is dispersed and decentred in the human rights field in the UK because of the way it is dispersed and decentred in the European system of human rights. There are more legitimate sites at which a sovereign decision to suspend fundamental human rights will be challenged, a further layer of courts beyond the national. As cosmopolitan political theorists argue, sovereignty is transformed in Europe as the Council of Europe and the European Union together create an overlapping 'set of interlocking institutions each responsible and accountable to each other' (Held 2003: 168; Benhabib 2007: 31).

It is only in the juridical sub-field, however, that differences between the US and UK were significant. In the governmental sub-field, the Legislature was similarly deferential to the Executive in both the US and UK. Although, in both cases, there was political opposition to the sovereign decision to suspend fundamental individual rights, in the end the Legislatures were fearful of appearing weak on terrorism and passed laws which have effectively legalised, consolidated and even extended the extraordinary powers taken by the Executive. Again, according to Ackerman, in terms of historical precedent, this is unsurprising (Ackerman 2004: 1047). As we noted above, in the UK the PTA allows control orders to be imposed on citizens as well as non-citizens. In the US, the Military Commissions Act has been widely criticised for stripping courts of fundamental powers, including suspending *habeus corpus*, and also for extending Executive powers to detain US citizens as well as non-citizens if they are designated 'unlawful enemy combatants' (CCR 2006b; HRF 2007).

In the mediated public, what was most interesting in both the US and UK was how sentiments of national pride were invoked. In both cases it proved possible to mobilise feelings of pride for the political life of the nation to defend the protection of rights for non-citizens as *individuals*, even when national security was felt to be threatened. The political life of the nation was accorded value and importance, even if the bare life of the nation was paramount. What proved very much more difficult, however, was harnessing feelings of national pride to realise global human rights that should be secured by a cosmopolitan state. It was practically impossible to represent the fundamental rights of non-citizens on an equal basis with the rights of citizens in conditions of heightened fears for security in the mediated publics of the US and UK.

Although human rights law abolishes the distinction between citizens and non-citizens in certain fundamental respects, what these case studies suggest is that nationalism continues to structure the cultural conditions within which sovereign decisions are made. In terms of Fraser's conception of frames of global justice, the meta-question of whose interests and rights are at stake is contested in these case studies, but only within limits that are firmly established by pride in the nation and national belonging. As we have seen in this chapter, invocations of national pride have come from judges committed to international human rights norms as well as journalists, from human rights activists as well as politicians. Nationalism is the norm for both defenders and opponents of human rights. Even within a member state of the European system of human rights, supporters of human rights judge that human rights will be better served if they are directly linked to nationalist rather than to cosmopolitan justifications. In actual fact, such strategies prove very problematic. In the UK, the successful use of human rights in the juridical sub-field has contributed to the abolition of the legal distinction between citizens and non-citizens following the letter rather than the spirit of international human rights law: the UK's control orders on terrorist suspects now apply equally to citizens and non-citizens alike. However, as we have seen, nationalist justifications of human rights as age-old British liberties have become entangled with demands for abolishing what are seen as the restrictions of European human rights on the popular will of the national political community, which would put public safety above the individual rights of terrorist suspects.

Although issues of national security surely raise the most difficult dilemmas where the guarantee of fundamental rights is concerned, human rights are supposed, in principle, to protect vulnerable people precisely when they are faced with state persecution, which is most likely when concerns for national security are heightened. As we have seen in the case studies analysed here, it is precisely when fundamental civil rights are most needed that they are most highly politicised. Moreover, the entanglement of human rights and nationalism is far from unique to cases in which the sovereign decision constructs a choice between national security and the fundamental human rights of terrorist suspects. As we shall see in Chapter 4, justifications for cosmopolitan norms, nationalism and human rights are entangled in complex ways in intermestic human rights cases even when such cases are celebrated by human rights activists as imagining a community of global citizens beyond nationality and beyond national borders.

4 Imagining a community without 'enemies of all mankind'

For cosmopolitans, we are human beings over and above anything else: nationalism is limited intellectually, morally and politically, and must be transcended, if not completely abolished. A diversity of identifications is possible for every individual – including those previously 'captured' by national identification, ethnicity, gender, sexuality and so on – so that a celebration of hybridity and inter-mingling is not only morally better than focus on national identity, it is also more satisfying and more enjoyable (see Phillips 2007: 68). In terms of claims for justice, cosmopolitanism begins from the idea that the national frame of politics is too parochial in a globalising world in which economic, social and cultural processes, and people and problems, cross territorial borders so readily (Held 1995; Beck 2006).

Cosmopolitanism is an attractive theory for our times. How-ever, in comparison with nationalism it can convincingly be argued that it is rather elitist, an ideal for 'frequent flyers' who are able to transcend the social and cultural ties of locality and nation (Calhoun 2003). It is for this reason that Craig Calhoun has set out to explore the continuing importance of nationalism. In *Nations Matter*, Calhoun's stated aim is to escape from the opposition of nationalism and cosmopolitanism, which he sees as damaging to those gains that have been made for ordinary people in the name of the nation, but also to the cosmopolitan ideal of the equal value of all human beings (Calhoun 2007: 24–5).

Calhoun argues that cosmopolitanism and nationalism share common roots in the liberal individualism that developed with the modern state.[1] Calhoun sees nations as collectivities of individuals (as we can see from the way statistics are gathered), who do not – at least in principle – require the mediation of family, community, region or class in order to be members of a society. This marks a significant break with feudal understandings of loyalty and honour in which there was no political identity outside immediate social relations. It is generally agreed that nationalism became a force in the world with the American and French Revolutions, which created modern states based on individual rights. However, Calhoun makes much of the fact that the political revolutions which officially inaugurated political modernity, breaking with imperialism in America and absolute monarchy in France, actually shared elements of both nationalism and cosmopolitanism. In America and France, states were established explicitly to guarantee 'the rights of man', especially to equal treatment before the law and to political representation.

Civic nationalism and cosmopolitanism differ, in Calhoun's view, only in terms of their respective evaluation of particularism and universalism. Nations are explicitly exclusive. This is clear in the great eighteenth-century declarations of the 'rights of man', which, having resoundingly called for the recognition that 'all men are created equal', born with inalienable natural rights, then go on to make it quite clear that by 'man' they mean the citizen of the national state.[2] Calhoun argues that cosmopolitanism begins from

---

[1] Calhoun prefers the formulation 'nation-state' over that of 'national state', presumably because he is precisely interested in the way in which nations are imagined in terms of a relatively coherent shared identity in relation to states. I prefer the latter, only because it seems to suggest better the view that states *make* nations, a view that Calhoun also shares.

[2] This is especially, and notoriously, evident in the formulation of the Declaration of the Rights of Man that followed the French revolution.

Article 1. Men are born and remain free and equal in rights. Social distinctions may be founded only upon the general good.
Article 2. The aim of all political association is the preservation of the natural and imprescriptible rights of man. These rights are liberty, property, security, and resistance to oppression.
Article 3. The principle of all sovereignty resides essentially in the nation.

the failure of civic nationalism in its own terms: if 'the right to rights' is that of all human beings by birth, why should citizens receive different treatment from non-citizens? Why should French or American citizens be privileged to live in societies that respect and uphold rights, while others are condemned to repression and destruction? However, if civic nationalism has a blind spot with regard to the putative universalism of the nation, Calhoun argues that cosmopolitanism has a similar blind spot with regard to particularism, being suspicious, and often dismissive, of relationships which appear to work against the formation of a world in which the rights of all human beings will be respected. This is especially true of the political community attached to the modern state, the nation.

The formation of the national political community, according to Calhoun, has been hugely significant in terms of the leverage it enables ordinary people to exercise over state elites concerning the conditions of common social life. Nationalism is a form of identification which has reinforced social bonds, produced deep experiences of belonging with strangers outside one's immediate circle, and mitigated the development of selfish individualism which is otherwise such a prominent feature of modernity. Of course, community here clearly does not involve anything like face-to-face relationships. Political communities are imagined communities (Anderson 1991). They involve a mediated sense of belonging amongst those who find themselves, through imaginative identification, to be in a particular

We move very rapidly here from abstract statements of the universal rights of man, to an assertion of the sovereignty of the nation, which is empowered to make such social distinctions as are deemed necessary for the good of all.

The move from universal to particular is perhaps less obvious in the wording of the American Declaration of Independence, which begins: 'We hold these truths to be self-evident, that all men are created equal, that they are endowed by their Creator with certain unalienable Rights, that among these are Life, Liberty and the pursuit of Happiness.' What is important here is the 'we', which – though it is not specified – is that of the American nation. The American Declaration presupposes rather than explicitly states that it is individuals who are members of the nation who are in possession of the universal rights of man.

community. A feeling of belonging to a national community of citizens is not 'natural', and nor does it relate only to the possession of citizenship rights. On the contrary, the national state has continually engaged in cultural projects to create and sustain a nation: through education, especially the teaching of a national language, in media communications, supporting arts, festivals celebrating national achievements, national museums and monuments and rituals and so on. As a result, as Calhoun argues, civic nationalism has become inextricably intertwined with ethnic nationalism – even if one or the other tends to dominate in different places at different times (Calhoun 2007: 117–46). Feelings of belonging to a nation, and citizens' sense of their entitlements and obligations in relation to national states, are not rationalist: they are always entangled with a sense of the nation as distinctive and special in respect of the geographical origin of its founders, its territorial base, its religion, language, food.

Imagined communities involve a shared understanding of the symbolic meanings around which they are organised, and they also involve practices that make the community a reality insofar as 'we' feel ourselves to be participating in it. The national community has been spectacularly successful. Far from involving a thin sense of belonging compared to some original notion of community as involving face-to-face relationships, the nation inspires an incredible degree of emotional attachment that has made extraordinary sacrifices quite customary. It is not so much, as Anderson points out, that citizens are prepared to kill for the nation that is astonishing; what is remarkable is how willing they have been to die for it (Anderson 1991: 7).

Although not necessarily impossible, it is difficult to see how a cosmopolitan project could replace such passions and commitments, even where what inspires attachment is predominantly civic nationalism which is halfway towards cosmopolitanism. In part this is because, in the absence of a world-state, cosmopolitanism lacks institutions which are uniquely dedicated to promoting cosmopolitan feeling in the world. The United Nations, which comes closest to a world-state, is actually – as its name suggests – created out of national states. The UN is based on 'the sovereign equality of all its Members' (UN Charter, Article 2). These states may now be undergoing transformation in so far as they are bound into structures of global governance in which, eventually, public policy may be made for the world (Held 2003: 167). However, such states have very little incentive to drop the symbols and routine turns of phrase that Billig identifies with 'banal nationalism', which routinely 'flag' the nation, and which help form a political community amongst citizens (Billig 1995). The emotional content of nationalism is closely linked to its particularism. It is not necessary to agree with Schmitt that 'whoever invokes humanity wants to cheat' to find his argument that where everyone is in principle a friend, where there are no enemies, it is far from obvious that there can be a political community at all (Schmitt 1996: 54). How can humanity inspire ongoing passionate attachments to rival the nation where every single human being would be equally entitled to call themselves a citizen of the world? With no 'them', where is the emotional attachment to 'us'?

The problem, then, is that in transcending nationalism, there is a risk of dissipating political community altogether, leaving individuals exposed, as it were, without experiencing social ties to strangers as in any way meaningful or valuable. However, despite the difficulties of imagining a global community of citizens, there is no doubt that the frame of justice that tied the state and nation together in a national political community is being disrupted. The question of how community may be formed if state and nation become detached is not only of interest to those engaged in normative political theory; it is also of pressing concern as a result of ongoing changes that are already taking place in the relationship between state and nation. It is just the way in which intermestic human rights are disrupting the national frame of justice that is the topic of this study. Besides the evident attractiveness of the way in which it takes modern universalism seriously – the claim that every single human being matters equally – these disruptions to the national frame of politics are what make cosmopolitanism especially relevant today.

HUMAN RIGHTS AGAINST 'ENEMIES OF ALL MANKIND'
In this chapter we will study two cases in which activists aimed directly at creating a community of global citizens around human rights cases. They aimed to mobilise sympathetic supporters of human rights in the US and UK for the civil rights of human beings in countries far away, supporters for whom such rights are not just morally relevant, but also important and compelling reasons for action. Using ground-breaking legal cases they attempted to create excitement and sympathy for human rights, to foster a global political community which would recognise obligations to realise international human rights encoded in international human rights law. Inevitably, however, because activists had to use the machineries of states which have historically been formed as national in order to further the project of creating a global community, the cosmopolitan justifications of human rights they mobilised had to compete with more conservative or simply more cautious actors in the human rights field, who defended the national community.

The Pinochet case has been celebrated by many as a turning point in the law of human rights (Habermas 1999; Sands 2005; Beck 2006: 223). It was the first time a former head of state was (almost) held internationally accountable for crimes against humanity committed during peacetime. Arrested in 1998 with a warrant from a Spanish magistrate demanding his extradition for crimes against humanity, including torture, hostage-taking and genocide, committed whilst he was President of Chile following a military coup, Pinochet was put under house arrest in the UK until he was finally declared medically unfit for trial and flown home to Chile in 2000. The case was ground-breaking because the highest court in the UK confirmed the principle that Pinochet's position as a former head of state did not legitimate his actions where they conflicted with human rights norms, nor protect him from prosecution for such crimes as torture and murder.

Uses of the Alien Tort Claims Act (ATCA) in the US have also been crucial to the human rights movement (Steinhardt and

D'Amato 1999; Stephens 2002; Earthrights International 2003). As noted in Chapter 2, ATCA is an obscure law from 1789, which has become hugely significant in the last twenty-five years because it allows foreigners to sue in federal courts for human rights abuses committed abroad using customary international law. I chose *Doe* v. *Unocal* as an example of the use of ATCA because it was roughly contemporaneous with the Pinochet case. Beginning in 1996 Burmese villagers sued the oil company Unocal for complicity in human rights abuses committed by the Burmese government and military during the building of the Yadana pipeline. Unocal finally settled out of court after a federal court had decided the case could go before a jury in 2003. As it made its long and complex way through the courts, *Unocal* was linked into a case heard in the Supreme Court, *Sosa* v. *Alvarez-Machain*, in which ATCA was tested against the opposition of the Bush Administration that it was unconstitutional and damaging to American national interests and security.

In both cases the defendants were referred to as 'the enemy of all mankind', '*hostis humani generis*'. Originally applied to pirates and the owners of slave ships, 'enemy of all mankind' is an 'extra-legal' term; it is used rhetorically to support legal arguments for universal jurisdiction, the pursuit and prosecution of those accused of committing offences so serious that any state is authorised to punish them. In modern times it was first used by a judge in the landmark Filartiga case in 1980 in which the family of a victim killed by state-sponsored torture in Paraguay was permitted to sue the perpetrator in the US (*Filartiga* v. *Pena-Irala*). According to this understanding, if Pinochet and Unocal are guilty of torture, genocide, slavery and other international crimes, they are 'enemies of all mankind'. They have put themselves outside the global community of civilised human beings, and they should be prosecuted for those crimes. Use of the term 'enemy of all mankind' vividly raises questions concerning what exactly the formation of a global community of justice might involve and what it means in relation to other, already-existing political communities.

Pinochet and ATCA cases were understood broadly – in the media, in subsequent commentaries by the legal profession, and by human rights organisations – in terms of human rights, though neither involves conventional human rights, law.[3] In terms of the effects of justifications that are made using human rights, ATCA cases and the Pinochet case are exemplary. They enable the study of how uses of the vocabulary of 'human rights' expand understandings of human rights, *exceeding the legal framework*, even when it is legal issues that are at stake. Besides their importance to the human rights movement, the cultural politics of Pinochet and ATCA cases are exemplary because both involve the use of customary international law in domestic courts to extend civil rights to distant others. In fact, it is this use of customary international law that makes ATCA so significant to the human rights movement in the US: it enables the introduction of human rights law into US courts, which is otherwise virtually impossible. Through ATCA, customary international law effectively becomes part of US law. The relevant section of the Judiciary Act of 1789 states that: 'The district courts shall have original jurisdiction of any civil action by an alien for a tort only, committed in violation of the law of nations or a treaty of the United

---

[3] As we noted in Chapter 1, the question of what kind of law covers what kinds of human rights claims is increasingly complex (see Steinhardt 1999; Ratner and Abrams 2001; Mekled-Garcia and Cali 2006). Moreover, intermestic human rights cases inevitably differ from country to country, and draw rather unconventionally on different bodies of law. In this respect, ATCA cases and the Pinochet case are actually *representative* of the peculiarities of intermestic human rights cases even though neither actually involve human rights law. Normally it is only states that are responsible for human rights. However, in cases brought under ATCA, very unusually, private individuals are sued for gross violations of human rights, thus allowing corporations to be found liable for human rights abuses (Meckled-Garcia and Cali 2006: 16). Such civil cases are very unlikely to be possible elsewhere in the world because US law, and indeed the US legal culture which favours civil suits as political tools, is unique in this respect (Stephens 2002). The Pinochet case was also not a conventional human rights case, which would normally involve only civil remedies in public law. Pinochet was actually arrested for extradition hearings to find out if he could legally be tried in a criminal court in Spain. However, the UK courts involved drew widely on interpretations of customary international law in order to present and judge the case. In this way, it becomes legally possible to find those who violate human rights criminally responsible.

States' (The Alien Tort Statute, 28 U.S.C. § 1350). Since the *Filartiga* case, the 'law of nations' has been interpreted in US courts as equivalent to customary international law. In the *Unocal* case the plaintiffs claimed that Unocal, through the Burmese military and police forces, used violence and intimidation to enslave villagers living in the area of the pipeline, and to commit rape, torture and murder. US federal courts were thus required to judge whether or not international crimes against humanity had been committed. In *Sosa* the Supreme Court confirmed that this was indeed the proper role of the federal courts.

Customary international law also played an important role in what was innovative about the Pinochet case. The initial finding by a Divisional Court that Pinochet was entitled to diplomatic immunity as a former head of state was appealed in the House of Lords where there were then three judgements by the Law Lords concerning the case, though only one legal decision. In the first judgement (Pinochet 1) the majority of the Lords found that Pinochet should be extradited to face criminal charges in Spain because customary international law, which would otherwise have prevented prosecution of a head of state for acts whilst committed in office, could not be understood to sanction crimes against humanity. This judgement was then set aside for reasons of alleged bias on the part of one of the judges (Pinochet 2), an unprecedented decision. Finally, the Lords decided that Pinochet should be extradited (Pinochet 3), but on much narrower technical grounds than Pinochet 1, based on national rather than international law.

IMAGINING A COMMUNITY OF GLOBAL CITIZENS

In the Pinochet and ATCA cases a global community formed by international law was imagined by human rights activists and innovative lawyers. In fact, international law in this conception becomes *cosmopolitan law*, which reaches inside states to create rights and responsibilities for everyone, regardless of nationality or place of residence (see pp. 38–40). A community of global citizens was imagined as 'always already' existing as a consequence of cosmopolitan law, even though the interpretation of international law on which this understanding of law depends is, in fact, contentious and, at best, in development. According to human rights activists and legal innovators, each and every individual in the world has the responsibility to avoid actions which contravene international human rights law, even if those actions might otherwise be considered a matter of internal domestic politics, and even if they are legal in national law. In addition, international human rights law requires states to pursue and prosecute those accused of acting in ways that violate human rights.

Cosmopolitan law therefore creates a global community of citizens. Global citizens happen to be resident in particular states, because there is no world-state. Their rights and responsibilities are nevertheless created by cosmopolitan law. Cosmopolitan law embodies universal moral principles of human dignity and autonomy, but it is also genuinely positive law, applicable and enforceable in national and international courts.

In the Pinochet case, activists and lawyers justified their use of human rights as if a community of global citizens already existed. In this way they attempted to imagine it into being. Advocates of global citizenship acted as if the UK state were a neutral political and legal apparatus – a carrier for global values of cosmopolitan law. The justifications for action produced by human rights organisations, especially Amnesty International (AI), represented their 'clients' (those who had been tortured and the relatives of the disappeared), as if cosmopolitan law defending individual entitlements regardless of national boundaries already existed. For example, in a report immediately following the Divisional Court's decision (before the case went to appeal), that Pinochet had diplomatic immunity from prosecution, AI stated that 'The UK *cannot* refuse to implement the rule of international law' in extraditing Pinochet to Spain for trial (Amnesty International 1998). In fact, however, precisely what was actually demanded by the rule of international law was highly contentious in the Pinochet case.

An imagined community of global citizens did gain a good deal of credibility with the Law Lords' decision in Pinochet 1, especially because of the unprecedented media coverage of the case. The judgement articulated a community of global citizenship insofar as it held that Pinochet's position as (former) head of state did not trump the legal entitlement of individuals to have their case heard in court, regardless of their nationality or residence. Thus all individuals are constituted as global citizens in customary international law which here upholds the norm of universal jurisidiction. However, the Law Lords' interpretation of customary international law actually came as a surprise to international lawyers, even if they hoped for this outcome (Bianchi 1999; Sands 2005). Pinochet 1 was decided by a majority of just three to two and justifications for majority and dissenting opinions turned to a large extent on different interpretations of international law, with dissenting Lords taking the traditional view that it regulates relations *between* sovereign states so that former heads of state *are* immune from prosecution, even in the case of crimes against humanity. The Lords staged a clash between fundamental principles of international law itself and Pinochet 1 was a landmark decision because it might so easily have gone the other way.

An imagined community of global citizens is also well-supported by ATCA law. This is directly as a result of the cases brought by legal advocacy organisations since 1980.[4] Human rights organisations see ATCA as contributing significantly to the 'worldwide movement to end impunity and hold human rights abusers accountable' (Brief of Amici Curiae International Human Rights Organisations and Religious Organisations in *Sosa* v. *Alvarez-Machain*, p. 1). Supporters of ATCA amongst human rights organisations and legal advocacy groups interpret international law as containing a cosmopolitan core which absolutely prohibits some crimes, including genocide, slavery, summary execution and torture, and

---

[4] See, for example, CCR 2003; Green and Stephens 2003; Earthrights International 2004; HRF 2004.

requires all states to exercise universal jurisdiction where these crimes are at issue, pursuing and prosecuting perpetrators and offering redress to victims. In *Sosa* v. *Alvarez-Machain*, the Supreme Court judgement confirmed this interpretation of a cosmopolitan core of international law, stating that it was clear that some norms of international law are 'specific, universal and obligatory', and that they must be enforced by US courts where remedies in the claimants' domestic courts have been exhausted. The Court also, however, strongly advised judicial caution (apparently accepting many of the (inter)nationalist arguments we will review in the next section). As Justice Souter put it in his writing up of the court opinion:

> [J]udicial power should be exercised on the understanding that the door is still ajar subject to vigilant doorkeeping, and thus open to a narrow class of international norms today.
>
> (*Sosa* v. *Alvarez-Machain, p. 35*)

Whilst the Supreme Court and human rights activists and lawyers agree, then, in their interpretation of ATCA as cosmopolitan law, the Court's caution, and the metaphor, suggest that 'the door' to hearing claims for damages in cases of the violation of even those human rights norms which enjoy the most deeply and widely held consensus could be closed in the future.

Although the discourse of global citizenship is primarily produced by and for legal professionals and human rights activists, it does create responsibilities for ordinary, individual citizens: we must avoid violating human rights if we act 'under colour of law' as state agents or in the name of the state (in the police force, for example, or the military). Also, more mundanely, but much more commonly, we are called on to support a state's pursuit and prosecution of those who have made themselves into 'the enemy of all mankind'. Global citizenship involves more than adherence to legal procedures in so far as it creates an affective community with which individuals identify, regardless of their citizenship status or where they live. As well as in activist interventions in courts, the imagined community of global citizenship was represented in the mediated public in the liberal media, principally in op-eds and expert opinions by activists and legal innovators and very occasionally in editorials.[5]

A phrase which sums up this affective identification and illustrates how ordinary people in the US and UK are called on as

---

[5] In the US it was represented in the *New York Times*: Dolly Filartiga, the brother of the young man tortured to death in the famous Filartiga case, wrote in impassioned support of ATCA in 'American Courts, Global Justice', 30 March 2004; Barbara Ehrenreich argued against the popular view that the 'constitution is not a suicide pact' and that the founding fathers *did* put principles before prudence, in 'Their George and Ours', 4 July 2004; the point of view of the *Center for Constitutional Rights* was represented in 'American Justice Tackles Rights Abuses Abroad', 3 September 2000. In the *Washington Post*: there were two articles sympathetically telling the story of Ka Hsaw Wa, Director of *Earthrights International* and his organisation's campaign in 'Rights Victims in Burma want a US Company to Pay', 13 April 1999 and 'Pipeline to Justice; a Burmese Activist has the Attention of the White House and, he Hopes, the World', 13 August 1999. In the *Los Angeles Times*: 'Foreign Torture Victims Seek Justice in US Courts', 28 February 1999, told the human stories behind the lawsuits sympathetically, thus 'humanising' the plaintiffs; Lisa Girion, in the news section, wrote several in-depth articles sympathetic to the plaintiffs: e.g. 'Judge OKs Unocal Abuse Lawsuit', 12 June 2002, 'US Ruling Says Firms Liable for Abuse Abroad', 19 September 2002, and, the story of ATCA told from the point of view of Peter Weiss, who led lawyers from the Center for Constitutional Rights in *Filartiga* '1789 Law Acquires Human Rights Role', 16 June 2003; an editorial, written by Michael O'Donnell, an expert in Third World law, argued strongly for ATCA, 'Capitalism vs Conscience; Companies Abuse Human Rights and the Feds don't Care', 9 June 2003; Ka Hswa Wa wrote 'Court is Villagers Only Hope', 9 June 2002; the villagers' stories were told in 'Pipeline to Justice?', 15 June 2003.

In the UK, there are a huge number of examples from the Pinochet case. Examples from the very beginning of the case, which set the tone for subsequent coverage, include: the *Guardian*: 'A Murderer Among Us', 15 October 1998; interview with Carlos Reyes (leader of Chile Democratico), 19 October 1998; letters page, 19 October 1998; the *Observer*: 'The Game is up for Pinochet', 18 October 1998, and an (untitled) editorial in the same edition; the *Mirror*: editorial 'Evil Pinochet Must Now Face Justice', 19 October 1998; letters page, 'The Right and Human Rights', 23 October 1998. Examples from the end of the case include: the *Mirror*: 'Betrayed; Torture Victims Round on Jack Straw after he Allows Chilean Tyrant Pinochet to Fly Home', and 'MP Anne Slams Pinochet Victory', 3 March 2000, after Straw announced Pinochet was unfit for trial; also the *Observer*: 'Only Tough Judicial Action can Halt the Torturer's Roll Call of Abuse' (written by M. Lattimer, Amnesty International's Director of Communications), 24 October 1999; the *Guardian* interview with Claudio Cordone, the leader of Amnesty International's Pinochet campaign on 4 March 2000.

global citizens is 'living amongst us', with reference to 'enemies of all mankind'. A form of words very like this was frequently used by NGO leaders in the mediated public both in the Pinochet cases and in relation to ATCA. It is a phrase which is a kind of performative declaration: ostensibly describing the reality of the community of global citizens it actually offers the possibility of imaginative iden-tification as a global citizen that, potentially, makes such a com-munity a reality: there are 'enemies of all mankind' living amongst 'us', whom, as global citizens, we should not ignore or tolerate.

In the Pinochet case a phrase equivalent to 'living amongst us' was used right at the beginning of the case in a very dramatic way to alert global citizens to the movements of an 'enemy of all mankind', General Pinochet. Hugh O'Shaughnessy, Chairman of the Latin American Bureau, wrote in the *Guardian* on 15 October 1998:

> There is a foreign terrorist in our midst who is in hiding somewhere in London . . . If this man escapes from Britain once again, a great many people here and abroad will want to know why . . . But possibly he may not get away this time. Keep your eyes peeled . . . If you are a patient in the London Clinic be particularly alert. Some people say he's holed up there for medical treatment. I shall be listening to the radio and television news today, waiting hopefully for the arrest of the former dictator of Chile, General Augusto Pinochet.
>
> ('*A Murderer Among Us*', Guardian, *15 October 1998*)

According to Geoffrey Robertson, O'Shaughnessy's article actually played a crucial role in Pinochet's arrest, alerting an investigating magistrate in Madrid, Balthasar Garzon, to his whereabouts. Garzon then successfully requested Pinochet's arrest through the Spanish Embassy in London (Robertson 2002: 396).

With reference to ATCA cases, the phrase 'living amongst us' was similarly used to describe how 'enemies of all mankind' should be captured and prosecuted in the US. Beginning their book on liti-gating international human rights in US courts, Beth Stephens and

Michael Ratner, both of whom have been prominently involved in ATCA cases, write:

> *Living amongst us* are former government officials from many nations who have committed gross violations of human rights. They should not live in impunity. The goal of this publication is to encourage lawyers throughout the country to litigate against human rights violators and on behalf of those murdered and tortured.
>
> *(Stephens and Ratner 1996: 5, my italics)*

Although the book from which this quote comes is aimed explicitly at lawyers, the sentiment is echoed again in the name of the coalition campaign to defend ATCA following the Department of Justice's attempt to limit it which led to *Sosa*: 'No Safe Haven'. Involving Amnesty International, Human Rights Watch, Human Rights First and Earthrights International amongst others, it aimed to prevent human rights abusers fleeing justice in their own countries, or simply ignoring international human rights, from finding a home in the US: those responsible for genocide, slavery and torture should not be 'living amongst us' with impunity (www.nosafehaven.org).

Global citizenship is constituted primarily through international law. It is unsurprising, then, that the leading citizens of the global community are human rights organisations and international human rights lawyers. However, 'we' ordinary citizens are called upon to take responsibility for human rights in the global community. Generally this does not involve avoiding or preventing the violation of human rights, though it does mean that we should be in possession of the knowledge that cosmopolitan law exists and that that everyone is bound to obey it or face punishment. Global citizenship more usually involves actively supporting human rights: by giving money or time to human rights organisations, demonstrating, signing petitions, writing letters, boycotting goods and so on. Or global citizenship may involve taking responsibility more passively, as it were, by simply supporting the extension of justice beyond the national community, using the resources and procedures of the cosmopolitanising state in order to make the global community of justice a reality. In supporting and upholding the rights and responsibilities delineated by cosmopolitan law *because it is the law*, we become citizens of a global political community.

RE-IMAGINING AN (INTER)NATIONAL COMMUNITY OF CITIZENS

An alternative response to the disruption of the frame which has tied the state and nation together as a political community is the attempt to *re*-imagine the national community and to *re*-fix the parameters of the national state, precisely to prevent their reformation along more cosmopolitan lines. This re-imagining, however, takes place in a context in which intermestic human rights are a reality, even if they are not (yet) routine. The national community is, therefore, re-imagined with an explicitly international inflection, as (inter) national citizenship, around factual and normative challenges to the national community of justice represented in intermestic human rights cases. Of course, as a relational term, nationalism was always international by definition. What is at issue now, however, is not so much the definition of 'the' nation as necessarily one amongst many, but rather the way in which the state is embedded in structures of global governance which impinge upon 'national affairs'. It is to the mobilisation of norms of universal international human rights, which potentially transform the state from national to cosmopolitan, that the re-imagining of the (inter)national community of citizens is a response.

In relation to intermestic human rights cases, the community of (inter)national citizens is re-imagined through the representation of international law as *politics*. Re-imagining the community of (inter)national citizens is led, above all, by conservative politicians. Conservative politicians justify their interventions in these cases by their representation of 'the people' who will suffer if the status quo of the national state is destroyed. In this case, they speak in the name of 'the nation'. They are supported in their efforts by op-eds and editorials in conservative papers. In fact, in the mediated publics of the US and UK the terms of the debate have tended to be set by conservative politicians, to which liberal politicians and liberal sectors of the media have then found themselves obliged to respond. Liberal politicians and journalists might reasonably be expected to be more sympathetic to the universalist claims of advocates of global citizenship. However, liberals often find themselves tempted by a hybrid between nationalism and cosmopolitanism that we will examine in the next section. There is also, moreover, a distinctively liberal version of the imagined community of (inter)national citizens.

In the US, the terms of the debate have been set by the Bush Administration. In the 'friend of the court' briefs which the Administration submitted in *Unocal* and *Sosa*, the justifications for an (inter)national community of citizens are very clearly represented.[6] Above all it is argued that customary international law is not really law at all, so that judicial interpretations that enable it to masquerade as such are simply allowing *Realpolitik* to be conducted by unrepresentative advocacy groups. This is judicial imperialism: it is not the place of the judiciary to conduct politics. Uses of ATCA in US courts to sue for violations of human rights are, therefore, undemocratic. They destroy the democratic separation of powers, usurping the proper role of the Executive to pursue foreign policy, especially dangerous whilst the US is engaged in the 'war against terrorism'. In addition, by depending on interpretations of customary international law involving unratified treaties and other non-binding documents, they also undermine the powers of the Legislature to make law in the name of the sovereign people. Judges should therefore treat ATCA as an historical relic, the origins and intentions of

---

[6] The relevant Administration legal briefs on which this analysis is based are as follows: Amici Curiae Brief for the United States of America in *Doe* v. *Unocal*; Petition for a Writ of Certiorari to the United Sates Court of Appeals for the Ninth Circuit in *USA* v. *Alvarez-Machain*; Brief for the United States as Respondent Supporting Petitioner in *Sosa* v. *Alvarez-Machain*.

which are obscure. Quoting Justice Story's observation from *US* v. *The La Jeune Eugenie* in 1822, the conservative position is that:

> No nation has ever yet pretended to be the custos morum of the whole world; and though abstractly a particular regulation may violate the law of nations, it may sometimes, in the case of nations, be a wrong without a remedy.
>
> *(Brief for the US as respondent supporting petitioner, Sosa v. Alvarez-Machain, p. 47)*

Conservative justifications of a re-imagined (inter)national community articulate, then, a realist vision of international relations which privileges reasons of state over the universal ideals of liberalism. However, this vision does have a normative dimension which is not typically associated with realism.[7] Conservatives have an alternative vision of global harmony to that of global citizenship based on how they see the facts of the place of individuals and nations in the international community. There is an international community, in which we (US citizens) participate as members of a democratic state within which it is elected politicians who have the responsibility for foreign affairs. Within the international community, good relations are to be promoted between and within states, especially with allies of the United States, but also, with states that maintain repressive regimes if necessary. The US Executive should act to change the internal politics of repressive regimes, but only as long as such strategy retains the primary aim of safeguarding national interests and national security. The proper relation between states is mutually respectful and tolerant pursuit of national interests.[8] Where the

---

[7] Thank you to George Lawson for pointing out to me that although realist theorists tend to ignore them, ethical dilemmas are nevertheless very important in realist politics (see Lebow 2003).

[8] In the 'friend of the court' briefs submitted by representatives of business, it is argued that commerce is one of the main ways in which national interests are reconciled and repressive states reformed. As well as damaging the US economy, ATCA cases also damage the prospects of states like Burma, to which businesses like Unocal bring the benefits of direct foreign investment and which have so few other opportunities for development (Brief for the National Association of

demands of national security require that other states are dealt with more harshly, as may be necessary in the war against terrorism, this is a decision for elected political leaders.

Conservative justifications of the re-imagined (inter)national community were made in response to intermestic human rights cases in detailed, technical ways to satisfy lawyers and judges in US courts. They were not widely rehearsed in the mediated public in relation to ATCA. In fact, there was not much discussion of the *Unocal* case at all in the US media. With the exception of the *LA Times*, where the story was closely followed from the beginning (Unocal is based in California) and which, by June 2003, was virtually campaigning against Unocal (in a way that is much more common in UK papers), in most papers the case only made it out of brief reports in the financial pages after February 2003 when the Court of Appeals for the Ninth Circuit agreed to re-hear it. It was only once the Supreme Court agreed, at the request of the Bush Administration, to hear *Sosa* that ATCA received mainstream coverage in this case. This lack of interest on the part of the mediated public may indicate that *re*-imagining the (inter)national community is hardly necessary for popular identification, as the contours of the existing national community have hardly been troubled by what are actually quite marginal events in US political life.[9]

The most striking positive indication that the terms of the debate are set by a model of political community that remains

Manufacturers as Amicus Curaie in Support of Reversal, *Sosa* v. *Alvarez-Machain*; Brief for the National Foreign Trade Council and others as Amici Curaie in Support of Petitioner in *Sosa* v. *Alvarezsuch-Machain*). This argument is at odds with that of the Executive, which claimed to be pursuing economic sanctions against Burma 'to promote positive political and economic change' (Brief for the US as respondent supporting petitioner, *Sosa* v. *Alvarez-Machain*, p. 45).

[9] The Bush Administration's arguments against ATCA were rehearsed by Robert Bork, a former federal judge, in the *Wall St Journal*, 'Judicial Imperialism', 12 July 2004, which received a response from Michael Posner, Executive Director of Human Rights First, 'The Use of US Courts for Human-Rights Cases', 13 July 2004. The National Foreign Trade Council took out a large advertisement on the op-ed page of the *New York Times* entitled 'The Business of Human Rights', 5 April 2004.

hegemonic comes from the justifications for pursuing ATCA cases by its liberal *supporters*. In a couple of editorials supporting ATCA from the *New York Times*, for example, it appears to be conceded that foreign policy concerns *do* trump human rights – though it is argued that this is not relevant in the Unocal case:

> As international human rights suits become more common in American courts, there will inevitably be tougher calls. If a court determined that foreign policy concerns were real in some future case, it would have at its disposal a variety of legal doctrines allowing it to avoid deciding the case. But . . . where such extraordinary circumstances are not present, the [court] should make it clear that the Myanmar villagers have a right to be heard.
>
> (*'An Important Human Rights Tool'*, New York Times, 8 August 2003; see also 'Legal Actions Over Foreign Misdeeds', New York Times, 30 March 2004).

What this quotation demonstrates is that even their liberal supporters in the US-mediated public tend to treat ATCA cases as rather ambiguously situated between politics and law. Unlike the activist advocates of global citizenship, they do not demand that courts should decide ATCA cases strictly following international human rights law. They suggest rather that the judiciary should defer to the Executive where there are genuine foreign policy concerns – regardless of the implications for universal human rights. It is sufficient here to compare, for example, the following statement from the lawyers representing the plaintiffs in *Doe* v. *Unocal* which imagines a community of global rather than national citizens in order to understand how much concession this liberal statement of support for ATCA from the *New York Times* makes to the conservative position:

> Even where a case has direct foreign policy impact '[judges] cannot shirk this responsibility [to apply congressional legislation] merely because [their] decision may have significant political

overtones', *Japan Whaling Ass'n v American Cetacean Soc.*, 478 US 221, 230 (1986).

> *(Plaintiffs-Appellants Supplemental Brief in Opposition to Amicus Curiae Brief Filed by the United States in* Doe v. Unocal, *p. 28)*

In the UK, justifications for re-imagining the community of (inter) national citizenship were also made in the name of opposition to judicial imperialism. They came primarily from Conservative politicians opposed to Pinochet's extradition, but also, in a somewhat different form, from liberal supporters of the decision to extradite Pinochet.

Conservative re-imaginings of the (inter)national community of citizens in the UK were very similar to those of the Bush Administration in the US. They were exemplified in Margaret Thatcher's dramatic speech to the Conservative Party, which reiterated themes widely covered by the conservative media throughout the case: 'our' obligations are as a nation to foster our 'national interests' rather than to consolidate and uphold universal principles of international human rights.[10] For Conservatives, Pinochet's brutality – and there was no dispute in the conservative media that Pinochet was responsible for torture and the disappearance of up to 4,000 people – is not our concern: the lives of 'our' national fellows are worth far more to 'us' than are the lives of those who belong to other nations. This was made explicit in Thatcher's arguments,

---

[10] Thatcher's speech to the Conservative Party Conference in 2000, in which she railed against it for abandoning him, produced a storm of media commentary (see www.guardian.co.uk/tory99/Story/0,,202256,00.html, last accessed 29 December 2007). Examples of conservative media defence of (inter)nationalism throughout the case include the *Daily Mail*: 'Jack's all Right . . . what about Chile?', 10 December 1998 and 'Tories and Chileans Pile the Pressure on Straw in Extradition Row', 27 November 1998; the *Sun* editorial, 'Why Has Britain Arrested a Friend in Need?' on 19 October 1998; and a report, 'Pinochet in Tears as He Faces Trial', 10 December 1998. The *Daily Telegraph* generally gave what appeared to be a more comprehensive and balanced account of the case, but it did orient stories towards anti-colonialism, featuring unrest in Chile as a result of Pinochet's arrest, with headlines like 'Tension Turns to Violence on the Streets of Santiago', 22 November 1998 and 'Pinochet's Return Puts Democracy Under Strain', 5 March 2000.

widely rehearsed from the beginning of the case in the conservative press, that Pinochet was entitled to respect and honour in the UK because he had been of invaluable help during the Falklands war, saving many British lives as a result.

In liberal sectors of the mediated public, anti-imperialist justifications of the re-imagined (inter)national community were much more conditional upon the ideal of ethical foreign policy articulated by the Foreign Secretary of the Labour government shortly after it was elected in 1997.[11] These justifications are similar to those expressed in liberal sectors of the US media in response to the Bush Administration that we saw exemplified in the quote from the *New York Times* above. The ideal of ethical foreign policy is that (inter) national citizens should support decisions of the UK state, in voluntary co-operation with other states, which contribute to establishing democracy and the rule of law within national states. If extraditing Pinochet to Spain to be prosecuted furthers this aim, it is the right thing to do. As a matter of ethical foreign policy rather than cosmopolitan law, however, interpretations of customary international law are inherently, and unashamedly, political. International law may form part of a political strategy, but it should not direct state conduct.

In the re-imagined (inter)national community, then, the emphasis is on the responsibilities of political leaders of national states who protect and defend the rights of national citizens to live in

---

[11] From the beginning of the case writers at the *Guardian* were critical of the British authorities for allowing Pinochet to enter the country (while he was not given leave to enter France); a criticism that assumes proper diplomatic relations between states are more important than the universal justice of international norms. Towards the end of the case there was consideration of how Chile had consolidated itself as a democratic state as a result of the actions of international elites in the Pinochet case to the point where Pinochet might even stand trial in Chile should he be returned. Several reports from Santiago that appeared in the *Guardian* towards the end of the case, for example, suggest that changes had been produced by Pinochet's arrest to make Chile freer and more democratic (e.g. 'People Find the Confidence to Face the Truth but Fear the General's Last Laugh', 16 October 1999, and 'Chilean Calls Grow for Pinochet Trial', 6 March 2000).

peace and prosperity. 'We' ordinary citizens of the (inter)national community have individual rights within national states, and only indirectly at the international level, through our national states. 'Our' responsibilities are to select our national leaders wisely, to ensure that they pursue our national interests prudently but energetically, maintaining good relations with other states wherever possible, but only insofar as peaceable relations are consistent with the overriding aim of national security. The question of how far foreign policy may be ethical requires political judgement; it is, therefore, debatable within the national mediated public. 'We' (inter)national citizens have no direct political responsibilities towards individuals in other national states, though our state may ethically support those states to achieve peace and prosperity for their citizens in so far as this is compatible with our own rights as national citizens.

COSMOPOLITAN NATIONAL CITIZENSHIP

The imagined community of the cosmopolitan nation is a creative compromise between global citizenship and (inter)nationalism, which competes directly with both. The basic motif of this somewhat paradoxical model of a community is that 'we' – who are unquestionably members of a national community first and foremost – take pride in our state in so far as it upholds universal human rights that are applicable across the world. Cosmopolitan nationalism presupposes that we are in a kind of transitional phase, which is moving towards a global community of justice insofar as states are no longer self-contained discrete units of jurisdiction. Gross violations of human rights both will be and should be a matter for international law rather than for politics or diplomacy. International law is both legally and morally just. However, the extension of universal human rights is not unfolding in any clear-cut way, though progress is possible, and it does not therefore constitute a global community of justice in which individuals find themselves to have rights and responsibilities as global citizens. *Some* national states are cosmopolitanising in terms of legal procedures which uphold, and *should* uphold, international human rights. This is especially the case where they have made international law their own, incorporating it into national law. In so doing, these exceptional cosmopolitanising states have formed exceptional communities of justice, centred within the state itself, which are uniquely able to judge 'enemies of all mankind' and to dispense justice without borders. 'We' cosmopolitan nationals are, therefore, called on to support the extension of international human rights by our cosmopolitan state.[12]

In both the US and UK, human rights organisations and legal advocacy groups justified their understanding of international law in the cases studied here *overwhelmingly*, and in the UK exclusively, in terms of the global community of justice. In the US, I found no unequivocal justifications of ATCA that were genuine expressions of cosmopolitan nationalism. On the rare occasions when NGOs in the US did adopt justifications of intermestic human rights that imagined a cosmopolitan national community of justice, it was a strategic response to attacks on ATCA. A very interesting example comes from the amicus brief submitted on behalf of international human rights organisations in *Sosa v. Alvarez-Machain*. The brief, prepared by Deena Hurwitz and Beth Stephens, quotes a senior official speaking on behalf of the Bush Administration, amongst others, to demonstrate that the US government has long been committed to the international effort to bring violators of human rights to justice. The words were clearly originally intended as (inter)nationalist; the argument is for the independence of national states against international institutions. Deployed in advice to the Supreme Court from

---

[12] 'Cosmopolitan nationalism' has a somewhat paradoxical ring, linking, as it does, two terms which are generally understood to refer to opposing perspectives based on reason and affect, universal morality and particularistic attachments. There are, however, many attempts to show how the two poles might be reconciled or combined anew in some way in contemporary thought; e.g. Appiah's 'cosmopolitan patriots' (Appiah 1998); Habermas's 'constitutional patriotism' (Habermas 2001: 74) (for interesting criticisms of these attempts see Fine 1994; Kostakopolou 2006). Moreover, such attempts may not be so new: it can be argued that Durkheim, for example, developed a conception very like 'cosmopolitan nationalism' based on human rights (Collier 2002).

international human rights organisations recommending that the domestic remedy provided by ATCA is crucial to the international community, however, they take on a much more ambiguous meaning. Deployed against the Administration's own intentions, they justify an imagined cosmopolitan national community:

> Here's what America believes in: We believe in justice and the promotion of the rule of law. We believe those who commit the most serious crimes of concern to the international community should be punished. We believe that states, not international institutions are primarily responsible for ensuring justice in the international system. We believe that the best way to combat these serious offences is to build domestic judicial systems, strengthen political will and promote human freedoms.
>
> *(Mark Grossman, Remarks to the Center for Strategic and International Studies, quoted in Brief on behalf of International Human Rights Organizations and Religious Organizations in* Sosa v. Alvarez-Machain, *p. 17)*

Strategically deployed in this context, these words support, not the imagined community of global justice that human rights NGOs articulate as 'always already existing', but rather an imagined community in which America, as an exemplary domestic system of justice, leads the international community towards the punishment of serious crimes against that community. This theme is carried through the document, which ends with the point that, 'Judicial repeal of the ATCA would undercut the US claim of leadership in the struggle to enforce human rights' (pp. 29–30).

At the same time, however, human rights organisations and legal advocacy NGOs were extremely careful to emphasise that ATCA does not involve the application of US law extraterritorially. They argue rather that in ATCA, US federal law provides a vital tool for furthering international human rights. However, it simply allows US courts to apply 'well-established, universally recognised norms of international law', the core of international law that is cosmopolitan, on which there is clearly worldwide consensus (see Brief of Amici

Curiae Lawyers Committee for Human Rights and the Rutherford Institute in *Sosa* v. *Alvarez-Machain*, p. 10).

Cosmopolitan nationalism is nevertheless dangerously close to imperialism, both in sentiment and effect. The imperialist effect of cosmopolitan nationalism is very evident in the Pinochet case. Cosmopolitan nationalism was confirmed in the legal reasoning of Pinochet 3 insofar as it drew on national rather than international law – albeit in such complicated ways as to be virtually unintelligible to non-lawyers. Pinochet 3 was far less dramatic and novel than Pinochet 1, though equally highly publicised in translations of the legal technicalities of the case in the mediated public. The Law Lords granted extradition on narrow technical grounds, allowing only those charges of crimes to stand which were committed after the date at which the Torture Convention was incorporated into English law in the Criminal Justice Act 1988. In this respect the decision was at odds with judges' interpretation in Pinochet 1 that some acts, including torture and hostage-taking, are crimes in international law, wherever and whenever they are committed. The reasoning of Pinochet 3 constructed, then, a much more equivocal endorsement of international customary law, and the enactment of 'quasi-universal' rather than universal jurisdiction, according to which obligations are only accepted by a state on the basis of international treaties in so far as they have become part of domestic law by ratification or incorporation (Shaw 2003: 598).

The consequence of the decision in Pinochet 3 was, therefore, a differentiation between Chilean and UK state sovereignty. Justice apparently required that international law should pierce the Chilean state, disallowing the immunity from prosecution that the democratically elected Chilean government had conferred on Pinochet for alleged international crimes. At the same time the Law Lords relied on traditional understandings of international law to confirm UK sovereignty in allowing only obligations that had been incorporated as domestic law to count as law. It appeared from this judgement that the UK was authorised to uphold justice across borders, reaching into

Chilean domestic politics, not because it was required by international (cosmopolitan) law, but because it was required by national (cosmopolitan) law. As a cosmopolitan state, the UK required its judiciary to disregard Chilean state sovereignty.

Liberal politicians are structurally situated in such a way that cosmopolitan nationalism is a tempting strategy for those who support the extension of international norms of justice but who must, necessarily, appeal to an electorate that is limited to those who posses nationality. In the UK, as we shall see in Chapter 5, it is a strategy that was very much favoured by the Blair government. In the Pinochet case this strategy was muted for technical reasons: ultimately the decision to extradite Pinochet lay with the Foreign Secretary of the UK government and, as this decision was officially 'quasi-judicial', there was a formal ban on speeches and comments on the case amongst members of the government.[13]

In the US liberal politicians have not prominently engaged in the political debate over ATCA. Democrat Senator for California Dianne Feinstein introduced an Alien Tort Statute Reform Act into Congress in October 2005, but it has never been debated in Senate, and nor did it become a topic of debate in the mediated public (GovTrack.us. S. 1874–109th Congress (2005): Alien Tort Statute Reform Act). In the only intervention I found in the US press in favour of ATCA by a politician throughout *Unocal* and *Sosa*, moderate Republican Arlen Specter of Pennsylvania ended his article with the words: 'Our credibility in the war on terrorism is only advanced when our government enforces laws that protect innocent

---

[13] Those few comments that were made on the case were the topic of enormous amounts of media conjecture and speculation. Widely discussed were those of Peter Mandelson, Trade Secretary, shortly after Pinochet's arrest, that it would be 'gut-wrenching' to see such a 'brutal dictator' like Pinochet escape justice – immediately declared 'emotional and unhelpful' by 'Cabinet sources' but widely suspected to have been made strategically; and Tony Blair's mention of Tory support for Pinochet in a speech to the Labour Party Conference in 1999 (see http://news.bbc.co.uk/1/hi/uk_politics/460009.stm, last accessed 29 December 2007).

victims. We then send the right message to the world: the United States is serious about human rights' ('The Court of Last Resort', *New York Times*, 7 August 2003).[14] Given the structural temptations and the resonance (as we saw in Chapter 3) of American national pride, it is to be expected that in the US, as in the UK, justifications of the use of intermestic human rights by politicians opposing (inter) nationalism would be made in the terms of cosmopolitan nationalism. Since, however, there is no wide-ranging mediated public debate on the use of human rights in US courts, this strategy can only be a matter of speculation here.

In the mediated public of the UK, cosmopolitan nationalism was more in evidence. The cosmopolitan nation was imagined in the populist press that supported Pinochet's arrest and pursuit in the UK.[15] Imagining the cosmopolitan nation was much more muted in the liberal broadsheet press, where it did not appear in news stories, op-eds or editorials, but only in letters.[16] In the US cosmopolitan nationalism was practically non-existent in media coverage of *Unocal* and *Sosa*. There are only a couple of examples where

[14] The *Wall Street Journal* reported that on 29 June 2002, sixteen Congressmen and two US senators asked the State Department not to intervene in the Exxon Mobil case, also filed under ATCA. As in the Unocal case, however, the State Department did intervene, writing a letter warning the Judge of the US District Court for the District of Columbia that the lawsuit against Exxon Mobil 'would impact adversely on the interests of the United States', economically and in the 'war on terrorism' ('A Global Journal Report: Administration Sets New Hurdles for Human Rights Cases', *Wall Street Journal*, 7 August 2002). I found no evidence of any such opposition in the cases with which we are concerned here.

[15] The *Daily Mirror*: 'You can Stick your Justice; Arrogant Pinochet Insults Britain', 12 December 1998; 'British justice can still shine like a beacon across the world', the opening line of an editorial headlined 'No Escape from Justice for Tyrant', 26 November 1998; and, when Straw announced Pinochet was unfit for trial, from a letter under the headline 'Day of Shame', 'It is a sad day for Britain and for justice', 3 March 2000.

[16] '[Pinochet's arrest] gives me hope that Britain can regain its reputation as a leading force for democracy and human rights' (*Guardian*, 19 October 1998); 'Britain can take the lead in providing a clear global signal to those who commit genocide and human rights abuses' (*Guardian*, 24 October 1998); and, when Pinochet was about to be released, 'For the first time in my life . . . I am ashamed of being British' (*Observer*, 12 March 2000).

cosmopolitan nationalism appeared to be strategically introduced, and taken up, in the mediated public by leaders of human rights organisations and human rights lawyers.[17] For the most part, however, cosmopolitan nationalism was remarkable by its absence in these debates, especially when we consider the important role played by national pride in debates over the legal conditions of arbitrary detentions in Guantanamo Bay.

Justifications for intermestic human rights that imagine a cosmopolitan national community of justice are problematic because cosmopolitan nationalism is very difficult to disentangle from imperialism. The superiority of the nation of which 'we' are citizens, who have individual human rights and responsibilities to uphold and support the realisation of human rights, largely through the activities of our state, justifies intervention in the affairs of another. The prominence of cosmopolitan nationalism in the Pinochet case compared to ATCA cases is surely, in part, because of the popularity of the Pinochet case, in that cosmopolitan nationalism was taken up by the populist press. In contrast, the ATCA cases were completely ignored in the populist press in the US. However, the judgement in Pinochet 3 also shows how legal judgements that observe the letter of the law can produce a state-sponsored, elite version of cosmopolitan nationalism. In this respect, taking the wider context of the Pinochet judgement into account, its celebration by the human rights movement should perhaps give us pause for thought.

---

[17] The examples that may be interpreted as strategically justifying cosmopolitan nationalism are as follows: Paul Hoffman, representing Alvarez, was quoted at the end of a *New York Times* article 'Justices Hear Case about Foreigners' saying: ' "Rather than undermine national security . . . use of the law only affirms the values that have made the country as strong as it is"', 31 March 2004; and Michael Posner in a letter to the *Wall Street Journal*, arguing that '[T]here is simply no evidence that US foreign policy has been adversely affected by any of these lawsuits. To the contrary, America's stature in the world has been enhanced by the availability of our courts to provide a remedy to those victims of gross human-rights abuses, for whom there is no remedy at home' (23 July 2004).

COSMOPOLITANISM-FROM-BELOW

In this chapter we have explored how activists seriously attempted to imagine a global community of citizens around the cosmopolitan law developed in ATCA cases and in the Pinochet case. They attempted to bring cosmopolitan ideals of global citizenship down from the abstract skies of philosophical thought, and also down from an idealised realm of global governance by international governmental organisations as a kind of proto-world state, into courts and mediated publics within states. Human rights activists attempted to imagine a popular global community of citizens that could seriously challenge the norm of national citizenship from within what has been historically constituted as the national state. This community of global citizens was not simply elitist, nor rationalist – though it did manifest elements of both. It is true that it was led by professionals in the human rights field: by activists employed as spokespersons for advocacy organisations, and by lawyers, who obviously have professional stakes in its success. And nor can we say that the global community articulated here received immense popular support. On the contrary, as we have seen, it was strongly contested in nationalist terms, and it was really only supported in some liberal sections of the mediated public. Nevertheless, the way in which the global community of citizens was imagined in these cases marks a different type of cosmopolitanism from that which Calhoun has criticised. It is not the cosmopolitanism of 'frequent flyers', the free-floating elites of global capitalism who are disengaging from nations and who have no interest in building popular support for new forms of citizenship. It is better understood as 'cosmopolitanism-from-below' (Kurasawa 2007).

The cosmopolitan project of imagining a global community of citizens differs from that of 'frequent flyer' cosmopolitanism because it attempted to gain popular understanding and acceptance of cosmopolitan legal norms in the mediated public within states. It tried to establish affective ties between individuals that are much wider than those of the national community, but it did so from within procedures and domains that are central to the political functioning of liberal-democratic states as such. The global community of citizens was imagined as tied to the legal and political procedures of states, which should be responsive to 'the people'. But 'the people' are now envisaged as cosmopolitans rather than, or perhaps as well as, nationals. Global citizenship is not imagined as something above, outside, or against the processes of liberal-democratic states; it is seen rather as emerging from within them.

Imagining the community of global citizens around Pinochet and ATCA involved modifying national states from below. It aimed to transform the national state into a cosmopolitan state with the consent of 'the people' the national state is supposed to serve. However, this does not mean that there is a seamless continuity between nationalism and cosmopolitanism in these cases, even for supporters of global citizenship. It is not because civic nationalism shares the ideal of equality between individual human beings with cosmopolitanism that passionate attachments to the nation can simply be transformed into ideals of global community. On the contrary, in the Pinochet case we see a direct conflict between nationalism and cosmopolitanism in the operation of cosmopolitan law itself. From the point of view of the national frame of justice, the way in which cosmopolitan law treats violations of human rights as absolute, thereby authorising intervention in the domestic affairs of states, including overriding the decisions of elected governments, is unacceptable. It is especially unacceptable because it is certain that, for reasons of *Realpolitik*, it will invariably be dominant states that will intervene in the affairs of weaker states, even if the intervention is done in the name of universal legal entitlements and obligations. Nationalism and cosmopolitanism contradict each other in cases where democratically elected leaders are tried for human rights violations.[18] The cosmopolitan ideal of multiple identities and scales

---

[18] This clash is evident in the statute of the International Criminal Court, which came into force in 2002 to try crimes under international humanitarian law. Although its status as an international forum no doubt involves particular cultural politics, it will resemble the cultural politics of intermestic human rights that we are examining here in so far as: (a) not all states will participate in the ICC (with the US leading the way in exempting itself); (b) the court is only authorised to bring cases where the will or the means are judged to be lacking in national

does not preclude, then, serious clashes of principle and interest in which nationalism will play a prominent part.

In the context of intermestic human rights cases, passionate attachments to the nation are in contradiction with cosmopolitanism because they negate the possibilities of international law as such. Politicians and journalists responded to activist imaginings of global community by re-imagining national citizenship in ways that could incorporate the challenges set by intermestic human rights cases to the national frame of justice. They either denied the validity of activist and legal justifications of human rights altogether, relying on the assumption that national citizenship is still paramount and the national frame of justice is still intact. Or they reasserted the primacy of the national frame, accepting that human rights for non-citizens are morally relevant but nevertheless privileging the rights, interests and values of national citizens. In the imagined (inter) national community and the cosmopolitan national community respectively, international law is seen as political; it is not really law at all. These imagined communities are premised on ideas of national superiority which have been so problematic in generating conflict between states and the oppression of minorities within them, and which have contributed to nationalism becoming discredited amongst social and political theorists as a form of legitimate social organisation. In terms of human rights norms, they are premised on the manipulation of ideals of international law in the name of national superiority, whether cynically, for reasons of personal gain or national interest, or for reasons of principle. Where intermestic human rights are seen as really matters of politics that are being speculatively framed as law, any possibility of the rule of international law (whether interpreted by legal innovators or traditionalists) is destroyed. Where international law is treated as an extension of national politics, it does not exist as law.

societies; (c) as a matter of statute the ICC will not recognise amnesties where crimes against humanity may have been committed (www.icc-cpi.int).

5 Global solidarity: justice not charity

of international & domestic concern

The emphasis of struggles over ~~intermestic~~ human rights is on civil rights, and this has also been the emphasis of this study so far. It reflects an historic Western privileging of civil rights as absolutely fundamental, in comparison with social, economic and cultural rights which are often not conceived of as *rights* at all – even if they are enumerated in the UDHR – but rather as political aspirations towards at least minimal conditions of human well-being and flourishing.[1] In this study, however, we are concerned with the *social forms* created by the cultural politics of intermestic human rights. Realising human rights in practice is always a collective endeavour; it is about the creation of new social forms. Human rights as civil rights require courts, education and training, intergovernmental agreements, international policing, communication networks and so on. They also require a cosmopolitan orientation towards justice, a reframing of issues of global justice as concerning citizens and non-citizens alike. In respect of the creation of cosmopolitan social forms, then, although social and economic rights are more explicitly about the

---

[1] Social, economic and cultural rights are associated insofar as they are included together in the International Covenant on Economic, Social and Cultural Rights. Together with the ICCPR and the UDHR, they make up what is sometimes referred to as 'the International Bill of Human Rights'. In fact, however, cultural rights ('the right to participation in the cultural life of the community' (Article 7, UDHR)) concern quite different matters from those of social and economic rights, and there is no compelling reason to put them all together, nor, indeed, to separate them from civil and political rights (for example, as Donnelly points out, many rights to culture are classic civil rights to freedom of expression and belief (Donnelly 1989: 36)). For the most part campaigns concerning social and economic rights do not directly concern cultural rights and vice versa, even though, in principle, they are indivisible (see Copelon 1998).

collective management and distribution of resources, they are not fundamentally different in kind from civil rights.

Solidarity is a key term in social theory and as a result it has various different uses (see Crow 2002; Kurasawa 2007). For my purposes in this analysis, it is important to distinguish between 'thinner' and 'thicker' solidarity. 'Solidarity' invariably denotes a 'we' who feel ourselves to share common bonds. In the 'thinner' version of solidarity 'we' experience ourselves as sharing common bonds simply as a result of shared social relationships, beliefs and values. This sense of solidarity is actually quite difficult to distinguish from 'community'. The thicker version of solidarity involves experience of 'we' accompanied by the sense that we belong together in a 'community of fate' and that we share a rough cost–benefit analysis (rarely fully calculated, and virtually never aimed at eliminating inequalities altogether) of what we owe each other in terms of a distribution of risks and resources. The difference between thinner and thicker solidarity is not that in the latter version people come together in order to realise rationally calculated aims; on the contrary, the durability of thicker solidarity depends at least as much as does thinner solidarity on affective ties. It is rather that 'our' sense of the 'we' is built in part around the expectation that material risks and resources *will be shared* and the understanding that this may result in greater benefits to some than to others in the community.

Sociologists sceptical of cosmopolitanism have pointed out that national states have enjoyed unrivalled success in organising this thicker sense of solidarity on a society-wide scale (Turner 2000, 2002; Calhoun 2003, 2007). To varying degrees, post-Second World War welfare states built on already established feelings of national belonging to enable re-distribution of wealth between citizens, setting up national systems of education, health, social assistance for those without paid work, and cultural institutions such as national broadcasting systems. Welfare states built on national communities that had long been fostered by states through education and communications media. Common bonds were strengthened as a result of citizens' mutual efforts, and national identity was consolidated by the military and propaganda battle against a national enemy in the Second World War.

Today, extending social and economic human rights requires something of the same sense of solidarity, but on a global scale. Article 2 of the International Convention on Economic Social and Cultural Rights requires that 'Each State Party to the present Covenant undertakes to take steps, individually and through international assistance and co-operation, especially economic and technical, to the maximum of its available resources, with a view to achieving progressively the full realization of the rights recognized in the present Covenant by all appropriate means'. The rights enumerated in the ICESCR include rights to fair wages, to be free from hunger, to an adequate standard of living, to education and to 'the enjoyment of the highest attainable standard of physical and mental health'. Given the overwhelming number of states which have ratified the ICESCR, it is arguable that even those Northern states which have not – most notably the US, which has signed but not ratified it – are bound by customary international law to do all they can to ensure the rights of persons in other states as well as in the US. If this were taken seriously it would mean a massive redistribution of resources from the global North to the South. If it is difficult to imagine a global community of citizens, however, it is even more difficult to imagine the global solidarity that such a redistribution of resources would seem to require as a precondition.

The solidarity on which welfare states built was not only that of feelings of national belonging fostered by the cultural practices of the state and strengthened in opposition to an enemy in wartime. It was also built on the principle of formal membership which excluded non-members. In national citizenship social rights are not simply legal entitlements; they have their corollary in legal *obligations* to contribute to the state for the collective good. When welfare states were established, these contributions were typically gendered: men contributed money through taxation on paid work, and physical strength if called upon to serve in the military; women typically contributed children and care for the family. The principle of welfare states was that of social insurance: citizens contributed to public goods on the basis that any member of the state would be entitled to access those goods when they needed them. Social insurance is based on a principle of reciprocity, not benevolence: the understanding that we are part of some sort of co-operative system in which each of us is making a contribution to the common good from which we all benefit (Brown *forthcoming*). Turner argues that the principle of social insurance that guided the welfare state has now been largely undermined with the rise of neo-liberal marketisation, the growth of large-scale unemployment, the decline in the need for soldier-citizens as warfare becomes more technical, and the erosion of the classic nuclear family. The principle that welfare states should provide minimum assistance to the very poorest has come to replace the principle that citizens are entitled to access to public goods to which they have contributed. Consequently, solidarity *within* the state is itself in decline (Turner 2000, 2002).

It is clearly not possible that anything like global solidarity will emerge 'all in one piece' as it were, even if national solidarity is in decline. The conditions that enabled solidarity to be fostered in the national state do not exist at a global scale. There is no world state to foster a strong sense of belonging together in a 'community of fate'; and without membership criteria, or clear, regular, social patterns of contribution and allocation, it would seem to be more difficult to establish any sense that each person is contributing fairly, if not equally, to the common good from which we all benefit.

Is it possible, however, that something like proto-global solidarity is nevertheless in the making at more limited scales? Fuyuki Kurasawa argues that this is just what we see in the alternative globalisation movement. He argues that the alternative globalisation movement consists of 'a mosaic of horizontal and transversal struggles' that *can* add up to a mode of social practice which constructs bonds of mutual commitment and reciprocity and which is oriented towards global justice (2007: 177). Kurasawa is here concerned with thick solidarity, the feeling that global injustice is a pressing issue for everyone involved, rather than with the thinner solidarity of 'planetary consciousness'. He sees solidarity as possibly emerging in discussions at the World Social Forum, and in such practices as the protests against World Trade Organisation in Seattle in 1999, the demonstrations in cities across the world against the invasion of Iraq in 2003, and so on. However, as his frequent use of the words 'can' and 'could' suggest, Kurasawa is more concerned with the theoretical possibilities of the alternative globalisation movement than with the investigation of its empirical successes and failures in relation to the aims and claims of actual participants (344). He does note, however, that the alternative globalisation movement has yet to impact on the formal decision-making of global governance (374).

I agree with Kurasawa that – in the absence of an already existing sense of belonging together and without formal membership in a global community that could only be guaranteed by a world state – if global solidarity is to be possible at all it will have to be built bit by bit from the bottom up. I also think, however, that any such form of proto-global solidarity will impact on global governance *only* if becomes genuinely popular in Northern states. We in the North are implicated in the poverty of people in the South, by structures of production, finance, trade and taxation. The question is whether and how those structures might be made visible, and whether mutual costs and benefits can be made a matter of global responsibility (see Young 2004).

Elected politicians are currently mandated to represent the interests of 'the people' within national states. Combined with the fact that negotiations at the international level are generally thought to be of very little interest to the mediated public, this makes radical global reform to realise universal social and economic rights extremely difficult. Only if popular global solidarity is generated *within* states is it conceivable that politicians and officials will stop treating international governmental organisations as outposts of national politics, and to begin to see them as making public policy for the world (Held 2003: 167).

POPULAR GLOBAL SOLIDARITY

The aim of this chapter is to explore the possibility of emergent forms of proto-global solidarity in popular campaigns against global poverty in the UK and US. The campaigns 'Make Poverty History' in the UK and 'ONE: the Campaign to Make Poverty History' in the US were both branches of the Global Call to Action Against Poverty (GCAAP) which was created in 2005 when the Millennium Development Goals were due to be reviewed.[2]

The strategy of GCAAP is 'think globally, act nationally'. Engaged in constructing global solidarity from below, it aims to target international governmental organisations through cosmopolitanising states. Different campaigns were launched in different countries with different names: 'Plus d'Excuses!' in France, 'Maak Het Waar' in the Netherlands, 'Zero Pobreza, Ya!' in Spain and so on. Throughout 2005, all the different national campaigns aimed to put pressure on their respective states to address global poverty at the G8 summit in July, the UN summit on Millennium Development Goals in September, and the WTO forum in December. At the G8 especially, pressure was created to force governments to achieve three clear and simple economic goals. Firstly, to increase aid to come close to the 0.7 per cent of GDP target promised in the 1970s. Secondly, to cancel 100 per cent of debt to multilateral institutions for those countries eligible under the Heavily Indebted Poor Country

---

[2] The UN Millennium Development Goals are concrete, measurable aims agreed at the United Nations Millennium Summit in 2000 to be achieved by 2015. They include: halving extreme poverty and hunger; achieving universal primary education; promoting gender equality, especially in education; reducing child mortality by two-thirds; reducing the maternal mortality rate by three-quarters; combating HIV/AIDS, malaria and other killer diseases; ensuring environmental sustainability; and developing a global partnership for development with targets for aid, trade and debt relief (see www.un.org/millenniumgoals/goals, last accessed 29 December 2007).

rules, to widen the criteria of eligibility for debt cancellation, and to set up fair and transparent processes for cancelling or repaying other debt. Thirdly, to realise 'trade justice', enabling developing countries to take control of their national economies by ending subsidies on Northern agricultural goods, tariffs on importing manufactured goods from the South, and the dumping of surpluses in the South.

Make Poverty History and ONE were intended as campaigns which would mobilise popular support to put pressure on the UK and US governments to address global poverty. To this end they were both very carefully managed media campaigns. All campaigns are necessarily mediated, in order to try to reach people who can make a difference (to persuade them to write letters, demonstrate, to knock on doors to persuade others and so on). But ONE and Make Poverty History were campaigns aimed at mobilising popular support that not only took place *through the media*; to a large extent, they took place *in the media*. For example, both campaigns made extensive use of celebrities to get their message across, culminating in Live8 in July 2005 which involved concerts in ten venues in nine different countries, was broadcast live on television, radio and through the Internet all around the world, and was received, according to the organisers, by three billion people. It would be wrong, however, to conclude that these campaigns created 'psuedo-events' (Boorstin 1992). There is no reason to suppose that the intentions of those involved were to create or to participate in a media event as such, rather than to bring about real change in the world. Indeed, the campaigns were genuinely grassroots insofar as they co-ordinated a number of NGOs in both countries, including many which receive their funding from donations and membership. In the US they included the Grameen Foundation USA, Action Against Hunger and Jubilee USA. In the UK they ranged from the large, international NGOs like Oxfam and Save the Children to smaller, more radical organisations, like the World Development Movement and Womankind.

Make Poverty History and ONE also used similar strategies to create a sense of global solidarity through symbolic politics. The best example of this was the white wristbands sold to supporters with 'Make Poverty History' or 'ONE' written on them. Wearing these bands was itself a kind of demonstration of global solidarity, of being part of a movement that encircled the globe. In the UK they were ubiquitous in 2005; on everyone's wrists, from those of schoolchildren and celebrities to that of the Prime Minister (in fact, they become so highly sought after that enterprising individuals sold them on eBay at a profit). The symbol of the white band was intended by campaign leaders to become absolutely synonymous with ending global poverty. At the G8 meeting in Edinburgh, marching demonstrators in white t-shirts encircled the centre of the city. Linking individuals wearing a white band across the world, the image of the white band was projected onto the UN General Assembly building in New York at the time of the summit meeting on the Millennium Development Goals on 15 September (www.one.org/node/68, last accessed 28 June 2007). Various other symbolic buildings have been 'wrapped' in the band at different times, including the European Commission building in Brussels. GCAAP plans a continuing programme of White Band Days across the world to keep building the solidarity generated by these campaigns (www.whiteband.org, last accessed 28 June 2007).

Another example of the attempt to build global solidarity symbolically came from Nelson Mandela's speech in Trafalgar Square in February 2005, which was broadcast around the world. In this case, the construction of solidarity was premised on the overcoming of previous injustices, agreed by the world to be insupportable, and the will to overcome the current scandal of global poverty. Introduced by Bob Geldof, the figurehead of the campaign in the UK, as 'President of the World', Mandela exhorted his audience to 'Make Poverty History' declaring that:

> [A]s long as poverty, injustice and gross inequality persist in our world, none of us can truly rest . . . The Global Call for Action Against Poverty can take its place as a public movement alongside

the movement to abolish slavery and the international solidarity against apartheid.

(www.makepovertyhistory.org/docs/mandelaspeech.doc, last accessed 28 June 2007)

Mandela's rhetoric here echoes that of activists working to mobilise supporters of human rights around the Pinochet and ATCA cases. Mandela too is making a performative declaration: mobilising support for the campaign to end global poverty as if worldwide awareness of movements to end injustice has *already* created global solidarity. In Mandela's speech, 'we' are attributed emotions that suggest that 'we' are already involved in the struggle against economic injustice in the under-development of the South. It is not that (as in charitable appeals) 'we' are to feel (or at least not predominantly) compassion. Compassion was an important sub-theme of the campaign, but in general the strategy was much closer to that outlined by Luc Boltanski in *Distant Suffering*: the denunciation of systematic injustice, for which the appropriate emotion is indignation and the desire to bring about change (Boltanski 1999). As Mandela put it, in phrases which were continually repeated throughout the campaign by activists and politicians in the UK:

> Sometimes it falls upon a generation to be great. You can be that generation. Let your greatness blossom . . . Make Poverty History in 2005. Make History in 2005. Then we can all stand with our heads high.
>
> *(www.makepovertyhistory.org/docs/mandelaspeech.doc, last accessed 28 June 2007)*

Make Poverty History was a good deal more successful in the UK in terms of generating interest and popular support than was ONE in the US. From the very beginning of 2005, progressive newspapers in the UK were themselves pledging to engage in the campaign to end poverty ('Africa: a Year for Change', *Guardian*, 1 January 2005; 'White Band Aid: Historic Chance to End Poverty', *Mirror*, 2 February

2005). (In the event, the *Guardian* left overt campaigning to its sister paper, the *Observer* while it ran more analytic, though still supportive, articles throughout the year; presumably advocating direct participation in the campaign was seen as more suitable for a Sunday paper.) As the campaign built towards Live8 these papers went further than just writing editorials in favour of Make Poverty History, urging readers to send emails and letters to politicians, and to join in the demonstrations at the G8 (see, for example, 'Let's Band Together and Make Poverty History', *Mirror*, 22 April 2005; 'Countdown to G8', *Observer*, 15 May 2005). The conservative press was also involved from the beginning, with the *Daily Telegraph* running 'Demand a Better Deal for the Poor' by Bill Gates and Bono on 3 January 2005, and the normally very sober *Financial Times* proposing a virtual demonstration at the G8 to encourage people to get involved ('A Bank of Ideas to End Inertia in the High Street', 3 May 2005). There were a number of articles critical of the campaign in those papers not actively involved in it. But even these tended to be balanced with op-eds admiring the sincerity of Make Poverty History's celebrity leaders and young supporters. 2005 was a General Election year in the UK and all three major parties pledged to work to end global poverty as a plank of their election campaigns. With no party political capital to be made by standing against it, by the time of Live8 even the *Daily Mail*, hitherto the paper which had been most critical of Make Poverty History, ran an editorial in support of the campaign: 'Live8 may not have all the right answers, but it is asking the right question. In all humanity, we can not ignore it' ('A Message that can't be Ignored', 2 July 2005).

In comparison, support for the campaign was far less prominent in US newspapers, where the campaign was not taken up as a set of concrete demands that should be achieved as a priority throughout the year. In part this is surely due to the different nature of newspapers in the US. *USA Today*, which is relatively populist by US standards, came closest to offering the kind of affirmation of the campaign that it received in the UK, mixing coverage of celebrity endorsement of its message with support for the aims of the campaign (e.g. 'Star Studded One Makes Case for Aid', 7 April 2005; 'After Failures, Backers of Africa Aid Change their Tune', 6 July 2005). The *New York Times* and the *Washington Post* strongly supported debt cancellation and increasing aid in editorials (*New York Times*: 'The Price of Gold', 3 June 2005; 'Crumbs for Africa', 8 June 2005; *Washington Post*: 'Mr Bush and Africa', 7 June 2005). In the populist local New York papers it was covered in the *New York Daily News* with critical distance and in the *New York Post* with overt hostility. A further explanation of the lack of sustained interest in the campaign in the US is that it tended to be seen as British-led, with Live8 also understood as peculiarly British (see 'Musically Saving the World: the dos and don'ts', *New York Times*, 9 June 2005). Indeed, in an interview in the *Washington Post* at the beginning of the campaign, Bob Geldof discussed the lack of brand impact of Live Aid (his previous venture into using celebrities and music to deal with poverty in Africa, in 1985) in the US, suggesting that the campaign would in part be about bringing issues to the awareness of American audiences through the US media ('Live 8 Concerts to Amplify Problem of Global Poverty', *Washington Post*, 1 June 2005). In the end Live8 was quite widely covered in the US, but the campaign was not supported in the US newspapers sampled to anything like the degree of its astonishing popularity in the UK.

US coverage of ONE was clearly not all the organisers had hoped for, then; especially in comparison with Make Poverty History in the UK, which surely exceeded all hopes in terms of the media coverage it received. From the point of view of strategy, however, both Make Poverty History and ONE, as branches of GCAAP, were astonishingly creative and novel campaigns, aiming to displace the taken-for-granted emphasis on 'national interests' in international politics to make genuinely global public policy for the benefit of people structurally disadvantaged by neo-liberal 'business as usual'. In this respect the campaigns aimed to realise a more just form of global governance in terms of the uneven realisation of social and economic rights.

RIGHTS AGAINST POVERTY

Social and economic rights have been part of the core schedule of international human rights since 1948. In Article 22 of the UDHR, it is stated that everyone is entitled to realisation 'through national effort and international co-operation' of his economic, social and cultural rights. In addition, and some would argue more fundamentally, in Article 25 it is stated that 'Everyone has the right to a standard of living adequate for the health and well-being of himself (sic) and of his family, including food, clothing, housing and medical care and necessary social services, and the right to security in the event of unemployment, sickness, disability, widowhood, old age, or other lack of livelihood in circumstances beyond his control' (Donnelly 1989: 38–41). Nevertheless, a clear distinction was drawn between social and economic rights and civil and political rights from the very beginning of the post-Second World War human rights regime, with socialists and liberals opposed during the Cold War over which set of rights should be ideologically and strategically prioritised (Forsythe 2000).

The contemporary controversy over whether civil and political rights are different in kind from social and economic rights is constitutive of the human rights field itself. Are human rights only and always legal rights? Or do they involve something more, or different from legal rights? Is the legalisation of human rights fundamental to their very nature? If human rights can not be legalised, does this mean that they are not really rights at all? The opposition is primarily between supporters and enemies of social and economic rights. However, supporters of social and economic rights are themselves divided over the relative advantages and disadvantages of conceiving of social and economic rights as either legal or political.

On one hand, in the UN, economic and social rights are understood as international law. In 2000, for example, the UN Development Programme's 'Human Development Report' stressed a human rights approach to development and poverty on the basis that human rights represent accepted international standards, and that they place concrete claims on individuals and institutions to fulfil their requirements (quoted in St Clair 2006). This understanding of social and economic rights draws on both customary international law and treaty law. It is, however, for the most part, 'soft law'; it is not intended to be adjudicated in court, but rather to influence policy-makers *as if* social and economic rights were law (Forsythe 2000: 12). The fact that international declarations and agreements on human rights have contained provisions for economic and social rights from the very beginning of the UN human rights system is used to argue that they should be treated as customary international law by international institutions and by national states.

On the other hand, there are those who doubt that such entitlements are logically possible. While states accept obligations by ratifying the ICESCR, for example, it is unclear what that might really mean for the hungry or homeless, especially when a state does not have resources to meet basic needs. Is it possible to address social and economic claims to duty-bearers who have clear, detailed obligations to respect and realise them as a matter of universal entitlement? Economic and social rights are often compared to civil rights in this respect: while civil rights also require state structures and resources, they enable the clear identification of specific obligations on the part of specific agents to *stop* acting in certain ways (Donnelly 1989: 33–4). It is argued by their detractors, therefore, that using a vocabulary of economic and social rights is no more than socialist political rhetoric masquerading as law. This argument has become somewhat less compelling since social and economic rights were made justiciable in the South African constitution, and the South African state has been called to account in its national courts for violations of the social and economic rights of people under its jurisdiction. In landmark cases, the Constitutional Court of South Africa has required the South African state to demonstrate that it is committing a reasonable level of resources to housing and health care (Sunstein 2004; Olivier and Jansen van Rensburg 2006). This indicates that social and economic rights are not *necessarily* different in logic to civil and political rights; they *can* be made into specific entitlements to concrete resources that are binding on states.

However, even if it is not logically impossible, there are no intermestic social and economic human rights of the kind we have explored in previous chapters in either the US or the UK. Even though the UK has ratified the ICESCR, its enforcement is confined to monitoring procedures in the UN. Social and economic rights are not embedded in the European system of human rights. Nor are there any mechanisms to bring cases of economic and social rights to domestic courts in European states. The European Social Charter, signed by a number of the member states of the Council of Europe, including the UK, is enforced only by the submission of periodic reports to the European Committee on Social Rights. It is not possible to use 'hard' law to bring claims for social and economic rights to court in the UK, nor in the US which has consistently refused to ratify the ICESCR at all, even though it was originally influenced by US conceptions of social justice (Sunstein 2004).

Alternatively, supporters as well as opponents of social and economic rights argue that they are better seen as *political* rather than legal. Abdullah An-Na'im, for example, argues that respect for human rights in the postcolonial states of Africa depends on the 'international community' for a radical re-structuring of international economic institutions (An-Na'im 2002). He focuses on structural obligations on the part of Northern states to provide assistance and co-operation, as stated in the ICESCR, to increase resources available to Southern states to meet the needs of their peoples. Similarly, Amartya Sen argues from his capabilities approach that whilst human rights may or may not be legislated for, they cannot be reduced to law. If human rights are understood in terms of actual capabilities rather than as formal or nominal entitlements, and if they are morally valuable, then the real conditions for the enjoyment of human rights must be created and sustained (Sen 1999, 2007). Creating legal entitlements that can be pressed in courts could only ever be *part* of a strategy for realising social and economic rights, since what is far more important is to ensure that states have the capacities and are directed by the political will to meet the demands placed upon them. The restructuring of international economic institutions is, therefore, a crucial step towards the realisation of universal entitlements to the basic means of life for all human beings.

At the UN Conference in Vienna on human rights in 1993, shortly after the end of the Cold War, it was reaffirmed that:

> All human rights are universal, indivisible and interdependent and interrelated. The international community must treat human rights globally in a fair and equal manner, on the same footing, and with the same emphasis. While the significance of national and regional particularities and various historical, cultural and religious backgrounds must be borne in mind, it is the duty of States, regardless of their political, economic and cultural systems, to promote and protect all human rights and fundamental freedoms.
>
> *(www.unhcr.bg/cis/n24.pdf, last accessed 29 December 2007)*

Whether social and economic rights are thought of as legal or political, there is no doubt that they are taken very seriously by the UN as indicating that states have obligations to do everything possible to end poverty – not just for their own citizens, but for those in other states. In addition, social and economic rights are increasingly the focus of human rights NGOs which have traditionally focussed on civil and political rights, especially Amnesty International and Human Rights Watch, as well as of specialist organisations set up to promote adherence to social and economic rights, such as the Center for Social and Economic Rights in New York.

In this context it was surprising to discover that Make Poverty History and ONE did not use a vocabulary of social and economic rights at all. It is still more surprising as the vocabulary of human rights had been used quite effectively in an earlier worldwide movement to address global poverty, the 'Drop the Debt' movement which also had local branches in Jubilee 2000 UK and Jubilee USA as well as elsewhere. This campaign amassed a great deal of support across the world for demands that the debt owed to wealthy states by poor nations should be cancelled entirely in 2000. 'Drop the Debt' used Christian language and mobilised primarily through networks of religious worshippers. The reference to 'Jubilee' comes from the Biblical injunction to treat each fifty years as 'the Sabbath's Sabbath', and as an occasion on which to free slaves and cancel obligations to repay debts. But in the UK 'Drop the Debt' also used a vocabulary of human rights to stress that cancelling debt was a matter of redressing historical injustice: people in indebted states are locked into paying back 'odious debt' from which they have not benefited, offered by Western banks at outrageous terms, often to leaders known to be corrupt. Attention to the *entitlements* of the poorest should result in sustained attention to how wealth is generated and distributed *within*, as well as *between* states. For example, Ann Pettifor, Director of Jubilee 2000, speaking at a United Nations Development Programme Forum in 2000 noted that:

> It has been the absence of the human rights 'scaffolding' that has resulted in the construction of 'cowboy' development policies that have proved to be both so flawed and exploitative of people in the poorest nations.
>
> *(Pettifor 2001)*[3]

ONE and Make Poverty History did not use the vocabulary of human rights at all. The only reference to social and economic rights I found throughout either campaign was to Bono's use of the UDHR as a backdrop for two songs in the opening concert of his world tour in San Diego ('How to Detonate a World Tour', *Daily Telegraph*,

---

[3] 'Drop the Debt' had an important impact: changing the argument from *whether* debt should be written off to *when* and *how*, and achieving pledges from world leaders – still so far unfulfilled – for 100 per cent cancellation (Buxton 2004). Unjust debt was also made an issue of social and economic rights at the UN level on the basis that it directly contravenes basic social and economic rights where repayment is made possible only by reducing state provision of essentials like water, food, health care and education (Millet and Toussaint 2004: 124–5).

31 March 2005). In his speech, Nelson Mandela did talk about global poverty as involving 'crimes against humanity'. This is a very interesting example of how legal categories circulate in popular culture, aquiring meanings that may be at odds with how they are used in courts. Describing global poverty as the result of 'crimes against humanity' is to strongly underline that it can be prevented and that not to do so is morally wrong; the description has no direct relevance, however, to how the international law of social and economic human rights is actually developing. There was no attempt at all elsewhere in the campaign, either in the US or the UK, to connect the aims of the campaign – to cancel debt, to increase aid and to restructure trade – to universal social and economic entitlements.

JUSTICE OR CHARITY

The aim of the Global Call to Action against Poverty was justice not charity. It appears, so far, to have resulted in neither justice nor a great deal of charity: whilst a little more money has been found by G8 states for developing countries, nothing at all has been done to restructure economic policies that produce the gross inequalities and suffering at which the campaign continues to aim (see World Development Movement 2006). Even Bob Geldof, slated by NGOs for acclaiming Make Poverty History as a success after the G8 summit in 2005, has since been publicly critical of the outcome (see www. live8live.com/datareport, last accessed 29 December 2007).

In terms of building proto-global solidarity, it is obviously harder to assess the success of Make Poverty History and ONE. However, it seems that the danger of narcissistic sentimentalism, which Boltanski warns is ever-present in the cultural politics of moral condemnation, was not avoided (Boltanski 1999). The creation of feeling for the suffering of distant people, which can generate a collective understanding of moral obligation to act to relieve that suffering, always risks degenerating into an emotionally indulgent admiration of one's own sensitivity, sincerity and strength of will. Make Poverty History and ONE undoubtedly achieved the expression of public sympathy for the suffering of people in far away countries. It also achieved, to a limited degree, a sense of collective responsibility. However, this fell well short of proto-global solidarity as a sense of mutual commitment and reciprocity oriented towards global justice. What it formed rather was a sense of collective responsibility that empowers and validates 'us': it is up to 'us' to do something for 'them'.

In part, the failure to build solidarity is linked, rather paradoxically, with the campaigns' strength in generating feelings of involvement amongst people in the North. The strategy of both Make Poverty History and ONE was very explicitly to elicit pride and joy, feelings of empowerment, rather than feelings of shame and guilt. As Stan Cohen has shown, the way in which NGOs elicit shame and guilt is often counterproductive: horrific and disturbing accounts produce denial; we'd rather 'not know what we know' (Cohen 2001). In contrast to those Cohen analysed, these campaigns continually emphasised pride: *you* are the one who can make a difference, as a member of a generation that is unique in history. As in the Nelson Mandela speech quoted above, there was a continual and extraordinarily un-ironic re-stating of the uncontested fact that *you* can change the world.[4] Such a strategy is surely effective – it certainly proved to be so in the UK – at mobilising support for short-term action, where the action to be taken is quite clear (wear wristbands, demonstrate, email leaders and so on). A strategy of individual emotional empowerment and pride seems less likely, however, to contribute to long-term reflection and analysis of how 'we' are bound into conditions from which some benefit more than others.

---

[4] This sentence from the *Mirror*, entreating people to buy a white wristband, symbol of the campaign, well exemplifies the theme: 'Join the celebrities by wearing a white band and help end poverty for ever . . . By wearing a white band, you can be part of the biggest anti-poverty drive, joining forces with 150 million people in 60 countries' ('White Band Aid', 5 February 2005) Again, from the *Observer*, 'In the next 50 days, you can change the world for good' ('Countdown to G8', 15 May 2005). And, from the Make Poverty History website, 'you can be part of it' (www.makepovertyhistory.org, 31 May 2005, last accessed 31 June 2006).

As well as individual pride and joy, eliciting national pride was also a prominent feature of both campaigns. Both in the US and the UK, as an individual 'you' were empowered, according to populist representations, as a member of a powerful and morally righteous nation that has the means, the goodwill and – if 'you' make it happen – the political will to establish global justice. Although Make Poverty History and ONE did not justify global social justice using human rights, they did construct a version of cosmopolitan nationalism. Ending global poverty was self-evidently justified in these campaigns because – for the first time in history – it is really possible, if we make it happen. Identifying with the cosmopolitan nation, 'we' take pride in our state and our nation because it is exercising moral leadership of the world and can, therefore, really end the obscenity of global poverty in an age where it is no longer necessary.

In the UK cosmopolitan nationalism was particularly evident in the speeches of politicians in the Labour government, especially Tony Blair and Gordon Brown. To the consternation of many of the NGOs involved in Make Poverty History, who were often at odds with the government's policies, especially on trade justice issues, the Prime Minister Tony Blair and the Chancellor of the Exchequer Gordon Brown managed to position themselves as the leaders of the campaign and were widely supported as such in the UK media.[5] British politicians certainly did call for global solidarity, and to some extent the Labour government was leading the initiatives at the G8 summit. For example, Gordon Brown proposed a Marshall Plan for Africa, using the response to the tsunami to show how global solidarity is *already* experienced:

> [D]oes not the response to the massive tidal wave in southeast Asia show just how closely and irrevocably bound together today

---

[5] Blair and Brown were so successful at taking over the campaign in the UK that many critics derided Make Poverty History as a PR exercise for the government. See Ann Talbot 'Live 8: Who Organised the PR Campaign for Blair and Bush', www.wsws.org, 11 July 2005; also Stuart Hodgkinson 'G8? Africa Nil', *Red Pepper*, November 2005).

and in our generation are the fortunes of the richest persons in the richest country to the fate of the poorest persons in the poorest country of the world, even when they are strangers and have never met.

(quoted in 'Business: a Moral Crusade – or War of Attrition?',
Observer, *9 January 2005)*

At the same time, however, British politicians also implied that the fact that Britain had the Presidency of the G8 in 2005 meant that the UK was literally leading the world in ending poverty. In fact, there were quite legitimate disagreements over how to cancel debt relief between British and, for example, Scandinavian leaders (who have traditionally taken the lead in the world on financial contributions to development); Britain has been one of the least generous countries with regard to aid, falling far short of its stated objectives; the UK is in a dominant position within the structures of global economic governance, with special voting rights in the IMF and the World Bank, membership of the G8 and so on, and yet trade justice is very rarely addressed in these institutions. In the terms of cosmopolitan nationalism, however, Britain's relative power in this respect is constructed as a matter of national pride rather than of shame; Britain is enhanced by its powerful position, its generosity and its moral righteousness: part of the solution, not part of the problem.

In the US, cosmopolitan nationalism was constructed very self-consciously by the leaders of ONE. Bono, who was behind the campaign in the US, was very clear that he aimed explicitly to appeal to national pride in US leadership of the world. He told *Time* magazine that he was advised not to appeal to the conscience of America, but to America's *greatness* ('Pooh Bahs of Poverty', 27 June 2005). Referring to America as, 'not just a country, but also an idea', that people who want to be free and equal should be 'embraced' ('10 Questions for Bono', *New York Times*, 21 September 2005), he drew on deep-rooted understandings of America as an exemplary nation for the world (see Lieven 2004). The ONE Declaration stated that 'We believe that in the best American tradition of helping others to help themselves, now is the time to join with other countries in a historic pact for compassion and justice to help the poorest people of the world overcome AIDs and extreme poverty' (www.one.org, last accessed 5 December 2005). ONE's slogan, which appeared frequently in their press releases, was: 'ONE is a new effort by Americans to rally Americans, ONE by ONE, to fight AIDs and extreme poverty'.

In the support they offered for the aims of the campaign to Make Poverty History (though they never explicitly named it as such), editorials and articles in liberal US papers also played on American national pride. In contrast to the official campaign, however, they mobilised shame: US political leaders should be *ashamed* not to be taking the lead in ending global poverty. The *New York Times*, for example, suggested that the President was behaving in a way that was positively un-American by withholding aid for Africa: 'The American people have a great heart. President Bush needs to stop concealing it' ('Crumbs for Africa', 8 June 2005).

In cosmopolitan nationalism, 'you', the empowered individual, are joined with others to create 'we', the powerful and proud cosmopolitan nation. 'We' are empowered because we are a cosmopolitan nation. Cosmopolitan nationalism is a form of narcissistic sentimentalism because it is largely concerned with how well one's feelings, and even one's actions, reflect on one's own self. In this case, it is one's self as a member of a nation to be proud of because of its moral leadership in the world. A good illustration of narcissistic sentimentalism in the context of the Make Poverty History campaign for global justice is this quote from a Scottish student responding to John Kamau, a Nairobi journalist in Edinburgh for the G8 summit, who asked him whether he should be hopeful about the outcome: 'This is not only about you, it is about our humanity' ('Trading Places', *Guardian*, 4 July 2005). Making global poverty history is primarily about how 'we' feel about the way in which we express our global leadership to benefit 'you', African nationals. Obviously such a stance, whilst possibly displaying a strong (if perhaps fleeting) sense of responsibility for the world, at the same time also displays a self-love that hardly reaches for global solidarity.

Make Poverty History and ONE aimed to build global solidarity in order to realise very specific goals: to increase aid, abolish unjust debt and liberalise trade. Although the goals were not actually realised, it may be that the emotional tone of the campaign was highly suitable for a short, sharp campaign that aimed to galvanise popular public support for those goals. It does also seem to have contributed to feelings that 'we' are part of a wider, interdependent humanity. However, *feelings* that humanity is interdependent are clearly not enough. A longer-term project of building global solidarity would surely also require *understanding* of how social relationships of interdependence amongst us are lived differently and what that means for 'us' as a global community. Global solidarity requires dialogue and in-depth analysis, neither of which is facilitated by narcissistic sentimentalism.

There was a lack of dialogue between Africans and the white Western organisers of Make Poverty History and ONE in the mediated publics of the UK and US (see, for example, 'African British Perspective on the Politics of Live8, G8 and the UK Media', Pambazuka News, 20 October 2005, www.pambazuka.org, last accessed 26 June 2007). Despite the slogan 'justice not charity' Africans were represented in very conventional ways as helpless victims of the calamities of their continent (Stevenson 1999, 2007). To some extent lack of dialogue is the inevitable consequence of existing media structures. Genuine dialogue across continents would surely require a popular transnational media, without which such alternative voices as are allowed to speak in the mediated public are bound to be structured by editorial decisions to fit dominant national narratives. There is generally a dominance of white elite perspectives in the mediated publics of the UK and US. In addition, the absence of African voices in this campaign was in part a consequence of its uncritical, celebratory tone in the UK, which meant that there was very little scope for critical perspectives at all. Those Africans who were permitted to contribute in the UK mediated public were either leaders of countries allied with the government, or poor villagers who were grateful recipients of the help promised by the campaign. In the US, newspapers' greater commitment to balancing points of view to achieve 'objectivity' might have been expected to create more space for African contributions to the debate. However, I found only one article which covered a range of African perspectives in the US papers ('Among Ordinary Africans, G8 Seems Out of Touch', *Washington Post*, 3 March 2005).

Perhaps even more importantly, however, the campaign's emotional tone of celebration did not facilitate in-depth analysis of the different socio-economic positions occupied in structures of global poverty. Whilst there was a surprising willingness in the UK media to 'educate' the public into some of the technical details of the campaign's demands, evident even in the tabloids, what was significantly lacking was analysis of the structures of global inequality and the way in which they are premised on, and at the same time produce, economic conflict. Make Poverty History and ONE mobilised support for policies *beyond* national interests, but the difficulties of *conflicts* of interests between rich Northerners and poor Southerners was not addressed. Cancelling debt and increasing aid cost very little in proportion to national income in the North. Media coverage focussed *overwhelmingly* on these two demands. Trade justice, on the other hand, would require the end of protectionism in Northern economies and the protection of developing ones to enable them to grow, and this would undoubtedly increase prices and threaten jobs in the North. There was very little consideration of what this would mean in practice, how it might be achieved, or what the effects of such a restructuring might be on workers in the North, either in the UK or the US. Above all, there was certainly no sustained discussion in the mediated public over politicians' responsibilities to citizens as compared to non-citizens where there is a *conflict* of interests between them. There was, therefore, no construction of a consensus on how rights and responsibilities should be balanced and distributed when it came to making policies on global poverty. And without sure knowledge of such a consensus, which 'world leader' could be expected to put the interests of non-citizens above those of citizens in drawing up or putting into practice such policies? It is in this context that George Bush's announcement on arriving at the G8 summit that, 'I come with an agenda that I think is best for our country' (interview with Trevor McDonald on *Tonight*, ITV, 3 July 2005, www.guardian.co.uk/g8/story/0,13365,1521149,00. html, last accessed 29 December 2007) makes perfect political sense.

CAMPAIGNING FOR SOCIAL AND ECONOMIC RIGHTS

The bold and original attempt to build global solidarity from the 'bottom up' in order to achieve specific goals represented by the Global Call for Action Against Poverty was unsuccessful then, in the case of Make Poverty History and ONE. Would it have been more successful if proposals for structural changes in global governance had been justified in the vocabulary of universal social and economic rights?

It was clearly necessary for GCAAP to challenge (inter) nationalism. In Chapter 4, we saw how (inter)nationalism attempts to re-fix the parameters of the national state which are challenged by structures of global governance – especially by 'intermestic' human rights. Building global solidarity from below in order to challenge international structures of inequality necessarily challenges (inter) nationalism because it involves putting pressure on politicians and civil servants of Northern states to *systematically*, not just occasionally, put national interests to one side in their political negotiations in international governmental organisations for the benefit of those people who happen to live in less powerful, subordinate states.

Claiming universal social and economic rights for all individuals as global citizens, regardless of nationality, is one way to challenge (inter)nationalism. As we saw in Chapter 4, activists imagined the community of global citizens *as if* cosmopolitan law already existed. Arguments for universal social and economic rights on behalf of global citizens might have been possible in the Global Call for Action Against Poverty campaigns in the US and UK. Although, as we have seen, the international law supporting social and economic rights established in the UN system is 'soft' rather than 'hard', this only prevents cases being brought to court; it does not mean that a rhetoric of human rights could not have been used in the mediated public. Indeed, in the UK at least, the relatively successful 'Drop the Debt' campaign had already used a vocabulary of human rights to make the argument that debt cancellation was a matter of justice, not charity. Make Poverty History and ONE did appeal to some kind of an understanding of global citizenship, the idea of the world as a single place occupied by a single global community of individuals with responsibilities towards each other as human beings. The symbol of the white wristband and the rhetoric of Nelson Mandela's speech were performative declarations of global solidarity in order to bring it into being (see Nash 2008). However, for the most part, both Make Poverty History and ONE imagined cosmopolitan nationalism rather than global citizenship.

One reason for this is surely the structure of the human rights field itself. As we saw in Chapter 4, it was mostly activists and innovative lawyers who imagined a community of global citizens possessing rights and obligations in cosmopolitan law. In the absence of 'hard' law through which cases of social and economic rights can be brought into domestic courts, it is governments who are the direct target of campaigns against global poverty. But politicians are elected to represent the interests of 'the people' within national states. This campaign relied much more directly on the mediated public than the civil rights cases studied in previous chapters. From newspapers to national public broadcasting systems, the media has long been closely tied to the imagining of the national political community (Anderson 1991; Billig 1995).

The mobilisation of sentiments of cosmopolitan nationalism is intended to shift the definition of 'national interest' in a more altruistic direction. Cosmopolitan nationalism can be articulated around the passionate support of human rights. As we saw in the Pinochet case, where human rights are invoked in cosmopolitan nationalism it is in the name of a powerful and morally righteous nation that acts *on behalf* of victims of human rights abuses. Whereas activists imagine a global community made up of a universal 'we' of individuals who are global citizens, the leaders of populist campaigns conducted in the name of the cosmopolitan nation are far more likely to link, and therefore to distinguish and to separate, 'we' who are actively engaged in the struggle for human rights, and 'they' who are the beneficiaries of our action. 'We' may be prepared to give up our national interest in order to help 'them'; or 'we' may re-interpret our national interests as compatible with helping 'them'. In either case the world continues to be divided along national lines, with some nations more outward looking and willing to take on global leadership than others.

Is cosmopolitan nationalism necessarily articulated, then, around benevolence, around charity, not justice? This quote from Bob Geldof exemplifies the construction of 'we' and 'they' which was prominent throughout both Make Poverty History and ONE:

> It is tempting hubris to say it is actually a Marshall Plan but it is similar to what Marshall asked in 1945. He said 'We are going to give you the money; but you have got to have democracy, and we are giving it for real and we are doing it partly for our national economic and national security, plus we can not tolerate you in poverty'.
>
> ('We've Got the Script, Now Let's Make the Film',
> Guardian, 12 March 2005)

And from Tony Blair (with a similar inflection in terms of combining morality and enlightened self-interest):

> The lesson of the past few years is that we can't, for our national interests, ignore other countries and continents. Famine and instability thousands of miles away lead to conflict, despair, mass

migration and fanaticism that can affect us all. So for reasons of self-interest as well as morality, we can no longer turn our back on Africa.

('I Believe this is African's Best Chance for a Generation',
Guardian, 12 March 2005).

In fact, as these quotes indicate, there is a rough and ready idea of reciprocity at work here. To return to the comparison between global redistribution and redistribution within welfare states, it is as if nations here are counted as individuals. Where individuals contributed to and received from common goods and services in welfare states, here it is nations that both contribute and receive. This is not a straightforward appeal to charity: 'we who are morally superior and powerful do this for them'. There is also an appeal to enlightened self-interest here that makes co-operation 'fair': 'in exchange they will reform their societies in such a way as to increase global security for the good of all'. This version of reciprocity is, however, an attenuated form of justice compared to the far greater egalitarianism envisaged by national welfare states, and by the imagined global community of human rights activists. It does not create concrete obligations on the part of individuals, nor enable the recognition of individual entitlements, nor contribute to the de-legitimation of the structures of production and distribution that create and sustain violations of social and economic human rights.

Given the difficulties of using human rights to end global poverty in formal procedures of the internationalising state, what conclusions can we draw about what difference human rights *rhetoric* might have made to the Global Call to Action Against Poverty in the US and UK? In fact, as we saw in Chapter 4, human rights claims can be mobilised in discourses of cosmopolitan nationalism; they do not necessarily give rise to an imagined community of global citizens in which each individual has equal entitlements and obligations. There is no reason to suppose, then, that human rights would not equally have been mobilised in the populist imagined community of cosmopolitan nationalism that was the primary orientation of ONE and Make Poverty History.

'Thicker' solidarity requires more than feelings of benevolence towards people suffering disadvantage. It also requires more than a rough and ready model of reciprocity between nations which largely leaves structures that maintain that disadvantage untouched. It requires understanding and acceptance of social relationships across differences which implicate each and every individual in that disadvantage; the shared appreciation of material risks and benefits that are unevenly distributed and yet experienced as of common concern. 'Thinner' global solidarity may now exist. There are mediated experiences that are shared across the world. These largely concern 'aesthetic cosmopolitanism': world music, literature and cinema (Kurasawa 2007). There are also political images that circulate globally: the Berlin Wall being torn down by jubilant crowds, Nelson Mandela walking out of Robben Island, the jet plunging into the Twin Towers. But, of course, such events are seen and discussed, and move people, in quite different ways in different contexts.

What we learn above all from Make Poverty History and ONE as attempts to build global solidarity from below is that a cosmopolitan project that interprets events and images to build global solidarity is in fierce competition with nationalist framings of those same events. These campaigns did begin to challenge the ill-effects of conceiving national interests in excessively narrow economic terms. They did introduce a rough and ready understanding of reciprocity: serious inequalities in global wealth threaten security and well-being in the North now as well as in the South. It is not obvious that use of a rhetoric of human rights would have contributed anything significantly different to the success of GCAAP in the US and UK. Given how universal human rights themselves can become incorporated into cosmopolitan nationalism, it is difficult to conclude with any certainty that a campaign that adopted justifications for action to end global poverty based on human rights would have fared any better, either in achieving the specific goals of the campaign, or in building popular global solidarity from below. The conclusion seems to be that nationalism can retain its dominance, and at the same time renew its vitality, by incorporating the attractions of cosmopolitanism in a globalising world.

6   Conclusion

Can human rights become a framework for global justice? It is only through cultural politics that human rights might become more than abstract moral ideals, that they might be institutionalised in concrete ways to protect human beings from arbitrary detention, torture and disappearance and to advance protection from starvation and the social destruction of poverty.

The cultural politics in which human rights activists are engaged to realise human rights in practice from within states is 'cosmopolitanism-from-below'. While 'cosmopolitanism-from-above' concerns above all the design and construction of institutions of global governance by elites, the cultural politics of the human rights activists I have analysed in these pages is oriented towards imagining a political community of global citizens from within the state, historically constituted in popular terms as national. 'Cosmopolitanism-from-below' intersects with 'cosmopolitanism-from-above' insofar as activists draw on international human rights norms developed initially in the UN and the Council of Europe to bring cases in domestic courts. However, using intermestic human rights in the national context, they aim to persuade state officials of the government and judiciary, but also, through the mediated public, the ordinary people, the voters and taxpayers in whose name state officials act, to think and act as global citizens with rights and responsibilities towards individual human beings regardless of nationality. In this way, human rights activists use intermestic human rights to reform the state, to transform it from a national state, which is legitimate insofar as it serves its citizens, into a cosmopolitan state, which is only legitimate insofar as it *also* serves human beings, regardless of their citizenship status.

The concept of 'human rights field' has proved invaluable to the study of 'cosmopolitanism-from-below' in relation to competing strategies and definitions of human rights, to explore how different actors involved in human rights are organised around privileged sites of contestation, especially courts and the mediated public, and the kinds of justifications they use in competition over the effective authority to define human rights. It has enabled detailed investigation of the cultural politics of human rights across the distinction between state and civil society – in relation to governmental and legal procedures and also in relation to wider questions of how political community and solidarity beyond the nation must be imagined in these procedures and in the mediated public if human rights are to be realised in practice. Can a general conclusion now be reached on the basis of these analyses?

It is always difficult to interpret a direction of general change out of a small number of detailed case studies. It is all the more difficult where change in one area is implicated in so many others. We appear to be in a transitional period in which social forms are being completely re-shaped in a range of interrelated changes as a result of globalisation. There is no area of social life of which this is truer than the state which, albeit partially and in complex ways, is becoming increasingly extended in networks of global governance that link state functions across borders (Sassen 2006: 403; Slaughter 2007). As their realisation depends on state transformation, this re-shaping is vital to human rights practices. By the same time token, however, especially in the current conditions of expanding neo-liberalism and heightened state security as a result of the global war on terror, the form states take, whether they simply become more oppressive and less responsive to the needs of human beings, or whether there is any hope that they may be restructured around norms of global justice, depends on the cultural politics of human rights.

I have argued throughout this study that the cultural politics of the intermestic human rights field concerns the state, the domains of law and government, *and* the mobilisation of human rights activists and the representation of human rights in the mediated public in civil society. However, in order now to weigh up whether it is possible to identify any progressive trend towards the realisation of the cosmopolitan state in the cultural politics of intermestic human rights, it is useful to separate out assessment of achievements in their institutional–legal realisation from achievements in creating an ethical framework for the understanding of human rights. While the institutional–legal dimension of human rights concerns only the legal and governmental procedures of the state, the ethical framework of human rights concerns an orientation towards globalising human rights in both state procedures and civil society. Ultimately, it is only if we can identify a cosmopolitan ethical framework in the making that we can be optimistic about the long-term prospects of realising cosmopolitan states.

Clearly, as I noted in Chapter 1, and as we have now analysed in some detail, the conditions of cultural politics in terms of the institutional–legal dimensions of human rights are quite different in the US and UK. It is difficult, though as we have seen not impossible, for human rights activists and juridical innovators to bring pressure to bear on state officials using intermestic human rights in the US. In contrast, because of the way in which the UK is embedded in the European human rights system, state officials in the UK are relatively responsive to legal strategies that use intermestic human rights. What is all the more striking, therefore, in the face of differences in the institutional–legal dimension of human rights in these two states, is the similarity between the US and the UK in terms of the success, or rather lack of success, of activists in the human rights field in creating an ethical framework for reform of the state in a cosmopolitan direction.

THE INSTITUTIONAL–LEGAL REALISATION OF HUMAN RIGHTS

Human rights in court

Human rights activists see legalising human rights through courts as vital to their concrete realisation: bringing international human rights norms, which are otherwise unenforceable, into national courts is a way of making law which is routine, technical, and objectively administered. In principle, as international norms of human rights are tested in national courts, judges should confirm the status of international law, making it increasingly precise and increasingly detailed concerning which activities states are legally required to undertake or to give up. Legalising human rights through judges' decisions in national courts is the most significant way in which human rights activists attempt to bring about the cosmopolitan state through cultural politics in the national context. It is, however, a risky strategy.

Human rights activists bring test cases using human rights into courts because it appears to offer the best possible means to realise human rights in practice. However, in a context in which human rights are so contentious, in so doing they contribute directly to the politicisation of law. In one sense law is always political as it is, like any other social institution, the outcome of cultural politics. The codification of law *as* law never simply involves the neutral regulation of social relations objectively administered; as the outcome of cultural political conflict, law is the naturalisation of power relations that made that particular outcome possible. In order to function as such, however, law must be *de-politicised*. To function effectively, law must appear to be nothing but neutral regulation, impartially administered through the proper procedures by designated officials who act independently of any particular interests, beliefs or values outside their professional investments in legal reasoning. Of course, the technical details of the law itself are often in dispute where it is called on to adjudicate conflicts between members of society. Where law is successfully de-politicised, however, no questions are raised concerning whether legal procedures are the appropriate means by which particular conflicts should be regulated. If the law appears to be political, on the other hand, to be inappropriately intervening in areas that are seen as more properly within the domain of other branches of the state, then the status of the law itself may be called into question.

When test cases are brought in national courts to confirm or extend the law in relation to international state obligations, the law is invariably politicised. Conor Gearty argues that this is actually recognised in the legal procedures that are used to adjudicate controversial human rights cases. That the highest courts of appeal in both the US (the Supreme Court) and UK (the Law Lords) are made up of a *number* of judges indicates that what is involved in adjudicating these cases is more than a technical interpretation of the law. Such cases are clearly seen as requiring, as Gearty puts it, 'the wisdom of the crowd' rather than the logic of legal argument. Whilst this is a feature of long-standing in the US Supreme Court, it is relatively recent in the UK. Similarly, in allowing 'friend of the court' briefs, including those submitted by representatives of other branches of the state, courts also indicate that there is more at stake in such cases than technicalities. Gearty argues that judges allow 'friends of the court' briefs from those who are seen to have an interest in the wider repercussions of the case – again a relatively recent innovation in the Law Lords, but long familiar in the US Supreme Court – because they know very well that in such cases they are involved in *law-making* rather than in *truth-finding* (Gearty 2006: 86–91).

The legitimacy of law depends on its appearance as solely reliant on principles of legal reasoning rationally administered according to the fundamental principles of the legal system in question. It is the prestige of law, its legitimacy, as well as the capacity to enforce agreement through the courts, on which activists depend when they bring controversial test cases in order to extend human rights norms as cosmopolitan law. To the extent, however, that law comes to be *seen* as political, rather than as neutrally administered regulation, legitimacy is not gained for human rights and it may, in the long-term, be lost for law itself. If some judges appear to be using law to arbitrate disputes where, as in intermestic human rights cases that draw upon international law, the status of the law *as* law is itself in dispute, especially where there are marked disagreements between senior judges themselves, the result is not necessarily a confirmation of the prestige and authority of human rights. On the contrary, it may result in other political actors, especially governmental officials, treating both the law and international human rights norms with contempt (Gearty 2006: 91).

As we have seen, activists have enjoyed some success in winning intermestic human rights cases in the domestic courts of the US and UK. What is most striking about the cases in which they have been successful, however, is that these cases have involved the affirmation of the relative importance of national over international law. Where human rights are *not* encoded in national law, they prove to be of very little use as a resource for activists in furthering the globalisation of human rights from within domestic courts in the US and the UK. It is as national law that human rights may gain legitimacy in national courts. In the US, in campaigns against the violations of the human rights of prisoners in Guantanamo Bay, activists were not able to make use of well-established international human rights law concerning fundamental civil rights of due process in domestic courts because of the long-standing resistance of US political elites to incorporating it into national law. Instead, activists relied on obscure national law to bring the government to court. In contrast, ATCA cases, although they appear to have had very little support from those in the government, judiciary and the mediated public who did not actively oppose the use of customary international law in US courts, were not so easily dismissed. ATCA is national law; indeed, passed as part of the Judiciary Act of 1789 through which the US federal judiciary was created in the very first US Congress, it is part of the very foundations of the US law as such.

In the UK, although the Executive is constrained by cultural politics that makes use of the European system of human rights, the preference for national law over international law also remains strong. In the Belmarsh case, passionate support for British civil liberties was far more in evidence than for European human rights, and human rights activists and innovators in the judiciary tried to build on that support in court as well as in the mediated public. Even in the Pinochet case, often seen as a turning point for cosmopolitan law because of the way customary international law was drawn upon in the UK's highest court in Pinochet 1 to confirm that torture and murder are crimes that must be tried when, where and by whomever they are committed, the final judicial decision in Pinochet 3 was made using law which had been passed by parliament, the Criminal Justice Act 1988, under which Pinochet's crimes were specified, and the Extradition Act 1870, which limited those crimes for which he might be extradited to torture and conspiracy to torture which were committed after the Criminal Justice Act was passed (Woodhouse 2003: 100). Withdrawal from the resounding commitment to cosmopolitan law in the Pinochet case was undoubtedly the result of reluctance on the part of the judges to make an unequivocal ruling on the issue of universal jurisdiction (Davis 2003: 11). Pinochet 3 was, in other words, a withdrawal from the commitment to restructuring the state along cosmopolitan lines that was endorsed by Pinochet 1.

In terms of the institutional–legal dimension of realising human rights in practice, then, their codification in national law is clearly hugely important. There is no necessary contradiction between national and cosmopolitan law. Legislatures can, and do, pass cosmopolitan law that in significant respects abolishes the distinction between citizens and non-citizens on which national states have historically been founded. As it has been interpreted in courts since 1980 to allow for US judges to decide tort claims in human rights cases when neither party has any connection to the United States, ATCA is cosmopolitan law. Similarly, it was on the basis of the UK's commitments under the ECHR, incorporated into national law in the UK parliament as the Human Rights Act, that the Law Lords found that the detention of non-citizens as terrorist suspects involved illegal discrimination.

As we have seen in all the case studies analysed here, however, judges are almost invariably reluctant to definitively pronounce for cosmopolitan law. In all cases, intermestic human rights cases are hard-fought in the courts at every turn by powerful state actors, and judges are cautious in upholding international human rights norms in the face of strong and vocal domestic political opposition. This means that intermestic human rights cases are highly contested within the judicial system itself, and the law does not appear to be the rational, technical, and therefore predictable process it is supposed to be. In all the legal cases covered here legal judgements were reversed more than once, legal commentators were astonished at decisions – where human rights advocates were successful just as much as when they failed – and, in each case, it appeared that the law in these areas was undeveloped, contentious, possibly even quixotic. We saw, for example, how surprised lawyers were when judges delivered their judgement in Pinochet 1, and how those same judges altered the substance of that decision – whilst leaving it formally intact – in Pinochet 3. We saw too, in *Sosa* v. *Alvarez-Machain*, how the judge, whilst delivering a judgement that confirmed ATCA as a tool for bringing cases against the gross violation of human rights, commented that 'the door was ajar ... subject to vigilant door-keeping', which suggests that the legal struggle *against* such cases is justified and may succeed in the future. The law is hardly de-politicised where there is effectively judicial encouragement to contest it.

Democratic human rights

The relative success of cosmopolitan law passed by Legislatures in the intermestic human rights cases studied here compared to the failure of human rights activists to make international norms effective through the courts where such law was absent, suggests that legislation by elected representatives rather than law-making by judges may ultimately be the only means by which human rights can be secured. It may, therefore, also be the only route by which the national state might practically be transformed into a cosmopolitan state. Most human rights organisations do try to influence government officials as well as judges, by creating reports, lobbying politicians, attempting to represent human rights favourably in the mediated public and so on. Despite these efforts, however, democracy and human rights are still commonly understood as opposed in principle and in practice.

As we have seen in the contestation of intermestic human rights in national courts, one of the principal arguments used against international human rights is that they are undemocratic. Human rights are criticised by the Executive as undemocratic where they appear to require that states simply comply with universal norms that do not take into account current circumstances, or that are not flexible enough to adapt to the demands of 'the people' who have elected government officials to represent their interests and values. Human rights are criticised as undemocratic where international norms appear to give undue power to unelected judges to make important decisions about the parameters of political life, even when it is democratically elected leaders who have signed and ratified international human rights agreements.

Whilst such arguments are clearly politically motivated in intermestic human rights cases in national courts, the suspicion that human right are undemocratic is much more widespread. Democracy and human rights appear, on the face of it, to be concerned with very different aspects of political life. Democracy appears above all to involve institutional arrangements for popular control over decision-making, while human rights concern the protection of scope for individuals to pursue their own goals (Beetham 2000). Moreover, as fundamental moral principles, human rights actually appear to be beyond democratic consent. As Ulrich Beck puts it, the human rights regime is self-legitimating: based not on popular consent but on the exercise of reason, it seems to open up the possibility of a cosmopolitan regime without democracy (Beck 2006: 297; see also Jacobson and Ruffer 2003; Jacobson 2004).

This understanding of human rights as undemocratic is mistaken. Human rights are actually designed *for* democracy: they are generally formulated in quite abstract and general terms, precisely in order to facilitate their adoption through democratic processes. There are very few international human rights that are absolute. Those that are absolute, that are not designed to be adapted to particular circumstances but rather to be respected without question, are supposed to provide the conditions for democracy itself; they are fundamental to any form of democracy as popular rule. In the UDHR, the basis of all international human rights law, there are very few Articles which take the absolute form 'No one shall . . .'. What is absolutely prohibited is enslavement; torture; cruel, inhuman or degrading treatment or punishment; arbitrary arrest, detention or exile; arbitrary interference with privacy. Such rights are the foundation of democratic participation as such; they are fundamental to individuals' capacities to express opinions and organise against the re-election of a government they oppose. In fact, even in the case of these absolute rights there is scope for interpretation: what counts as torture, as arbitrary arrest, as cruel, inhuman or degrading punishment? Although there are strong precedents to establish the limits of interpretation of these norms in international law, their meaning can not ultimately be fixed in abstraction; it must, of necessity, be defined in concrete regulations and practices. All other Articles take the form 'Everyone has the right to . . .', for example, 'life, liberty and security of person' (UDHR, Article 3), 'recognition everywhere as a person before the law' (Article 4), and so on. Human rights specified in this form, which is not that of absolute prohibition, have been developed precisely to enable the tailoring of standards to particular social and political circumstances whilst retaining their core conception of the value of the human person as an individual (Merry 2006: 8).

International human rights are designed to be interpreted and defined in democratic processes precisely in order to safeguard democracy. Indeed, it seems that it is only if human rights are institutionalised through democratic processes that they may become effective. Human rights may become democratically legitimate in the institutional—legal dimension of the state where it is the

Legislature that takes the lead rather than the judiciary in authoritatively defining human rights.

This is not to say that judicial activism with regard to human rights should be seen as undemocratic. On the contrary, judicial review of legislation will surely always be necessary precisely because human rights are so open-ended in permitting broad interpretations of fundamental principles and because Legislatures may be tempted into law-making that is oppressive, whether of minorities or of the majority. In most such cases the judiciary should only have to review legislation, returning it to the Legislature to make new law if it is so deeply flawed as to be clearly unacceptable in a democratic society. In extreme cases, however, the judiciary might even make law to safeguard democracy. Where the Executive is determined to override fundamental individual rights to participate in political life, it may be that judges are the only state officials who may call those violations into question in cosmopolitan law (using customary international law, for example), even where they have been agreed upon by elected representatives.

Safeguarding fundamental civil rights is just as important where it is the rights of non-citizens to participate in democratic politics that is at stake. The question of who can or should have voting rights in a state which is properly democratic and in which both citizens and non-citizens are resident is beyond the scope of this study (see Benhabib 2004; Kostakopoulou 2006). It is clear, however, that at any particular time there will be people, possibly relatively new arrivals, who are resident within the jurisdiction of a particular state in which they have no right to vote. In such cases it is vital that newly arrived non-citizens are able to engage in political activities in order to influence those members of the state who do have more direct influence over the actions of elected representatives and therefore over the conditions of their residence in that state. In addition, as we saw in Chapter 5 especially, there may be those who are affected by public policy instituted by a state who are not, and can not be, resident within its jurisdiction. For a cosmopolitan state to be genuinely capable of making law and public policy in the interests of 'all affected' by particular regulations, it is necessary that citizens and non-citizens alike are able to exercise influence on decisions that directly affect their lives without fear of state repression.

Of course, such a possibility requires a very complex set of conditions which goes far beyond formal civil rights guaranteed in law.[1] We can not address the general conditions that are required for democracy in the cosmopolitan state here. It would surely have to include, for example, at least some kind of representation of the perspectives of non-citizens in the mediated public concerning issues which affect them, both those resident within and outside the territory of the state. The media itself would need to be reformed to make it more ethically responsive to meta-questions of global justice. The media would have to adopt a different orientation from that formed in its historic role as 'the Fourth Estate', watching over and addressing the state on behalf of the people. Such an orientation, while it need not be, and indeed it is not in more liberal sectors of the media, unsympathetic to claims of universal human rights, does tend to privilege the status of citizens. A genuinely popular transnational media would be necessary, in which commonalities and differences were debated from divergent perspectives of citizens and non-citizens alike. The restructuring of media along these lines in terms of both

---

[1] Indeed, as Conor Gearty argues, given that law itself may be oppressive, at odds with the political freedoms necessary to democracy, it is vital to keep open the possibility of civil disobedience in order to change it (Gearty 2007). Gearty is especially sensitive to interpretations of human rights law in the UK which have been and continue to be at odds with civil liberties (for example, the Law Lords' endorsement of the control orders we considered in Chapter 3 as not breaching European human rights, though they may be applied to terrorist suspects without charging and trying them). For this reason he separates human rights as law conceptually from civil liberties which are political. In my view, however, there is nothing in the theory of civil liberties that Gearty proposes which is not also covered by principles of human rights; it is not because human rights law has been interpreted in ways that are oppressive that human rights activists will give up trying to challenge those interpretations. Indeed, it seems odd to give up on the language of human rights to contest oppression when it is precisely for this purposes that it was designed.

production and consumption both seem unlikely, however, without a huge transformation in citizens' conception of themselves as the 'people' in relation to 'the state'. And where is such a transformation to take place except in the popular media?

In order for human rights to be institutionalised in a cosmopolitan state, then, it seems that they must be interpreted and defined for the most part by the Legislature rather than the judiciary. At the moment, however, it is rare that Legislatures make human rights law. As we saw in the cases examined here, even when the judiciary required the Legislature to create law, to balance respect for human rights with concerns for national security in the Guantanamo and Belmarsh cases, although civil rights as the foundation of democratic political life were actually debated both in the UK parliament and the US Congress, the law that emerged did *not* respect fundamental human rights to due process of law. Both the judiciary *and* the Legislature have been reluctant to endorse fundamental rights for all human beings, regardless of nationality, even after they have been violated by the Executive in the 'war on terror', and even after the judiciary has drawn attention to lack of respect for fundamental rights as a problem. The Legislature will inevitably be too timid to pass legislation to ensure that the human rights of noncitizens are respected where politicians fear that supporting human rights will make them unpopular, or at the very least, where they fear it will not win them any votes.

Intermestic human rights in the global war on terror
It is especially likely that both Legislature and the judiciary will be reluctant to endorse the principles of cosmopolitan law in practice in the current climate of fear generated by the 'global war on terror'. Although the very few fundamental human rights that are absolute are designed precisely to constrain the Executive and its military command structure in times of crisis, where the Executive has successfully argued that national security is concerned there is no doubt

that its power relative to the other branches of the state has increased.[2]

The contestation of Executive power in the US and UK was directly implicated in a number of the cases we have examined here in which human rights activists and juridical innovators brought intermestic human rights cases in domestic courts. It was directly contested in challenging the arbitrary detentions of Guantanamo and Belmarsh which were authorised by a sovereign decision that increased Executive power relative to the Legislature and the judiciary. It was indirectly contested in the ATCA cases, in which the US Executive intervened effectively to defend human rights violations of non-citizens, their torture, murder and enslavement, on the grounds that foreign policy, especially at times of heightened risk in the global war against terror, required that such practices should be prudently ignored for the sake of diplomatic relations with other states. Although, as we have noted, 'the global war on terror' has no legal status, it has clearly made a difference, both in the US and the UK, to the cultural political context in which legal judgements are made.

In the US, legal judgements concerning the Executive violation of human rights in the case of Guantanamo, and the indirect support of the Bush Administration for human rights violations in *Sosa* v. *Alvarez-Machain*, were ambiguous at best. Although the over-reach of Executive power demanded by the Bush Administration was not condoned by Supreme Court judges in *Sosa* v. *Alvarez-Machain*, their

---

[2] In her study of state transformation through globalisation, Sassen argues that there is a general trend towards the concentration of power in the Executive as a result of the de-regulation and privatisation of the economy. Globalisation is leading to increased constraints on representative democracy, not because there is a lack of control over forces that impinge upon the state, but because states are both enabling and adapting to globalisation by hollowing out the oversight and law-making functions of the Legislature (Sassen 2006). It is not just in the context of the global war on terror that the Executive gains authority; it is also through neo-liberal economic practices.

decision was not as unequivocal as might have been expected concerning the absolute duty of US courts to uphold core principles of universal human rights. The Supreme Court was clearly reluctant to enact principles of universal jurisdiction, even though the judges had a clear mandate to do so in the venerable domestic law of the Alien Tort Claims Act. The decisions in the numerous cases brought on behalf of the Guantanamo detainees over the six years they have been imprisoned which have reached the Supreme Court have also been equivocal. Although in *Rasul* v. *Bush* there was a clear decision, against the Executive, that the detention centre in Guantanamo Bay was effectively under their jurisdiction and that the prisoners did, therefore, have *habeus corpus* rights in US courts, the judges declined to assert unequivocally that they should, therefore, have full access to US courts. Similarly, in *Hamdan* v. *Rumsfeld*, whilst Supreme Court judges ruled against the Executive that the military tribunals they had set up to try the prisoners satisfied neither US nor international military standards of due process, they did not rule either that the detainees must be granted prisoner of war status, or that they should be brought before US courts.

In neither case did the Supreme Court clearly state what the law required in terms of the treatment of the detainees in Guantanamo Bay. Despite the absolutely fundamental prohibition against arbitrary detention on which the rule of law is premised, whether national or international, the judges effectively passed the decision on to Congress to make legislation that would cover the situation in which these prisoners find themselves. Congress similarly ducked making a clear challenge to the Executive's sovereign decision that the global war on terror required the indefinite detention without charge or trial of terrorist suspects deemed 'unlawful combatants'. The fundamental nature of absolute rights in a democratic polity was debated in Congress, but in making legislation in response to the Court's ruling, the Legislature deferred to the Executive decision by passing the Military Commissions Act 2006 which definitively barred Guantanamo detainees from challenging their detention in US courts.

In the UK the Law Lords have been bolder in challenging the Executive than has the Supreme Court in the US. This is undoubtedly due to the way in which the UK is embedded in the European system of human rights rather than to the wider context of cultural politics concerning the global war on terror. The wider cultural political context is somewhat different in the US and UK: the UK is only an ally of the US in the global war on terror rather than its chief prosecutor; there is a great deal of opposition to it in the mediated public in the UK, and as a consequence politicians very rarely use the term 'global war on terror' as such. However, there are also similarities: there are similar concerns about the security of citizens faced with terrorism in the UK and the US, and very little sympathy in the mediated public for those non-citizens suspected of terrorism who are detained without charge. Nevertheless, in *A and others* v. *Home Secretary*, 2004, the Law Lords found that it was illegal to treat non-citizens differently from citizens by arbitrarily detaining those suspected of terrorism, even when 'normal' law had been suspended by the Executive declaration of a state of national emergency.

The UK parliament was, however, just as deferential to the Executive's sovereign decision to suspend normal law as a response to terrorist threats as was the US Congress. Again, although there was much political rhetoric concerning fundamental rights in a democratic polity when legislation required as a result of the Law Lords' decision was debated, the Prevention of Terrorist Act 2005 adheres to the letter rather than the spirit of the human rights law, and actually allows the extension of Executive power rather than its limitation. In addition, parliamentary debates over this legislation and representations of the issues at stake in the mediated public undoubtedly contributed to growing calls for the reform, even the abolition, of the UK Human Rights Act itself, the very basis of the Law Lords' ruling against the sovereign decision.

HUMAN RIGHTS AS A COSMOPOLITAN ETHICAL FRAMEWORK

In liberal-democratic states human rights will only become important to democratically elected politicians in the Executive and Legislature once they are important to citizen-voters. It is only when people with political rights within the state elect and support government officials who understand states to be accountable to humanity rather than exclusively to citizens that states may gradually be reformed along cosmopolitan lines. In effect, citizens must dissolve the conditions of their own privileged position in relation to national states if cosmopolitan states are to become a reality.

This is not quite as impossible as it sounds if we consider that, in supporting the human rights of non-citizens, a minority of citizens already do encourage the extension of cosmopolitan law. However, as we have seen in the case studies, cosmopolitan understandings of human rights are highly contested in the national contexts of the US and UK. For citizens to dissolve their own privileged status *as* citizens, human rights will have to be contested within a much narrower range of possibilities than at present.

There will be no end to competition over authoritative definitions of human rights as long as they are of any value. We have already noted that in legal terms, the meaning of most human rights is quite open-ended, designed for democratic debate. Even where human rights are absolute, designed to safeguard the conditions of that debate, because they are, like all symbolic communication, the product of ongoing practices of cultural politics, their definition can not finally be fixed. The meaning of human rights is essentially contestable. In addition, the meaning of human rights is also highly contested for empirical reasons: designed to be adaptable to different circumstances, human rights are also supposed to guide actors who occupy objectively powerful positions of authority and who are likely to resist being constrained in unfamiliar ways, especially where they have interests in preferring a course of action that does not respect human rights. Whilst the meaning of human rights can not be finally fixed, however, it is, in principle, possible to establish an ethical framework of relatively stable limits on the *range* within which human rights are contested in cultural politics.

A cosmopolitan ethical framework would limit the contestation of human rights to those meanings which abolish the significance of the moral and legal distinction between citizens and non-citizens, eliminating discrimination in fundamental entitlements that currently exist on the grounds of nationality and residency. It would support only practices of human rights that systematically abolish the discrimination between citizens and non-citizens. As we noted in Chapter 1, the contestation of human rights can be understood as raising meta-questions about the frame of global justice in terms of 'what', 'how' and 'who' (pp. 15–19). While human rights issues invariably concern first-order conflicts over substance, what is ultimately at stake in the cultural politics of human rights is the framing of justice as predominantly of concern to the national political community or as cosmopolitan; a matter for global citizens with rights and responsibilities across borders. In a cosmopolitan ethical framework, debates over justice would be situated within shared understandings that justice must encompass 'all affected' by a particular issue: it can not be arbitrarily applied only to citizens but must include all those for whom the issue is relevant, citizens and non-citizens alike.

What are human rights?

In a cosmopolitan ethical framework human rights would be continually re-confirmed as legitimately and properly concerning *global* justice. Within such a framework, first-order questions of substance would concern only which of the comprehensive schedule of international human rights norms were to be applied in a particular case. As we have noted, there is a wide-ranging list of human rights in international human rights law, including extensive measures to address social and economic misery as well as the details of civil and political rights with which we are more familiar in Europe and North

America. In a cosmopolitan ethical framework of human rights, the 'what' question of global justice would concern only 'which human rights are relevant to this issue?'.

In the current cultural politics of intermestic human rights the 'what' of human rights is much more likely to concern the question 'what is more relevant here, human rights or other considerations?' than the question 'what kinds of human rights are relevant here (civil, political, social, economic or cultural)?'. The meta-question of justice that is most commonly addressed is not 'what kinds of human rights?' but rather *whether* human rights are important at all. This is especially evident, of course, in the cases of national security we have examined. In these cases, human rights activists are engaged in contesting the view that it is citizens' security that matter, while the rights of non-citizens suspected of terrorism to due process of the law are irrelevant. How 'what' becomes 'whether' is also evident in relation to the social and economic rights we examined in Chapter 5; in these cases the question of 'what' human rights mean was settled in advance of the campaign against global poverty with the prior decision that representing claims on global structures that create severe economic inequality as a matter of human rights was unlikely to gain popular support in the US and UK.

Who is the subject of human rights?

I have stressed throughout this study that what intermestic human rights introduce that is radically new into national political life is the principle that it is not exclusively citizens who are the bearers of entitlements but individual human beings, regardless of their citizenship status or where they live in relation to jurisdictional boundaries. In a cosmopolitan ethical framework of human rights, 'who' is reasonably contested where it is a matter of who, as a bearer of universal entitlements, is being treated unjustly in this particular case, and who, as a bearer of human rights obligations, is responsible for that treatment. In the current cultural politics of human rights, however, the question 'who is the subject of human rights?' is contested in ways that go beyond what would be acceptable within the limits of a cosmopolitan ethical framework of human rights. The idea that citizens and non-citizens should have equal rights appears to be difficult to countenance except by human rights activists and their supporters. Certainly, when it comes to making law in accordance with international human rights norms which abolish this distinction in significant ways, state officials clearly find it a very difficult ideal to live up to in practice.

How are human rights to be decided?

As I have been arguing in this conclusion on the basis of the analysis of the human rights field in previous chapters, intermestic human rights cases raise issues of concern to all branches of government: 'how' decisions concerning human rights are to be settled is appropriately disputed between the judiciary, the Legislature and the Executive. Above all I have argued that what is most necessary, and most difficult, is the making of human rights law by the Legislature. Courts are currently the principal site at which human rights activists have been able to achieve a hearing for human rights cases. However, there is a problem of circularity in arguing that the Legislature must take more responsibility for human rights that makes it virtually impossible for human rights to be secured: it is only if the Legislature makes human rights law that universal human rights will become democratically legitimate; it is only if the electorate values universal human rights that the Legislature will make law that respects human rights for all individuals, regardless of nationality or residence. It is difficult for the Legislature to engage in a cultural politics of human rights to ensure the institutionalisation of equal rights for citizens and non-citizens when politicians are answerable to an electorate which undoubtedly privileges their own individual and collective rights over those of non-citizens.

TOWARDS A COSMOPOLITAN STATE?

The national frame of justice is being called into question in cosmopolitanism-from-below using intermestic human rights. The state is currently in transformation as a result of multiple processes of globalisation, political, economic and legal, as it is extended in networks of global governance. The project of cosmopolitanism-from-below in which human rights activists are engaged is in part a response to that transformation, which seems to offer opportunities to extend norms of justice beyond the national state that were previously difficult to conceive of putting into practice. Cosmopolitanism-from-below using intermestic human rights is also, however, essential if norms of global justice are to have any effect on the state formation that is currently taking place.

Human rights activists construct cosmopolitanism-from-below as a project that simply aims to bring state actors to account in the name of a political community of global citizens which already exists as a consequence of rights and obligations that are clearly laid out in international law. Human rights activists speak, write and act as if the global political community of international law is an 'always already' existing fact as well as being of indisputable normative value. As we have seen, however, activist interpretations of international law are actually highly contested; international law as a global constitution is, at best, in development as a result of the cultural politics in which human rights activists are engaged. The political and legal apparatuses of states, even those that ostensibly have long-standing commitments to the international rule of law like the US and UK, are far from neutral carriers for global values of cosmopolitan law. They are, on the contrary, the sites of vigorous contestation over the meaning and applicability of human rights in particular national contexts.

Contrary to the assertions of those human rights activists engaged in trying to bring about cosmopolitanism-from-below, nationalism seems to remain dominant in all domains of the human rights field outside that of committed human rights activists themselves. In fact, it would not be too strong to say that nationalism may even be given new life through the cultural politics of inter-mestic human rights.

Nationalism, and the importance of the national state to its citizens, is re-stated in the perspective of (inter)nationalism. (Inter)nationalism encodes quite a traditional perspective on political life, though it is carried by liberal and conservative governmental offi-cials, lawyers, judges and journalists in somewhat different ways. In both versions, (inter)nationalism emphasises the contested nature of international law, the way in which it results in the politicisation of law in domestic courts. In its conservative version it may, as we have seen, accommodate itself ethically to a ruthlessness towards non-citizens in the name of safeguarding the security and economic well-being of citizens who belong within the boundaries of the only legitimate political community, that of the nation. In its liberal version, (inter)nationalism is more likely to emphasise a politics of international law that should support decisions by state officials that foster democracy and the rule of law within national states. International law is resolutely seen, however, as a tool of political strategy rather than, as it is by human rights activists engaged in imagining a political community beyond the nation, as cosmopolitan law for global citizens. (Inter)nationalism may update nationalism for our globalising times, emphasising co-operation between states in response to the factual and normative challenges to the national community of justice represented in intermestic human rights cases. Above all, however, it re-iterates the ideal of the national state as sovereign, self-determining and democratically responsive to the interests and values of national citizens.

Nationalism is modified, extended and given new meaning as cosmopolitan nationalism. Cosmopolitan nationalism takes con-cerns about the violation of human rights at home and abroad ser-iously, and supports legal and political action to deal with them. However, effectively treating international law as politics by any other means, cosmopolitan nationalism is imperialist: cosmopolitan nationalists take the moral high ground with regard to the rights of non-citizens, but, counselling prudence, unlike advocates of global citizenship, they do not categorically demand that these rights are to be universally respected as a matter of international law in every case.

There is no doubt that international human rights are potentially imperialist where they allow for interference in the affairs of small and weak states which would not be, and are not, tolerated by more powerful states. Whereas human rights activists try to counteract these imperialist tendencies by insisting that human rights must be applied rigorously and universally to protect the fundamental freedoms and well-being of each and every individual human being, regardless of the consequences in terms of international politics, cosmopolitan nationalism takes up the imperialist logic that they should be protected only when it is prudent for national interests to do so. Cosmopolitan nationalism frames human rights in terms of what is possible in a given situation during what is understood to be a transitional period toward the full realisation of human rights. Cosmopolitan nationalism, like (inter)nationalism, constructs international law as a political tool rather than as routinely administered, technical, cosmopolitan law for global citizens.

Cosmopolitan nationalism is symptomatic of one of the most difficult dilemmas faced by human rights activists: it is necessary to translate human rights into the vernacular in order to gain public support for their institutionalisation; to create, in the terms I have used here, a cosmopolitan ethical framework of human rights. But this is inherently risky. As nationalism remains dominant, activists campaign to mobilise national pride, and not just shame, for human rights causes. The risk then, however, is that human rights will be co-opted by nationalism. Cosmopolitan nationalism is pro-human rights, but without respect for international law it may actually be positively dangerous for the bearers of human rights. The view that international human rights agreements can be treated as nothing more than political tools in the short-term means that the aim of achieving the routine predictability to which law aspires actually becomes impossible to realise in the long-term, if it is possible to maintain it as an ideal at all. The dangers of treating international human rights instrumentally are clear, for example, in the case of the Belmarsh detainees examined in Chapter 3: they were detained without charge (in clear violation of their fundamental human rights) because they could not be returned to the states of which they were nationals where they had well-founded fear of persecution (out of respect for their human rights) (Nash forthcoming).

States are undergoing transformation in networks of global governance. As we have seen in these case studies of intermestic human rights, cosmopolitan law does exist and it is being enforced through national courts, albeit to a far lesser extent than human rights activists imagining a political community of global citizens would have us understand. However, in the US and UK at any rate, and there is no reason to think they are exceptional in this respect, the legitimacy of state institutions and procedures continues to be coded as national. Actually existing states *may* be in transition towards the ideal-type of the cosmopolitan state. However, it is clear from the dilemmas and challenges that are thrown up by the cultural politics of human rights in the globally dominant liberal-democracies studied here that the progressive potential of human rights to become a framework for global justice will be extremely difficult to realise in practice.

References

Abbott, K. and Snidal, D. (2001), 'Hard and Soft Law in International Governance', in J. Goldstein, M. Kahler, R. Keohane and A.-M. Slaughter (eds), *Legalization and World Politics*, Cambridge, Massachusetts: MIT Press.

Ackerman, B. (2004), 'The Emergency Constitution', *The Yale Law Journal* 113: 1029–91.

Agamben, G. (1998), *Homo Sacer: Sovereign Power and Bare Life*, Stanford: Stanford University Press.

Agamben, G. (2005), *State of Exception*, Chicago: Chicago University Press.

Alexander, J. (1995), 'The Reality of Reduction: the Failed Synthesis of Pierre Bourdieu', in *Fin de Siecle Social Theory: Relativism, Reduction, and the Problem of Reason*, London: Verso.

Alexander, J. (2003), *The Meanings of Social Life: A Cultural Sociology*, Oxford: Oxford University Press.

Alexander, J. and Smith, P. (2003), 'The Strong Program in Cultural Sociology: Elements of a Structural Hermeneutics', in J. Alexander, *The Meanings of Social Life: A Cultural Sociology*, Oxford: Oxford University Press.

American Civil Liberties Union (2002), *Insatiable Appetite: The Government's Demand for New and Unnecessary Powers After September 11*, Washington, DC: ACLU.

American Civil Liberties Union (2004), *Conduct Unbecoming: Pitfalls in the President's Military Commissions*, Washington, DC: ACLU.

American Civil Liberties Union (2006a), 'Dimming the Beacon of Freedom: US Violations of the International Covenant on Civil and Political Rights', shadow report for the UN Human Rights Committee. www.aclu.org. Last accessed 3 January 2008.

American Civil Liberties Union (2006b), 'Enduring Abuse: Torture and Cruel Treatment by the United States at Home and Abroad', report to the UN Committee Against Torture. www.aclu.org. Last accessed 3 January 2008.

Amnesty International (1998), *USA: The Inescapable Obligation of the International Community to Bring to Justice those Responsible for Crimes Against Humanity Committed During the Military Government in Chile* (AI Index: AMR 22/16/98).

Amnesty International (2002a), *USA: Memorandum to the US Government on the Rights of Detainees in US Custody in Afghanistan and Guantánamo Bay* (AI Index: AMR 51/050/2002).

Amnesty International (2002b), *UK: Rights Denied: the UK's Response to 11 September 2001* (AI Index: EUR 45/019/2002).

Amnesty International (2003), *UK: Justice Perverted under the Anti-terrorism, Crime and Security Act 2001* (AI Index: EUR 45/029/2003).

Amnesty International (2004), *USA: Restoring the Rule of Law – The Right of Guantánamo Detainees to Judicial Review of the Lawfulness of their Detention* (AI Index: AMR 51/093/2004).

Amnesty International (2005a), *USA: Guantánamo and Beyond: The Continuing Pursuit of Unchecked Executive Power* (AI Index: AMR 51/063/2005).

Amnesty International (2005b), *USA: Guantánamo – an Icon of Lawlessness* (AI Index: AMR 51/002/2005).

Amnesty International (2005c), *USA: Guantánamo: Trusting the Executive, Prolonging the Injustice* (AI Index: AMR 51/030/2005).

Amnesty International (2005d), *USA: Human Rights not Hollow Words – An Appeal to President George W. Bush on the Occasion of his Re-inauguration* (AI Index: AMR 51/012/2005).

Amnesty International (2006a), *USA: Military Commissions Act of 2006 – Turning Bad Policy into Bad Law* (AI Index: AMR 51/154/2006).

Amnesty International (2006b), *UK: Human Rights: a Broken Promise* (AI Index: EUR 45/004/2006).

Anderson, B. (1983), *Imagined Communities: Reflections on the Origin and Spread of Nationalism*, London: Verso.

Anderson, B. (1991), *Imagined Communities: Reflections on the Origin and Spread of Nationalism*, revised edition, London: Verso.

An-Na'im, A. (2002), 'The Legal Protection of Human Rights in Africa: How to do More with Less', in A. Sarat and T. Kearns (eds), *Human Rights: Concepts, Contests, Contingencies*, Ann Arbor: University of Michigan Press.

Apodaca, C. (2007), 'The Whole World can be Watching: Human Rights and the Media', *Journal of Human Rights* 6: 147–64.

Appiah, K. (1998), 'Cosmopolitan Patriots', in P. Cheah and B. Robbins (eds), *Cosmopolitics: Thinking and Feeling Beyond the Nation*, Minneapolis: University of Minnesota.

Arendt, H. (1968), *The Origins of Totalitarianism*, San Diego: Harvest Books.

Barbalet, J. (2002), 'Introduction: Why Emotions are Crucial', in J. Barbalet (ed.), *Emotions and Sociology*, Oxford: Blackwell.

Bauman, Z. (1999), *In Search of Politics*, Cambridge: Polity.

Beck, U. (2006), *Power in the Global Age*, Cambridge: Polity.

Beetham, D. (2000), *Democracy and Human Rights*, Cambridge: Polity Press.

Begg, M. (2006), *Enemy Combatant: A British Muslim's Journey to Guantanamo and Back*, London: Free Press.

Bellamy, R. (1999), *Liberalism and Pluralism: Towards a Politics of Compromise*, London and New York: Routledge.

Benhabib, S. (2004), *The Rights of Others: Aliens, Residents and Citizens*, Cambridge: Cambridge University Press.

Benhabib, S. (2007), 'Twilight of Sovereignty or the Emergence of Cosmopolitan Norms? Rethinking Citizenship in Volatile Times', *Citizenship Studies* 11/1: 19–36.

Benson, E. and Neveu, E. (2005), *Bourdieu and the Journalistic Field*, Cambridge: Polity.

Bianchi, A. (1999), 'Immunity versus Human Rights: The Pinochet Case', *European Journal of International Law* 10/2: 237–77.

Bickerton, C., Cunliffe, P., and Gourevitch, A. (2007), *Politics without Sovereignty: A Critique of Contemporary International Relations*, London: University College Press.

Biersteker, T. and Weber, C. (eds) (1996), *State Sovereignty as Social Construct*, Cambridge: Cambridge University Press.

Billig, M. (1995), *Banal Nationalism*, London: Sage.

Bognador, V. (2006), 'Judges and the Constitution', speech at Gresham College, London, 30 May.

Boli, J. (1987), 'Human Rights or State Expansion? Cross-National Definitions of Constitutional Rights', in G. Thomas, J. Meyer, F. Ramirez and J. Boli (eds), *Institutional Structure: Constituting State, Society and the Individual*, Newbury Park, California: Sage.

Boltanski, L. (1999), *Distant Suffering: Morality, Media and Politics*, Cambridge: Cambridge University Press.

Boltanski, L. and Thevenot, L. (2006), *On Justification: Economies of Worth*, Princeton: Princeton University Press.

Boorstin, D. (1992), *The Image: a Guide to Pseudo-Events in America*, New York: Vintage Books.

Bourdieu, P. (1977), *Outline of a Theory of Practice*, Cambridge: Cambridge University Press.

Bourdieu, P. (1987), 'The Force of Law: Toward a Sociology of the Juridical Field', *Hastings Law Journal* 38/5: 805–53.

Bourdieu, P. (1990), *In Other Words: Essays Towards a Reflexive Sociology*, Cambridge: Polity.

Bourdieu, P. (1991), *Language and Symbolic Power*, Cambridge: Polity.

Bourdieu, P. (1992), *An Invitation to Reflexive Sociology*, Chicago: Chicago University Press.

Brown, C. 'Bob Dylan, Live Aid, and the Politics of Popular Cosmopolitanism', in D. Boucher and G. Browning (eds), *The Political Art of Bob Dylan*, 2nd edn, Basingstoke: Palgrave, forthcoming.

Brysk, A. (ed.) (2002), *Globalization and Human Rights*, Berkeley, California: University of California.

Buergenthal, T., Shelton, D. and Stewart, D. (2002), *International Human Rights*, St Paul, Minnesota: West Publishing Co.

Bush, G. W. (2001), 'Address to a Joint Session of Congress and the American People', 10 September 2001. www.whitehouse.gov/news/releases/2001/09/20010920–8.html. Last accessed 29 December 2007.

Butler, J. (2004), *Precarious Life: The Power of Mourning and Violence*, London: Verso.

Buxton, N. (2004), 'Debt Cancellation and Civil Society: a Case Study of Jubilee 2000', in P. Gready (ed.), *Fighting for Human Rights*, London and New York: Routledge.

Calhoun, C. (2003), 'The Class Consciousness of Frequent Travellers: Towards a Critique of Actually Existing Cosmopolitanism', in D. Archibugi (ed.), *Debating Cosmopolitics*, London: Verso.

Calhoun, C. (2007), *Nations Matter: Culture, History and the Cosmopolitan Dream*, London and New York: Routledge.

Campbell, K. (2007), 'The Balance of Terror: Torture, Terrorism, and Security', *Law, Culture and the Humanities* 3: 155–69.

Cassese, A. (2001), *International Law*, Oxford: Oxford University Press.

Castles, S. and Davidson, A. (2001), *Citizenship and Migration*, Basingstoke, Hampshire: Macmillan.

Center for Constitutional Rights (2002), *Secret Trials and Executions*, New York: Seven Stories Press.

Center for Constitutional Rights (2003), *Plain Responses to Attacks on ATCA*, New York: Center for Constitutional Rights.

Center for Constitutional Rights (2004), *Report of Former Guantanamo Detainees ("The Tipton Report")*, New York: Center for Constitutional Rights.

Center for Constitutional Rights (2006a), *Articles of Impeachment Against George W. Bush*, Hoboken, New Jersey: Melville House Publishing.

Center for Constitutional Rights (2006b), *The Military Commissions Act: Questions and Answers*, New York: Center for Constitutional Rights.

Chakrabarti, S. (2003), 'Anti-terror Laws Ride Roughshod over Human Rights'. www.poptel.org.uk/scgn/issues/0502.htm. Last accessed 25 May 2007.

Chandler, D. (2006), *From Kosovo to Kabul and Beyond: Human Rights and International Intervention*, 2nd edn, London: Pluto.

Charlesworth, H. and Chinkin, C. (2000), *The Boundaries of International Law: a Feminist Analysis*, Manchester: Manchester University Press.

Chomsky, N., Glasbeek, D. and Sempill, J. (1999), *Latin America: from Colonization to Globalization*, Lancing, Sussex: Ocean Press.

Chouliaraki, L. (2006), *The Spectatorship of Suffering*, London: Sage.

Cohen, S. (2001), *States of Denial: Knowing about Atrocities and Suffering*, Cambridge: Polity.

Coicaud, J.-M., Doyle, M. and Gardner, A.-M. (eds) (2003), *The Globalization of Human Rights*, Tokyo: The United Nations University Press.

Collier, J. (2002), 'Durkheim Revisited: Human Rights as the Moral Discourse for the Postcolonial, Post-Cold War World', in A. Sarat and T. Kearns (eds), *Human Rights: Concepts, Contests, Contingencies*, Ann Arbor: University of Michigan Press.

Comaroff, J. (2007), 'Terror and Territory: Guantanamo and the Space of Contradiction', *Public Culture* 19/2: 381–405.

Copelon, R. (1998), 'The Indivisible Framework of International Human Rights: Bringing it Home', in D. Kairys (ed.), *The Politics of Law: a Progressive Critique*, New York: Basic Books.

Couldry, N. (2000), *The Place of Media Power: Pilgrims and Witnesses of the Media Age*, London and New York: Routledge.

Couldry, N. (2003a), *Media Rituals: a Critical Approach*, London and New York: Routledge.

Couldry, N. (2003b), 'Media Meta-Capital: Extending the Range of Bourdieu's Field Theory', *Theory and Society* 32/5–6: 653–77.

Cowan, J., Dembour, M.-B., and Wilson, R. (eds) (2001), *Culture and Rights: Anthropological Perspectives*, Cambridge: Cambridge University Press.

Crawford, J. and Marks, S. (1998), 'The Global Democracy Deficit: an Essay in International Law and its Limits', in D. Archibugi, D. Held and M. Kohler (eds), *Re-imagining Political Community: Studies in Cosmopolitan Democracy*, Stanford: California: Stanford University Press.

Crow, G. (2002), *Social Solidarities: Theories, Identities and Social Change*, Buckingham: Open University Press.

Cushman, T. (2005), 'The Human Rights Case for the War in Iraq: a Consequentialist View', in R. Wilson (ed.), *Human Rights in the 'War on Terror'*, Cambridge: Cambridge University Press.

Davis, M. (2003), 'Introduction: Law and Politics in the Pinochet Case', in M. Davis (ed.), *The Pinochet Case: Origins, Progress, Limitations*, London: The Institute of Latin American Studies.

Dayan, D. (2001), 'The Peculiar Public of Television', *Media, Culture and Society* 23/6: 743–65.

Demobour, M. (2006), *Who Believes in Human Rights: Reflections on the European Convention*, Cambridge: Cambridge University Press.

Donnelly, J. (1989), *Universal Human Rights in Theory and Practice*, Ithaca: Cornell University Press.

Dudley, W. (2005), *Opposing Viewpoints: Mass Media*, Farmington Hills, Michigan: Greenhaven Press.

Earthrights International (2003), *Legal Manual: Litigation*, Washington, DC: Earthrights International.

Earthrights International (2004), *In Our Court: ATCA, Sosa and the Triumph of Human Rights*, Washington, DC: Earthrights International.

Favell, A. (2001), *Philosophies of Integration: Immigration and the Idea of Citizenship in France and Britain*, Basingstoke, Hampshire: Macmillan.

Fine, R. (1994), 'The New Nationalism and Democracy: a Critique of Pro Patria', *Democratization* 1/3: 423–43.

Fish, S. (1994), *There's No Such Thing as Free Speech and It's a Good Thing Too*, Oxford: Oxford University Press.

Forsythe, D. (2000), *Human Rights in International Relations*, Cambridge: Cambridge University Press.

Fortier, A.-M. (2005), 'Pride Politics and Multiculturalist Citizenship', *Ethnic and Racial Studies* 28/3: 559–78.

Foucault, F. (1977), 'Nietzsche, Genealogy, History', in D. Bouchard (ed.), *Language, Counter-Memory, Practice*, Ithaca: Cornell University Press.

Foucault, F. (2000), 'Confronting Governments: Human Rights', in J. D. Fabion (ed.), *Essential Works of Foucault 1954–1984: vol 3: Power*, Harmondsworth: Penguin.

Fraser, N. (2005), 'Reframing Justice in a Globalizing World', *New Left Review* 36: 69–88.

Fraser, N. (2007), 'Interview with Kate Nash and Vikki Bell', *Theory, Culture and Society* 24/4: 73–86.

Fraser, N. (2008), 'Abnormal Justice', *Critical Inquiry* 34/3: 393–422.

Friel, H. and Falk, R. (2004), *The Record of the Paper: How The New York Times Misreports US Foreign Policy*, London: Verso.

Gans, H. (2003), *Democracy and the News*, Oxford: Oxford University Press.

Gearty, C. (2006), *Can Human Rights Survive?*, Cambridge: Cambridge University Press.

Gearty, C. (2007), *Civil Liberties*, Oxford: Oxford University Press.

Gilroy, P. (1993), *The Black Atlantic: Modernity and Double Consciousness*, London: Verso.

Goffman, E. (1986), *Frame Analysis: an Essay on the Organisation of Experience*, York, Pennsylvania: Northeastern University Press.

Gould, C. (2004), *Globalizing Democracy and Human Rights*, Cambridge: Cambridge University Press.

Green, J. and Stephens, B. (2003), *An Activist's Guide: Bringing International Human Rights Claims in United States Courts*, New York: Center for Constitutional Rights.

Greenberg, K. and Dratel, J. (eds) (2005), *The Torture Papers: the Road to Abu Ghraib*, Cambridge: Cambridge University Press.

Guilhot, N. (2005), *The Democracy-Makers: Human Rights and the International Order*, New York: Columbia University Press.

Habermas, J. (1989), *The Structural Transformation of the Public Sphere: an Inquiry into a Category of Bourgeois Society*, Cambridge: Polity.

Habermas, J. (1996), *Between Facts and Norms: Contributions to a Discourse Theory of Law and Democracy*, Cambridge: Polity.

Habermas, J. (1999), 'Bestiality and Humanity: a War on the Border between Legality and Morality', *Constellations* 6/3: 263–72.

Habermas, J. (2001), *The Postnational Constellation*, Cambridge: Polity.

Harre, R. (1986), 'An Outline of the Social Constructionist Viewpoint', in R. Harre (ed.), *The Social Construction of Emotions*, Oxford: Basil Blackwell.

Held, D. (1995), *Democracy and the Global Order: from the Modern State to Cosmopolitan Governance*, Cambridge: Polity Press.

Held, D. (2002), 'Law of States, Law of Peoples: Three Models of Sovereignty', *Legal Theory* 8/1: 1–44.

Held, D. (2003), 'Global Social Democracy', in A. Giddens (ed.), *The Progressive Manifesto*, Cambridge: Polity.

Hersh, S. (2005), *Chain of Command*, Harmondsworth: Penguin.

Hirsh, D. (2003), *Law against Genocide: Cosmopolitan Trials*, London: Glasshouse Press.

Human Rights First (2000), *Behind the Wire*, New York: Human Rights First.

Human Rights First (2002), *A Year of Loss: Re-examining Civil Liberties since September 11*, New York: Human Rights First.

Human Rights First (2003a), *Imbalance of Powers*, New York: Human Rights First.

Human Rights First (2003b), *Assessing the New Normal*, New York: Human Rights First.

Human Rights First (2004), *The Future of the Alien Tort Claims Act*, New York: Human Rights First.

Human Rights First (2006), 'Questions and Answers about the Military Commissions Act'. hrw.org/backgrounder/usa/qna1006. Last accessed 3 January 2008.

Human Rights First (2007), 'Analysis of Proposed Rules for Military Commissions Trials'. www.humanrightsfirst.info/pdf/07125-usls-hrf-rcm-analysis.pdf. Last accessed 3 January 2008.

Human Rights Watch (2004a), *Detainee Accounts*, New York: Human Rights Watch.

Human Rights Watch (2004b), *Above the Law: Executive Power after September 11 in the United States*, New York: Human Rights Watch.

Human Rights Watch (2004c), *Neither Just nor Effective*, New York: Human Rights Watch.

Human Rights Watch (2006), *Statement of Human Rights Watch to the United Nations Human Rights Committee: United States Compliance with the ICCPR*, New York: Human Rights Watch.

Ignatieff, M. (ed.) (2005), *American Exceptionalism and Human Rights*, Princeton: Princeton University Press.

Jacobson, D. (1996), *Rights Across Borders: Immigration and the Decline of Citizenship*, Baltimore: John Hopkins University.

Jacobson, D. (2004), 'Cosmopolitan Promises: the Rising Struggle over Human Rights and Democracy', *Journal of Human Rights* 3/2: 215–24.

Jacobson, D. and Ruffer, G. (2003), 'Courts Across Borders: the Implications of Judicial Agency for Human Rights and Democracy', *Human Rights Quarterly* 25/1: 74–92.

Jetschke, A. (1999), 'Linking the Unlinkable? International Norms and Nationalism in Indonesia and the Phillipines', in T. Risse, S. Ropp and K. Sikkink (eds), *The Power of Human Rights: Institutional Norms and Domestic Change*, Cambridge: Cambridge University Press.

Johns, F. (2005), 'Guantanamo Bay and the Annihilation of the Exception', *The European Journal of International Law* 16/4: 613–35.

Kahn, P. (2005), 'American Exceptionalism, Popular Sovereignty, and the Rule of Law', in M. Ignatieff (ed.), *American Exceptionalism and Human Rights*, Princeton: Princeton University Press.

Kant, I. (1991), *Political Writings*, Cambridge: Cambridge University Press.

Keane, J. (1991), *The Media and Democracy*, Cambridge: Polity.

Keck, M. and Sikkink, K. (1998), *Activists beyond Borders: Advocacy Networks in International Politics*, Ithaca, New York: Cornell University Press.

Kennedy, H. (2000), 'Foreward', in F. Klug, *Values for a Godless Age: the Story of the UK's New Bill of Rights*, London: Penguin.

Khan, I. (2005), 'Close Guantanamo and Disclose the Rest', 22 June 2005, Amnesty International press release. http://web.amnesty.org/library/Index/ENGAMR511012005?open&of=ENG-USA. Last accessed 29 December 2007.

Klug, F. (2000), *Values for a Godless Age: the Story of the UK's New Bill of Rights*, London: Penguin.

Kostakopoulou, D. (2006), 'Thick, Thin and Thinner Patriotisms: is this all there is?' *Oxford Journal of Legal Studies* 26/1: 73–106.

Kovach, W. and Rosentiel, T. (2001), *The Elements of Journalism*, London: Atlantic Books.

Krasner, S. (1999), *Sovereignty: Organized Hypocrisy*, Princeton: Princeton University Press.

Kurasawa, F. (2007), *The Work of Global Justice: Human Rights as Practices*, Cambridge: Cambridge University Press.

Lakoff, G. (2004), *Don't Think of an Elephant! Know your Values and Frame the Debate: the Essential Guide for Progressives*, White River Junction: Chelsea Green.

Lamont, M. and Thevenot, L. (eds) (2000), *Rethinking Comparative Cultural Sociology*, Cambridge: Cambridge University Press.

Lasso, J. (1997), 'A Culture of Respect for Human Rights', *UN Chronicle* 4: 28–9.

Lawson, G. (2008), 'A Realistic Utopia?: Nancy Fraser, Cosmopolitanism and the Making of a Just World Order', *Political Studies* 56/4: 881–906.

Lebow, R. (2003), *The Tragic Vision of Politics: Ethics, Interests and Orders*, Cambridge: Cambridge University Press.

Liberty (2004), 'Reconciling Security and Liberty in an Open Society'. www.liberty-human-rights.org.uk/pdfs/policy04/liberty-and-security.pdf. Last accessed 3 January 2008.

Liberty (2006), 'The Human Rights Act; Exploding the Myths'. www.liberty-human-rights.org.uk/issues/pdfs/the-human-rights-act-exploding-the-myths. PDF. Last accessed 3 January 2008.

Lieven, A. (2004), *America Right or Wrong: an Anatomy of American Nationalism*, Hammersmith: HarperCollins.

Livingstone, S. (2005), 'On the Relation between Audiences and Publics: Why Audience and Public?'. http://eprints.lse.ac.uk/archive/00000437. Last accessed 12 February 2006.

Madsen, M. and Dezalay, Y. (2002), 'The Power of the Legal Field: Pierre Bourdieu and the Law', in R. Banakar and M. Travers (eds), *An Introduction to Law and Social Theory*, Oxford: Hart.

Mahoney, J. (2007), *The Challenge of Human Rights: Origin, Development and Significance*, New York: Wiley-Blackwell.

Mazower, M. (2004), 'The Strange Triumph of Human Rights, 1933–50', *The Historical Journal* 47/2: 379–98.

McChesney, R. (2004), *The Problem of the Media: US Communication Politics in the 21st Century*, New York: Monthly Review Press.

Meckled-Garcia, S. and Cali, B. (2006), *The Legalization of Human Rights: Multidisciplinary Perspectives on Human Rights and Human Rights Law*, London: Routledge.

Merry, S. (2006), *Human Rights and Gender Violence: Translating International Law into Local Justice*, Chicago: University of Chicago Press.

Mertus, J. (2004), *Bait and Switch: Human Rights and U.S. Foreign Policy*, London and New York: Routledge.

Mertus, J. (2005), 'Human Rights and Civil Society in a New Age of American Exceptionalism', in R. Wilson (ed.), *Human Rights in the 'War on Terror'*, Cambridge: Cambridge University Press.

Millet, D. and Toussaint, E. (2004), *Who Owes Who? 50 Questions about World Debt*, London: Zed Books.

Montgomery, J. (2002), 'Sovereignty in Transition', in J. Montgomery and N. Glazer (eds), *Sovereignty Under Challenge*, New Brunswick: Transaction.

Moravscik, A. (1994), 'Lessons from the European Human Rights Regime', in *Inter-American Dialogue: Advancing Democracy and Human Rights in the Americas: What Role of the OAS?* Washington, DC: Inter-American Dialogue.

Nash, K. (2000), *Contemporary Political Sociology: Globalization, Politics and Power*, Oxford: Blackwell.

Nash, K. (2001), 'The "Cultural Turn" in Social Theory: Towards a Theory of Cultural Politics', *Sociology* 35/1: 77–92.

Nash, K. (2008), 'Global Citizenship as Showbusiness: the Cultural Politics of Make Poverty History', *Media, Culture and Society* 30/1: 167–81.

Nash, K. 'Between Citizenship and Human Rights', *Sociology*, forthcoming.

Negrine, R. (1989), *Politics and the Mass Media in Britain*, London: Routledge.

Nussbaum, M. (2003), *Upheavals of Thought: The Intelligence of Emotions*, Cambridge: Cambridge University Press.

Nyer, P. (2006), 'The Accidental Citizen: Acts of Sovereignty and (un)Making Citizenship', *Economy and Society* 35/1: 22–41.

Olivier, M. and Jansen van Rensburg, L. (2006), 'South African Poverty Law: the Role and Influence of International Human Rights Instruments', in L. Williams (ed.), *International Poverty Law: an Emerging Discourse*, London: Zed Books.

Ortener, S. (2006), *Anthropology and Social Theory: Culture, Power, and the Acting Subject*, Durham and London: Duke University Press.

Parekh, B. (2000), *The Future of Multi-Ethnic Britain: Report of the Committee on the Future of Multi-Ethnic Britain*, London: Profile.

Pettifor, A. (2001), 'Global Economic Justice: Human Rights for Debtor Nations', *Journal of Human Development* 2/1: 47–51.

Phillips, A. (2007), *Multiculturalism without Culture*, Princeton: Princeton University Press.

Poole, T. (2005), 'Harnessing the Power of the Past? Lord Hoffman and the *Belmarsh Detainees* Case', *Journal of Law and Society* 32/4: 534–61.

Preis, A. (1996), 'Human Rights as Cultural Practice: An Anthropological Critique', *Human Rights Quarterly* 18/2: 286–315.

Prime Minister's press conference with Tony Blair, 5 August 2005. www.number10.gov.uk/output/Page8041.asp. Last accessed 12 June 2007.

Ratner, M. and Ray, E. (2004), *Guantánamo: What the World Should Know*, Moreton in Marsh, Gloucestershire: Arris Books.

Ratner, S. and Abrams, J. (2001), *Accountability for Human Rights Atrocities in International Law: Beyond the Nuremberg Legacy*, Oxford: Oxford University Press.

Risse, T. and Ropp, S. (1999), 'International Human Rights Norms and Domestic Change: Conclusions', in T. Risse, S. Ropp and K. Sikkink (eds), *The Power of Human Rights: Institutional Norms and Domestic Change*, Cambridge: Cambridge University Press.

Risse, T., Ropp, S. and Sikkink, K. (1999), *The Power of Human Rights: Institutional Norms and Domestic Change*, Cambridge: Cambridge University Press.

Robertson, G. (2002), *Crimes against Humanity: the Struggle for Global Justice*, 2nd edn, London: Penguin.

Rorty, R. (1993), 'Human Rights, Rationality, and Sentimentality', in S. Shute and S. Hurley (eds), *On Human Rights*, New York: Basic Books.

Rosenau, J. (2003), *Distant Proximities: Dynamics Beyond Globalization*, Princeton: Princeton University Press.

Roth, K. (2000), 'The Charade of US Ratification of International Human Rights Treaties', *Chicago Journal of International Law* 1/2: 347–54.

Sands, P. (2005), *Lawless World: America and the Making and Breaking of Global Rules*, London: Allen Lane.

Sassen, S. (2006), *Territory, Authority, Rights: from Medieval to Global Assemblages*, Princeton: Princeton University Press.

Schmitt, C. (1996), *The Concept of the Political*, Chicago: Chicago University Press.

Schmitt, C. (2005), *Political Theology: Four Chapters on the Concept of Sovereignty*, Chicago: Chicago University Press.

Sen, A. (1999), *Development as Freedom*, Oxford: Oxford University Press.

Sen, A. (2007), 'Human Rights and the Limits of Law', *Cardozo Law Review* 26/5: 2913–27.

Sewell, W. (1992), 'A Theory of Stucture: Duality, Agency and Transformation', *American Journal of Sociology* 98/1: 1–25.

Shaw, M. (2003), *International Law*, Cambridge: Cambridge University Press.

Silverstone, R. (1999), *Why Study the Media?*, Thousand Oaks, California and London: Sage.

Slaughter, A.-M. (2004), *A New World Order*, Princeton: Princeton University Press.

Slaughter, A.-M. (2007), 'Values-based Foreign Policy', *Democratiya* 10. www.democratiya.com. Last accessed 12 September 2007

Snow, D. and Benford, R. (1988), 'Ideology, Frame Resonance and Participating Mobilization', in B. Klandermans, H. Kriesi and S. Tarrow (eds), *From Structure to Action: Social Movement Research across Different Cultures*, Greenwich, Connecticut and London: JAI Press.

Snow, D., Rocheford, E., Worden, S. and Benford R. (1986), 'Frame Alignment Processes, Micromobilization and Movement Participation', *American Sociological Review* 51/4: 464–81.

Soysal, Y. (1994), *Limits of Citizenship: Migrants and Postnational Membership in Europe*, Chicago: Chicago University Press.

Soysal, Y. (2001), 'Postnational Citizenship: Reconfiguring the Familiar Terrain', in K. Nash and A. Scott (eds), *The Blackwell Companion to Political Sociology*, Oxford: Blackwell.

St Clair, A. (2006), 'How can Human Rights Contribute to Poverty Reduction? A Philosophical Assessment of the *Human Development Report 2000*', in L. Williams (ed.), *International Poverty Law: an Emerging Discourse*, London: Zed Books.

Steiker, C. (2005), 'Capital Punishment and American Exceptionalism', in M. Ignatieff (ed.), *American Exceptionalism and Human Rights*, Princeton: Princeton University Press

Steiner, H. and Alston, P. (eds) (2000), *International Human Rights in Context: Law, Politics, Morals*, 2nd edn, Oxford: Oxford University Press.

Steinhardt, R. (1999), 'The Internationalization of Domestic Law', in R. Steinhardt and A. D'Amato (eds), *The Alien Tort Claims Act: an Analytical Anthology*, Ardsley, New York: Transnational Publishers.

Steinhardt, R. G. and D'Amato, A. (1999), *The Alien Tort Claims Act: an Analytical Anthology*, Ardsley, New York: Transnational Publishers.

Stephens, B. (2002), 'Translating Filartiga: A Comparative and International Law Analysis of Domestic Remedies for International Human Rights Violations', *Yale Journal of International Law* 27/1: 1–58.

Stephens, B. and Ratner, M. (1996), *International Human Rights Litigation in the US Courts*, New York: Transnational Publishers.

Stevenson, N. (1999), *The Transformation of the Media: Globalisation, Morality and Ethics*, Harlow, Essex: Pearson Education.

Stevenson, N. (2007), 'Cosmopolitan Europe, Post-colonialism and the Politics of Imperialism', in C. Rumford (ed.), *Cosmopolitanism and Europe*, Liverpool: Liverpool University Press.

Steyne, J. (2003), 'Guantanamo Bay: the Legal Black Hole', 27th F. A. Mann Lecture, London.

Street, J. (2001), *Mass Media, Politics, and Democracy*, New York and Basingstoke: Palgrave.

Sunstein, C. (2004), *The Second Bill of Rights: FDR's Unfinished Revolution and why we need it more than ever*, New York: Basic Books.

Sznaider, N. and Levy, D. (2006), 'Sovereignty Transformed: a Sociology of Human Rights', *The British Journal of Sociology* 57/4: 657–76.

Thompson, J. (1995), *The Media and Modernity: a Social Theory of the Media*, Cambridge: Polity.

Tonkiss, F. (2007), *Contemporary Economic Sociology*, London and New York: Routledge.

Turner, B. (2000), 'Liberal Citizenship and Cosmopolitan Virtue', in A. Vandenberg (ed.), *Citizenship and Democracy in a Global Era*, Basingstoke, Hampshire: Macmillan.

Turner, B. (2002), 'Cosmopolitan Virtue, Globalization and Patriotism', *Theory, Culture and Society* 19/1–2: 45–63.

UN Human Rights Commission Report (2006), 'Situation of Detainees at Guantanamo', Economic and Social Council GENERAL Future E/CN. 4/2006/ 120. 15 February 2006.

UN press release (2004), 'General Assembly Proclaims World Programme for Human Rights Education', GA/10317. 10 December 2004.

Weber, M. (1970), 'The Social Psychology of World Religions', in H. H. Herth and C. W. Mills (eds), *From Max Weber: Essays in Sociology*, London: Routledge and Kegan Paul.

White House press release (2006), 'President Discusses Creation of Military Commissions to Try Suspected Terrorists', 6 September 2006. www.whitehouse. gov/news/releases/2006/09/20060906-3.html. Last accessed 29 December 2007.

Wilson, R. (ed.) (1999), *Human Rights, Culture and Context: Anthropological Perspectives*, London: Pluto.

Woodhouse, D. (2003), 'The Progress of Pinochet through the UK Extradition Procedure; an Analysis of the Legal Challenges and Judicial Decisions', in M. Davis (ed.), *The Pinochet Case: Origins, Progress, Limitiations*, London: The Institute of Latin American Studies.

Woodiwiss, A. (2005), *Human Rights*, London and New York: Routledge.

World Development Movement (2006), *Small Change*, London: World Development Movement.

Young, I. (1996), 'Communications and the Other: Beyond Deliberative Democracy', in S. Benhabib (ed.), *Democracy and Difference*, Princeton, New Jersey: Princeton University Press.

Young, I. (2004), 'Responsibility and Global Labor Justice', *The Journal of Political Philosophy* 12/4: 365–88.

Index

Made in the USA
Lexington, KY
08 January 2015